AMERICAN FAMILY LAWS
VOLUME III

AMERICAN FAMILY LAWS

A Comparative Study of the Family Law
of the Forty-eight American States,
Alaska, the District of Columbia,
and Hawaii (to Jan. 1, 1935)

VOLUME III
[*Husband and Wife*]

By
CHESTER G. VERNIER

Assisted by
JOHN B. HURLBUT

1935
STANFORD UNIVERSITY PRESS
STANFORD UNIVERSITY, CALIFORNIA
LONDON: HUMPHREY MILFORD
OXFORD UNIVERSITY PRESS

STANFORD UNIVERSITY PRESS
STANFORD UNIVERSITY, CALIFORNIA

LONDON: HUMPHREY MILFORD
OXFORD UNIVERSITY PRESS

———

THE BAKER AND TAYLOR COMPANY
55 FIFTH AVENUE, NEW YORK

MARTINUS NIJHOFF
9 LANGE VOORHOUT, THE HAGUE

THE MARUZEN COMPANY
TOKYO, OSAKA, KYOTO, SENDAI

PREFACE

EACH VOLUME of this work covers a distinct field of family law. In order to make this volume usable as an entity there will be found herein a table of contents, table of cases cited, table of statutory sources, table of abbreviations, list of analytical tables, and index for this volume. Cross references are made to other parts of this work for the benefit of those interested in other branches of family law.

In this work, of which this book comprises Volume III, an effort has been made to present in comparative form a portion of the family law of the forty-eight states, Alaska, the District of Columbia, and Hawaii. While the method of treatment varies somewhat from section to section, dependent upon the kind and amount of material, it has been the purpose, wherever possible, to do four things: (1) make a brief summary of the common law; (2) state the statutory law, first in summary form, second in detail, showing variations, resemblances, and omissions; (3) add such comment and criticism as seems pertinent; (4) collect under each head a selected list of references, including texts, case books, annotations, reports, articles, and case notes from law magazines. Wherever it seemed helpful, comparative tables have been used; and wherever possible, the key words of the statute have been reproduced. The work partakes, therefore, somewhat of the nature of a commentary, a digest, an annotation, and a work of reference.

Acknowledgment of general assistance in the preparation of this work has been made in the preface to Volume I. Additional acknowledgment for Volume III is made to John B. Hurlbut, J. Rex Dibble, Homer B. Kidwell, and Mary E. Rechif, research assistants. Mr. Kidwell and Miss Rechif assisted in the collection of recent statutes and references. Mr. Dibble aided in the final revision of this volume and in the formulation of the text of twenty sections. Mr. Hurlbut is entitled to joint authorship of Volume III by reason of two years' work devoted to the selection and classification of statutory material and for his aid in the formulation of the major portion of the text.

CHESTER G. VERNIER

STANFORD UNIVERSITY
March 15, 1935

v

TABLE OF CONTENTS

PAGE

LIST OF TABLES IN THE TEXT xi
TABLE OF CASES CITED xiii
TABLE OF STATUTORY SOURCES xxv
TABLE OF ABBREVIATIONS xxix

PART VII. HUSBAND AND WIFE

SECTION

149. INTRODUCTION 3
150. GENERAL PRINCIPLES 24
151. WIFE'S ANTENUPTIAL DEBTS AND CONTRACTS 30
152. WIFE'S POSTNUPTIAL DEBTS AND CONTRACTS—IN GENERAL . . . 34
153. WIFE'S POSTNUPTIAL DEBTS AND CONTRACTS—NECESSARIES . . . 47
154. WIFE'S POSTNUPTIAL CONTRACTS—WHEN LIVING APART FROM
      HUSBAND 50
155. WIFE'S CONTRACTS WITH HUSBAND BEFORE MARRIAGE 51
156. WIFE'S CONTRACTS WITH HUSBAND AFTER MARRIAGE 65
157. WIFE'S TORTS 72
158. TORTS BY THIRD PERSONS 85
159. THE HUSBAND'S DEBTS—IN GENERAL 100
160. FAMILY EXPENSES 102
161. DUTY OF SUPPORT—CIVIL LIABILITY 108
162. DUTY OF SUPPORT—CRIMINAL LIABILITY 112
163. FAMILY COURTS AND COURTS OF DOMESTIC RELATIONS 139
164. DOMICILE OF WIFE 145
165. CRIMES BY WIFE—COERCION 156
166. CRIMES BY ONE SPOUSE INJURIOUS TO THE OTHER 162
167. WIFE'S PROPERTY—IN GENERAL 166
168. WIFE'S REAL PROPERTY AT MARRIAGE 186
169. WIFE'S PERSONAL PROPERTY AT MARRIAGE 186
170. WIFE'S PARAPHERNALIA 187
171. WIFE'S REAL PROPERTY ACQUIRED AFTER MARRIAGE 189
172. WIFE'S PERSONAL PROPERTY ACQUIRED AFTER MARRIAGE 192
173. WIFE'S EARNINGS 192
174. RECORDING OF SEPARATE PROPERTY OF WIFE 196
175. EFFECT OF RECORDING SEPARATE PROPERTY OF WIFE 201
176. HUSBAND'S PROPERTY 202

vii

SECTION   PAGE

177. PROPERTY ACQUIRED OUTSIDE THE STATE—CONFLICT OF LAWS . . . 204
178. COMMUNITY PROPERTY 207
179. SUITS BY AND AGAINST THE WIFE 255
180. SUITS BETWEEN SPOUSES 268
181. WIFE'S POWER TO MAKE A WILL 273
182. CONVEYANCES AND TRANSFERS BETWEEN HUSBAND AND WIFE . . . 281
183. WIFE'S CONVEYANCES OF HER REAL PROPERTY TO THIRD PERSONS . 293
184. SEPARATE EXAMINATION OF THE WIFE 317
185. WIFE'S TRANSFERS OF PERSONAL PROPERTY TO THIRD PERSONS . . 318
186. POWER OF ATTORNEY OF HUSBAND AND WIFE 322
187. WIFE AS A SOLE TRADER 333
188. DOWER—IN GENERAL 345
189. DOWER—ABOLITION AND STATUTORY SUBSTITUTES 351
190. DOWER—EXTENT 371
191. DOWER—REAL PROPERTY SUBJECT TO 375
192. DOWER—WASTE 394
193. DOWER—REPAIRS 396
194. DOWER—EMBLEMENTS 397
195. DOWER—METHODS OF BARRING IN GENERAL 397
196. DOWER—BARRING BY JOINTURE OR SETTLEMENT 401
197. DOWER—BARRING BY CONTRACT OR SETTLEMENT BEFORE MARRIAGE . 411
198. DOWER—BARRING BY CONTRACT OR SETTLEMENT AFTER MARRIAGE . 412
199. DOWER—BARRING BY WILL 414
200. DOWER—BARRING BY DEED 423
201. DOWER—BARRING BY OTHER MEANS 435
202. DOWER—FORFEITURE OF 439
203. DOWER—FORFEITURE OF PROVISION IN LIEU OF DOWER 446
204. DOWER—FAILURE OF PROVISION IN LIEU OF DOWER 447
205. DOWER—ELECTION AND WAIVER, IN GENERAL 448
206. DOWER—TIME LIMIT FOR AND MANNER OF ELECTION AND WAIVER . 464
207. DOWER—ELECTION AND WAIVER, MISCELLANEOUS 466
208. ASSIGNMENT OF DOWER—IN GENERAL 471
209. ASSIGNMENT OF DOWER—POSSESSION OF DWELLING, ETC., PENDING
    ASSIGNMENT 488
210. ASSIGNMENT OF DOWER—BY NON-JUDICIAL ACTION 493
211. ASSIGNMENT OF DOWER—BY SUMMARY PROCEEDINGS 496
212. ASSIGNMENT OF DOWER—ACTION TO COMPEL, AND DAMAGES FOR
    WITHHOLDING 498
213. ASSIGNMENT OF DOWER—METHOD OF 503

SECTION	PAGE
214. Dower—Miscellaneous Provisions	514
215. Curtesy—In General	527
216. Curtesy—Abolition and Statutory Substitutes	532
217. Curtesy—Extent	553
218. Curtesy—Real Property Subject to	556
219. Curtesy—Election	557
220. Curtesy—Methods of Barring	560
221. Curtesy—Forfeiture of	567
222. Curtesy—Waste	571
223. Curtesy—Miscellaneous Provisions	572
224. Assignment of Wages by Husband and Wife	575
225. Other Limitations on Transfer of Property by Husband and Wife	579
226. Husband and Wife as Witnesses for and against Each Other	583
227. Descent and Distribution	603
228. Homestead, Exempt Property, and Family Allowance	628
229. Statute of Limitations	664
230. Miscellaneous Provisions	670

INDEX

Index to Volume III	681

LIST OF TABLES IN THE TEXT

TABLE		PAGE
LXXVIII.	The Wife's Postnuptial Contracts	37
LXXIX.	Marriage Contracts and Settlements	55
LXXX.	Contracts between the Husband and Wife	67
LXXXI.	Wife's Torts	77
LXXXII.	Suit by Spouse for Furnishing Liquor	92
LXXXIII.	Husband's Criminal Liability for Desertion and Non-Support of the Wife	118
LXXXIV.	Family Courts and Courts of Domestic Relations	141
LXXXV.	Domicile of Wife	147
LXXXVI.	Coercion by Husband of Wife in the Commission of Crime	158
LXXXVII.	Wife's Separate Property	171
LXXXVIII.	Recording of the Wife's Separate Property	197
LXXXIX.	Community Property of Husband and Wife	236
XC.	Suits by and against a Wife	256
XCI.	Conveyances and Transfers between Spouses	285
XCII.	Wife's Conveyances of Her Real Property to Third Persons	298
XCIII.	Power of Attorney of Husband and Wife	325
XCIV.	Wife as a Sole Trader	336
XCV.	Dower and Statutory Substitutes Therefor	355
XCVI.	Real Property Subject to Dower	380
XCVII.	Barring Dower by Jointure or Settlement	404
XCVIII.	Barring Dower by Deed	426
XCIX.	Statutory Election between Will and Dower, etc.	450
C.	Assignment of Dower	474
CI.	Possession of Dwelling, etc., Pending Assignment of Dower	489
CII.	Method of Assignment of Dower	506
CIII.	Dower—Miscellaneous Provisions	518
CIV.	Share of Survivor as against Will of Deceased Spouse	533
CV.	Curtesy and Statutory Substitutes Therefor	538
CVI.	Assignment of Wages by Husband or Wife	576
CVII.	Husband and Wife as Witnesses for and against Each Other	590
CVIII.	Descent and Distribution	612
CIX.	Homestead and Exempt Property—Widow's Allowance	638
CX.	Wife and Statutes of Limitations	665

TABLE OF CASES CITED

PAGE

Abbott v. *Wetherby, Administrator,* 6 Wash. 507; 33 P. 1070 (1893) . . . 246
American Blower Company v. *MacKenzie,* 197 N. C. 152; 147 S. E. 829
    (1929) 517, 527
Anderson v. *Hilker,* 38 Wash. 632; 80 P. 848 (1905) 225
Anderson v. *Medbery,* 16 S. D. 324; 92 N. W. 1089 (1902) 201
Andrews v. *Andrews,* 116 Wash. 513; 199 P. 981 (1921) 210
Archer v. *Moulton,* 183 Minn. 306; 236 N. W. 455 (1931) 64
Arnold v. *Leonard,* 114 Tex. 535; 273 S. W. 799 (1925) . . . 211, 212, 214, 215
Austin v. *Austin,* 136 Miss. 61; 100 So. 591 (1924) 29
Austin v. *Collins,* 317 Mo. 435; 297 S. W. 36 (1927) 463

Bagg v. *Schoenfelt,* 71 Okla. 195; 176 P. 511 (1918) 201
Baker v. *Cailor* (Ind. App.); 176 N. E. 854 (1931) 111
Baledes v. *Greenbaum,* 112 Conn. 64; 151 A. 333 (1930) 50
Balster v. *Cadick,* 29 App. D. C. 405 (1907) 528
Bancker, Succession of, 154 La. 77; 97 So. 321 (1923) 660
Banfield v. *Small,* 139 Ore. 134; 8 P. (2d) 779 (1932) 662
Barber v. *People,* 203 Ill. 543; 68 N. E. 93 (1903) 585
Barker v. *Jenkins,* 84 Va. 895; 6 S. E. 459 (1888) 662
Barkley, Estate of, 91 Cal. App. 388; 267 P. 148 (1928) 632
Barlow v. *Barlow,* 49 R. I. 117; 140 A. 467 (1928) 535
Basler v. *Sacramento Gas and Electric Company,* 158 Cal. 514; 111 P. 530 (1910) 215
Bay District Claim Service, Ltd. v. *Jones,* 136 Cal. App. 789; 24 P. (2d) 977
    (1933) 111
Bayes v. *Howes,* 113 Ky. 465; 68 S. W. 449 (1902) 454
Beasley v. *State,* 138 Ind. 552; 38 N. E. 35 (1894) 163, 165
Bechtol v. *Ewing, Administrator,* 89 Ohio St. 53; 105 N. E. 72 (1913) . . . 194
Belt v. *Bush,* 74 Okla. 94; 176 P. 935 (1918) 662
Bender v. *Pfaff,* 282 U. S. 127; 51 Sup. Ct. 64; 75 L. Ed. 252 (1930) . . . 233
Berman v. *Beaudry,* 118 Me. 248; 107 A. 708 (1920) 369
Beville, Ex parte, 58 Fla. 170; 50 So. 685 (1909) 600
Blair v. *Seitner Dry Goods Company,* 184 Mich. 304; 151 N. W. 724 (1915) . 98
Blair v. *Stewart,* 49 F. (2d) 257 (1931) 231
Blakely v. *Kanaman,* 107 Tex. 206; 175 S. W. 674 (1915) 296
Blatt v. *Blatt,* 79 Colo. 57; 243 P. 1099 (1926) 610
Boehringer v. *Schmid,* 254 N. Y. 355; 173 N. E. 220 (1930) 191
Bomar v. *Wilkins,* 154 S. C. 64; 151 S. E. 110 (1930) 416
Booker v. *Booker,* 225 Ala. 626; 144 So. 870 (1932) 583
Bozich v. *First State Bank of Buhl,* 150 Minn. 241; 184 N. W. 1021 (1921) . 583
Bradford v. *Stone,* 20 R. I. 53; 37 A. 532 (1897) 516
Brandenburg v. *Petroleum Exploration Company,* 218 Ky. 557; 291 S. W. 757
    (1927) 663

PAGE

Breen v. *Breen*, 102 Kan. 766; 173 P. (2d) 2 (1918) 660
Brown v. *Brown*, 88 Conn. 42; 89 A. 889 (1914) 272
Brown v. *Cousens*, 51 Me. 301 (1864) 667
Brown v. *Pridgen*, 56 Tex. 124 (1882) 248
Bruggemeyer's Estate, In re, 115 Cal. App. 525; 2 P. (2d) 534 (1931)   205, 206, 253
Brunnert v. *Boeckmann's Estate*, 226 Mo. App. 494; 258 S. W. 768 (1924) . . 667
Brunswick Bank and Trust Company v. *Valentine*, 158 Va. 512; 164 S. E. 569
    (1932) 293
Bubb's Executors, In re, 132 Misc. 61; 229 N. Y. S. 567 (1928) 48
Buckeye v. *Buckeye*, 203 Wis. 248; 234 N. W. 342 (1931) 271
Bullen's Estate, In re, 47 Utah 96; 151 P. 533 (1915) 518
Bunker v. *Bunker*, 130 Me. 103; 154 A. 73 (1931) 610, 627
Burdick's Estate, In re, 112 Cal. 387; 44 P. 734 (1896) 226, 233

Caldwell v. *Blount*, 193 N. C. 560; 137 S. E. 578 (1928) 283
Campbell v. *Durant*, 110 Kan. 30; 202 P. 841 (1921) 660
Campbell v. *Johnson* (Tex. Civ. App.); 284 S. W. 261 (1926) 223
Case Threshing Machine Company, J. I., v. *Wiley*, 89 Wash. 597; 154 P. 437
    (1916) 224
Caudle v. *Morris*, 160 N. C. 168; 76 S. E. 17 (1912) 661
Circonte v. *Barba*, ... Del. . . . . ; 161 A. 925 (1932) 192
C.I.T. Corporation v. *Sanderson*, 43 F. (2d) 985 (1930) 46
Clements v. *Marston*, 52 N. H. 31 (1872) 601
Cole v. *Marvin*, 98 Ore. 175; 193 P. 828 (1920) 498
Colorado Fuel & Iron Company v. *Industrial Commission of Colorado*, 93 Colo.
    188; 24 P. (2d) 1117 (1933) 156
Commonwealth v. *Moore*, 162 Mass. 441; 38 N. E. 1120 (1894) 601
Commonwealth v. *Rutherfoord*, 160 Va. 524; 169 S. E. 909 (1933) 156
Commonwealth v. *Spencer*, 212 Mass. 438; 99 N. E. 266 (1912) 601
Cooke v. *Bremond*, 27 Tex. 457 (1864) 218
Cook's Estate, In re, 34 Nev. 217; 117 P. 27 (1911) 661
Cooper v. *Pearce*, 222 Ala. 540; 133 So. 583 (1931) 296
Cosper v. *Valley Bank*, 28 Ariz. 373; 237 P. 175 (1925) 224
Council v. *Pridgen*, 153 N. C. 443; 69 S. E. 404 (1910) 315
Cousins v. *Sun Life Assurance Society*, (1933) 1 Ch. 126; 174 L. Times 339–40
    (1932) 677
Crim v. *Austin* (Tex. Comm. of App.) ; 6 S. W. (2d) 348 (1928) . . . 217, 225
Crosby v. *Turner*, 200 Ala. 189; 75 So. 937 (1917) 283
Crouch v. *Edwards*, 52 Ark. 499; 12 S. W. 1070 (1890) 374
Curtis v. *Ashworth*, 165 Ga. 782; 142 S. E. 111 (1928) 26, 76

Daggett v. *State*, 86 Tex. Cr. 98; 215 S. W. 454 (1919) 602
Dahlman v. *Dahlman*, 28 Mont. 373; 72 P. 748 (1903) 609
Davis v. *Davis*, 101 Va. 230; 43 S. E. 358 (1903) 662
Davis v. *Davis*, 138 Va. 682; 123 S. E. 538 (1924) 463
Davis v. *Fyfe*, 107 Cal. App. 281; 290 P. 468 (1931) 50
Davis v. *State*, 157 Miss. 669; 128 So. 886 (1930) 601

PAGE

Dayton v. *Donart,* 22 Kan. 256 (1879) 660
Dayton Spice Mills Company v. *Sloan,* 49 Neb. 662; 68 N. W. 1040 (1896) . . 283
De Kyne v. *Lewis,* 5 N. J. Misc. 948; 139 A. 434 (1927) 295
Deutsch v. *Rohlfing,* 22 Colo. App. 534; 126 P. 1123 (1912) 276
DeVries v. *Conklin,* 22 Mich. 255 (1871) 45
Dinquel v. *Dacco,* 273 Ill. 117; 112 N. E. 337 (1916) 660
Dodgen v. *DeBorde,* 43 Ga. App. 131; 158 S. E. 64 (1931) 76
Donalson v. *Yeates,* 173 Ga. 30; 159 S. E. 856 (1931) 659
Dorn v. *Stidham,* 139 S. C. 66; 137 S. E. 331 (1926) 662
Dowell v. *Gray Von Allmen Milk Company,* 221 Ky. 780; 299 S. W. 965 (1927) 669
Dreamer v. *Oberlander,* 122 Neb. 335; 240 N. W. 435 (1932) 108
Dreier v. *Pomeroy,* 104 N. J. Eq. 504; 146 A. 178 (1929) 295, 316
Drishaus' Estate, In re, 199 Cal. 369; 249 P. 515 (1926) 205, 253
Druhl's Estate, In re, 61 N. D. 168; 237 N. W. 697 (1931) 634, 661
Dummir v. *Davis Bros. Lumber Company, Ltd.,* 17 La. App. 309; 135 So. 684
   (1931) 232
Dunn v. *Mullan,* 211 Cal. 583; 269 P. 604 (1931) 217
Dutton v. *Buckley,* 116 Ore. 661; 242 P. 626 (1926) 316

Ehler v. *Ehler,* 214 Ia. 789; 243 N. W. 591 (1932) 660
Eliason v. *Draper,* 25 Del. 1; 77 A. 572 (1910) 98
Ellis v. *Abbott,* 69 Ore. 234; 138 P. 488 (1914) 316
Emig v. *Daum,* 1 Ind. App. 146; 27 N. E. 322 (1890) 165
Engen v. *Union State Bank of Harvard,* 121 Neb. 257; 236 N. W. 741 (1931) 663
Evan's Estate, In re, 145 Minn. 252; 177 N. W. 126 (1920) 420
Evans v. *Morris,* 234 Mo. 177; 136 S. W. 408 (1911) 315
Everett v. *Ballard,* 174 N. C. 16; 93 S. E. 385 (1917) 296, 314

Falligant v. *Barrow,* 133 Ga. 87; 65 S. E. 149 (1909) 369, 450
Farmers' Exchange Bank v. *Hageluken,* 165 Mo. 443; 65 S. W. 728 (1901) . 315
Farrow v. *Farrow,* 172 N. J. Eq. 421; 65 A. 1009 (1907) 188
Feiner v. *Boynton,* 73 N. J. L. 136; 162 A. 420 (1905) 47
Fiedler v. *Fiedler,* 42 Okla. 124; 140 P. 1022 (1914) 25, 29, 272
First National Bank v. *Hallquist,* 48 N. D. 263; 184 N. W. 269 (1921) . . . 583
First National Bank v. *Leonard,* 36 Ore. 390; 59 P. 873 (1900) 45
First National Bank of Wahoo v. *Havlik,* 51 Neb. 668; 71 N. W. 291 (1897) . 283
First Wisconsin National Bank v. *Jahn,* 179 Wis. 117; 190 N. W. 822
   (1922) 24, 29, 46
Fisher v. *Marsh,* 69 Wash. 570; 125 P. 951 (1912) 225
Fitzmaurice v. *Fitzmaurice,* 62 N. D. 191; 242 N. W. 526 (1932) . . 24, 29, 272
Flandermeyer v. *Cooper,* 85 Ohio St. 327; 98 N. E. 102 (1912) . . . 87, 99
Fletcher v. *Wakefield,* 75 Vt. 257; 54 A. 1012 (1903) 283
Florida Citrus Exchange v. *Grisham,* 65 Fla. 46; 61 So. 123 (1913) . . 45, 184
Fontaine v. *Fontaine,* 205 Wis. 570; 238 N. W. 410 (1931) 30
Forsythe v. *Paschal,* 34 Ariz. 380; 271 P. 865 (1928) 225
Foster v. *Marshall,* 22 N. H. 491 (1851) 528
Foust v. *Hill,* 215 Ky. 364; 285 S. W. 235 (1926) 316

PAGE

Fowlie v. *First Minneapolis Trust Company*, 184 Minn. 82; 237 N. W. 846
(1931) 99
Frame v. *Frame*, 120 Tex. 61; 36 S. W. (2d) 152 (1931) 231
Frees, Estate of, 187 Cal. 150; 201 P. 112 (1921) 206, 253
Fritz v. *Tudor*, 64 Ky. (1 Bush) 28 (1866) 504
Funk v. *United States*, 290 U. S. 371; 54 Sup. Ct. 212; 78 L. Ed. 369
(1933) 584, 602

Garrett v. *State*, 109 Ind. 527; 10 N. E. 570 (1886) 165
Garza v. *Kenedy* (Tex. Comm. of App.); 299 S. W. 231 (1927) 669
George v. *Ransom*, 15 Cal. 322; 76 Amer. Dec. 490 (1860) 211
Gimenez v. *Great Atlantic and Pacific Tea Company*, 240 App. Div. 238; 269
N. Y. S. 463 (1934) 99
Globe Indemnity Company v. *J. R. Quesenberry*, 1 La. App. 364 (1924) . . . 75
Glover v. *Glover*, 45 S. C. 51; 22 S. E. 739 (1895) 627
Glover v. *Summerour*, 165 Ga. 513; 141 S. E. 211 (1928) 282
Goessling's Estate, In re, 287 Mo. 663; 230 S. W. 613 (1921) 415
Golden v. *State*, 22 Tex. App. 1; 2 S. W. 531 (1886) 165
Goodell v. *Kock*, 282 U. S. 118; 51 Sup. Ct. 62; 75 L. Ed. 247 (1930) . . . 233
Gorman v. *Gause* (Tex. Civ. App.); 36 S. W. (2d) 279 (1931) . . . 229, 231
Gotliffe v. *Edelston*, (1930) 2 K. B. 378 271
Gowin v. *Gowin* (Tex. Civ. App.); 264 S. W. 529 (1924) 272
Gray v. *Perlis*, 76 Cal. App. 511; 245 P. 221 (1926) 231
Greenwood v. *Martin's Bank*, (1932) 1 K. B. 371 161
Gridley v. *Wood*, 344 Ill. 153; 176 N. E. 356 (1931) 514
Guice v. *Lawrence*, 2 La. Ann. 226 (1847) 224
Gutierrez, In re, 33 F. (2d) 987 (1929) 225

H——, A., v. *H——, G. M.*, 139 L. T. Rep. 412 (1928) 156
Hagerman v. *Wigent*, 108 Mich. 192; 65 N. W. 756 (1896) 600
Hagert v. *Hagert*, 22 N. D. 290; 133 N. W. 1035 (1911) 109
Haines v. *Fort*, 93 Ga. 24; 18 S. E. 994 (1893) 315
Hall v. *Hall*, 236 Ky. 42; 32 S. W. (2d) 536 (1930) 284
Hamblin v. *Marchant*, 103 Kan. 508; 175 P. 678 (1918) 611
Hammett v. *Farrar* (Tex. Civ. App.); 8 S. W. (2d) 236 (1928) 296
Haning v. *United States*, 59 F. (2d) 942 (1932) 161
Harris v. *Brown*, 187 F. 6 (1911) 601
Hart v. *Stinger*, 46 F. (2d) 321 (1930) 282
Hartford-Connecticut Trust Company v. *Lawrence*, 106 Conn. 178; 138 A. 159
(1927) 463
Hawkins v. *Britton State Bank* (Tex. Comm. of App.); 52 S. W. (2d) 243
(1932) 254
Hawkins v. *Corbit*, 83 Okla. 275; 201 P. 649 (1921) 583
Hentges v. *Hoye*, 158 Minn. 402; 197 N. W. 852 (1924) 450
Herbert v. *Wren*, 7 Cranch 369 (1813) 504
Hernandez v. *Becker*, 54 F. (2d) 542 (1931) 254
Higgins v. *Stokes*, 116 Ky. 664; 74 S. W. 251 (1903) 669

PAGE

Hinson v. *Booth,* 39 Fla. 333; 22 So. 687 (1897) 659

Hipp v. *Dupont de Nemours Company,* 182 N. C. 9; 108 S. E. 316 (1921) . . 98

Hirsch v. *United States,* 62 F. (2d) 128 (1932) 254

Holland v. *Moon,* 39 Ark. 120 (1882) 323

Holleman v. *Harward,* 119 N. C. 150; 25 S. E. 972 (1896) 86

Holmes v. *Holmes,* 27 Okla. 140; 111 P. 220 (1910) 662

Hopkins v. *Bacon,* 282 U. S. 122; 51 Sup. Ct. 62; 75 L. Ed. 249 (1930) . . . 233

Hughes v. *Holman,* 110 Ore. 415; 223 P. 730 (1924) 30

Hulsman v. *Ireland,* 205 Cal. 345; 270 P. 498 (1928) 253

Hunt v. *State,* 72 Ark. 241; 79 S. W. 769 (1904) 165

Hunter v. *State,* 10 Okla. Cr. 119; 134 P. 1134 (1913) 602

Jackson v. *Griffen,* 39 Ariz. 183; 4 P. (2d) 900 (1931) 228

Jackson v. *Wilson,* 117 Ala. 432; 23 So. 521 (1897) 659

Jacobin v. *Pope and Talbot,* 214 Cal. 758; 7 P. (2d) 1017 (1932) 663

Jameson v. *Tully,* 178 Cal. 380; 173 P. 577 (1918) 98

Jefferson County Bank v. *Hale,* 152 Tenn. 648; 280 S. W. 408 (1925) . 316, 318

Johnson, Estate of, 175 Wis. 248; 185 N. W. 180 (1921) 471

Johnson v. *Taylor,* 120 Cal. App. 771; 4 P. (2d) 999 (1931) 34, 225

Jones v. *Commonwealth,* 252 Ky. 341; 67 S. W. (2d) 480 (1934) 601

Jones v. *Davies,* 5 H. and N. 766 (1860) 528

Jones & Company v. *Black* (Tex. Civ. App.); 42 S. W. (2d) 151 (1931) . . . 46

Jordan v. *State,* 142 Ind. 422; 41 N. E. 817 (1895) 165

Jorgenson v. *Minneapolis Threshing Company,* 64 Minn. 489; 67 N. W. 364
(1896) 282

June v. *LaBadie,* 132 Mich. 135; 92 N. W. 937 (1903); 100 N. W. 996 (1904) . 45

Katzenberg v. *Katzenberg,* 183 Ark. 626; 37 S. W. (2d) 696 (1931) . . 29, 272

Keeney v. *McVoy,* 206 Mo. 42; 103 S. W. 946 (1907) 370

Kelley v. *Proctor,* 41 N. H. 139 (1860) 588

Kemph v. *Belknap,* 15 Ind. App. 77; 43 N. E. 891 (1895) 555

Kennedy v. *Duncan,* 224 Mo. 661; 123 S. W. 856 (1909) 486

Kennedy v. *Kennedy,* 74 S. C. 541; 54 S. E. 773 (1906) 662

Kennington v. *Hemmingway,* 101 Miss. 259; 57 So. 809 (1912) 284

Kilgore v. *Hanley,* 27 W. Va. 451 (1886) 601

Kindly v. *Spraker,* 72 Ark. 228; 79 S. W. 766 (1904) 581

King v. *City of Owensboro,* 187 Ky. 21; 218 S. W. 297 (1920) 161

King v. *Merritt,* 67 Mich. 194; 34 N. W. 689 (1887) 496

Kittredge v. *Grau,* 158 La. 154; 103 So. 723 (1925) 213

Kneuven v. *Berliner's Estate* (Mo. App.); 54 S. W. (2d) 494 (1932) . . . 667

Kollar v. *Noble,* 184 Ark. 297; 42 S. W. (2d) 408 (1931) 415

Kopcyznski v. *State,* 137 Wis. 358; 118 N. W. 863 (1908) 165

Kosanke v. *Kosanke,* 137 Minn. 115; 162 N. W. 1060 (1917) 103

Kosciolek v. *Portland Railway, Light and Power Company,* 81 Ore. 517;
160 P. 132 (1916) 25, 29, 88

Krueger v. *Groth,* 190 Wis. 387; 209 N. W. 773 (1926) 663

PAGE

Lamphier v. *State*, 70 Ind. 317 (1880) 165

Landwehr v. *Barbas*, 241 App. Div. 769; 270 N. Y. S. 534 (1934) 86, 99

Lee v. *Hall Music Company*, 120 Tex. 14; 35 S. W. (2d) 685, 687 (1931) . . 45

Lee v. *Hempy*, 35 Ohio App. 402; 172 N. E. 421 (1929) 677

Leffin v. *Jeffers* (Tex. Comm. of App.) ; 52 S. W. (2d) 81 (1932) 253

Leonetti v. *Tolton*, 264 Mich. 618; 250 N. W. 512 (1933) 583

Lerch v. *Barnes*, 61 Fla. 672; 54 So. 763 (1911) 314

Leucht v. *Leucht*, 129 Ky. 700; 112 S. W. 845 (1908) 600

Levell v. *Metropolitan Life Insurance Company*, 118 Cal. App. 426; 5 P. (2d)
   430 (1931) 234

Lillienkamp v. *Rippetoe*, 133 Tenn. 57; 179 S. W. 628 (1915) 29

Little v. *Simmons*, 222 Ala. 206; 131 So. 561 (1930) 659

Livingston v. *Superior Court*, 117 Cal. 633; 49 P. 836 (1897) 109

Lob's Sons v. *Karnofsky* (La. App.) ; 144 So. 164 (1932) ; Reversed in 177
   La. 229; 148 So. 34 (1933) 345

Lord Advocate v. *Jaffrey*, 124 L. T. R. 129 (1920) 23

Lord Audley's Case, 3 How. State Trials 402 (1631) 165

Loughran v. *Loughran*, 66 F. (2d) 567 (1933) 445

Lovejoy v. *Cockrell* (Tex. Comm. of App.) ; 63 S. W. (2d) 1009 (1933) . . . 254

Luse v. *Reed*, 63 Minn. 5; 65 N. W. 91 (1895) 282

McArthur, Estate of, 210 Cal. 439; 292 P. 469 (1930) 253, 628

McCaffrey v. *Benson*, 40 La. Ann. 10; 3 So. 393 (1888) 251

McCarthy v. *Walsh*, 123 Me. 157; 122 A. 406 (1923) 463

McCord v. *Bright*, 44 Ind. App. 275; 87 N. E. 654 (1909) 284

McCormick v. *State*, 135 Tenn. 218; 186 S. W. 95 (1915) 601

McCoy v. *Niblick*, 228 Pa. 342; 77 A. 551 (1910) 296

McCoy v. *State*, 221 Ala. 466; 129 So. 21 (1930) 600

McGehee v. *McGehee*, 152 Md. 661; 136 A. 905 (1927) 463

McHugh's Estate, In re, 165 Wash. 123; 4 P. (2d) 834 (1931) 228

McIrvin v. *Lincoln Memorial University*, 138 Tenn. 260; 197 S. W. 862 (1917) 664

McKay v. *Lauriston*, 204 Cal. 557; 269 P. 519 (1928) 234

McKinney v. *Merritt*, 35 Idaho 600; 208 P. 244 (1922) 220

McMahon v. *Gray*, 150 Mass. 289; 22 N. E. 923 (1889) 471

McMillan v. *United States Fire Insurance Company*, 48 Idaho 163; 280 P. 220
   (1929) 225

Mains v. *Webber's Estate*, 131 Mich. 213; 91 N. W. 172 (1902) 189

Mann v. *Nies*, 213 Ia. 121; 238 N. W. 601 (1932) 292

Mark v. *Title Guarantee and Trust Company*, 122 Cal. App. 301; 9 P. (2d)
   839 (1932) 221, 253

Marri v. *Stamford Street Railway Company*, 84 Conn. 9; 78 A. 582 (1911) 86, 99

Marston v. *Norton*, 5 N. H. 205 (1830) 274

Marston v. *Rue*, 92 Wash. 129; 159 P. 111 (1916) 222

Martin v. *Martin*, 313 Mo. 476; 285 S. W. 92 (1926) 661

Martin v. *Robson*, 65 Ill. 129 (1872) 3

Masson, Templier & Company v. *De Fries*, (1909) 2 K. B. (C. A.) 831 . . . 188

Matt v. *Smith*, 16 Cal. 533 (1860) 323

PAGE

Mayo v. *Hutchinson,* 57 Me. 546 (1870) 45
Messimer v. *Echols* (Tex. Civ. App.) ; 194 S. W. 1171 (1917) 214
Metzler v. *Metzler,* 8 N. J. Misc. 821 ; 151 A. 847 (1930) 72
Micou v. *McDonald,* 55 Fla. 776 ; 46 So. 291 (1908) 45
Minchew v. *Hankins* (Tex. Civ. App.) ; 278 S. W. 306 (1925) 284
Mock v. *Neffler et al.,* 148 Ga. 25 ; 95 S. E. 673 (1918) 194
Moffitt's Estate, In re, 153 Cal. 359 ; 95 P. 653 (1908) 226
Moffitt v. *Kelly,* 218 U. S. 400 ; 31 Sup. Ct. 79 ; 54 L. Ed. 1086 (1910) . . . 226
Monahan v. *Monahan,* 77 Vt. 133 ; 59 A. 169 (1903) 194
Morris v. *Masters,* 349 Ill. 455 ; 182 N. E. 406 (1932) 64
Morris v. *Pennsgrove National Bank and Trust Company,* 115 N. J. Eq. 219 ;
    170 A. 16 (1934) 669
Morton v. *State,* 141 Tenn. 357 ; 209 S. W. 644 (1918) 29
Moulin v. *Monteleone,* 165 La. 169 ; 115 So. 447 (1927) 29
Muskogee Electric Traction Company v. *Green,* 91 Okla. 200 ; 217 P. 155 (1923) 194

Nash v. *Mobile & Ohio Railroad Company,* 149 Miss. 823 ; 116 So. 100 (1928) 25, 88
Neasham v. *McNair,* 103 Ia. 695 ; 72 N. W. 773 ; 38 L. R. A. 847 (1897) . . . 103
Nick v. *Nick,* 195 Ia. 351 ; 189 N. W. 829 (1922) 369
Nickerson v. *Nickerson,* 65 Tex. 281 (1886) 215
Nieberg v. *Cohen,* 88 Vt. 281 ; 92 A. 214 (1914) 98
Nissley v. *Brubaker,* 192 Pa. St. 388 ; 43 A. 967 (1899) 668
Noble's Estate, In re, 194 Ia. 733 ; 190 N. W. 511 (1922) 369, 610
Nolan v. *Moore,* 96 Tex. 341 ; 72 S. W. 583 (1903) 323
Northern Texas Traction Company v. *Hill* (Tex. Civ. App.) ; 297 S. W.
    778 (1927) 214, 246

O'Brien v. *Galley-Stockton Shoe Company,* 65 Colo. 70 ; 173 P. 544 (1918) . . 104
Offenbacker v. *Offenbacker* (Ind. App.) ; 187 N. E. 903 (1933) 196
O'Hagan v. *Fraternal Aid Union,* 144 S. C. 84 ; 141 S. E. 893 (1927) . . . 677
Oppenheim v. *Kridel,* 236 N. Y. 156 ; 140 N. E. 227 (1923) 87
O'Rourke v. *Cleary,* 104 Vt. 312 ; 163 A. 583 (1933) 634
Osborne v. *Cooper,* 113 Ala. 405 ; 21 So. 320 (1896) 283
Osborne v. *Osborne,* 40 F. (2d) 800 (1930) 72
Osgood v. *Breed,* 12 Mass. 525 (1815) 274
O'Shea, In re Estate of, 85 Neb. 156 ; 122 N. W. 881 (1909) 661
Ostheller v. *Spokane and Inland Empire Railroad Company,* 107 Wash. 678 ;
    182 P. 630 (1919) 215
Overby v. *Williams,* 170 Ky. 140 ; 185 S. W. 822 (1916) 660
Overton v. *State,* 43 Tex. 616 (1875) 165

Pauley v. *Knouse,* 109 Neb. 716 ; 192 N. W. 195 (1923) 315
People v. *Chapman,* 62 Mich. 280 (1886) 165
People v. *Graff,* 59 Cal. App. 706 ; 211 P. 829 (1922) 165, 166
People v. *Kirkpatrick,* 77 Cal. App. 104 ; 246 P. 84 (1926) 165
People v. *McClelland,* 146 Misc. 545 ; 263 N. Y. S. 403 (1933) 166
People v. *MacMullen,* 134 Cal. App. 81 ; 24 P. (2d) 794 (1933) . . . 164, 166

PAGE

People v. *Sybisloo,* 261 Mich. 1; 184 N. W. 410 (1921) 161
People ex rel. Troare v. *McClelland,* 146 Misc. 545; 263 N. Y. S. 403
   (1933) 163, 165
Perkins v. *Sunset Telephone and Telegraph Company,* 155 Cal. 712; 103 P.
   190 (1909) 231
Pfaff v. *Bender,* 38 F. (2d) 642 (1929) 230
Phillips v. *Phillips,* 141 Ark. 583; 217 S. W. 794 (1920) 285
Place v. *Searle,* (1932) 2 K. B. 497 98
Poe v. *Seaborn,* 282 U. S. 101; 51 Sup. Ct. 58; 75 L. Ed. 239 (1930) . . 233, 254
Pollock v. *Columbia Bank,* 193 Wis. 389; 214 N. W. 363 (1927) 471
Ponder v. *Morris & Brothers,* 152 Ala. 531; 44 So. 651 (1906) 48
Pons v. *Yazoo and M.V.R. Company,* 122 La. 156; 47 So. 449 (1908) . . . 282
Pretzer v. *Pretzer,* 215 Cal. 659; 12 P. (2d) 429 (1932) 220
Price v. *Brittain,* 80 Ind. App. 294; 137 N. E. 620 (1923) 284
Pritchard v. *Pritchard,* 93 Ind. App. 89; 177 N. E. 502 (1931) 601
Pumphrey v. *Pumphrey,* 52 Ark. 193; 12 S. W. 390 (1889) 451

Radl v. *Radl,* 72 Minn. 81; 75 N. W. 111 (1898) 450
Raines v. *Mercer,* 165 Tenn. 415; 55 S. W. (2d) 263 (1932) 29
Ralston v. *Ralston,* (1930) 2 K. B. 238 271
Ray v. *Bushakra,* 237 Ky. 178; 35 S. W. (2d) 19 (1931) 284
Real v. *Hollister,* 17 Neb. 661; 24 N. W. 333 (1885) 315
Reid v. *Reid,* 216 Ia. 882; 249 N. W. 387 (1933) 196
Rex v. *Creamer,* 35 Times L. R. 281 (1919) 166
Rex v. *Lapworth,* (1931) 1 K. B. 117 602
Rhode Island Hospital Trust Company v. *Briggs,* 52 R. I. 254; 160 A. 197 (1932) 416
Rice v. *McCarthy,* 73 Cal. App. 655; 239 P. 56 (1925) 221
Rice v. *Rice,* 12 Del. Ch. 245; 111 A. 439 (1920) 415
Richardson v. *State,* 103 Md. 112; 63 A. 317 (1906) 601
Riley v. *Wilson,* 86 Tex. 240; 24 S. W. 394 (1893) 284
Roan v. *Holmes,* 32 Fla. 295; 13 So. 339 (1893) 501
Roberge v. *Town of Troy,* 105 Vt. 134; 163 A. 770 (1933) 185
Robert v. *Haines,* 112 Ga. 842; 38 S. E. 109 (1901) 194
Roco v. *Green,* 50 Tex. 483 (1878) 629
Root v. *Root,* 164 Mich. 638; 130 N. W. 194 (1911) 336
Ruby v. *Ruby,* 112 W. Va. 62; 163 S. E. 717 (1932) 439

Sacknoff v. *Sacknoff,* 131 Me. 280; 161 A. 669 (1932) 272
Saks v. *Huddleston,* 36 F. (2d) 537 (1929) 50
Sanders v. *McMillan,* 98 Ala. 144; 11 So. 750 (1892) 503
Sanders v. *Wallace,* 118 Ala. 418; 24 So. 354 (1898) 416
Sanger v. *Sanger,* 132 Kan. 596; 296 P. 355 (1931) 64
Schelling v. *Thomas,* 96 Cal. App. 682; 274 P. 755 (1929) 220
Schenk's Estate, In re, 53 Utah 381; 178 P. 344 (1919) 662
Schoeffner v. *Schoeffner,* 163 La. 146; 111 So. 655 (1927) 213
Schofield v. *Gold,* 26 Ariz. 296; 225 P. 71 (1924) 232
Schramm v. *Steele,* 97 Wash. 309; 166 P. 634 (1917) 224

PAGE

Schreffler v. *Chase*, 245 Ill. 395; 92 N. E. 272 (1910) 587
Schultz v. *Christopher*, 65 Wash. 496; 118 P. 629 (1911) 29
Scott v. *Scott*, 324 Mo. 1055; 26 S. W. (2d) 598 (1930) 435, 552
Scott v. *Vaughn*, 83 S. C. 362; 65 S. E. 269 (1909) 416
Selaster v. *Simmons*, 39 Ariz. 432; 7 P. (2d) 258 (1932) 223, 233
Sharp v. *Zeller*, 110 La. 61; 34 So. 129 (1902) 213
Sheard v. *Oregon Electric Company*, 137 Ore. 341; 2 P. (2d) 916 (1931) . . 99
Shearin v. *Shearin*, 161 Tenn. 172; 29 S. W. (2d) 254 (1930) 535
Sherman v. *Weber*, 113 N. J. Eq. 451; 167 A. 517 (1933) 191
Sherry v. *Moore*, 258 Mass. 420; 155 N. E. 441 (1927) 98
Shields v. *Barton*, 60 F. (2d) 351 (1932) 254
Shields v. *Parsons*, 230 Ky. 143; 18 S. W. (2d) 961 (1929) 660
Shore v. *Holt*, 185 N. C. 212; 117 S. E. 165 (1923) 267
Siberell v. *Siberell* (Cal.); 295 P. 385 (1931) 253
Siberell v. *Siberell*, 214 Cal. 767; 7 P. (2d) 1003 (1932) 218, 231
Sill's Estate, In re, 121 Cal. App. 202; 9 P. (2d) 243 (1932) 231
Slater v. *Slater*, 124 Va. 370; 98 S. E. 7 (1919) 526
Sloss-Sheffield Steel and Iron Company v. *Yancey*, 202 Ala. 458; 80 So. 842
   (1919) 494
Smith v. *Martin*, 124 Mich. 34; 82 N. W. 662 (1900) 32
Smith v. *Meyers*, 52 Neb. 70; 71 N. W. 1006 (1897) 601
Smith v. *Nicholas Building Company*, 93 Ohio St. 101; 112 N. E. 204 (1915) . 98
Smith v. *State*, 198 Ind. 156; 152 N. E. 803 (1926) 602
Snortium v. *Snortium*, 155 Minn. 230; 193 N. W. 304 (1923) 282
Snyder v. *People*, 26 Mich. 105 (1872) 165
Solko v. *Jones*, 117 Cal. App. 372; 3 P. (2d) 1028 (1931) 215
Sparks v. *Kuss*, 195 Wis. 378; 216 N. W. 929; 218 N. W. 208 (1928) 46
Speer v. *Speer*, 67 Ga. 748 (1881) 415
Spreckels v. *Spreckels*, 116 Cal. 339; 48 P. 228 (1898) 234
State v. *Arnold*, 182 Minn. 313; 235 N. W. 373 (1931) 29, 165, 166
State v. *Asper*, 35 N. M. 203; 292 P. 225 (1930) 161
State v. *Banks*, 48 Ind. 197 (1874) 165
State v. *Bramlett*, 114 S. C. 389; 103 S. E. 755 (1920) 601
State v. *Clayton*, 162 Tenn. 368; 38 S. W. (2d) 551 (1931) 518
State v. *Dowell*, 106 N. C. 722; 11 S. E. 525 (1890) 165
State v. *Edens*, 95 N. C. 693; 59 Amer. Rep. 294 (1886) 165
State v. *Fulton*, 149 N. C. 485; 63 S. E. 145 (1908) 165
State v. *Garris*, 98 N. J. L. 608; 121 A. 292 (1914) 136
State v. *Haines*, 51 La. Ann. 731; 25 So. 372 (1889) 165
State v. *Hogg*, 126 La. 1053; 53 So. 225 (1910) 165
State v. *Jackson*, 143 Miss. 745; 109 So. 724 (1926) 136
State v. *Jaroslowski*, 30 Del. 108; 103 A. 657 (1918) 600
State v. *Kirby*, 167 Tenn. 307; 69 S. W. (2d) 886 (1934) 165
State v. *Koontz*, 124 Kan. 216; 257 P. 944 (1927) 165
State v. *Lankford*, 6 Boyce (Del.) 594; 102 A. 63 (1917) 166
State v. *Parker*, 3 Ohio Dec. (Reprint) 551 (1882) 165
State v. *Phillips*, 85 Ohio St. 317; 97 N. E. 976 (1912) 165

PAGE

State v. *Pitts*, 12 S. C. 180; 32 Amer. Rep. 508 (1879) 189
State v. *Ralston*, 131 Kan. 138; 289 P. 409 (1930) 601
State v. *Renslow*, 209 Ia. 982; 230 N. W. 316 (1930) 161
State v. *Reynolds*, 48 S. C. 384; 26 S. E. 679 (1896) 601
State v. *Roth*, 117 Minn. 404; 136 N. W. 12 (1912) 165
State v. *Sansome*, 133 Miss. 428; 97 So. 753 (1923) 136
State v. *Shaw*, 79 Kan. 396; 100 P. 78 (1909) 162, 165
State v. *Snyder*, 93 N. J. L. 18; 107 A. 167 (1919) 601
State v. *Todd*, 173 La. 23; 136 So. 76 (1931) 601
Stayton v. *State*, 46 Tex. Cr. 205; 78 S. W. 1071 (1904) 165
Stephens v. *Stephens* (Tex. Civ. App.); 292 S. W. 290 (1927) 212
Stevens v. *Hush*, 104 Misc. 69; 171 N. Y. S. 41 (1918) 47
Stewart v. *Stewart*, 199 Cal. 318; 249 P. 197 (1926); 204 Cal. 546; 269 P.
    439 (1928) 233, 234
Stone v. *Stone*, 185 Ark. 390; 47 S. W. (2d) 50 (1932) 659
Stout v. *Van Zante*, 109 Ore. 430; 219 P. 804 (1923) 29
Strand, Ex parte, 123 Cal. App. 170; 11 P. (2d) 89 (1932) 602
Street v. *Bertolone*, 193 Cal. 751; 226 P. 913 (1924) 225
Strom v. *Strom*, 98 Minn. 427; 107 N. W. 1047 (1906) 25, 29
Suiter v. *Suiter*, 323 Ill. 519; 154 N. E. 337 (1926) 463
Sumner v. *Conant*, 10 Vt. 9 (1836) 323
Sutton v. *Harvey*, 24 Tex. Civ. App. 26; 57 S. W. 879 (1900) 248
Syndergaard's Estate, In re, 31 Utah 490; 88 P. 616 (1907) 662

Taylor v. *Murphy*, 50 Tex. 291 (1883) 225
Teague v. *Fairchild* (Tex. Comm. of App.); 15 S. W. (2d) 585 (1929) 214, 246, 253
Teckenbrock v. *McLaughlin*, 246 Mo. 711; 152 S. W. 38 (1912) 529
Terry v. *Humphrey*, 27 N. M. 564; 203 P. 539 (1922) 220
Thiebeault v. *Poole*, 283 Mass. 480; 186 N. E. 632 (1933) 99
Thomas v. *James*, 84 Okla. 91; 202 P. 499 (1921) 583
Thomas v. *Thomas*, 51 Ill. 162 (1869) 165
Thompson v. *Société Catholique d'Education Religieuse et Littéraire*, 157 La.
    875; 103 So. 247 [1925] 247
Thompson v. *Thompson*, 218 U. S. 611; 31 Sup. Ct. 111; 54 L. Ed. 1180 (1910) 272
Thompson v. *Union and Mercantile Trust Company*, 164 Ark. 411; 262 S. W.
    324 (1924) 374
Thornton's Estate, In re, 221 Cal. 1; 33 P. (2d) 1 (1934) 205, 216
Tillie v. *Finley*, 126 Ohio St. 578; 186 N. E. 448 (1933) 50
Tillotson v. *Foster*, 310 Ill. 52; 141 N. E. 412 (1923) 493
Todok v. *Union State Bank of Harvard*, 281 U. S. 449; 50 Sup. Ct. 363; 74
    L. Ed. 956 (1930) 663
Tomasello v. *State*, 91 Ind. App. 970; 173 N. E. 235 (1930) 161
Torlonia v. *Torlonia*, 108 Conn. 292; 142 A. 843 (1928) 156
Trimble v. *Kentucky River Coal Corporation*, 235 Ky. 301; 31 S. W. (2d) 367
    (1930) 394
Tucker v. *Tucker*, 224 Mo. App. 669; 31 S. W. (2d) 238 (1930) 601
Turner v. *Heavrin*, 182 Ky. 65; 206 S. W. 23 (1918) 98

PAGE

Union National Bank of Greeley v. *Wright*, 78 Colo. 346; 242 P. 54 (1925) . . 659

Union Securities Company v. *Smith*, 93 Wash. 115; 160 P. 304 (1916) . . . 230

United States v. *Malcolm*, 282 U. S. 792; 51 Sup. Ct. 184; 75 L. Ed. 714
(1931) 234, 253

United States v. *Robbins*, 269 U. S. 315; 46 Sup. Ct. 148; 70 L. Ed. 285
(1926) 233, 234

Urquhart v. *Oliver*, 56 Ga. 345 (1876) 276

Vandegrift's Estate, In re, 105 Pa. Super. Ct. 293; 161 A. 898 (1932) . . . 292

Van Maren v. *Johnson*, 15 Cal. 308 (1860) 225, 233

Vann v. *Edwards*, 135 N. C. 661; 47 S. E. 784 (1904) 320

Van Veen v. *Van Veen*, 213 Ia. 323; 238 N. W. 718 (1931) 471

Villescas v. *Arizona Copper Company*, 20 Ariz. 268; 179 P. 963 (1919) . . 224

Volz v. *Zang*, 113 Wash. 378; 194 P. 409 (1920) 230

Vosburg v. *Mallory*, 155 Ia. 165; 135 N. W. 577 (1912) 552

Voss v. *Stortz*, 177 Ky. 541; 197 S. W. 964 (1917) 558

Vukodonovich v. *State*, 197 Ind. 169; 150 N. E. 56 (1926) 601

Wadsworth v. *Webster*, 257 N. Y. S. 386 (1932) 272

Wait v. *Pierce*, 191 Wis. 202; 209 N. W. 475 (1926) 25, 30, 272

Walker v. *Reamy*, 36 Pa. St. 410 (1860) 165

Wallace v. *Mason*, 100 Ky. 560; 38 S. W. 887 (1897) 184

Walston v. *Allen*, 82 Vt. 549; 74 A. 225 (1909) 283

Ward v. *Wolf*, 56 Ia. 465; 9 N. W. 350 (1881) 369

Warren v. *Dail*, 170 N. C. 406; 87 S. E. 126 (1915) 296

Watkins, Succession of, 156 La. 1000; 101 So. 395 (1924) 213

Webster v. *Snyder*, 103 Fla. 1131; 138 So. 755 (1932) 271

Weddington v. *Adkins*, 245 Ky. 747; 54 S. W. (2d) 331 (1932) 660

Weidman v. *Weidman*, 274 Mass. 118; 174 N. E. 206 (1931) 271

Westerman v. *Westerman*, 25 Ohio St. 500 (1874) 601

White, Succession of, 170 La. 403; 127 So. 883 (1930) 660

White v. *State*, 44 Ohio App. 331; 185 N. E. 64 (1933) 138

White v. *Stump*, 266 U. S. 310; 45 Sup. Ct. 103; 69 L. Ed. 301 (1924) . . 663

Whitehead v. *Brownsville Bank*, 166 Tenn. 249; 61 S. W. (2d) 975 (1933) . . 527

Whitfield v. *State*, 85 Fla. 142; 95 So. 430 (1923) 600

Williams v. *Paine*, 169 U. S. 55 (1897) 323

Wimmer v. *Nicholson*, 151 Wash. 199; 275 P. 699 (1929) 224

Wolff v. *Meyer*, 75 N. J. L. 181; 66 A. 959 (1907) 296

Wright & Webb v. *Cennandale*, 46 T. L. R. 403 (1930) 50

Y and O Coal Company v. *Paszka*, 20 Ohio App. 248; 152 N. E. 31 (1925) . . 32

Zitlow v. *State*, 213 Wis. 493; 252 N. W. 358 (1934) 138

TABLE OF STATUTORY SOURCES

In the following table are listed the statutory sources which were examined for the material used in Volume III of *American Family Laws*. The list is substantially the same as the list in Volume II. In eleven states (California, Illinois, Massachusetts, North Carolina, Ohio, Oklahoma, Tennessee, Texas, Utah, Wisconsin, Wyoming) later compilations became available and are cited in this volume.

In all states the constitutions, together with the latest amendments, have also been examined.

For abbreviations used in citing statutory material, see Table of Abbreviations. In citing the annual laws, variously called "Acts," "Session Laws," "Laws," etc., one uniform term will be used, viz., Session Laws, abbreviated, Sess. L.

TABLE OF STATUTORY SOURCES

Jurisdiction	Revision or Code Edition	Latest Annual Statute
Alabama	Code, 1923	General and Local Acts, extra session, 1933
Alaska	Compiled Laws, 1913	Session Laws, 1933
Arizona	Revised Code, 1928	Session Laws, first special session, 1931–32
Arkansas	Crawford and Moses, Digest of the Statutes, 1921 Castle's Supplement to Crawford and Moses, Digest, 1927	Acts, special sessions, 1933–34
California	Civil Code, 1933 (Lake) Code of Civil Procedure, 1933 (Lake) Penal Code, 1933 (Lake) Probate Code, 1933 (Lake) Deering, Political Code, 1931 Deering, General Laws, 1931	Statutes and Amendments to the Codes, 1933
Colorado	Compiled Laws, 1921	Session Laws, second extraordinary session, 1933–34

Jurisdiction	Revision or Code Edition	Latest Annual Statute
Connecticut	General Statutes, Revision of 1930 Cumulative Supplement to same, January sessions, 1931, 1933	Public Acts, 1933
Delaware	Revised Code, 1915	Laws, 1933
District of Columbia..	Code of the District of Columbia, 1929	Statutes of the United States, 1931–33
Florida	Revised General Statutes, 1920	Laws, 1933 (General Laws)
Georgia	Code, 1926; Annotated 1930 Supplement to Code	Laws, 1933
Hawaii	Revised Laws, 1925	Session Laws, regular session, 1933 Session Laws, special session, 1933
Idaho	Compiled Statutes, 1919	General Laws, extraordinary session, 1933
Illinois	Cahill, Revised Statutes, 1931	Laws, 1933 Laws, special session, 1933
Indiana	Burns's Annotated Statutes, 1926 (Watson's Revision), and Supplement of 1929	Acts, special session, 1932
Iowa	Code, 1927	Acts, extra session, 1933–34
Kansas	Revised Statutes, 1923 Supplement to same, 1931	Laws, special session, 1933–34
Kentucky	Carroll's Statutes, 1922 Baldwin's Statute Service, 1926 (supplementing Carroll's Statutes) Codes of Practice, 1906	Acts, 1934 Acts, special session, 1934
Louisiana	Revised Civil Code, 1920 Marr's Revised Code of Practice, 1927 Marr's Annotated Revised Statutes, 1915; Supplement of 1926 to Marr's Statutes	Acts, regular session, 1934; extra sessions, 1933–34
Maine	Revised Statutes, 1930	Acts and Resolves, special session, 1934

Jurisdiction	Revision or Code Edition	Latest Annual Statute
Maryland	Bagby, Annotated Code, 1924 Supplement to same, 1929	Laws, 1933 Laws, special session, 1933
Massachusetts	General Laws (Tercentenary Edition), 1932	Acts and Resolves, 1933 Acts, extra session, 1933
Michigan	Compiled Laws, 1929	Public Acts, extra sessions, 1933–34
Minnesota	General Statutes, 1923 Appendix and Addenda to same, 1926	Laws, 1933
Mississippi	Code, 1930, Annotated	General Laws, 1934 (including extraor- dinary session, 1932)
Missouri	Revised Statutes, 1929	Laws, extra session, 1933–34
Montana	Revised Codes, 1921 Supplement to same, 1927	Laws, extraordinary session, 1933–34
Nebraska	Compiled Statutes, 1929	Laws, 1933
Nevada	Compiled Laws, 1929 (Hillyer)	Statutes, 1933
New Hampshire	Public Laws, 1926	Laws, 1933
New Jersey.........	Compiled Statutes, 1910 Cumulative Supplement to same, 1911–24 Supplement to same, 1925–30	Laws, 1933
New Mexico.........	Statutes, Annotated, Compilation of 1929	Laws, 1933
New York...........	Cahill's Consolidated Laws, 1930 Cahill, Civil Practice, 1931; Cumu- lative Supplement to same, 1932 Cahill, Criminal Code, 1928	Laws, 1934 (including extraordinary session)
North Carolina	Code, 1927 Supplement to same, 1929	Public Laws, 1933 Public-Local and Private Laws, 1933
North Dakota........	Compiled Laws, 1913 Supplement to same, 1925	Laws, 1933
Ohio	Page's Complete General Code, 1931 Supplement to same, 1932	Laws, 1933

Jurisdiction	Revision or Code Edition	Latest Annual Statute
Oklahoma	Statutes, 1931	Session Laws, regular and extraordinary sessions, 1933
Oregon	Code, Annotated (Official Edition), 1930	Laws, special and regular sessions, 1933
Pennsylvania	Statutes, 1920 (West) Cumulative Supplement to same, 1928 (West)	Acts and Vetoes, special session, 1933–34
Rhode Island	General Laws, 1923	Acts and Resolves, 1933
South Carolina	Code of Laws, 1922	Acts, 1934
South Dakota	Compiled Laws, 1929	Session Laws, 1933 Laws, special session, 1933
Tennessee	Code, 1932	Public Acts, 1933
Texas	Complete Statutes, 1928 Supplement to same, 1931	General and Special Laws, third and fourth called sessions, 1934
Utah	Revised Statutes, 1933, Annotated	Laws, 1933 Laws, second special session, 1933
Vermont	General Laws, 1917	Laws, 1933 Laws, special session, 1933
Virginia	Code of 1930, Annotated	Acts of Assembly, extra session, 1933; regular session, 1934
Washington	Remington's Compiled Statutes, 1922 Supplement to same, 1927	Laws, 1933 Laws, special session, 1933
West Virginia	Official Code, 1931	Acts, regular and first extraordinary sessions, 1933; extraordinary session, 1932
Wisconsin	Statutes, 1931	Laws, 1933
Wyoming	Revised Statutes, 1931, Annotated	Session Laws, 1933 Special Session Laws, 1933

TABLE OF ABBREVIATIONS

[The usual abbreviations are used for citations to law magazines, legal reports, and encyclopedias]

Amd. ....Amended or Amendment
Ann. C. ....Annotated Code
Ann. St. ....Annotated Statute
App. ....Appendix
Art. ....Article

B. R. ....Bill of Rights

C. ....Code
C. C. ....Civil Code
C. C. P. ......Code of Civil Procedure
C. Cr. P. ..Code of Criminal Procedure
C. of L. ....Code of Law
C. of Prac. ....Code of Practice
Ch. ....Chapter
Civ. Prac. Act......Civil Practice Act
Cl. ....Clause
Comp. L. ....Compiled Laws
Comp. St. ....Compiled Statutes
Consol. L. ....Consolidated Laws
Consol. St. ......Consolidated Statutes
Const. ....Constitution
Cr. C. ....Criminal Code

Dig. ....Digest
Div. ....Division

Enab. Act.............. Enabling Act

G. C. ....General Code

G. L. ....General Laws
G. S. ....General Statutes

L. ....Laws

Org. Act.................Organic Act

P. ....Part
P. C. ....Penal Code
Pol. C. ....Political Code
Prac. C. ....Practice Code
Prob. C. ....Probate Code
Pub. L. ....Public Laws

R. C. ....Revised Code
R. G. S. ......Revised General Statutes
R. L. ....Revised Laws
Rules of Civ. Prac.
        Rules of Civil Practice

S. ....Statutes
Sched. ....Schedule
Sec. ....Section
Sess. L. ....Session Laws
St. ....Statutes
Subd. ....Subdivision
Supp. ....Supplement
Sur. Ct. Act......Surrogate Court Act

T. ....Title

PART VII.　HUSBAND AND WIFE

Section 149. Introduction

CROSS REFERENCES: General principles, **Sec. 150**; Wife's property, in general, **Sec. 167**; Suits by and against the wife, **Sec. 179**; Dower, in general, **Sec. 188**; Curtesy, in general, **Sec. 215**; Descent and distribution, **Sec. 227**; Homestead, **Sec. 228**; Miscellaneous provisions, **Sec. 230**

The ancient landmarks are gone. The maxims and authorities and adjudications of the past have faded away. The foundations hitherto deemed so essential for the preservation of the nuptial contract, and the maintenance of the marriage relation, are crumbling. The unity of husband and wife has been severed . . . . She no longer clings to and depends upon man, but has the legal right and aspires to battle with him in the contests of the forum; to outvie him in the healing art; to climb with him the steps of fame; and to share with him in every occupation . . . . His legal supremacy is gone, and the sceptre has departed from him.[1]

GENERAL COMMENT

The foregoing quotation from the opinion of Mr. Justice Thornton, written in 1872, undoubtedly represents the ultimate goal sought to be attained by the wave of married women's legislation started in the United States about 1844. At the time it was written it was more eloquent than true. Have all the states attained this goal even now, almost a century after the beginning of the legislative movement for equal rights?

In the present volume the writer has attempted to give a comparative picture of the existing statutory situation. The material has been placed under eighty main heads. Statutes regulating the rights and duties of husband and wife are very numerous and often very complicated. Only by a detailed study of the entire legislative field, topic by topic, can a fair conclusion be reached. General statements are likely to be misleading. Nevertheless, for the benefit of the student who wishes to see the picture in broad outline, an attempt will be made in this introductory section to: (1) state some general observations; (2) summarize the more important results of present legislation; (3) point out some of the more important trends; (4) criticize certain omissions, contradictions, and inequalities; (5) list the more important recommendations for future law-making.

The two fundamental objectives of the Married Women's Acts have been: (1) to remove the wife's common-law disabilities; (2) to equalize the rights of husband and wife. Recent legislation has developed a

---

[1] Justice Thornton, in *Martin* v. *Robson*, 65 Ill. 129 (1872).

third objective—equalization of burdens as between spouses. That husband and wife should be on a plane of equality of rights is no longer seriously disputed. In the heat of the struggle to take from the husband some of his common-law powers and perquisites and thus equalize the rights of the two spouses, the need to lighten the burden placed upon the husband by the common law for the reason that he was so favored has been somewhat obscured. Fortunately the tendency of recent legislation is also toward equalization of burdens. It is hardly probable that it will be necessary for men to organize a countermovement to restore the rights of downtrodden husbands.

Despite the fact that general statements are likely to be misleading, an attempt will now be made to answer the question raised at the beginning of this section—have married women won their struggle for equality? In the writer's opinion they have succeeded very substantially, but not completely. More specifically, it is believed that even the most progressive states may still improve their family legislation; many changes are still needed in the more conservative states; and in practically all, the need for equalization of burdens deserves further consideration. In the summary which follows, the general validity of the foregoing statements will be clearly indicated. The detailed comparison in the sections which follow will furnish convincing proof.

General Summary

The movement to improve the legal status of married women has proceeded along two general lines: (1) by way of piecemeal legislation increasing the rights of the wife and decreasing the rights of the husband; (2) by way of broad "equal rights" statutes recently adopted in twelve states (see **Sec. 150**). On the other hand, nine states still declare that the husband is the "head of the family." However, as aptly said by a **Georgia** judge (see **Sec. 150**), "he, like the King of England, is largely a figurehead."

Though present-day legislation clearly establishes the separate legal personality of the spouses, many recent cases can be found which still pay lip service to the Blackstonian statement that, "by marriage, the husband and wife are one person in law." This misleading statement was not true even at common law. It is high time that it be given decent burial as one of the outworn relics of an older jurisprudence.

To a person favoring equality of rights for the two sexes the broad equal-rights statutes make a strong appeal. These statutes have, however, given rise to numerous doubts and difficulties. It is believed that

§ 149]

the desirable goal of equality can best be attained by specific legislation of a detailed nature. (See **Sec. 150** and references thereto.)

The common-law liability of the husband for the antenuptial debts of the wife has almost universally disappeared. There are a few minor limitations in some states. Though the wife was never liable for the husband's antenuptial debts, nine states today quite unnecessarily provide that she shall not be so liable (**Sec. 151**).

The common-law inability of a wife to make contracts has been removed, at least generally, in all jurisdictions. Until recently many states continued this disability as to certain onerous types of contracts, such as contracts of suretyship. Today even these limitations have largely disappeared. In this respect **Florida** and **Texas** are the most backward states and stand in conspicuous disharmony with their neighbors. The inability of the wife to contract at common law was a natural consequence of a lack of capacity under the unity conception. Today women demand equality of capacity and resent even those limitations based upon a theory of protection or privilege (see **Sec. 152**).

No statutes have been found which substantially lighten the husband's common-law liability for the support of his wife (see **Sec. 153**). While there seems to be no reason to decrease this burden of the husband, there are strong reasons for imposing upon the wife an analogous duty of sharing in the burden of family support. Statutes imposing such a duty upon the wife now exist in twenty-three jurisdictions, constituting one of the striking developments of recent familial legislation (**Sec. 160**). Modern legislation has stripped the husband of many property rights and has conferred them upon the wife. Placing a duty of support upon her is therefore fair to creditors and is a recognition of her equal and independent status. Furthermore in some situations such statutes are a protection to a wife, enabling her to buy on credit. The common-law rule authorizing her to buy necessaries on the credit of her husband was of doubtful assistance to her.

Aside from the family-expense statutes just mentioned, modern statutes have not made a wife liable for her husband's debts. In fact the statutes which create the wife's separate estate generally expressly provide that such separate estate shall not be liable for the debts of the husband (**Sec. 159**). The reader's attention may be called to the **West Virginia** statute which provides that if real or personal property is transferred by the husband to the wife before or after marriage the wife shall be liable for the husband's existing obligations in tort or contract, to the extent of the property transferred (**Sec. 159**). (See also

[§ 149

Sec. 182 for transfers and conveyances between spouses in fraud of creditors.)

In addition to the family-expense statutes and as further evidence of the tendency to equalize burdens, statutes may now be found in seventeen states which under certain circumstances impose a burden upon the wife to support the husband. The wife was under no such obligation at common law (**Sec. 161**). These statutes, being in line with the policy of equalizing burdens as well as rights, deserve attention in other states.

Recent legislation has greatly strengthened the marital duty of support in another direction, viz., by criminal or quasi-criminal statutes relating to desertion and non-support. Statutes of this type are popularly known as "Lazy Husband Laws." Mere neglect or abandonment of a wife was not criminal at common law. Some of the present statutes seem designed primarily to prevent the wife and children from becoming public charges. This was even more marked in the earlier statutes. While society has an obvious interest in protecting itself from the financial burden of pauperism, the later statutes are mainly on a broader basis, viz., that of compelling the husband by more effective means to fulfill the obligation of support incurred by the marriage.

The Uniform Desertion and Non-Support Act has been adopted wholly or substantially in about one-third of the fifty-one American jurisdictions. Others have adopted parts of it. Several, notably **Alabama,** seem to have improved upon it. The most significant feature of these statutes is the authority to release the husband on probation upon his undertaking to support the wife or comply with the terms of an order of support. There are surprising omissions in a few jurisdictions, and the laws of many could be improved in the matter of administrative detail. Detailed suggestions for improvements will be found in **Section 162.**

Only eleven states expressly authorize antenuptial contracts. In the others the right to make such contracts rests upon a common-law basis. Thirty-five jurisdictions recognize this type of contract by fragmentary regulation of some of its incidents, e.g., recording, form, etc. It is recommended that all states which have not done so should require recording of marriage contracts respecting real property, as a protection to subsequent bona fide purchasers and creditors (**Sec. 155**).

The common-law inability of husband and wife to contract with each other has been removed in sixteen jurisdictions by statutes expressly permitting such contracts. In most of the others the same result has been reached by statutes conferring upon a wife the general power to make contracts. The effect of such statutes is not always clear. Even in some of the jurisdictions conferring express power there are unnecessary limitations. In curious disharmony with modern thought, four jurisdictions expressly forbid husband and wife to contract with each other (**Sec. 156**). There seems to be no sound reason why the wife should not be allowed complete freedom to contract with the husband, subject only to those limitations which the law imposes on persons occupying a confidential relationship. As a matter of clarity, all states should provide that a wife's contractual capacity extends to transactions with the husband. This is superior to the prevailing type of statute which says that she may contract as if unmarried.

In the majority of states the common-law liability of the husband for the wife's premarital torts and contracts has been abrogated. It is doubtful if any of them would now recognize this form of liability. The reasons which justified the husband's liability no longer exist under our changed legal order. The matter should not be left to implications, however, as it still is in many states. Just as obviously there is no room in this age of equal rights for the common-law rule making the husband liable for the wife's postnuptial torts, except where he is a joint wrongdoer. Especially absurd is the common-law presumption of coercion for torts committed under certain circumstances. In sixteen jurisdictions no express abrogation of these common-law rules relating to postnuptial torts is found. In many states where the intent was to abolish this liability the statutes are poorly drawn and need revision (see **Sec. 157**). One state, **Georgia,** has expressly codified the ancient common-law rule making the husband liable for the wife's torts.

Express legislation is singularly lacking on one subject which has sharply divided the courts, viz., whether one spouse may sue a third person who commits a tort upon the other spouse, or a tort injurious to the marriage relation. The common law gave such a right to the husband, whether the injury consisted of a wilful or negligent tort to the wife, an alienation of affections, or a criminal conversation. Such legislation as exists in this field is fragmentary, and the courts are left to draw implications from the effect of general statutory changes upon the common-law situation. The result is doubt and disharmony. Much of the fragmentary legislation is ambiguous or merely suggests certain implications. Only twenty-one jurisdictions have been found with even this poor type of legislation. Either the wife should be given an express equality to sue for torts to the husband, both wilful and negligent, and for alienation of affections and criminal conversation, or the husband's similar rights

[§ 149

should be abrogated. Much could be said for complete abrogation of the action for criminal conversation and for limitation or abolition of the right to sue for alienation of affections. Very little can be said in favor of the inequality which still exists in practically all states. Without hesitation it is recommended that all states should pass statutes equalizing the rights of the spouses in this regard (see **Sec. 158**).

The success of the purely statutory juvenile courts in the United States has resulted in a definite trend toward the establishment of family or domestic relations courts with somewhat similar procedural methods. To date only fifteen states have expressly established such courts with jurisdiction over controversies between husband and wife. In general these courts, where authorized, have been confined to centers of population where the frequency of relevant cases makes their work more valuable. The principal benefits of such courts are: (1) the unity of jurisdiction over family problems, contrasted with the present practice in many jurisdictions of requiring suits in several courts; (2) the more or less informal procedure normally followed in these courts; (3) the advantage of the usual scheme of having social agencies, probation officers, and specially trained investigators provide the court with an insight into the character of the particular home involved; (4) the increased efficiency of a court which specializes in family problems (see **Sec. 163**). For these reasons the authorization of such courts is recommended.

The common law gave the wife little choice in the matter of her domicile. Upon marriage the domicile of the husband became hers, and in general he had the sole right to change it. Even without express statutory authority the courts have made some exceptions to the rigorous application of this rule. Thus it is generally agreed that she may acquire a separate domicile for divorce; and probably she may do so for any purpose if she have cause for divorce. That the common-law rule should be abolished in its entirety has found some following among the writers, but little favor in the cases. Thirty-three of the fifty-one jurisdictions have legislated on the subject. Classified by subjects, thirty-three of these statutes relate to the wife's settlement for poor relief, eleven to residence for divorce, and eleven to residence for voting, jury service, etc. Many of these statutes have codified common-law rules substantially or in part. In others a tendency to break away from the common law is shown. Under some of the broad equal-rights statutes it may well be contended that a wife's power to choose her domicile is as great as that of her husband. Most of the statutes giving a wife power to choose her domicile for a particular purpose make no distinction between an

§ 149]

innocent and a guilty wife. The philosophy of the present day demands that a wife have the freedom of her husband in the choice of her domicile, irrespective of the fact that she may be derelict in her duty to him. Undoubtedly the law is headed in this direction. A frank admission by express statute of equality on this point would be a desirable forward step (see **Sec. 164**).

In most respects the common law was harsh to the married woman. The statutory problem has in general been one of extending to her much needed relief. In one respect, however, she was favored over the husband, and given a virtual immunity from punishment for the commission of many crimes. The common law of England by an ancient rule, apparently not known in other countries, presumed that a wife committing a crime in the presence of her husband was acting under his coercion. This presumption, at first absolute, later became rebuttable, and did not apply to certain major crimes. In this latter form the rule came to the United States. It is now generally conceded that the rule is artificial and illogical, even as modified. To the writer it seems utterly indefensible, in view of our prevailing view of social responsibility.

In only nineteen states, however, are there statutes dealing with this ancient rule. In only three of the nineteen is the rule abolished in toto; the legislation in the other sixteen merely limits the common-law rule in various ways (see **Sec. 165**). In five more states the courts have held that the presumption of coercion is abolished by implication from the passage of laws placing husband and wife upon a more equal footing. These decisions, like the majority of the statutes, do not go far enough. All states, except the three which have already done so, should not only abolish the presumption of coercion, but should also provide that actual coercion of a wife by a husband shall no longer be an excuse for the commission of a crime except to the extent that any person is excused when acting under the compulsion of a third party.

The common-law fiction that husband and wife were one produced certain other difficulties in the law of crimes. The courts of some jurisdictions still hold that a husband and wife cannot conspire together, steal or embezzle from each other, or be guilty of arson by burning the other's dwelling house. In many other jurisdictions the law on these points is not clear because there are no express statutes and no decisions. The existing cases draw conflicting implications from substantially similar general laws. Very little express legislation was found. Despite the conflicting cases on larceny, only one American jurisdiction (**Hawaii**) has expressly legislated on this matter. And unfortunately the statute

in this territory has simply codified the common-law rule. Only ten jurisdictions have express legislation in regard to arson. While all of these
evince an intent to abolish the fiction of unity, only four of them do so
in clear and express language (**Sec. 166**).

It is surprising that the legislatures have not exploded the myth of
unity as applied to these crimes upon the failure of the courts to do so.
It seems obvious that the general legislation increasing the rights of the
married woman, permitting her to own property, contract, sue and be
sued, etc., is unmistakable evidence of a fundamental change in the
concept of the marital relationship. If the common law is to justify its
vaunted claims to flexibility, it should view the crimes of either spouse
in the same light as those of a third person. Since the courts have failed
to make this clear, it should be done by express and explicit legislation.

In no field of family law has there been a more complete revolution,
in both form and philosophy, than in the field of property rights. Here
the common law was very harsh. Courts of equity with their invention
of the wife's equity to a settlement and the wife's separate estate in
equity laid the foundation for an even better statutory separate estate.
While progress in many jurisdictions has been piecemeal, with attendant
confusion and uncertainty of judicial decision, the legislation of all jurisdictions has been more or less consistently directed toward the establishment of the wife upon a complete property equality with the husband
(see **Sec. 167** *et seq.*).

In the property field, as elsewhere, there are numerous variations in
details. It seems, however, that one may safely say that the wife in
practically all jurisdictions now retains for her own enjoyment the
property which she brings to the marriage and the property which she
acquires thereafter. With but few exceptions the husband has been
shorn of his right to control and manage the wife's property. (See **Sec.
178** for special rules as to community property in eight states.) In the
property field many states have indeed arrived at the goal of equality.
Florida is the most notable exception. On the other hand it may be
argued that certain states in some respects now unduly favor the wife.
The struggle for equality will probably be an unending one. The chief
need in this field, however, is no longer for equality, but for simplification. A recodifying housecleaning to sweep out the outmoded phraseology of a past era may well be the next step. In fact a beginning has
already been made in some states.

Early statutes giving the wife enlarged rights in property were widely
held to give her no legal right to her earnings, which at common law

belonged to her husband. A working woman with no property was therefore placed at a disadvantage. Today in all states except two the wife is probably entitled in her own right to her earnings for services rendered to third persons outside the household. The eight community-property states are not included here. They will be discussed separately. In only twenty-eight states are the statutes in regard to earnings clear and satisfactory. One jurisdiction (**Hawaii**) rather strangely forbids the wife to contract for personal services without the written consent of the husband. In many jurisdictions two points still remain in considerable doubt: (1) May the wife contract with the husband for services to be performed for him? Twelve jurisdictions expressly deny or qualify her right to do so. Three states forbid contracts in general between husband and wife. (2) May the wife contract with third persons for services to be performed within the household? The only specific statute found on this point was that of **Maryland,** allowing the wife to contract with boarders and lodgers as if unmarried.

Few will deny that the wife should be entitled to her earnings for services rendered to third persons outside the household. The two states which deny her this right are backward indeed. As a matter of social policy it is doubtful if we should allow the wife to barter and bicker with the husband over household services. On the other hand it is hardly consistent with modern standards to require her to serve the husband without pay outside the household. On some points it seems clear that many states need further legislation relative to the wife's earnings (see **Sec. 173**).

The wife's separate personal property is often found in the possession of the husband or in the joint possession of husband and wife, thus presenting a misleading picture of ownership and giving the husband an opportunity to practice fraud upon the wife or third parties. Under the circumstances one might well expect to find a well-developed statutory policy of registration of the wife's separate personal property. Recording acts of a general nature relating to such property were found in eight states only. Two others have statutes of limited application. Furthermore, in a majority of the states having recording acts, recording is permissive and not mandatory. Two states which formerly had recording acts have recently repealed them. Compelling a wife to record her separate personal property seems inconsistent with the modern idea of equality. As a matter of protection to the wife and to third parties who deal with the husband, it seems that permissive registration at least is worthy of a wider legislative consideration (see **Secs. 174, 175**).

[§ 149

Since at common law the husband's property rights were fully protected, the modern process of equalizing rights has not called for much legislative thought in his behalf. Except for relief from liability for the wife's obligations not founded upon his duty of support, the process for him has been mainly one of negation and delimitation. Only in the eight community-property states do we find any definition of the husband's separate property (see **Sec. 178**). Statutes in five states giving the husband express authority to sue the wife to recover his property which has fallen into the control and possession of the wife give indications of a changing order. Not without subtle irony, these statutes give notice that today a husband may need protection for usurpation on the part of a wife (**Sec. 176**).

Only seven jurisdictions have attempted to legislate on the difficult subject of marital rights in property acquired outside the domicile of the spouses. In only two of these (**Louisiana** and **California**) does such legislation depart from what would normally be recognized by the courts as the guiding rule in the absence of statute. The **California** attempt to change rights vested according to the law of other states has recently been held invalid (see **Sec. 177**).

The community-property system existing in eight states (**Arizona, California, Idaho, Louisiana, Nevada, New Mexico, Texas, Washington**) is foreign to anything known to the common law. Fundamentally it is an institution of the civil law. (See **Sec. 178** and references there for history and details.) In these eight states there are three classes of property: (1) separate property of the husband; (2) separate property of the wife; (3) common or community property. It is this third classification which formally differentiates these states from their neighbors. The fundamental purpose of this odd creation of the civil law seems to have been to guarantee to the wife, at least upon dissolution of the marriage, her fair share of the marital gains. In spite of a common origin, the community-property system varies greatly in these eight states. Furthermore the courts have developed radically different conceptions of the system even where the statutes are substantially similar.

Under this system the husband is the dominant figure in the management of the community property. With minor exceptions the wife is without power to manage or dispose of the community property during marriage. Under this system we find the wife sometimes discriminated against and sometimes curiously favored.

One of the serious disadvantages of the community-property system is the possible disruption of the husband's business activities upon the

§ 149]

wife's death. The husband may have spent years in building a successful business enterprise, only to find it suddenly broken up by the untimely death of his spouse and the interference of her heirs or devisees. **Nevada** and **New Mexico** avoid this difficulty by giving all community property to the surviving husband. In the others it has been found necessary to give the husband some special control over the dissolved community.

That the community-property system was an advance over the grotesque and unfair common-law system of marital rights cannot be doubted. Whether it is to be preferred to the more enlightened modern statutory systems is a different question. It is not likely that any legislator from a common-law state who delves into the perplexities of the community system will feel the urge to adopt it (**Sec. 178**).

The emancipation of the wife has now reached a point where, in most jurisdictions, her procedural disabilities have been completely abolished. Stimson, writing in 1886, found only nineteen jurisdictions with express statutes permitting the wife to sue and be sued alone. Today this is the rule in all but eight jurisdictions. In the matter of procedural freedom **North Carolina** and **Texas** are the most backward states (see **Sec. 179**).

Very little express legislation can be found on the more difficult problem of whether and to what extent the spouses may sue each other. Divorce actions are allowable of course (see Vol. II). To what extent may husband and wife sue each other for injury to and recovery of property, for breach of contract, and for personal tort? In most jurisdictions the answer to these questions must be one of implication from statutes which are not explicit. Where the statutes permit contracts and property transactions between spouses, the right to enforce the same by legal action is clearly implied. Statutes giving the wife separate property rights generally have been construed to allow her to protect such rights by suits against the husband. Broad statutes permitting the wife to sue and be sued as if sole have in some states been construed to authorize suits by her against her husband. The field where there is even yet the greatest doubt and confusion is that of actions for personal tort. In most of the cases where this difficult problem of family policy has arisen, the right of one spouse to sue the other has been denied. Several late cases have strengthened the minority view. Though this is one of the most debated points today in family law, not a single state has settled the argument by an express statute. It is the opinion of the writer that even personal-tort actions, with some limitations, should be permitted (see **Sec. 180**).

All jurisdictions have completely emancipated the married woman from her common-law incapacity to make a valid will. The earlier statutes often required that the husband's written consent be annexed or that the wife be separately examined, or exempted the husband from the list of persons whom the wife could make the object of her bounty. As late as 1882 a **Georgia** statute provided that "married women are incapable of making wills for want of perfect liberty of action, being presumed to be under the control of their husbands." Today married women may generally make wills, subject only to such requirements as apply to other persons. In a number of states the married woman is favored, being able to make a valid will at a lower age than applies to a single woman (**Sec. 181**).

While the common law allowed the wife to retain the fee to her lands, she was unable to make a binding conveyance thereof to a third person until custom developed a method by which the husband and wife could pass title by joining in a fictitious action to levy a fine or suffer a common recovery. In America, even in Colonial times, local custom or statutes made this grotesque method of conveyancing unnecessary. A deed in which the husband joined and which the wife separately acknowledged was sufficient. For many years after the creation of the wife's separate statutory estate the husband's joinder in the wife's deed and her separate examination was universally retained. As late as 1886 Stimson lists only eighteen jurisdictions which authorized the wife to convey her real property by her sole deed. The philosophy of our legislation in this respect has been rather intricate. To protect the wife against the unconscionable conduct of third parties, the law forced upon her the husband's counsel and consent. For fear that the husband's counsel might in fact amount to coercion, her separate examination upon that point was required. This latter formality has now been discarded by most jurisdictions for all purposes (see **Sec. 184**). It is not surprising to find that the necessity for the husband's joinder has likewise been generally abandoned, except as to conveyances of the wife's homestead (**Secs. 183, 228**).

Where the husband has a contingent interest in the wife's land in the nature of curtesy, it is still necessary for him to join in the wife's deed in order to bar his own claim, or to release it by separate instrument. In some of the minority states where the husband's joinder and her separate examination are still needed to pass the wife's interest in land, a peculiar situation exists. In these states she has full power to contract and may by her sole act lay herself open to damages and her prop-

§ 149]

erty to execution for a failure to convey. By her sole act she cannot convey, but she can contract to convey and thus deprive herself of her property. A **North Carolina** justice aptly likens this incongruous result to "whipping the devil around the stump." It is another unfortunate result of the patchwork evolution of the law. To require the husband to join in the wife's deed is a superficial gesture of the past and should be dispensed with. The artificial formality of the wife's separate examination, though theoretically useful, is practically futile. This antiquated and discriminatory practice should also be abolished by the few states which still retain it.

The statutory situation in regard to conveyances of land and transfers of personal property between spouses is even less satisfactory. At common law such transactions were utterly impossible. The wife could own no personal property, and the unity theory precluded a conveyance of real property from the husband to the wife directly. Various indirect ways of evading these harsh rules were later worked out. Today twenty-seven jurisdictions have statutes expressly authorizing direct transfers of property from one spouse to the other. In most of the others the same result may be reached by implication from general legislation. **Minnesota** has the most archaic provision to be found in a progressive state. The statute there provides that "no contract between husband and wife relative to the real estate of either, or any interest therein," shall be valid. An indirect conveyance through the medium of a third party has been held effectual, though it is in pursuance of an invalid contract between the spouses. In several other states an effective conveyance from the wife directly to the husband is still impossible at law (**Sec. 182**).

There seems to be no reason for denying the husband and wife complete freedom to deal with each other respecting property, subject only to the rules applicable to persons occupying a confidential relationship, and to the rules protecting the rights of creditors. To remove possible doubts and to put the matter beyond the reach of occasional archaic reasoning, it would be well for states not having express statutes to adopt the broad statute approved in **Section 182**.

A recognition of the basic difference between real and personal property, and the practical necessity of allowing the wife greater freedom in the control of the latter, led most jurisdictions at an early date to authorize the wife to dispose of her personal property to third persons without the intermeddling of the husband. In all but seven of the fifty-one jurisdictions this is now made clear by express statute (**Sec. 185**). In a few jurisdictions both spouses must still join in a transfer or mort-

[§ 149

gage of household goods, whether owned by the husband or by the wife
(**Sec. 225**).

At common law the basic incapacity of the wife obviously rendered
her completely unable to act through an agent. She could, however, be
an agent, since this did not involve contractual capacity. As a general
rule one may do by agent whatever he can do in person. Hence, in so far
as statutes have given a married woman capacity to do various acts, no
statutory authority to do these same acts by agent is needed. Nevertheless thirty-four jurisdictions have legislation dealing with the wife's
power to act through an agent (**Sec. 186**). Most of these statutes are
surplusage in that they vest the wife with a particular authority, where
by implication she is vested with a general authority. They should be
broadened in scope or entirely omitted. As is usually true, there are a
few backward jurisdictions (**Hawaii, Minnesota**) which by their statutes impose agency limitations hard to justify under modern standards.

A married woman could not at common law carry on a trade or business, except under the "Custom of London," or under extreme circumstances in which the husband was regarded as civilly dead. From an
early date legislatures have permitted the wife in certain special situations (as when deserted by her husband) to become a sole trader. With
the removal of the common-law incapacities of the wife such legislation
has become unnecessary. Many of the early statutes have disappeared
from the books. There is, however, a lingering sentiment in some jurisdictions that to allow a wife to engage in business involves special hazards
and demands legislative attention. At present twenty-three jurisdictions
still have legislation of this nature (**Sec. 187**). These statutes vary
widely in scope, in purpose, and in the formalities prerequisite to the
wife's obtaining the status of a sole trader. In general they seem to be
inspired by a desire to enable the wife to secure a livelihood when the
husband fails her or to protect the husband's creditors. For the most
part these statutes are antiquated relics of the past. They are furthermore seldom used. Except in the few states where the wife's general
capacity to contract is still limited, they serve no useful purpose. They
should be removed from the codes and, where necessary, the wife's
capacity to contract, etc., should be enlarged.

The law of dower and curtesy is so complex that many sections are
required for an adequate presentation (see **Secs. 188–214** for dower and
Secs. 215–23 for curtesy). In **Sections 188** and **215** an attempt has
been made: (1) to summarize this body of law; (2) to point out the
modern tendencies; (3) to offer pertinent criticism; and (4) to make a

§ 149]

series of recommendations for suggested reforms. No field of family law is more deserving of a complete renovation. It is sufficient here to say merely that the desirable remedy is the complete abolition of dower and curtesy and the substitution of a new system free of dower and curtesy formulae and dogma. A few states have already done this. In many more the tendency is in that direction.

The assignment of wages by husband or wife, or both, is the subject of legislation in twenty-five states (**Sec. 224**). Many of these statutes are of limited application. In thirteen states they apply to the husband's assignments only; in eight to assignment of future wages only. As a protection to the wife against an improvident husband some limitation of the right to assign future wages seems theoretically desirable. Discussion of the effect and desirability of such legislation seems to be almost totally lacking in legal magazines. Here is a situation where a factual survey by some foundation or organization is needed as a basis for a sound recommendation for future legislation.

At an early period the common law definitely refused to permit one spouse to testify for the other. This refusal, based chiefly on bias and interest, is indefensible, since bias and interest affect only the credibility not the capacity of a witness. Fifty jurisdictions have legislated on this subject in reference to criminal cases and forty-five in reference to civil cases. Only four in each category retain the common-law rule. The statutes of the other jurisdictions sum up as follows: In civil cases the spouse is privileged in sixteen jurisdictions, competent in thirteen, competent and compellable in twelve; in criminal cases the spouse is privileged in twenty-two jurisdictions, competent in fifteen, competent and compellable in nine.

Whether a spouse could testify against the other at common law was in dispute. Some authorities said the spouse was incompetent for this purpose, others said privileged. The practical effect was the same, since the privilege was accorded to the one against whom the testimony was offered. These rules were formulated to protect the marital peace and to shield a spouse from the necessity of giving evidence repugnant to normal feelings. A summary of the present statutory situation is as follows: In civil cases the spouse is privileged in fifteen jurisdictions, competent in eleven, competent and compellable in eleven; in criminal cases the spouse is privileged in twenty-five jurisdictions, competent in six, competent and compellable in four, incompetent in sixteen.

As to marital communications, the husband and wife at common law were usually said to be privileged but not incompetent. The reason given

[§ 149

was the desirability of protecting marital trust and confidence. The statutes have usually retained this supposed protection. Twenty-four jurisdictions provide that the spouse as to marital communications is privileged, seven not compellable, and sixteen incompetent. (See **Sec. 226** for special statutes and limitations relating to the husband and wife as witnesses.)

It is gratifying to see that the great majority of jurisdictions have modified the common law in varying degrees. But it is believed that progress has been checked too quickly. Enabling the law to ascertain the truth by all available evidence is a more important consideration than the protection of marital peace. It is therefore recommended that the husband and wife as witnesses be governed by the same rules as third persons, with the reservation that their credibility be weighed in the light of their relationship. This is the manifest tendency of the law, but to put it into full effect would require some change in the statutes of every state.

At common law the husband and wife did not inherit real property from each other, but were confined to the rights of curtesy and dower, respectively. As to personal property, the husband's marital rights, or rights as administrator, were so great as to make inheritance unimportant. Today in all of the fifty-one jurisdictions statutes of descent and distribution exist. This legislation is too complicated to permit of brief summary. (See **Sec. 227** and the elaborate table therein contained.) For the purpose of this introductory section a few brief observations must suffice. The modern tendency is to treat husband and wife alike, a practice that should be universal. In so far as a widow needs added protection, she obtains it by means of dower, homestead, and family-allowance legislation. Some statutes in this field are needlessly ambiguous and involved. Here again the modern trend is toward simplicity and clarity. In **Section 227** a detailed recommendation is made which it is believed represents a desirable goal for future legislation.

Homestead, viz., the statutory exemption of real property from attachment and execution, was unknown to the common law. From its inception in 1839 in the old Republic of Texas, it has spread over the United States. Though this exemption has sometimes been abused and used to defraud creditors, its general beneficial effect has been universally admitted. Forty-four jurisdictions have what may properly be called homestead laws for the benefit of a surviving spouse or widow. Two others have similar provisions not called homestead. In one additional state the provision is for the benefit of minor children only. Hence in only four jurisdictions is relevant legislation lacking. The wealth of

§ 149]

homestead legislation is too great to permit of brief summary. (See **Sec. 228** for such presentation as the limitations of this volume permit.)

The same benevolent spirit which has prompted the protection of the family homestead has also provided for the support of the family after decedent's death by means of legislation relating to allowances, exemptions, etc. Praiseworthy in spirit as this legislation is, it may be suggested that it is sometimes so generous that the rights of creditors have been seriously impaired. In a few jurisdictions the allowance granted is so niggardly as to afford little protection. This legislation is also collected in **Section 228.**

As a further protection to the homestead, forty-one jurisdictions have statutes limiting its disposal. Twenty-seven require the consent of both husband and wife for an alienation or encumbrance of the homestead; ten require the consent of the wife. Eleven jurisdictions similarly protect exempt personal property. Nine have analogous statutes concerning household goods (see **Sec. 225**). The purpose of these restrictions is praiseworthy. The benefit of the homestead and exemption laws may be seriously endangered if one spouse is permitted to convey such property against the wishes of the other.

Wherever the wife may sue alone the statute of limitations should run against her as against any other litigant. In twelve jurisdictions, however, the wife is given a preferred status. The explanation is historical. At a time when the wife could not sue alone statutes were passed in most jurisdictions suspending the limitation during coverture or giving her a specified time after discoverture in which to file her suit. Curiously some states which have not given the wife full power to sue have repealed the statutes giving her this protection, while others in which she has been given full procedural freedom have retained the privilege. These latter states should remove the limitation privilege from the books. Some courts have already held that these statutes are repealed by implication. No express legislation was found relating to limitations as applied to suits between spouses. Logically the usual statute of limitation should be a bar, but expressions to the contrary may be found in some texts and cases (see **Sec. 229**).

In **Section 230** a large number of miscellaneous statutes are collected. Because of their number and diversity they need no further reference in a general summary.

In the sections which follow, detailed recommendations for changes in the law are made. In this introductory section the more important ones only are listed. Following each recommendation is a reference to the section of this volume in which the problem is discussed. A study of the section referred to will in each case indicate the states to which the recommendation is applicable.

List of Recommendations

1. Equalization of rights between husband and wife should be promoted by statutes relating to particular rights and duties, rather than by vague equal-rights legislation. (**Sec. 150.**)

2. A few states should remove the remaining disabilities of a married woman to contract. (**Sec. 152.**)

3. About half the states should adopt broad family-expense statutes. (**Sec. 160.**)

4. Many states should require recording of marriage contracts respecting real property, as a protection to bona fide purchasers. (**Sec. 155.**)

5. Four states should repeal their statutes forbidding contracts between husband and wife. Many others should confer the power by more explicit language. (**Sec. 156.**)

6. Many states need legislation for the purpose of more clearly abrogating the husband's common-law liability for antenuptial and postnuptial torts. One state should repeal its statute codifying the common-law rule. (**Sec. 157.**)

7. Practically all states need legislation to clarify the wife's rights respecting suits against third persons for wilful and negligent torts to the husband, and for alienation of affections and for criminal conversation. These latter two might well be limited or even abolished. In any event, equality between the spouses should be the goal. (**Sec. 158.**)

8. The **West Virginia** statute, providing that if real or personal property is transferred by the husband to the wife before or after marriage the wife shall be liable for the husband's existing obligations in tort or contract to the extent of the property transferred, deserves consideration in other states. (**Sec. 159.**)

9. Two-thirds of the states should pass statutes compelling the wife to support the husband when he is unable to support himself and she has the ability or means to furnish such support. (**Sec. 161.**)

10. Two-thirds of the states should adopt the Uniform Desertion and Non-Support Act with suggested improvements. (**Sec. 162.**)

11. Two-thirds of the states should establish family or domestic relations courts. (**Sec. 163.**)

§ 149]

12. All states need legislation to confer upon the wife the same power to choose her domicile that the husband has. (**Sec. 164.**)

13. All but three jurisdictions need legislation to abolish in toto the common-law rules in regard to coercion of a wife by the husband where she commits a crime in his presence. She should be excused only to the extent that any person is excused when acting under the compulsion of a third party. (**Sec. 165.**)

14. Most jurisdictions need further legislation to abolish the fiction of unity as applied to the commission, by the husband and wife, of such crimes as conspiracy, larceny, embezzlement, and arson. (**Sec. 166.**)

15. In many states the law relating to the property rights of married women could well be recodified and simplified. (**Sec. 167.**)

16. A few states should pass statutes giving the wife a right to her own earnings. In many others the existing statutes need clarification. (**Sec. 173.**)

17. Eight states need further legislation to give the wife procedural freedom. (**Sec. 179.**)

18. In most of the states express statutes authorizing suits between spouses for injury to property, for recovery of property, and on contracts are needed. (**Sec. 180.**)

19. No state has an express statute regulating the right of the one spouse to sue the other for personal torts. Such suits should be allowed with some limitations. (**Sec. 180.**)

20. One-half the states might well clarify the right of one spouse to convey land and transfer personal property to the other by the passage of a statute such as already exists in eight states. (**Sec. 182.**)

21. A few states still requiring the husband's joinder in the wife's deeds and her separate examination should abolish these discriminations. (**Secs. 183, 184.**)

22. Sole-trader statutes no longer serve any useful purpose and might well be repealed in the twenty-three states still having them. A few of these states should at the same time give the wife general power to make contracts. (**Sec. 187.**)

23. Dower and curtesy should be completely abolished. A new statutory system should be substituted free of dower and curtesy formulae and dogma, as has already been done in a few states. (**Secs. 188** and **215.**)

24. A factual survey is needed to determine whether there should be further legislation regulating the assignment of wages by husband and wife. (**Sec. 224.**)

[§ 149

25. Husband and wife as witnesses should be governed by the same rules of evidence as affect third persons, with the reservation that their credibility should be weighed in the light of their relationship. This would require changing more or less the law of every state. (**Sec. 226.**)

26. The law relating to husband and wife as heirs and distributees could be improved in many states. (Detailed suggestions made in **Sec. 227.**)

27. Homestead and exemption statutes could be improved in many states. (Detailed suggestions made in **Sec. 228.**)

28. Statutes in a few states giving married women special favors in respect to the statute of limitations should be repealed. (**Sec. 229.**)

REFERENCES

Books

BARON and FEME. *A Treatise of the Common Law concerning Husbands and Wives,* 3d ed. (1738).

BELL, SIR SYDNEY SMITH. *The Law of Property Arising from the Relation of Husband and Wife* (1850).

BISHOP, JOEL PRENTISS. *Commentaries on the Law of Married Women under the Statutes of the Several States, and at Common Law, and in Equity,* 2 vols. (1873–75).

BRECKENRIDGE, SOPHRONISBA P. *Marriage and the Civic Rights of Women* (1931). (A monograph on domicile and citizenship of women as affected by marriage.)

——. *The Family and the State* (1934).

BRIGHT, JOHN EDWARD. *The Law of Husband and Wife, as Respects Property* (1849).

CORD, WILLIAM H. *A Treatise on the Legal and Equitable Rights of Married Women,* 2d ed., 2 vols. (1885).

JACOB, CHARLES M. *Litigation of Husband and Wife* (1928).

JESSUP, HENRY W. *Law for Wives and Daughters* (1927).

MACQUEEN, JOHN F. *The Rights and Liabilities of Husband and Wife,* 4th ed. (1905).

MORRIS, RICHARD BRANDON. *Studies in the History of American Law, with Special Reference to the Seventeenth and Eighteenth Centuries,* ch. iii, pp. 126–97 (1930).

PEDERSON, VICTOR C. *The Woman a Man Marries, an Analysis of Her Standard* (1927).

POLLOCK, SIR FREDERICK, and FREDERICK WILLIAM MAITLAND. *History of English Law before the Time of Edward I,* Vol. 2, 2d ed. (1899).

SCHOULER, JAMES. *A Treatise on the Law of Husband and Wife* (1882).

——. *A Treatise on the Law of Marriage, Divorce, Separation and Domestic Relations,* 6th ed., 3 vols. (1921).

§ 149]

SMITH, MARY PHLEGAR. *Special Legal Relations of Married Women in North Carolina as to Property, Contracts and Guardianship,* University of North Carolina Extension Bulletin, Vol. VII, No. 9 (1928).

STEWART, DAVID. *The Law of Husband and Wife, as Established in England and the United States* (1885).

Articles

DOLAN, MRS. JULIA B. "Another Version of the Legal Status of Women in Wisconsin," 15 Marq. L. Rev. 139–57 (1931).

GRACE, W. P. "Unreasonable Disabilities of Married Women," 1883 Ark. St. Bar Assoc. Rep. 19.

HITCHCOCK, HENRY. "Modern Legislation Touching Marital Property Rights," 8 So. L. Rev. (N.S.) 633–62 (1880).

HOLBROOK, EVANS. "The Change in the Meaning of Consortium," 22 Mich. L. Rev. 1–9 (1923).

HOLMES, JOHN. "Changes in the Law of Coverture," 1889 Mo. St. Bar Assoc. Rep. 118.

POLLARD, CLAUDE. "The Law of Married Women in Texas," 46 Amer. L. Rev. 241–52 (1912).

POUND, ROSCOE. "Individual Interests in the Domestic Relations," 14 Mich. L. Rev. 177–96 (1916).

RIDDELL, LORD. "Ancient Laws and Modern Women" (address), 168 L. T. 352–53 (1929).

RUFFIN, THOMAS. "Married Women before the Law in North Carolina," 1 N. C. Jour. of L. 230 (1904).

STOUT, CLAUDE D. "The Legal Status of Women in Wisconsin," 14 Marq. L. Rev. 66–80, 121–69, 199–211 (1930).

SURVEYER, E. F. "Husband and Wife in Louisiana and Quebec," 28 La. Bar Assoc. Rep. 55–78 (1928).

THEOBALD, THOMAS D., JR. "Does Equity Protect Property Rights in Domestic Relations?" 19 Ky. L. Jour. 57–68 (1930).

Notes

"Amateur Legislation on Rights and Wrongs of Married Women," 22 Jour. Jur. 266–70 (1878).

"The Chaos of Our Family Law," 71 Sol. J. 816–18 (1927).

"Equalizing the Legal Status of the Sexes," 21 Col. L. Rev. 712–14 (1921).

"Failure of the Married Women's Acts to Place Husband and Wife on an Equal Basis," 17 Va. L. Rev. 398–402 (1931).

"The Law as to Married Women in Missouri," 11 Cent. L. Jour. 41–43 (1880).

"Marriage in Missouri: Is It Advisable to Abolish the Disabilities of Coverture?" 1887 Mo. St. Bar Assoc. Rep. 118, 139.

"Progress in Removing the Disabilities of Married Women," 17 Amer. L. Rev. 269–70 (1883).

"Husband and Wife—Fiction of Unity," *Lord Advocate* v. *Jaffrey and Another* (H. L. 1920), 124 L. T. R. 129—21 Col. L. Rev. 488 (1921).

[§ 149

Section 150. General Principles

CROSS REFERENCES: Introduction, **Sec. 149**; Duty of support, civil liability, **Sec. 161**; Duty of support, criminal liability, **Sec. 162**; Wife's domicile, **Sec. 164**; Wife's property, in general, **Sec. 167**

It is the purpose of the present section to call attention to a few statutes of rather general application. Most important are the so-called "equal rights statutes"—broad provisions which have been adopted in twelve jurisdictions and which seem to have been intended as the culmination of the married women's legislation. These broad equalizing statutes are of four types, viz., those which provide that (1) the wife is on an equality with her husband; (2) the wife is on an equality with an unmarried woman; (3) all disabilities of coverture are abolished; (4) women are on an equality with men. The first three types have been combined in the statutes of some jurisdictions, presumably in an effort to make the language more emphatic. Thus, six jurisdictions provide, in effect, that a wife has the same legal rights as the husband (**Alaska, Arizona, Minnesota, Oklahoma, Oregon, Washington**), is under no further disabilities (**Alaska, Oregon, Washington**), and is subject to the same legal liabilities (**Arizona**). Four provide, in effect, that a wife has the same rights as an unmarried woman (**Arkansas, Minnesota, Oklahoma, South Dakota**), and is subject to the same laws (**Arkansas**). Four states provide generally that all disabilities (and incapacities, in **Louisiana**) of coverture are abolished (**Arkansas, Louisiana, Mississippi, Tennessee**). The fourth type is found only in **Wisconsin**, and, while the statute does not specifically mention married women, it is interpreted to include them (see *First Wisconsin National Bank* v. *Jahn,* 179 Wis. 117; 190 N. W. 822 [1922]). The summary following should be consulted for the wording of the foregoing statutes, and also for minor limitations upon them.

Other jurisdictions, in addition to the foregoing twelve, have statutes which, in varying degrees, give the wife equal rights with respect to her property, contracts, torts, or her capacity to sue. In general these statutes have been collected and discussed in subsequent sections of this volume under the particular subjects with which they deal, and have not been included in this section. However, in a personal-injury action in **North Dakota** by the wife against the husband (*Fitzmaurice* v. *Fitzmaurice,* 62 N. D. 191; 242 N. W. 526 [1932]), the court said of a statute of this type: ". . . . It recognizes her legal individuality, and preserves for her every right that she had prior to her marriage."

§ 150]

It has been pointed out in **Section 149** that in general a married woman should have the same legal rights and be subject to the same liabilities as her husband. The question is, how may that result best be obtained? On first impression, the broad equal-rights statutes appear to be the logical method; but there are certain objections to such statutes that should not be overlooked.

It is fundamental that the legislative intent to place the wife on an equal basis should be certain and unambiguous, and the broad statutes that have been adopted are not free from uncertainty. The **Wisconsin** provision is particularly subject to such criticism. (See summary following; and see also *Wait* v. *Pierce,* 191 Wis. 202; 209 N. W. 475 [1926].) The terms of most of the other statutes seem to evince an intent to effect a complete emancipation of the wife. In practice, however, there has been a great deal of controversy regarding their effect, particularly as they relate to rights and liabilities between spouses. Contrary decisions have been reached under virtually identical statutes (see *Fiedler* v. *Fiedler,* 42 Okla. 124; 140 P. 1022 [1914]; and *Strom* v. *Strom,* 98 Minn. 427; 107 N. W. 1047 [1906]), and until the provisions are judicially construed on each question presented their meaning often is in doubt. At least two courts have gone so far as to hold that these statutes do not confer new substantive rights upon the wife, but merely remove common-law procedural disabilities (*Nash* v. *Mobile & Ohio Railroad Company,* 149 Miss. 823; 116 So. 100 [1928]; *Kosciolek* v. *Portland Railway,* 81 Ore. 517; 160 P. 132 [1916]; contra *Wait* v. *Pierce,* 191 Wis. 202; 209 N. W. 475 [1926]).

A further objection is that in the majority of the equal-rights statutes nothing is expressly said regarding the liabilities of the wife. It is true that most of the foregoing jurisdictions recognize, in varying degrees, that the wife is liable on her contracts (**Sec. 152**) and for her torts (**Sec. 157**), or that she may be sued alone (**Sec. 179**). But if a broad equal-rights statute is adopted, such statute logically should place an equality of burden upon the wife. If the statute uses language to the effect that the wife has the same rights as the husband and is subject to the same liabilities (see the **Arizona** provision), it should also reserve the special privileges accorded women in general: for example, the separate classification for women in laws relating to hours and conditions of work. If, on the other hand, it is said that the wife has the same rights and is subject to the same liabilities as a single woman, the reservation of special privileges of women is unnecessary. But in such case, to avoid uncertainty, it is very essential that the statute define the

[§ 150

rights and obligations between spouses; for how can it be said that the wife is in the same position as a feme sole in controversies concerning her husband? A minor objection to the equal-rights statutes is that, when such broad provisions are enacted, inconsistent laws limiting the rights of the wife are often retained in the statute books.

On the whole, unless a broad statute is more carefully worded and is more explicit than are the equal-rights statutes which have been adopted, it is better to confine legislation to particular rights and obligations of the wife.

Two other types of statutes may be mentioned briefly. Nine jurisdictions provide that the husband is the "head of the family" (**California, Georgia, Idaho, Montana, New Mexico, North Dakota, Ohio, Oklahoma, South Dakota**). For many purposes such statutes are unimportant, as is indicated in subsequent sections of this volume. They are material, however, in regard to the domicile of the wife (see **Sec. 164**). The **Georgia** statute further provides that the wife's legal civil existence in general is merged in the husband, except so far as the law recognizes her separately (see summary following). In the light of the modern concept of the marital relation, such a statute is unjustified; but other express statutes in **Georgia** have abrogated much of the effect of the foregoing provision. The reader is referred to *Curtis* v. *Ashworth,* 165 Ga. 782; 142 S. E. 111 (1928), for a good discussion of the present situation in **Georgia.** It was correctly said in that case: "While the husband is still declared by statute to be head of the family (Civil Code, Sec. 2992), he, like the King of England, is largely a figurehead." Eight of the foregoing states (**Georgia** excepted) have another general statute of little practical significance. It is said that husband and wife contract toward each other obligations of mutual respect, fidelity, and support. **Louisiana** has a similar statute. Miscellaneous provisions of a general nature were found in **Hawaii, North Dakota,** and **Oklahoma** (see summary).

In the summary following, the words of the statutes have been reproduced as far as is practicable.

SUMMARY

Alaska (Comp. L. 1913, Sec. 495) : All laws which impose or recognize civil disabilities upon a wife not imposed or recognized upon the husband are hereby repealed; and for any unjust usurpation of her property or natural rights she has the same right to appeal in her own name alone to all courts for redress that he has.

§ 150]

Arizona (R. C. 1928, Sec. 2174) : Married women of the age of twenty-one and upwards have the same legal rights as men of that age, except the right to make contracts binding the common property of husband and wife, and are subject to the same legal liabilities as men of such age.

Arkansas (Crawf. and Moses, Dig. 1921, Sec. 5577) : Every married woman has all the rights to contract and be contracted with, to sue and be sued, and in law and equity shall enjoy all rights and be subjected to all laws of this State as though she were a femme sole. It is expressly declared to be the intention of this act to remove all statutory disabilities of married women as well as common law disabilities, such as the disability to act as executrix or administratrix, and all other statutory disabilities.

California (C. C. 1933 [Lake], Secs. 155–56) : Husband and wife contract toward each other obligations of mutual respect, fidelity and support. Husband is head of the family.

Georgia (C. 1926, C. C., Sec. 2992) : The husband is head of the family and the wife is subject to him; her legal civil existence is merged in him except so far as the law recognizes her separately, either for her own protection or benefit, or for the preservation of public order.

Hawaii (R. L. 1925, Sec. 3119) : All married women shall adopt the names of their husbands as a family name.

Idaho (Comp. St. 1919, Secs. 4654–55) : Same provisions as those in **California.**

Louisiana (Sess. L. 1928, Act 283, p. 583) : All married women are fully emancipated from all disabilities and relieved from all incapacities to which, as such, they are now subject. In no case shall any act, contract or obligation of a married woman require, for the validity thereof, the authority of her husband or of the Judge. The above does not apply to married women until they reach the age of eighteen, nor does it affect the law relating to the matrimonial community of *acquêts* and gains. (C. C., Art. 119) : Husband and wife owe to each other mutually, fidelity, support and assistance.

Minnesota (G. S. 1923, Sec. 8616) : Women shall retain the same legal existence and legal personality after marriage as before, and every married woman shall receive the same protection of all her rights as a woman which her husband does as a man, including the right to appeal to the courts in her own name alone for protection or redress. This section does not confer upon the wife a right to vote or hold office except as is otherwise provided by law.

[§ 150

Mississippi (Const., Sec. 94): Married women are fully emancipated from all disability on account of coverture, but the legislature is not prevented from regulating contracts between spouses. (C. 1930, Sec. 1940): The common law as to disabilities of married women and its effect upon rights of property of the wife is totally abrogated; and she has the same capacity to acquire, own and dispose of property, real and personal, in possession or expectancy, and to make any contract in reference to it, and to bind herself personally, and to sue and be sued with all the rights and liabilities incident thereto, as if she were not married.

Montana (R. C. 1921, Secs. 5782–83): Same provisions as those in **California**.

New Mexico (St. Ann. 1929, Secs. 68[101]–68[102]): Same provisions as those in **California**.

North Dakota (Comp. L. 1913, Sec. 4411): The wife after marriage has with respect to property, contracts, and torts the same capacity and rights and is subject to the same liabilities as before marriage, and in all actions by or against her she shall sue and be sued in her own name. (Secs. 4407–8): Same positions as those in **California**. (Supp. 1913–25, Sec. 4414): Neither husband nor wife, as such, is answerable for the acts of the other.

Ohio (Complete G. C. 1931 [Page], Secs. 7995–96): Same provisions as those in **California**.

Oklahoma (St. 1931, Sec. 1665): Woman shall retain the same legal existence and legal personality after marriage as before, and shall receive the same protection of all her rights as a woman which her husband does as a man; and for any injury to her reputation, person, property, character, or any natural right, she shall have the same right to appeal in her own name alone to the courts of law or equity for redress and protection that her husband has; provided that this does not confer upon the wife a right to vote or hold office except as otherwise provided by law. (Secs. 1651–52): Same provisions as those in **California**. (Sec. 1659): Neither husband nor wife, as such, is answerable for the acts of the other.

Oregon (C. 1930, Sec. 33[215]): All laws which impose or recognize civil disabilities upon a wife not imposed or recognized upon the husband are repealed, and for any unjust usurpation of her property or natural rights she has the same right to appeal in her own name alone to courts of law or equity for redress that he has; provided that this does not confer upon the wife the right to vote or hold office except as otherwise provided by law.

§ 150]

South Dakota (Comp. L. 1929, Sec. 178) : The wife shall have and retain after marriage all the civil and property rights of a single woman; and for any injury to her reputation, person, or property, she may sue in her own name without joining her husband, and in like manner actions founded upon her separate contracts or torts or relating to her individual property may be brought against her without joining him; provided that this does not confer upon the wife the right of suffrage or of holding office except as otherwise expressly provided. (Secs. 167–68) : Same provisions as those in **California.**

Tennessee (C. 1932, Secs. 8460–61) : Married women are fully emancipated from all disability on account of coverture, and the common law as to the disabilities of married women and its effect on their property rights is totally abrogated, except that tenancies by the entirety and curtesy consummate are not thereby affected.

Washington (Remington, Comp. St. 1922, Sec. 6901) : Same provision as that in **Oregon.**

Wisconsin (St. 1931, Sec. 6.015) : Women shall have the same rights and privileges under the law as men in the exercise of suffrage, freedom of contract, choice of residence for voting purposes, jury service, holding office, holding and conveying property, care and custody of children, and in all other respects. Statutes where the masculine gender is used are construed as including the feminine gender unless that will deny females the special protection and privileges which they now enjoy for the general welfare.

CASES

The following cases contain statements relative to the effect of the equal-rights statutes. Many of them involve personal-injury actions by a wife against her husband, and demonstrate vividly some of the uncertainty referred to in the text. The numerous and vigorous dissents should be noted:

Katzenberg v. *Katzenberg,* 183 Ark. 626; 37 S. W. (2d) 696 (1931); *Moulin* v. *Monteleone,* 165 La. 169; 115 So. 447 (1927); *State* v. *Arnold,* 182 Minn. 313; 235 N. W. 373 (1931); *Strom* v. *Strom,* 98 Minn. 427; 107 N. W. 1047 (1906); *Austin* v. *Austin,* 136 Miss. 61; 100 So. 591 (1924); *Fitzmaurice* v. *Fitzmaurice,* 62 N. D. 191; 242 N. W. 526 (1932); *Fiedler* v. *Fiedler,* 42 Okla. 124; 140 P. 1022 (1914); *Kosciolek* v. *Portland Railway,* 81 Ore. 517; 160 P. 132 (1916); *Stout* v. *Van Zante,* 109 Ore. 430; 219 P. 804 (1923); *Lillienkamp* v. *Rippetoe,* 133 Tenn. 57; 179 S. W. 628 (1915); *Morton* v. *State,* 141 Tenn. 357; 209 S. W. 644 (1918); *Raines* v. *Mercer,* 165 Tenn. 415; 55 S. W. (2d) 263 (1932); *Schultz* v. *Christopher,* 65 Wash. 496; 118 P. 629 (1911); *First Wisconsin National Bank* v. *Jahn,* 179

Wis. 117; 190 N. W. 822 (1922); *Fontaine* v. *Fontaine,* 205 Wis. 570; 238 N. W. 410 (1931); *Wait* v. *Pierce,* 191 Wis. 202; 209 N. W. 475 (1926).

REFERENCES
Articles

STOUT, CLAUDE D. "The Legal Status of Women in Wisconsin," 14 Marq. L. Rev. 66–80, 121–69, 199–211 (1930).

THEOBALD, THOMAS D., JR. "Does Equity Protect Property Rights in Domestic Relations?" 19 Ky. L. Jour. 57–68 (1930).

TURNER, JENNIE McMULLIN. "Women's Rights by Blanket Legislation," 2 Wis. L. Rev. 103–9 (1922).

Notes

"Liability of One Spouse to the Other for Personal Torts under the Married Women's Acts," 38 Harv. L. Rev. 383–89 (1925).

"Right of a Wife to Maintain an Action against Her Husband for Injuries to Her Person Caused by His Negligence," *Wait* v. *Pierce,* 191 Wis. 202; 209 N. W. 475 (1926)—4 Wis. L. Rev. 37–40 (1926); 11 Minn. L. Rev. 79–80 (1926).

"Wife May Choose Her Own Form of Religious Worship," *Hughes* v. *Holman,* 110 Ore. 415; 223 P. 730 (1924)—10 Va. L. Reg. (N.S.) 843 (1925).

Section 151. Wife's Antenuptial Debts and Contracts

CROSS REFERENCES: Wife's antenuptial torts, **Sec. 157;** Liability of community property for wife's antenuptial obligations, **Sec. 178;** Suits against wife, **Sec. 179**

At common law, the husband became liable by virtue of the marriage for the antenuptial obligations of his wife. His liability, being created by the assumption of the marital status, ended with the dissolution of the marriage. He was answerable for her antenuptial obligations regardless of how little property she brought to him; for, in the words of Blackstone, "he has adopted her and all her circumstances" (1 Black. 443). It is obvious that the common law operated unfairly upon all concerned.

In forty-four of the jurisdictions examined, the husband's common-law liability in this respect is either entirely abrogated or greatly limited by express statute. In the other seven jurisdictions, it seems hardly probable that this burden is now imposed upon him. Statutes in the following thirty-six jurisdictions expressly provide that the husband (or his property) is not answerable for the debts or liabilities of the wife contracted or incurred before marriage: **Alabama, Alaska, Arizona, California, Connecticut, District of Columbia, Florida, Hawaii, Idaho, Illinois, Iowa, Maine, Maryland, Massachusetts, Minnesota, Montana, Nebraska, Nevada, New Hampshire, New Jersey, New Mexico, North Carolina, North Dakota, Oklahoma, Oregon, Pennsylvania, Rhode Island, South Carolina, South Dakota, Tennessee, Texas, Utah, Vermont, Virginia, Washington, and Wisconsin.** In five of the foregoing jurisdictions where the community-property system obtains (**Arizona, California, Idaho, New Mexico, Texas**), it is provided that the "separate property" of the husband is not liable for the wife's antenuptial debts. The courts are in conflict as to whether the community property is liable (see **Sec. 178**). If the community property is liable, it is to be observed that the common law is not completely abrogated, but that the husband's liability persists to the extent of his interest in the community.

Two jurisdictions free the husband of the burden of his wife's antenuptial debts unless he assumes it in writing. **Arkansas** requires "an express written contract," and **Wyoming,** "an assumption in writing."

Six jurisdictions limit the liability of the husband for the antenuptial debts of the wife to the extent or value of property he may receive from her. **Colorado** makes the husband liable "to the extent of the real and personal property he may receive with or through her, or derive from the rent or sale of her lands, and no further." The **Indiana** statute is the same, except that it covers only personal property received with or through the wife, or derived from the rent or sale of her lands. Both states expressly provide that such liability of the husband shall not be extinguished by the death of the wife. **Kentucky** exempts the husband, "except to the amount or value of the property he may receive from or by her by virtue of the marriage," and **Missouri** exempts the property of the husband "except such as may be acquired from the wife." In **New York** his liability extends to the property acquired "of his wife by antenuptial contract or otherwise." The **West Virginia** statute is the broadest and operates on husband and wife alike. It provides that if real or personal property is transferred or conveyed by either spouse to the other, before or after marriage, by reason of antenuptial agreement or otherwise, the spouse receiving the property is liable for the obligations of the other created before the transfer or conveyance to the extent of the value of the property so transferred or conveyed. Obviously, these six statutes are open to varying constructions. The husband's common-law rights in the wife's property solely by virtue of the marriage have

[§ 151

been universally abrogated (**Sec. 167**). If the foregoing statutes are significant today, it must be mainly because they operate on marriage settlements. They seem to be designed to protect the wife's creditors from transfers which fall short of being fraudulent conveyances, and to perpetuate the theory that if the husband gets the wife's property he should be liable for the debts she brings with it. The soundness of this position is certainly open to question.

No statutes expressly abrogating the common law on the subject were found in the other seven jurisdictions (**Delaware, Georgia, Kansas, Louisiana, Michigan, Mississippi, Ohio**). The husband's liability was never regarded as that of a debtor, but grew out of the peculiar legal consequences of marriage at common law. When the wife is given the substantive rights and liabilities of a single woman as to property, and her procedural disabilities are removed, the foundation of the husband's liability is gone. In at least two of the foregoing states, the courts have held that the common-law rule is abrogated (*Smith* v. *Martin,* 124 Mich. 34; 82 N. W. 662 [1900]; *Y and O Coal Company* v. *Paszka,* 20 Ohio App. 248; 152 N. E. 31 [1925]). Both jurisdictions, however, have general statutes to the effect that the husband is not liable for the contracts or conduct of the wife. Finally, the common-law rule never did obtain in **Louisiana.**

Coverture itself did not extinguish the wife's responsibility for her antenuptial obligations. Upon the husband's death, her liability revived. If the common-law disabilities of coverture are removed by statute, the wife's liability on her antenuptial contracts would seem to follow naturally. The following jurisdictions, however, have seen fit to provide specifically that she or her property shall be so liable: **Alabama, California, Colorado, Delaware, District of Columbia, Florida, Idaho, Indiana, Kentucky, Maine, Maryland, Missouri, Montana, Nevada, New Jersey, New Mexico, North Carolina, North Dakota, Oklahoma, South Dakota, West Virginia, Wisconsin, Wyoming.** The statutes of **California, Idaho, Nevada,** and **New Mexico** (all community-property states) refer to the "separate property" of the wife. In three states, if a woman with liabilities marries, and has or acquires lands, judgment may be rendered against her (**Wyoming**) or against her and her husband jointly (**Colorado, Indiana**) to be levied on such lands "only." These latter provisions seem strangely out of place even in the jurisdictions in which they are found.

Apparently as a matter of formal reciprocity, the following jurisdictions expressly provide that the wife is not liable for the antenuptial obligations of the husband (**Alaska, Arizona, Arkansas, Illinois, Iowa, Nevada, Oregon, Utah, Washington**). The same is true, of course, without the aid of statute. The unusual **West Virginia** legislation, to which reference has already been made, operates in the opposite direction and imposes upon the wife a limited liability for the husband's premarital obligations.

Citations for the statutes discussed above follow:

Alabama, C. 1923, Sec. 8625; **Alaska,** Comp. L. 1913, Sec. 443; **Arizona,** R. C. 1928, Sec. 2175; **Arkansas,** Crawf. and Moses, Dig. 1921, Secs. 5577, 5589–90; **California,** C. C. 1933 (Lake), Secs. 170–71; **Colorado,** Comp. L. 1921, G. S., Secs. 5580–82; **Connecticut,** G. S. 1930, Sec. 5154; **Delaware,** R. C. 1915, Sec. 3060; **District of Columbia,** C. 1929, T. 14, Ch. 2, Sec. 45; **Florida,** R. G. S. 1920, Sec. 3950; **Georgia,** C. 1926, C. C., Secs. 2993, 3007; **Hawaii,** R. L. 1925, Sec. 3001; **Idaho,** Comp. St. 1919, Sec. 4664; **Illinois,** Cahill, R. S. 1931, Ch. 68, Sec. 5; **Indiana,** Burns, Ann. St. 1926, Secs. 8747–49; **Iowa,** C. 1927, Sec. 10465; **Kansas,** R. S. 1923, Secs. 23(201), 23(203); **Kentucky,** Carroll, St. 1922, Secs. 2127, 2130; **Maine,** R. S. 1930, Ch. 74, Sec. 4; **Maryland,** Bagby, Ann. C. 1924, Art. 45, Secs. 5, 14; **Massachusetts,** G. L. 1932, Ch. 209, Sec. 8; **Michigan,** Comp. L. 1929, Sec. 13059; **Minnesota,** G. S. 1923, Sec. 8620; **Mississippi,** C. 1930, Sec. 1940; **Missouri,** R. S. 1929, Secs. 3003–4; **Montana,** R. C. 1921, Secs. 5790, 5798–99; **Nebraska,** Comp. St. 1929, Sec. 42(206); **Nevada,** Comp. L. 1929 (Hillyer), Sec. 3370; Sess. L. 1933, Ch. 96, p. 118; **New Hampshire,** Pub. L. 1926, Ch. 288, Sec. 3; **New Jersey,** Comp. St. 1910, p. 3235, Sec. 10; **New Mexico,** St. Ann. 1929, Secs. 68(306)–68(307); **New York,** Cahill, Consol. L. 1930, Ch. 14, Sec. 54; **North Carolina,** C. 1927, Sec. 2517; **North Dakota,** Comp. L., Supp. 1913–25, Sec. 4414; **Ohio,** Complete G. C. 1931 (Page), Secs. 7998, 8002; **Oklahoma,** St. 1931, Sec. 1659; **Oregon,** C. 1930, Sec. 33(205); **Pennsylvania,** St. 1920 (West), Secs. 8690, 14586; **Rhode Island,** G. L. 1923, Sec. 4204; **South Carolina,** C. of L. 1922, C. C., Sec. 5540; **South Dakota,** Comp. L. 1929, Sec. 175; **Tennessee,** C. 1932, Sec. 8459; **Texas,** Complete St. 1928, Civ. St., Art. 4613, as amended in Supp. 1931, Sec. 4613; **Utah,** R. S. 1933, 40-2-5; **Vermont,** G. L. 1917, Sec. 3526; **Virginia,** C. 1930, Sec. 5134, as amended by Sess. L. 1932, Ch. 25, p. 21; **Washington,** Remington, Comp. St. 1922, Sec. 6905; **West Virginia,** C. 1931, Ch. 48, Art. 3, Secs. 14, 15; **Wisconsin,** St. 1931, Sec. 246.08; **Wyoming,** R. S. 1931, Secs. 69(106), 69(107).

REFERENCES

Books

BLACKSTONE, SIR WILLIAM. *Commentaries on the Laws of England,* I, 443 (1765–66).

MADDEN, JOSEPH WARREN. *Handbook of the Law of Persons and Domestic Relations,* pp. 233–41 (1931).

SCHOULER, JAMES. *A Treatise on the Law of Marriage, Divorce, Separation and Domestic Relations,* 6th ed., I, 99–104 (1921).

[§ 151

Note

"Husband's Liability for Wife's Antenuptial Debts," *Johnson* v. *Taylor,* 120 Cal.
App. 771; 4 P. (2d) 999 (1931)—18 Va. L. Rev. 795–96 (1932).

Annotations

"Liability of Community Property for Antenuptial Debts of Husband and Wife,"
19 L. R. A. 235 (1893).
"Liability of Husband for Antenuptial Debts of Wife," 60 Amer. Dec. 259–61
(1884).
"What Amounts to Laches or Delay on Part of Wife or Widow in Attacking Antenuptial Settlement Which Will Prevent Relief," 74 A. L. R. 559–61 (1931).

Section 152. Wife's Postnuptial Debts and Contracts—In General

CROSS REFERENCES: Wife's antenuptial contracts, **Secs. 151, 155**; Contracts of
abandoned wife, **Sec. 143**; Wife's contracts for necessaries, **Sec. 153**; Wife's
contracts with husband, **Sec. 156**; Family expenses, **Sec. 160**; Power of wife
to bind community property, **Sec. 178**; Wife's conveyances and transfers of her
real and personal property, **Secs. 182, 183, 185**; Wife as a sole trader, **Sec. 187**;
Wife as stockholder, bank depositor, etc., **Sec. 230**; Contracts of infant, **Sec.
273**

Except in certain extreme situations in which the husband was regarded as civilly dead, the wife's promise at common law was void. It
was thus of less weight than an infant's promise. The almost complete
loss of her property rights upon coverture left her with little occasion
to contract. With certain limitations, however, the wife could bind her
separate estate in equity by contracts made in reference thereto. Her
power in this respect was an equitable incident to her separate estate.

Statutes in the past have often followed the old equitable outlines,
and permitted the wife to contract only in reference to her separate
statutory estate. Until recently, even many of the more liberal jurisdictions expressly denied the wife's power to bind herself on contracts
of suretyship, and other particularly onerous and non-beneficial contracts. The last twenty-five years, however, have brought a considerable
wave of legislation completely removing the disability of the wife to
bind herself and her property by contract. Her common-law incapacity
is gone in all jurisdictions, and her power to contract is that of a feme
sole in most jurisdictions. Even the special limitations relative to surety-

ship and kindred matters have now largely disappeared from the statutes.

Legislation which unequivocally invests the wife with a broad power to contract with others than the husband was found in forty-six of the jurisdictions examined. These statutes may be classified as follows:

1. In twenty-seven jurisdictions, by express statute, the wife may apparently contract as if unmarried without limitation (**Alaska, Arizona, Arkansas, Colorado, Connecticut, Delaware, District of Columbia, Illinois, Iowa, Louisiana, Maryland, Massachusetts, Minnesota, Missouri, Montana, New Jersey, North Dakota, Ohio, Rhode Island, South Carolina, Utah, Vermont, Virginia, Washington, West Virginia, Wisconsin, Wyoming**).

2. In nine jurisdictions (**California, Mississippi, Nevada, New Mexico, New York, Oklahoma, Pennsylvania, South Dakota, Tennessee**), she may contract in reference to or respecting property as if unmarried, except that in **Pennsylvania** she cannot become accommodation endorser, maker, guarantor, or surety for another. The fact that the wife must confine her contracts to those in "reference" to or "respecting" property does not seem to limit her contractual power materially.

3. In six jurisdictions, the wife may contract as if unmarried subject to the limitations specified. Her power to bind herself or her property as surety for her husband, or for others, is either limited or denied (**Alabama, Georgia, Kentucky, New Hampshire**). She cannot make an executory contract to sell or mortgage her lands without the husband's joinder (**Indiana, Kentucky**); or contract for personal service without the written consent of the husband (**Hawaii**); or be agent for another than her husband without his consent (**Georgia**). Several other jurisdictions do not permit the wife to contract with the husband (**Sec. 156**), or convey her lands without his joinder (**Sec. 183**). A number of statutes are also express to the effect that she cannot by her sole act during coverture deprive the husband of his survivor's share of her lands. That, of course, is true in all jurisdictions which retain curtesy or a similar substitute (see **Secs. 215** *et seq.*).

4. The statutes of four jurisdictions seem to limit the wife's contracts to those made with reference to her separate property (**Idaho, Kansas, Nebraska, North Carolina**). One must go to the cases to determine the ultimate extent of the wife's power to contract in these states.

In the remaining five jurisdictions (**Florida, Maine, Michigan,**

[§ 152

Oregon, Texas), no legislation expressly investing the wife with a general power to contract was found. Under the **Oregon** equal-rights statute, the wife may apparently contract as a feme sole. **Maine** seems to reach the same result by providing that she is liable for her debts contracted in her own name for any lawful purpose. In **Florida, Michigan,** and **Texas,** the wife's disability has been only partially removed (see table and notes following). **Florida** and **Texas** are by far the most backward states in this respect, and stand conspicuously out of harmony with all the other American jurisdictions.

The liability of the wife on her contracts follows as an incident from her statutory power to contract. The table following, however, will indicate that most jurisdictions have express legislation to that effect. In the community-property states, the wife is generally without power to bind the community (**Sec. 178**). A majority of jurisdictions have taken the precaution to provide that the husband and his property are not answerable for the debts contracted by the wife (except for necessaries, etc.; see **Secs. 153, 160**). The statutes of **Kentucky** and **West Virginia** are unique in this respect. **Kentucky** ambiguously provides that the husband is not liable except to the amount or value of property he may receive from or by the wife by virtue of the marriage. In **West Virginia,** if the wife transfers property to the husband, he is liable for her contractual obligations created prior to the transfer to the extent of the value of the property so transferred. In terms, the statute is not confined to fraudulent transfers, or to those without consideration. Finally, **Georgia** archaically provides that the wife cannot be an agent for another than her husband without his consent, in which case he is bound by her acts.

It seems needless to suggest that the wife should be given the same power to bind herself by contract that the husband enjoys. Her common-law immunity from liability on her promises was never regarded as a privilege or protection, but rather as the natural consequence of a total incapacity. The wife neither needs nor desires privilege or protection today. To restrict her power to contract upon either theory is hardly consistent with modern standards. The rapid evolution of the wife's statutory power to contract in recent years is an acknowledgment of that fact.

The table follows.

§ 152]

TABLE LXXVIII*

The Wife's Postnuptial Contracts

Jurisdiction and Citation	Wife's Power to Contract	Wife's Liability	Husband's Liability
Alabama .... C. 1923, Secs. 8266–67, 8272, 8274–75	Wife over eighteen years of age has full legal capacity to contract as if sole, except that she cannot directly or indirectly become a surety for her husband. Contracts of non-resident wife concerning real or personal property in **Alabama** have same force as if made by resident wife	Wife is liable as if sole	Husband is not liable
Alaska .... Comp. L. 1913, Secs. 439, 443, 494	Contracts may be made by the wife in same manner as if sole	Wife's contracts may be enforced against her as if she were sole	Neither the husband nor his property is liable
Arizona .... R. C. 1928, Sec. 2174	Wife of twenty-one years or more has the same legal rights as men of that age, except the right to make contracts binding the community property	Wife of twenty-one years or more has the same liabilities as men of that age	
Arkansas .... Crawf. and Moses, Dig. 1921, Secs. 5577, 5581–82	Wife may contract and be contracted with as if sole	Wife is liable as if sole	Wife's contracts in respect to her separate property, or trade, or business do not bind the husband or his property
California .... C. C. 1933 (Lake), Secs. 158, 167, 171	Wife may enter into any engagement or transaction respecting property which she might if sole	Separate property of the wife is liable	Community property is not liable unless contract is secured by pledge or mortgage thereof executed by husband
Colorado .... Comp. L. 1921, G. S., Secs. 2451, 5584–86	Wife may enter into any contract the same as if she were sole. Wife may be a special partner	Judgment may be rendered and enforced against her as if she were sole	
Connecticut .... G. S. 1930, Secs. 5154–55	Wife may contract as if unmarried (in case of marriage on or after April 20, 1877)	Wife is liable and her property may be attached and taken on execution	Husband is not liable

* See pages 45–46 for all numbered footnotes to this table.

[§ 152

TABLE LXXVIII *(Continued)*

Jurisdiction and Citation	Wife's Power to Contract	Wife's Liability	Husband's Liability
Delaware .... R. C. 1915, Sec. 3048, amd. by Sess. L. 1919, Ch. 197, p. 524; Sec. 3052, amd. by Sess. L. 1919, Ch. 197, p. 526; Sec. 3060	Wife may contract as if sole, but she cannot affect husband's right to curtesy. Wife may purchase land and secure purchase money by mortgage, etc.	Wife's contracts are a charge on her separate property, and a personal judgment may be recovered against her	Husband is not liable on wife's purchase-money mortgage, etc., unless he is a party thereto
District of Columbia C. 1929, T. 14, Secs. 22, 43, 44	Wife may contract and be contracted with as if sole. Wife's contracts deemed to be made in reference to her statutory and equitable separate estate as a source of credit unless a contrary intent is expressed. Wife as grantee or lessee may bind herself and assigns by covenant running with the land	Judgment may be recovered against wife, and execution issued as if she were sole	Husband is not liable upon wife's contract made in her own name and upon her own responsibility
Florida .... Const., Art. 11, Sec. 2; R. G. S. 1920, Secs. 3218–22, 3948, 4222	See footnote 1 following	See footnote 1 following	
Georgia .... C. 1926, C. C., Secs. 3007, 3011, ˄573	Wife is a feme sole as to her separate estate unless controlled by settlement. She may contract, but cannot bind her separate estate by any contract of suretyship, or by any assumption of husband's debts. Wife cannot be agent for another than her husband without his consent		Husband is bound by wife's acts when she is agent for third party with his consent
Hawaii .... R. L. 1925, Sec. 2994, amd. by Sess. L. 1931, Act 146, p. 142; Secs. 2997, 3002	Wife may contract as if sole, except that she cannot contract for personal service without written consent of husband, or contract with husband. Wife, otherwise qualified, may act as surety on all bonds, etc., required under laws of territory	Wife and her property are liable as if she were sole for her contracts in respect to her separate property, trade, business, labor, or services	Neither husband nor his property is liable (except in certain cases when wife becomes a sole trader—see **Sec. 187**)

§ 152]

TABLE LXXVIII *(Continued)*

Jurisdiction and Citation	Wife's Power to Contract	Wife's Liability	Husband's Liability
Idaho .... Comp. St. 1919, Secs. 4657, 4665	Wife may contract with reference to her separate estate in the same manner, to the same extent, and with like effect as husband may contract in relation to his property	Separate property of the wife is liable	Husband is bound by wife's contracts to no greater extent than wife is bound by his contracts
Illinois .... Cahill, R. S. 1931, Ch. 68, Secs. 5, 6	Wife may contract to the same extent as if unmarried	Wife's contracts may be enforced against her to same extent as if she were sole	Neither the husband nor his property is liable
Indiana .... Burns, Ann. St. 1926, Secs. 8738–39, 8741–42, 8744	Wife may contract as if sole, but she cannot enter into any executory contract to sell or mortgage her real estate without husband's joinder	Wife is bound as if sole by her covenants of title and as principal on her official bond	Husband is not liable for wife's contracts, including those made in carrying on her separate trade or business, or when in partnership with another than husband, or for improvement or repairs made on her lands by her order or authority
Iowa .... C. 1927, Secs. 10447, 10465–66	Wife may contract to the same extent as if sole	Wife's contracts may be enforced against her to the same extent as if she were sole	Neither the husband nor his property is liable
Kansas .... R. S. 1923, Sec. 23(202)	Wife may contract with reference to her real and personal property in the same manner, to the same extent, and with like effect as husband may contract in relation to his property	See preceding column	
Kentucky .... Carroll, St. 1922, Secs. 2127–28, 2130	Wife may contract as if sole, except that she cannot make an executory contract to convey or mortgage her lands without husband's joinder	Wife's separate estate is liable, except that upon a contract to answer for the debt, default, or misdoing of another, including her husband, her estate must have been set aside for that purpose by mortgage or other conveyance	Husband is not liable except to the amount or value of the property he may receive from or by her by virtue of the marriage

[§ 152

TABLE LXXVIII *(Continued)*

Jurisdiction and Citation	Wife's Power to Contract	Wife's Liability	Husband's Liability
Louisiana .... Sess. L. 1928, Act 283, p. 583	Wife of eighteen years may make contracts of all kinds and assume obligations of all kinds permitted by law for other persons, without authority of husband or judge. Wife of eighteen years may bind herself or her property by way of security or otherwise for benefit of husband or the community. (The foregoing does not modify the laws relating to the community)	See preceding column	
Maine .... R. S. 1930, Ch. 74, Secs. 1, 4	Wife may manage her separate property without joinder or assent of husband[2]	Wife is liable for her debts contracted in her own name for any lawful purpose.[2] Her property may be taken on execution as if she were sole, but she cannot be arrested	Husband is not liable for debts of wife contracted in her own name for any lawful purpose
Maryland .... Bagby, Ann. C. 1924, Art. 45, Secs. 5, 18, 20; Art. 71, Sec. 9	Wife may engage in business, form a co-partnership with any person, and make other contracts as fully as if unmarried. Wife as grantee or lessee may bind herself and assigns by covenant running with the land[3]	Judgment may be recovered and execution issued as if she were sole	Husband is not liable upon any contract made by wife in her own name and upon her own responsibility
Massachusetts ...... G. L. 1932, Ch. 209, Secs. 2, 9	Wife may make contracts as if she were sole, except that she is not authorized to contract with husband	Wife's contracts relative to her separate property, trade, labor, or services bind her and her separate estate as if she were sole	Wife's contracts relative to her separate property, trade, labor, or services do not bind husband or his property (except in certain cases when wife becomes a sole trader—see **Sec. 187**)
Michigan .... Comp. L. 1929, Secs. 13057, 13059, 13061, 13062–66	Wife's statutory separate estate may be "contracted" by her to same extent as if she were sole.[4] She may contract in relation to her personal earnings as if sole. Wife may bind and make herself jointly liable with husband upon any written instrument[4]	Wife is liable upon any contract made by her in cases where husband is not in law liable or where he refuses to perform such contract[4]	Husband is not liable upon any contract made by wife in relation to her sole property

§ 152]

TABLE LXXVIII *(Continued)*

Jurisdiction and Citation	Wife's Power to Contract	Wife's Liability	Husband's Liability
Minnesota .... G. S. 1923, Secs. 8618, 8620	Wife may make any contract which she could if sole	Wife is bound by her contracts and her property is liable for her debts as if she were sole	Husband is not liable
Mississippi .... Const., Sec. 94; C. 1930, Sec. 1940	Wife is fully emancipated from all disability on account of coverture. She may contract in reference to property as if she were sole	Wife may contract in reference to property and bind herself personally with all liabilities incident thereto as if she were sole	
Missouri .... R. S. 1929, Secs. 2998, 3484	Wife may contract and be contracted with as if she were sole[3]	Wife and her property are liable as if she were sole; but she may invoke exemption and homestead laws unless husband has already invoked same	
Montana .... R. C. 1921, Secs. 5786, 5790, 5799, 5810–11	Wife may make contracts in the same manner, to same extent, and with like effect as if she were sole	Wife and her separate property are liable	Husband, as such, is not answerable for acts of wife on debts contracted by her
Nebraska .... Comp. St. 1929, Sec. 42(205)	Wife may enter into any contract with reference to her real and personal property in the same manner, to the same extent, and with like effect as husband may contract in relation to his property	See preceding column	
Nevada .... Comp. L. 1929 (Hillyer), Secs. 3371, 3373	Wife may enter into any contract, engagement, or transaction respecting property which she might if sole	Separate property of wife is liable for her debts contracted after marriage	
New Hampshire..... Pub. L. 1926, Ch. 288, Sec. 2; Ch. 366, Sec. 26	Wife may contract as if sole, except that no contract or conveyance as surety or guarantor for husband, or any undertaking by her in his behalf, is binding on her, except a mortgage releasing her dower and homestead[3]	Wife and her property are liable as if she were sole	

[§ 152

TABLE LXXVIII (*Continued*)

Jurisdiction and Citation	Wife's Power to Contract	Wife's Liability	Husband's Liability
New Jersey Comp. St. 1910, p. 3226, Sec. 5, amd. by Supp. 1925–30, Sec. 124(5); p. 3235, Sec. 10; p. 3237, Sec. 14; p. 3238, Sec. 16	Wife may bind herself by contract in the same manner and to same extent as if she were sole, but she cannot affect husband's right to curtesy	Wife and her property are liable as if she were sole	Husband is not liable for debts contracted by wife in her own name
New Mexico St. Ann. 1929, Secs. 68(201), 68(307), 68(402), 100(219)	Wife may enter into any agreement or transaction respecting property which she might if sole. She may become a special partner	Separate property of wife is liable	Community property is not liable unless contract secured by pledge or mortgage thereof executed by husband
New York Cahill, Consol. L. 1930, Ch. 14, Secs. 51, 55	Wife has all rights in respect to the acquisition, use, enjoyment, and disposition of property and to make contracts in respect thereto as if she were sole	Wife is liable as if sole	Husband and his property are not bound
North Carolina C. 1927, Sec. 2507	Wife may contract and deal so as to affect her real and personal property in the same manner and with the same effect as if she were sole	See preceding column	
North Dakota Comp. L. 1913, Sec. 4411; Sec. 4414, amd. by Supp. 1913–25, p. 928	Wife has same capacity with respect to contracts as before marriage	Wife is subject to same liabilities with respect to contracts as before marriage	Husband, as such, is not answerable for acts of wife
Ohio Complete G. C. 1931 (Page), Secs. 7999, 8002	Wife may enter into any engagement or transaction which she might if sole		Husband, as such, is not answerable for acts of wife
Oklahoma St. 1931, Secs. 1655, 1659	Wife may enter into any engagement or transaction respecting property which she might if sole	Separate property of wife is liable	Husband, as such, is not answerable for acts of wife
Oregon C. 1930, Secs. 33(201), 33(205), 33(211), 33(215)	All laws which impose or recognize civil disabilities upon wife which are not imposed or recognized as existing as to husband are repealed.[5] Wife may manage her property to same extent as husband can his property	See preceding column	Neither husband nor his property is liable

TABLE LXXVIII *(Continued)*

Jurisdiction and Citation	Wife's Power to Contract	Wife's Liability	Husband's Liability
Pennsylvania .... St. 1920 (West), Secs. 8690, 14570, 14573, 14586	Wife may, as if single, make any contract which is necessary, convenient, or advantageous to the exercise and enjoyment of her right and power to acquire, own, control, and dispose of property; but she cannot become accommodation endorser, maker, guarantor, or surety for another[3]	Property of wife is liable	
Rhode Island....... G. L. 1923, Secs. 4195, 4204	The wife may make any contract whatsoever the same as if she were sole	Wife is liable as if she were sole	Husband is not liable
South Carolina...... Const., Art. XVII, Sec. 9; C. of L. 1922, C. C., Sec. 5540	Wife may bind herself by contract in the same manner and to the same extent as though she were sole	Wife's contracts may be enforced against her in law or equity, and execution may issue against her property as if she were sole	Husband is not liable
South Dakota....... Comp. L. 1929, Secs. 171, 175, 178	Wife may enter into any engagement or transaction respecting property which she might if sole. Wife retains after marriage all the civil and property rights of a single woman	Separate property of wife is liable	Husband, as such, is not answerable for the acts of wife
Tennessee .... C. 1932, Sec. 8460	Wife is fully emancipated from all disability on account of coverture. She may contract in reference to property, and bind herself personally as if sole, except that she cannot affect husband's curtesy	Wife may bind herself personally and sue and be sued with all the rights and incidents thereof as if she were sole	
Texas .... Complete St. 1928, C. Cr. P., Art. 276; Civ. St., Art. 1985; Arts. 4613, 4614, amd. by Supp. 1931, p. 381; Arts. 4620–21, 4623	Wife has sole management and control of her separate property (but husband must join in conveyances of land and transfer of stocks and bonds). Wife may never be the joint maker of a note, or a surety on any bond or obligation of another without joinder of husband[3,6]	Husband and wife are sued jointly for separate debts and demands against wife, but no personal judgment is rendered against the husband[6]	Separate property of husband is not liable (except for necessaries)[6]

[§ 152

TABLE LXXVIII (*Continued*)

Jurisdiction and Citation	Wife's Power to Contract	Wife's Liability	Husband's Liability
Utah .... R. S. 1933, 40-2-2, 40-2-5	Wife may contract to the same extent and in the same manner as if she were sole	Wife's contracts may be enforced against her to the same extent and in the same manner as if she were sole	Neither husband nor his property is liable
Vermont .... G. L. 1917, Sec. 3521; Sec. 3523, amd. by Sess. L. 1919, No. 90, p. 98, and Sess. L. 1929, No. 48, p. 63; Sess. L. 1933, No. 20, p. 21	Wife may contract with any person, other than the husband, in the same manner as if she were sole	Wife may bind herself and her separate property; execution may issue against her separate property as if she were sole	Husband living with or supporting wife is liable for poll tax or flood tax assessed against wife
Virginia .... C. 1930, Sec. 5134, amd. by Sess. L. 1932, Ch. 25, p. 21	Wife may contract, and be contracted with, in the same manner as if she were sole, but she cannot by her sole act deprive husband of his curtesy	Wife may contract with the "same consequences" as if sole	Husband is not liable
Washington .... Remington, Comp. St. 1922, Secs. 6890, 6902, 6905	Wife may contract in the same manner as if she were sole	Wife's contracts may be enforced against her to the same extent and in the same manner as if she were sole	Neither husband nor his separate property is liable for the separate debts of wife
West Virginia...... C. 1931, Ch. 48, Art. 3, Secs. 3, 8, 15, 18	Wife may contract the same as if sole. Wife may enter into partnership with any person	Wife is liable as if sole, and such liability may be enforced during coverture or after its termination. Wife's contracts to convey may be specifically enforced	If wife transfers or conveys real or personal property to husband before or after marriage, by reason of antenuptial contract or otherwise, husband is liable for wife's contractual obligations created before the transfer to the extent of the value of the property so transferred
Wisconsin .... St. 1931, Sec. 6.015	Women have the same rights and privileges under the law as men in the exercise of freedom of contract .... and in all other respects[7]	See footnote 7 following	
Wyoming .... R. S. 1931, Sec. 69(102)	Wife may make contracts in the same manner as if sole	Wife's contracts may be enforced against her as if she were sole	

§ 152]

TABLE LXXVIII (Continued)

[1] The wife in **Florida** has no general power to contract; her separate property remains under the care and management of the husband (R. G. S. 1920, Sec. 3948). By force of the constitutional provision defining her separate estate, she may at pleasure terminate the husband's control of her property (*Florida Citrus Exchange* v. *Grisham,* 65 Fla. 46; 61 So. 123 [1913]). In Revised General Statutes of 1920, Sections 3218–22 permit the wife to petition to the circuit court in the circuit of her residence praying for license to take charge and control of her separate estate, to contract freely, and to bind herself in all respects as fully as if she were unmarried. After notice and hearing, and inquiry before a master, the court, if satisfied as to her capacity and qualifications, may empower her by decree to contract as if unmarried.

Article 11, Section 2, of the **Florida** constitution provides that a married woman's separate estate may be charged in equity and sold for the purchase money thereof, for money or thing due upon any agreement made by her in writing for the benefit of her separate estate, or for the price of any property purchased by her, or for labor and materials used with her knowledge or assent in the construction of buildings, repairs, etc., upon her property, or for agricultural or other labor bestowed on her property with her knowledge and consent. In *Micou* v. *McDonald,* 55 Fla. 776; 46 So. 291 (1908), the court held that this provision enables the wife, in the cases therein specifically enumerated, to assume obligations that can be charged in equity and enforced out of her separate estate. Thus, she may obligate herself by an agreement in writing for the payment of money or thing of value that inures to the benefit of her separate estate. Revised General Statutes of 1920, Section 4222, provides that the wife may procure loans upon the security of her separate real estate by uniting with the husband in executing a mortgage thereon.

[2] No statute expressly authorizing married women to contract was found in **Maine**, although formerly there was such a statute permitting her to bind herself by contract made for any lawful purpose (see *Mayo* v. *Hutchinson,* 57 Me. 546 [1870], and Pub. L. 1866, Ch. 52).

[3] Wife as landlady may contract with boarders and lodgers and have all the legal rights and remedies given to persons conducting a boarding or lodging house, as if she were sole (**Maryland**); contracts by her in the purchase of sewing machines for her own use are valid without husband joining in the contract (**Pennsylvania**); wife is deemed capable in law of binding herself by recognizance for appearance at preliminary examination as prosecutrix or material witness in felony cases (**Missouri**); wife and her surety is bound by recognizance in the same manner as if she were sole (**New Hampshire**); wife cannot be surety on recognizance or bail bond, but, if she is the accused, the undertaking is binding on both principal and surety (**Texas**).

[4] No statute conferring upon the wife a general power to contract was found in **Michigan**. Under the provision cited in the table, she may contract in relation to her separate estate, but apparently that is the extent of her general power to contract (see *DeVries* v. *Conklin,* 22 Mich. 255 [1871]; *June* v. *LaBadie,* 132 Mich. 135; 92 N. W. 937 [1903]; 100 N. W. 996 [1904]). The 1929 Act giving the wife power to bind herself jointly with the husband upon any written instrument obviously extends her power to contract; but her liability on such contracts is confined to real estate owned by the spouses as tenants by the entirety, real estate acquired by either as survivor, and personal property and choses in action owned by them jointly with right of survivorship.

[5] The **Oregon** statutes formerly expressly provided that the wife might contract as if sole (L. 1920, Sec. 9758). This provision, along with many others, was repealed in 1927 (G. L. 1927, Ch. 144, p. 161). It seems clear, however, that the wife may contract freely under the equal-rights statute outlined in the table. See also *First National Bank* v. *Leonard,* 36 Ore. 390; 59 P. 873 (1900).

[6] The statutes of **Texas** neither expressly nor impliedly confer upon the wife a general power to contract. In *Lee* v. *Hall Music Company,* 120 Tex. 14; 35 S. W. (2d) 685, 687 (1931), the wife's power to contract was described as follows: "Our statutes impliedly invest the wife with power to contract for necessaries for herself and children as well as for such expenses as are incidental to the management and control of her separate estate and such community property as the statutes commit to her charge . . . . She also has the implied power under Article 4623 to become, jointly with her husband, the joint maker of a note or a surety on any bond or obligation of another. Save in the above respects the statutes do not give her power to bind herself to personal liability for debts." Neither the separate property of the husband nor the community property, other than the personal earnings of the wife and the income, rents, and revenues from her separate property, is subject to the payment of debts contracted by the

[§ 152

TABLE LXXVIII (*Concluded*)

wife, except those contracted for necessaries (Art. 4623). The community property is not liable for debts or damages resulting from contracts of the wife, except for necessaries, unless the husband joins in the execution of the contract (Art. 4621). See also **Sec. 178.**

⁷ Prior to the adoption of the sweeping **Wisconsin** equal-rights statute, the wife did not possess a general power to contract. She may now contract as freely as a man, and her liabilities, contractual or otherwise, may be enforced as similar liabilities may be enforced against men (see *First Wisconsin National Bank* v. *Jahn,* 179 Wis. 117; 190 N. W. 822 [1922]; *Sparks* v. *Kuss,* 195 Wis. 378; 216 N. W. 929; 218 N. W. 208 [1928]).

REFERENCES

Books

BLACKSTONE, SIR WILLIAM. *Commentaries on the Laws of England,* I, 442–45 (1765–66).

MADDEN, JOSEPH WARREN. *Handbook on the Law of Persons and Domestic Relations,* pp. 244 *et seq.* (1931).

SCHOULER, JAMES. *A Treatise on the Law of Marriage, Divorce, Separation and Domestic Relations,* 6th ed., I, 239 *et seq.* (1921).

STIMSON, F. J. *American Statute Law,* Secs. 6403, 6412 (1886).

Article

READER, F. E. "Married Women's Contracts of Suretyship," 38 Dickinson L. Rev. 230–54 (1934).

Notes

"Contracts of Married Woman, Validity Determined by Law of State Where Completed," *C.I.T. Corporation* v. *Sanderson,* 43 F. (2d) 985 (1930)—29 Mich. L. Rev. 773–74 (1931) ; 17 Va. L. Rev. 388–89 (1931).

"Contracts of Wife as Charge upon Her Separate Estate under Limited Statutes," *Jones & Company* v. *Black* (Tex. Civ. App.) ; 42 S. W. (2d) 151 (1931)—18 Va. L. Rev. 329–30 (1932).

Annotations

"Authority of Husband to Bind Wife by Assent to Account Stated," 2 A. L. R. 81–3 (1919).

"Conflict of Laws as to Capacity of Married Woman to Contract," 18 A. L. R. 1516–61 (1922) ; 71 A. L. R. 744–49 (1931).

"Disability of Married Woman under Common Law," 2 L. R. A. 345–48 (1889).

"Enforceability of a Mechanic's Lien against the Property of a Married Woman for Work Performed or Materials Furnished under a Contract Made with Her Husband," 4 A. L. R. 1025–66 (1919).

"Incapacity of Principal to Contract as Affecting Liability of Guarantor or Surety for Married Woman," 24 A. L. R. 841–44 (1923) ; 43 A. L. R. 589–90 (1926).

"Liability of Wife for Husband's Torts," 12 A. L. R. 1459–86 (1921).

"Married Woman Incapable to Contract as Surety," 8 L. R. A. 406–7 (1890).

"Married Woman's Power to Contract and Bind Her Separate Estate Therefor," 99 Amer. Dec. 598–610 (1888).

"Partnership between Husband and Wife in Business," 2 L. R. A. 343–44 (1889) ; 9 L. R. A. 593 (1890) ; 16 L. R. A. 526–28 (1892).

"Personal Liability of Married Woman for Domestic or Household Services," 36 A. L. R. 389–93 (1925).

"Scope and Effect of 'Special Protection and Privilege' in an Act Giving Women the Same Rights as Men," 26 A. L. R. 356 (1923).

"Suretyship of Wife under Mortgage of Separate Property for Husband's Debt," Ann. Cas. 1912D 108.

"Validity and Effect of Transfer of Expectancy by Married Woman," 17 A. L. R. 603 (1922).

"Validity of New Promise by Woman after Discoverture to Pay Debt Incurred during Coverture," 53 L. R. A. 366–70 (1902); 7 L. R. A. (N.S.) 1053–55 (1907); 33 L. R. A. (N.S.) 741–42 (1911); 17 A. L. R. 1341–52 (1922).

"Validity of Postnuptial Agreement Releasing or Waiving Rights of Surviving Spouse on Death of Other Spouse," 49 A. L. R. 116–53 (1927).

"Wife's Liability for Husband's Funeral Expenses," 57 A. L. R. 400–402 (1928).

●

Section 153. Wife's Postnuptial Debts and Contracts—Necessaries

CROSS REFERENCES: Family expenses, **Sec. 160**; Liability of community property for debts of wife, **Sec. 178**

At common law a married woman was so completely disabled by coverture that she could not bind herself by contract even for necessaries. If the husband did not adequately support her, however, she could bind him by contracting for necessaries upon his credit. The husband's liability in this respect arose from his duty to support his spouse so long as they lived together or lived apart by agreement or by reason of his own misconduct.

The common-law liability of the husband for necessaries furnished to the wife is affirmed in whole or in part by the statutes of sixteen jurisdictions. No statutes were found which substantially lighten the husband's duty in this respect.

Within the limits of her statutory power to contract (see **Sec. 152**), a married woman may today bind herself or her property by her own special contract for necessaries. It is still presumed, however, that she purchases necessaries on the credit of her husband (see *Stevens* v. *Hush,* 104 Misc. 69; 171 N. Y. S. 41 [1918]; *Feiner* v. *Boynton,* 73 N. J. L. 136; 162 A. 420 [1905]). **Georgia** has codified this presumption, while **Connecticut** and **West Virginia** have expressly provided that purchases made by the wife are presumed to be made on her own account and liability. The fact that the wife is given a separate statutory estate, free from the control of the husband, and the power to contract, does not lessen the husband's liability for necessaries furnished to her. (See *Ponder* v. *Morris & Brothers,* 152 Ala. 531; 44 So. 651 [1906]; *In re Bubb's Executors,* 132 Misc. 61; 229 N. Y. S. 567 [1928].)

The statutes of the **District of Columbia, Hawaii, Kentucky, Maryland,** and **Minnesota** merely state that the husband shall be liable for necessaries furnished to the wife or contracted by the wife. By implication **South Carolina** and **Texas** reach the same result by providing that the husband shall not be liable for the debts of the wife, except those contracted for her necessary support. **California, Ohio, Oklahoma, Montana, New Mexico, Nevada, North Dakota,** and **South Dakota** all provide that if the husband does not make adequate provision for the wife a third person in good faith may supply her with necessaries and recover the reasonable value thereof from the husband. The husband is not liable, however, if the wife has abandoned him, unless she offers to return or unless she was justified in leaving him because of his own misconduct. All of the foregoing jurisdictions except **Nevada** and **Ohio** venture beyond the common law at that point and free the husband of liability if the parties are living apart by agreement, unless such liability is stipulated in the agreement.

Georgia charges the husband with liability for necessaries furnished to the wife while the spouses are separated (until provision is made for separate maintenance, voluntarily or by decree), unless the wife lives in adultery or leaves him without cause. In the latter case "notice by the husband shall relieve him of all liability" for necessaries furnished to her. If the statute requires notice to free the husband of liability in such a case, it imposes a duty upon him which did not exist at common law. In **Oregon,** the husband is chargeable with debts contracted by the wife for the support and education of their minor children even though she wrongfully abandons him.

Maryland gives a rather unique statutory protection to a husband who believes that his wife is abusing her right to contract for necessaries on his credit. He may petition the court in equity in the county in which he resides for an order prohibiting the wife from pledging his credit, which order may be made if, after a hearing, the court is satisfied that the husband is properly supporting her. A tradesman who attempts to collect from the husband for goods furnished to the wife after written notice of the order is subject to an action by the husband for the annoyance and mortification caused. The wife is entitled to counsel, paid for by the husband, and may apply to the court for a rescission of the order if the husband does not continue reasonably to provide for her.

In many jurisdictions today the wife is made jointly liable with the husband for necessaries furnished to the family, or for family expenses, regardless of her assent (**Sec. 160**). There is nothing in the modern status of the wife to warrant lightening the husband's common-law duty of support. There do seem, however, to be strong considerations for imposing an analogous duty upon her in keeping with her modern status.

Citations to the statutes discussed in this section follow:

California, C. C. 1933 (Lake), Secs. 174–75; **Connecticut,** G. S. 1930, Secs. 5155, 5172; **District of Columbia,** C. 1929, T. 14, Sec. 46; **Georgia,** C. 1926, C. C., Secs. 2988, 2996–97; **Hawaii,** R. L. 1925, Sec. 3000; **Kentucky,** Carroll, St. 1922, Sec. 2130; **Maryland,** Bagby, Ann. C. 1924, Art. 16, Secs. 45, 49–51; **Minnesota,** G. S. 1923, Sec. 8620; **Montana,** R. C. 1921, Secs. 5800–5801; **Nevada,** Comp. L. 1929 (Hillyer), Secs. 3376–77; **New Mexico,** St. Ann. 1929, Ch. 68, Secs. 103–4; **North Dakota,** Comp. L. 1913, Secs. 4415–16; **Ohio,** Complete G. C. 1931 (Page), Secs. 8003–4; **Oklahoma,** St. 1931, Secs. 1660–61; **Oregon,** C. 1930, Sec. 33(206); **South Carolina,** C. of L. 1922, C. C., Sec. 5540; **South Dakota,** Comp. L. 1929, Secs. 176–77; **Texas,** Complete St. 1928, Civ. Sts., Arts. 4613, 4623; **West Virginia,** C. 1931, Ch. 48, Art. 3, Sec. 22.

REFERENCES

Books

MADDEN, JOSEPH WARREN. *Handbook on the Law of Persons and Domestic Relations,* pp. 190–98 (1931).

SCHOULER, JAMES. *A Treatise on the Law of Marriage, Divorce, Separation and Domestic Relations,* 6th ed., I, 105–47 (1921).

STIMSON, F. J. *American Statute Law,* Secs. 6403, 6412 (1886).

Articles

BROWN, ROBERT C. "The Duty of the Husband to Support the Wife," 18 Va. L. Rev. 823–44 (1932).

WRIGHT, CECIL A. "Implied Agency of the Wife for Necessaries," 8 Can. B. R. 722–28 (1930).

Annotations

"Duty of Husband to Provide Necessaries for Wife as Affected by Her Possession of Independent Means," 18 A. L. R. 1131–40 (1922).

"Estoppel of Man Representing Woman as His Wife to Deny Liability for Purchases by Her," Ann. Cas. 1913D 1062–63.

"Furniture and Household Goods as Necessaries for Which Husband Is Liable," 24 A. L. R. 1483–87 (1923).

"Husband's Liability for Legal Services in Attempting to Restore Wife's Capacity after Adjudication of Insanity," 26 A. L. R. 559 (1923).

"Husband's Liability for Money Loaned to Wife to Buy Necessaries," 23 L. R. A. 132 (XII) (1894).

"Liability of Husband for Necessaries as Affected by Question Whether or Not They Were Purchased on His Credit," 27 A. L. R. 554–79 (1923).

"Liability of Husband for Necessaries Furnished Wife while Living with Him," 47 L. R. A. (N.S.) 280–83 (1914); L. R. A. 1917F 861.

"Liability of Husband for Necessaries Furnished Wife while Living Apart from Him," L. R. A. 1917A 958.

"Liability of Husband for Services of Detective Employed by Wife to Shadow Him," 41 A. L. R. 1437 (1926).

"Liability of Husband in Independent Action for Services Rendered by Attorney to Wife in Divorce Suit," 25 A. L. R. 354–67 (1923); 42 A. L. R. 315–16 (1926).

"Liability of Husband for Support and Care of Insane Wife," 4 A. L. R. 1109–15 (1919).

"Liability of Married Woman for Necessaries," 15 A. L. R. 833–60 (1921).

"Right to Recover from Husband for Support Furnished to Wife after Clandestine Marriage," 30 A. L. R. 802 (1924).

"Wearing Apparel as Necessaries for Which Husband Is Liable," 60 A. L. R. 1185–91 (1929).

"Wife as Agent for Her Husband to Employ Physician," 71 A. L. R. 659–60 (1931).

Notes

"Legal Costs as Necessaries, Wife Guilty of Adultery," *Wright & Webb* v. *Cennandale,* 46 T. L. R. 403—4 Aust. L. Jour. 124–25 (1930).

"Liability for Expenses of Wife as Litigant," 42 Jurid. Rev. 257–58 (1930).

"Liability of Husband for Wife's Necessaries When He Has Furnished Her with Money," *Saks* v. *Huddleston,* 36 F. (2d) 537 (1929)—43 Harv. L. Rev. 961–62 (1930); 16 Va. L. Rev. 599–604 (1930); 15 St. Louis L. Rev. 298–99 (1930).

"Husband's Liability for Necessaries, Money Loaned to Wife," *Davis* v. *Fyfe,* 107 Cal. App. 281; 290 P. 468 (1931)—4 So. Calif. L. Rev. 244–45 (1931).

"Duty of Husband to Provide Necessaries," *Baledes* v. *Greenbaum,* 112 Conn. 64; 151 A. 333 (1930)—25 Ill. L. Rev. 712–15 (1931).

"Liability of Husband for Necessaries," *Tillie* v. *Finley,* 126 Ohio St. 578; 186 N. E. 448 (1933)—7 U. of Cinn. L. Rev. 428–30 (1933).

Section 154. Wife's Postnuptial Contracts—When Living Apart from Husband

CROSS REFERENCES: Powers and rights of abandoned and separated wives, **Sec. 143;** Powers and rights of abandoned and separated husbands, **Sec. 144;** Wives of aliens and non-residents, **Sec. 146**

At common law, the fact that the wife lived apart from the husband because of his desertion or other sufficient reason did not release her from the disabilities of coverture. It was only in certain unusual situations, in which the husband was regarded as civilly dead, that she acquired the capacity to contract. To obviate this extreme hardship, early statutes commonly conferred upon her the power to contract as a feme sole when living apart from the husband by reason of his misconduct. As the general statutory capacity of married women to contract matured, these early statutes became unnecessary. Many of them have been repealed. Those that remain in the present statutory compilations are summarized in **Section 143,** Volume II, of this series.

REFERENCES
Note

"Liability of a Husband for His Wife's Contracts while Apart," 74 Law Jour. 39–40, 58 (1932).

Section 155. Wife's Contracts with Husband before Marriage

CROSS REFERENCES: Statute of Frauds, **Sec. 7;** Wife's contracts with husband after marriage, **Sec. 156;** Barring dower by jointure, **Sec. 196;** Barring dower and curtesy by contract before marriage, **Secs. 197, 220**

At common law, the fictional merger of the spouses upon marriage, with its attendant consequences, rendered useless any attempt of a betrothed couple to contract respecting rights to accrue during coverture. Indeed, all debts between the parties, whether due at coverture or which might become due during coverture, were extinguished by the marriage. The common law did, however, permit the betrothed couple to contract respecting property rights to accrue after the dissolution of the marriage. In fact, the law looked with favor upon this class of contracts, which came to be known as marriage contracts or marriage settlements.

In only eleven of the jurisdictions examined is there any express statutory authority for the making of marriage contracts. In most jurisdictions, therefore, marriage contracts still rest upon a common-law basis. The so-called Statute of Frauds in forty-six of the jurisdictions examined requires agreements in consideration of marriage to be in writing. Thirty-five jurisdictions recognize the subject of marriage contracts in a fragmentary or incidental manner. The great bulk of the legislation found on the subject deals with requirements of form, recording, or both. Twenty-six jurisdictions have legislated in this respect. The tendency is to require that marriage contracts be acknowledged or

[§ 155

proved, and recorded in the manner prescribed for conveyances. It is generally provided that the contract is ineffective against bona fide purchasers and creditors if not recorded. Of the nine jurisdictions making some statutory provision for witnesses, five require the contract to be either executed in the presence of at least two witnesses or attested to by at least two witnesses. Two jurisdictions make all marriage contracts void as against prior creditors.

The statutes of **Arizona, Connecticut, Delaware, Louisiana, Maine, Massachusetts, Nebraska, New Hampshire, New York, North Carolina,** and **Texas** expressly authorize the making of marriage contracts. Attention is also directed to the jointure statutes collected in **Section 196.** The parties intending marriage may make such stipulations as they desire, not contrary to good morals or rule of law (**Arizona, Louisiana** [in relation to property], and **Texas**) ; but they cannot alter the legal order of descent with respect to themselves or the inheritance of their children or posterity (**Arizona**), or with respect to themselves in what concerns the inheritance of their children or posterity (**Louisiana** and **Texas**). Neither can the parties impair the legal rights of the husband over the persons of their common children (**Texas**) ; nor impair the legal rights of the husband over the persons of his wife and children, nor impair those rights which belong to the husband as head of the family (**Louisiana**). The parties may determine what rights each shall have in the property of the other during marriage and after its dissolution by death (**Delaware** and **Maine**) ; or determine whether the property of which each is possessed at the time of marriage shall remain or become the property of either (**Massachusetts**) ; or bar each other in the rights of dower and curtesy, and other rights which otherwise might be acquired in the property of the other (**New Hampshire** and **North Carolina**). A spouse by contract (**Connecticut, Nebraska**) or by an agreement (**New York**) may release the statutory share given a surviving spouse (**Connecticut**), may bar his or her right to inherit lands of the other (**Nebraska**), or may waive the right to elect to take against the will of the other (**New York**).

It is to be observed that none of these statutes expressly states that the subject matter of a marriage contract must be property. The **Arizona** and **Texas** statutes, however, are the only ones which do not refer specifically to property. It is well settled, however, that in the absence of express statutory authority the parties cannot by antenuptial agreement alter the fundamental duties and obligations which grow out of the marital status.

§ 155]

Nine jurisdictions (**Arizona, California, Georgia, Idaho, Louisiana, Montana, Nevada, New Mexico, Texas**) expressly allow a minor capable of contracting matrimony to make a valid marriage contract. In **Arizona** and **Texas,** however, the minor must have the written consent of his parents, or of the surviving parent, or of his guardian if both parents be dead; and in **Louisiana** he must be "assisted" in the agreement by those persons whose consent is necessary to his marriage. In the other six jurisdictions named above, a minor may apparently make a valid marriage contract in his own right, although he may need the consent of his parents to contract matrimony. Also, in **Massachusetts,** a female of eighteen years or more may join with her guardian in making and executing a marriage contract.

Texas, Arizona, and **Louisiana** provide that no matrimonial agreement may be altered after the marriage is celebrated. At common law, the unity conception of the spouses undoubtedly prevented them from making any new stipulations during coverture. Where the husband and wife are now authorized to make postnuptial contracts, it would seem to follow, in the absence of legislation to the contrary, that they can alter and modify their antenuptial agreement at will.

All of the fifty-one jurisdictions examined, except **Louisiana, Maryland, New Mexico, North Carolina,** and **Pennsylvania,** have adopted in substance that part of the English Statute of Frauds requiring agreements in consideration of marriage to be in writing. Of the exceptions, **Louisiana** and **New Mexico** specifically provide that marriage contracts must be in writing; and **North Carolina** provides for the recording of marriage contracts whereby money or other estate is secured to either spouse. Obviously, to the extent that recording is required, to that extent at least the contract must be in a formal writing. Apart from the Statute of Frauds, **California, Idaho, Montana,** and **Nevada** require that all marriage contracts must be in writing; and **Arkansas, Massachusetts,** and **Missouri** provide that marriage contracts affecting property shall be in writing. **Georgia** is unique in the sense that it limits the operation of the Statute of Frauds, and expressly allows a parol antenuptial agreement contemplating a future settlement upon the wife to be enforced by a court of equity.

At common law, marriage was regarded as a consideration "of the highest value." An antenuptial settlement made upon one or both of the parties to the marriage could not be impeached by prior creditors of the settlor unless both parties to the contract concurred in a fraudulent intent or in the knowledge of intended fraud. Three jurisdictions radically

[§ 155

depart from the common law in this respect. In **North Carolina,** marriage settlements are void as to creditors prior to the marriage; and in **Virginia** such contracts are void as to creditors existing prior to the execution of the agreement. In **Tennessee,** a marriage contract is not effective against creditors when a greater value is secured to the intended wife and children of the marriage than the portion actually received by the wife on marriage plus such property as the husband has at the time of the marriage less the just debts by him then owing.

In **New York,** the husband is liable for the wife's antenuptial obligations to the extent of the value of property he receives from her by antenuptial contract; and in **West Virginia,** if real or personal property is transferred by either spouse to the other by antenuptial agreement, the spouse receiving the property is liable for the prior obligations of the other to the extent of the value of the property so transferred. These statutes seem eminently fair and theoretically sound. For the statutes of several other jurisdictions which only partially abrogate the husband's common-law liability for the wife's antenuptial debts, and which probably have similar applications, see **Section 151.**

Under modern statutes which universally and with but few exceptions completely cast aside the unity conception of the spouses, parties intending marriage may now effectively contract relative to rights to accrue during coverture. Indeed, in all but a very few jurisdictions, husband and wife may contract together (see **Sec. 156**). Likewise, under the modern statutes which secure to the wife the property which she brings to the marriage (**Sec. 167**), the great weight of authority and the better view secures to either spouse the antenuptial debts owing to him by the other. **Georgia,** however, harks back to the old law by providing that "intermarriage of the parties generally releases a debt." The **Georgia** statute adds, however, that such is not the case when the obligation is given in contemplation of marriage.

As a protection to subsequent bona fide creditors and purchasers, all jurisdictions might well require the marriage contracts respecting real property to be recorded in the manner prescribed for conveyances.

The table following contains in detail the statutory material found on the subject of marriage contracts, together with citations for the same.

TABLE LXXIX*

MARRIAGE CONTRACTS AND SETTLEMENTS[1]

Jurisdiction and Citation	Recording	Form-Acknowledgments, Witnesses, etc.	Failure to Record or Observe Required Form	General and Miscellaneous
Alabama C. 1923, Sec. 6892	Conveyance of personal property in consideration of marriage, if possession remains with husband or husband and wife, shall be recorded in county of husband's residence within twelve months after possession commenced		If not so recorded, the property must be taken as property of the husband in favor of purchasers without notice and creditors	
Arizona R. C. 1928, Secs. 970, 2171	Agreements in consideration of marriage shall be recorded in manner and form required for deeds	Marriage contracts must be acknowledged before officer authorized to take acknowledgments to deeds, in manner required for deeds	The contract shall be invalid against a purchaser for value or creditor without notice unless so recorded and acknowledged	The parties[2] may enter into any obligation not contrary to good morals or rule of law; but they cannot alter legal order of descent.[3] Agreement cannot be altered after marriage
Arkansas Crawf. and Moses, Dig. 1921, Secs. 7028–35	If real estate is conveyed or secured, contract with certificate of proof, etc., shall be recorded in every county in which real estate affected is situated	Marriage contracts shall be acknowledged or proved before a court of record, or judge or clerk thereof, in manner required for deeds. Marriage contracts affecting real or personal estate shall be in writing, and acknowledged by each party or proved by one or more witnesses	Until deposited for record, the contract shall be invalid except as between the parties and those with notice. Depositing for record deemed full notice	Marriage contracts duly proved or acknowledged, certified or recorded, shall be received in any court of record without further proof of execution. Certificate of acknowledgment or proof, or record, is not conclusive but may be rebutted
California C. C. 1933 (Lake), Secs. 178–81	All contracts for marriage settlements must be recorded in every county in which real estate affected is situated	Marriage contracts must be in writing, executed, acknowledged or proved in manner required for grant of land	Recording or non-recording has like effect as recording or non-recording of a grant of real property	A minor capable of contracting marriage may make a valid marriage settlement

* See pages 62–63 for all numbered footnotes to this table.

TABLE LXXIX (*Continued*)

Jurisdiction and Citation	Recording	Form-Acknowledgments, Witnesses, etc.	Failure to Record or Observe Required Form	General and Miscellaneous
Connecticut .... G. S. 1930, Sec. 5156		See last column		Statutory share of surviving spouse may be released by written contract before marriage whereby either has received from other what is intended as a provision in lieu thereof
Delaware ...... R. C. 1915, Sec. 3003; Sec. 3050, amd. by Sess. L. 1919, Ch. 197, p. 525	If contract affects liability of lands or tenements, it shall be recorded in every county where such lands are situated within one year from the making thereof	Marriage contract, determining rights in the estate of other, shall be executed in the presence of two witnesses at least ten days before marriage; and if acknowledged before an authorized officer, it may be recorded in deed records	If not recorded, the contract shall be of no avail against one without notice of the execution of the same	The parties may determine what rights each shall have in the other's estate during marriage and after its dissolution by death
Georgia .... C. 1926, C. C., Secs. 2999– 3008, 4236, 4243, 4310	Every marriage contract or voluntary settlement by husband on wife, whether in execution of marriage articles or not, must be recorded in office of clerk of superior court in the county of husband's residence (or county where property is situated if parties are non-residents) within three months after the execution thereof	Every marriage contract in writing must be attested by at least two witnesses	Until recorded, the contract shall be of no effect against a prior bona fide purchaser, creditor, or surety without notice[4]	Marriage contracts in writing shall be liberally construed to carry out intention of the parties. No want of form or technical expression shall invalidate the same. Minors capable of contracting matrimony may make a valid marriage contract[5]
Hawaii .... R. L. 1925, Secs. 3004, 3171	All articles of marriage settlement for the transfer of real estate within the territory shall be recorded		If not recorded, the contract shall not be binding to the detriment of third parties or conclusive upon their rights	Nothing in the chapter on property, contracts, and suits of married women shall invalidate any marriage settlement or contract

§ 155]

TABLE LXXIX (*Continued*)

Jurisdiction and Citation	Recording	Form-Acknowledgments, Witnesses, etc.	Failure to Record or Observe Required Form	General and Miscellaneous
Idaho .... Comp. St. 1919, Secs. 4658, 4671–74	All contracts for marriage settlements must be recorded in every county in which real estate affected is situated	All marriage contracts must be in writing and executed, acknowledged, or proved in manner required for conveyance of land	Recording or non-recording has like effect as recording or non-recording of a conveyance of real property	A minor capable of contracting marriage may make a valid marriage settlement. The statutes creating a separate estate for the wife shall not invalidate any marriage settlement
Kentucky .... Carroll, St. 1922, Secs. 494–95	Agreement in consideration of marriage must be recorded in the county in which the property affected is situated	Marriage contracts shall be acknowledged by the party executing the same, or proved	Unless so recorded, acknowledged, or proved, the contract shall not be binding against a purchaser for value without notice	
Louisiana ...... C. C., Arts. 540, 1888, 2265, 2325–33, 2336, 2352–53, 2360, 2395, 2424, 3333; Marr, Ann. R. S. 1915, Sec. 1578	All marriage contracts affecting the estates of the parties shall be recorded in the parish where the immovable property is situated[6]	Every matrimonial agreement must be by an act before a notary and two witnesses		The parties[2] may contract respecting property with few limitations.[7] They may modify or limit the community of acquests or gains, or even agree that it shall not exist. Marriage contracts cannot be altered after the marriage celebration
Maine .... R. S. 1930, Ch. 74, Secs. 8, 14		Marriage settlements shall be executed in presence of two witnesses		The parties may by marriage settlement determine what rights each shall have in the other's estate during marriage, and after its dissolution by death. Statutory provisions on judicial separation shall not invalidate any marriage settlement or contract

[§ 155

TABLE LXXIX (*Continued*)

Jurisdiction and Citation	Recording	Form-Acknowl- edgments, Wit- nesses, etc.	Failure to Record or Observe Re- quired Form	General and Miscellaneous
Massachusetts G. L. 1932, Ch. 209, Secs. 13, 25–27	The marriage con- tract, with schedule of property to be affected annexed thereto, shall be recorded either be- fore the marriage or within ninety days thereafter in the county of the husband's residence at time of record[8]	The Statute au- thorizes only writ- ten contracts. Schedule of prop- erty intended to be affected must be annexed to the contract	If not so re- corded, the con- tract is void except as be- tween the parties, their heirs and repre- sentatives	The parties may provide that the whole or any part of the property of which either is seized at time of marriage shall re- main or become the property of either.[9] General provisions relating to property, con- tracts, debts, etc. (see Statute), of wife shall not invalidate a mar- riage settlement or contract
Michigan Comp. L. 1929, Sec. 13060				All contracts made by persons in con- templation of mar- riage remain in full force after the mar- riage takes place
Mississippi C. 1930, Sec. 2143	Covenants or agree- ments in considera- tion of marriage shall be recorded in the manner directed for conveyances of real or personal estate	Marriage con- tracts shall be acknowledged by the party bound, or proved by one or more witnesses, as is required for conveyances of real or personal estate	Unless so ac- knowledged or proved, and re- corded, the con- tract shall not be good against a purchaser for value without notice, or any creditor	
Missouri R. S. 1929, Secs. 1706–7, 2986–88	Marriage contracts whereby any estate, real or personal, may be affected in law or in equity shall be recorded in each county where such estate is situated	If the contract affects any estate, real or personal, it shall be in writing, acknowledged or proved, and certi- fied as is required for conveyances of land	Until deposited with recorder, the contract shall be invalid, except between parties and those with notice. De- positing with recorder deemed full notice	A marriage con- tract duly proved or acknowledged, certified, and re- corded may be received in evi- dence in any court without further proof of execution
Montana R. C. 1921, Secs. 5804–7	All contracts for marriage settlements must be recorded in every county in which real estate affected thereby is situated	All contracts for marriage settle- ments must be in writing, and ex- ecuted, acknowl- edged, or proved in manner re- quired for grants of land	Recording or non-recording has like effect as recording or non-recording of conveyance of real property	A minor capable of contracting marriage may make a valid mar- riage settlement

§ 155]

TABLE LXXIX (*Continued*)

Jurisdiction and Citation	Recording	Form-Acknowledgments, Witnesses, etc.	Failure to Record or Observe Required Form	General and Miscellaneous
Nebraska ...... Comp. St. 1929, Sec. 30(106)		Such contracts (see last column) shall be in writing, signed by both parties to the marriage and acknowledged as required for conveyances of lands		Man or woman may bar his or her right to inherit lands of spouse by contract in lieu thereof made before marriage
Nevada .... Comp. L. 1929 (Hillyer), Secs. 3381–85	All marriage contracts must be recorded in every county in which real estate affected thereby is situated	All marriage contracts must be in writing, executed and acknowledged or proved in manner required for conveyances of land	No marriage contract shall be valid as to any real estate, except between the parties thereto, until deposited for record. Depositing with recorder deemed full notice	A minor capable of contracting marriage may make a valid marriage contract or settlement
New Hampshire. Pub. L. 1926, Ch. 306, Secs. 15, 16				By settlement before marriage, the parties may effectively bar right of dower, curtesy, homestead right, or distributive share in the other's estate. Such settlement shall be enforced by court of probate
New Jersey ..... Comp. St. 1910, p. 3237, Sec. 13				"That all contracts made between persons in contemplation of marriage shall remain in full force after such marriage takes place"
New Mexico ... St. Ann. 1929, Secs. 68(203)– 68(206), 68(409)	Contracts for marriage settlement must be recorded in every county in which real estate affected thereby may be situated	All contracts for marriage settlement must be in writing, executed and acknowledged or proved as is required for a grant of land	Recording or non-recording has like effect as the recording or non-recording of a grant of real property	A minor capable of contracting marriage may make a valid marriage settlement

[§ 155

TABLE LXXIX (*Continued*)

Jurisdiction and Citation	Recording	Form-Acknowledgments, Witnesses, etc.	Failure to Record or Observe Required Form	General and Miscellaneous
New York ...... Cahill, Consol. L. 1930, Ch. 13, Sec. 18(9); Ch. 14, Secs. 53, 54				Right to elect to take against any last will of spouse may be waived by agreement, subscribed and duly acknowledged, made before marriage. Contract in contemplation of marriage remains in full force after marriage. Husband is liable for wife's antenuptial debts to extent of property acquired from her by antenuptial contract
North Carolina.. C. 1927, Secs. 1008, 2516, 3314	All marriage contracts whereby any money or other estate is secured to the wife or husband shall be registered in same manner as required for deeds of land	All marriage contracts whereby any money or other estate is secured to the wife or husband shall be proved or acknowledged in manner required for deeds of land	Such contracts shall be valid against creditors and purchasers for value only from registration[10]	Any person of full age about to be married may release and quitclaim dower, tenancy by the curtesy, and other rights which each might acquire in the property of the other
South Carolina.. C. of L. 1922, C. C., Sec. 5541	All marriage contracts, deeds, and settlements shall be recorded with schedule of property intended to be conveyed or passed annexed thereto	The contract, deed, or settlement shall describe the property intended to be comprehended, or shall have a schedule of such property annexed thereto, which shall be executed at the same time and subscribed by the same witnesses as the contract, deed, or settlement	The contract, deed, or settlement shall be deemed null and void as against creditors and bona fide purchasers and mortgagees if not recorded as prescribed	

TABLE LXXIX (*Continued*)

Jurisdiction and Citation	Recording	Form-Acknowledgments, Witnesses, etc.	Failure to Record or Observe Required Form	General and Miscellaneous
Tennessee ...... C. 1932, Secs. 7621, 7627–28, 7839–40	Marriage contracts in which the wife's property before marriage is settled on her or on a trustee for her use shall be recorded in the county where the husband resides at the time of the marriage[11]			See footnote 12 following
Texas .... Complete St. 1928, Civ. St., Arts. 4610–12, 6632–33	Covenants or agreements in consideration of marriage shall be recorded in manner required for deeds and other conveyances	Every matrimonial agreement must be acknowledged before an officer authorized to take acknowledgment to deeds in the manner required for deeds, and attested by at least two witnesses[13]	The contract shall not be good against a purchaser for value or creditor without notice unless acknowledged or proved and recorded in manner prescribed	The parties[2] may make any stipulations not contrary to good morals or rule of law; but they cannot alter the legal order of descent,[3] or impair the legal right of the husband over the persons of their common children. The agreement cannot be altered after celebration of the marriage
Virginia .... C. 1930, Sec. 5185				Every gift, conveyance, assignment, transfer, or charge made upon consideration of marriage is void as to prior creditors, but not as to subsequent purchasers and creditors
West Virginia... C. 1931, Ch. 40, Art. 1, Secs. 8, 9; Ch. 48, Art. 3, Sec. 15	Contracts in consideration of marriage respecting real estate or chattels shall be recorded in the county in which the property is situated		After recording, the contract is as valid as if it were a deed; but before recording, it is void as to creditors and subsequent purchasers for value without notice	If real or personal property is transferred by either spouse to the other by antenuptial agreement or otherwise, the spouse receiving the property is liable for the prior obligations of the other to the extent of the value of the property transferred

[§ 155

TABLE LXXIX (Continued)

[1] With the exception of **Louisiana, Maryland, New Mexico, North Carolina,** and **Pennsylvania,** all of the fifty-one jurisdictions examined have adopted in substance that portion of the English Statute of Frauds requiring agreements in consideration of marriage to be evidenced by a writing. But, as indicated in the table above, **Louisiana** and **New Mexico,** apart from the Statute of Frauds, require marriage contracts to be in writing; and **North Carolina** reaches the same result to the extent that marriage contracts are required to be recorded. Nothing was found in the statutes of **Maryland** and **Pennsylvania** dealing with the subject of this section.

Also, six jurisdictions not included in the table above otherwise recognize the subject of marriage contracts. **Colorado** (Comp. L. 1921, G. S., Sec. 5579), **Kansas** (R. S. 1923, Sec. 23[207]), and **Minnesota** (G. S. 1923, Sec. 8623) provide that nothing in the statutes defining the status of married women shall invalidate any marriage contract or settlement. **Washington** (Remington, Comp. St. 1922, Sec. 10601) requires the county auditor to record marriage contracts upon the payment of his fees for the same. **Oklahoma** (St. 1931, Sec. 1539) provides that a will shall be subservient to any antenuptial marriage contract in writing; and in **Utah** (R. S. 1933, 101-1-25) a will made by testator before marriage is revoked unless provision was made for the surviving wife in a marriage contract or settlement, showing testator's intention to substitute such provision for a legacy, or unless she is provided for in the will or so mentioned therein as to show an intention not to make a bequest to her.

[2] A minor capable of contracting marriage may: (a) make a valid matrimonial agreement with the written consent of both parents, of the surviving parent, or of his guardian if both parents are dead (**Arizona, Texas**); (b) give his consent to a marriage contract provided that, if he is not emancipated, he has been "assisted" by those persons whose consent is necessary to his marriage (**Louisiana**).

[3] With respect to themselves or the inheritance of their children or posterity which either may have by any other person, or in respect to their common children.

[4] If trustee or husband, having possession of the contract, refuses to have the same recorded, the wife or her next friend may apply to the judge of the superior court for an order compelling a record to be made. Such application is notice equivalent to recording. The trustee, refusing to record after demand, shall be personally liable to cestui qui trust for all damages sustained by reason of such failure to record.

[5] The **Georgia** Code covers the subject of marriage contracts and settlements in more detail than the statutes of any other jurisdiction examined except **Louisiana.** Marriage is expressly stated to be a valuable consideration. Hence, the wife stands as a purchaser for value as to property settled on her by the husband under the contract, provided he "does not incapacitate himself from paying his existing, just debts." The Code provides that "intermarriage of the parties generally releases a debt," but that such is not the effect when the obligation is given in contemplation of marriage.

Any agreement, whether by parol or in writing, may be executed and enforced by a court of equity at the instance of the wife during the life of the husband, provided the rights of third persons, purchasers, or creditors in good faith without notice are not affected thereby. To that extent marriage contracts are taken out of the Statute of Frauds. The husband may voluntarily execute such agreement or he may, at any time during coverture, either through trustees or directly to his wife, convey property to which he has title, subject to the rights of prior purchasers or creditors without notice. Marriage contracts will be enforced at the instance of all persons in whose favor there are limitations of the estate. Marriage articles, however, will be enforced or executed only at the instance of persons coming within the scope of the marriage consideration, but, when executed at their instance, the court may execute also in favor of volunteers (i.e., all persons except the parties to the contract and the offspring of the wife). The judge of the superior court of the county of the wife's domicile may, upon petition, exercise the powers of a chancellor in appointing, removing, or substituting trustees or in granting any order for the protection of the wife's trust estate created by marriage settlement.

[6] "All marriage contracts made within this state, tending in anywise to convey, transfer, assure, or affect the estates of the parties, or being only intended to ascertain the dotal rights of the wife, or that her marriage portion is liable to some reserves, or stipulated to be paraphernal or extradotal property . . . . shall be recorded in the parish where the immovable property is situated" (**Louisiana,** C. C., Art. 2265). It is also provided that, when by marriage contract the parties, being of age, shall agree that the recording shall exist only on one or more immovables belonging to the husband, the immovable and other property not included shall remain

§ 155]

TABLE LXXIX (*Concluded*)

free and released from mortgage for the wife's dowry; but it cannot be stipulated that no recording shall be made.

[7] **Louisiana** has an abundance of statutory material on the subject of marriage contracts. The parties may stipulate as they please, in relation to property, not contrary to good morals; but they cannot alter the legal order of descent either with respect to themselves, in what concerns the inheritance of their children or posterity, or with respect to their children between themselves, "without any prejudice to the donations inter vivos or morta causa which may take place . . . . in cases determined by this Code." Neither can the parties derogate from the rights resulting from the power of the husband over the person of his wife and children, or which belong to him as head of the family. As stated above, the parties may even agree that the community shall not exist. They may stipulate and limit the dowry to be brought by the wife; they may make donations to each other under marriage contract as freely as either might give to a stranger; they may agree that a future succession shall be dotal or paraphernal; they may establish usufruct by marriage contract; they may stipulate that the wife shall receive annually, upon her own acquittances, a part of her revenue (from her dotal effects) for her maintenance and personal wants. The husband is not bound to give security upon his receiving the dowry, unless he has been bound to do so by the marriage contract; and if permitted by the contract, he may alienate with his wife's consent immovables settled as dowry, but their value must be reinvested in other immovables. It is provided that each of the spouses, if separate in property, contributes to the expense of the marriage in the manner agreed in their contract; but if they had no agreement on the subject, the wife contributes to the amount of one-half her income. (See, in addition, C. C., Arts. 1564, 1743–48, on the subject of donations between married persons by marriage contract.)

[8] Or, if he is not a resident of the state, then in the county or district where the wife resides at the time of the record, if it is made before the marriage; or where she last resided, if it is made after the marriage (**Massachusetts**).

[9] Such contract may limit to the husband or wife an estate in fee or for life in the whole or any part of the property, and may designate any other lawful limitations. All such limitations shall take effect at the time of the marriage as if they had been contained in a deed conveying the property limited.

In **Massachusetts** a female minor of eighteen years or more may join with her guardian in making a marriage contract, and convey her real and personal property to trustees approved by the probate court having jurisdiction, to be held upon the trusts declared in such contract.

[10] **North Carolina** provides that every contract and settlement of property made by any man and woman in consideration of a marriage between them, for the benefit of themselves or their issue, shall be *void* as against creditors of the parties making the same respectively, existing at the time of the marriage. Obviously, this is a departure from the common law.

[11] And in every county in the state to which he may remove with the property. If the contract is made outside the state, it shall be registered in every county in the state to which the husband and wife remove with the property. Deeds for the settlement of personal property in consideration of marriage shall be registered in the county where the grantor or bargainor resides, and all marriage settlements and contracts "may" be recorded.

[12] The **Tennessee** Code provides that no marriage settlement or other marriage contract shall be good against creditors, where a greater value is secured to the intended wife, and the children of the marriage, than the portion actually received with the wife in marriage plus such estate as the husband is possessed of at the time of the marriage after deducting the just debts which he then owes. When a creditor attacks the marriage contract, the burden of proof is upon the one claiming under the contract. Any legacy given to the wife in general words and not in trust, or any distributive share in an estate during coverture, shall be taken as part of the portion received with the wife, and secured to those claiming under the contract to make up any deficiency created by the claims of creditors on the property conveyed in the marriage contract.

[13] When the wife reserves to herself any property, or rights to property, whether in esse or expectancy, such reservation must be acknowledged and recorded as provided by law to be valid as to subsequent purchasers or creditors of her husband.

REFERENCES

Book

STIMSON, F. J. *American Statute Law,* Secs. 6440–45, 6480–83 (1886).

Articles

JUDAH, NOBLE B., JR. "Antenuptial Contracts in Illinois," 6 Ill. L. Rev. 503–17 (1912).

STONE, JULIAN. "Law Governing Rights in Property under a Prenuptial Contract, According to the English and American Cases," 13 B. U. L. Rev. 219–33 (1933).

Notes

"Antenuptial Contracts, After-Acquired Real Property," *Sanger* v. *Sanger,* 132 Kan. 596; 296 P. 355 (1931)—27 Ill. L. Rev. 202–3 (1932).

"Consideration in Antenuptial Contracts," *Morris* v. *Masters,* 349 Ill. 455; 182 N. E. 406 (1932)—21 Geo. L. Jour. 236–37 (1933).

"Effect of Marriage on Contract Existing at Time of Marriage," *Archer* v. *Moulton,* 183 Minn. 306; 236 N. W. 455 (1931)—16 Minn. L. Rev. 108 (1931).

Annotations

"Antenuptial Agreement as Defense in Civil Suit by Wife for Support," 6 A. L. R. 80–81 (1920).

"Conveyance of Interest in Community Property by One Spouse to Other," 37 A. L. R. 282–308 (1925).

"Divorce or Judicial Separation as Affecting Marriage Settlement," 47 A. L. R. 473–76 (1927).

"Effect of Agreement between Parents as to Religious Education and Nurture of Child," 12 A. L. R. 1153–57 (1921).

"Marriage Settlement or Gift from One Spouse to the Other as Affected by Marital Misconduct," 29 A. L. R. 198–220 (1924).

"Specific Performance of Contract to Provide for Intended Husband or Wife," 12 L. R. A. (N.S.) 232–34 (1908).

"Validity of Antenuptial Agreement for Release of Dower and Like Interests in Property of Intended Spouse," Ann. Cas. 1914B 620.

"Validity of Antenuptial Contract by Husband or Wife to Support the Other," 15 L. R. A. (N.S.) 491 (1908).

"Validity of Contract Relinquishing Rights in Intended Husband's Estate Signed by Intended Wife in Ignorance of Her Legal Rights," 9 L. R. A. (N.S.) 953–54 (1907).

"What Amounts to Laches or Delay on Part of Wife or Widow in Attacking Antenuptial Settlement," 74 A. L. R. 559–61 (1931).

"Rule Regarding Revocation of Will by Marriage as Affected by Antenuptial Agreement or Settlement," 92 A. L. R. 1010–23 (1934).

Section 156. Wife's Contracts with Husband after Marriage

CROSS REFERENCES: Separation agreements, **Sec. 138;** Wife's contracts, in general, **Sec. 152;** Conveyances and transfers between husband and wife, **Sec. 182;** Power of attorney between husband and wife, **Sec. 186;** Barring dower and curtesy by postnuptial contract or settlement, **Secs. 196, 198, 220**

The inability of the wife to make a binding promise, coupled with the fictional merger of her legal identity with that of her spouse, obviously rendered her incapable in law of contracting directly with the husband. The unity idea of the spouses is foreign to modern statutes. Unless a contrary legislative intent appears, the broad statutes authorizing the wife to contract as if sole, found in most jurisdictions today (**Sec. 152**), undoubtedly enable her to contract with the husband as well as with third persons. Some of the earlier decisions, however, have suggested that the removal of the wife's disability to contract does not of itself remove her disability to contract with the husband.

General statutes which expressly authorize the spouses to contract with each other were found in only sixteen jurisdictions (**Alabama, California, Colorado, Connecticut, Maryland, Minnesota, Montana, Nevada, New Mexico, New York, North Carolina, North Dakota, Ohio, Oklahoma, South Dakota, West Virginia**). Some of the foregoing, as well as **Washington,** also have legislation which expressly recognizes contracts of a particular kind. Curiously out of harmony with modern thought, four jurisdictions expressly forbid husband and wife to contract with each other (**Hawaii, Louisiana, Massachusetts, Vermont**). These statutes, together with others which indirectly recognize the capacity of the spouses to contract inter se, or which are otherwise directly pertinent, are outlined in the table at the end of this section. Reference is also made to **Section 182,** where the matter of conveyances and transfers between husband and wife is discussed.

Eight jurisdictions expressly authorize the spouses to contract for an immediate separation. Attention is directed to **Section 138** for a discussion of the subject.

It will be observed that the authority of the spouses to contract together is variously qualified in all but three of the sixteen jurisdictions. Eight jurisdictions allow them to contract "respecting property," and in eight their contracts are made subject to the general rules controlling the acts of parties standing in a confidential relationship. The latter qualification would, of course, ordinarily be made by the courts without

[**§ 156**

express statute. **West Virginia** is the only state which requires all contracts between the spouses to be evidenced by a writing. **Minnesota** strangely provides that contracts between husband and wife relative to the real estate of either are not valid. In **Iowa** and **Oregon,** the survivor's dower, curtesy, or statutory share apparently cannot be the subject of a postnuptial contract. **Georgia** provides that the wife's contract of sale with the husband of her separate estate necessitates a court order. Also, as was indicated in **Section 155,** several jurisdictions forbid the alteration of antenuptial marriage contracts after marriage.

It is clear that the husband and wife cannot contract so as to alter the fundamental duties incident to the marital status. Such contracts are void as against public policy, and in many instances are said to be without consideration. Limitations of this nature are found in several statutes. Eight jurisdictions provide that the spouses cannot alter their legal relation except as to property, or by separation agreement, or both. In **New York** and **West Virginia,** it is expressly stated that they cannot by contract alter or dissolve the marriage, or (**New York**) relieve the husband of his duty to support. Statutes of doubtful wisdom which seem to prevent personal-service contracts, even though respecting services outside the household, are found in **Illinois** and **Mississippi** (see also **Sec. 173**).

The courts have often been confronted with the question whether, under the various Married Women's Acts, the wife may form a partnership with the husband. It is interesting to note that **Maryland** and **West Virginia** expressly provide that the wife may form a partnership with him, and that in **Colorado** and **New Mexico** she may become his special partner; while in **Rhode Island,** the spouses are expressly forbidden to enter any trading partnership together.

There seems to be no sound reason why the wife should not be allowed complete freedom to contract with the husband, subject only to those limitations which the law would impose regardless of statutory restriction. Even though the wife is given a general power to contract as if unmarried, as a matter of clarity all jurisdictions ought to provide expressly that the wife's contractual capacity extends to transactions with the husband.

The table follows.

§ 156]

TABLE LXXX

Contracts between the Husband and Wife

Jurisdiction and Citation	May the Husband and Wife Contract?	General Provisions, Limitations	Miscellaneous
Alabama .... C. 1923, Sec. 8272	Yes	Contracts between husband and wife are subject to the rules of law as to contracts between persons standing in confidential relations	
California .... C. C. 1933 (Lake), Secs. 108, 159–60	Yes	Husband and wife may contract respecting property subject to general rules which control the actions of persons occupying confidential relations with each other. They cannot alter their legal relations, except as to property, and except that they may agree in writing to an immediate separation	Mutual consent of the parties is sufficient consideration for a contract of separation
Colorado .... Comp. L. 1921, G. S., Sec. 2451	Yes	The wife may contract with the husband the same as though she were unmarried	The wife may become a special partner with the husband
Connecticut .... G. S. 1930, Secs. 5154, 5156	Yes	The wife may contract with the husband as if unmarried	Statutory share of surviving spouse may be released by written contract after marriage whereby either has received from other what is intended as a provision in lieu thereof[1]
Delaware .... R. C. 1915, Sec. 3003	....		To avail against persons without notice postnuptial contracts concerning lands belonging to either spouse, affecting the liability of such lands, must be recorded
Georgia .... C. 1926, C. C., Secs. 2998, 3009, 3011	....	No contract of sale of a wife as to her separate estate with her husband or her trustee shall be valid unless allowed by order of court. The wife may act as attorney and agent for the husband, but proof of such authority must be made as in other cases (except in case of her purchase of necessaries)	When a transaction between husband and wife is attacked for fraud by the creditors of either, the onus is on the husband and wife to show that the transaction is fair
Hawaii .... R. L. 1925, Sec. 2994, amd. by Sess. L. 1931, Act 146, p. 142	No	The wife "shall not be authorized" to contract with her husband (see **Sec. 182**)	

[1] A husband and wife in **Connecticut** married before April 20, 1877, may by contract, properly recorded, abandon all rights in the other's property under former laws and accept the rights granted by present statutes.

[§ 156

TABLE LXXX (*Continued*)

Jurisdiction and Citation	May the Husband and Wife Contract?	General Provisions, Limitations	Miscellaneous
Illinois .... Cahill, R. S. 1931, Ch. 68, Sec. 8	....		Neither husband nor wife shall be entitled to recover any compensation for any labor performed or services rendered for the other, whether in the management of property or otherwise
Iowa .... C. 1927, Sec. 10447	....		When property is owned by the husband or wife, the other has no interest therein which can be the subject of a contract between them
Kansas .... R. S. 1923, Sec. 22(238)	....		Either spouse may consent in writing, executed in the presence of two witnesses, that the other may bequeath more than one-half of his property from the one consenting
Louisiana .... C. C., Arts. 1790, 2329, 2446; Marr, Ann. R. S., Supp. 1926, p. 1104	....	Contracts between husband and wife are forbidden. A contract of sale between spouses can take place only in three situations[2]	Married persons settling in this state from other states may within one year after such settlement make a valid marriage contract
Maine .... R. S. 1930, Ch. 74, Sec. 2; Ch. 76, Sec. 61	....	The wife may release to husband the right to control her property and to dispose of income thereof, for their mutual benefit, and may in writing revoke the same	Executors and administrators may pay debts due between spouses, as if the marriage relation had never existed between them
Montana .... R. C. 1921, Secs. 5786–88	Yes	Either husband or wife may make any contract with the other respecting property which either might if unmarried, subject to the general rules which control the actions of persons occupying confidential relations with each other. They cannot alter their legal relations, except as to property, and except that they may agree to an immediate separation	Mutual consent is sufficient consideration for a contract of separation

[2] (*a*) When one of the spouses makes a transfer of property to the other, who is judicially separated from him or her, in payment of his or her rights; (*b*) when the transfer made by the husband to his wife, even though not separated, has a legitimate cause, as the replacing of her dotal or other effects alienated; (*c*) when the wife makes a transfer of property to her husband, in payment of a sum promised to him as a dowry.

The writer is uncertain whether the broad statute passed in 1928 (Act 283, p. 583) removing the disabilities of the wife to contract operates to repeal the prohibition against inter-spousal contracts. See also Civil Code, Articles 1743–55 on donations between married persons either by marriage contract or during marriage.

§ 156]

TABLE LXXX (*Continued*)

Jurisdiction and Citation	May the Husband and Wife Contract?	General Provisions, Limitations	Miscellaneous
Nevada .... Comp. L. 1929 (Hillyer), Secs. 3373–75	Yes	Husband and wife may contract respecting property subject to general rules controlling actions of persons occupying confidential relations with each other. They cannot alter their legal relations, except as to property, and except that they may agree in writing to an immediate separation	Mutual consent of the parties is sufficient consideration for a contract of separation
New Hampshire .... Pub. L. 1926, Ch. 288, Sec. 2	....		The statutory authority given to the wife to contract "shall not affect the laws heretofore in force as to contracts between husband and wife"
New Jersey .... Comp. St. 1910, p. 3237, Sec. 14	....		It is provided in the Married Women's Act: "Nor shall anything herein enable husband or wife to contract with, or to sue each other, except as heretofore" (see **Sec. 152**)
New Mexico .... St. Ann. 1929, Secs. 68(201), 68(203)–68(205), 68(510)–68(511), 100(219)	Yes	The spouses may contract respecting property subject to the general rules of common law which control the actions of persons occupying confidential relations with each other. They cannot alter their legal relations, except in regard to their property, and except that they may agree in writing to an immediate separation	Mutual consent is a sufficient consideration for a contract of separation. Such contracts must be recorded. The wife may become a special partner with her husband
New York .... Cahill, Consol. L. 1930, Ch. 13, Sec. 18(9); Ch. 14, Sec. 51	Yes	The wife may contract respecting property with the husband. The spouses cannot contract to alter or dissolve the marriage or to relieve the husband from his liability to support his wife	Husband or wife may waive right to take against will of spouse by postnuptial contract subscribed and duly acknowledged

[§ 156

TABLE LXXX (*Continued*)

Jurisdiction and Citation	May the Husband and Wife Contract?	General Provisions, Limitations	Miscellaneous
North Carolina ..... C. 1927, Secs. 1008, 2515–16	Yes	Contracts between spouses not inconsistent with the public policy are valid; but no contract which affects wife's real estate, or income thereof, or which impairs or changes the body or capital of wife's personal estate, or income thereof, for more than three years thereafter is valid unless such contract is in writing and is proved as required for conveyances. Separate examination of wife is required	The husband and wife may release and quitclaim dower, tenancy by the curtesy, and all other rights which they may have acquired by marriage in the property of the other[3]
North Dakota ...... Comp. L. 1913, Secs. 4411–13	Yes	Either husband or wife may make any contract with the other respecting property which either might if unmarried. The spouses cannot alter their marital relation except that they may agree in writing to an immediate separation	Mutual consent of the parties is sufficient consideration for a contract of separation
Ohio .... Complete G. C. 1931 (Page), Secs. 7999, 8000	Yes	A husband or wife may make any contract with the other which either might if unmarried, subject to the general rules which control the action of persons occupying confidential relations with each other. They cannot alter their legal relations except that they may agree in writing to an immediate separation	
Oklahoma .... St. 1931, Secs. 1655–57	Yes	Either husband or wife may make any contract with the other respecting property which either might if unmarried, subject to the general rules which control the actions of persons occupying confidential relations with each other. The spouses cannot alter their legal relations, except as to property, and except that they may agree to an immediate separation	Mutual consent of the parties is sufficient consideration for a contract of separation
Oregon .... C. 1930, Sec. 33(201)	....		When property is owned by either husband or wife, the other has no interest therein which can be the subject of a contract between them

[3] Contracts and settlements of property made by any man and woman "in consideration of a marriage between them" for the benefit of such man and woman, or of their issue, are void as against creditors of the parties making the same existing at the time the contracts or settlements are made (**North Carolina**).

§ 156]

TABLE LXXX (*Concluded*)

Jurisdiction and Citation	May the Husband and Wife Contract?	General Provisions, Limitations	Miscellaneous
Pennsylvania ...... St. 1920 (West), Sec. 14589	....		The wife may loan the husband money belonging to her separate estate, and take as security a judgment or mortgage against the estate of the husband in the name of a third person, who shall act as trustee for the wife
Rhode Island .... G. L. 1923, Sec. 4201	....	"Nothing herein contained, however, shall be construed to allow any husband and wife to enter into any trading partnership together"	
South Dakota ...... Comp. L. 1929, Secs. 171–73	Yes	Either husband or wife may enter into any contract with the other respecting property which either might if unmarried, subject to the general rules which control the actions of persons occupying confidential relations with each other. The spouses cannot alter their legal relations, except as to property, and except that they may agree in writing to an immediate separation	Mutual consent of the parties is sufficient consideration for a contract of separation
Vermont .... G. L. 1917, Sec. 3521	No	A married woman may make contracts with any person other than her husband	
Washington .... Remington, Comp. St. 1922, Secs. 5828, 6894	Yes	The husband and wife may make any agreement concerning the status or disposition of the whole or any portion of the community property, then owned or afterward to be acquired, to take effect upon the death of either[4]	When any question arises as to the good faith of any transaction between husband and wife, the burden of proof is on the party asserting the good faith
West Virginia ..... C. 1931, Ch. 48, Art. 3, Secs. 8, 9, 18, 24	Yes	The wife may contract with the husband, but such contract shall not be enforceable at law, unless it or some memorandum or note thereof be in writing and signed by the party to be charged thereby. The spouses cannot contract to alter or dissolve the marriage. The wife may enter into a partnership with any person, including her husband	

[4] Such agreement must be in writing under their hands and sealed, witnessed, acknowledged, and certified as is required for deeds of land, and may at any time thereafter be altered.

[§ 156

REFERENCES

Books

MADDEN, JOSEPH W. *Handbook of the Law of Persons and Domestic Relations,* pp. 244 *et seq.* (1931).

SCHOULER, JAMES. *A Treatise on the Law of Marriage, Divorce, Separation and Domestic Relations,* 6th ed., I, 544–56 (1921).

STIMSON, F. J. *American Statute Law,* Secs. 6445–46, 6467 (1886).

Notes

"The Effect of Misconduct upon Gifts Received from a Spouse," *Osborne* v. *Osborne,* 40 F. (2d) 800—44 Harv. L. Rev. 276–78 (1930) ; 79 Univ. of Pa. L. Rev. 89–90 (1930).

"Contracts between Husband and Wife, Full Faith and Credit," *Metzler* v. *Metzler,* 8 N. J. Misc. 821; 151 A. 847 (1930)—31 Col. L. Rev. 316–17 (1931).

Annotations

"Liability of Husband for Services Rendered by Wife in Carrying on His Business," 23 A. L. R. 18–24 (1923).

"Validity of Contract to Pay Wife for Services," L. R. A. 1917D 268–73.

"Validity of Partnership Agreement between Husband and Wife," 20 A. L. R. 1304–17 (1922) ; 38 A. L. R. 1264 (1925).

Section 157. Wife's Torts

CROSS REFERENCES : Wife's antenuptial contracts, **Sec. 151**; Crimes by the wife, **Sec. 165**; Liability of community property for wife's torts, **Sec. 178**; Suits against wife, **Sec. 179**; Suits between spouses, **Sec. 180**

I. ANTENUPTIAL TORTS OF THE WIFE

As one of the incidents of marriage at common law, the husband became immediately liable for the wife's premarital obligations, whether in tort or in contract. This burden in some measure offset his marital rights in his bride's property, but it was in no sense measured thereby. The husband's liability, being created by the marriage, was discharged by the dissolution of the marriage. Upon the husband's death, the wife did not recover the property which went to her spouse at marriage, but her liability for her antenuptial obligations revived in full force. Obviously, the common law operated unfairly upon all concerned.

§ 157]

Statutes expressly abrogating or greatly limiting the husband's common-law liability were found in all of the fifty-one jurisdictions examined except seven (**Delaware, Georgia, Kansas, Louisiana, Michigan, Mississippi, Ohio**). **Louisiana** never did recognize the common-law rule. In twenty-one jurisdictions the statutes refer specifically to the wife's premarital torts or to her premarital obligations in general, but in twenty-three jurisdictions the statutes refer to the wife's debts or liabilities "contracted" before marriage. The choice of language in these latter statutes is unfortunate. There is no reason to believe that a distinction between tortious and contractual obligations is intended, but a literal construction might lead to such a distinction. Of the forty-four jurisdictions with legislation on the subject, thirty-six provide that the husband, or his property, is not liable for the wife's antenuptial obligations as described, and two (**Arkansas, Wyoming**) that he is not liable without an assumption thereof in writing. The statutes of the community-property states are silent as to the liability of the community property. The remaining six jurisdictions (**Colorado, Indiana, Kentucky, Missouri, New York, West Virginia**) have not completely discarded the common law, but ambiguously measure the husband's liability by the amount of property he receives from the wife. The statutes in these jurisdictions vary in terminology, and are outlined in the table following. Several of them appear to be vestiges of the era in which the husband was still secure in his common-law marital rights in the wife's property. If they are of much significance today, it must be because of their relation to marriage contracts.

Whatever the reasons may have been which justified the husband's common-law liability for the wife's premarital torts and contracts, those reasons do not exist today. Even in the absence of express statute, it is not probable that an enlightened court would enforce the common-law rule. But the matter ought not to be left to implication. The statutes of all jurisdictions should contain an express abrogation of the common-law rule as to both contractual and tortious obligations of the wife incurred before marriage.

At common law, coverture did not extinguish the wife's liability for her antenuptial wrongs. Her liability was temporarily suspended because of the disabilities incident to coverture. With the statutory removal of those disabilities, and in particular her incapacity to be sued alone, her present liability cannot be questioned. Many jurisdictions, however, have seen fit to provide expressly that she is so liable.

[§ 157

Attention is called to the strange legislation found in **Colorado, Indiana,** and **Wyoming** providing that a judgment recovered against the wife, or the wife and husband, on account of an antenuptial liability may be levied on her lands "only." These statutes seem mere relics, strangely out of place even in the jurisdictions in which found, and are doubtless of little present significance.

II. Postnuptial Torts of the Wife

Although the wife at common law was powerless to create a binding contract, coverture did not render her incapable of committing civil and criminal offenses. Somewhat analogous to the odd rule which developed in respect to her crimes (**Sec. 165**), an equally curious rule developed in respect to her torts. The husband was liable either jointly or alone for all of the wife's civil wrongs. For those not committed in his presence by his direction or under his coercion he was jointly liable with the wife. In this respect he was not regarded as a tort feasor, but his liability existed solely by virtue of the marriage, and hence ended with the dissolution of the marriage. For the wife's torts committed in his presence by his direction he was solely liable, and the wife was excused on grounds of coercion. The wife, however, was thought to be so susceptible to domination by her spouse that the torts committed in his presence were prima facie presumed to have been committed under his coercion. One exception to the foregoing rules was made: if the wife's tort was committed in connection with an attempted contract, so that to enforce tort liability would indirectly enforce the void contract, the law gave no relief to the injured party. Various reasons have been advanced to justify the husband's general liability for the wife's misconduct. Among them are a supposed duty on the part of the husband to keep his spouse in good behavior, the wife's common-law incapacity to be sued alone, and the fact that a judgment against the wife was practically worthless because of the husband's marital rights in her property. Bishop acrimoniously remarks that the common-law rule might be more consonant with common sense "if the law gave to husbands the power, and cast upon them the duty, to chastise their wives in order to make them good, and kill them when the chastisement failed to produce its intended fruits."[1]

In this age of equal rights by statute there is obviously no room for a rule of law which makes the husband liable for the wife's torts except

---

[1] *Law of Married Women,* Sec. 909 (1873).

§ 157]

as a joint tort feasor. Whatever may have been the reasons which sustained the common-law rule, those reasons do not exist today. Neither is there any room for a rule of law which makes the husband a joint tort feasor by the application of the absurd common-law presumption of coercion. One might expect to find the common law on the subject universally abrogated by express statute. On the contrary, no statutes of general application in respect to the husband's liability for the wife's civil wrongs were found in sixteen jurisdictions (**Arizona, Arkansas, Colorado, Connecticut, Florida, Idaho, Kansas, Louisiana, Massachusetts, Mississippi, Nebraska, Nevada, New Hampshire, New Mexico, South Carolina, Tennessee**). In **Louisiana,** however, the husband never was liable solely by virtue of the marriage (*Globe Indemnity Company* v. *J. R. Quesenberry,* 1 La. App. 364 [1924]). One state (**Georgia**) has codified the common law. The statutes of two states (**Pennsylvania, Wyoming**) imply that the husband's common-law liability persists. The remaining thirty-two jurisdictions have statutes which either completely or partially abrogate the common law. Some of them are inartistically drafted, do not anticipate all the ramifications of the common-law rule, and probably do not accurately express the legislative intent.

Ten jurisdictions (**Alaska, California, Delaware, Illinois, Iowa, Missouri, New Jersey, Oregon, Utah, Washington**) have substantially the same legislation to the following effect: "For civil injuries committed by a married woman, damages may be recovered from her alone, and her husband shall not be liable therefor, except in cases where he would be jointly liable with her if the marriage did not exist." This statute is an admirable one because it completely covers the subject. It is worthy of adoption elsewhere. Equally as efficacious is the legislation in two states (**New York, West Virginia**) to the effect that the husband is not liable for the wife's torts unless done by his actual coercion or instigation, which is not presumed but must be proved. Five jurisdictions (**Montana, North Dakota, Ohio, Oklahoma, South Dakota**) probably reach the same result by providing that the husband "as such" is not answerable for the acts of the wife. Finally, fifteen jurisdictions (**Alabama, District of Columbia, Hawaii, Indiana, Kentucky, Maine, Maryland, Michigan, Minnesota, North Carolina, Rhode Island, Texas, Vermont, Virginia, Wisconsin**) have statutes of varying phraseology which simply state that the husband (or his separate property) is not liable for the wife's torts, or which excuse him from liability unless he participates

[§ 157

therein. Most of these latter statutes do not seem to preclude the application of the presumption of coercion. Some of them (notably in the **District of Columbia, Hawaii, Indiana, Maryland**) do not on their face completely abrogate the common law. In two states (**Kentucky, West Virginia**) what is said above is qualified. Under a freak **Kentucky** statute, the husband is still liable for the wife's obligations to the extent of property received from her "by virtue of the marriage"; and **West Virginia** has a most unique statute which makes the husband liable to the extent of property transferred to him by the wife subsequent to the creation of the liability. This statute is doubly unique because under it the wife is liable for the husband's torts by a like measure, and because it does not in express terms require the transfer to be without consideration. It must also be observed that the statutes are silent as to the liability of community property for the torts of the wife (see **Sec. 178**).

In those jurisdictions which have not clarified the matter by statute, the courts have differed as to the extent to which the husband's common-law liability has been impliedly abrogated by the modern legislation establishing the legal personality of the wife. Some courts have courageously refused to hold the husband for the independent torts of the wife. One of the most enlightened decisions is found in **Georgia**. Successive re-enactments of the **Georgia** code have contained a codification of the common law (see table), yet it has been recently held that the husband is no longer liable for the independent torts of the wife not committed by his command or with his consent and in which he does not participate, because, "as all the reasons for which the husband was made liable . . . . have been swept away, the rule thereof has been done away with" (*Curtis* v. *Ashworth,* 165 Ga. 782; 142 S. E. 111 [1928]; *Dodgen* v. *DeBorde,* 43 Ga. App. 131; 158 S. E. 64 [1931]). Other courts have limited the husband's liability to the wife's personal torts, or to her personal torts committed in his presence. The great weight of authority refuses to apply the common law to torts committed by the wife in the management of her separate property. The whole matter, however, should be taken out of the hands of the judges by the enactment of legislation expressly abolishing every phase of the ridiculous common-law rule.

Statutes dealing with the wife's liability for her own torts, found in twenty-nine jurisdictions, are collected in the table following. **Maine** and **Pennsylvania** strangely provide that she cannot be arrested on account of her torts. Even at common law, she was jointly liable for her civil wrongs which were not committed in the husband's presence under his coercion, and in most jurisdictions under general statutes she may now be sued as if unmarried without the joinder of the husband (**Sec. 179**). **West Virginia** is the only jurisdiction which expressly abrogates the common-law rule which excused the wife when acting under the husband's coercion, but the necessary effect of most of the other statutes is in the same direction. Coercion obviously should not excuse the wife except when it is a recognized excuse for any defendant. It remains to add that the wife may now generally contract as if unmarried (**Sec. 152**), and hence her torts committed in connection with her contracts may be enforced against her in the same manner as her other torts are enforced against her.

The table follows.

TABLE LXXXI

WIFE'S TORTS

Jurisdiction and Citation	Antenuptial Torts		Postnuptial Torts	
	Husband's Liability	Wife's Liability	Husband's Liability	Wife's Liability
Alabama .... C. 1923, Secs. 8265–66	Husband is not liable for wife's torts committed before marriage	Wife remains liable and suable as if sole for her torts committed before marriage	Husband is not liable for wife's torts in commission of which he does not participate	Wife is liable for her torts and suable therefor as if sole
Alaska .... Comp. L. 1913, Secs. 443, 493	Husband is not liable for wife's liabilities incurred before marriage		Husband is liable only when he would be jointly responsible if marriage did not exist	Damages for wife's torts may be recovered from her alone
Arizona .... R. C. 1928, Secs. 2174–75	Husband's separate property is not liable for debts of wife "contracted" before marriage	Wife of twenty-one years is subject to the same legal liabilities as men of twenty-one years		Wife of twenty-one years is subject to the same legal liabilities as men of twenty-one years
Arkansas .... Crawf. and Moses, Dig. 1921, Secs. 5577, 5590	Husband is not liable for wife's "antenuptial debts" except by virtue of express written contract	Wife's common-law disabilities are removed		Wife's common-law disabilities are removed

[§ 157

TABLE LXXXI (*Continued*)

Jurisdiction and Citation	Antenuptial Torts		Postnuptial Torts	
	Husband's Liability	Wife's Liability	Husband's Liability	Wife's Liability
California C. C. 1933 (Lake), Secs. 170–71a	Husband's separate property is not liable for debts of wife "contracted" before marriage	Wife's separate property is liable for her debts "contracted" before marriage	Husband is liable only when he would be jointly liable if marriage did not exist	Damages for wife's torts may be recovered from her alone
Colorado Comp. L. 1921, G. S., Secs. 5580–82	Husband is subject to wife's liabilities "contracted" before marriage to the extent of the property he may receive with or through her or derive from the sale or rent of her lands. Such liability is not extinguished by wife's death	If wife has lands, judgment on her antenuptial liability may be rendered against her and husband jointly, to be levied on such lands only		
Connecticut G. S. 1930, Secs. 5154, 5172	Husband is not liable for debts of wife "contracted" before marriage	Wife may be sued "for a tort"	Husband of wife married before April 20, 1877, is not liable for her torts committed without his actual coercion	Wife married after April 20, 1877, may be sued "for a tort." Wife married before April 20, 1877, may be sued and her property attached, etc., for any tort committed by her without the actual coercion of the husband
Delaware R. C. 1915, Sec. 3060; Sess. L. 1925, Ch. 228, p. 534		Wife and her property are liable for her debts "contracted" before marriage	Husband is liable only when he would be jointly responsible if the marriage did not exist	Damages for wife's tort may be recovered against wife alone
District of Columbia C. 1929, T. 14, Secs. 43, 45	Husband is not liable for claims or demands against wife arising prior to marriage	Wife and her property are liable for her antenuptial obligations as if unmarried	Husband is not liable for tort committed by wife separately out of his presence without his participation or sanction	Wife is liable for her torts as if unmarried

TABLE LXXXI (*Continued*)

Jurisdiction and Citation	Antenuptial Torts		Postnuptial Torts	
	Husband's Liability	Wife's Liability	Husband's Liability	Wife's Liability
Florida R. G. S. 1920, Sec. 3950	Husband is not liable to pay the debts of the wife "contracted" before marriage	The property of the wife is subject to her debts "contracted" before marriage		
Georgia C. 1926, C. C., Sec. 4413			"Every person shall be liable for torts committed by his wife, and for torts committed by his child, or servant, by his command . . . ."	
Hawaii R. L. 1925, Secs. 3000–3001	Husband is not liable upon a cause of action which originated against the wife prior to marriage		Husband is personally responsible for the wife's torts done by and with his authority or consent, and for none other	
Idaho Comp. St. 1919, Secs. 4664–65	Husband's separate property is not liable for debts of wife "contracted" before marriage	Wife's separate property is liable for her debts "contracted" before marriage		
Illinois Cahill, R. S. 1931, Ch. 68, Secs. 4, 5	Husband is not liable for wife's liabilities incurred before marriage		Husband is liable only when he would be jointly responsible if marriage did not exist	Damages for wife's torts may be recovered from wife alone
Indiana Burns, Ann. St. 1926, Secs. 8742–43, 8747–49	Husband is subject to wife's liabilities "contracted" before marriage to the extent of the personal property he may receive with or through her or derive from the sale or rent of her lands. Such liability is not extinguished by wife's death	If wife has lands, judgment on her antenuptial liabilities may be rendered against her and husband jointly, to be levied on such lands only	Husband is not liable for wife's torts; if wife commits tort by direction of husband or in his presence with his consent, both spouses are jointly liable therefor	Wife, without reference to her age, is liable for her torts, and an action may be prosecuted against her therefor as if she were sole

[§ 157

TABLE LXXXI (*Continued*)

Jurisdiction and Citation	Antenuptial Torts		Postnuptial Torts	
	Husband's Liability	Wife's Liability	Husband's Liability	Wife's Liability
Iowa C. 1927, Secs. 10465, 10467	Husband is not liable for wife's liabilities incurred before marriage		Husband is not liable except when he would be jointly liable if marriage did not exist	Damages for wife's torts may be recovered from her alone
Kentucky Carroll, St. 1922, Secs. 2127, 2130	Husband is not liable for debts or responsibility of wife incurred before marriage, "except to the amount or value of the property he may receive from or by her by virtue of the marriage"	Wife's estate is liable for her debts and responsibilities incurred before marriage	Husband is not liable for debts or responsibility of wife incurred after marriage, "except to the amount or value of the property he may receive from or by virtue of the marriage"	Wife's estate is liable for her debts and responsibilities "contracted" after marriage, except as otherwise provided
Louisiana C. C., Art. 2403		Debts of wife anterior to the marriage must be acquitted out of her own personal and individual effects		
Maine R. S. 1930, Ch. 74, Sec. 4	Husband is not liable for debts of wife "contracted" before marriage	Wife is liable for her debts "contracted" before marriage	Husband is not liable for wife's torts in which he takes no part	Wife is liable for her torts as if she were sole, but she cannot be arrested
Maryland Bagby, Ann. C. 1924, Art. 45, Secs. 5, 14	Husband is not liable for claims or demands against wife arising prior to the marriage	Wife is liable for her wrongs independent of contract committed before marriage, as if she were sole	Husband is not liable for tort committed by wife separately out of his presence, without his participation or sanction	Wife is liable for her wrongs independent of contract as if she were sole
Massachusetts G. L. 1932, Ch. 209, Secs. 6, 8	Husband is not liable upon a cause of action originating against wife prior to the marriage		Husband is not liable "to pay a judgment" recovered against wife (except as otherwise provided)	

§ 157]

TABLE LXXXI (*Continued*)

Jurisdiction and Citation	Antenuptial Torts		Postnuptial Torts	
	Husband's Liability	Wife's Liability	Husband's Liability	Wife's Liability
Michigan .... Comp. L. 1929, Sec. 14015			"No suit shall be brought against husband and wife jointly, or against the husband alone, for any tort of the wife, unless such tort was committed under such circumstances as to render them both liable"	
Minnesota ...... G. S. 1923, Secs. 8618, 8620	Husband is not liable for wife's torts committed before coverture	Wife and her property are liable for her torts as if she were sole	Husband is not liable for wife's torts committed during coverture	Wife and her property are liable for her torts as if she were sole
Missouri .... R. S. 1929, Secs. 3004, 3290	Husband's property, "except such as may be acquired from the wife," is exempt from liabilities incurred by wife before marriage		Husband is liable only when he would be jointly responsible if the marriage did not exist	Damages for wife's torts may be recovered against her alone
Montana .... R. C. 1921, Secs. 5790, 5798–99	Husband's property is not liable for wife's debts "contracted" before marriage. Husband, as such, is not answerable for the acts of the wife	Wife's property is liable for her debts "contracted" before marriage	Husband, as such, is not answerable for the acts of the wife	
Nebraska .... Comp. St. 1929, Sec. 42(206)	Husband's property is not liable for debts of wife "contracted" before marriage			
Nevada .... Comp. L. 1929 (Hillyer), Secs. 3370–71	Husband's separate property is not liable for debts of wife "contracted" before marriage	Wife's separate property is liable for her debts "contracted" before marriage		
New Hampshire . Pub. L. 1926, Ch. 288, Secs. 2, 3	Husband is not liable for debts of wife "contracted" before marriage			Wife may be sued for any wrong by her done as if she were sole

[§ 157

TABLE LXXXI (*Continued*)

Jurisdiction and Citation	Antenuptial Torts		Postnuptial Torts	
	Husband's Liability	Wife's Liability	Husband's Liability	Wife's Liability
New Jersey Comp. St. 1910, p. 3235, Sec. 10; Supp. 1925–30, Sec. 124(20)	Husband is not liable for debts of wife "contracted" before marriage	Wife is liable for her debts "contracted" before marriage	Husband is liable only when he would be jointly responsible if the marriage did not exist	Damages for wife's torts may be recovered against her alone
New Mexico St. Ann. 1929, Secs. 68(306)– 68(307)	Husband's separate property is not liable for debts of wife "contracted" before marriage	Wife's separate property is liable for her debts "contracted" before marriage		
New York Cahill, Consol. L. 1930, Ch. 14, Secs. 54, 57	Husband is liable for wife's debts "contracted" before marriage to the extent of property acquired from her by antenuptial contract or otherwise		Husband is not liable for wife's torts unless done by his actual coercion or instigation. Coercion or instigation is not presumed, but must be proved	Wife is liable for her tortious acts
North Carolina C. 1927, Secs. 2517–18	Husband is not liable for wrongs done by wife before marriage	Wife's liability for her antenuptial wrongs is not impaired by marriage	Husband is not liable for damages accruing from wife's torts	
North Dakota Comp. L. 1913, Sec. 4411; Supp. 1913– 25, Sec. 4414	Husband's separate property is not liable for debts of wife "contracted" before marriage. Husband, as such, is not answerable for the acts of the wife	Wife's separate property is liable for her debts "contracted" before marriage	Husband, as such, is not answerable for the acts of the wife	Wife with respect to torts is subject to the same liability as before marriage
Ohio Complete G. C. 1931 (Page), Sec. 8002	Husband, as such, is not answerable for the acts of the wife		Husband, as such, is not answerable for the acts of the wife	
Oklahoma St. 1931, Secs. 1659, 1665	Husband's separate property is not liable for debts of wife "contracted" before marriage. Husband, as such, is not answerable for the acts of the wife	Wife's separate property is liable for her debts "contracted" before marriage. Wife retains same legal personality as before marriage	Husband, as such, is not answerable for the acts of the wife	Wife retains same legal personality as before marriage

§ 157]

TABLE LXXXI (*Continued*)

Jurisdiction and Citation	Antenuptial Torts		Postnuptial Torts	
	Husband's Liability	Wife's Liability	Husband's Liability	Wife's Liability
Oregon C. 1930, Secs. 33(205), 33(214)	Husband is not liable for wife's liabilities incurred before marriage		Husband is liable only when he would be jointly responsible if marriage did not exist	Damages for wife's torts may be recovered from her alone
Pennsylvania St. 1920 (West), Secs. 8690, 14586, 14602	Husband is not liable for debts of wife "contracted" before marriage		Execution on judgment recovered against husband for wife's torts shall be first had against the property of the wife	See preceding column. Wife may be sued civilly with same consequences as if unmarried, but she may not be arrested or imprisoned for her torts
Rhode Island G. L. 1923, Secs. 4204–5	Husband is not liable for torts of wife committed before marriage	Wife's property is subject to levy for judgment in any action of tort against her as if she were single	Husband is not liable for wife's torts unless he participates therein or coerces her thereto	Wife's property is subject to levy for judgment in any action of tort against her as if she were single
South Carolina C. of L. 1922, C. C., Sec. 5540	Husband is not liable for debts of wife "contracted" before marriage			
South Dakota Comp. L. 1929, Secs. 175, 178	Husband's separate property is not liable for debts of wife "contracted" before marriage. Husband, as such, is not answerable for acts of wife	Actions for wife's separate torts may be brought against her without joining the husband	Husband, as such, is not answerable for the acts of the wife	Actions for wife's separate torts may be brought against her without joining the husband
Tennessee C. 1932, Sec. 8459	Husband is not liable for obligations of wife incurred before marriage			
Texas Complete St. 1928, Civ. St., Art. 4613	Husband's separate property is not liable for debts of wife "contracted" before marriage		Separate property of husband is not liable for wife's torts	
Utah R. S. 1933, 40-2-5, 40-2-7	Husband is not liable for wife's liabilities incurred before marriage		Husband is liable only when he would be jointly liable if marriage did not exist	Damages for wife's torts may be recovered from her alone

[§ 157

TABLE LXXXI (*Concluded*)

Jurisdiction and Citation	Antenuptial Torts		Postnuptial Torts	
	Husband's Liability	Wife's Liability	Husband's Liability	Wife's Liability
Vermont .... G. L. 1917, Sec. 3526	Husband is not liable for debts of wife "contracted" before marriage		Husband is not liable for wife's torts unless committed by his authority or direction	
Virginia .... C. 1930, Sec. 5134, amd. by Sess. L. 1932, Ch. 25, p. 21	Husband is not liable for wife's torts committed before marriage	Wife may be sued with same consequences as if unmarried	Husband is not liable for wife's torts committed after marriage	Wife may be sued with same consequences as if unmarried
Washington .... Remington, Comp. St. 1922, Secs. 6904–5	Husband is not liable for wife's liabilities incurred before marriage		Husband is not liable except when he would be jointly responsible if marriage did not exist	Damages for wife's torts may be recovered from her alone
West Virginia .. C. 1931, Ch. 48, Art. 3, Secs. 14, 15, 20	Husband or his property is not liable for wife's torts committed before marriage (but see footnote 1)	Wife is liable for her torts committed before marriage	Husband is not liable for wife's torts unless done as his agent, or by his actual coercion or instigation. The latter is not presumed but must be proved (but see footnote 1)	Wife is liable for her torts, whether under the coercion or instigation of husband or not
Wisconsin ...... St. 1931, Secs. 246.08, 272.05	Husband is not liable for wife's "antenuptial debts"	Wife and her property are liable for her "antenuptial debts" as if sole	When judgment is entered against both spouses in action for tort committed by wife alone, execution is levied upon the property of the wife alone	See preceding column
Wyoming .... R. S. 1931, Sec. 69(106)	Husband is not liable for the wife's liabilities "contracted" before marriage without an assumption thereof in writing	If wife has lands, judgment on her antenuptial liabilities may be rendered against her to be levied on such lands only	When judgment is rendered against both spouses for wife's tort, execution thereon is first levied on the wife's lands, if any	See preceding column

[1] **West Virginia** has a unique statute which provides: "If any property real or personal has been heretofore, or shall hereafter be, conveyed or transferred by either husband or wife to the other, before or after marriage, by reason of any antenuptial contract or otherwise, the grantee or transferee shall be liable for the obligations, whether based on contract or tort, of the grantor or transferor of such property created before such conveyance or transfer, to the extent of the value of the property so conveyed or transferred" (C. 1931, Ch. 48, Art. 3, Sec. 15).

§ 157]

REFERENCES

Books

MADDEN, JOSEPH W. *Handbook of the Law of Persons and Domestic Relations,* pp. 206 *et seq.* (1931).

STIMSON, F. J. *American Statute Law,* Secs. 6404, 6414 (1886).

Articles

MILLER, ROBERT W. "Liability of a Husband for Wife's Torts," 18 Ia. L. Rev. 30–42 (1932).

STONHAM, R. M. "Liability of Husband for Wife's Torts," 8 Aust. L. Jour. 12–13 (1934).

Notes

"Husband and Wife—Postnuptial Torts—Liability of Husband under Married Women's Property Act (England)," 20 Ill. L. Rev. 80–83 (1925).

"Liability of Husband for the Torts of His Wife," 83 Univ. of Pa. L. Rev. 66–73 (1934).

Annotations

"Liability of Husband for Independent Tort of Wife," 20 A. L. R. 528–42 (1922); 27 A. L. R. 1218–19 (1923); 59 A. L. R. 1468–73 (1929).

"Liability of Owner of Automobile for Injury while Spouse Is Using Car," 64 A. L. R. 873–77 (1929).

Section 158. Torts by Third Persons

CROSS REFERENCES: Damages in suits by the wife, **Sec. 167;** Wife's right to her earnings, **Sec. 173;** Nature of damages recovered in community-property states, **Sec. 178;** Suits by the wife, **Sec. 179**

This section deals with the right of action of husband or wife against third persons for: (*a*) "criminal conversation" (i.e., wrongful sexual intercourse) and alienation of affections; (*b*) other wilful or negligent torts or injuries to the other spouse; and (*c*) the wrongful death of the other spouse. Express legislation on this subject is singularly lacking except as to actions for wrongful death and for the sale of intoxicating liquor. The so-called "case law" is of more importance, although a detailed discussion of it is not within the scope of this work. (For cases, see references following this section.)

[§ 158

I. Actions at Common Law and under the General Married Women's Legislation

Legislation increasing the wife's rights (**Secs. 149–50**) has not abrogated the common-law right of the husband to sue a third person for criminal conversation or for alienation of the wife's affections. The great majority of courts also allow his action for a negligent or wilful tort to her which causes a loss of "consortium" (her companionship, care, attention, society, and services due him). The earlier common law considered loss of services as the theoretical basis of such action, damages being increased by the loss of the other elements of consortium. The recent statutes giving the wife a right to certain of her earnings and services (**Secs. 167, 173**) must reduce the husband's recovery for a tort to her—otherwise, by her action, double recovery would be given. Moreover, a few courts have held that such statutes destroy the peg on which the common-law action was hung, and have thus denied the husband's action for the more sentimental elements of consortium (*Marri* v. *Stamford Street Railway Company,* 84 Conn. 9; 78 A. 582 [1911]); although he may still recover for actual expenses incurred by him through injury to her. He is also generally permitted to sue for an act designed or apt to injure the marital relation, as, for example, a sale of drugs to the wife, resulting in an impairment of consortium (*Holleman* v. *Harward,* 119 N. C. 150; 25 S. E. 972 [1896]).

Because of the peculiarly inferior position of the wife under the earlier common law, the causes of action discussed above were not given to her. However, the fact that today a married woman in general is on an equal basis with her husband has resulted in judicial recognition that the right of a spouse to the affections and exclusive marital intercourse of the other is mutual. Thus, even without express statutes, actions for alienation of affections and criminal conversation are now available to the wife. But she still is not permitted to sue for a negligent injury to the husband. It is said that she has no legal right to his services; that the pecuniary damage is recoverable in his action; and that the loss of other elements of consortium (society, etc.) is too remote or uncertain a basis for her action. A striking illustration of this latter rule is shown by a recent New York case (*Landwehr* v. *Barbas,* 241 App. Div. 769; 270 N. Y. S. 534 [1934]), where the court refused recovery by the wife for a negligent injury to the husband which resulted in his emasculation (see, however, the dissenting opinion). The majority view which thus gives the husband an action for a negligent injury to the

§ 158]

wife, yet which denies a similar action to her, is logically inconsistent in view of the equality of married women. A few courts have therefore denied such action to either spouse. Since the damage to consortium from a wilful tort to the husband is very similar to that arising from a negligent injury to him, the courts, to be consistent, should hold that the wife has no action. Contrary statements, however, have been made by some courts in cases where there was also the probability that the marital relation would be injured if the act were done. Where the latter is true, it is generally held that the wife may sue (*Flandermeyer* v. *Cooper,* 85 Ohio St. 327; 98 N. E. 102 [1912]).

II. Statutes Expressly or Impliedly Recognizing Rights of Action for Torts by Third Persons

The relevant statutes may be classified according to the type of action involved, as follows: (*a*) actions for criminal conversation and alienation of affections; (*b*) actions for a negligent or wilful tort to the other spouse, or for an act designed or apt to injure the marital relation; (*c*) actions for wrongful death.

Express statutes were found in five states permitting the husband (**Alabama, Florida, Georgia**) or the wife (**Maine**) to sue for criminal conversation; or permitting the wife to sue for alienation of affections (**Maine, Wisconsin**). Six states have rather vague provisions which do not, in terms, mention either action, but under which both actions have been brought by the husband and by the wife (**California, Montana, North Dakota, Oklahoma, South Dakota**), or by the husband (**Georgia**) (see summary following this section). An ambiguous **New York** statute permits the wife to sue for an injury to her person, or an injury arising out of the marital relation. Relying in part on this provision and on a statute which includes criminal conversation in a definition of "personal injury," the court in *Oppenheim* v. *Kridel,* 236 N. Y. 156; 140 N. E. 227 (1923), permitted the wife to sue for criminal conversation.[1] Statutes relating to witnesses indirectly refer to actions for alienation of affections (**Arizona, Iowa, Wyoming**) and for criminal conversation (**Arizona**) brought by either spouse; and to an action

---

[1] The present volume covers statutes to January 1, 1935, only. Since that date **New York** and **Indiana** have passed statutes abolishing suits for criminal conversation and alienation of affections. As this book goes to press, similar legislation is being considered in at least ten other states. See Nathan P. Feinsinger's article, "Legislative Attack on 'Heart Balm'," in 33 Mich. L. Rev. 979–1009 (1935).

for criminal conversation brought by the husband (**Wyoming**). A peculiar **Hawaii** statute provides that the wife of a husband who sues for criminal conversation with her is not liable criminally for adultery. It is significant that the only express statutes found permitting the wife's action (**Maine, Wisconsin**) were passed after the courts in those states had persistently denied her relief. Other jurisdictions apparently have achieved the result of such statutes by judicial decision. The **Maine** statute respecting alienation of affections is peculiar (see summary following), and by its terms would allow recovery against the wife's mother-in-law, but not against her father-in-law.

Thirteen jurisdictions have legislation pertaining to actions by one spouse against a third person for a negligent or wilful tort to the other spouse. In **Georgia** and **Hawaii,** statutes apparently declaratory of the common law permit the husband to sue for torts to his wife. Four states (**California, Florida, New Jersey, Pennsylvania**) have provisions allowing a joinder of the separate actions of husband and wife for her injury, thus implying that he may sue. A statute in **Connecticut** clearly implies that the husband has an action for expenditures made or indebtedness incurred by him as a result of injury to the wife (see summary following). A **Wisconsin** statute contains an implication that the husband may sue. In **Maryland,** a husband may sue for slander of his wife relating to her character or reputation for chastity. On the other hand, three states (**Kansas, Utah, Virginia**) expressly declare that the husband cannot sue for an injury to his wife, although in **Kansas** the damages recovered by the wife which are based on the impairment of her ability to perform household services inure to the husband's benefit. However, **Utah** and **Virginia** have gone even farther than the minority rule as to injury to the wife (see above, subdivision I), since they allow her to recover for her own use all damages from her injury, even though expenses have been incurred by the husband. A statute in **Iowa** enumerates certain elements of damage as recoverable in the wife's action, thereby impliedly precluding recovery for them by the husband.

It is possible that the broad statutes in some states (see **Sec. 150**) giving the wife rights equal to her husband may be construed as allowing her to sue on the cause of action discussed above. It has been held, however, in some cases that such provisions do not create new substantive rights of action in the wife, but only affect her procedural rights. (See *Nash* v. *Mobile & Ohio Railroad Company,* 149 Miss. 823; 116 So. 100 [1928]; and *Kosciolek* v. *Portland Railway, Light and Power Company,* 81 Ore. 517; 160 P. 132 [1916].)

§ 158]

Under certain circumstances, the furnishing of intoxicating liquor by a third person to one spouse, although it is not tortious to him or her, may seriously impair the marital relation and so injure the other spouse. Thirty jurisdictions have statutes under which a spouse so injured may recover damages. Presumably directed toward the protection of a wife and children, they sometimes have a broader scope and often extend to "any person injured in person, property, or means of support" (see table following for details).

The husband, at common law, had no cause of action for a tort which resulted in the wife's death, unless he could show a loss of consortium in the interval between the injury and death, and, obviously, the wife had no cause of action for death of her husband. Enactments commonly called "wrongful death statutes" have been passed in every jurisdiction under which husband and wife are usually treated alike, either as beneficiaries of a new cause of action created by the statute or as distributees of the damages recovered by the representative on the deceased's cause of action. In general, the statutes say nothing of changing the common-law rule as to the action by the survivor for loss of consortium. A special **Arkansas** statute, however, does enable the husband to sue for loss of services and companionship caused by the wife's death. Citations to these "death statutes" are collected following Table LXXXII on pages 96–97, but the provisions are not sufficiently germane to justify setting forth their substance.

III. CONCLUSION

Excluding the death and liquor statutes which are incidental to this subject, only twenty-one jurisdictions have been found with even fragmentary legislation; and much of it merely implies certain rights or is ambiguous. It is unfortunate that this field of law has not received more legislative attention. Rights of marital relations have changed fundamentally since the time of Blackstone, yet the evolution of the law in this field has been left primarily to the courts. A certain desirable unanimity of opinion has developed relative to criminal conversation and alienation of affections, but the clarity possible through proper legislation is lacking. In the writer's opinion, the majority view of the cases in respect to actions by one spouse for a tortious injury to the other should be changed. If the husband may sue, the wife should be able to do so; or if the legislature feels that the damages are too sentimental or uncertain, then the husband's action should be abrogated. The writer holds no brief for the vague statutes of some jurisdictions but feels that

[§ 158

a broad and clear definition of the rights of either spouse against a third person for torts connected with the marital relation is needed.

The statutory material discussed in this section, other than that relating to wrongful death and injuries caused by intoxicating liquor, is summarized below. Following this summary will be found a table of liquor statutes and finally a compilation of citations to the wrongful-death statutes.

SUMMARY OF STATUTES

(EXCLUSIVE OF DEATH AND LIQUOR STATUTES)

Alabama (C. 1923, Sec. 5672) : Husband may sue for criminal conversation.

Arizona (R. C. 1928, Sec. 4412[3]) : Either spouse may testify for or against the other, in actions for alienation of affections or criminal conversation.

California (C. C. 1933 [Lake], Sec. 49) : Rights of personal relations forbid abduction of husband from wife . . . . abduction or enticement of wife from husband . . . . seduction of wife. (C. C. P. 1933 [Lake], Sec. 427) : In an action by husband and wife for her injury, all consequential damage of the husband, including loss of wife's services, money expended, or debts incurred by reason of injury, may be alleged and recovered without separately stating husband's cause of action.

Connecticut (Cum. Supp. 1931, 1933, Ch. 293, p. 519, Sec. 1154*b*) : If husband has made expenditures or contracted indebtedness as a result of personal injury to wife, amount of such expenditures, etc., may be recovered by wife in her action; provided the husband endorses his consent upon the complaint prior to service upon defendant; except in action in which husband is a defendant.

Florida (R. G. S. 1920) : The declaration in criminal conversation is "that the defendant debauched and carnally knew the plaintiff's wife" (Sec. 2648[25]) ; in an action by husband and wife for her injury in respect of which she is necessarily joined as co-plaintiff, he may add his own claims; and separate actions in respect of such claims may be consolidated if the court shall think fit (Sec. 2586).

Georgia (C. 1926, C. C.) : If a tort be committed upon the person or reputation of the wife, the husband or wife may recover therefor (Sec. 2994) ; a person may recover for torts committed to himself or to his wife . . . . (Sec. 4412) ; husband may sue another for abducting or harboring his wife, except for assisting wife driven from home by cruel treatment (Sec. 4464) ; same as the **Alabama** statute (Sec. 4465).

§ 158]

Hawaii (R. L. 1925) : Except as otherwise provided, persons in the Territory are liable for trespass or injury to the wives of others (Sec. 2365) ; a woman who is the subject of action for criminal conversation is not liable criminally for adultery (Sec. 4443).

Iowa (C. 1927) : Any woman in an action for her wrongful injury may recover for loss of time, medical attendance, and expenses incurred, in addition to elements of damage recoverable by common law (Sec. 10462) ; either spouse may testify against the other in action for alienation of affections (Sec. 11260[3]).

Kansas (R. S. 1923, Sec. 23[205]) : Wife has the sole right of action for wrongful personal injury to her, except that recovery based on impairment of her ability to perform household services and domestic duties is for husband's benefit as far as he is entitled thereto.

Maine (R. S. 1930, Ch. 74, Sec. 7) : Whoever, being a female over eighteen, carries on criminal conversations with, alienates affections of, the husband, or by enticement deprives wife of his aid, comfort, and society, is liable to wife.

Maryland (Bagby, Ann. C. 1924, Art. 88, Sec. 4) : Husband may sue after marriage for slander touching wife's character or reputation for chastity before or during marriage.

Montana (R. C. 1921, Sec. 5693) : Same as the **California** statute (C. C. 1933, Sec. 49).

New Jersey (Comp. St. 1910, p. 3236, Sec. 12*a*; p. 4057, Sec. 21) : Substantially like the **Florida** statute (R. G. S. 1920, Sec. 2586).

New York (Cahill, Consol. L. 1930) : Wife may sue as if unmarried for an injury to her person . . . . or for an injury arising out of the marital relation (Ch. 14, Sec. 57) ; "personal injury" includes criminal conversation (Ch. 23, Sec. 37*a*).[1]

North Dakota (Comp. L. 1913, Sec. 4355) : Same as the **California** statute (C. C. 1933, Sec. 49).

Oklahoma (St. 1931, Sec. 17) : Same as the **California** statute (C. C. 1933, Sec. 49).

Pennsylvania (St. 1920 [West], Sec. 30) : Rights of action of wife and of husband accruing from wrongful injury to her shall be redressed in only one action in the names of husband and wife.

South Dakota (Comp. L. 1929, Sec. 100) : Substantially like the **California** statute (C. C. 1933, Sec. 49).

---

[1] Since the foregoing statutes were summarized, **New York** has adopted a statute abolishing civil actions for criminal conversation (Cahill, Civ. Prac. Act 1931, Secs. 61*a*–61*i,* added by Sess. L. 1935, Ch. 263).

[§ 158

Utah (R. S. 1933, 40-2-4) : Husband cannot recover for personal injury or wrong to wife, or for expenses connected therewith; but she may recover against third person for injury or wrong as if unmarried; such recovery shall include expenses paid or assumed by husband.

Virginia (C. 1930, Sec. 5134, as amended by Sess. L. 1932, Ch. 25, p. 21) : Husband cannot sue for personal injury to wife, nor for expenses, loss of services or consortium. She may recover entire damage, including expenses arising from injury (whether chargeable to her or husband).

Wisconsin (St. 1931, Sec. 246.07) : Wife may sue in her own name and for her benefit, for alienation and loss of affection and society of husband. Statute giving wife a right of action for injury to her person or character does not affect the husband's right to maintain a separate action for any such injuries as are now provided by law.

Wyoming (R. S. 1931, Sec. 89[1702]) : Husband or wife may testify against other in action by husband for criminal conversation with wife, or in action by either spouse for alienation of other's affections.

TABLE LXXXII*

SUIT BY SPOUSE FOR FURNISHING LIQUOR

Jurisdiction and Citation	Person by Whom Suit May Be Brought	Person Liable[1]	Damages	Is Illegal Sale Necessary for Liability
Alabama .... C. 1923, Sec. 5674	Every wife, or other person, who shall be injured[2]	Vendor is liable	Actual as well as exemplary	Yes
Colorado .... Comp. L. 1921, G. S., Secs. 3719, 6308	For an illegal sale, any wife or other person injured.[2] For a sale to a habitual drunkard, every husband, wife, or other person injured[2]	Vendor is liable for furnishing to habitual drunkard, if written notice is given; or to any person illegally		....[3]
Delaware ...... R. C. 1915, Sec. 177	Wife or husband of an intoxicated person who has suffered personal injury	Vendor is liable for furnishing to a person of known intemperate habits for any injury to the person of one intoxicated	Actual as well as exemplary	No

* See page 96 for all numbered footnotes to this table.

§ 158]

TABLE LXXXII (*Continued*)

Jurisdiction and Citation	Person by Whom Suit May Be Brought	Person Liable[1]	Damages	Is Illegal Sale Necessary for Liability
Hawaii .... R. L. 1925, Sec. 2130	A husband, wife . . . . or other injured person,[2] or the legal representative of the intoxicated who is injured. A wife may sue in her own name	Vendor is liable for furnishing to a person twice convicted of drunkenness	Wife's recovery is her own separate property	No
Illinois .... Cahill, R. S. 1931, Ch. 43, Sec. 20	Any person who may be injured[4]	Vendor is liable	Actual as well as exemplary. A wife's recovery is her own separate property	Yes
Indiana .... Burns, Ann. St. 1926, Sec. 2753	Any wife . . . . or other person injured[2]	Vendor is liable	All damages sustained	Yes
Iowa .... C. 1927, Sec. 2055	Every wife . . . . or other person injured[2] may sue in his or her own name	Vendor is liable	Actual as well as exemplary	Yes
Kansas .... R. S. 1923, Secs. 21(2150)– 21(2153), 21(2155)	Every wife . . . . or other person injured[2]	Vendor is liable. Owner of premises is liable if he had knowledge that liquor was sold in violation of law. City officials are liable if they were not in good faith in enforcing the law, and knew, or could by reasonable diligence have known, that liquor was being sold in violation of law	Actual as well as exemplary	....[3]
Kentucky ...... Carroll, St. 1922, Sec. 1307	The wife . . . . of the intoxicated person	Vendor is liable for furnishing to an inebriate, if written notice has been given to vendor	Actual and punitive	No
Maine .... R. S. 1930, Ch. 137, Sec. 19	Every wife . . . . or husband . . . . who is injured[4]	Vendor is liable. Owner of premises is liable if he had knowledge of the furnishing	Actual and exemplary	No

[§ 158

TABLE LXXXII (*Continued*)

Jurisdiction and Citation	Person by Whom Suit May Be Brought	Person Liable[1]	Damages	Is Illegal Sale Necessary for Liability
Massachusetts G. L. 1932, Ch. 138, Sec. 49	A wife or husband . . . . injured[2]	Vendor is liable. Owner of building is liable if he had knowledge, unless the lessee had a license for the sale	A wife's recovery is her separate property	No
Michigan Comp. L. 1929, Sec. 9193	Every wife or husband . . . . injured[4]	Vendor is liable	Actual and exemplary, not less than fifty dollars. A wife's recovery is her own separate property	Yes
Minnesota G. S. 1923, Sec. 3239	Every husband or wife . . . . injured[2]	Vendor is liable	All damages sustained	Yes
Missouri R. S. 1929, Sec. 4487	Every wife or husband . . . . injured[4]	Vendor is liable	Actual and exemplary. A wife's recovery is her own separate property	Yes
Montana R. C. 1921, Sec. 11065	Any person injured[4]	Vendor is liable	Actual and exemplary. A wife's recovery is her separate property	Yes
Nebraska Comp. St. 1929, Secs. 53(147)– 53(149)	Any person injured in any manner. Loss of companionship is specially mentioned[5]	Vendor is liable. City or county law-enforcing officers are liable unless they acted in good faith, or did not know, or by reasonable diligence could not have known, that such illegal sales were being made	All damages and the expenses of any civil or criminal proceeding brought	Yes
New Hampshire Pub. L. 1926, Ch. 144, Secs. 52, 53	Any husband or wife . . . . may recover for a sale to a habitual drunkard. Any person injured[2] may recover for an illegal sale	Vendor is liable for an illegal sale, or for a legal sale if written notice was given him not to furnish liquor	Not less than fifty and not more than five hundred dollars, from a legal sale. All damages from an illegal sale	. . . .[3]
New Jersey Cum. Supp. 1911–24, Sec. 100(309)	Any person injured[4]	Vendor is liable	Actual and exemplary	Yes

§ 158]

TABLE LXXXII (*Continued*)

Jurisdiction and Citation	Person by Whom Suit May Be Brought	Person Liable[1]	Damages	Is Illegal Sale Necessary for Liability
New York ...... Cahill, Consol. L. 1930, Ch. 7, Sec. 16	Any person injured . . . .[4]	Vendor is liable	Actual and exemplary. A wife's recovery is her separate property	Yes
North Dakota .. Comp. L. 1913, Sec. 10121	Every wife . . . . or other person injured[2]	Vendor is liable	Actual and exemplary. The wife may control her recovery as if unmarried	No
Ohio .... Complete G. C. 1931 (Page), Secs. 6203–5	A husband or wife . . . . injured[2]	Vendor is liable if a notice has been given to him not to furnish liquor. The owner or lessee of building where liquor is sold is liable if he has knowledge		No
Oklahoma ...... St. 1931, Sec. 2652	Every wife . . . . or other person injured[2]	Vendor is liable. In any action by a married woman or other person to recover for loss of support, it shall only be necessary to prove that the defendant has furnished liquor during the period when such cause of action shall have accrued	Actual damages sustained	**Yes**
Oregon .... C. 1930, Sec. 15(708)	The wife or husband	Vendor is liable for furnishing liquor to an intoxicated person or habitual drunkard	All resulting damages	No
Pennsylvania ... St. 1920 (West), Secs. 14029–31	Any wife or husband . . . . may sue for a sale after notice has been given. He or she may also recover a fine for each offense. Any person injured in person or property may sue for an illegal sale	Vendor is liable for an illegal sale without notice, or any sale if notice has been given not to furnish the liquor	Damage caused if an illegal sale. The fine (see first column) is five dollars for each offense. For a sale after notice, damages are limited to not less than fifty and not more than five hundred dollars	....[3]

[§ 158

TABLE LXXXII (*Concluded*)

Jurisdiction and Citation	Person by Whom Suit May Be Brought	Person Liable[1]	Damages	Is Illegal Sale Necessary for Liability
South Dakota Comp. L. 1929, Sec. 10309	Every wife or husband . . . . injured[4]	Vendor is liable)	Actual and exemplary. Damages may be recovered for mental suffering though no actual injury can be shown	Yes
Vermont G. L. 1917, Sec. 6579	A husband or wife injured[2]	Vendor is liable. Owner of building is liable if he knew or had reason to know liquor was sold there in violation of law		. . . .[3]
Virginia C. 1930, Sec. 4675(26)	Every wife . . . . or other person injured[2]	Vendor is liable	Actual and exemplary. A wife may control the recovery as if unmarried	No
Washington Remington, Comp. St. 1922, Secs. 1713, 7348	Any person injured[2] . . . . or every husband or wife injured	Vendor is liable for furnishing to a habitual drunkard. Vendor is liable for furnishing to any person if it reasonably could be anticipated that the sale would result in intoxication	A wife's recovery shall inure to her separate use	No
West Virginia C. 1931, Ch. 60, Art. 1, Sec. 22	Every husband or wife . . . . injured[2]	Vendor is liable. Owner of building is liable if he had knowledge liquor was sold	Actual and exemplary	Yes
Wyoming R. S. 1931, Sec. 59(119)	Any person injured[4]	Vendor is liable	Actual and exemplary	Yes

[1] The word "vendor" as afterward used refers to any person who sells, gives, or otherwise furnishes liquor.

[2] Injured in person, property, or means of support.

[3] Statutes in these states make distinctions in the extent of liability or persons liable depending on whether or not sale is legal or illegal.

[4] Injured in person, property, means of support, or otherwise.

[5] Injured in person, property, means of support, health, loss of companionship, care or attention, or in any other manner whatever (**Nebraska**).

Citations to statutes covering actions for wrongful death follow:

Alabama, C. 1923, Sec. 5696; **Alaska,** Comp. L. 1913, Sec. 1185; **Arizona,** R. C. 1928, Secs. 944–46; **Arkansas,** Const., Art. 5, Sec. 32; Crawf. and Moses, Dig. 1921, Secs. 1072–75; **California,** C. C. P. 1933 (Lake), Sec. 377; **Colorado,**

§ 158]

Comp. L. 1921, G. S., Secs. 6302–5; **Connecticut,** G. S. 1930, Secs. 4983, 5987; **Delaware,** R. C. 1915, Sec. 4155; **District of Columbia,** C. 1929, T. 21, Secs. 1–3; **Florida,** R. G. S. 1920, Secs. 4960–61; **Georgia,** C. 1926, C. C., Secs. 4424–26, 4462; **Hawaii,** R. L. 1925, Sec. 2681, as amended by Sess. L. 1933, Act 139, p. 136; **Idaho,** Comp. St. 1919, Sec. 6644; **Illinois,** Cahill, R. S. 1931, Ch. 70, Secs. 1, 2; **Indiana,** Burns, Ann. St. 1926, Sec. 292; **Iowa,** C. 1927, Secs. 10463–64; **Kansas,** R. S. 1923, Secs. 60(3203)–60(3204); **Kentucky,** Const., Secs. 54, 241; Carroll, St. 1922, Secs. 4–6; **Louisiana,** C. C., Art. 2315; **Maine,** R. S. 1930, Ch. 101, Sec. 9; Sec. 10, as amended by Sess. L. 1933, Ch. 113, p. 247; **Maryland,** Bagby, Ann. C. 1924, Art. 67, Secs. 1–4; **Massachusetts,** G. L. 1932, Ch. 229, Secs. 1–5; **Michigan,** Comp. L. 1929, Secs. 14061–63; **Minnesota,** G. S. 1923, Sec. 9657; **Mississippi,** C. 1930, Secs. 510–11; **Missouri,** R. S. 1929, Secs. 3262–64; **Montana,** R. C. 1921, Sec. 9076; **Nebraska,** Comp. St. 1929, Secs. 30(809)–30(810); **Nevada,** Comp. L. 1929 (Hillyer), Secs. 9194–95; **New Hampshire,** Pub. L. 1926, Ch. 302, Secs. 10–14; **New Jersey,** Comp. St. 1910, pp. 1907–11, Secs. 7–9; Sec. 8, as amended by Cum. Supp. 1911–24, Secs. 55(8), 55(10); **New Mexico,** Const., Art. 20, Sec. 16; St. Ann. 1929, Secs. 36(101)–36(104); **New York,** Const., Art. 1, Sec. 18; Cahill, Consol. L. 1930, Ch. 13, Secs. 130–34; **North Carolina,** C. 1927, Secs. 160–61; **North Dakota,** Comp. L. 1913, Secs. 8321–22; Sec. 8323, as amended by Supp. 1913–25, Sec. 8323; Secs. 8324–26; **Ohio,** Complete G. C. (Page), Supp. 1932, Secs. 10509(166)–10509(169); **Oklahoma,** Const., Art. 23, Sec. 7; St. 1931, Secs. 570–71; **Oregon,** C. 1930, Sec. 5(703); **Pennsylvania,** St. 1920 (West), Secs. 15977–80; Sec. 15981, as amended by Cum. Supp. 1928, Sec. 15981*a;* **Rhode Island,** G. L. 1923, Sec. 4862; Sec. 4863, as amended by Sess. L. 1932, Ch. 1912, p. 186; **South Carolina,** Const., Art. 9, Sec. 15; C. of L. 1922, C. C. P., Secs. 367–70; **South Dakota,** Comp. L. 1929, Secs. 2929–31; **Tennessee,** C. 1932, Secs. 8236–41; **Texas,** Const., Art. 16, Sec. 26; Complete St. 1928, Civ. Sts., Arts. 4671–78; **Utah,** Const., Art. 16, Sec. 5; R. S. 1933, 104-3-11; **Vermont,** G. L. 1917, Sec. 3314; Sec. 3315, as amended by Sess. L. 1919, No. 85, p. 92; **Washington,** Remington, Comp. St. 1922, Secs. 183, 183(1); Supp. 1927, Secs. 194, 6384; **West Virginia,** C. 1931, Ch. 55, Art. 7, Secs. 5–7; **Wisconsin,** St. 1931, Secs. 331.03–331.05; **Wyoming,** Const., Art. 9, Sec. 4; R. S. 1931, Secs. 89(403)–89(404).

REFERENCES

IN GENERAL

Book

PECK, EPAPHRODITUS. *Law of Persons and Domestic Relations,* pp. 201–13 (1930).

Articles

HOLBROOK, EVANS. "The Change in the Meaning of Consortium," 22 Mich. L. Rev. 1–9 (1923).
LIPPMAN, JACOB. "The Breakdown of Consortium," 30 Col. L. Rev. 651–73 (1930).
SHRIMAN, H. "Use of Injunctions in Family Relations," 27 Ill. L. Rev. 440–43 (1932).

[§ 158

CRIMINAL CONVERSATION AND ALIENATION OF AFFECTIONS

Article

BROWN, ROBERT C. "Action for Alienation of Affections," 82 Univ. of Pa. L. Rev. 472–506 (1934).

FEINSINGER, NATHAN P. "Legislative Attack on 'Heart Balm'," 33 Mich. L. Rev. 979–1009 (1935).

Notes

"Actions for Enticement and Criminal Conversation," *Jameson* v. *Tully,* 178 Cal. 380; 173 P. 577 (1918)—6 Calif. L. Rev. 379–82 (1918).

"Criminal Conversation—Right of Wife to Sue," *Turner* v. *Heavrin,* 182 Ky. 65; 206 S. W. 23 (1918)—32 Harv. L. Rev. 576 (1919).

"Loss of Consortium—Alienation of Affections," *Sherry* v. *Moore,* 258 Mass. 420; 155 N. E. 441 (1927)—22 Ill. L. Rev. 557–58 (1928).

"Alienation of Affections," *Place* v. *Searle,* (1932) 2 K. B. 497—66 U. S. L. Rev. 300–302 (1932).

"Alienation of Husband's Affections, Enabling Acts," *Eliason* v. *Draper,* 25 Del. 1; 77 A. 572 (1910)—10 Col. L. Rev. 775–76 (1910).

Annotations

"Wife's Action for Alienation of Affections," 6 L. R. A. 554–55 (1889) ; 4 L. R. A. (N.S.) 643–45 (1906).

"Wife's Right of Action for Criminal Conversation," 4 A. L. R. 569 (1919) ; 28 A. L. R. 327 (1924).

"Excessiveness or Inadequacy of Damages for Criminal Conversation or Alienation of Affections," 69 A. L. R. 1282–95 (1930).

TORT TO OTHER SPOUSE

Articles

DRAPER, C. M. "A Wife's Right to Recover for Personal Injuries to Husband," 6 Rocky Mt. L. Rev. 66–69 (1933).

HANNIGAN, JOHN E. "Damages Recoverable by Husband for Injury to Wife," 16 Col. L. Rev. 122–32 (1916).

Notes

"Consortium," *Blair* v. *Seitner Dry Goods Company,* 184 Mich. 304; 151 N. W. 724 (1915)—13 Mich. L. Rev. 704–5 (1915).

"Loss of Consortium," *Smith* v. *Nicholas Building Company,* 93 Ohio St. 101; 112 N. E. 204 (1915)—14 Mich. L. Rev. 689–90 (1916).

"Recovery by Wife for Loss of Consortium Due to Negligent Injury to Husband," *Hipp* v. *Dupont de Nemours Company,* 182 N. C. 9; 108 S. E. 316 (1921)—35 Harv. L. Rev. 343 (1922).

"Recovery for Indirect Injury Caused by Action of a Third Person," *Nieberg* v. *Cohen,* 88 Vt. 281; 92 A. 214 (1914)—28 Harv. L. Rev. 511–13 (1915).

§ 158]

"Rights and Liabilities of Husband as to Third Parties—Effect of Married Women's Property Acts on Husband's Action for Loss of Consortium," *Marri* v. *Stamford Street Railway Company*, 84 Conn. 9; 78 A. 582 (1911)—24 Harv. L. Rev. 501 (1911).

"Recovery by Wife for Injury to Husband: Opportunity to Bear Children as a Marital Right," *Landwehr* v. *Barbas*, 241 App. Div. 769; 270 N. Y. S. 534 (1934)—20 Cor. L. Quar. 106–10 (1934).

"Right of Wife to Sue for Loss of Consortium from Physical Injury," *Sheard* v. *Oregon Electric Company*, 137 Ore. 341; 2 P. (2d) 916 (1931)—9 N. Y. Univ. L. Quar. Rev. 235–36 (1931).

"Contributory Negligence of Wife as Bar to Action by Husband for Consequential Damages," *Thiebeault* v. *Poole*, 283 Mass. 480; 186 N. E. 632 (1933)—13 B. U. L. Rev. 725–28 (1933).

"Survival of the Cause of Action for Loss of Services at Common Law and under Modern Statutes," *Fowlie* v. *First Minneapolis Trust Company*, 184 Minn. 82; 237 N. W. 846 (1931)—9 N. Y. Univ. L. Quar. Rev. 344–53 (1932).

Annotations

"Husband's Right to Damages for Loss of Consortium Due to Personal Injury to Wife," 21 A. L. R. 1517–28 (1922).

"Wife's Right of Action for Loss of Consortium," L. R. A. 1916E 703; 37 A. L. R. 897–98 (1925); 59 A. L. R. 680–81 (1929).

"Workmen's Compensation Act as Barring Husband's Right of Action for Injury to Infant Wife," 60 A. L. R. 849–50 (1929).

"Damages on Account of Medical Expenses Past or Future, Due to Injury to Wife, as Recoverable by Her or by Husband," 66 A. L. R. 1189–97 (1930).

INJURY TO MARITAL RELATION

Notes

"Wife's Right of Action for Loss of Consortium," *Flandermeyer* v. *Cooper*, 85 Ohio St. 327; 98 N. E. 102 (1912)—26 Harv. L. Rev. 74–75 (1912).

"Husband's Action for Loss of Consortium Based on Implied Warranty to Wife," *Gimenez* v. *Great Atlantic and Pacific Tea Company*, 240 App. Div. 238; 269 N. Y. S. 463 (1934)—47 Harv. L. Rev. 1443–44 (1934).

Annotation

"Right of Action against One Selling Habit-Forming Drugs to Child or Spouse," 3 A. L. R. 1152–53 (1919).

WRONGFUL DEATH

Articles

SCHUMACHER, B. E. "Right of Action under Death and Survival Statutes," 23 Mich. L. Rev. 114–37 (1925).

"Inadequacies of English and State Survival Legislation," 48 Harv. L. Rev. 1008–13 (1935).

[§ 158

Section 159. The Husband's Debts—In General

CROSS REFERENCES: Husband's liability for wife's debts, Secs. 152, 153; Family expenses, Sec. 160; Wife's property, Secs. 167 *et seq*.

The wife, as such, was not liable at common law for the debts of her husband. The bulk of her property rights became his upon marriage, to dissipate as he desired. When the husband was shorn of his marital rights in the wife's property and the wife was given a separate statutory estate, most jurisdictions expressly provided, as an added security to the wife, that such separate estate should not be liable for the debts of her spouse. Thus, the following thirteen jurisdictions have felt the matter of sufficient importance to give the wife protection by constitutional provision: **Alabama, Arkansas, Florida, Georgia, Maryland, Michigan, North Carolina, North Dakota, Oregon, South Carolina, South Dakota, Utah, West Virginia.**

In only seven jurisdictions was no express legislation of this nature found (**Delaware, Indiana, Louisiana, Maine, Mississippi, New Hampshire, Tennessee**). The statutes of forty-three of the fifty-one jurisdictions examined expressly provide either that the wife or her separate property is not liable for the debts of the husband. In addition, the **Ohio** Code states that the wife, as such, is not answerable for the acts of the husband. About half of the jurisdictions specifically protect the wife's earnings from liability for the husband's debts (see footnote 2, p. 184, Table LXXXVII, **Sec. 167**; also **Sec. 178**); and nine states provide either that the wife or her property is not liable for the antenuptial obligations of the husband (**Sec. 151**).

At common law, the husband's interest in the wife's property jure uxoris or as tenant by the curtesy initiate was subject to execution against him. Not only have his marital rights been abolished (**Sec. 167**), but his right of curtesy, where the same remains, has been reduced to a mere possibility during coverture, similar to the wife's inchoate dower (**Secs. 215** *et seq*.). **Alaska, Iowa,** and **Oregon** expressly provide that the husband has no such interest in the wife's property as to make the same subject to his liabilities; and **Connecticut, Missouri, Pennsylvania,** and **Vermont** expressly protect the wife's property from interference by way of execution against any interest which he may have therein.

The protection given to the wife is qualified in many jurisdictions. Thus, there is a growing sentiment that she should be liable for family support regardless of which spouse contracts the obligation (**Secs. 160,**

§ 159]

161). In **Hawaii** and **Massachusetts**, if the wife goes into business on her separate account and fails to file the proper certificate as prescribed by law, the personal property employed in the business may be taken as the property of the husband. In **Montana**, the wife's personal property not included in her inventory of her separate estate, and which is in the sole and exclusive possession of the husband, may be subject to the debts of the husband as against one who deals with the husband on the credit of such property in good faith and without notice.

The **West Virginia** legislation is unique in the unusual liability imposed upon the wife. It is there provided that if real or personal property is transferred by husband to wife, before or after marriage, by reason of antenuptial contract or otherwise, the wife shall be liable for the husband's obligation, whether in tort or contract, created before the transfer, to the extent of the value of the property transferred.

It should also be observed that in the community-property states the wife's interest in the community, even though it be regarded as a present vested interest, may in most jurisdictions be taken to satisfy the husband's obligations, whether contracted for the benefit of the community or not (**Sec. 178**).

Citations to the statutory and constitutional provisions referred to above follow:

Alabama, Const., Sec. 209; C. 1923, Sec. 8261; **Alaska,** Comp. L. 1913, Secs. 439, 443; **Arizona,** R. C. 1928, Secs. 2174–75; **Arkansas,** Crawf. and Moses, Dig. 1921, Secs. 5580, 5589; Const., Art. IX, Sec. 7; **California,** C. C. 1933 (Lake), Secs. 168, 171; **Colorado,** Comp. L. 1921, G. S., Sec. 5576; **Connecticut,** G. S. 1930, Secs. 5154, 5792; **District of Columbia,** C. 1929, T. 14, Sec. 27; **Florida,** Const., Art. XI, Sec. 1; R. G. S. 1920, Sec. 3947; **Georgia,** Const., Art. III, Sec. 11, Par. 1; C. 1926, C. C., Sec. 2993; **Hawaii,** R. L. 1925, Sec. 2999; **Idaho,** Comp. St. 1919, Secs. 4665, 6919; **Illinois,** Cahill, R. S. 1931, Ch. 68, Sec. 5; **Iowa,** C. 1927, Secs. 10052, 10447, 10465; **Kansas,** R. S. 1923, Sec. 23(201); **Kentucky,** Carroll, St. 1922, Sec. 2127; **Maryland,** Const., Art. III, Sec. 43; Bagby, Ann. C. 1924, Art. 45, Sec. 1; **Massachusetts,** G. L. 1932, Ch. 209, Secs. 7, 10; **Michigan,** Const., Art. XVI, Sec. 8; Comp. L. 1929, Sec. 13057; **Minnesota,** G. S. 1923, Secs. 8617, 8620; **Missouri,** R. S. 1929, Secs. 3002–3; **Montana,** R. C. 1921, Secs. 5790, 5795, 5799; **Nebraska,** Comp. St. 1929, Sec. 42(201); **Nevada,** Comp. L. 1929 (Hillyer), Secs. 3367, 3371; **New Jersey,** Comp. St. 1910, p. 3238, Sec. 15; **New Mexico,** St. Ann. 1929, Sec. 68(307); **New York,** Cahill, Consol. L. 1930, Ch. 14, Sec. 50; **North Carolina,** Const., Art. X, Sec. 6; C. 1927, Sec. 2506; **North Dakota,** Const., Sec. 213; Comp. L. 1913, Sec. 4414, as amended by Supp. 1913–25, p. 928; **Ohio,** Complete G. C. 1931 (Page), Sec. 8002; **Oklahoma,** St. 1931, Sec. 1659; **Oregon,** Const., Art. XV, Sec. 5; C. 1930, Secs. 33(201), 33(205), 33(211)– 33(212); **Pennsylvania,** St. 1920 (West), Secs. 8690, 14586–87, 14593; **Rhode Island,** G. L. 1923, Sec. 4202; **South Carolina,** Const., Art. XIV, Sec. 8; C. of L.

1922, C. C., Sec. 5537; **South Dakota,** Const., Art. XXI, Sec. 5; Comp. L. 1929, Sec. 175; **Texas,** Complete St. 1928, Civ. St., Arts. 4616, 4620; **Utah,** Const., Art. XXII, Sec. 2; R. S. 1933, 40-2-1, 40-2-5; **Vermont,** G. L. 1917, Secs. 3524-25; **Virginia,** C. 1930, Sec. 5134, as amended by Sess. L. 1932, Ch. 25, p. 21; **Washington,** Remington, Comp. St. 1922, Secs. 6891, 6905; **West Virginia,** Const., Art. VI, Sec. 49; C. 1931, Ch. 48, Art. 3, Secs. 1, 2, 8, 15, 16; **Wisconsin,** St. 1931, Secs. 246.02, 246.03, 246.05; **Wyoming,** R. S. 1931, Sec. 69(101).

REFERENCES

Book

STIMSON, F. J. *American Statute Law,* Sec. 6410 (1886).

Annotations

"Estate by Curtesy Initiate as Subject to Payment of Debts of Husband," Ann. Cas. 1914C 1187–89.

"Liability for Funeral Expenses of Married Woman," 15 A. L. R. 852–53 (1921); 31 A. L. R. 1499–1509 (1924).

"Liability of Husband for Funeral Expenses as Affected by the Fact That Wife Was Living Apart from Him," 34 A. L. R. 812–13 (1925).

Section 160. Family Expenses

CROSS REFERENCES: Alimony to the husband, **Sec. 109;** Wife's contracts for necessaries, **Sec. 153;** Liability of community property for debts of wife, **Sec. 178;** Support of child, **Sec. 234**

As has already been observed, the wife at common law was in nowise liable for the support of herself or her family. This burden fell upon the husband alone. One of the striking developments in the field of family legislation has been the adoption of statutes rendering the wife or her property liable with the husband for necessaries furnished to the family or for family expenses. Legislation of this kind was found in twenty-three jurisdictions.

These statutes, which are set out in the summary below, vary in scope and application. In four jurisdictions, the liability imposed upon the wife is confined to debts for necessaries contracted by herself. In two jurisdictions, the statute refers only to the husband's contracts for necessaries. In the balance of the twenty-three jurisdictions, the liability of the wife attaches regardless of which spouse contracts the obligation.

§ 160]

Of these, the broader statutes have come to be known as family-expense statutes. The most common type, adopted in almost identical form by eight jurisdictions (**Colorado, Illinois, Iowa, Montana, Oregon, Utah, Washington, Wyoming**), provides in substance that the expenses of the family and the education of the children are chargeable upon the property of both husband and wife, and that in relation thereto they may be sued either jointly or severally. Similarly, in **Arkansas,** the support of their unmarried minor children is chargeable jointly and severally upon the property of both husband and wife, and in relation thereto they may be sued either jointly or severally. A glance at the summary following will indicate that in a number of jurisdictions the statutes impose upon the husband and wife a liability much broader than the husband's common-law liability for necessaries. **Connecticut** and **West Virginia** have the broadest legislation in this sense. In those two jurisdictions, the liability of the husband and wife extends to any article purchased by either which in fact goes to the support of the family or for the joint benefit of the spouses. It is obvious, also, that under these so-called family-expense statutes the wife becomes liable for articles which go to the maintenance and upkeep of the husband. Under the **Iowa** statute, it has been held that a diamond shirt stud used by the husband for personal adornment is a family expense (*Neasham* v. *McNair,* 103 Ia. 695; 72 N. W. 773; 38 L. R. A. 847 [1897]). **Wyoming,** which provides that the personal expenses of the husband are not chargeable to the wife's separate estate, is the only jurisdiction having a statute of this type which expressly limits its operation in this respect.

Five jurisdictions expressly make the husband primarily liable. In **Connecticut,** the wife is entitled to an indemnity in equity from the property of the husband if she is compelled to satisfy the obligation imposed by the statute; and in **West Virginia,** she is entitled to be subrogated to the rights of the creditor thus satisfied. In **Nebraska** and **Pennsylvania,** the wife's property is liable only after execution against the husband has failed for want of property; and in **Arizona,** execution must first be levied upon the common property and the separate property of the husband. Under the broader statutes, each spouse is a principal as to the creditor; yet as between the spouses, it has been held that the primary duty of the husband for necessaries has not been changed. (See *Kosanke* v. *Kosanke,* 137 Minn. 115; 162 N. W. 1060 [1917].) In the case just cited, the **Minnesota** court said: "Although this statute makes both husband and wife liable to third parties for such necessaries, it does not relieve the husband from the duty to support the family which has

[§ 160

rested upon him from time immemorial, and as between husband and wife the duty to furnish such necessaries still rests upon the husband." It may well be doubted whether the final conclusion of the court is sound today. The recent family-expense legislation reflects the sound philosophy that equality of burden is the correlative of equal rights. This new liability which is thrown upon the wife recognizes that the husband has now been shorn of those marital rights which not only enabled him to support the wife, but which forced the wife to look to the husband for support. If the wife may now be made to pay but can then recoup her loss from her husband, it is evident that her emancipation is either incomplete or overcomplete and inequitable.

In four jurisdictions (**California, Minnesota, North Dakota, South Dakota**), it is specified that the obligations to which the statute applies must be contracted while the spouses are living together; and it has been .held by the courts of several states that the term "family expense" implies that the spouses are living together as a family, or, at least, that they are no more than temporarily separated. (See *O'Brien* v. *Galley-Stockton Shoe Company,* 65 Colo. 70; 173 P. 544 [1918].) If the family relation does not exist, it seems that the creditor must fall back upon the common-law liability of the husband. The statutes of **Connecticut** and **West Virginia,** however, expressly provide that both spouses shall be liable for the reasonable support of the wife while abandoned by the husband.

It will be observed that most of these statutes, if read literally, impose no personal liability on the wife, but render her property liable only. In some jurisdictions, only a limited part of the wife's property is thus liable. Under the **California** statute, it seems that the wife's liability is practically confined to that part of her separate estate acquired after marriage by gift from the husband. In **Missouri,** only her personal property is liable. The **Vermont** statute covers only the annual products of her lands and her interest in property held by the entireties.

Every jurisdiction might well adopt a broad family-expense statute. That the wife should share the burden of family expenses seems only fair to creditors and consistent with the independent property status now universally accorded to married women. Too, a statute of this kind is in reality a protection to the wife, as well as a burden. The common-law liability of the husband for necessaries is of doubtful assistance to her in dealing with a cautious trader.

The substance of the statutes discussed in this section, together with the citations therefor, will be found in the summary which follows.

§ 160]

SUMMARY OF STATUTES DEALING WITH WIFE'S LIABILITY FOR
FAMILY EXPENSES

Arizona (R. C. 1928, Secs. 2176, 3729) : The husband and wife shall
be sued jointly for debts contracted for necessaries by the wife on the
husband's credit. Execution shall be levied on the common property,
the separate property of the husband, and the separate property of the
wife in the order named.

Arkansas (Crawf. and Moses, Dig. 1921, Sec. 5580; Supp. 1927,
Sec. 4980[d]) : The wife's separate property is not liable for the husband's debts "except such debts as may have been contracted for the
support of herself or her children by her as his agent." The support of
their unmarried minor children is chargeable jointly and severally upon
the property of both husband and wife, and in relation thereto they may
be sued either jointly or severally.

California (C. C. 1933 [Lake], Sec. 171) : The separate property
of the wife is liable for debts contracted by either while living together
for the necessaries of life; but the separate property of the wife held at
the time of marriage or that acquired after marriage by devise, succession or gift, other than by gift from the husband, is exempt from such
liability.

Colorado (Comp. L. 1921, G. S., Sec. 5575) : The expenses of the
family and the education of the children are chargeable upon the property of both husband and wife, or either of them, and in relation thereto
they may be sued jointly or separately.

Connecticut (G. S. 1930, Sec. 5155) : The husband and wife are
both liable when any article purchased by either shall have in fact gone
to the support of the family or for the joint benefit of both, or for the
reasonable apparel of the wife or for her reasonable support while
abandoned by her husband.[1]

Illinois (Cahill, R. S. 1931, Ch. 68, Sec. 15) : The expenses of the
family and the education of the children shall be chargeable upon the
property of both husband and wife, in favor of creditors therefor, and
in relation thereto they may be sued jointly or separately.

Iowa (C. 1927, Sec. 10459) : The reasonable and necessary expenses
of the family and the education of the children are chargeable upon the

[1] The **Connecticut** statute specifically includes the reasonable and necessary services of a
physician rendered the husband, wife, or their minor child while residing in the family of its
parents; and the rental of any premises actually occupied by husband and wife as a residence,
and reasonably necessary for that purpose. The husband is primarily liable, and the wife is
entitled to an indemnity in equity from the property of the husband if her own property is taken
in satisfaction of any such claim. The statute applies only to marriages after April 20, 1877.

[§ 160

property of both the husband and wife, or either of them, and in relation thereto they may be sued jointly or separately.

Louisiana (C. C., Arts. 2389, 2395, 2435) : When the wife is ad-
ministering her own separate estate, or if she has obtained a separation
of property, she may be liable in some cases for family expenses.[2]

Massachusetts (G. L. 1932, Ch. 209, Sec. 7) : A married woman
with property to the amount of two thousand dollars or more is jointly
liable with her husband for debts, to the amount of one hundred dollars
in each case, incurred for necessaries furnished with her knowledge or
consent to herself or her family.

Minnesota (G. S. 1923, Sec. 8620) : When husband and wife are
living together, they shall be jointly and severally liable for all necessary
household articles and supplies furnished to and used by the family.

Missouri (R. S. 1929, Secs. 3002–3) : The personal property of the
wife and the "annual products" of her lands·are subject to execution
for the payment of debts of the husband created for necessaries for the
wife or family.

Montana (R. C. 1921, Secs. 5790, 5799) : The expenses for necessaries of the family and of the education of the children are chargeable
upon the property of both husband and wife, or either of them, and
in relation thereto they may be sued jointly or separately.[3]

Nebraska (Comp. St. 1929, Sec. 42[201]) : All property of the
wife not exempt by law from sale on execution or attachment shall be
liable for necessaries furnished her family, after execution against the
husband for such indebtedness has been returned unsatisfied for want
of property.

North Dakota (Comp. L. 1913, Sec. 4415, as amended by Supp.
1913–25, p. 928) : The husband and wife shall be jointly and severally
liable for debts contracted by either while living together for necessary
household supplies of food, clothing and fuel, and for shelter for themselves and family, and for the education of their minor children.

---

[2] "If all the property of the wife be paraphernal, and she have reserved to herself the administration of it, she ought to bear a proportion of the marriage charges, equal, if need be, to one-
half her income" (C. C., Art. 2389). "Each of the married persons separate in property, contributes to the expenses of the marriage in the manner agreed on by their contract; if there be
no agreement on the subject, the wife contributes to the amount of one-half of her income"
(C. C., Art. 2395). "The wife, who has obtained the separation of property, must contribute, in
proportion to her fortune and to that of her husband, both to the household expenses and to those
of the education of their children. She is bound to support those expenses alone, if there remains
nothing to her husband" (C. C., Art. 2435).

[3] The **Montana** Code also provides that the separate property of the wife shall be exempt
from the husband's debts "unless for necessary articles procured for the use and benefit of herself and her children under the age of eighteen years."

§ 160]

Oregon (C. 1930, Sec. 33[206]) : The expenses of the family and the education of the children are chargeable upon the property of both husband and wife, or either of them, and in relation thereto they may be sued jointly or separately.[4]

Pennsylvania (St. 1920 [West], Secs. 14606, 14608) : In the case of debts contracted for necessaries for the support and maintenance of the family of any married woman, the creditor may sue both spouses, with judgment to be executed against the husband alone. If no property of the husband can be found, an alias execution may issue and be levied on the wife's separate property.[5]

South Dakota (Comp. L. 1929, Sec. 175) : The husband and wife shall be jointly and severally liable for all the necessaries of life consisting of food, clothing and fuel purchased by either of them for their family while they are living together as husband and wife.

Texas (Complete St. 1928, Civ. St., Arts. 1984, 4623–24) : The husband and wife shall be jointly sued for all debts contracted by the wife for necessaries furnished herself or children. If the debts so contracted are reasonable and proper, the court shall decree that execution may be levied upon either the common property or the separate property of the wife, at the discretion of the plaintiff.

Utah (R. S. 1933, 40-2-9) : The expenses of the family and the education of the children are chargeable upon the property of both husband and wife, or of either of them, and in relation thereto they may be sued jointly or separately.

Vermont (G. L. 1917, Sec. 3525 ; Sess. L. 1927, No. 48, p. 52) : The "annual products" of the wife's lands may be attached or levied upon for the husband's debts created for necessaries for the wife and family. Real estate and tangible personal property held by the husband and wife by the entirety is chargeable with the debts contracted by the husband for necessaries as if he owned such property in his sole name.

Washington (Remington, Comp. St. 1922, Sec. 6916) : The expenses of the family and the education of the children are chargeable upon the property of both husband and wife, or either of them, and in relation thereto they may be sued jointly or separately.

---

[4] After divorce, the wife is not liable for debts or family expenses contracted by the husband while they were living together.

[5] But judgment shall not be rendered against the wife in such joint action unless it is shown that the debt was contracted by the wife and incurred for articles necessary for the support of the family; if the husband has absented himself from the country for a year or more, suit may be brought against the wife alone; and judgment obtained in such action shall have the same force as if recovered against the husband and wife jointly.

[§ 160

West Virginia (C. 1931, Ch. 48, Art. 3, Sec. 22) : The husband and wife are both liable when any article purchased by either goes to the support of the family or for the joint benefit of both, or for the reasonable apparel of the wife and minor children, or for the reasonable support of such wife and children while abandoned by the husband.[6]

Wyoming (R. S. 1931, Sec. 69[101]) : The necessary expenses of the family and the education of the children are chargeable upon the property of both husband and wife, or either of them, and in relation thereto they may be sued jointly or separately. But the personal expenses of the husband are not chargeable to the wife's separate estate.

REFERENCES

Book

STIMSON, F. J. *American Statute Law*, Sec. 6410 (1886).

Note

"Personal Liability of Wife for Debt Incurred by Husband for Family Necessaries," *Dreamer* v. *Oberlander*, 122 Neb. 335; 240 N. W. 435 (1932)—18 Va. L. Rev. 680–81 (1932).

Annotations

"Articles or Services for Husband Personally as 'Family Expenses' or 'Necessaries,' within Statute Making Wife Liable Therefor," 13 A. L. R. 1396–1402 (1921).

"Liability of Wife for Household Expenses," Ann. Cas. 1917C 561–76.

"Personal Liability of Married Woman for Domestic or Household Services," 36 A. L. R. 389–93 (1925).

Section 161. Duty of Support—Civil Liability

CROSS REFERENCES: Separate maintenance, **Secs. 139, 140;** General principles, **Sec. 150;** Wife's contracts for necessaries, **Sec. 153;** Family expenses, **Sec. 160;** Duty of support, criminal liability, **Sec. 162;** Support of child, **Sec. 234**

In spite of the fact that the husband has lost many of the property rights which at common law accrued to him by reason of the marriage,

---

[6] The **West Virginia** statute also includes the reasonable and necessary services of a physician rendered the husband or wife while living together or rendered to a minor child while residing with its parents; the rent of premises actually occupied by the spouses as a residence and reasonably necessary to them for that purpose; the reasonable services of any domestic laborer, or other person from which the family or both husband and wife benefit. Under this statute the property of the husband is primarily liable. If the wife's property is taken in satisfaction of any such claim, she may be subrogated to the rights of the creditor whose claim is thus satisfied.

§ 161]

his duty to support the wife has not been lightened by statute. Generally speaking, it has been strengthened. Statutes now very generally authorize the wife herself to bring civil proceedings to enforce this duty; and in most jurisdictions, a delinquent husband has been made criminally liable. On the other hand, the wife, who at common law was under no duty to support the husband, is now often subject to such a duty. Express legislation imposing upon the wife a duty to support the husband under certain circumstances was found in seventeen jurisdictions.

The statutes of **California, Idaho, Montana, New Mexico, North Dakota, Ohio, Oklahoma,** and **South Dakota** all state that the husband and wife contract toward each other "obligations of mutual respect, fidelity and support." Practically the same statement is found in the **Louisiana** Code. **California, Idaho, Montana, Nevada, New Mexico, North Dakota, Oklahoma,** and **South Dakota** expressly provide that when the husband has not deserted her the wife must support him out of her separate property if he has no separate property (and there is no community property [**California, Idaho, Nevada, New Mexico**]) and he is unable because of infirmity to support himself. **Ohio** provides that the husband must support himself and family, but that, if he is unable, the wife must assist him "so far as she is able." Apparently none of these jurisdictions have provided for the enforcement of this duty by the husband. The courts of both **North Dakota** and **California** have held, however, that the statute imposes more than a mere unenforceable duty, and that an equitable action will lie to compel the wife to furnish support to the husband. (See *Livingston* v. *Superior Court,* 117 Cal. 633; 49 P. 836 [1897]; *Hagert* v. *Hagert,* 22 N. D. 290; 133 N. W. 1035 [1911].) The action seems to be in analogy to a suit in equity by the wife for separate maintenance.

A different type of legislation was found in **California, Connecticut, Iowa, Kentucky, Michigan, New Jersey, New York, Pennsylvania,** and **Wisconsin.** While the statutes in these jurisdictions differ in detail, they all impose upon the husband or wife of a person likely to become a public charge, or who is a public charge, a duty to support such person, if the husband or wife is of sufficient ability. Upon proceedings instituted by the poor authorities or other appropriate persons, the duty may be enforced by execution against the property of the spouse charged or by a court order to pay stipulated sums. Also, in **Connecticut,** the estate of one dying without issue, and leaving a destitute husband or wife surviving, is liable for the support of such husband or wife until remarriage. The heirs or devisees of the deceased may be

[§ 161

compelled to contribute to the support of the distressed spouse to an amount equal to the estate received. It is to be observed that the duty of support under these statutes is enforceable equally on both husband and wife.

In addition to the legislation above, it is to be noted that the statutes rendering the wife or her property liable for family necessaries or family expenses, discussed in **Section 160,** in effect impose upon the wife a duty to support herself, her family, and her husband to the extent that such liability may be enforced by the creditor.

We have seen that the fact that the wife is given an independent property status with the power to contract does not alter the primary duty of the husband to support his spouse. Nor do the family-expense statutes lighten his burden in this respect. Civil statutes have left practically unchanged the husband's common-law liability for necessaries (**Sec. 153**). The creditor who furnishes necessaries to the wife in effect enforces the husband's duty of support. We have also seen that in most jurisdictions the courts have been given statutory power to compel the husband to support the wife (**Sec. 139**). In addition, most of the statutes providing for the criminal enforcement of the husband's duty give civil relief to the wife as an incident thereto (**Sec. 162**). It remains to notice briefly several statutes, not discussed elsewhere, dealing with the husband's civil liability for support.

The statutes of **Connecticut, Georgia, Hawaii, Louisiana, Ohio, Oklahoma,** and **West Virginia** state that it is the duty of the husband to support the wife. In **Hawaii** he must support her "in the same style and manner in which he supports himself," and in **Louisiana** he is "obliged to furnish her with whatever is required for the convenience of life, in proportion to his means and condition." In **Delaware, Michigan, New Jersey, Pennsylvania,** and **Wisconsin,** if the husband deserts the wife, leaving her a public charge or likely to become a public charge, the poor authorities may initiate proceedings to compel the husband to support the wife if he is able, and to seize his property. **North Dakota** and **Oregon** statutes allow the wife to bring an action against the husband if he fails to support her properly. After hearing, the court may render such judgment as is equitable under the circumstances. In **Indiana,** after complaint and hearing, if it appears that the husband has abandoned the wife and fails to support her, an order may be made directing the sequestration and sale of his property. **Vermont** expressly provides that if a husband of sufficient ability allows the wife to become a public charge the town may recover in an action of contract against the

§ 161]

husband the expenses so incurred. Such recovery is, however, limited to the expenses incurred within one year previous to the bringing of the action.

It is to be observed that under the statutes outlined in this section the wife is under duty to support the husband only if he is poor. The fact that the wife may be financially independent does not, however, lighten the husband's duty to support her if he is able.

Citations for the statutory material covered in this section are as follows:

California, Deering, G. L. 1931, Act 5814, p. 3133, Secs. 6, 7; C. C. 1933 (Lake), Secs. 155, 176; Connecticut, G. S. 1930, Secs. 1717–19, 5155; Delaware, R. C. 1915, Sec. 1464; Georgia, C. 1926, C. C., Sec. 2996; Hawaii, R. L. 1925, Sec. 3000; Idaho, Comp. St. 1919, Secs. 4654, 4669; Indiana, Burns, Ann. St. 1926, Secs. 8760–61; Iowa, C. 1927, Secs. 5306–9; Kentucky, Sess. L. 1928, Ch. 16, p. 100, Sec. 37; Louisiana, C. C., Arts. 119–20; Michigan, Comp. L. 1929, Secs. 8209–23; Montana, R. C. 1921, Secs. 5782, 5802; Nevada, Comp. L. 1929 (Hillyer), Sec. 3378; New Jersey, Cum. Supp. 1911–24, Secs. 161(197), 161(211); New Mexico, St. Ann. 1929, Secs. 68(101), 68(105); New York, Cahill, Consol. L. 1930, Ch. 49½, Sec. 125; Sess. L. 1933, Ch. 578, p. 1225; North Dakota, Comp. L. 1913, Secs. 4407, 4409, 8169–74; Ohio, Complete G. C. 1931 (Page), Secs. 7995, 7997; Oklahoma, St. 1931, Secs. 1651, 1653; Oregon, C. 1930, Secs. 33(207)–33(210); Pennsylvania, St. 1920 (West), Sec. 17034; Cum. Supp. 1928 (West), p. 724, Secs. 16811A(1009)–16811A(1015); South Dakota, Comp. L. 1929, Secs. 167, 169; Vermont, G. L. 1917, Sec. 4230; West Virginia, C. 1931, Ch. 48, Art. 3, Secs. 22, 24; Wisconsin, St. 1931, Secs. 49.11, 49.13.

REFERENCES
Articles
BROWN, ROBERT C. "The Duty of the Husband to Support the Wife," 18 Va. L. Rev. 823–44 (1932).
CROZIER, BLANCHE. "Marital Support," 15 B. U. L. Rev. 28–58 (1935).

Notes
"Rights of Wife against Husband and in His Property, Validity of Sale of Husband's Interest in Tenancy by Entirety for Support," Baker v. Cailor (Ind. App.); 176 N. E. 854 (1931)—45 Harv. L. Rev. 588–89 (1932); 7 Ind. L. Jour. 194–96 (1931).
"Wife's Right to Support," 77 L. Jour. 425 (1934).
"Separation Agreements, Duty to Support, Failure to Pay Allowance," Bay District Claim Service, Ltd. v. Jones, 136 Cal. App. 789; 24 P. (2d) 977 (1933)— 7 So. Calif. L. Rev. 342–44 (1934).

Annotation
"Defenses Available to Husband in Civil Suit by Wife for Support," 6 A. L. R. 6–88 (1920).

[§ 161

Section 162. Duty of Support—Criminal Liability

CROSS REFERENCES: Duty of support, civil liability, **Sec. 161;** Parent's duty to support child, civil and criminal liability, **Sec. 234**

At common law, it was not an indictable offense for the husband to abandon or neglect to provide for the wife. In this respect, the husband's duty of support has been greatly strengthened by statute. All of the fifty-one jurisdictions examined, except **Mississippi,** now impose by means of abandonment, desertion, and non-support statutes a criminal or quasi-criminal liability upon the husband who, under certain circumstances, breaches such duty. Statutes of this type have come to be popularly known as "Lazy Husband Laws." **Mississippi** appears to be without legislation covering desertion and non-support of the wife by the husband. Within the last ten years the courts of the state have declared two distinct enactments to be unconstitutional (see Table LXXXIII, footnote 35, p. 136).

The subject of desertion and non-support of the wife and family is not new in the field of penal legislation. Only in comparatively recent years, however, has it been given the study it deserves, or has the social problem involved been fully recognized. Like many other phases of family law, it has been neglected in favor of more pressing problems of commerce and industry. It is more than a matter of private concern when the husband deserts or fails to provide for the wife and family. Society has the obvious interest to protect itself from the financial burden of pauperism. The earlier laws and many of the existing statutes seem designed primarily to prevent the wife and family from becoming public charges. Society has, however, a deeper and broader interest. While the social wisdom of an attempt to keep unwilling spouses together may be questioned, it can hardly be doubted that society should offer direct protection to the wife by compelling the husband to fulfil the obligation to support which the marital status throws upon him. Thus, in recent years, enlightened legislatures have sought to give the wife an avenue of relief additional to her civil remedies, which are often so ineffective, and to provide directly for her by compelling the husband through fear of punishment to support her.

It is evident, then, that desertion and non-support legislation should be regarded as only quasi-criminal in character. The primary purpose should not be to punish. The interests of the parties are such that to punish the husband severely by confining him in an institution, no matter how deserving of such punishment he may be, only augments the hard-

§ 162]

ship at which the statute is aimed. A failure to recognize the peculiarities
of the problem involved probably explains the fragmentary legislation
found in some jurisdictions.

The Uniform Desertion and Non-Support Act, approved by the National Conference of Commissioners on Uniform State Laws in 1910,
has been wholly or substantially adopted in about a third of the jurisdictions examined. Parts of the Act have been adopted in other jurisdictions. Several jurisdictions, notably **Alabama,** in adopting the Act seem
to have considerably improved upon it. In general, there is a rather fundamental similarity, but a wide variation of detail, in the various statutes
on this subject. There are, however, surprising omissions in a few jurisdictions, and, in the matter of administration, many of the statutes are
incomplete and fragmentary, and do not reflect any well-reasoned legislative or social policy.

The statutes of thirty-nine jurisdictions create two distinct offenses—
desertion or abandonment of the wife, and non-support of the wife. Four
jurisdictions (**Connecticut, Illinois, Iowa, New Hampshire**) penalize non-support only. In **New York,** one who abandons or neglects to
support the wife is, under certain circumstances, declared to be a disorderly person. The **Minnesota** and **North Dakota** statutes cover non-
support of the wife, and desertion and non-support of a pregnant wife.
The **Oklahoma** statute covers abandonment coupled with neglect. Abandonment or neglect of a pregnant wife is penalized in **Ohio.** The only
legislation on the subject found in **Georgia** and **Kentucky** is contained
in statutes declaring one who leaves his wife without means of subsistence
to be a vagrant. Just what constitutes desertion or non-support varies
with the several statutes. The definition contained in Section 1 of the
Uniform Act has been widely adopted. Though desertion is set up as a
distinct offense, the statutes seem mainly directed at the failure to provide which ordinarily follows in the wake of desertion. It will be observed that under most of the statutes the desertion or non-support is not
complete unless the wife be in dangerous or necessitous circumstances, or
without means of subsistence, or in danger of becoming a public charge.
The term "destitute and necessitous circumstances," used by the Uniform
Act, has been given a liberal meaning by the courts. Thus, it has been
held that the wife need not be "naked and starving."

The tendency seems to be to make desertion or non-support of the
wife a felony. At least thirteen jurisdictions have felony statutes. In
Maine, the offense may be either a felony or a misdemeanor depending
upon the aggravated nature of the husband's conduct. The **Washington**

[§ 162

statute labels the offense a gross misdemeanor. **Nevada** has both a felony and a misdemeanor statute. All of those jurisdictions which penalize desertion or non-support of a pregnant wife make the offense a felony. Two jurisdictions (**Arkansas, Tennessee**) raise the offense to a felony if the husband leaves the state after leaving the wife. In addition, the vagrancy statutes of several jurisdictions cover the case of a husband who fails to provide for his wife.

The most significant feature of the various desertion and non-support statutes is the authority given to release the husband on probation upon his promise or undertaking to furnish proper support for his spouse or to comply with the terms of an order of support issued by the court. All of the fifty jurisdictions except **Georgia, Kentucky, Missouri, New Mexico, Rhode Island,** and **Texas** have some provision to this effect. **Oklahoma** provides that the governor may parole the husband or suspend his sentence upon recommendation of the trial judge and upon the husband's entering into an approved undertaking. Thirteen jurisdictions also provide for a temporary order of support either before the trial or pending appeal (see Table LXXXIII, footnote 6, p. 133).

Some of the more or less common features found in the different jurisdictions follow. (See Table LXXXIII, footnotes 7, 9, 10, pp. 133, 134.) In seventeen jurisdictions, if a fine is imposed, it shall or may be paid in whole or in part to the wife or for her benefit. The Uniform Act contains no similar provision. In twenty-five, a like disposition of the proceeds recovered on forfeited recognizances is authorized. In **Minnesota** and **North Dakota,** the wife herself may sue upon the recognizance. Twenty-nine jurisdictions authorize a sentence at hard labor or to the workhouse. In **Colorado,** the husband may be committed to the workhouse as a condition of a suspended sentence. Twenty-two jurisdictions make some provision for the payment of a nominal sum to be made to the wife or for her benefit when the husband is confined at hard labor. In twenty-four, no other evidence is necessary to prove the fact of marriage than is necessary to prove such fact in civil action. Twenty-one provide that existing statutes or rules of law prohibiting the disclosure of confidential communications between the spouses do not apply to prosecutions for desertion and non-support. Twenty-eight expressly make the wife a competent witness to testify either as to all relevant matters or against the husband, but in **Iowa** and **South Dakota** her consent is necessary. Nine jurisdictions expressly make the wife a "compellable" witness. The Uniform Act merely provides that she is a "competent witness" to testify against the husband. Twenty-five jurisdictions set

§ 162]

up a presumption of wilfulness on proof of certain facts. Ten recognize the offense created as subject to extradition.

New Hampshire has an interesting statute which rather reverses the situation, and which provides that a wife who separates herself from her husband without cause is subject to punishment by imprisonment or fine. If a fine is imposed, it may be applied for the husband's benefit.

The provisions of the Uniform Act might well be adopted in those jurisdictions which do not have equivalent legislation. While uniformity in a matter of this kind is not essential, it is of course desirable. The Uniform Act leaves open the question whether desertion and non-support ought to be made a felony or a misdemeanor. The mistaken belief that extradition in the case of misdemeanors is either impossible or impracticable has apparently influenced some legislatures to create a felony. If the husband is to be charged with a felony, it is inevitable that proceedings will be more protracted and conviction more difficult. Bearing in mind that the husband will be incarcerated only as a last resort, it would seem that the possibility of a county jail sentence with hard labor will supply the necessary coercive element.

In several particulars the Uniform Act can be amplified. Proceedings in non-support cases ought to be as simple and rapid as is possible under the various court systems. Most jurisdictions have given no special attention to this matter. The lowest courts ought to be authorized to hear and try desertion and non-support cases, to render judgment (at least within the extent of their general jurisdiction, subject to the defendant's right of appeal and trial de novo as in other cases), and to release the husband on probation under an order of support. This usually is not possible if the statute creates a felony. In any event, however, local magistrates and justices ought to be authorized to release the accused, with his consent, under an order of support rather than to bind him over for trial.

Success of legislation of this type depends in the final analysis on the manner in which it is administered. The tendency to place desertion and non-support matters within the jurisdiction of family or domestic relations courts should of course be continued. Any court hearing cases of this kind should have the benefit of information and assistance of a competent probation officer. This is especially true after the husband is released on probation. His case should be studied individually, not only to determine proper corrective methods, but also to encourage and stimulate reformation. An adequate statute ought to provide for the role to be played by the probation officer.

[§ 162

All jurisdictions should expressly recognize desertion and non-support as extraditable offenses, should definitely place the responsibility of instituting extradition proceedings, and should provide for the costs of such proceedings. Obviously, it is more to the interest of the public to extradite the husband than it is to extradite the ordinary misdemeanant.

Several minor suggestions may also be appropriate here. The wife should be expressly made a compellable witness as well as a competent witness. An express provision that venue may be laid in any county in which the wife may be when the complaint is made seems desirable. If the husband is sentenced at hard labor, it seems only reasonable that the wife should receive nominal payments on account of such labor. Under many of the statutes, there is little assurance that funds will be available for this purpose. Provision might be made whereby such payments become a general charge on the county if the finances of the particular institution to which the husband is sentenced prove inadequate to meet them.

The more significant features of the criminal legislation dealing with abandonment, desertion, and non-support of the wife by the husband are presented in the table and notes which follow. The Uniform Act is here given in full.

§ 1. Any husband who shall, without just cause, desert or wilfully neglect or refuse to provide for the support and maintenance of his wife in destitute or necessitous circumstances; or any parent who shall, without lawful excuse, desert or wilfully neglect or refuse to provide for the support and maintenance of his or her child or children under the age of sixteen years in destitute or necessitous circumstances, shall be guilty of a crime and, on conviction thereof, shall be punished by fine not exceeding five hundred dollars, or imprisonment . . . . not exceeding two years, or both, with or without hard labor, in the discretion of the court.

§ 2. Proceedings under this act may be instituted upon complaint made under oath or affirmation by the wife or child or children, or by any other person, against any person guilty of either of the above-named offenses.

§ 3. At any time before the trial, upon petition of the complainant and upon notice to the defendant, the court, or a judge thereof in vacation, may enter such temporary order as may seem just, providing for support of the deserted wife or children, or both, pendente lite, and may punish for violation of such order as for contempt.

§ 4. Before the trial, with the consent of the defendant, or at the trial, on entry of a plea of guilty, or after conviction, instead of imposing the penalty hereinbefore provided, or in addition thereto, the court in its discretion, having regard to the circumstances, and to the financial ability or earning capacity of the defendant, shall have the power to make an order, which shall be subject to change by the court from time to time, as circumstances may require, directing the defendant to pay a certain

§ 162]

sum periodically, for a term not exceeding two years, to the wife or to the guardian, curator or custodian of the said minor child or children, or to an organization or individual approved by the court as trustee; and shall also have the power to release the defendant from custody on probation for a period so fixed, upon his or her entering into a recognizance, with or without surety, in such sum as the court or a judge thereof in vacation, may order and approve. The condition of the recognizance shall be such that if the defendant shall make his or her personal appearance in court whenever ordered to do so, and shall further comply with the terms of such order of support, or of any subsequent modification thereof, then such recognizance shall be void, otherwise of full force and effect.

§ 5. If the court be satisfied by information and due proof under oath, that at any time during said period of two years the defendant has violated the terms of such order, it may forthwith proceed with the trial of the defendant under the original charge, or sentence him or her under the original conviction, or enforce the suspended sentence, as the case may be. In case of forfeiture of recognizance, and enforcement thereof by execution, the sum recovered may, in the discretion of the court, be paid, in whole or in part, to the wife, or to the guardian, curator, custodian or trustee of the said minor child or children.

§ 6. No other or greater evidence shall be required to prove the marriage of such husband and wife, or that the defendant is the father or mother of such child or children, than is or shall be required to prove such facts in a civil action. In no prosecution under this act shall any existing statute or rule of law prohibiting the disclosure of confidential communications between husband and wife apply, and both husband and wife shall be competent witnesses to testify against each other to any and all relevant matters, including the fact of such marriage and the parentage of such child or children; provided that neither shall be compelled to give evidence incriminating himself or herself. Proof of the desertion of such wife, child or children in destitute or necessitous circumstances or of neglect or refusal to provide for the support and maintenance of such wife, child or children shall be prima facie evidence that such desertion, neglect or refusal is wilful.

§ 7. It shall be the duty of the sheriff, warden, or other official in charge of the county jail, or of the custodian of the reformatory, workhouse, or house of correction, in which any person is confined on account of a sentence at hard labor, under this act, to pay over to the wife, or to the guardian, curator or custodian of his or her minor child or children, or to an organization or individual approved by the court as trustee, at the end of each week, for the support of such wife, child or children, a sum equal to . . . . for each day's hard labor performed by said person so confined.

§ 8. This act shall be so interpreted and construed as to effectuate its general purpose to make uniform the law of those states which enact it.

[§ 162

TABLE LXXXIII*

Husband's Criminal Liability for Desertion and Non-Support of the Wife

Jurisdiction and Citation	Nature of the Offense	The Crime and Punishment	Probation of Husband, Relief to Wife, etc.	Miscellaneous
Alabama .... C. 1923, Secs. 4479–95, 5571–72	Without good cause, to desert or wilfully neglect or refuse or fail to provide for the support and maintenance of the wife, she being then and there in destitute or necessitous circumstances[1]	A misdemeanor, punishable by a fine not exceeding $100, or by a term in county jail or at hard labor for not more than twelve months, or by both fine and sentence[1]	On entry of plea of guilty, or after conviction and after judgment and sentence is imposed, the court[2] may suspend judgment and sentence, make[3] an order[4] directing the payment of certain sums into court periodically for the wife's use, and release defendant on probation upon his entering into recognizance approved by the court.[5] Defendant may be likewise released after serving part of sentence[12]	See footnotes 6, 7, 8, 9, 10, 11
Alaska .... Sess. L. 1919, Ch. 49, p. 156	Without lawful justification, to wilfully abandon and leave the wife, or refuse or neglect to provide her with necessary food, clothing, shelter or medical attendance	A misdemeanor, punishable by fine not exceeding $500, or by imprisonment for not more than twelve months, or by both. If a jail sentence is imposed, the prisoner may be compelled to work on the roads, etc.	Before the trial, with consent of the defendant, or after conviction[13] the court[3] may make an order[4] directing defendant to pay a certain definite sum or a certain sum weekly into court for the benefit of the wife, and release him on probation upon his entering into undertaking with one or more sufficient sureties[5]	See footnotes 7, 8, 10
Arizona .... R. C. 1928, Secs. 4636–37	Having sufficient ability to provide for the wife's support, or able to earn the means thereof, to wilfully abandon and leave her in a destitute condition, or to refuse or neglect to provide her with necessary food, clothing, shelter or medical attendance, unless justified in so doing by her misconduct	A felony[14]	After arrest, conviction, or plea of guilty and before sentence, if defendant shall enter into an undertaking, to be binding one year, with sureties approved by the court, conditioned that he will furnish the wife with necessary food, clothing, etc., the court may suspend proceedings or sentence[15]	

* See pages 132–38 for all numbered footnotes to this table.

§ 162]

TABLE LXXXIII (*Continued*)

Jurisdiction and Citation	Nature of the Offense	The Crime and Punishment	Probation of Husband, Relief to Wife, etc.	Miscellaneous
Arkansas Crawf. and Moses, Dig. 1921, Sec. 2596, amd. by Supp. 1927, p. 171	Without good cause, to abandon or desert the wife, or to fail, neglect or refuse to maintain or provide for such wife[16]	Punishable by imprisonment in county jail for not more than one year, or by fine not less than $50 or more than $1,000, or by both[16]	The court may suspend sentence "upon probation, employment and support"	See footnote 7
California P. C. 1933 (Lake), Secs. 270a, 270b, 270d, 270e, 273h	Having sufficient ability to provide for the wife's support, or able to earn the means thereof, to wilfully abandon and leave the wife in a destitute condition, or to refuse or neglect to provide such wife with necessary food, clothing, shelter or medical attendance, unless justified by her misconduct in abandoning her	Punishable by imprisonment in the state prison or county jail not exceeding two years, or by fine not exceeding $1,000, or by both	Before plea or trial, or after conviction or plea of guilty, and before sentence, the court may suspend proceedings or sentence, if defendant enters into an undertaking, valid for two years, with sufficient sureties in such sum as the court may fix, conditioned that defendant will pay to the wife such sum per month as the court may direct[15]	See footnotes 7, 10
Colorado Comp. L. 1921, G. S., Secs. 5566–74, 8879	To wilfully neglect, fail or refuse to provide reasonable support and maintenance for the wife, or to wilfully fail, refuse or neglect to provide proper care, food and clothing in case of sickness for the wife, or to leave the wife with intent to abandon her[17]	A felony, punishable by imprisonment in the penitentiary for not to exceed one year[18]	The court may suspend sentence and release the defendant on probation, not to exceed two years, upon his giving bond with sufficient surety upon conditions named by the court, which conditions shall require defendant to perform his duty toward the wife[15, 19]	See footnotes 7, 8, 9, 10
Connecticut G. S. 1930, Secs. 6265–69	To unlawfully neglect or refuse to support the wife	A felony, punishable by imprisonment for not more than one year[18]	The court may suspend execution of any jail sentence upon execution and acceptance of a bond with sufficient surety, conditioned for the payment of such sum for the support of the wife as the court may direct, for a term not more than one year from conviction[20]	See footnotes 6, 10

[§ 162

TABLE LXXXIII (*Continued*)

Jurisdiction and Citation	Nature of the Offense	The Crime and Punishment	Probation of Husband, Relief to Wife, etc.	Miscellaneous
Delaware .... R. C. 1915, Secs. 3033–45	Without just cause, to desert or wilfully neglect or refuse to provide for the support and maintenance of the wife in destitute or necessitous circumstances	A misdemeanor, punishable by a fine not exceeding $500 or by imprisonment with hard labor for not exceeding one year, or by both	Before the trial, with the consent of the defendant, or on entry of plea of guilty or after conviction,[13] the court[3] may make an order[4] directing the defendant to pay a certain sum periodically to the wife or trustee named, and release defendant on probation upon his entering into recognizance with or without surety[5, 21]	See footnotes 6, 7, 8, 9, 10, 11
District of Columbia ..... C. 1929, T. 6, Secs. 271–74	Without just cause, to desert or wilfully neglect or refuse to provide for the support and maintenance of the wife in destitute or necessitous circumstances	A misdemeanor, punishable by a fine not exceeding $500, or by imprisonment in the workhouse for not more than twelve months, or by both	Before the trial with consent of defendant, or after conviction,[13] the court[22] may make an order[3, 4] directing defendant to pay a certain sum weekly for one year to the wife or trustee named, and release him on probation for one year upon his entering into a recognizance with or without sureties[5]	See footnotes 7, 10
Florida .... R. G. S. 1920, Secs. 5496–98	To desert the wife, or withhold from her the means of support	A felony, punishable by imprisonment in state prison for not exceeding twelve months, or by a fine not exceeding $1,000, or by both[23]	If the husband either before or after conviction enters into a sufficient bond conditioned that he will provide the wife with necessary and proper home, food, clothing and care, or will for such purposes pay to a trustee appointed by the court such sums periodically as the court may direct, he shall be released from custody or further punishment	

§ 162]

TABLE LXXXIII (*Continued*)

Jurisdiction and Citation	Nature of the Offense	The Crime and Punishment	Probation of Husband, Relief to Wife, etc.	Miscellaneous
Georgia .... C. 1926, P. C., Sec. 449	All able - bodied persons who quit their houses and leave their wives without means of subsistence are vagrants	A misdemeanor		
Hawaii .... R. L. 1925, Secs. 3014–16; Sess. L. 1925, Act 164, p. 189, Sec. 3016*A*	To desert or wilfully neglect the wife, or to refuse to provide for her support or maintenance, thereby reducing her to destitute or necessitous circumstances	A misdemeanor, punishable by a fine not exceeding $500 or by imprisonment not exceeding one year	The court may release the defendant under suspended sentence for such period as the court may fix, and such terms as to the payment, weekly or otherwise, of money for the support of the wife, and as to giving security therefor, as the court may fix[24]	See footnotes 7, 8
Idaho .... Sess. L. 1923, Ch. 190, p. 297, amd. by Sess. L. 1931, Ch. 112, p. 193	Having sufficient ability to provide for the wife's support, or able to earn the means thereof, to wilfully abandon and leave the wife in a destitute condition, or to refuse or neglect to provide such wife with necessary food, clothing, shelter or medical attendance, unless justified by her misconduct in abandoning her	A misdemeanor, punishable by a fine of not more than $500, or by imprisonment in the county jail not to exceed one year, or both	Before the trial, or after conviction, with the consent of defendant, the court[3] may make an order[4] directing the defendant to pay a certain sum weekly to the wife or person named, and release defendant on probation during such time as the court may direct, upon his entering into recognizance with or without sureties[5]	See footnotes 7, 10
Illinois .... Cahill, R. S. 1931, Ch. 38, Secs. 2–12	Without reasonable cause, to neglect or refuse to provide for the support or maintenance of the wife in destitute or necessitous circumstances	A misdemeanor, punishable by a fine not to exceed $600, or by imprisonment in the county jail, house of correction, or workhouse not to exceed one year, or by both fine and imprisonment	Before the trial,[25] with the consent of defendant, or after conviction or plea of guilty,[13] the court[3] may make an order[4] directing the defendant to pay a certain sum periodically, for a period not to exceed one year, to the wife or trustee named, and release defendant on probation upon his entering into recognizance with or without surety[5]	See footnotes 6, 7, 10

[§ 162

TABLE LXXXIII (*Continued*)

Jurisdiction and Citation	Nature of the Offense	The Crime and Punishment	Probation of Husband, Relief to Wife, etc.	Miscellaneous
Indiana .... Burns, Ann. St. 1926, Secs. 2866, 2869–74, 12457	To neglect to support the wife and provide her with necessary food, clothing and medical attention[26]	A misdemeanor, punishable by fine not to exceed $500 to which may be added imprisonment in the county jail or workhouse for a period not exceeding six months[26]	Before the trial or after conviction or sentence, with the consent of the defendant, the court[3] may make an order[4] directing the defendant to pay a certain sum weekly to the wife or trustee named for a period not exceeding two years, and release defendant on probation upon his entering into recognizance with approved surety[5, 27]	See footnotes 7, 8, 10
Iowa .... C. 1927, Secs. 13230–35	Without good cause, to wilfully neglect or refuse to maintain or provide for the wife, she being in a destitute condition	Desertion, punishable by imprisonment in the penitentiary for not more than one year, or in the county jail for not more than six months	If after arrest and before trial, or after conviction and before sentence, the husband enters into a sufficient bond with or without sureties, conditioned that he will furnish the wife with a necessary and proper home, food, care and clothing, the court may release him	See footnote 7
Kansas .... R. S. 1923, Secs. 21(442)– 21(448)	Without just cause, to desert or neglect or refuse to provide for the support and maintenance of the wife in destitute or necessitous circumstances	Punishable by imprisonment in the reformatory or penitentiary at hard labor for not exceeding two years	Before the trial, with the consent of defendant, or on plea of guilty or after conviction,[13] the court[3] may make an order[4] directing defendant to pay a certain sum periodically for not to exceed two years to the wife or trustee named, and release defendant on probation on his entering into recognizance with or without surety[5]	See footnotes 6, 7, 8, 10

§ 162]

TABLE LXXXIII (*Continued*)

Jurisdiction and Citation	Nature of the Offense	The Crime and Punishment	Probation of Husband, Relief to Wife, etc.	Miscellaneous
Kentucky .... Carroll, St. 1922, Secs. 4758(1), 4758(2)	Any able-bodied male who purposely deserts his wife, leaving her without suitable subsistence or suitable means of subsistence, he himself being idle and dissolute, is a vagrant[28]	Punishable by fine of $10, or imprisonment in the workhouse or county jail for thirty days, or both		
Louisiana ...... Sess. L. 1932, Act 77, p. 332	Without just cause, to desert or wilfully neglect to provide for the support of the wife in destitute or necessitous circumstances	A misdemeanor, punishable by fine not exceeding $100, or by imprisonment in parish prison not exceeding one year, or by both	Before the trial, with the consent of defendant, or after conviction,[13] the court[3] may make an order[4] directing the defendant to pay a certain sum weekly to the wife, and release defendant on probation upon his entering into recognizance with or without sureties[5]	See footnote 10
Maine .... R. S. 1930, Ch. 129, Secs. 44–48	Without lawful excuse, to desert the wife when she is in destitute or necessitous circumstances, or to wilfully neglect or refuse to provide necessary support and maintenance to such wife[29]	A felony if the offense is of a high and aggravated nature, punishable by not more than $500 or imprisonment with or without hard labor for not more than two years, or by both; otherwise, a misdemeanor, punishable by fine of not more than $300 or by imprisonment with or without hard labor for not more than eleven months, or by both	Before the trial,[30] with the consent of the defendant, or after conviction,[13] the court[3] may make an order[4] directing the defendant to pay a certain sum weekly for one year to the wife or trustee named, and release the defendant on probation for one year upon his entering into recognizance with sureties[5]	See footnote 10
Maryland ...... Bagby, Ann. C. 1924, Art. 27, Secs. 87–89, amd. by Sess. L. 1931, Ch. 448, pp. 1137–41	Without just cause to desert or wilfully neglect to provide for the support and maintenance of the wife[31]	A misdemeanor, punishable by a fine not exceeding $100, or by imprisonment in the house of correction for not more than three years, or by both[31]	Before the trial,[32] with the consent of the defendant, or after conviction,[13] the court[3] may pass an order[4] directing the defendant to pay a certain sum weekly for three years to the wife and release defendant on probation for three years upon his entering into recognizance with or without sureties[5]	See footnote 10

[§ 162

TABLE LXXXIII (*Continued*)

Jurisdiction and Citation	Nature of the Offense	The Crime and Punishment	Probation of Husband, Relief to Wife, etc.	Miscellaneous
Massachusetts .. G. L. 1932, Ch. 273, Secs. 1–10	Without just cause, to desert the wife and leave her without reasonable provision for her support, or to unreasonably neglect or refuse to provide for the support and maintenance of the wife, or to abandon or leave the wife in danger of becoming a burden on the public	Punishable by a fine of not more than $200, or by imprisonment for not more than one year, or by both	Before trial with the consent of the defendant, or after plea of guilty or nolo contendere, or after conviction, the court[3] may make an order[4] directing the defendant to pay certain sums periodically for not exceeding six years to the probation officer for the benefit of the wife, and release defendant on probation. The court may require a recognizance with or without surety[5]	See footnotes 6, 7, 8, 10
Michigan .... Sess. L. 1931, No. 328, pp. 654–56, Secs. 161–63, 166	To desert and abandon the wife without providing necessary and proper shelter, food, care and clothing for her, or, being of sufficient ability, to fail, neglect or refuse to provide necessary and proper shelter, food, care and clothing for the wife	A felony, punishable by imprisonment in the state prison for not more than three years or less than one year, or by imprisonment in the county jail for not more than one year or less than three months	If before sentence, defendant enters into a bond in such sum and with such surety as the court may fix, conditioned that he will furnish the wife with necessary and proper shelter, food, etc., the court may place defendant on probation for a term not exceeding the maximum sentence possible[15]	See footnotes 7, 8, 10
Minnesota ...... G. S. 1923, Secs. 10135–38	Without lawful excuse, to wilfully fail to furnish proper food, shelter, clothing, or medical attendance to the wife, such wife being in destitute circumstances[33]	A misdemeanor[34]	If the person convicted gives bond in such sum and with sureties as the court may approve, conditioned to furnish the wife with proper food, shelter, etc., for a period not exceeding five years, the court shall suspend judgment. The bond may be conditioned upon the payment of a specified sum at stated intervals	See footnotes 7, 8, 10

TABLE LXXXIII (*Continued*)

Jurisdiction and Citation	Nature of the Offense	The Crime and Punishment	Probation of Husband, Relief to Wife, etc.	Miscellaneous
Mississippi[35]				
Missouri .... R. S. 1929, Secs. 4026–28, 4433	Without good cause, to abandon or desert the wife, or to fail, neglect or refuse to maintain and provide for her[36]	Punishable by imprisonment in the county jail for not more than one year or by fine not exceeding $1,000, or by both		See footnotes 7, 9
Montana .... R. C. 1921, Secs. 11017–20	Having sufficient ability to provide for the wife's support or able to earn the means thereof, to wilfully abandon and leave the wife in a destitute condition, or to refuse or neglect to provide such wife with necessary food, clothing, shelter or medical attendance, unless justified in abandoning her by her misconduct	A misdemeanor[37]	Before trial or after conviction, with the consent of the defendant, the court[3] may make an order[4] directing the defendant to pay a certain sum weekly to the wife or trustee named, during such time as the court may direct, and release defendant on probation upon his entering into a recognizance with or without sureties[5]	See footnotes 7, 10
Nebraska .... Comp. St. 1929, Secs. 28(458)– 28(461)	Without good cause, to abandon the wife and wilfully neglect or refuse to maintain or provide for her[38]	Desertion, punishable by imprisonment in the penitentiary for not more than one year, or by imprisonment in the county jail for not more than six months[38]	If before conviction, the accused pays or secures to the wife not less than $200 or more than $1,000, or property of equal value, the court may discharge him upon payment of costs. If, after conviction and before sentence, the accused executes a bond approved by the courts conditioned that he shall furnish the wife the support required by law, the court may suspend sentence on the payment of costs[39, 15]	

[§ 162

TABLE LXXXIII (*Continued*)

Jurisdiction and Citation	Nature of the Offense	The Crime and Punishment	Probation of Husband, Relief to Wife, etc.	Miscellaneous
Nevada .... Comp. L. 1929 (Hillyer), Secs. 10128, 10516–23	Without just cause, to desert or wilfully neglect or refuse to provide for the support and maintenance of the wife in destitute or necessitous circumstances⁴⁰	Punishable by a fine not exceeding $500 or by imprisonment in the county jail not exceeding six months, or by both⁴⁰	Before the trial with the consent of the defendant, or on entry of plea of guilty or after conviction,¹³ the court³ may make an order⁴ directing the husband to pay a certain sum periodically for not exceeding two years to the wife or trustee named, and release the defendant on probation upon his entering into recognizance with or without surety⁵	See footnotes 6, 7, 8
New Hampshire . Pub. L. 1926, Ch. 288, Secs. 15–19	To wilfully neglect or refuse to maintain the wife when such wife is destitute or dependent wholly or in part on her earnings for adequate support, or to neglect his employment or misspend his earnings so as not to provide properly for the support of the wife	Punishable by imprisonment for not more than six months, or by fine of not more than $100, or by both	The court may make an order of support, subject to modification, and suspend sentence during compliance with such order or with such order as may theretofore have been made against the husband. No conviction under the act shall affect an order for support previously made	See footnote 10
New Jersey ..... Comp. St., Cum. Supp. 1911–24, Secs. 52(73e)– 52(73i), 160(213)	To desert or wilfully neglect or refuse to provide for the support and maintenance of the wife in destitute or necessitous circumstances⁴¹	A misdemeanor, punishable by fine not exceeding $500, or by imprisonment, with or without hard labor, as the court may direct, for any term not exceeding one year, or by both⁴¹	Before the trial,⁴² with the consent of the defendant, or on entry or plea of guilty or after conviction,¹³ the court³ may make an order⁴ directing the husband to pay a certain sum periodically to the wife or trustee named, and release defendant on probation upon his entering into recognizance with or without sureties⁵	See footnotes 6, 7, 8, 10

§ 162]

TABLE LXXXIII (*Continued*)

Jurisdiction and Citation	Nature of the Offense	The Crime and Punishment	Probation of Husband, Relief to Wife, etc.	Miscellaneous
New Mexico ... St. Ann. 1929, Sec. 35(4604)	To abandon the wife leaving her without sufficient means of support; or, being able to work, to fail to provide for the support of the wife as far as his ability extends, and to thereby leave her destitute	Punishable by imprisonment for such period not exceeding one year as the court may fix. On a second offense, the imprisonment may be for any period not exceeding two years		
New York ...... Cahill, Consol. L. 1930, Ch. 41, Sec. 50; Cahill, Cr. C. 1928, Secs. 899–913; Inferior Cr. Courts Act, Sec. 74, Cahill, Cr. C. 1928, p. 371	Persons who actually abandon their wives without adequate support, or leave them in danger of becoming a burden upon the public or who neglect to provide for them according to their means, or who threaten to run away and leave their wives a burden upon the public, are disorderly persons[43]	See footnote 44	Upon confession or proof that the husband is a disorderly person, the magistrate may require him to give security by a written undertaking with one or more approved sureties that he will pay to poor authorities weekly for one year a specified sum for the support of the wife. If the undertaking be given, he must be discharged. Otherwise, the magistrate must convict him as a disorderly person[44]	
North Carolina .. C. 1927, Secs. 4447–50; Supp. 1929, Sec. 1461(*h*)	To wilfully abandon the wife without providing adequate support for her and the children begotten upon her; while living with the wife, to wilfully neglect to provide adequate support for her	A misdemeanor[45]	Upon conviction of abandonment the court may make such order as will best provide for the support of the wife, as far as necessary, from the property or labor of the defendant. Upon conviction of non-support, the court may make such order as will best provide for the support of the wife, and may commit the husband to the county jail to be hired out, his wages to be paid to the wife	See footnote 7

[§ 162

TABLE LXXXIII (*Continued*)

Jurisdiction and Citation	Nature of the Offense	The Crime and Punishment	Probation of Husband, Relief to Wife, etc.	Miscellaneous
North Dakota[46].. Comp. L., Supp. 1913–25, Secs. 9594(*a*1)– 9594(*a*3)	Without lawful excuse, to wilfully fail to furnish proper food, shelter, clothing or medical attendance to the wife; without lawful excuse, to desert and fail to support the wife while pregnant with intent wholly to abandon her	A felony, punishable by imprisonment in the state penitentiary for not more than five years	Before the trial, with consent of the defendant, or on entry of plea of guilty or after conviction,[13] the court[3] may make an order accepting defendant's bond with approved sureties conditioned to furnish the wife with proper food, shelter, etc., for not exceeding five years, and suspend judgment (in case of plea of guilty or conviction). The bond may be conditioned upon the payment of specified sums at stated intervals[47]	See footnote 7
Ohio .... Complete G. C. 1931 (Page), Secs. 13008–11	To fail, neglect or refuse to provide a pregnant wife with the necessary or proper home, care, food and clothing; to leave a pregnant wife with intent to abandon her	Punishable by imprisonment in jail or workhouse at hard labor for not less than six months nor more than one year, or in the penitentiary for not less than one year nor more than three years[48]	If the husband, after conviction and before sentence, enters into bond in sufficient sum and with approved sureties conditioned that he will furnish the wife with necessary and proper home, care, food and clothing, or will pay a certain sum weekly to a trustee for such purpose, sentence may be suspended	See footnote 8
Oklahoma ...... St. 1931, Secs. 1830–32, 2526	Without good cause, to abandon the wife in destitute or necessitous circumstances and neglect and refuse to maintain or provide for her	A felony, punishable by imprisonment in the state penitentiary for any period of time not less than one year or more than ten years	Upon conviction the governor may parole the defendant upon recommendation of the trial judge upon defendant's entering into an approved undertaking with two or more sufficient sureties, conditioned that he will periodically pay to the clerk of court such sums as the court may fix for the support of the wife[49]	See footnotes 7, 8, 10

§ 162]

TABLE LXXXIII (*Continued*)

Jurisdiction and Citation	Nature of the Offense	The Crime and Punishment	Probation of Husband, Relief to Wife, etc.	Miscellaneous
Oregon .... C. 1930, Secs. 13(304), 14(845)– 14(851)	Without just or sufficient cause, to desert or abandon the wife without providing necessary and proper shelter, food, care or clothing for her, or to fail or neglect to support the wife	A felony, punishable by confinement in the state prison for not more than one year or by imprisonment in the county jail for not more than one year	If, before sentence, defendant enters into a bond approved by the court, conditioned that he will furnish the wife with necessary and proper shelter, food, care and clothing, the court may suspend sentence[15]	See footnotes 7, 8, 10
Pennsylvania[50] .. St. 1920 (West), Secs. 9066–68, 9071– 74, 9077–79; Cum. Supp. 1928 (West), Sec. 9079a	To separate from the wife without reasonable cause or/and to wilfully neglect to maintain her, such wife being destitute or dependent wholly or in part on her earnings for adequate support[51]	A misdemeanor, punishable by imprisonment not exceeding one year, or by fine not exceeding $100, or by both	Upon conviction, the court may suspend sentence upon compliance with order of support before made against defendant, or which the court trying him may make, on entry of bond by him conditioned on compliance with such order[52]	See footnotes 6, 7, 10, 11
Rhode Island ... G. L. 1923, Sec. 6182	To abandon the wife, leaving her in danger of becoming a public charge, or to neglect to provide according to his means for the support of the wife; or being an habitual drunkard, to neglect or refuse to aid in the support of the family	A misdemeanor, punishable by imprisonment for not less than six months nor more than three years in the state workhouse and house of correction, or not more than one year in the county jail		
South Carolina .. C. of L. 1922, Cr. L., Sec. 20, amd. by Sess. L. 1925, No. 98, p. 143	Being able-bodied or capable of earning or making a livelihood, to abandon or fail to supply the actual necessaries of life to the wife, without just cause or excuse	A misdemeanor, punishable by imprisonment for a term not exceeding one year, or by fine of not less than $300 nor more than $1,500, or by both fine and imprisonment	If defendant, before or after conviction, gives bond with one or more sureties under such terms and conditions as the court may deem proper for the maintenance and support of the wife, he shall not be imprisoned or fined until the condition is broken	See footnote 10

[§ 162

TABLE LXXXIII (*Continued*)

Jurisdiction and Citation	Nature of the Offense	The Crime and Punishment	Probation of Husband, Relief to Wife, etc.	Miscellaneous
South Dakota ... Comp. L. 1929, Secs. 4108-12	Without good cause, to wilfully abandon the wife, leaving her in a destitute condition; or, without good cause, to wilfully neglect or refuse to provide for the wife, she being in a destitute condition	Desertion punishable by imprisonment in the state penitentiary for not exceeding one year, or by imprisonment in the county jail for not exceeding six months	If, before trial, or after conviction and before sentence, the defendant enters into an undertaking approved by the court with or without sureties, conditioned that he will furnish the wife with a necessary and proper home, food, care, and clothing, the court may release him[15]	See footnote 7
Tennessee ...... C. 1932, Secs. 11370-78	Wilfully and without good cause, to neglect or fail to provide for the wife according to his means, or to leave the wife destitute or in danger of becoming a public charge[53]	A misdemeanor, punishable by sentence to the workhouse for a period not exceeding eleven months and twenty-nine days[54]	If the defendant pleads guilty or is found guilty, the court may require him to give an undertaking with approved sureties, conditioned that he will pay a certain sum periodically to the clerk of the court for the benefit of the wife[55]	See footnotes 7, 8, 9, 10
Texas[56] .... Complete St. 1928, P. C., Art. 507; Arts. 602 and 604, amd. by Supp. 1931, p. 624; Arts. 603, 605-6	To wilfully desert, neglect or refuse to provide for the support and maintenance of the wife who may be in necessitous circumstances	Punishable by confinement in the penitentiary for not more than two years, or in jail for not more than six months, or by fine of not less than $25 nor more than $500, or by both fine and imprisonment	See footnote 57	See footnotes 6, 7, 8, 9
Utah .... R. S. 1933, 103-13-1, 103-13-2	Without just cause, to desert or wilfully neglect or refuse to provide for the support and maintenance of the wife in destitute or necessitous circumstances	A felony, punishable by imprisonment in the state prison at hard labor for not exceeding eighteen months	Before the trial, with the consent of the defendant, or after conviction, in lieu of the punishment provided, the court[3] may make an order[4] directing the defendant to pay a certain sum weekly for one year into the county treasury for the benefit of the wife, and release defendant on probation upon his entering into a recognizance with or without security[5]	See footnotes 7, 10

§ 162]

TABLE LXXXIII (*Continued*)

Jurisdiction and Citation	Nature of the Offense	The Crime and Punishment	Probation of Husband, Relief to Wife, etc.	Miscellaneous
Vermont .... G. L. 1917, Sec. 3536, amd. by Sess. L. 1921, No. 80, p. 77, and further amd. by Sess. L. 1925, No. 52, p. 59; Secs. 3537–43, 6831	Without just cause, to desert or wilfully neglect or refuse to provide for the support and maintenance of the wife in destitute circumstances[58]	Punishable by imprisonment at hard labor for not more than two years or by fine of not more than $300, or by both[58]	Before the trial, with the consent of the defendant, or on entry of plea of guilty, or after conviction,[13] the court[3] may make an order[4] directing the defendant to pay a certain sum periodically to the wife or trustee named and release defendant on probation upon his entering into a recognizance with or without surety[5]	See footnotes 6, 7, 8, 10
Virginia .... C. 1930, Secs. 1936–38; Sec. 1939, amd. by Sess. L. 1932, Ch. 262, p. 466; Secs. 1940–44	Without just cause, to desert or wilfully neglect or refuse or fail to provide for the support and maintenance of the wife, such wife being then and there in destitute or necessitous circumstances	A misdemeanor, punishable by fine not exceeding $500 or by sentence to the state convict road force for a period of not less than ninety days or more than twelve months, or by both; or in lieu of such fine, defendant may be required to suffer a forfeiture of not more than $500	Before the trial, with the consent of the defendant, or on plea of guilty or after conviction,[13] the court[59] may make an order[4] directing defendant to pay a certain sum or a certain percentage of his earnings periodically to the wife directly or through the court or probation officer, and suspend sentence and release defendant on probation, upon his entering into a recognizance with or without surety[5]	See footnotes 6, 7, 8, 9, 10, 11
Washington .... Remington, Comp. St. 1922, Sec. 6908; Sec. 6909, amd. by Supp. 1927; Secs. 6910–12	Having sufficient ability to provide for the wife's support, or able to earn the means thereof, to wilfully abandon and leave the wife in a destitute condition, or to refuse or neglect to provide such wife with necessary food, clothing, shelter, or medical attendance, unless justified by her misconduct in abandoning her	A gross misdemeanor[60]	Before or after trial, conviction, or sentence, with the consent of the defendant, the court[3] may make an order[4] directing the defendant to pay a certain sum weekly during such time as the court may direct to the wife or trustee named, and release defendant on probation upon his entering into a recognizance with or without sureties[5]	See footnotes 7, 10, 61

[§ 162

TABLE LXXXIII (*Continued*)

Jurisdiction and Citation	Nature of the Offense	The Crime and Punishment	Probation of Husband, Relief to Wife, etc.	Miscellaneous
West Virginia C. 1931, Ch. 48, Art. 8, Secs. 1–6	Without just cause, to desert or wilfully neglect or refuse to provide for the support and maintenance of the wife in destitute and necessitous circumstances	A misdemeanor punishable by a fine not exceeding $500 or by imprisonment in the county jail not exceeding one year with hard labor, or by both	The justice of peace before whom conviction is had[3, 13] may require the defendant to pay a certain sum periodically to the wife or trustee,[4] and release the defendant upon his entering into sufficient bond[62]	See footnotes 7, 8, 9, 10
Wisconsin St. 1931, Secs. 351.30, 351.31	Without just cause, to desert or wilfully neglect or refuse to provide for the support and maintenance of the wife in destitute or necessitous circumstances	Punishable by a fine not exceeding $500 or by imprisonment in the state prison, county jail, or county workhouse not exceeding two years, or by both	Before the trial,[63] with the consent of the defendant or on entry of plea of guilty or after conviction,[13] the court[3] may make an order[4] directing the defendant to pay a certain sum weekly, for not exceeding two years, to wife or trustee named, and release the defendant on probation upon his entering into a recognizance with or without surety[5]	See footnotes 6, 7, 8, 10
Wyoming R. S. 1931, Secs. 32(803)– 32(808)	Without just cause, to desert or wilfully neglect or refuse to provide for the support and maintenance of the wife in destitute or necessitous circumstances	Punishable by a fine not exceeding $500 or by imprisonment in the county jail not exceeding two years, or both, with or without hard labor	Before the trial, with the consent of the defendant or on entry of plea of guilty or after conviction,[13] the court[3] may make an order[4] directing the defendant to pay a certain sum weekly, for not exceeding two years, to the wife or trustee named, and release defendant on probation upon his entering into a recognizance with or without surety[5]	See footnotes 6, 7, 8, 10

[1] The **Alabama** Code also provides that an able-bodied person who abandons his wife, without just cause, leaving her without sufficient means of subsistence or in danger of becoming a public charge is a vagrant, punishable by fine not exceeding five hundred dollars or by a term at hard labor for not more than twelve months.

[2] In **Alabama**, original jurisdiction is lodged in the domestic relations and juvenile courts where established, but otherwise in probate courts. The court determines both law and fact. Defendant after conviction may appeal to the circuit court where he is entitled to a jury trial

§ 162]

TABLE LXXXIII (*Continued*)

and trial de novo. Such appeals are given a preferred place on the calendar to facilitate a speedy trial.

[3] In making the order, the court shall have regard to the circumstances, and to the financial ability, etc., of the defendant.

[4] The order is subject to change as circumstances may require.

[5] The recognizance is conditioned that the defendant shall make his personal appearance in court at stated times or when ordered, and that he shall further comply with the terms of the order of support.

[6] The following jurisdictions provide for the issuance of a temporary order of support: **Delaware, Illinois, Kansas, Nevada, Texas, Vermont, Virginia, Wisconsin,** and **Wyoming** (before the trial); **Alabama** (before the trial or pending appeal); **Connecticut** (pending appeal); **Massachusetts** (after arraignment and before appeal is perfected, and on appeal before final determination); **New Jersey** (after complaint and before consideration thereof by the grand jury). (See Sec. 3 of the Uniform Act.)

[7] **Alabama, Alaska, Arkansas, California, Delaware, District of Columbia, Hawaii, Idaho, Illinois, Kansas, Massachusetts, Minnesota, Missouri, Nevada, New Jersey, North Dakota, Oklahoma, Texas, Utah, Vermont, Washington, West Virginia, Wisconsin,** and **Wyoming** provide that no other evidence is required to prove marriage than is or shall be required to prove such fact in a civil action.

In **Alabama, Alaska, California, Delaware, District of Columbia, Hawaii, Idaho, Illinois, Indiana, Iowa, Kansas, Massachusetts, Nevada, New Jersey, Oregon, Texas, Utah, Vermont, Washington, Wisconsin,** and **Wyoming** the statute expressly provides that existing rules of law prohibiting the disclosure of confidential communications between the spouses do not apply. (See Sec. 6 of the Uniform Act.) In the jurisdictions above and in **Oklahoma, Pennsylvania, South Dakota, Virginia,** and **West Virginia** the wife is expressly made a competent witness to testify to all relevant matters, or to testify against her husband as to all relevant matters. **Alabama, Delaware, District of Columbia, Hawaii, Indiana, New Jersey, Oregon, Texas,** and **Wisconsin** make the wife a "compellable" witness as well. It will be observed that the Uniform Act does not expressly make the wife a compellable witness. **Iowa** and **South Dakota** qualify the foregoing by providing that the wife shall not be called against the husband without her consent. In addition, **Colorado** and **Michigan** provide that the wife may testify against the husband without his consent. **Delaware, Illinois, Indiana, Kansas, Nevada, Vermont, Virginia, Wisconsin,** and **Wyoming** add that the wife cannot be made to incriminate herself.

The statutes of **Alabama, Alaska, California, Delaware, District of Columbia, Hawaii, Idaho, Indiana, Iowa, Kansas, Massachusetts, Montana, Nevada, New Jersey, North Carolina, Oregon, South Dakota, Texas, Utah, Vermont, Virginia, Washington, West Virginia, Wisconsin,** and **Wyoming** set up a presumption of wilfulness on proof of desertion or neglect, etc. For example, **Delaware, Hawaii, Kansas, Nevada, New Jersey, Texas, Vermont, West Virginia, Wisconsin,** and **Wyoming** have adopted the last sentence of Section 6 of the Uniform Act. **District of Columbia, Idaho, Iowa, Massachusetts,** and **Utah** set up substantially the same presumption. In **Alaska, California, Idaho, Montana,** and **Washington** proof of abandonment or (and) non-support is prima facie evidence that such conduct is wilful. In **North Dakota,** desertion or failure to support a pregnant wife for a period of three months is prima facie evidence of an intention wholly to abandon. Upon proof of certain facts, a presumption of desertion or abandonment or an intention to desert or abandon is raised in **Alabama, Oregon,** and **Virginia. Oregon** provides that the fact that a man lives and cohabits with a woman or holds her out as his wife is prima facie evidence that he is her husband. **Tennessee** sets up a rebuttable presumption that the husband is possessed of means adequate to support the wife.

[8] The offense is committed in any county where the wife may be when the complaint is made (**Alabama, Colorado, Delaware, Ohio**); or in any county in which the wife has been an actual resident for not less than sixty days while the failure and neglect to support has continued (**Oregon**); or in any county in which the wife may have been at the time the abandonment occurred or in which the wife has resided for six months next preceding the filing of the complaint, indictment or information (**Texas**); or in any county or city in which the wife may be at the time of the desertion and where the accused may be found (**Virginia**); or in any county in which the wife may be at the time the desertion, neglect, etc., or any part thereof,

[§ 162

TABLE LXXXIII (*Continued*)

took place, or where the husband may be found when the complaint is made (**West Virginia**). Proceedings shall be begun in the county where the husband and wife last lived together, or where the husband or wife is living, or in the court having such place in its judicial district (**Massachusetts**). Complaint may be made in the precinct where the wife or defendant may be at the time (**Alaska**).

Proceedings may be instituted by complaint, etc., by the wife or any other person (**Delaware, Kansas, Nevada, Wyoming**), or any other person, persons, or organization (**Hawaii, Wisconsin**); by the wife or any reputable person (**Minnesota**); by the deserted wife or any one personally cognizant of the facts (**Alaska, West Virginia**); by the wife or certain designated officers upon information received, or any person with knowledge of the facts (**Alabama, Virginia**); by the wife, the prosecuting attorney or any person or organization (**Indiana**). Complaint may be made by any of the superintendents of poor of the city or county or the county agent of the state welfare commission for the county wherein the wife resides (**Michigan**). Proceedings may be instituted by any prosecuting officer upon complaint made by the wife or any other person (**Vermont**). **Oklahoma** has the rather unique provision that no person shall inform against the husband except the wife or any public officer of the county.

[9] Ten jurisdictions have some provision as to extradition. **Alabama** and **Virginia** provide that when the judge certifies that in his opinion the case is a proper one for extradition, or in any event if the cost of extradition is borne by the parties interested, the husband shall be returned. **Idaho** and **West Virginia** expressly state that the offense created by the statute is subject to extradition. **Tennessee** provides that, if the husband wilfully leaves the state after abandoning the wife with intent to leave her destitute or liable to become a public charge, it is the duty of the governor to demand his return upon the proper warrant being issued, etc. **Colorado, Delaware, Missouri, Texas,** and **West Virginia** make provision for the expenses of extradition.

[10] About half the jurisdictions provide for an incidental financial relief to the wife by an appropriation for her benefit of fines imposed or of money collected on forfeited recognizances, or by providing for certain definite sums to be paid to her or for her benefit, or appropriated for that purpose, in case the husband is sentenced to hard labor. Statutory authority whereby the fine may be directed to be paid in whole or in part to the wife or someone for her benefit was found in **Alabama, California, District of Columbia, Idaho, Illinois, Louisiana, Maine, Maryland, Massachusetts, Montana, New Hampshire, New Jersey, Pennsylvania, South Carolina, Vermont, Virginia,** and **Washington.** The Uniform Act contains no provision of this sort. Provision for a similar disposition of sums recovered on forfeited recognizances was found in **Alabama, Alaska, Colorado, Connecticut, Delaware, District of Columbia, Idaho, Illinois, Indiana, Louisiana, Maine, Maryland, Massachusetts, New Jersey, New York, Pennsylvania, Tennessee, Utah, Vermont, Virginia, Washington, West Virginia, Wisconsin,** and **Wyoming.** Upon violation of the terms of the order of support, the sureties become liable for the payments in **Oklahoma.** In **Minnesota** and **North Dakota,** the wife or anyone furnishing her with food, etc., may sue upon the bond for breach of the conditions thereof.

The husband, upon conviction and sentence, may be compelled to do hard labor (or sent to the workhouse, etc.) in **Alabama, Alaska, California, Delaware, District of Columbia, Idaho, Indiana, Kansas, Maine, Maryland, Massachusetts, Michigan, Montana, New Jersey, New York, North Carolina, Oklahoma, Ohio, Oregon, Pennsylvania, Rhode Island, Tennessee, Utah, Vermont, Virginia, Washington, West Virginia, Wisconsin,** and **Wyoming.** All of these jurisdictions, except **Alaska, New York, Ohio, Rhode Island, Tennessee, Wisconsin,** and **Wyoming,** have some provision for financial assistance to be given to the wife on account of such labor. These provisions differ in many details. The amount to be paid to the wife or her benefit for each day's labor varies from forty cents in **Vermont** to not to exceed two dollars and a half in **Oklahoma.** In **Colorado,** as a part of the conditions of a suspended sentence, the court may direct that the prisoner be committed to any common jail or workhouse for not over ninety days. When so confined, provision is made for payments by the county toward the support of the wife if she otherwise would be a public charge.

[11] The **Alabama, Delaware, Pennsylvania,** and **Virginia** acts provide for the appointment of probation officers to assist the court. In **Alabama** and **Virginia** the statute directs the probation officer to study defendant's antecedent history, to determine proper corrective measures, and to use every effort to encourage and stimulate reformation.

§ 162]

TABLE LXXXIII (*Continued*)

[12] The **Alabama** Code provides that "this chapter shall be liberally construed in order to accomplish the beneficent purposes herein provided for."

[13] Instead of imposing the penalties prescribed, or in addition thereto.

[14] If no other punishment is prescribed, a felony in **Arizona** is punishable by imprisonment in the state prison for not exceeding five years (R. C. 1928, Sec. 4485).

[15] The statutes of **Arizona, California, Colorado, Michigan, Nebraska, Oregon,** and **South Dakota** authorize the court, upon defendant's failure to comply with his undertaking, to modify the order and take a new undertaking rather than to continue proceedings against him.

[16] The **Arkansas** statute provides, however, that, if the husband after leaving the wife removes from the state, he is guilty of a felony, punishable by sentence to the penitentiary for not to exceed one year.

[17] That part of the **Colorado** statute relative to abandonment of the wife reads as follows: "or any man being the father of a child or children, under sixteen years of age, who shall leave such child or children or his wife with intent to abandon such wife, or child or children . . . ."

[18] Unless, owing to physical incapacity or other good cause, he is unable to furnish the support, etc.

[19] In **Colorado**, all courts of record have jurisdiction. Complaint or information may be filed in such court or before any justice of the peace of the county where the offense is committed. The justice before binding the accused over may release him upon his giving bond as above.

[20] The **Connecticut** statute provides that any justice of the peace, or any town, city, or borough court before which complaint is brought, may hold a trial thereon; but if in the opinion of the court a greater punishment should be inflicted than is within its jurisdiction, defendant shall be bound over to the superior court having criminal jurisdiction.

[21] In that section corresponding to Section 5 of the Uniform Act, the **Delaware** Code provides that if the court is satisfied, etc., that defendant has violated the order of support it may proceed with "the trial of the defendant under the original conviction"—an obvious error.

[22] The Juvenile Court is given concurrent jurisdiction with the Supreme Court of the **District of Columbia.**

[23] The husband shall not be prosecuted if there exists at the time of the desertion grounds for divorce recognized by the **Florida** statutes. One who misspends what he earns without providing for himself or family is a vagrant under the **Florida** statutes.

[24] The **Hawaii** Act provides for the sequestration of any money belonging to the husband, after the latter has been absent for six months continuously without making provision for the support of the wife.

[25] The **Illinois** statute provides that the husband may be prosecuted for non-support at any time during the existence of the marriage relation. Proceedings may be by indictment or information. The offenses under the Act are to be construed as continuing offenses.

[26] **Indiana** also provides that one who deserts his wife except for the cause of adultery or other vicious or immoral conduct, leaving her without reasonable means of support, is guilty of a felony, punishable by sentence to state prison for not less than one year nor more than three years, and by disfranchisement and incapacity to hold any office of trust or profit for three years.

[27] The **Indiana** statute also allows the court, after conviction, to suspend judgment and release defendant on probation on condition that he will appear before the court and provide for the neglected wife as directed.

[28] An able-bodied male who is without visible means of support and who habitually fails or refuses to engage in honest labor for his own support or for the support of his family is a vagrant under the **Kentucky** statutes.

[29] Being able by means of his property or labor to provide for the necessary support and maintenance of the wife.

[30] The **Maine** Act gives the judges of municipal and police courts and trial justices original and concurrent jurisdiction with the Superior Court in all prosecutions for misdemeanor.

[31] See also Session Laws of Maryland, 1927, Chapter 334, page 604, for a desertion and non-support act applying to persons in Alleghany County.

[§ 162

TABLE LXXXIII (*Continued*)

[32] The **Maryland** Act allows a justice of the peace to release the defendant, with the latter's consent, after making an order and taking a recognizance as above, instead of committing him pending action by the grand jury.

[33] **Minnesota** also makes desertion and failure to support a pregnant wife, without lawful excuse and with intent wholly to abandon her, a felony punishable by imprisonment in the state prison not exceeding five years. Desertion and failure to support for three months is presumptive evidence of such intention.

[34] When not otherwise prescribed, the punishment for a misdemeanor under the **Minnesota** statutes is imprisonment in the county jail for not more than three months or a fine of not more than one hundred dollars.

[35] The Uniform Act as adopted by **Mississippi** in 1920 (Sess. L. 1920, Ch. 212, p. 304) was declared wholly invalid on the ground that it authorized prosecution of a felony merely upon complaint under oath by any person, thus violating the constitutional provision requiring indictment (*State* v. *Sansome,* 133 Miss. 428; 97 So. 753 [1923]). The law was substantially re-enacted in 1924, providing for the prosecution by indictment (Sess. L. 1924, Ch. 155, p. 208). This Act was in turn held wholly invalid on the ground that the power given to the court to suspend sentence is an invasion of the sole pardoning power vested in the governor (*State* v. *Jackson,* 143 Miss. 745; 109 So. 724 [1926]). The 1924 Act repealed Subsection (*k*), Section 3332, Hemingway's Annotated Code, 1917, which made one who abandons his wife under certain circumstances a vagrant. In 1928 (Sess. L. 1928, Extra Sess., Ch. 89, p. 141) a statute was passed covering desertion and non-support of child by the parent. It appears, however, that at the present time **Mississippi** is without legislation covering desertion and non-support of the wife by the husband.

[36] If the husband leaves his wife in **Missouri,** and takes up his abode elsewhere, and without just cause fails to provide for her, he is deemed to have abandoned her within the state of **Missouri.**

[37] When not otherwise prescribed, a misdemeanor in **Montana** is punishable by imprisonment in the county jail for not exceeding six months, or by fine not exceeding five hundred dollars, or by both (R. C. 1921, Sec. 10725).

[38] The **Nebraska** statute also makes a wilful failure, refusal or neglect to provide proper food, etc., for the wife a misdemeanor. Provision is made for suspension of sentence on defendant's furnishing proper bond, or parole upon condition that he assign his wages to the one to whom paroled.

[39] In **Nebraska,** the juvenile court presided over by the district judge has exclusive original jurisdiction, except when the district judge is absent, in which case the county court has concurrent jurisdiction with the right of appeal to the district court.

[40] In **Nevada,** Section 10128, Compiled Laws, 1929 (Hillyer), makes desertion or non-support a felony. The definition of the offense is almost identical with that of the Uniform Act adopted in 1923, referred to above. This section also authorizes the release of the defendant before the trial with his consent, or, after conviction, upon his entering into recognizance conditioned that he will pay weekly such sum as the court may direct for the support of the wife.

[41] See also **New Jersey,** where Compiled Statutes, 1910, page 1770, Section 73*a,* desertion and non-support act, was held not to be repealed by implication by adoption of the Uniform Act (*State* v. *Garris,* 98 N. J. L. 608; 121 A. 292 [1914]). See also Compiled Statutes, 1910, page 1931, Section 17 (as amended by Cum. Supp. 1911–24, p. 947, Sec. 59[17]); page 1932, Sections 18, 19, 20; page 1933, Sections 21, 22, 23; page 1934, Sections 24, 25, 26, 27; page 1935, Sections 28, 29, 30; and Cumulative Supplement 1911–24, Sections 161(211)–161(217), for other acts which penalize desertion and non-support and which seem primarily designed to protect the community from the expense of supporting the deserted wife.

[42] Jurisdiction is in the **New Jersey** "Family Courts" where established.

[43] The **New York** statutes also provide that a man who abandons his wife, while she is pregnant and in destitute circumstances or liable to become a burden upon the public, is guilty of a felony. Unless otherwise prescribed, a felony in **New York** is punishable by imprisonment for not more than seven years, or by fine of not more than $1,000, or by both (Cahill, Consol. L., Ch. 41, Secs. 50, 1935).

[44] The proceedings against "disorderly persons" are of a quasi-criminal nature, and said to be for the purpose of suppressive prevention rather than punishment. Complaint on oath may be made to a justice of the peace or police justice of a city, village or town, or to the mayor,

§ 162]

TABLE LXXXIII (*Continued*)

recorder, city judge, or judge of the general sessions of the city. The domestic relations court in the city of New York has sole and exclusive jurisdiction to try, hear, and determine charges against persons in the city alleged to be disorderly. Upon failure to give the undertaking described above, the magistrate must commit the husband to not exceeding six months' hard labor, or until he gives such security. A return is made to the county court, which must examine the record and hear any proof offered, and which may discharge the husband absolutely or on parole under a probation officer, or upon his giving security as above, or order him retained in jail, etc., when committed for a term not exceeding six months at hard labor. Proceeds from the undertaking, when forfeited, are to be applied for the benefit of the wife.

[45] Unless prescribed, a misdemeanor in **North Carolina** is punished as at common law (unless it be infamous, done in secrecy, etc.) (C. 1927, Sec. 4173).

[46] **North Dakota** after adopting the Uniform Act in 1911 (Sess. L. 1911, Ch. 123) repealed the same in 1923 (Sess. L. 1923, Ch. 166) and substituted the present act therefor.

[47] Section 9594(*a*1) of the **North Dakota** statutes penalizing desertion of a pregnant wife contains no similar provision for defendant's release upon his furnishing bond as above.

[48] The **Ohio** statute provides that defendant shall be acquitted if it appears that because of lack of property, physical incapacity, etc., he is unable to provide for the wife.

[49] The governor may suspend sentence upon the same terms, etc. Under the **Oklahoma** statute, any interested party may sue on the bond for violation of the conditions thereof.

[50] The reader is directed to **Pennsylvania** Statutes 1920 (West), Sections 9057–80, for a picture of the rather confused and ill-organized statutory situation in **Pennsylvania**. See especially Sections 9057–65, 9069–70, and 9075 respecting civil relief to the wife.

[51] Separation, under the **Pennsylvania** statute, includes every case where a husband has caused his wife to leave him by conduct which is grounds for divorce. One who deserts or refuses without cause to support the wife is also a vagrant in **Pennsylvania**.

[52] See also **Pennsylvania** Statutes 1920 (West), Sections 7490–91, 8208, 15714, 15716, for some procedural details.

[53] **Tennessee** also provides that if the husband wilfully leave the state, after abandoning the wife with intent to leave her destitute or liable to become a public charge, he shall be guilty of a felony.

[54] Under the **Tennessee** Act, complaint may be made to the judge of any juvenile court. If the husband pleads not guilty, he is bound over for action by the grand jury and trial in the criminal court.

[55] According to the **Tennessee** Act, upon giving the undertaking, the defendant "must" be discharged, or the court may, if the case warrants leniency, release defendant on his own recognizance on bond as above but without sureties. If the defendant is bound over and pleads guilty or is found guilty, it is the "duty" of the court to require the above undertaking, etc., and, if it is given, defendant "must" be released, but, if not given, the court "must" sentence him to the above punishment and costs.

[56] A 1929 amendment to the **Texas** Act raised the crime from a misdemeanor to a felony (Sess. L. 1929, Ch. 195, p. 427).

[57] Rather curiously, **Texas** seems to have made no special provision for a permanent order of support, and for release of defendant on probation.

[58] **Vermont** also provides that one of sufficient ability who neglects or refuses to provide necessary food and maintenance for the wife shall be imprisoned for not more than six months or fined not more than $20, or both.

[59] The **Virginia** statute gives the juvenile and domestic relations courts, where established, exclusive original jurisdiction. If the accused fails to appear when summoned, the court may proceed with the trial in his absence, but, if a judgment of conviction is entered, he has thirty days to make application to have the case reopened. The statute also makes provision for taking a plea of guilty and a recognizance when the accused is outside the jurisdiction of the court.

[60] Unless otherwise prescribed, a gross misdemeanor in **Washington** is punishable by imprisonment in the county jail for not more than one year, or by fine of not more than $1,000, or by both.

[61] The **Washington** statute makes provision, as an ancillary remedy during pendency, for the seizure, etc., of money due the defendant by third parties or personal effects of the defendant held by third parties.

[§ 162

TABLE LXXXIII (*Concluded*)

[62] The **West Virginia** statute provides that "juvenile, circuit, intermediate and criminal courts shall have original, concurrent, and appellate jurisdiction . . . ." Proceedings may be instituted, however, before any justice of the peace of the county in which the wife may be. If defendant appeals and is found guilty, the payments fixed by the justice relate back to the date of the appeal.

[63] In **Wisconsin**, the county and municipal courts have concurrent jurisdiction with the circuit courts. If the defendant is bound over and pleads not guilty, he is entitled to a jury trial. If no regular panel of jurors is in attendance, the court shall order a special venire. Proceedings follow the regular practice of the circuit court in criminal cases.

REFERENCES

[See also references to Secs. 166 and 234]

Articles

BALDWIN, WILLIAM H. "The Most Effective Methods of Dealing with Cases of Desertion and Non-Support," 8 J. Crim. L. 564–75 (1917).

———. "Non-Support and Its Remedies in Massachusetts," 7 J. Crim. L. 743–51 (1917).

———. "The Present Status of Family Desertion and Non-Support Laws," Address Delivered at National Conference of Charities and Corrections, Boston, Massachusetts, June 10, 1911.

Notes

"Abandonment of Pregnant Wife, Ignorance as a Defense," *White* v. *State,* 44 Ohio App. 331 ; 185 N. E. 64 (1933)—11 N. Y. Univ. L. Quar. Rev. 104–6 (1933).

"Wilful Non-Support of Wife and Children," *Zitlow* v. *State,* 213 Wis. 493 ; 252 N. W. 358 (1934)—9 Wis. L. Rev. 425–26 (1934).

Annotations

"Abandonment of Wife or Children as Vagrancy," 14 A. L. R. 1485–87 (1921).

"Criminal Responsibility of Husband for Abandonment or Non-Support of Wife, Who Refuses to Live with Him," 3 A. L. R. 107–14 (1919) ; 8 A. L. R. 1314–16 (1920).

"Extent or Character of Support Contemplated by Statute Making Non-Support of Wife or Child Offense," 36 A. L. R. 866–76 (1925).

"Misconduct of Wife as Affecting Criminal Charge of Abandonment against Husband," 17 A. L. R. 999–1001 (1922).

"Non-Support as Infamous Offense within Constitutional or Statutory Provision in Relation to Presentment or Indictment by Grand Jury," 24 A. L. R. 1014–15 (1923).

"Power to Make Abandonment, Desertion or Non-Support of Wife or Family a Criminal Offense," 14 A. L. R. 1485–87 (1921) ; 48 A. L. R. 1193–98 (1927).

§ 162]

Section 163. Family Courts and Courts of Domestic Relations

CROSS REFERENCES: Jurisdiction over divorce actions, **Sec. 81;** Lazy husband laws, **Sec. 162;** Juvenile court laws, **Sec. 277**

The terms "family court" and "court of domestic relations" have been applied in a few jurisdictions to special courts which deal only with minor children or with adults in their relations with such children. The present section is not concerned with courts of that nature, but with "family courts" or "courts of domestic relations" which have a jurisdiction, at least in part, over marital rights of husband and wife. Hereafter, these latter courts will be called "courts of domestic relations."

The success of the purely statutory juvenile courts in the United States (**Sec. 277**) has resulted in a definite trend toward the establishment of courts with somewhat similar procedural methods but with a jurisdiction over other legal problems of the family, including those of husband and wife. This movement, however, is still in its infancy, only fifteen jurisdictions having been found with legislation relevant to husband and wife. It is probable that a few other jurisdictions, by rule of court, have segregated actions involving domestic relations into special sessions or divisions of the court.

There are two general classes of statutes. In the first place, fifteen jurisdictions have statutes which specifically enumerate the type of action concerning husband and wife which is within the jurisdiction of the court of domestic relations. Thus, such jurisdiction extends in varying degrees (see Table LXXXIV following) to: desertion and non-support of the wife by her husband (**Alabama, Hawaii, New Jersey, New York, North Carolina, Oregon, Tennessee, Virginia, West Virginia**); divorce (**Hawaii, Missouri, Ohio, Oklahoma, Oregon, Tennessee, West Virginia**); prosecution for assault or assault and battery by one spouse upon the other (**Alabama, North Carolina**); and prosecution for adultery if defendant waives indictment and trial by jury (**New Jersey**). In three jurisdictions the so-called "juvenile court" has jurisdiction over desertion and non-support of the wife by her husband (**District of Columbia, Nebraska, Pennsylvania**), and over divorce in **Nebraska.** In the exercise of such jurisdiction, these courts are in effect, if not in name, courts of domestic relations.

In the second place, broad statutes in **New Jersey** and **Virginia,** in conferring jurisdiction on the court, have not been limited to specific actions. Such provisions are more consistent with the premise underlying the establishment of courts of domestic relations, viz., that these courts, in general, are better able to cope with problems of domestic relations. However, certain limitations on the courts in these two states which reduce their effectiveness should be noted (see Table LXXXIV).

In **New Jersey** and **Virginia** the establishment of these special courts has not been limited by the population factor. In general, however, these courts have been confined in varying degrees to the centers of population, where the frequency of relevant cases makes their work more valuable. As their advantages are proved, no doubt such courts will be extended, as far as is practicable, to other sections of the several jurisdictions.

The table following indicates other phases of these statutes which cannot be given in detail in the text; for example, whether the court of domestic relations has exclusive jurisdiction or concurrent jurisdiction with other courts; and whether the court is a separate one or merely a special division or department of another court.

An extended discussion of the principles involved in the establishment of these special courts, of arguments for and against them, or of their procedure is not within the scope of this work. For such material the reader is referred to the references at the end of this section. However, the principal benefits of courts of domestic relations may be mentioned very briefly: (*a*) the unity of jurisdiction over family problems, contrasted with the present practice in many jurisdictions of requiring suits in several courts; (*b*) the more or less informal procedure normally followed in these courts; (*c*) the advantage of the usual scheme of having social agencies, probation officers, and specially trained investigators provide the court with an insight into the character of the particular home involved; (*d*) the increased efficiency of a court which deals entirely with domestic relations. The latter benefit of course is possible only through the retention of the same personnel for a reasonable time. In the writer's opinion such advantages point toward the early adoption of these special courts by an increasing number of jurisdictions.

The reader is referred to a valuable monograph on the subject published by the United States Department of Labor, Children's Bureau, *Publication No. 193* (1929), compiled by Bernard Flexner, Reuben Oppenheimer, and Katherine F. Lenroot. At page 71 is a very complete bibliography relating to family courts. A further publication by the same Bureau, *Chart No. 17* (1930), compiled by Freda R. Lyman, relating to jurisdiction over children's cases and cases of domestic relations, should also be of help.

Citations to the statutes discussed are collected in the table following.

§ 163]

TABLE LXXXIV*

Family Courts and Courts of Domestic Relations

Jurisdiction and Citation	Name and Place Where Found[1]	Jurisdiction of Court[2]
Alabama .... Sess. L. 1927, No. 225, pp. 238–50	Juvenile and Domestic Relations Court established in each county now or hereafter having a population of two hundred thousand or more	Original and exclusive jurisdiction over prosecution and punishment: of assaults or of assaults and batteries by one spouse on the other; or of offense of abandonment or failure to support wife, by husband
District of Columbia .... C. 1929, T. 6, Sec. 271	Juvenile Court[3]	Concurrent jurisdiction with Supreme Court over prosecutions for desertion or non-support of wife by husband
Hawaii .... R. L. 1925, Secs. 2236–37	Division of Domestic Relations comprises part of First Circuit Court	Jurisdiction (unless case is especially assigned to one of the other judges) over divorce, separation, annulment of marriage, separate maintenance, alimony, desertion and non-support of wife by husband (the above does not limit powers of other circuit judges)[4]
Missouri .... R. S. 1929, Sec. 2132	Two divisions of Circuit Court of city of St. Louis are designated as Court of Domestic Relations	Said divisions (see preceding column) shall be assigned all actions for divorce, separate maintenance, annulment of marriage, and all proceedings growing out of such actions
Nebraska .... Comp. St. 1929, Secs. 28(459), 43(203)	Juvenile Court[3]	Exclusive original jurisdiction over prosecutions for desertion or non-support of wife by husband. Jurisdiction over all cases for divorce or alimony
New Jersey .... Comp. St., Cum. Supp. 1911–24, Sec. 160(213); Supp. 1925–30, Sec. 53(215b[2])	a) Juvenile and Domestic Relations Court established in each county b) In any city of the first class in which there are three criminal courts, one of such courts shall be known as the Family Court	a) Jurisdiction over disputes involving the domestic relation, jurisdiction over which is now or may hereafter be vested in any court, except Chancery or Orphans' Court. Included in such jurisdiction are cases where gravamen of complaint is the failure of one member of family to discharge his legal obligation to another member; or to provide adequate support b) Jurisdiction over non-support or desertion cases; and over adultery cases if defendant, in writing, waives indictment and jury trial
New York .... Sess. L. 1924, Ch. 424, pp. 777–79; Sess. L. 1933, Ch. 482, pp. 1038–80[5]	a) One division of the Domestic Relations Court of the city of New York is the Family Court b) One or more parts of the City Court of Buffalo shall be designated as the Domestic Relations Court	a) Jurisdiction over proceedings to compel support of a wife or to punish for failure to do so. In exercising its jurisdiction, court has power to order either spouse to remain away from the other, to abstain from offensive conduct against other, to give proper attention to the home, to refrain from acts which tend to make the home an improper place for other b) Equity jurisdiction in addition to existing criminal jurisdiction to compel support of wife by the husband

* See page 143 for all numbered footnotes to this table.

TABLE LXXXIV (*Continued*)

Jurisdiction and Citation	Name and Place Where Found[1]	Jurisdiction of Court[2]
North Carolina ..... C. 1927, Supp. 1929, Secs. 1461(*f*)–1461(*h*), 1461(*o*)	Domestic Relations Court may be established in counties or in cities with population of twenty-five thousand or over; or such court may be a joint county and city court. Above provision does not apply to eleven named counties	Exclusive original jurisdiction over all cases where either spouse is charged with abandonment, non-support or desertion of the other, or with assault or assault and battery upon other. In divorce actions where there is a minor child involved, court shall make recommendations to the Superior Court as to the disposition of child
Ohio .... Complete G. C. 1931 (Page), Secs. 1532(1), 1532(2), 1532(4), 1532(6)– 1532(8), 1639	Domestic Relations Division of the Court of Common Pleas, established in six named counties[6]	Said division (see preceding column) shall be assigned all divorce and alimony cases[6]
Oklahoma .... St. 1931, Secs. 3858–59, 3867	Family Court established in every county now or hereafter having a population of more than ninety thousand	Concurrent jurisdiction and power with District Court over divorce, separate maintenance, and alimony cases, and proceedings arising out of divorce cases
Oregon .... C. 1930, Secs. 28(845)–28(849)	Department of Domestic Relations of the Circuit Court is substituted for independent court of domestic relations and established in all judicial districts comprising only one county and having population of over one hundred thousand[7]	Jurisdiction over proceedings against husband for failure to support wife. Said department shall also be assigned all uncontested divorce actions, and all divorce actions involving child under eighteen years of age[7]
Pennsylvania ...... St. 1920 (West), Sec. 13453	Juvenile Court[3]	Court may enforce law relative to desertion and non-support of wife by husband
Tennessee .... Private Acts 1929, Vol. II, Ch. 675, pp. 1979–91	Juvenile and Domestic Relations Court established in Hamilton County	Original and concurrent jurisdiction with Circuit and Chancery Courts over all divorce actions, including alimony and maintenance of wife. Original and exclusive jurisdiction over divorce actions involving disposition of minor children, and over cases involving desertion and non-support of wife by husband

§ 163]

TABLE LXXXIV (*Concluded*)

Jurisdiction and Citation	Name and Place Where Found[1]	Jurisdiction of Court[2]
Virginia .... C. 1930, Secs. 1937a, 1945, 1950, 1953a, 1953e	Juvenile and Domestic Relations Court established in every county, and in every city having a separate circuit court or a corporation court. In cities with population less than twenty-five thousand, the same court may be established for city and one or more counties	Exclusive original jurisdiction over all offenses except murder and manslaughter[8] committed by one member of family against another member of said family, and trial of all criminal warrants in which one member of family is complainant against another; provided that, in prosecutions for felonies other than murder and manslaughter,[8] jurisdiction is limited to that of examining magistrate. Also exclusive original jurisdiction over the prosecution and punishment of persons who knowingly contribute in any way to disruption of marital relation or the home. Exclusive original jurisdiction over cases involving desertion and non-support of a wife by her husband
West Virginia ...... Sess. L. 1921, Ch. 168, pp. 610–15; Sess. L. 1923, Ch. 134, pp. 488–92	*a*) Domestic Relations Court established in Cabell County *b*) Domestic Relations Court established in Monogalia County	*a*) Concurrent jurisdiction with Circuit Court over all causes pertaining to divorce, annulment of marriage, alimony and related proceedings, and to desertion and non-support of wife by husband *b*) Full and exclusive jurisdiction over all causes pertaining to desertion and non-support of wife by husband

[1] A few jurisdictions have courts called "courts of domestic relations" which have jurisdiction over children and over adults in their relations with children, but which do not have jurisdiction over relations between husband and wife as such. These courts are not included in the table above.

[2] Only the jurisdiction of the court is given as it affects rights of husband and wife as husband and wife. The reader should not assume that such is the sole jurisdiction of the court.

[3] The juvenile court is included because, in exercising the jurisdiction set forth above, it is in effect, if not in name, a family court (see **Sec. 277** for a general discussion of juvenile courts).

[4] **Hawaii:** See Revised Laws, 1925, Sections 2238–39, as to appointment of probation officers.

[5] **New York** (Const., Art. VI, Sec. 18): The legislature may establish courts of domestic relations as separate courts or as parts of other courts; and may confer (among other powers) jurisdiction upon them necessary to compel support of wife by husband.

[6] **Ohio** (Complete G. C. 1931 [Page], Sec. 1532[2]): A division of domestic relations was also established for Summit County, but the statute does not specifically provide for divorce jurisdiction and was therefore omitted in the table.

[7] **Oregon:** A statute providing for a court of domestic relations in every county which now or hereafter has a population of two hundred thousand or more still remains on the statute books, and may apply to a situation not covered by the provision set forth in the table. Such court, if established, has concurrent jurisdiction with the Circuit Court in proceedings against husband for failure to support wife (see C. 1930, Secs. 33[601], 33[605]).

[8] **Virginia** (C. 1930): The jurisdiction given in the table is that of a special justice of said court, as elected in cities of more than twenty-five thousand (Sec. 1950). When the special justice is appointed in counties and smaller cities, the word "rape" should be added to the words "murder, manslaughter" of the table (Sec. 1953e).

[§ 163

REFERENCES

Book

GOLDSTEIN, JONAH J. *The Family in Court* (1934). Reviewed in 34 Col. L. Rev. 1381–84 (1934).

Pamphlet

FLEXNER, B., R. OPPENHEIMER, and K. F. LENROOT. *The Child, the Family and the Court,* Part I (1929). (See pp. 71–72 of this pamphlet for numerous additional references.)

Reports

"Bibliography: Probation, Juvenile and Domestic Relations Courts, Crime, Psychiatric Treatment and Related Subjects"—*Proceedings of the National Probation Association* (1925), pp. 236–50. (Reprint: National Probation Association, New York, 1926. 15 pp.)

"Report of the Special Committee of the Florida State Bar Association Appointed to Consider Creation of Domestic Relations Courts and Needed Changes in Juvenile Laws," 4 Fla. S. Bar Assoc. L. Jour. 303–5 (1930).

Articles

AUMANN, F. R. "Domestic Relations Court in Ohio," 15 J. A. J. S. 89–93 (1931).

DAY, L. B. "The Development of the Family Court," Annals of Amer. Acad. of Pol. and Soc. Sci., Vol. 136, No. 225, pp. 105–11 (March, 1928).

HEILKER, HELEN. "Domestic Relations Court of Cincinnati," 3 Univ. of Cin. L. Rev. 458–61 (1929).

KANZLER, JACOB. "The Court of Domestic Relations of the State of Oregon for the County of Multnomah," 1 Ore. L. Rev. 41–47 (1921).

LIECK, ALBERT. "The English Police Court as a Court of Family Relations," 3 Idaho L. Jour. 136–42 (1933).

MORRISON, C. "Courts of Domestic Relations," 72 L. Jour. 235–36; 172 L. T. 303–5 (1931).

NORTH, V. L. "Milwaukee's Approach to Juvenile and Domestic Relations Cases," 18 Marq. L. Rev. 241–47 (1934).

SCHMIDT, W. A. "Ohio Domestic Relations Court," 16 Marq. L. Rev. 49–51 (1931).

WAITE, EDWARD F. "Courts of Domestic Relations," 5 Minn. L. Rev. 161–71 (1921).

Note

"Why Not a Court of Domestic Relations?" 72 Sol. Jour. 670–71, 786–87 (1928).

§ 163]

Section 164. Domicile of Wife

CROSS REFERENCES: Absolute divorce, residence qualifications, **Sec. 82**; Limited divorce, residence qualifications, **Sec. 123**; Domicile of child, **Sec. 238**; Domicile of infants, **Sec. 281**

The common law gave the wife little choice in the matter of her domicile. Upon marriage, the domicile of the husband became hers, and, if in the reasonable exercise of his rights as head of the family he changed it, hers followed. This rule of law is still generally recognized, but the rigor and absurdity of its application in certain situations led the courts to make exceptions to it. In varying degrees most courts now recognize that the wife should be allowed to acquire a separate domicile if she is under no duty to live with her spouse. Thus, it is generally conceded that she may establish a separate domicile for the purpose of bringing a divorce action; and probably she may do so for any purpose if she has cause for divorce. There is also some authority to the effect that she may acquire a domicile of her own if she lives apart from the husband for cause, though insufficient for divorce. Finally, that the common-law rule should be abolished in its entirety has found some following among the writers, but little favor in the cases.

Statutes dealing expressly with the subject of this section were found in thirty-three jurisdictions. Twelve jurisdictions have legislation of a general nature, and thirty have statutes dealing particularly with the wife's domicile or residence for the purpose: (1) of bringing a divorce action (eleven); (2) of voting, jury service, etc. (eleven); (3) or with the wife's "settlement" for poor relief (twenty-two). Only a small part of this legislation reflects the general emancipation of married women.

Five jurisdictions (**California, Georgia, Louisiana, Montana, North Dakota**) have substantially codified the general common-law rule in express terms. The same is implied by the statutes of nine jurisdictions (**California, Idaho, Louisiana, Montana, New Mexico, North Dakota, Ohio, Oklahoma, South Dakota**) which provide that the wife is bound to follow the husband in his change of residence. In addition, nineteen jurisdictions expressly recognize the general rule in respect to the wife's settlement for the purpose of poor relief, and one (**California**) in respect to her residence for the purpose of voting. An interesting exception to the husband's common-law right to change the family domicile is found in three jurisdictions to the effect that neither spouse can remove the other from the homestead without his consent

[§ 164

(**Illinois, Iowa, Utah**) unless the owner provides another one suitable to the condition in life of the family (**Illinois, Utah**).

Ten states expressly recognize the right of the wife to establish a separate domicile or residence for divorce purposes. Most of the jurisdictions defining the wife's settlement for purposes of poor relief make exception to the general rule that her settlement is that of the husband. The most common of these is to the effect that her premarital settlement continues if the husband has no settlement within the state (twelve jurisdictions) or within the United States (**Rhode Island**). **Pennsylvania** stands alone in allowing the wife to gain a settlement in the same manner as others, and a few other jurisdictions give her the same privilege if the husband has no settlement within the state (**Iowa, Massachusetts, New Jersey, Oklahoma**), or in the case of certain other specified situations (**Iowa, New Hampshire, New York**). In **Connecticut**, marriage of a pauper does not affect the settlement of either party, and **Maine** provides that a marriage induced by the collusion of town authorities does not change the wife's settlement.

The attention of the reader is particularly directed to the progressive legislation found in **Georgia, Hawaii, Maine, Massachusetts, Michigan, New Jersey, New York, North Carolina, Ohio, Pennsylvania, Virginia,** and **Wisconsin,** most of which is of recent origin. The statute in **Hawaii** broadly provides that marriage does not change the domicile of a woman domiciled in the Territory at the time of marriage, unless she assumes the actual domicile of the husband. A reasonable construction of the **Wisconsin** equal-rights statute would permit a wife to establish a separate domicile as if single. Some of the broad statutes containing a blanket removal of the disabilities of coverture seem to reach a similar result. **Georgia,** after laying down the general common-law rule, proceeds to emasculate it by providing that in case of voluntary separation the wife's domicile is determined as if she were single. **Michigan** provides that for political purposes the domicile of the wife is established by the same facts and rules of law as that of any other person. Other statutes expressly permitting the wife to acquire a separate domicile or residence for particular purposes may be classified as follows: for voting (**Maine, Massachusetts, Michigan, New Jersey, New York, North Carolina, Ohio, Pennsylvania, Virginia, Wisconsin**); for holding office (**Maine, Michigan, New Jersey, New York, Pennsylvania, Wisconsin**); for jury service (**Maine, New Jersey, Wisconsin**); for testacy, intestacy, taxation (**New Jersey**). None of these statutes purport to distinguish between a guilty or an innocent wife, but

§ 164]

in three jurisdictions the operation of the statute is confined to instances in which the spouses are living apart (**Massachusetts, North Carolina, Ohio**), or in which the husband has no residence within the state (**North Carolina**). As a practical matter, this limitation is not a serious one.

It is apparent that the legislation on the subject of the wife's domicile is both fragmentary and unsatisfactory. With the general abolition of the disabilities of coverture, the common-law rule that the wife's domicile follows that of the husband can no longer find support in the unity conception of husband and wife. If the rule can be supported at all today, it must be because of some theoretical utility which it has as a matter of public policy in preserving the integrity of the home. As a practical matter, it is doubtful if a penalty of this type inflicted upon the wife who leaves the husband's home without cause is of any influence in shaping her course of conduct. The philosophy of the present day demands that the wife have the freedom of a single woman in establishing a separate domicile, and enjoying the rights incident thereto, irrespective of the fact that she may be derelict in her duty toward the husband. Express legislation to that effect would be not only a frank admission of physical facts but also a forward step consistent with the modern status of married women.

A tabular summary of the statutory material outlined above and citations for the same follow.

TABLE LXXXV
DOMICILE OF WIFE

Jurisdiction and Citation	In General	Domicile for Divorce	Settlement for Poor Relief	Residence for Voting, Jury Service, etc.
California ......C. C. 1933 (Lake), Secs. 129, 156; Deering, Pol. C. 1931, Secs. 52, 1239; Sess. L. 1931, Ch. 110, p. 146, Sec. 2½	Husband is head of family. He may choose any reasonable place or mode of living, and the wife must conform thereto. The residence of husband is residence of wife	For purposes of divorce action, each spouse may have separate domicile or residence, depending upon proof of the fact, and not upon legal presumption	Residence of husband is residence of wife	Residence of husband is residence of wife (voting)

TABLE LXXXV (*Continued*)

Jurisdiction and Citation	In General	Domicile for Divorce	Settlement for Poor Relief	Residence for Voting, Jury Service, etc.
Connecticut ..... G. S. 1930, Secs. 1687–88			Wife's premarital settlement continues till husband gets settlement in state. If either party to marriage is a pauper or within one year prior thereto has been a pauper, such marriage does not affect settlement of either	
Delaware .... R. C. 1915, Sec. 1461			Legal settlement of head of family is the settlement of his wife	
Georgia .... C. 1926, C. C., Secs. 2183, 2187	Domicile of wife is that of husband, but in case of a voluntary separation and living apart, her domicile is determined as if she were single	In case of a pending application for divorce, the wife's domicile is determined as if she were single		
Hawaii .... Sess. L. 1931, Act 51, p. 43	Marriage does not change domicile of woman domiciled in this Territory at time of marriage, unless she assumes actual domicile of husband after marriage			
Idaho .... Comp. St. 1919, Secs. 4640, 4655	Husband is head of family. He may choose any reasonable place or mode of living, and wife must conform thereto	In divorce action, presumption of law that domicile of husband is domicile of wife does not apply. After separation, each may have separate domicile depending upon actual residence and not upon legal presumption		

§ 164]

TABLE LXXXV (*Continued*)

Jurisdiction and Citation	In General	Domicile for Divorce	Settlement for Poor Relief	Residence for Voting, Jury Service, etc.
Illinois .... Cahill, R. S. 1931, Ch. 68, Sec. 16				Neither spouse can remove the other from their homestead without his consent unless the owner provides another homestead suitable to the condition in life of the family
Indiana .... Burns, Ann. St. 1926, Sec. 12259			Wife has settlement of husband if he has any in state; otherwise, her own at time of marriage is not lost; but if spouses reside for six months in state before husband abandons wife, her settlement is in township where she resided at time of abandonment	
Iowa .... C. 1927, Secs. 5311, 10149			Wife has settlement of husband if he has one in state. If not, or if she lives apart from or is abandoned by him, she may acquire a settlement as if single. In case of divorce, death of husband or abandonment by him, wife may resume her premarital settlement if both settlements were in the state	Neither spouse can remove the other from the homestead without his consent
Kansas .... R. S. 1923, Sec. 39(305)			Wife's settlement follows that of husband if he has any in state; otherwise, her own at time of marriage is not lost or suspended by the marriage	

[§ 164

TABLE LXXXV (*Continued*)

Jurisdiction and Citation	In General	Domicile for Divorce	Settlement for Poor Relief	Residence for Voting, Jury Service, etc.
Louisiana ...... C. C., Arts. 39, 120	Wife is bound to live with husband and follow him wherever he chooses to reside. She has no other domicile than that of her husband			
Maine .... R. S. 1930, Ch. 6, Sec. 5; Ch. 33, Sec. 1			Wife has settlement of husband if he has one in state, otherwise her own settlement is not affected by the marriage. Her settlement is not affected by a marriage procured by collusion of town authorities	For purposes of voting, office holding, or jury service, each spouse may have a separate residence, to be determined as in the case of other persons
Massachusetts .. G. L. 1932, Ch. 51, Sec. 1; Ch. 116, Sec. 1			Wife has settlement of husband, but, if he has none in state, she retains her premarital settlement or may acquire one in manner provided for others	Wife dwelling or having her home separate and apart from husband is deemed to reside at the place where she dwells or has her home, for the purpose of voting and registration
Michigan .... Comp. L. 1929, Sec. 8255; Sess. L. 1931, No. 265, p. 449			Woman of full age acquires settlement of husband by marrying if he have any	Domicile of wife for purpose of voting, office holding or other political purpose is established by same facts and rules of law as that of any other person, unaffected by domicile of husband
Montana .... R. C. 1921, Secs. 33, 5783	Residence of husband is presumptively the residence of wife. Husband is head of family. He may choose any reasonable place or mode of living and wife must conform thereto			

§ 164]

TABLE LXXXV (*Continued*)

Jurisdiction and Citation	In General	Domicile for Divorce	Settlement for Poor Relief	Residence for Voting, Jury Service, etc.
Nebraska .... Comp. St. 1929, Sec. 42(339)		If wife brings suit for limited divorce, she is deemed an inhabitant of the state if she resides in it, although the husband resides elsewhere		
New Hampshire . Pub. L. 1926, Ch. 105, Sec. 1			Wife has settlement of husband if he have one in state; otherwise her own at time of marriage continues. But she may gain a settlement of her own by the ownership of property and payment of taxes thereon	
New Jersey ..... Comp. St., Supp. 1925–30, Sec. 124(19); Cum. Supp. 1911–24, Sec. 161(164)			Wife has settlement of husband if he has one in state. If not, her settlement is that which she had at time she became a resident and domiciliary of county or municipality wherein relief is sought; provided she has not in lieu thereof gained a settlement in manner provided for others	Domicile of wife is established by the same facts and rules of law as that of any other person, for the purpose of voting, office holding, testacy, intestacy, jury service, taxation
New Mexico .... St. Ann. 1929, Secs. 68(102), 68(504)	Husband is head of family. He may choose any reasonable place or mode of living and wife must conform thereto	If wife is plaintiff, residence by husband in state inures to her benefit		

[§ 164

TABLE LXXXV (*Continued*)

Jurisdiction and Citation	In General	Domicile for Divorce	Settlement for Poor Relief	Residence for Voting, Jury Service, etc.
New York ...... Cahill, Consol. L. 1930, Ch. 14, Sec. 61; Ch. 49½, Sec. 54; Cahill, Civ. Prac. Act 1931, Sec. 1166		If wife dwells within state when she commences action against husband for divorce or separation, she is deemed a resident thereof, although husband resides elsewhere	Domicile of wife is that of husband, except that widow or woman divorced or separated by judicial decree has settlement she had at time of husband's death, divorce, or separation; but she may subsequently gain a new settlement. On desertion, wife retains settlement of husband at time of desertion and if his whereabouts remain unknown she may after one year acquire a separate settlement which continues till husband is located and is shown to have new settlement	Domicile of wife is established by same facts and rules of law as that of any other person for purposes of voting and office holding
North Carolina .. C. 1927, Secs. 1342, 5937(*a*)			Wife's settlement is that of husband if he has one in state; otherwise, her own at time of marriage is not lost or suspended	For purpose of voting and registration, residence of wife living with husband is where husband resides; if wife lives separate and apart or if husband has no legal residence in state, then her residence is where she actually resides
North Dakota ... Comp. L. 1913, Secs. 14, 2501, 4399, 4408	Residence of husband is presumptively the residence of wife. Husband is head of family. He may choose any reasonable place or mode of living and the wife must conform thereto	In divorce actions, presumption of law that domicile of husband is that of wife does not apply. After separation each may have separate domicile depending for proof upon actual residence and not legal presumption	Residence of wife follows that of husband if he has any in state; otherwise her own at time of marriage is not lost	

§ 164]

TABLE LXXXV (*Continued*)

Jurisdiction and Citation	In General	Domicile for Divorce	Settlement for Poor Relief	Residence for Voting, Jury Service, etc.
Ohio .... Complete G. C. 1931, Secs. 4785(31), 7996, 11982	Husband is head of family. He may choose any reasonable place or mode of living and wife must conform thereto	When wife sues for divorce or alimony, the residence of husband shall not be so construed as to preclude her from the provisions of the chapter on divorce and alimony		In determining residence for voting purposes, the place where family of wife resides is considered her place of residence; but when spouses live apart, the place where either resides for the required period is his or her place of residence[1]
Oklahoma ...... St. 1931, Secs. 680, 1652, 7562	Husband is head of family. He may choose any reasonable place or mode of living and wife must conform thereto	Wife who resides in state at time of applying for divorce is deemed a resident of the state, though her husband resides elsewhere	Wife has settlement of husband if he has one in state; otherwise, she may obtain one by six months' continuous residence in any county	
Pennsylvania ... St. 1920 (West), Sec. 16996, amd. by Cum. Supp. 1928 (West), p. 733; Cum. Supp. 1928 (West), Sec. 14582(*a*)			Wife during marriage, whether living with husband or apart, or after husband's death, is deemed to be settled in place where she has gained settlement in manner provided by law for any other person	Domicile of wife for purpose of voting or holding office is determined for all purposes as if single
Rhode Island ... G. L. 1923, Sec. 1508			Wife's settlement is that of husband if he has any in state or United States; otherwise, wife retains her premarital settlement	

[1] By a 1923 amendment, **Ohio** provided that "the voting residence of a married woman may be determined in the same manner as that of a married man" (Sess. L. 1923, p. 119; Page, Ann. G. C. 1926, Sec. 4865). In 1929, this provision with others was repealed and a new election code was adopted, which contains the provision given in the table but does not seem to carry forward the 1923 legislation (Sess. L. 1929, p. 307).

[§ 164

TABLE LXXXV (*Continued*)

Jurisdiction and Citation	In General	Domicile for Divorce	Settlement for Poor Relief	Residence for Voting, Jury Service, etc.
South Carolina .. C. of L. 1922, C. C., Sec. 2284			Wife has settlement of husband if he has any in state; otherwise, her own at time of marriage is not lost or suspended by the marriage	
South Dakota ... Comp. L. 1929, Secs. 160, 168, 10038	Husband is head of family. He may choose any reasonable place or mode of living and wife must conform thereto	In divorce actions, presumption of law that husband's domicile is domicile of wife does not apply after separation; each may have separate domicile, depending for proof upon actual residence and not legal presumption	Wife's settlement follows that of husband if he has one in state; otherwise, her own at time of marriage is not lost or suspended by the marriage	
Utah .... R. S. 1933, 19-5-60, 40-2-10			Wife has settlement of husband if he has one in state; if not, or if she lives apart from or is abandoned by him, she may acquire a settlement as if unmarried. Wife's premarital settlement may, at her election, be resumed upon husband's death, or if she is divorced or abandoned by him, if both settlements were in the state	Neither spouse can remove the other from their homestead without his consent unless the owner provides another homestead suitable to the condition in life of the family
Vermont .... G. L. 1917, Sec. 4216			Wife who lived with husband in town where he last resided for three years, supporting himself and family, is deemed to have gained a residence in such town	

§ 164]

TABLE LXXXV (*Concluded*)

Jurisdiction and Citation	In General	Domicile for Divorce	Settlement for Poor Relief	Residence for Voting, Jury Service, etc.
Virginia .... C. 1930, Sec. 82a				For purpose of registering and voting, the residence of wife is not controlled by residence or domicile of husband
Wisconsin ...... St. 1931, Secs. 6.015, 49.02	"Women shall have the same rights and privileges under the law as men in . . . . the choice of residence for voting purposes, jury service, holding office, ... and in all other respects"		Wife follows and has settlement of husband if he has one in state; otherwise, her own at time of marriage is not lost or suspended by the marriage (but see first column)	Women have same rights as men in choice of residence for voting purposes, jury service, holding office
Wyoming ...... R. S. 1931, Sec. 35(133)		If at time wife exhibits bill for divorce she resides in the state, she is deemed a resident thereof, although husband resides elsewhere		

REFERENCES

Books

GOODRICH, HERBERT F. *Handbook on the Conflict of Laws,* pp. 44–50 (1927).

MADDEN, JOSEPH W. *The Law of Persons and Domestic Relations,* pp. 146–47 (1931).

SCHOULER, JAMES. *Marriage, Divorce, Separation and Domestic Relations,* 6th ed., Vol. II, Sec. 1642 (1921).

STIMSON, F. J. *American Statute Law,* Secs. 6030–31 (1886).

Articles

BEALE, JOSEPH HENRY. "Domicil of a Married Woman," 2 So. L. Quar. 93–111 (1917).

HOGG, F. D. "Domicil of a Married Woman in Relation to Divorce," 6 Can. B. R. 655–69 (1928).

LEVIT, ALBERT. "Domicil of a Married Woman," 91 Cent. L. Jour. 4–14, 24–33 (1920).

———. "Recent Domicil Cases," 20 Ill. L. Rev. 146–52 (1926).

PARKS, JAMES LEWIS. "Domicil of a Married Woman," 8 Minn. L. Rev. 28–39 (1923).

[§ 164

Annotations

"Inability of Husband to Support Wife as Excuse for Her Refusal to Live with Him," L. R. A. 1915A 222–23.

"Separate Domicil of Wife for Purposes Other than Suit for Divorce, Separation, or Maintenance," 75 A. L. R. 1254–73 (1931).

Notes

"Desertion—Antenuptial Contracts as to Residence," 15 Col. L. Rev. 277–78 (1915).

"Divorce and Changed Domicile," *H——, A.,* v. *H——, G. M.,* 139 L. T. Rep. 412 (1928)—165 L. T. 558 (1928) ; 2 So. Calif. L. Rev. 188–89 (1928) ; *Torlonia* v. *Torlonia,* 108 Conn. 292 ; 142 A. 843 (1928)—2 So. Calif. L. Rev. 188–89 (1928) ; 38 Yale L. Jour. 381–85 (1929).

"Domicile—Agreement between Husband and Wife to Live Apart," 9 Ore. L. Rev. 393–95 (1930).

"The Domicile of a Wife," 28 Harv. L. Rev. 196–98 (1914).

"Right of Married Woman Living Amicably with Husband to Acquire Separate Domicile," 20 Va. L. Rev. 244–52 (1933).

"Maintenance of Separate Domicile by Married Woman," *Commonwealth* v. *Rutherfoord,* 160 Va. 524 ; 169 S. E. 909 (1933)—82 Univ. of Pa. L. Rev. 55–56 (1933) ; 19 Cor. L. Quar. 82–85 (1933) ; 47 Harv. L. Rev. 348–49 (1933) ; 18 Minn. L. Rev. 476–78 (1934) ; 20 Va. L. Rev. 244–50 (1933).

"Presumption as to Domicile of a Married Woman for Purpose of Workmen's Compensation," *Colorado Fuel & Iron Company* v. *Industrial Commission of Colorado,* 93 Colo. 188 ; 24 P. (2d) 1117 (1933)—6 Rocky Mt. L. Rev. 80–81 (1933).

Section 165. Crimes by Wife—Coercion

CROSS REFERENCE : Torts by wife, **Sec. 157**

One of the curiosities of the common law was the rule that a wife committing a crime in the presence of her husband was presumed to be acting under his coercion and should be excused, unless shown to be acting of her own free will. It was a curious rule because it was apparently peculiar to common-law countries and was not recognized in Scotland. The origin, the limits, and the reasons for the rule are all more or less obscure. The reason most commonly given, that the wife should be excused because she acts in fear of or out of affection for her husband, would seem to apply in whole or in large part to the relationship of parent and child, master and servant, overlord and retainer, etc. But in none of these cases was mere coercion an excuse for criminal acts. Doubtless the common law wished to encourage obedience by the wife,

§ 165]

but this policy applies to other relationships where obedience has received no such reward. It is generally admitted that this common-law rule was illogical and artificial at the time of its origin. At present with our changed legal and economic situation this presumption seems indefensible. One is even tempted to agree with the bitter statement of Dickens[1] that, "if the law presumes that, the law is an ass—an idiot."

Modern decisions have modified the ancient rule. Originally the rule of coercion applied to all crimes and the presumption was absolute. Today wherever the presumption still exists it is rebuttable. It is generally agreed that the presumption will not be inferred in the more serious crimes of treason, murder, homicide, and robbery. Decisions may be found in which it is held that the presumption does not apply to perjury, keeping a gaming or bawdy house, or to certain illegal dealings in intoxicating liquors. (See references at end of section.)

Five states (**Colorado, Iowa, Kansas, Kentucky, Tennessee**) and some federal courts have held that the presumption of coercion is abolished by implication by the passage of legislation placing husband and wife upon a more or less equal legal basis.

In only nineteen states have statutes been found dealing expressly with this ancient rule. These statutes do not follow any general pattern, and some of them are obscure in meaning. The express statutes are set out in the table following. In only three states (**Minnesota, New York, Washington**) is the defense of coercion abolished in toto. In **Texas** coercion is made ground for mitigating the punishment. Six states (**Arkansas, Colorado, Georgia, Illinois, Maryland, Nevada**) have abolished the presumption of coercion, but recognize coercion as a defense in some modified form, if actual coercion is shown. The statutes of six states (**Arizona, California, Idaho, Montana, Texas, Utah**), while modifying the common-law rule, are silent as to the presumption of coercion. Four other states (**North Dakota, Oklahoma, Oregon, South Dakota**) have passed modifying statutes but expressly provide that coercion shall be presumed.

As shown in the table, coercion as a defense does not apply to any felony in three states (**Arizona, California, Montana**); nor to capital offenses in five states (**Colorado, Idaho, Illinois, Nevada, Utah**). In one (**Oregon**) it does not apply to murder and in another (**Georgia**) to offenses punishable by death or life imprisonment. In three states it is provided that coercion shall be no defense in a long list of crimes

---

[1] *Oliver Twist,* chap. 51.

specifically named: **North Dakota** (twenty offenses), **Oklahoma** (eighteen offenses), **South Dakota** (twenty-two offenses).

Most of the foregoing statutes seem unsatisfactory because they do not go far enough. If the ancient rule ever had any reason for being, that reason is no longer in existence. It seems perfectly obvious that all states not only should abolish the presumption of coercion but should also provide that actual coercion of a wife by her husband shall no longer be an excuse except to the extent that any person is excused when acting under compulsion of a third party. The equalizing process of modern legislation should apply in general to duties as well as to rights. There is no reason to continue an ancient privilege to violate the criminal law.

The table follows.

TABLE LXXXVI

COERCION BY HUSBAND OF WIFE IN THE COMMISSION OF CRIME

Jurisdiction and Citation	Coercion a Defense	Extent of Defense and Limitations Thereon	Presumptions; Other Provisions
Arizona R. C. 1928, Sec. 4489	Yes	All crimes except felonies; where wife acts "under the threats, command or coercion" of husband	Statute silent on presumption of coercion
Arkansas Crawf. and Moses, Dig. 1921, Sec. 2304	Yes	All crimes, "if it appear from all the facts and circumstances of the case that violence, threats or coercion were used"	No presumption of coercion. Husband shall be prosecuted as principal and receive the punishment which would have been inflicted on the wife if she had been found guilty
California P. C. 1933 (Lake), Sec. 26	Yes	All crimes except felonies; where wife acts under husband's "threats, command or coercion"	Statute silent on presumption of coercion
Colorado Comp. L. 1921, G. S., Sec. 6641	Yes	All crimes except those punishable by death: "provided it appears from all the facts and circumstances of the case that violent threats, command or coercion were used"	No presumption of coercion. Husband shall be prosecuted as principal and receive the punishment which would otherwise have been inflicted on the wife if she had been found guilty
Georgia C. 1926, P. C., Sec. 38	Yes	All crimes except those punished by death or perpetual imprisonment: "provided, it appears, from all the facts and circumstances of the case, that violent threats, command or coercion were used"	Husband shall be prosecuted as principal, and, if convicted, shall receive the punishment which otherwise would have been inflicted on the wife, if she had been found guilty. No presumption of coercion
Idaho Comp. St. 1919, Sec. 8090	Yes	All crimes except those punishable by death, where wife acts under "threats, commands or coercion"	Statue silent on presumption of coercion

§ 165]

TABLE LXXXVI (*Continued*)

Jurisdiction and Citation	Coercion a Defense	Extent of Defense and Limitations Thereon	Presumptions; Other Provisions
Illinois .... Cahill, R. S. 1931, Ch. 38, Sec. 625	Yes	All crimes except those punishable with death; "provided, it appear, from all the facts and circumstances of the case, that violent threats, command or coercion were used"	Husband shall be prosecuted as principal, and receive the punishment which would otherwise have been inflicted on the wife if she had been found guilty. No presumption of coercion
Maryland .... Bagby, Ann. C. 1924, Art. 35, Sec. 4A, added by Sess. L. 1931, Ch. 398, p. 988	Yes	All crimes, except treason and murder, when committed in the presence of and under the coercion of the husband	Presumption of coercion abolished
Minnesota ...... G. S. 1923, Sec. 9911	No	"It is no defense for a married woman charged with crime that the alleged act was committed by her in the presence of her husband"	
Montana .... R. C. 1921, Sec. 10729	Yes	All crimes except felonies, where wife acts under husband's "threats, command or coercion"	Statute silent on presumption of coercion
Nevada .... Comp. L. 1929 (Hillyer), Sec. 9952	Yes	All crimes except those punishable with death; "provided, it appear, from all the facts and circumstances of the case, that violent threats, command or coercion were used"	No presumption of coercion
New York ...... Cahill, Consol. L. 1930, Ch. 41, Sec. 1092	No	"It is not a defense to a married woman charged with crime that the alleged criminal act was committed by her in the presence of her husband"	
North Dakota ... Comp. L. 1913, Secs. 9211–15	Yes	All crimes, except twenty, viz.: treason, murder, manslaughter, maiming, attempt to kill, rape, abduction, abuse of children, seduction, abortion either upon herself or another female, concealing the death of an infant whether her own or that of another, fraudulently producing a false child whether as her own or that of another, bigamy, incest, the crime against nature or sodomy, indecent exposure, obscene exhibition of books and prints, keeping a bawdy or other disorderly house, misplacing a railway switch, and obstructing a railway track	Presumption of subjection, but may be rebutted by any facts showing that the wife acted freely. When rebutted, subjection to husband is no excuse unless there is actual compulsion by use of force and fear

[§ 165

TABLE LXXXVI (*Continued*)

Jurisdiction and Citation	Coercion a Defense	Extent of Defense and Limitations Thereon	Presumptions; Other Provisions
Oklahoma ...... St. 1931, Secs. 1800–1804	Yes	All crimes except eighteen, viz.: treason, murder, manslaughter, maiming, attempt to kill, rape, abduction, abuse of children, seduction, abortion either upon herself or upon another female, concealing the death of an infant whether her own or that of another, fraudulently producing a false child whether as her own or that of another, bigamy, incest, crime against nature, indecent exposure, obscene exhibition of books and prints, keeping a bawdy or other disorderly house	Wife's subjection is inferred from the fact that she committed the act in the presence and with the assent of her husband. This presumption rebuttable by any facts showing that the wife acted freely. Compulsion must be actual and by use of force or fear
Oregon .... C. 1930, Sec. 9(807)	Yes	All felonies, except murder. (Statute silent as to misdemeanors: by implication coercion would be a defense)	The presumption of coercion is disputable and may be overcome by other evidence
South Dakota ... Comp. L. 1929, Secs. 3587–91	Yes	All crimes except twenty-two, viz.: treason, misprision of treason, criminal syndicalism, murder, manslaughter, maiming, attempt to kill, rape, abduction, abuse of children, seduction, abortion either upon herself or another female, concealing death of an infant whether her own or that of another, fraudulently producing a false child whether as her own or that of another, bigamy, incest, crime against nature, indecent exposure, obscene exhibitions of books and prints, keeping a bawdy or other disorderly house, misplacing a railway switch, and obstructing a railway track	Presumption of coercion exists when wife acts in the presence of and with the assent of the husband. It is rebuttable by any facts showing that the wife acted freely. Subjection does not exist unless there be actual compulsion by use of force or fear
Texas .... Complete St. 1928, P. C., Arts. 32, 33	No	Wife who commits an offense by command or persuasion of her husband shall in no case be punished with death and in cases not capital she shall receive only one-half the punishment to which she would otherwise be liable	A husband who instigates or aids a wife in the commission of an offense shall, at the discretion of the jury, be punished by death in capital cases and in other cases the punishment shall be doubled
Utah .... R. S. 1933, 103-1-40	Yes	All crimes, except those punishable by death, where wife acts under husband's "threats, command or coercion"	Statute silent on presumption of coercion

TABLE LXXXVI (*Concluded*)

Jurisdiction and Citation	Coercion a Defense	Extent of Defense and Limitations Thereon	Presumptions; Other Provisions
Washington .... Remington, Comp. St. 1922, Sec. 2255	No	"It is no defense for a married woman charged with the commission of crime, that the alleged act committed by her was committed in the presence of her husband"	

REFERENCES

Books

BISHOP, JOEL PRENTISS. *Criminal Law,* 9th ed., Vol. 1, Secs. 356–66 (1923).

RUSSELL, SIR WILLIAM OLDNALL. *Crimes and Misdemeanors,* 8th ed., Vol. 1, pp. 94–103 (1923).

Article

PERKINS, R. M. "Doctrine of Coercion," 19 Ia. L. Rev. 507–20 (1934).

Notes

"Effect of Married Women's Acts upon Presumption of Husband's Coercion," 22 Ill. L. Rev. 674 76 (1928)

"Husband Liable for Wife's Crime in Home," *People* v. *Sybisloo,* 261 Mich. 1; 184 N. W. 410 (1921)—20 Mich. L. Rev. 547–48 (1922).

"Presence of Husband When Unlawful Acts Committed by Wife, Presumption of Coercion," *State* v. *Renslow,* 209 Ia. 982; 230 N. W. 316 (1930)—17 Va. L. Rev. 191–92 (1930).

"Presumption of Coercion—Effect of Married Women's Act," *King* v. *City of Owensboro,* 187 Ky. 21; 218 S. W. 297 (1920)—34 Harv. L. Rev. 89–90 (1920).

"Presumption of Coercion—Rebuttal," *Tomasello* v. *State,* 91 Ind. App. 970; 173 N. E. 235 (1930)—6 Notre Dame Lawy. 264–65 (1931).

"Forgery of Cheques by Wife," *Greenwood* v. *Martin's Bank,* (1932) 1 K. B. 371— 48 L. Quar. Rev. 304–6 (1932).

"Is the Presumption of Marital Coercion Vanishing as a Defense?" *State* v. *Asper,* 35 N. M. 203; 292 P. 225 (1930)—3 Rocky Mt. L. Rev. 220–22 (1931).

"Responsibility of a Husband for the Crime of His Wife Committed in His Presence," *Haning* v. *United States,* 59 F. (2d) 942 (1932)—11 Tenn. L. Rev. 57– 59 (1932).

Annotations

"Coercion as a Defense to Crime—Husband and Wife," 106 Amer. St. Rep. 725–27 (1906).

"Criminal Responsibility of Husband for Violation of Liquor Law by Wife," 19 A. L. R. 136–40 (1922); 27 A. L. R. 312 (1923).

"Effect of Coverture upon Criminal Responsibility of a Woman," 4 A. L. R. 266– 83 (1919); 71 A. L. R. 1116–30 (1931).

"Liability of a Married Woman for Crimes Committed in Her Husband's Presence," 33 Amer. St. Rep. 89–96 (1893).

[§ 165

Section 166. Crimes by One Spouse Injurious to the Other

CROSS REFERENCES: Relationship of husband and wife in general, **Sec. 149;**
Criminal liability for desertion and non-support, **Sec. 162;** Suits by one spouse
against the other, **Sec. 180;** Husband and wife as witnesses for and against
each other, **Sec. 226**

In general, husband and wife are criminally liable at common law
for offenses directed against the other spouse; for example, for murder,
manslaughter, mayhem, aggravated assault. However, because of the
husband and wife relationship there are certain exceptions to the general
rule, and it is with such exceptions that the present section is concerned.
The crimes to be discussed fall into two groups: first, crimes against
the property of the other spouse (arson, larceny, and embezzlement);
second, crimes against the person of the other spouse (assault and
battery, rape, with incidental mention of libel and slander). In Volume
I, **Section 46** is a discussion of bigamy, so far as it concerns the marital
relation. Adultery, so far as it concerns divorce, is discussed in Volume
II, **Sections 65, 118.** Other aspects of adultery though interesting to the
student of criminal law may be dismissed with a reference to the excel-
lent article of Geoffrey May (see references at end of section). Criminal
liability for desertion and non-support as contained in the "Lazy Husband Laws" has been discussed in **Section 162.** The reader's attention
is also called to the fact that many jurisdictions have statutes making
criminal the placing of the wife in a house of prostitution by the husband.

The fiction of the earlier common law that, in legal contemplation,
husband and wife were one resulted in the rule that neither spouse was
guilty of arson for burning the property of the other. However, a contrary result has been reached in the majority of the later cases in the
United States (*State* v. *Shaw,* 79 Kan. 396; 100 P. 78 [1909]; see also
citations following this section); and in two states (**Michigan, Wisconsin**), when judicial decisions adopted the older common-law rule, that
view was changed by statutes making the husband or wife guilty. Ten
jurisdictions have been found with express legislation on this point. In
four (**Alabama, Michigan, Oregon, Wisconsin**) it is provided that
either spouse may be convicted of arson for burning the other's property.
In five (**Alaska, Hawaii, Iowa, Maine, Massachusetts**) the statutes
provide that a wife is guilty for burning her husband's property. Probably the courts in these jurisdictions would hold that the husband is
similarly guilty. **Vermont** provides that a wife who burns a building
owned by herself or husband or by them jointly with intent to defraud
an insurance company is guilty of arson.

§ 166]

The most frequent offenses against the property of the other spouse are those which would constitute larceny if done by a third person. Again the "unity" fiction of the earlier law resulted in the rule that neither spouse was guilty of larceny for such acts. Later cases in the United States have been divided. A few courts, relying on the Married Women's Property Acts, have held that a spouse may be guilty (*Beasley* v. *State,* 138 Ind. 552; 38 N. E. 35 [1894]; see also references at end of this section). But according to the majority view, a unity of a social relationship, though not of property, still exists; consequently neither spouse is guilty (*People ex rel. Troare* v. *McClelland,* 146 Misc. 545; 263 N. Y. S. 403 [1933]); and the more recent cases have adopted this view (see citations following this section). Only one jurisdiction, **Hawaii,** has been found with express legislation; and, unfortunately, the statute adopts the rule of no liability for larceny. Logically, if the unity fiction still exists as to larceny, it should also apply to embezzlement by one spouse of the property of the other. The few cases found on this question, cited at the end of the section, are divided.

The rule of the early English law that a husband had a right to chastise his wife was not adopted in this country; and it is generally true today that either spouse may be convicted of a criminal assault or assault and battery upon the other. However, there has been a tendency in some jurisdictions to refuse to prosecute for a technical but not very serious assault or battery, a tendency reflected in part in the terms of the express legislation on the subject found in six states. Thus, the husband is guilty if he brutally (**Maryland**) strikes or beats the wife (**Delaware, Georgia, Maryland**), or otherwise cruelly mistreats her (**Georgia**); or if he unlawfully, wilfully, or wantonly assaults or treats her with cruelty or violence (**New Mexico**). In **Tennessee** the statute merely states that he is to be punished for an assault and battery upon the wife; and in **Massachusetts,** if he is convicted of an assault upon her, the court may require him to give a recognizance for his good behavior. **Georgia** has a statute somewhat similar to the **Massachusetts** provision. **Delaware** and **Maryland** provide that a husband who is guilty as above may be punished by whipping. Statutes in **Alabama** and **North Carolina** which give the court of domestic relations jurisdiction over an assault or an assault and battery by one spouse upon the other (**Sec. 163**) impliedly recognize a criminal liability.

A husband cannot directly rape his wife even though she be unwilling, for he is deemed to have a legal right to sexual intercourse. But he may be guilty of rape for aiding and abetting the rape of his wife

[§ 166

by a third person, or for forcing the third person to do so. At common law neither spouse is guilty for a criminal libel directed against the other. It has been held, however, that the husband may be criminally liable for a libel or slander of the wife under the general libel and slander statutes, although the contrary has also been held (see cases cited at the end of this section relating to rape and to libel and slander).

Although the homicide of a spouse has not been considered in this section, statutes in **North Dakota** and **South Dakota** are of interest. It is there provided that, whenever the grade or punishment of homicide depends on its having been committed under circumstances evincing a depraved mind or unusual cruelty, the jury may consider the fact that any domestic relation existed between the accused and the person killed, in determining the moral quality of the act.

The recognition given the unity fiction by modern courts (for a late case, see *People* v. *MacMullen,* 134 Cal. App. 81; 24 P. (2d) 794 [1933]) is unfortunate; and it is surprising that the legislatures have not exploded the myth upon the failure of the courts to do so. The larceny cases furnish the most striking example of the retention of the fiction; and according to the majority view, either spouse may still steal from the other with impunity. It is true that the married women's legislation, in and of itself, technically does not destroy the common-law theory of unity; but it seems obvious to the writer that the legislation permitting a wife to own her own property, to contract, to sue and to be sued as if single, to act as executrix or administratrix, etc., is unmistakable evidence of a fundamental change in the concept of the husband and wife relationship. It is a recognition of the understanding today that husband and wife have separate legal entities. And if the common law is to justify its claim of flexibility, it should view the crimes of either spouse in the same light as those of a third person. It is sometimes argued that public policy is against legal interference with controversies between spouses. That may have weight as applied to torts between them, but it should not operate to justify criminal offenses which injure the state.

Citations to the statutes discussed are given below, followed by a collection of a few of the more interesting cases on the subject.

Alabama, C. 1923, Sec. 3295; Sess. L. 1927, No. 225, p. 239, Sec. 2; **Alaska,** Comp. L. 1913, Sec. 1914; **Delaware,** R. C. 1915, Sec. 4712; **Georgia,** C. 1926, P. C., Secs. 104, 1324; **Hawaii,** R. L. 1925, Secs. 4178, 4291; **Iowa,** C. 1927, Sec. 12991(b6); **Maine,** R. S. 1930, Ch. 130, Sec. 5; **Maryland,** Bagby, Ann. C. 1924, Art. 27, Secs. 15, 16; **Massachusetts,** G. L. 1932, Ch. 266, Sec. 6; Ch. 279, Sec. 12; **Michigan,** Comp. L. 1929, Sec. 16939; **New Mexico,** St. Ann. 1929, Sec. 35(608); **North Carolina,** C. 1927, Supp. 1929, Sec. 1461(h); **North Dakota,** Comp. L.

1913, Sec. 9461; **Oregon,** C. 1930, Sec. 14(305); **South Dakota,** Comp. L. 1929, Sec. 4011; **Tennessee,** C. 1932, Sec. 10800; **Vermont,** G. L. 1917, Sec. 6854; **Wisconsin,** St. 1931, Sec. 343.06.

CASES

1. A spouse may be guilty of arson for burning the other's property: *Garrett* v. *State,* 109 Ind. 527; 10 N. E. 570 (1886); *Emig* v. *Daum,* 1 Ind. App. 146; 27 N. E. 322 (1890); *Jordan* v. *State,* 142 Ind. 422; 41 N. E. 817 (1895); *State* v. *Shaw,* 79 Kan. 396; 100 P. 78 (1909); *State* v. *Roth,* 117 Minn. 404; 136 N. W. 12 (1912). Contra: *Snyder* v. *People,* 26 Mich. 105 (1872); *Kopcyznski* v. *State,* 137 Wis. 358; 118 N. W. 863 (1908). (The rule in **Michigan** and **Wisconsin** has been changed by statute—see text above.)

2. A spouse is not guilty of larceny for stealing the other's property: *Thomas* v. *Thomas,* 51 Ill. 162 (1869); *State* v. *Banks,* 48 Ind. 197 (1874); *Lamphier* v. *State,* 70 Ind. 317 (1880) (see below for later **Indiana** case contra); *State* v. *Arnold,* 182 Minn. 313; 235 N. W. 373 (1931); *People ex rel. Troare* v. *McClelland,* 146 Misc. 545; 263 N. Y. S. 403 (1933); *State* v. *Parker,* 3 Ohio Dec. (Reprint) 551 (1882); *State* v. *Phillips,* 85 Ohio St. 317; 97 N. E. 976 (1912); *Walker* v. *Reamy,* 36 Pa. St. 410 (1860) (Dictum); *Overton* v. *State,* 43 Tex. 616 (1875). Contra: *Hunt* v. *State,* 72 Ark. 241; 79 S. W. 769 (1904); *Beasley* v. *State,* 138 Ind. 552; 38 N. E. 35 (1894); *State* v. *Koontz,* 124 Kan. 216; 257 P. 944 (1927).

3. A spouse may be guilty of embezzlement of the other's property: *People* v. *Graff,* 59 Cal. App. 706; 211 P. 829 (1922); *People* v. *Kirkpatrick,* 77 Cal. App. 104; 246 P. 84 (1926); *State* v. *Hogg,* 126 La. 1053; 53 So. 225 (1910). Contra: *Golden* v. *State,* 22 Tex. App. 1; 2 S. W. 531 (1886).

4. A husband may be guilty of rape for aiding and abetting rape of wife: *Lord Audley's Case,* 3 How. State Trials 402 (1631); *State* v. *Haines,* 51 La. Ann. 731; 25 So. 372 (1899); *People* v. *Chapman,* 62 Mich. 280 (1886); *State* v. *Dowell,* 106 N. C. 722; 11 S. E. 525 (1890).

5. A husband may be guilty of libel or slander directed against his wife: *State* v. *Kirby,* 167 Tenn. 307; 69 S. W. (2d) 886 (1934); *Stayton* v. *State,* 46 Tex. Cr. 205; 78 S. W. 1071 (1904). Contra: *State* v. *Edens,* 95 N. C. 693; 59 Amer. Rep. 294 (1886). See also *State* v. *Fulton,* 149 N. C. 485; 63 S. E. 145 (1908), for an opinion by an evenly divided court.

[§ 166

REFERENCES
Book

MADDEN, JOSEPH W. *Handbook of the Law of Persons and Domestic Relations,* pp. 225–27 (1931).

Article

MAY, GEOFFREY. "Experiments in the Legal Control of Sex Expression," 39 Yale L. Jour. 219–44 (1929).

Notes

"Assault—Disease Communicated by Husband to Wife," *State* v. *Lankford,* 6 Boyce (Del.) 594; 102 A. 63 (1917)—18 Col. L. Rev. 81–82 (1918); 18 Yale L. Jour. 409 (1918).

"Embezzlement by Wife of Husband's Property," *People* v. *Graff,* 59 Cal. App. 706; 211 P. 829 (1922)—11 Calif. L. Rev. 282–85 (1923).

"Larceny of Husband's Property by Wife," *Rex* v. *Creamer,* 35 Times L. R. 281 (1919)—3 Minn. L. Rev. 431–34 (1919).

"Larceny by Wife from Husband," *State* v. *Arnold,* 182 Minn. 313; 235 N. W. 373 (1931)—30 Mich. L. Rev. 622–23 (1932); 15 Minn. L. Rev. 589–90 (1931).

"Penal Code—Effect of Common Law—Defences," *People* v. *McClelland,* 146 Misc. 545; 263 N. Y. S. 403 (1933)—34 Col. L. Rev. 171–72 (1934).

"Conspiracy, Husband and Wife," *People* v. *MacMullen,* 134 Cal. App. 81; 24 P. (2d) 794 (1933)—7 So. Calif. L. Rev. 234–36 (1934).

Annotations

"Arson—Ownership—Burning by Husband or Wife of Owner," 17 A. L. R. 1173–75 (1922).

"Criminal Responsibility of Husband for Rape or Assault of Wife," 18 A. L. R. 1063–66 (1922).

"Larceny or Embezzlement by One Spouse of Other's Property," 55 A. L. R. 558–62 (1928).

"Right of Injured Spouse to Discontinue Prosecution for Adultery," 4 A. L. R. 1340 (1919).

Section 167. Wife's Property—in General

CROSS REFERENCES: Wife's power to bind her separate property by contract, **Sec. 152**; Right of action for personal injury to wife, **Sec. 158**; Husband's debts, **Sec. 159**; Wife's liability for family expenses, etc., **Secs. 160, 161**; Wife's property, in particular, **Secs. 168** *et seq.;* Wife's earnings, **Sec. 173**; Recording wife's separate property, **Secs. 174, 175**; Property acquired outside the state, **Sec. 177**; Community property, **Sec. 178**; Suits by and against wife and between spouses, **Secs. 179, 180**; Wife's power to make a will, **Sec. 181**; Wife's conveyances, transfers of property, power of attorney, etc., **Secs. 182** *et seq.;* Wife as a sole trader, **Sec. 187**; Curtesy, **Secs. 215** *et seq.;* Miscellaneous, **Sec. 230**

§ 167]

Marriage at common law might be a very costly undertaking for a woman with property, for the common law was most generous to the husband in the matter of his rights in the property which the wife held at marriage or thereafter acquired. So long as coverture lasted, the husband was entitled to the usufruct of her real property. He could alienate his interest therein, and the same was subject to execution against him. If the wife had an estate of inheritance, and if during coverture issue capable of inheriting such estate was born alive, his interest became enlarged to a life estate. He then held as tenant by the curtesy initiate until the wife's death, and thereafter for his life as tenant by the curtesy consummate. Title to the wife's personal property in possession vested absolutely in him merely by force of the marriage, and, with the exception of a few odds and ends which might be included in the wife's paraphernalia, the same passed to his personal representative after his death. While coverture lasted, he was entitled to reduce her choses in action to possession, and thereby vest title in himself; but if he neglected to do so, he lost all right to them. The wife's chattels real followed a slightly different course. The husband was entitled to the use and income thereof, with the power of disposition during coverture; but, unlike choses in action, undisposed of chattels real became his absolutely if he survived the wife. These were the rights which the law gave him solely by virtue of the marriage. Needless to say, with but few exceptions, he has been shorn of these rights by modern statutes.

In no other field of family law has there been a more complete revolution, both in form and in the philosophy which the form reflects. The courts of equity with their invention of the wife's separate estate in equity, and the wife's equity to a settlement, laid the foundation for that wave of legislation beginning about 1844 which carried forward the liberation of the wife from the harsh dogmas of the common law. Progress in many jurisdictions was piecemeal, with the attendant confusion and uncertainty of judicial decision. Some states lagged behind, while others, irritated perhaps at the distrustful attitude of the courts toward legislative efforts at reform, sought at one blow to emancipate the wife from the chains of the past. Regardless of these differences, however, the legislation of all jurisdictions has been directed toward a delimitation of the husband's marital rights in the wife's property, and the establishment of the wife on a complete property equality with the husband. The revolution in this respect, today practically complete, reached its culmination in the 1921 **Wisconsin** "equal rights" statute, which grants to "women" all privileges and rights under the law enjoyed by men.

[§ 167

In the table at the end of this section the general statutes abolishing the husband's marital rights in the wife's property are collected. The eight community-property states are omitted. The definition of the wife's separate property in those jurisdictions is treated in **Section 178.** Other sections of this volume deal in some detail with the power of the wife to acquire, control, and dispose of her property.

Fifteen jurisdictions (**Alabama, Arkansas, Florida, Georgia, Kansas, Maryland, Massachusetts, Michigan, North Carolina, North Dakota, Oregon, South Carolina, South Dakota, Utah, West Virginia**) have seen fit to define the wife's separate property, or give protection to the same, by constitutional provision. The table following reveals the various types of legislation by which the several jurisdictions have sought to deprive the husband of his marital rights in the wife's property. In a general way they may be classified as follows: (1) statements that the wife's property held at marriage, or afterward acquired, remains her own, or her separate property, etc. (as in **Alabama**); (2) statements expressly cutting off the husband's rights in the wife's property (as in **Connecticut**); (3) statements defining the wife's capacity as to property (as in **Illinois** and **Virginia**); (4) broad statements removing the disabilities of coverture or establishing the independent legal personality of the wife (as in **Oklahoma, Oregon,** and **Mississippi**). The first type is the oldest and most common, while the fourth type is of more recent innovation. The older statutes commonly employ the equitable term "sole and separate." The use of this expression has been unfortunate because of the confusion of thought it engenders.

While legislation on this subject exhibits no special degree of uniformity, and while the full import of many of the statutes can only be determined by a resort to the cases, it seems clear in most instances that the wife retains for her own separate enjoyment the property which she brings to the marriage and the property which she acquires after marriage. In this latter connection, five jurisdictions (**Colorado, Kansas, Nebraska, New Hampshire, Vermont**) except gifts from the husband, while **Alabama** expressly includes the same. As to the effect of the former, see **Section 182. Vermont** appears to have been one of the last jurisdictions to break away from the doctrine that the husband has a freehold interest in land not held by the wife to her sole and separate use by reason of the instrument through which such land was acquired (see footnote 11 of Table LXXXVII, p. 185). Roughly, about a fourth of the statutes specifically designate the rents, issues, and profits of the wife's separate property as likewise her separate property. A normal

§ 167]

construction ought to reach the same result. Express provision to that effect is, however, of special importance in the community-property states (**Sec. 178**). A few jurisdictions also expressly provide that damages recovered by the wife for personal injury belong to her in her own right.

With but few exceptions, it is also evident that the husband has been shorn of his right to control and manage the wife's property, either by express statutory statement to that effect or by reason of the affirmative control given to the wife. Until quite recently, it was not uncommon for legislatures to give a statutory control to the husband, apparently on the theory that the wife was not as yet sufficiently hardened and experienced to meet her new responsibilities. **Florida** is unique in this respect. The husband there is given the management of the wife's property, but she may oust him at will (see footnote 6, p. 184). A number of jurisdictions, perhaps impliedly recognizing a propensity on the part of the husband to assume control of the wife's property, expressly authorize her to maintain an action to recover property which has fallen within his control (**Sec. 180**). On the other hand, under the **Florida** statute referred to above, she cannot sue the husband for the rents and profits of her separate property.

There is, of course, little present necessity for the doctrine of the wife's separate estate in equity. Two jurisdictions (**District of Columbia, Virginia**), however, expressly provide that equitable separate estates may still be created.

It should be observed that because some of the statutes expressly apply only to persons thereafter married, and because of the incapacity of the legislatures to disturb vested rights, there may be different strata of law applicable to different factual situations. This is of little importance, however, in most jurisdictions today because of the years which have intervened since the drastic changes in the law were made.

Reform in this field of family law has not always been encouraged by the courts. Early decisions are colored with a distrust for such severe innovations in the property relations of the spouses. Following the familiar rule of construction that statutes in derogation of the common law are to be strictly construed, full effect to legislative intent has often not been accorded. Even today, some of our legal presumptions of title do not reflect the spirit of the age. There has been a growing tendency, however, for the courts to recognize that a revolution in fact has occurred, and that, except as to specified limitations, the wife in most jurisdictions is intended to be sui juris as to property.

[§ 167

As far-reaching as have been the changes in the property relations of the spouses, personal rights and duties remain practically unchanged. The legislation considered in this section does not purport to redefine the family relation. Thus the husband may possess the wife's property when necessary to enjoy his right to cohabit with her. Several jurisdictions expressly provide that he cannot be ousted from her dwelling. However, many of the statutes if literally read would make him a trespasser should he assert such right. The common law threw upon the husband the duty of support, but gave him those resources of the wife which could be made readily available for that purpose. He now stands shorn of his marital property rights, yet his duty of support has not been mitigated. Indeed, it has been strengthened, as is evidenced by the almost universal introduction of the quasi-criminal Lazy Husband Laws (**Sec. 162**). To illustrate that the economic emancipation of the wife without a mitigation of the husband's burdens was not without some opposition, we quote the following colorful and acrimonious observations of Bishop concerning the modern policy,

. . . . which yields to wives the double advantages of matrimony and single bliss, and lifts from the shoulders of their husbands none of the burdens borne when the law gave them compensatory advantages. It remains only to add a provision compelling every young man to marry instantly the girl who chooses him, and the end of domestic woe will have come . . . . Then she can have as she can have now if the man will submit to the marriage, for her sole and separate use, to accumulate till her husband dies, all that she owned before marriage, all that comes to her afterward, and all that she can acquire by her labor and skill; while he provides for her houseroom, meals, clothing, and the other necessaries of life . . . . If she chooses, she may employ her time with domestic cares; or if she chooses, she may leave her babes for him to look after and nurse, and her meals for him to prepare with his own, while she engages in business on her separate account, and accumulates money not a cent of which or its increase is she required to appropriate to the support of her family or even of herself—all must be borne by the husband.[1]

Viewed with an unprejudiced eye, the modern statutory system undoubtedly does contain an element, or at least a potentiality, of unfairness. There never has been, however, any serious movement to retrace our steps of the last seventy-five years. Indeed, we can anticipate that the few remaining economic disabilities of married women will soon be swept away. We cannot be blind to the fact that the emancipation of the wife from her common-law disabilities as to property has only been a part of a larger and more inclusive movement—the political, social, and economic emancipation of woman from the bondage of the past. The

---

[1] *The Law of Married Women*, Vol. 2, p. 526 (1875).

§ 167]

wave of "equal rights" has not been confined to husband and wife, but extends to man and woman. If as between husband and wife we have been unfair to the husband in our attempt to be fair to the wife, the solution is not in a retreat, if that were possible, but lies in the direction of more extensive family-expense statutes. Equality of rights ought to carry with it an equality of duty. A wife with property ought to be saddled with a joint duty to maintain the household, and a duty to support the husband when she is able and he is unable.

Some of the statutes discussed in this section are loosely drawn and not entirely free from ambiguity, especially as to the powers of the wife over her property. The statute chapters on the property rights of married women are in many instances cluttered with fragments and phraseology of the past. House cleaning might well be in order, with the substitution of a few concise statements of the wife's rights, powers, and liabilities. This has been done in some jurisdictions. In the 1932 **Tennessee** Code, for instance, seven sections take the place of twenty-three former sections. Repeal and substitution as suggested ought not only to make the statute law clearer, but also to divorce the courts from outworn precedents. The tendency will no doubt be in the direction of broad statements of emancipation and legal personality. We may also expect to see the extension of "equal rights" legislation similar to that adopted in **Wisconsin.**

The table follows.

TABLE LXXXVII*

WIFE'S SEPARATE PROPERTY[1]

Jurisdiction[1] and Citation	In General	Wife's Earnings[2] (See Sec. 173)	Miscellaneous
Alabama .... Const., Sec. 209; C. 1923, Secs. 8261–62, 8264, 8273	Real and personal property of female in this state acquired before marriage, or to which she may become entitled after marriage in any manner including gift from or contract with husband, is her separate property	Wife's earnings are her separate property; but she is not entitled to compensation for services rendered to or for the husband or family	Damages which wife is entitled to recover for injury to her person or reputation are her separate property. Property conveyed to an active trustee for wife's benefit is not her separate property in this sense

* See pages 183–85 for all numbered footnotes to this table.

TABLE LXXXVII (*Continued*)

Jurisdiction[1] and Citation	In General	Wife's Earnings[2] (See Sec. 173)	Miscellaneous
Alaska Comp. L. 1913, Secs. 439, 489–90, 495	The wife may manage, sell, convey or devise her property and pecuniary rights held at marriage or acquired after marriage by gift, devise or inheritance to the same extent and in the same manner that husband may manage, etc., his property (see last column)	Real or personal property acquired by wife by her own labor is subject to same exemptions and liabilities as her property held at marriage or acquired afterward by gift, devise or inheritance	All laws which impose or recognize civil disabilities upon wife not imposed or recognized as existing as to husband are repealed. Neither husband nor wife has any interest in property of other as will make the same liable for contracts or liabilities of spouse not the owner (except as expressly provided)
Arkansas Const., Art. IX, Sec. 7; Crawf. and Moses, Dig. 1921, Secs. 5574, 5577, 5580–81	Real and personal property which wife in this state holds or owns at marriage or acquires after marriage by gift, grant, inheritance, devise, or otherwise, and the rents, issues, and proceeds of the same, are her separate property, free from the interference or control of husband	Wife's earnings from her trade, business, labor, or services are her sole and separate property and may be used or invested by her in her own name	Wife enjoys all rights and is subjected to all the laws of the state as though she were a feme sole
Colorado Comp. L. 1921, G. S., Secs. 5576, 5578	Real and personal property which wife in this state owns at marriage (together with the rents, issues, profits, and proceeds thereof) or which comes to her by descent, devise, or bequest, or the gift of any person except her husband, including presents or gifts from husband as jewelry, table ware, watches, money and wearing apparel, remains her sole and separate property not subject to husband's disposal	Wife's earnings from her trade, business, labor, or services are her sole and separate property and may be used and invested by her in her own name	
Connecticut G. S. 1930, Secs. 5154, 5157, 5165–70	Neither husband nor wife acquires by marriage any right to or interest in any property held by the other before or acquired after marriage, except as to the survivor's share as provided by law[3]	The separate earnings of the wife are her sole property[3]	

§ 167]

TABLE LXXXVII (*Continued*)

Jurisdiction[1] and Citation	In General	Wife's Earnings[2] (See Sec. 173)	Miscellaneous
Delaware .... R. C. 1915, Sec. 3048, amd. by Sess. L. 1919, Ch. 197, p. 524; Sec. 4207	Wife's property, whether real, personal or mixed, and the choses in action which she may have acquired in any manner, and all the income, rents, and profits thereof, are deemed to be her sole and separate property	See footnote 4	
District of Columbia ..... C. 1929, T. 14, Ch. 2, Secs. 21, 24, 26, 27	The property, real, personal, and mixed, belonging to wife at marriage, or acquired or received from any person (except from husband in prejudice of creditors) by purchase, gift, devise, grant, bequest, descent, distribution, as proceeds of a judgment in law or equity, or in any other manner, is her own property as absolutely as if she were single	The property, real, personal, and mixed, which wife acquires by her own skill, labor, or personal exertions is her own property as absolutely as if she were unmarried	Wife shall hold all her property of every description for her separate use as fully as if single. Equitable separate estates may, however, be created and shall be governed by the rules of equity applicable[5]
Florida .... Const., Art. XI, Sec. I; R. G. S. 1920, Secs. 3218–22, 3806, 3947, 3948; Sec. 3949, amd. by Sess. L. 1927, Ch. 12254, p. 1137; Secs. 3951–52	Real and personal property of wife owned before marriage or lawfully acquired after marriage by gift, devise, bequest, descent or purchase is her separate property	Wife's wages and earnings acquired in any employment separate from husband are her separate property subject to her own disposal	The wife's property remains in the care and management of the husband.[6] He is not entitled to charge for his services, nor is the wife entitled to sue him for the rents and profits of her property
Georgia .... Const., Art. III, Sec. 11, Par. 1; C. 1926, C. C., Secs. 2993, 2995	Property of wife at marriage whether real, personal, or choses in action, and property given to, inherited, or acquired by her during coverture, is her separate property	When living apart from husband, the acquisitions of wife, and children living with her, vest in her for her separate use, free from control of husband	

TABLE LXXXVII (*Continued*)

Jurisdiction[1] and Citation	In General	Wife's Earnings[2] (See Sec. 173)	Miscellaneous
Hawaii .... R. L. 1925, Sec. 2993, amd. by Sess. L. 1925, Act 274, p. 392; Sec. 2995	Upon marriage, the real and personal property of wife remains her separate property, free from husband's control	All work or labor performed, or services rendered by wife for or to a person other than husband and children, is presumed to be performed on her separate account unless there is an express agreement on her part to the contrary. Wife cannot contract for personal service without written consent of husband	Wife may receive, receipt for, hold, manage, and dispose of real and personal property, in the same manner as if she were sole
Illinois .... Cahill, R. S. 1931, Ch. 68, Secs. 7–9	Wife may own in her own right real and personal property obtained by descent, gift, or purchase; and may manage, sell, and convey the same to the same extent and in the same manner that husband can property belonging to him	Wife may receive, use and possess her own earnings and sue therefor, free from interference of husband or his creditors; but she is not entitled to recover compensation for labor or services performed for husband, whether in the management of property or otherwise	
Indiana .... Burns, Ann. St. 1926, Secs. 3346, 8739–40, 8751	Wife may take, acquire, and hold real or personal property by conveyance, gift, devise, descent, or by purchase with her separate means; and the same together with the rents and profits thereof is her separate property under her own control as if she were single. Personal property held by wife at marriage or afterward acquired remains her own "to the same extent and under the same rule as her real estate so remains"	Wife's earnings and profits from her trade, business, services and labor, other than labor for her husband or family, are her sole and separate property	Money recovered as damages for injury to wife's person or character is her separate property

TABLE LXXXVII (*Continued*)

Jurisdiction[1] and Citation	In General	Wife's Earnings[2] (See Sec. 173)	Miscellaneous
Iowa .... C. 1927, Secs. 10446–47, 10461–62, 10465	Wife may own in her own right real and personal property acquired by descent, gift, or purchase; and manage, sell and convey the same to the same extent and in the same manner as the husband can property belonging to him	Wife may receive the wages for her personal labor, maintain an action therefor in her own name, and hold the same in her own right	Wife may recover for loss of time, medical attendance, etc., incurred as a result of wrongful injury to herself, in addition to elements of damage recoverable at common law. Neither husband nor wife has any interest in property of other which will make the same liable for contracts and liabilities of spouse not the owner (except as expressly provided)
Kansas .... Const., Art. XX, Sec. 6; R. S. 1923, Secs. 23(201), 23(204)– 23(205)	Real and personal property owned by wife in this state at marriage, and the rents, issues, and profits thereof, and any real or personal property which shall come to her by descent, devise, bequest, or the gift of any person except her husband is her sole and separate property not subject to the husband's disposal	Wife's earnings from her trade, business, labor or services are her sole and separate property, and may be used and invested by her in her own name	Right of action to recover damages for personal injuries causing loss of ability to perform services vests solely in wife; but recovery so far as based upon loss or impairment of ability to perform household services shall be for benefit of husband so far as he is entitled thereto
Kentucky .... Carroll, St. 1922, Secs. 2127–28, 2339	Marriage gives the husband during life of the wife no estate or interest in the real or personal property of wife owned at marriage or acquired thereafter. During coverture wife holds and owns all her estate to her separate and exclusive use, free from husband's control. She may take, acquire and hold real or personal property by gift, devise, descent or purchase. She may rent her real estate and collect in her own name the rents thereof	See footnote 4	No judgment of eviction suffered by husband or conveyance by him of the inheritance or freehold of the wife, or other act done by him, operates as a discontinuance or impairs her right of action.

[§ 167

TABLE LXXXVII (*Continued*)

Jurisdiction[1] and Citation	In General	Wife's Earnings[2] (See Sec. 173)	Miscellaneous
Maine .... R. S. 1930, Ch. 74, Secs. 1-3, 5	A woman having property is not deprived of any part of the same by marriage, and the husband by marriage acquires no right to any property of the wife. A wife of any age may own in her own right real and personal estate acquired by descent, gift or purchase, and may manage the same without the assent of the husband	Wife may receive the wages of her personal labor, not performed for her own family, maintain an action therefor in her own name, and hold the same in her own right against her husband or any other person	Wife may release to husband the right to control her property, and may in writing revoke the same. The husband alone cannot maintain an action respecting the wife's property
Maryland .... Const., Art. III, Sec. 43; Bagby, Ann. C. 1924, Art. 45, Sec. 1, amd. in Supp. 1929, p. 270; Art. 45, Secs. 3-5; Art. 71, Sec. 9	Wife may hold all her property of every description for her separate use as fully as if single. Real and personal property belonging to wife at marriage or afterward acquired by her is not liable for husband's debts	Wife may engage in any business. She may conduct a boarding or lodging house as if single. The property which she acquires by her own skill, labor or personal exertions is not liable for husband's debts[4]	See footnote 5
Massachusetts .. G. L. 1932, Ch. 209, Secs. 1, 4, 12, 29; Ch. 215, Sec. 4; Ch. 246, Sec. 32	The real and personal property of a woman remains her separate property upon her marriage. Wife may receive, receipt for, hold, manage, and dispose of real and personal property as if single (subject to husband's curtesy consummate)	Work and labor performed by wife for a person other than her husband and children shall, unless there is an express agreement on her part to the contrary, be presumed to be performed on her separate account[7]	See footnote 5
Michigan .... Const., Art. XVI, Sec. 8; Comp. L. 1929, Secs. 13057–58, 13061	Wife's real and personal property acquired before marriage or to which she may after marriage become entitled by gift, grant, inheritance, devise, or in any manner remains the estate and property of such wife	Wife is absolutely entitled to have, hold, own, retain and enjoy any and all earnings acquired by her as the result of her personal efforts, and to sell or otherwise dispose of the same as if unmarried	See footnote 5

§ 167]

TABLE LXXXVII (*Continued*)

Jurisdiction[1] and Citation	In General	Wife's Earnings[2] (See Sec. 173)	Miscellaneous
Minnesota ...... G. S. 1923, Secs. 8616–17	All property, real, personal, and mixed, and all choses in action, owned by wife at marriage, remains her separate property. Wife may receive, acquire and enjoy property of every description, and the rents, issues and profits thereof, free from husband's control, as fully as if single (see last column)	Wife may receive, acquire and enjoy all avails of her contracts and industry free from husband's control, as fully as if single	A woman shall retain the same legal existence and legal personality after marriage as before, and receive the same protection of all her rights as a woman which her husband does as a man
Mississippi .... Const., Sec. 94; C. 1930, Secs. 1940, 1943, 1945	Marriage imposes no disability or incapacity on a woman as to the ownership, acquisition, or disposition of property. Wife may acquire, hold, manage, control, use, enjoy, and dispose of all property, real and personal, in possession or expectancy, as if single (see last column)	Any contract between the husband and wife whereby one claims or shall receive compensation from the other for services rendered is void	Wife is fully emancipated from all disability on account of coverture. The common law as to disabilities of married women and its effect on the rights of property of the wife is totally abrogated[8]
Missouri .... R. S. 1929, Sec. 3003	Real and personal property, including rights in action, belonging to the wife at marriage or which may come to her during marriage by gift, bequest, inheritance, or purchase with her separate means, together with all income, increase, and profits thereof, remains her separate property under her sole control[9]	Property, including rights in action, due as the wages of the wife's separate labor is her separate property	Property, including rights in action, which has grown out of any violation of the wife's personal rights is her separate property

[§ 167

TABLE LXXXVII (*Continued*)

Jurisdiction[1] and Citation	In General	Wife's Earnings[2] (See Sec. 173)	Miscellaneous
Montana .... R. C. 1921, Sec. 5785; Sec. 5792, amd. by Sess. L. 1933, Ch. 63, p. 119, Secs. 5795–97	All the property of the wife owned before marriage and that acquired afterwards is her separate property under her own control	All work and labor performed by wife for a person other than her husband and family shall, unless there is a written agreement on her part to the contrary, be presumed to be performed on her separate account. The earnings and accumulations of wife and minor children living with her or in her custody, while she is living separate from husband, are her separate property	Neither husband nor wife has any interest in the property of the other (except as to duty of support), but neither can be excluded from the other's dwelling
Nebraska .... Comp. St. 1929, Secs. 42(201), 42(203)	Real and personal property owned by wife in this state at marriage and the rents, issues and profits thereof, and any real, personal, or mixed property which comes to her by descent, devise, the gift of any person except her husband, or by purchase or otherwise, remains her sole and separate property not subject to husband's disposal	Wife's earnings from her trade, business, labor, or services are her sole and separate property, and may be used and invested by her in her own name	
New Hampshire . Pub. L. 1926, Ch. 288, Sec. 1; Ch. 356, Sec. 20	Every woman shall hold to her own use, free from husband's control, all property at any time earned, acquired or inherited by, bequeathed, given or conveyed to her, either before or after marriage, if such earning, acquisition, etc. were not occasioned by payment or pledge of the husband's property	See preceding column and footnote 7	

§ 167]

TABLE LXXXVII (*Continued*)

Jurisdiction[1] and Citation	In General	Wife's Earnings[2] (See Sec. 173)	Miscellaneous
New Jersey ..... Comp. St. 1910, p. 2266, Sec. 24; p. 3223, Sec. 1; p. 3224, Sec. 2; p. 3225, Secs. 3, 4; p. 3238, Sec. 15; Supp. 1925–30, Sec. 124(4)	Wife's real and personal property owned at marriage, or which she receives or obtains by purchase, gift, grant, devise, descent, bequest, or in any manner, and the rents, issues and profits thereof, is her sole and separate property as if she were single	Wages and earnings of wife in any employment, occupation or trade, and all investments thereof, are her sole and separate property. All work and labor performed by wife for third persons shall, unless there is an agreement on her part to the contrary, be deemed to be performed on her separate account	Widow may demand from deceased husband's personal representative personal property which she owned at marriage or subsequently acquired and which was in the husband's possession at death
New York ...... Cahill, Consol. L. 1930, Ch. 14, Secs. 50, 51, 60	Real and personal property owned by wife at marriage or acquired after marriage, and the rents, issues, and profits thereof, remains her sole and separate property as if single, not subject to the husband's control or disposal	Wife has a cause of action in her sole and separate right for all wages, salary, etc., for which she renders work, labor or services or which are derived from her trade, business or occupation. The husband has no right of action therefor unless wife, or husband with her consent, has otherwise expressly agreed with obligor. In any action to recover such wages, or for the loss thereof, the presumption of law is that the wife alone is entitled thereto, unless the contrary expressly appears	Wife has all rights in respect to the acquisition, use, enjoyment, and disposition of real and personal property as if single. All sums recovered in actions or special proceedings by wife to recover damages to her person, estate, or character are her separate property
North Carolina .. Const., Art. X, Sec. 6; C. 1927, Secs. 2506, 2513–14	Real and personal property of wife in this state acquired before marriage, or to which she becomes entitled after marriage in any manner, remains her sole and separate property	Earnings of wife by virtue of any contract for her personal service may be recovered by her suing alone, and are her sole and separate property as fully as if single	Damages for personal injury or other tort may be recovered by wife suing alone, and such recovery is her sole and separate property as fully as if single. The savings from income of wife's separate estate are her separate property

[§ 167

TABLE LXXXVII (*Continued*)

Jurisdiction[1] and Citation	In General	Wife's Earnings[2] (See Sec. 173)	Miscellaneous
North Dakota ... Const., Sec. 213; Comp. L. 1913, Secs. 4410–11; Sec. 4414, amd. by Supp. 1913–25, p. 928	Real and personal property of wife in this state acquired before marriage or to which after marriage she becomes in any manner rightfully entitled is her separate property	Earnings and accumulations of wife and minor children living with her or in her custody, while she is living separate from husband, are her separate property	After marriage, wife has with respect to property the same capacity and rights as before marriage. Neither husband nor wife has any interest in the property of the other (except as to duty of support), but neither can be excluded from the other's dwelling
Ohio .... Complete G. C. 1931 (Page), Secs. 7998, 8001	Married person may take, hold, and dispose of real and personal property as if single		Neither husband nor wife has any interest in property of other (except as to duty of support, right to dower, and to remain in mansion house after death of spouse), but neither can be excluded from other's dwelling except upon decree or order of injunction
Oklahoma ...... St. 1931, Secs. 1654, 1659, 1665	Wife shall retain the same legal existence and legal personality after marriage as before marriage, and receive the same protection of her rights as a woman which her husband does as a man	Earnings and accumulations of wife and minor children living with her or in her custody, while she is living separate from husband, are her separate property	Neither husband nor wife has any interest in the separate property of the other (except as to duty of support), but neither can be excluded from the other's dwelling. For injury to her reputation, person, property, character, or any natural right, wife has same right as husband to appeal to courts in her own name
Oregon .... Const., Art. XV, Sec. 5; C. 1930, Secs. 33(201), 33(211)– 33(212), 33(215)	All laws which impose or recognize civil disabilities upon wife not existing as to husband are repealed. Wife may manage, sell, etc., the property and pecuniary rights owned at marriage or afterward acquired to same extent, and in same manner, that husband can manage, etc., property belonging to him	Real or personal property acquired by wife during coverture by her own labor is subject to the same exemptions and liabilities as property owned at marriage or afterward acquired by gift, devise or inheritance	Neither husband nor wife has any interest in property of other as will make the same liable for contracts or liabilities of spouse who is not the owner (except as expressly provided)

§ 167]

TABLE LXXXVII (*Continued*)

Jurisdiction[1] and Citation	In General	Wife's Earnings[2] (See Sec. 173)	Miscellaneous
Pennsylvania ... St. 1920 (West), Secs. 8690, 14569, 14574–75, 14586	Every species of property owned by wife at marriage continues to be her property as fully as before marriage. All property accruing to wife during coverture by will, descent, deed, or otherwise shall be owned, used, and enjoyed by her as her own separate property	Wife's separate earnings, whether as wages, for labor, salary, property, business or otherwise, accrues to her separate benefit and use, as if she were single, free from the husband's control[10]	Wife has the right and power of a feme sole to acquire, own, possess, control, and dispose of real and personal property (except that husband must join in her conveyance or mortgage of lands)
Rhode Island ... G. L. 1923, Sec. 4193	Real estate, chattels real, and personal estate owned by wife before marriage or acquired after marriage, and the proceeds thereof, are her sole and separate property free from control of husband	Property of wife acquired by her own industry, and the proceeds thereof, is her sole and separate property, free from husband's control	Damages recovered in suits for wife's benefit, and compensation for her property taken for public use, and the proceeds thereof, are her sole and separate property
South Carolina .. Const., Art. XVII, Sec. 9; C. of L. 1922, C. C., Secs. 5537–38	Real and personal property of wife owned at marriage, or which accrues to her thereafter by gift, grant, inheritance, devise, purchase, or otherwise, is her separate property. She has all the rights incident thereto to which a single woman or man is entitled	All the earnings and income of wife are her separate estate, governed by the same law as applies to her other separate estate	
South Dakota ... Const., Art. XXI, Sec. 5; Comp. L. 1929, Secs. 170, 175, 178	Real and personal property of wife in this state acquired before marriage or to which she may after marriage become in any manner rightfully entitled is her separate property	Earnings and accumulations of wife, and minor children living with her or in her custody, while she is living separate from husband are her separate property	Wife retains after marriage all the civil and property rights of a single woman. She may sue in own name for injury to her reputation, person, or property. Neither husband nor wife has any interest in other's property (except as to duty of support) but neither can be excluded from other's dwelling

[§ 167

TABLE LXXXVII (*Continued*)

Jurisdiction[1] and Citation	In General	Wife's Earnings[2] (See Sec. 173)	Miscellaneous
Tennessee ...... C. 1932, Sec. 8460	Marriage imposes no disability or incapacity on wife as to the ownership, acquisition, or disposition of property of any sort. Wife has same capacity to acquire, hold, manage, control, use, enjoy, and dispose of all property in possession as if single		Wife is fully emancipated from all disability on account of coverture. The common law as to disability of married women and its effects on rights of property of wife is totally abrogated (except as to tenancies by entirety and curtesy consummate)
Utah .... Const., Art. XXII, Sec. 2; R. S. 1933, 40-2-1, 40-2-4, 40-2-5	Real and personal estate of wife acquired before marriage, or to which she afterward becomes entitled by purchase, gift, grant, inheritance or devise, remains her estate and property	Wife may receive wages for her personal labor, maintain an action therefor in her own name, and hold same in her own right as if unmarried	Wife may recover against third person for personal injury or wrong to her as if single, and such recovery includes medical treatment and other expenses paid or assumed by husband
Vermont .... G. L. 1917, Sec. 1944, amd. by Sess. L. 1919, No. 74, p. 85; Sec. 3523, amd. by Sess. L. 1919, No. 90, p. 98, and Sess. L. 1929, No. 48, p. 63; Secs. 3524–25	Personal property and rights of action acquired by wife before marriage, or during coverture, except by gift from husband, shall be held to her sole and separate use[11]	"Nothing herein contained shall authorize a claim by either husband or wife against the other for personal services"[7]	Neither the wife's separate property nor the rents, issues, income, and products of same is subject to husband's disposal[11]
Virginia .... C. 1930, Sec. 5134, amd. by Sess. L. 1932, Ch. 25, p. 21; Sec. 5139	Wife has the right to acquire, hold, use, control, and dispose of property (subject to husband's curtesy) acquired since April 4, 1877, as if single. Neither husband's curtesy nor his marital rights entitle him to possession, or use, or rents, issues, and profits of wife's lands during coverture		In action by wife to recover for personal injury, she may recover the entire damage sustained, including expenses arising out of the injury (whether chargeable to her or husband) even though husband may be entitled to her services about domestic affairs and consortium. Equitable separate estates may be created as heretofore

§ 167]

TABLE LXXXVII (*Continued*)

Jurisdiction[1] and Citation	In General	Wife's Earnings[2] (See **Sec. 173**)	Miscellaneous
West Virginia .. Const., Art. VI, Sec. 49; C. 1931, Ch. 48, Art. 3, Secs. 1, 2, 11, 12, 16, 17	Real and personal property owned by wife at marriage or acquired as statute prescribes, and the rents, issues, and profits thereof, remains her property in all respects as if single, free from husband's control or disposal. Wife may take property by inheritance, gift, grant, devise, or bequest from any person	Wife's earnings and all property purchased by her with proceeds thereof is her own property, free from husband's control or disposal	See footnote 5
Wisconsin ...... St. 1931, Secs. 6.015, 246.01– 246.03, 246.05, 246.07	Real and personal property of wife owned at marriage, and the rents, issues, and profits thereof, is her sole and separate property, not subject to husband's disposal. Wife may receive real and personal property by inheritance, gift, grant, devise, or bequest from any person, and hold the same to her sole and separate use free from husband's disposal, as if she were single (see last column)	Individual earnings of wife, except those accruing for labor for husband, or in his employ or payable by him, is her separate property free from the husband's control	Women shall have the same rights and privileges under the law as men in holding and conveying property, and in all other respects. Judgment recovered by wife for injury to her person or character is her separate property
Wyoming ...... R. S. 1931, Secs. 69(101), 69(105)	Real and personal property owned by wife at marriage and that acquired afterward in good faith from any person, or by descent or otherwise, together with rents, issues, and profits thereof, remain during coverture her sole and separate property under her sole control as if she were single	Wife's earnings from her trade, business, labor or services are her sole and separate property, and may be used and "entrusted" by her in her own name	

[1] The community-property states are omitted from the table above. What constitutes the separate property of the spouses in those jurisdictions is discussed in **Section 178**. Specific powers of the wife in respect to her separate property, in both the community-property and the so-called common-law states, are treated in other sections of this volume. General statements found in the community-property states follow: Married women are fully emancipated from the disabilities and relieved from all incapacities to which, as such, they were subject (**Louisiana**, Sess. L. 1928, Act 283, p. 583). All laws which impose or recognize civil disabilities upon the wife, not existing as to husband, are abolished (**Washington**, Remington, Comp. St. 1922, Sec. 6901). The wife has exclusive control of her separate property (**Arizona**, R. C. 1928, Sec. 2174;

TABLE LXXXVII (*Continued*)

Idaho, Comp. St. 1919, Sec. 4657). Neither husband nor wife has any interest in the property of the other, but neither can be excluded from the other's dwelling (**California,** C. C. 1933 [Lake], Sec. 157; **New Mexico,** St. Ann. 1929, Sec. 68[106]. Neither husband nor wife has any interest in the property of the other (**Nevada,** Comp. L. 1929 [Hillyer], Sec. 3373).

[2] Seventeen jurisdictions specify that the wife's earnings are not liable for the husband's debts (**Alaska, Arkansas, District of Columbia, Illinois, Iowa, Maryland, Minnesota, Missouri, Montana, North Dakota, Oklahoma, Oregon, Pennsylvania, South Dakota, Utah, West Virginia, Wisconsin**). **Georgia** provides that the wife's acquisitions when living apart from the husband are free from his debts.

[3] The **Connecticut** provisions above govern the property rights of persons married since April 20, 1877. A separate set of provisions, of little practical significance today, governs the rights of persons married before that date (unless, by contract, rights under the old law are relinquished for those under the new law). Under the old law, the husband is made a statutory trustee of the wife's personalty. He may receive and enjoy the income thereof during life, subject to the duty of supporting the wife and children.

[4] **Delaware** formerly expressly provided that the wife might receive the wages of her personal labor not performed for the family, maintain an action therefor in her own name, and hold the same in her own right (R. C. 1915, Sec. 3059). This section was repealed in 1919, when a new chapter on married women was adopted (Sess. L. 1919, Ch. 197, p. 524). Section 4207 of the Revised Code, 1915, allows the wife to sue to recover the wages for her personal labor "as provided by Sec. 27, Ch. 87"—the latter section being Section 3059, repealed as above. **Kentucky** formerly provided that the wages of the wife for her services and labor should be free from the debts and control of the husband (Act of April 11, 1873; see also *Wallace* v. *Mason,* 100 Ky. 560; 38 S. W. 887 [1897]). A former **Maryland** statute allowed the wife to hold her earnings to her sole and separate use as a feme sole (Acts of 1842, Ch. 293, Sec. 8, as amended by Acts of 1882, Ch. 265; Pub. G. L. 1888, Art. 45, Sec. 7).

[5] The **District of Columbia** and **Maryland** provide that it is not necessary for the wife to have a trustee to secure to her the sole and separate use of her property, but that she may "make" a trustee by deed, or apply to equity for the appointment of one. In **Massachusetts,** the Probate Court, which is given exclusive jurisdiction of petitions of married women relative to their separate estates, may upon petition of the wife appoint a trustee to hold her separate property for her and to prosecute and defend all actions brought by or against her. **Michigan** provides that one holding property for the wife may convey the same to her by deed or otherwise, for her sole and separate use. In **West Virginia,** the wife is expressly given all the benefits of the law available to any person in respect to property held in trust for her; and she may have trusts in her favor terminated and extinguished to the same extent as if she were unmarried.

[6] The **Florida** court has held that under the constitutional provision establishing the wife's rights to her separate property the wife may at her pleasure terminate the control over her property given to the husband by statute (*Florida Citrus Exchange* v. *Grisham,* 65 Fla. 46; 61 So. 123 [1913]). Also, she is authorized by statute to petition in chancery to the circuit court of the circuit of her residence for a license to take charge and control of her separate property. After notice and hearing, and inquiry before a master, the court, if satisfied as to her capacity and qualifications, may so decree. She is also authorized to take charge of her property if the husband has been adjudged insane and has continued so for one year.

[7] **Massachusetts, New Hampshire,** and **Vermont** provide that the earnings of the wife of a defendant are not subject to trustee process; which is of no significance if the wife's earnings belong to her.

[8] **Mississippi** provides that it is unlawful for the husband to rent the wife's plantation, houses, horses, etc., or operate any business in his own name with her means. Business done with her property is deemed to be on her account and for her use by the husband as her agent, as to those without notice, unless the contract between the spouses changing this relation is in writing properly recorded. If the husband appropriates the wife's property, he is liable to the wife, but he is not accountable for the income and profits of her estate after one year from the receipt thereof. If the wife permits the husband to employ the income of her estate or use her estate in support of the family, he is not chargeable therefor.

[9] The **Missouri** statutes provide, however, that the provision above shall not affect the title of the husband to personal property reduced to his possession with the express assent of the

§ 167]

TABLE LXXXVII (*Concluded*)

wife. Personal property is not deemed to have been reduced to possession by his use, occupancy, care, or protection thereof unless the wife in writing give him full authority to dispose of the same for his own use and benefit.

[10] Under the **Pennsylvania** statute, the person claiming title to such property is compelled in the first instance to show title when the same is brought in issue. "To prevent any fraudulent practices," the wife is required to file a petition with the court of common pleas stating her intention to claim the benefits of the provision above, which petition is recorded and is conclusive evidence of her right to such benefits.

[11] In **Vermont**, General Laws, 1917, Section 3523 provides that the wife may convey real estate acquired by her under a deed or decree made to her sole and separate use and to the exclusion of the marital rights of the husband. At least until 1919, **Vermont** was committed to the doctrine that real estate not conveyed to her sole and separate use is not her separate estate and that the husband has a freehold interest therein. By an amendment to Section 3523 (Sess. L. 1919, No. 90, p. 88) the wife may convey, manage, and control "any other real estate hereafter acquired by her." While this amendment seems to abolish the old doctrine, no cases have been found which discuss the matter (see *Roberge* v. *Town of Troy,* 105 Vt. 134; 163 A. 770 [1933]).

REFERENCES
Books

PECK, E. *The Law of Persons and Domestic Relations,* 3d ed., chap xi, pp. 214 *et seq.* (1930).

POMEROY, JOHN NORTON. *A Treatise on Equity Jurisprudence,* 4th ed., Vol. III, Secs. 1098–1120 (1918).

SCHOULER, JAMES. *A Treatise on the Law of Marriage, Divorce, Separation and Domestic Relations,* 6th ed., I, 344–489 (1921).

STIMSON, F. J. *American Statute Law,* Sec. 6420 (1886).

TIFFANY, HERBERT THORNDIKE. *Real Property and Other Interests in Land,* 2d ed., Vol. 1, Sec. 206, "Equitable Modifications of Husband's Rights" (1920).

Article

HITCHCOCK, HENRY. "Modern Legislation Touching Marital Property Rights," 6 So. L. Rev. (N.S.) 633–62 (1880).

Annotations

"Character of Interests of Husband and Wife in Purchase-Money Mortgage on Sale of Estate by Entireties," 30 A. L. R. 905–7 (1924).

"Divorce as Affecting Estate by Entireties," 59 A. L. R. 718–19 (1929).

"Estate by Entireties as Affected by Statute Declaring Nature of Tenancy under Grant or Devise to Two or More Persons," 43 A. L. R. 1081–85 (1926).

"Estates by Entireties in Personal Property," 8 A. L. R. 1017–23 (1920).

"Right of Murderer in Property Owned as Tenant by Entirety with His Victim," 51 A. L. R. 1106 (1927).

Notes

"Marital Property Rights and the Conflicts of Laws," 43 Harv. L. Rev. 1286–89 (1930).

"Property of Married Women in Florida," 4 Fla. S. Bar Assoc. L. Jour. 154–67 (1930).

[§ 167

Section 168. Wife's Real Property at Marriage

CROSS REFERENCES: Wife's property, in general, **Sec. 167**; Community property, **Sec. 178**

The common-law marital rights of the husband in the real property which the wife may hold at marriage have been uniformly legislated away. Most jurisdictions have express statutory affirmations to the effect that the wife's real property (or the wife's property) owned at marriage remains her separate property under her control. The statutes of a few jurisdictions take the form of expressly denying the husband's marital rights in such property. The remaining jurisdictions reach the same result by expressly removing the disabilities of the wife as to property, or defining her capacity as to property.

Attention is directed to **Section 167,** and the table therein contained, for an outline of the statutory material on this subject.

REFERENCES

Books

MADDEN, JOSEPH W. *Handbook of the Law of Persons and Domestic Relations,* pp. 91 *et seq.* (1931).
STIMSON, F. J. *American Statute Law,* Secs. 6420–21, 6450–51 (1886).

Section 169. Wife's Personal Property at Marriage

CROSS REFERENCES: Wife's personal property, in general, **Sec. 167**; Wife's paraphernalia, **Sec. 170**; Community property, **Sec. 178**

It is probable that in none of the fifty-one jurisdictions today does the husband retain his common-law right to the personal property which the wife owns at marriage. The statutes of most jurisdictions are express to the effect that such property continues to belong to the wife after marriage, or that the husband acquires no right therein by reason of the marriage. In the other jurisdictions the same result is reached by broad legislation establishing the wife's capacity as to property or removing her disabilities as to property. The statutes of five jurisdictions (**Delaware, Georgia, Minnesota, Missouri, Vermont**) specifically include the matter of the wife's choses in action; and one jurisdiction (**Rhode Island**), the wife's chattels real. Of course, both are included in the generic term "property" or "personal property." The

§ 169]

statutes cutting off the husband's rights to the wife's personalty may be found in Table LXXXVII, **Section 167.**

REFERENCES

Books

MADDEN, JOSEPH W. *Handbook of the Law of Persons and Domestic Relations,* pp. 85 *et seq.* (1931).

SCHOULER, JAMES. *A Treatise on the Law of Marriage, Divorce, Separation and Domestic Relations,* 6th ed., I, 167–203 (1921).

STIMSON, F. J. *American Statute Law,* Secs. 6420–21, 6450–51 (1886).

Section 170. Wife's Paraphernalia

CROSS REFERENCES: The wife's personal property before and after marriage, **Secs. 169, 172;** Widow's allowance, **Sec. 228;** Homestead and exemptions, **Sec. 228**

The peculiar common-law doctrine which enabled a widow to demand her "paraphernalia" (that is, her wearing apparel, personal ornaments, etc., commensurate with her rank in life) constituted a limited exception to the general rights of the husband in the personal property of his spouse. Like her other personal property, the wife's wearing apparel, ornaments, etc., which she brought into the marriage or which she later acquired from the husband or third persons theoretically belonged to the husband and were subject to his disposal during coverture. He was, however, incapacitated to alienate the wife's paraphernalia by will, and, if he died without having disposed of it, title thereto passed to the widow subject only to the claims of the husband's creditors.

No statute expressly retaining or abrogating the common-law doctrine of the wife's paraphernalia as such was found. Several odd bits of legislation, however, seem to have their foundation in this common-law idea. **Alabama** provides that "the wearing apparel of the wife, however acquired, is her separate property" (C. 1923, Sec. 8263). A 1915 **New Jersey** statute provides that "the paraphernalia of a married woman, being the suitable ornaments and wearing apparel of a married woman which have come to her through her husband during coverture, now possessed by her and which she may hereafter attain, shall be her sole and separate property as though she were a single woman" (Comp. St., Cum. Supp. 1911–24, Sec. 124[18]). Literally construed, these provisions might preclude the husband from furnishing wearing apparel

[§ 170

to the wife with the intent to retain title thereto in himself. The **Colorado** statute creating a separate estate for the wife free from the disposal of the husband expressly excepts gifts from the husband from its operation, but as an exception to such exception expressly includes "presents or gifts from her husband, as jewelry, silver, table ware, watches, money and wearing apparel" (Comp. L. 1921, G. S., Sec. 5576). **Georgia** formerly protected the wife's paraphernalia by name from the debts and contracts of the husband, and expressly included therein her wearing apparel, watch, ornaments, etc., as may have been given to her for her own use and comfort (C. 1882, Sec. 1773). In **California,** the husband cannot sell the clothing or wearing apparel of the wife which belongs to the community without her written consent (C. C. 1933 [Lake], Sec. 172). This constitutes a limited exception to the husband's general power of control over the community personal property. Finally, "the wife's paraphernalia" is expressly excepted from the operation of a **Virginia** statute requiring a change of possession for the validity of a gift of chattels unless made by deed or will (C. 1930, Sec. 5142).

The wife's "paraphernalia" at common law should not be confused with the wife's "paraphernal property" in **Louisiana.** The latter, a much broader term, comprehends all of the separate property of the wife which she does not bring to the husband to assist him in bearing the expenses of the marriage establishment. The wife may control her paraphernal property unassisted by the husband (see C. C., Arts. 2335, 2383).

There are few, if any, cases arising under modern statutes which involve the right of a widow to claim her paraphernalia. Indeed, the question is not likely to arise in view of the extensive property rights now given to the wife. In a fairly recent case, one of the judges on the King's Bench expressed the opinion that the English Married Women's Act of 1882 impliedly abrogates the doctrine of the wife's paraphernalia on the theory that, when the husband's common-law right to the wife's chattels is abolished, an exception to that right must also fall. The two other members of the court declined to express an opinion as to whether the widow might in a proper case still claim her paraphernalia (*Masson, Templier & Company* v. *De Fries,* [1909] 2 K. B. [C. A.] 831). On the other hand, the **New Jersey** court, in holding that the husband might during his life claim jewels purchased by him for the ornament of his wife and not shown to be a gift to her, took the position that the **New Jersey** legislation does not impliedly abolish the paraphernalia doctrine (*Farrow* v. *Farrow,* 172 N. J. Eq. 421; 65 A. 1009 [1907] ;

§ 170]

see also *Mains* v. *Webber's Estate,* 131 Mich. 213 ; 91 N. W. 172 [1902] ;
State v. *Pitts,* 12 S. C. 180 ; 32 Amer. Rep. 508 [1879]).

Whether there is any place for the ancient doctrine of the wife's
paraphernalia under modern legislation establishing the property rights
of married women is a question of little practical significance. The
personal property which a wife brings to the marriage or which she
afterward acquires with her own means or from third persons universally remains her own. The problem is significant only in so far as it
concerns wearing apparel, etc., furnished by the husband during coverture under his duty to support or otherwise, without intention to make
a gift of the same to her. There seems to be nothing in the modern
statutes (unless it be the **Alabama** provision above referred to) which
prevents a husband from supplying the wife with clothing, ornaments,
etc., with intent to retain title thereto in himself. Assuming, then, that
a gift from the husband (which was, of course, an utter impossibility
at common law) cannot be established, the wife is given far greater protection today than the common law offered. Statutes now commonly
provide that the reasonable wearing apparel of the debtor and his family,
or of the debtor and his wife, shall be exempt from attachment or
seizure on execution. And upon the death of the husband, the widow
is almost universally given an allowance which includes her reasonable
wearing apparel, and personal ornaments, or which includes rights more
extensive than her common-law right to claim her paraphernalia (**Sec.
228**).

REFERENCES
Books

SCHOULER, JAMES. *A Treatise on the Law of Marriage, Divorce, Separation and
Domestic Relations,* 6th ed., I, 173 (1921).
STIMSON, F. J. *American Statute Law,* Sec. 6428 (1886).

Section 171. Wife's Real Property Acquired after Marriage

CROSS REFERENCES : Wife's property, in general, **Sec. 167** ; Community property,
Sec. 178

That the husband's rights jure uxoris in the wife's real property
acquired during coverture have been universally abolished seems evident
from the statutes outlined in Table LXXXVII, **Section 167.**

[§ 171

At common law, a devise or conveyance to husband and wife created a tendency by the entireties at least in the absence of a manifestation of intention to create a joint tenancy or tenancy in common. The chief difference between tenancies by the entireties and joint tenancies is that in the former the right of survivorship cannot be defeated by a voluntary or involuntary conveyance by one spouse to a stranger. A few jurisdictions have refused to recognize this peculiar common-law creation. Some courts have held the same to be impliedly abolished by the Married Women's Acts establishing the independent legal personality of the wife, but the general view seems to be to the contrary. There is little express legislation on the matter. **Kansas** and **Virginia** clearly abolish tenancies by the entireties. Six jurisdictions seem to impliedly reach the same result by specifying the manner in which the spouses may hold property jointly and not including therein estates by the entireties (**California, Montana, Nevada, New Mexico, Oklahoma, South Dakota**). On the other hand, **Alaska** and **Tennessee** expressly retain such estates; and **Mississippi** and **West Virginia** expressly permit their creation if the intention to do so is sufficiently expressed. Legislation tacitly recognizing the present possibility of tenancies by the entireties is found in jurisdictions as follows: the spouses may create the same (**Oregon**) or terminate the same (**Michigan**) by conveyance inter se; when the spouses convey property held by entireties, both are bound on covenants (**Missouri**); such estates are liable for the debts of husband contracted for necessaries (**Vermont**) or to satisfy a decree for support of wife (**Pennsylvania**). Most jurisdictions have statutes applying to joint grantees and devisees generally, reversing the common-law rule, and establishing a rule of construction favoring tenancies in common in the absence of express language of survivorship or other clear manifestation of intention to create a joint tenancy. These statutes are generally said to have no effect on transfers to husband and wife in jurisdictions in which estates by the entireties are otherwise recognized. Legislation of this kind found in four jurisdictions (**Arizona, Indiana, Michigan, Missouri**) expressly excepts transfers to husband and wife. In five jurisdictions (**District of Columbia, Kentucky, Massachusetts, Montana, Rhode Island**), however, transfers to husband and wife are expressly included within the operation of the statute. These latter statutes probably do not of themselves abolish estates by the entireties, or preclude the creation of the same if a proper expression of intention is employed.

Citations to the general statutes securing to the wife the real property

§ 171]

she acquires during coverture may be found in **Section 167.** Citations to the statutes referred to above on the matter of estates by the entireties follow:

Alaska, Comp. L. 1913, Sec. 488, as amended by Sess. L. 1929, Ch. 66, p. 147; **Arizona,** R. C. 1928, Sec. 2777; **California,** C. C. 1933 (Lake), Sec. 161; **District of Columbia,** C. 1929, T. 25, Sec. 276; **Indiana,** Burns, Ann. St. 1926, Sec. 13384; **Kansas,** R. S. 1923, Sec. 22(132); **Kentucky,** Carroll, St. 1922, Sec. 2143; **Massachusetts,** G. L. 1932, Ch. 184, Sec. 7; **Michigan,** Comp. L. 1929, Secs. 12965, 13069; **Mississippi,** C. 1930, Sec. 2113; **Missouri,** R. S. 1929, Secs. 3015, 3114; **Montana,** R. C. 1921, Secs. 5789, 6683; **Nevada,** Comp. L. 1929 (Hillyer), Sec. 3362; **New Mexico,** St. Ann. 1929, Sec. 68(301); **Oklahoma,** St. 1931, Sec. 1658; **Oregon,** C. 1930, Sec. 33(203); **Pennsylvania,** St., Cum. Supp. 1928 (West), Secs. 10172a(1) *et seq.;* **Rhode Island,** G. L. 1923, Sec. 4243; **South Dakota,** Comp. L. 1929, Sec. 174; **Tennessee,** C. 1932, Sec. 8461; **Vermont,** Sess. L. 1927, No. 48, p. 52; **Virginia,** C. 1930, Sec. 5159; **West Virginia,** C. 1931, Art. 36, Ch. 1, Secs. 19, 20.

REFERENCES

Book

STIMSON, F. J. *American Statute Law,* Secs. 6422, 6427 (1886).

Article

WILKERSON, W. A. "Creditor's Rights against Tenants by the Entireties," 11 Tenn. L. Rev. 139–48 (1933).

Notes

"Estates by Entirety, Effect of Husband's Deed to Himself and Wife," *Boehringer* v. *Schmid,* 254 N. Y. 355; 173 N. E. 220 (1930)—8 N. Y. Univ. L. Quar. Rev. 503–4 (1931).

"Tenancies by the Entirety under Massachusetts Decisions," 11 B. U. L. Rev. 396–99 (1931).

"Real Property, Tenancies in Entirety, Murder of the Ancestor," *Sherman* v. *Weber,* 113 N. J. Eq. 451; 167 A. 517 (1933)—11 N. Y. Univ. L. Quar. Rev. 298–300 (1933); 82 Univ. of Pa. L. Rev. 183–85 (1933).

Annotations

"Divorce as Affecting Estate by Entireties," 59 A. L. R. 718–19 (1929).

"Estate by Entireties as Affected by Statute Declaring Nature of Tenancy under Grant or Devise to Two or More Persons," 43 A. L. R. 1081–85 (1926).

"Estates by Entireties in Personal Property," 8 A. L. R. 1017–23 (1920).

"Right of Murderer in Property Owned as Tenant by Entirety with His Victim," 51 A. L. R. 1106 (1927).

"Character of Tenancy Created by Instrument Purporting to Convey One's Own Title or Interest to Another," 62 A. L. R. 514–21 (1929).

"Common-Law Rights and Disabilities of Both Husband and Wife as Attaching to Estate by Entireties," 63 A. L. R. 235–36 (1929).

[§ 171

Section 172. Wife's Personal Property Acquired after Marriage

CROSS REFERENCES: Wife's property, in general, **Sec. 167**; Wife's paraphernalia, **Sec. 170**; Wife's earnings, **Sec. 173**; Community property, **Sec. 178**

The statutes securing to the wife the personal property which she legitimately acquires during coverture are collected in Table LXXXVII, **Section 167,** to which reference may be made. It seems clear that in no jurisdiction does the husband's common-law marital right attach to such property. The statutes of three jurisdictions (**Delaware, Missouri, Vermont**) expressly cover the matter of the wife's choses in action; and one jurisdiction (**Rhode Island**), the wife's chattels real. The wife's earnings are generally expressly secured to her (**Sec. 173**), and in many jurisdictions damages recovered for personal injury are expressly made her separate property.

It will be observed that several jurisdictions (**Colorado, Kansas, Nebraska, New Hampshire, Vermont**) expressly except gifts of the husband from the operation of the statute (see also **Sec. 182**). **Colorado,** while making this general exception, rather curiously allows the wife to retain as her own presents from the husband "as jewelry, silver, table ware, watches, money, and wearing apparel."

REFERENCES

Note

"Estates by Entirety in Personalty," *Circonte* v. *Barba,* . . . . Del. . . . . ; 161 A. 925 (1932)—10 N. Y. Univ. L. Quar. Rev. 410–12 (1933).

Section 173. Wife's Earnings

CROSS REFERENCES: Wife's contracts with third persons, **Sec. 152**; Wife's contracts with husband, **Sec. 156**; Recovery for personal injury to wife, **Sec. 158**; Wife's property, in general, **Sec. 167**; Wife's earnings as community property, **Sec. 178**; Suits by the wife, **Sec. 179**; Wife as a sole trader, **Sec. 187**

At common law, the services and earning capacity of the wife belonged to the husband alone. He was accordingly entitled to all of her earnings, even before the same were reduced to possession. Ordinarily, only the husband or his personal representative could maintain an action for the wages of the wife's labor and services. If, however, the debtor

§ 173]

made an express promise to the wife, it seems that she could maintain an action therefor after the husband's death. The distrust with which the courts have looked upon the statutory emancipation of the wife may explain in part why the early statutes defining in general the wife's rights in property were widely held to confer upon her no right to her own earnings. A working woman with no property was thus placed at an unfair disadvantage. The hesitancy of the courts to extend by implication the effect of statutes creating the wife's separate estate stimulated the enactment of legislation expressly covering the matter of the wife's earnings.

Statutes expressly dealing with the wife's earnings were found in thirty-six of the so-called common-law jurisdictions. Excluding from consideration the eight community-property states, it is probable that in all jurisdictions except **Georgia,** and possibly **Vermont,** the wife is entitled in her own right to her earnings for services rendered to third parties outside the household. Twenty-eight jurisdictions expressly give her this right. To appreciate the full extent of the wife's right to her earnings, attention must also be directed to the statutes establishing the wife's capacity to contract with the husband and with third parties, to acquire property, and to carry on a business as a sole trader (see cross references above).

In the eight community-property states, the earnings of the wife, in the absence of agreement to the contrary, are normally community property. Though forming a part of the community, such property is in some respects given an unusual status (**Sec. 178**).

Although differing in terminology, statutes in twenty-eight of the remaining forty-three jurisdictions expressly provide that the wife is entitled to her earnings in her own right (**Alabama, Alaska, Arkansas, Colorado, Connecticut, District of Columbia, Florida, Illinois, Indiana, Iowa, Kansas, Maine, Michigan, Minnesota, Missouri, Nebraska, New Hampshire, New Jersey, New York, North Carolina, Oregon, Pennsylvania, Rhode Island, South Carolina, Utah, West Virginia, Wisconsin, Wyoming**).

Three jurisdictions (**Hawaii, Massachusetts, Montana**) provide that the wife's labor and services performed for others than her husband and family shall be presumed to be on her separate account unless there is an express agreement on her part to the contrary. **Hawaii,** however, rather strangely forbids the wife to contract for personal service without the written consent of the husband.

The statutory situation in **North Dakota, Oklahoma,** and **South Dakota** is not satisfactory. Each of these jurisdictions has generous

[§ 173

provisions emancipating the wife from the disabilities of coverture and exempting the wife's earnings from the debts of the husband, yet specifically provide that the wife's earnings while living separate from the husband are her separate property. The latter confusing provision seems to have been originally copied from **California,** a community-property state. In **Oklahoma,** however, the court has said that the wife has a statutory right to her separate earnings (*Muskogee Electric Traction Company* v. *Green,* 91 Okla. 200; 217 P. 155 [1923]).

The **Georgia** Code allows the wife to hold for her own separate use her "acquisitions" while living apart from the husband. The **Georgia** court seems bound to the doctrine that the wife's earnings while living with the husband belong to him in the absence of an agreement on his part that the wife may retain the same as her separate estate (*Robert* v. *Haines,* 112 Ga. 842; 38 S. E. 109 [1901] ; *Mock* v. *Neffler et al.,* 148 Ga. 25; 95 S. E. 673 [1918]).

The remaining eight jurisdictions (**Delaware, Kentucky, Maryland, Mississippi, Ohio, Tennessee, Vermont, Virginia**) apparently have no legislation expressly securing to the wife the right to her earnings. Of these, **Delaware, Kentucky,** and **Maryland** formerly had such statutes. It cannot be supposed that their legislatures intended a retreat in the matter. **Mississippi** and **Tennessee** have very broad statutes purporting to completely emancipate the wife from the disabilities of coverture, especially as to the ownership and acquisition of property. A **Virginia** statute, in addition to conferring generous property rights upon the wife, allows her to recover the entire damage sustained by reason of a personal injury inflicted upon her. The **Ohio** court has held that the wife may recover in her own right for services to a third party rendered outside the home and not in discharge of her household duties (*Bechtol* v. *Ewing, Administrator,* 89 Ohio St. 53; 105 N. E. 72 [1913]). A **Vermont** statute purports to secure to the wife in general her personal property and rights of action acquired after marriage. It seems doubtful, however, whether the wife has a right to her wages for services rendered to third parties without the husband's consent (see *Monahan* v. *Monahan,* 77 Vt. 133, 139; 59 A. 169, 170 [1903]).

The application of the statutes here considered to the matter of services which the wife may perform for the husband presents a distinct problem. At common law, the wife obviously could not contract to serve the husband for pay, either within or without the household, both because of her incapacity to contract generally and with her spouse

§ 173]

particularly, and because of his absolute right to her services. The statutes of twelve jurisdictions (**Alabama, Florida, Hawaii, Illinois, Indiana, Maine, Massachusetts, Montana, Mississippi, New Hampshire, Vermont, Wisconsin**) either qualify or deny the right of the wife to compensation for services performed for the husband. Also, in **Hawaii, Massachusetts,** and **Vermont,** the spouses by statute cannot contract together (**Sec. 156**). In the main the courts have jealously guarded the right of the husband to the wife's services in the household. Even in jurisdictions in which the spouses may freely contract inter se, the wife cannot contract for services to which the husband is entitled as implied in the marital relation. Whether the wife may recover for services rendered to the spouse in his business outside the household depends upon the attitude of the courts in interpreting the statutes discussed in this section and those statutes authorizing the wife to contract, etc. One must go to the cases to determine the exact extent to which the husband's personal right to the wife's labor remains uninvaded. Whether the wife may recover from third parties for services performed in the household also presents a distinct problem. There is a considerable authority to the effect that even under modern statutes she cannot do so in the absence of a renunciation on the part of the husband. In this connection, it is interesting to observe that **Maryland** expressly authorizes the wife to contract with boarders and lodgers as if sole.

Few will deny that the wife ought to be entitled to her earnings for services rendered to third parties outside the household. The two states which seem to deny her the same are backward, indeed. As a matter of social policy we ought to proceed cautiously in allowing the wife to barter and bicker with the husband over household services, but to enforce upon her a duty to serve the husband outside the household is hardly consistent with modern standards. While the legislation on the subject of the wife's earnings is not entirely satisfactory or free from ambiguity, the greatest confusion has come from those courts which still cling to the old order, especially in the matter of the relative rights of the spouses to damages for injury to the wife impairing her earning capacity.

The statutory material on the wife's earnings, together with the citations therefor, will be found in Table LXXXVII, **Section 167.**

REFERENCES
Book

MADDEN, JOSEPH W. *Handbook of the Law of Persons and Domestic Relations,* pp. 152–56 (1931).

[§ 173

Articles

CROZIER, BLANCHE. "Marital Support," 15 B. U. L. Rev. 28–58 (1935).
WARREN, JOSEPH. "Husband's Right to Wife's Services," 38 Harv. L. Rev. 421–26, 622–50 (1925).

Notes

"Wife's Right to Earnings," *Offenbacker* v. *Offenbacker* (Ind. App.); 187 N. E. 903 (1933)—9 Ind. L. Jour. 472–74 (1934).
"Workmen's Compensation, Wife as Employee of Husband," *Reid* v. *Reid,* 216 Ia. 882; 249 N. W. 387 (1933)—19 Ia. L. Rev. 130–31 (1933).

Annotations

"Right of Married Woman to Recover for Services Rendered outside the Home," L. R. A. 1917E, p. 282.
"Liability of Husband for Services Rendered by Wife in Carrying on His Business," 23 A. L. R. 18 (1923).
"Constitutionality of Provisions of Income Tax Law as Regards Income of Husband and Wife," 78 A. L. R. 352–53 (1932).
"Services by One Spouse to Other as Consideration for Latter's Promise," 73 A. L. R. 1518–23 (1931).

Section 174. Recording of Separate Property of Wife

CROSS REFERENCES: Recording requirements for marriage contracts, **Sec. 155;** Effect of recording separate property of the wife, **Sec. 175;** Community property, **Sec. 178;** Recording transfers and conveyances between husband and wife, **Sec. 182;** Wife as a sole trader, certificate requirements, **Sec. 187**

In the usual family setting, it is perhaps only natural that the wife's separate personalty should often be found in the possession of the husband or in the joint possession of the husband and wife. This misleading picture of ownership presents the husband with abundant opportunity to practice fraud upon both the wife and third parties. With the purpose of offering greater protection to the wife, as well as to put on notice those who would deal with the husband, one might expect to find a well-developed statutory policy of registration of the wife's separate personal property. Apparently, however, only eight jurisdictions have recording acts of this nature which are of general application. Four of these (**California, Idaho, Nevada, Texas**) are community-property jurisdictions. In addition to the eight states having general statutes, **Alabama** and **Louisiana** have statutes of a limited character.

§ 174]

As to those eight jurisdictions which have recording statutes of general application, the following observations may be made. The constitutions of **Arkansas, Nevada, Oregon,** and **Texas** direct that legislation be passed providing for the registration of the wife's separate property. **Oregon,** however, appears to be without such legislation at the present time. The statutes of at least five jurisdictions are in phraseology permissive and not mandatory. Six jurisdictions provide for the registration of the wife's separate personal property only, while two (**Nevada, Texas**) include her real property as well. **Nevada** makes express provision for registration by non-resident wives. Only **Texas,** and **Nevada** (in the case of non-resident wives), require that the wife's personal property be recorded in the county of its situs rather than in the county of the wife's residence.

The few statutes found on this subject appear in the table below. The effect of recording or failure to record is discussed in **Section 175** immediately following.

TABLE LXXXVIII

RECORDING OF THE WIFE'S SEPARATE PROPERTY

Jurisdiction and Citation	What Record May Be Made	Effect of Recording	Effect of Failure to Record
Alabama C. 1923, Sec. 6892	Personal property conveyed in consideration of marriage when possession remains with the husband or the husband and wife shall be recorded in the county of the husband's residence within twelve months after such possession commenced in the state. If the husband removes to another county, the record shall be made within four months thereafter		The personal property must be taken as the property of the husband in favor of purchasers without notice and creditors
Alaska[1]			

[1] An **Alaska** statute providing for the recording of an inventory of the wife's personal property was repealed by Session Laws, 1931, Chapter 16, page 64.

[§ 174

TABLE LXXXVIII (*Continued*)

Jurisdiction and Citation	What Record May Be Made	Effect of Recording	Effect of Failure to Record
Arkansas[2] ...... Const., Art. IX, Sec. 8; Crawf. and Moses, Dig. 1921, Secs. 5575, 5591–93, 5597, 8349	The wife may make a schedule of her separate personal property and file it with the recorder of the county in which she lives. Any person who shall bona fide sell or give any property to a married woman may schedule and record the same as her separate property with like effect	The schedule or certified copy thereof shall be prima facie evidence in all courts and places that the property therein mentioned together with the issue and increase of the same is, and was when the schedule was made, the separate property of the wife. A conveyance or will of property to the wife, on being duly recorded, shall have all the effect of a schedule	In any suit, action or proceeding relating to property not scheduled and recorded, the burden of proof shall rest on the wife to show that the same is her separate property. Failure to file such schedule shall not, however, render a forfeiture, or prejudice her right and title to her separate property
California ...... C. C. 1933 (Lake), Secs. 165–66	A full and complete inventory of the separate personal property of the wife may be made out and signed by her, acknowledged or proved in the manner required for a grant of real property by a single woman, and recorded in the county in which the parties reside	The filing of an inventory in the recorder's office is notice and prima facie evidence of the title of the wife	
Idaho .... Comp. St. 1919, Secs. 4661–62	A full and complete inventory of the separate personal property of the wife may be made out and signed by her, acknowledged or proved in the manner required for a conveyance of real property by a single woman, and recorded in the county in which the parties reside	The filing of an inventory in the recorder's office is notice and prima facie evidence of the title of the wife	

Louisiana[3] ......

[2] The constitutions of **Arkansas**, **Nevada**, **Oregon**, and **Texas** provide that laws shall be passed by the legislatures for the registration of the wife's separate property.

[3] **Louisiana** appears to have no general provision for the recording of the wife's separate estate. In the case of donations inter vivos of property that may be legally mortgaged, both the act of donation and the act of acceptance must be registered within the time prescribed for mortgages. When the donation is to the wife, it is the husband's duty to make the registry, but if he fails to do so the wife may make it herself. Want of registry may be pleaded by all persons concerned except the donor and those persons whose duty it was to cause the registry and their representatives. The wife is not entitled to relief for want of registry, but may have her recourse against her husband (C. C., Arts. 1554–55, 1557–58). Provision is also made for the preservation of the mortgages and privileges accorded by law to the wife for the protection of her dotal, paraphernal, or other rights against the husband by recording the evidence of such claim in the parish or parishes in which the husband may own mortgageable property.

§ 174]

TABLE LXXXVIII (*Continued*)

Jurisdiction and Citation	What Record May Be Made	Effect of Recording	Effect of Failure to Record
Montana .... R. C. 1921, Secs. 5793–94, 5799	A full and complete inventory of the separate personal property of the wife may be made out and signed by her, acknowledged or proved in the manner required for a grant of real property by a single woman, and recorded in the county in which the parties reside	The filing of an inventory in the clerk's office is notice and prima facie evidence of the title of the wife. Such property is exempt from all debts, etc., of the husband (unless for necessaries)	Even though not recorded, the separate property of the wife is not liable for the husband's debts unless such property is in the sole and exclusive possession of the husband, and then only as to such persons as deal with him on the credit of such property without knowledge or notice that it belongs to the wife
Nevada .... Const., Art. IV, Sec. 82; Comp. L. 1929 (Hillyer), Secs. 3357–59	A full and complete inventory of the separate property of the wife, exclusive of money in specie, must be made out and signed by her, acknowledged or proved in the manner required for a conveyance of real property by a single woman, and recorded, (*a*) if she is a resident, in the county of her residence, and in any other county in which she may have real estate; (*b*) if she is a nonresident, in each county wherein any of her property, real or personal, is located or used. Supplemental inventory shall be made out and filed, including all other separate property afterwards acquired, except money in specie	*a*) Resident wives: Filing for record in the county of her residence is notice of her title except as to real estate situate in another county. Filing for record the inventory of such real estate in the county wherein situated is notice of her title thereto *b*) Non-resident wives: Filing for record in any county is notice of her title to all property located or used in such county	Failure to file inventory for record as provided, or omission from the inventory as filed, is as to that property prima facie evidence as between the wife and purchasers in good faith for valuable consideration that such property is not the separate property of the wife
Oklahoma ...... St. 1931, Sec. 1658	A full and complete inventory of the separate personal property of the wife may be made out and signed by her, acknowledged or proved in the manner required for a grant of real property by a single woman and recorded in the county in which the parties reside	The filing of the inventory in the register's office is notice and prima facie evidence of the title of the wife	

[§ 174

TABLE LXXXVIII (*Concluded*)

Jurisdiction and Citation	What Record May Be Made	Effect of Recording	Effect of Failure to Record
Oregon[4]			
South Dakota ... Comp. L. 1919, Sec. 174	A full and complete inventory of the separate personal property of the wife may be made out and signed by her, acknowledged or proved in the manner provided for a grant of real property, and recorded in the county in which the parties reside	The filing of the inventory in the register's office is notice and prima facie evidence of the title of the wife	
Texas .... Complete St. 1928, Civ. St., Arts. 6647–51	All property, real and personal, which may be owned or claimed at the time of marriage by any woman, or which she may acquire after marriage by gift, devise or descent, shall be registered, (*a*) if real estate, in the county where situate; (*b*) if personal property, in the county where the same remains, and, in case such personal property is removed to another county, registration must be made in that county within four months after such removal[5]	The registration of a schedule of the wife's separate property, as provided, shall be conclusive as against all subsequent creditors of and purchasers from her husband	

[4] The **Oregon** Constitution, Article XV, Section 5, provides that laws shall be passed for the registration of the wife's separate property. **Oregon** formerly had a recording act almost identical to that of **Alaska** (L. 1920, Secs. 9760–62), but the same was repealed in 1927 (Sess. L. 1927, Ch. 103, p. 96, Sec. 1).

[5] The **Texas** statutes provide that the wife may prepare a schedule of all the property which she owned at marriage and make a statement under oath before an officer authorized to take acknowledgments that the property therein described is her separate property, and that such officer shall annex a certificate of the fact, which certificate shall be sufficient evidence for the recorder of any county to record the same. If the wife subsequently comes into possession of any property to which she had a claim at the time of marriage, or by gift, devise or descent, she may have a schedule of the same recorded in the same manner.

REFERENCES

Book

STIMSON, F. J. *American Statute Law,* Sec. 6431 (1886).

§ 174]

Section 175. Effect of Recording Separate Property of Wife

CROSS REFERENCES: Effect of recording or failure to record marriage contracts, **Sec. 155**; Recording of separate property of wife, **Sec. 174**; Wife as a sole trader, certificate requirements, **Sec. 187**

Of the eight jurisdictions having recording statutes of general application, only two (**Montana, Texas**) make the record or the filing for record more than notice or prima facie evidence of the wife's title. In **Montana,** the statute expressly exempts the wife's property included in her inventory from all debts and liabilities of the husband (unless for necessaries); and in **Texas,** registration of the wife's schedule is made conclusive as against all subsequent creditors of and purchasers from the husband.

Only four jurisdictions have any express statutory statement of the effect of a failure to record. Of these, only two expressly deny the wife the right to assert her ownership against third parties who deal with the husband. The narrow **Alabama** statute provides that personal property not included in the wife's inventory "must" be taken as the property of the husband in favor of bona fide purchasers and creditors; and in **Montana,** such property, if in the "sole and exclusive possession" of the husband, may apparently be taken for the husband's debts in favor of one who deals with the husband on the credit of such property without notice of the wife's ownership. In **Nevada,** a failure to record is prima facie evidence against the wife's claim of title; and in **Arkansas,** the statute leaves the wife with the burden of proving her title.

The statutes of **California, Idaho, Oklahoma, South Dakota,** and **Texas** are silent as to what effect shall be given to a failure to file the proper inventory. Apparently the wife is not prevented from asserting her title and proving it by other evidence subject to the burden of proof which would ordinarily be thrown upon her (see *Bagg* v. *Schoenfelt,* 71 Okla. 195; 176 P. 511 [1918]; *Anderson* v. *Medbery,* 16 S. D. 324; 92 N. W. 1089 [1902]).

To require the wife to record an inventory of her separate personal property is perhaps not consonant with our idea of equal rights of the spouses. It may of course also be said that some of the presumptions of ownership created by the courts are equally inconsistent with modern standards. But traditional family routine and inertia are not easily changed by a few generations of formal legislative emancipation. To the external eye, the wife's title to her personal property is often obscure or entirely hidden from view. As a matter of protection both to

[§ 175

the wife and to third parties who would deal with the husband, it does seem that some form of registration of her separate personal property is worthy of a wider legislative consideration. Perhaps the filing for record ought not to be made more than prima facie evidence of the wife's title or a failure to record preclude her from asserting and proving her title even as against bona fide intervenors. She ought, however, to be given an opportunity to put on notice those who would deal with the husband, and to minimize harassment from his creditors. It is interesting to observe, however, that of the few jurisdictions having had such recording statutes two (**Alaska, Oregon**) have recently repealed them.

The second and third columns of Table LXXXVIII, **Section 174,** contain in summarized form the statutory statements of the effect of recording, or failure to record, the wife's inventory of her separate property.

REFERENCES
Book

STIMSON, F. J. *American Statute Law,* Sec. 6432 (1886).

Annotation

"Estoppel of Wife Who Permits Record Title to Realty to Remain in Husband's Name to Assert Her Own Title as against One Extending Credit to Husband," 76 A. L. R. 1501–14 (1932).

Section 176. Husband's Property

CROSS REFERENCES: Effect of absolute divorce on husband's property, **Secs. 99** *et seq.;* Effect of limited divorce on husband's property, **Sec. 129;** Powers and rights of abandoned wife in husband's property, **Sec. 143;** Husband's liability for wife's obligations, **Secs. 151, 152, 153, 157, 187;** Family expenses, **Sec. 160;** Duty of support, **Sec. 161;** Estates by the entireties, **Sec. 171;** Community property, **Sec. 178;** Dower, **Secs. 188** *et seq.;* Assignment of wages, **Sec. 224;** Homestead and exempt property, **Secs. 225, 228**

Aside from her right of dower, which was inchoate until the husband's death, the common law gave the wife no present interest in the husband's property. The husband was the legal unit. Modern standards which stimulated the statutory emancipation of the wife as to

§ 176]

property did not necessitate any general restatement of the husband's capacity as to property. Except for relief from liability for the wife's obligations not founded upon his duty of support, the process for him has been mainly one of negation and delimitation. It is only in the community-property states that we find any affirmative definition of the husband's separate property. He remains the master of his own assets, except that he cannot generally bar the wife's dower or statutory substitute by his sole act (**Sec. 200**), and except as modern statutes limit his right to deal with the homestead and exempt property (**Sec. 225**) and assign his wages (**Sec. 224**).

Only the following more or less miscellaneous legislation not directly considered elsewhere need be dealt with here. **California, Montana, Nevada, New Mexico, North Dakota, Oklahoma,** and **South Dakota** provide that neither husband nor wife has any interest in property of the other (except as to support), but that neither can be excluded from the other's dwelling. **Ohio** has substantially the same provision. **Connecticut** provides that neither husband nor wife acquires by the marriage any interest in the property of the other owned at marriage or acquired thereafter, except to share as survivor. Three jurisdictions (**Alaska, Iowa, Oregon**) provide that when property is owned by either husband or wife the other has no such interest therein as will make the same liable for the contracts and liabilities of the spouse not the owner (except as otherwise provided), and in **Iowa** and **Oregon,** no such interest as can be the subject of a contract between the spouses.

In five jurisdictions (**Alaska, Illinois, Iowa, Oregon, Utah**) the husband is given express authority to maintain an action against the wife to recover his property which has fallen into the control and possession of the wife; and in **Maine,** he may bring a bill in equity to recover such property exceeding one hundred dollars in value. Not without subtle irony, these statutes seem to impliedly recognize that under the new order the husband may need protection from usurpation on the part of the wife.

An **Ohio** statute, rather unique in its phraseology, provides that a "married person" may take, hold, and dispose of property as if unmarried.

Citations for the foregoing statutes follow:

Alaska, Comp. L. 1913, Secs. 439–40; **California,** C. C. 1933 (Lake), Sec. 157; **Connecticut,** G. S. 1930, Sec. 5154; **Illinois,** Cahill, R. S. 1931, Ch. 68, Sec. 10; **Iowa,** C. 1927, Secs. 10447–48; **Maine,** R. S. 1930, Ch. 74, Sec. 6; **Montana,** R. C. 1921, Secs. 5785, 5789; **Nevada,** Comp. L. 1929 (Hillyer), Sec. 3372; **New Mexico,**

[§ 176

St. Ann. 1929, Sec. 68(306); **North Dakota,** Comp. L. 1913, Sec. 4410; **Ohio,** Complete G. C. 1931 (Page), Secs. 7998, 8001; **Oklahoma,** St. 1931, Sec. 1654; **Oregon,** C. 1930, Secs. 33(201)–33(202); **South Dakota,** Comp. L. 1929, Sec. 170; **Utah,** R. S. 1933, 40-2-6.

REFERENCES

Book

STIMSON, F. J. *American Statute Law,* Sec. 6423 (1886).

Annotation

"Authority of Wife to Consent to Search and Seizure of Husband's Property," 58 A. L. R. 740–41 (1929).

Section 177. Property Acquired Outside the State— Conflict of Laws

CROSS REFERENCE: Wife's property, in general, **Sec. 167**

A determination of marital rights in property acquired outside the domicile of the spouses involves a difficult question of conflict of laws. The problem is too ramified to warrant more than a statement of the following elementary and generally accepted principles. In the absence of a marriage contract or settlement, marital rights in immovables are governed by the law of the situs; and marital rights in movables owned at marriage are governed by the law of the matrimonial domicile at the time (ordinarily considered to be the domicile of the husband), and, in the case of movables thereafter acquired, by the law of the domicile of the parties at the time of the acquisition. Presumably, however, a jurisdiction may by appropriate legislation control rights to movables acquired therein by non-residents. Finally, vested rights are not divested by the removal of the spouses to another jurisdiction.

Express legislation on the subject of this section was found in only seven jurisdictions, and in only two instances (**Louisiana, California**) does such legislation depart from what would normally be recognized by the courts as the guiding rule in the absence of statute. Obviously, in respect to rights which the husband acquires in the wife's property

§ 177]

by virtue of the marriage, the problem here considered is not as significant now as it was before the legislative emancipation of the wife had reached the present uniform degree of maturity. As between the community-property states and the so-called common-law jurisdictions, however, the conflict of property laws presents a vital problem.

Three jurisdictions (**Kansas, Massachusetts, Nebraska**) provide that a woman married elsewhere shall, if the husband becomes a resident of the state, enjoy all the property rights acquired under the law of another state or by virtue of a marriage contract made in another state. Presumably, these statutes merely recognize what is well settled at common law.

Arizona provides that "the marital rights of persons married out of this state, who may move to this state, shall in regard to property acquired in this state during the marriage be regulated by the laws of this state." **Texas** has substantially the same provision. In **Louisiana,** "a marriage contracted out of this state, between persons who afterward come here to live, is also subjected to community of acquests, with respect to such property as is acquired after their arrival." These express statutory statements of the normal rule obviously preclude the doctrine sometimes advanced that the law of the matrimonial domicile follows the parties to a new domicile.

Louisiana also stipulates that "every marriage contracted in this state superinduces of right partnership or community of acquests or gains," if there be no agreement to the contrary, and expressly extends the community law to rights in both movables and immovables acquired within the state by non-residents. So far as the latter provision affects movables, it is a statutory departure from the unwritten law.

California has a most unusual provision to the effect that ". . . . personal property wherever situated, heretofore or hereafter acquired (by either husband or wife) while domiciled elsewhere, which would not have been the separate property of either if acquired while domiciled in this state is community property . . . ." This statute represents a bald attempt to divest property of its separate character and to convert it into community property. It squarely raises the question whether **California** can prescribe such a condition of residence in respect to personal property brought into a state by non-residents. In a recent decision, the **California** court met the grave constitutional question involved, and held the attempted metamorphosis invalid (*In re Thornton's Estate,* 221 Cal. 1; 33 P. [2d] 1 [1934]; see also *In re Bruggemeyer's Estate,* 115 Cal. App. 525; 2 P. [2d] 534 [1931]; *In re Drishaus' Estate,* 199

[§ 177

Cal. 369; 249 P. 515 [1926]; *Estate of Frees,* 187 Cal. 150; 201 P. 112 [1921]).

It will be observed that most of the statutes securing to the wife her property, and excluding the husband's common-law rights therein, are so worded as to be equally applicable to resident and non-resident wives, though some are in express terms confined to "married women in this state" (see Table LXXXVII, **Section 167**).

Citations to the statutes considered in this section are as follows:

Arizona, R. C. 1928, Sec. 2177; **California,** C. C. 1933 (Lake), Sec. 164; **Kansas,** R. S. 1923, Sec. 23(206); **Louisiana,** C. C., Arts. 2399–2401; **Massachusetts,** G. L. 1932, Ch. 209, Sec. 29; **Nebraska,** Comp. St. 1929, Sec. 42(204); **Texas,** Complete St. 1928, Civ. St., Art. 4627.

REFERENCES

Books

GOODRICH, H. F. *Conflict of Laws,* pp. 272–82 (1927).
STIMSON, F. J. *American Statute Law,* Sec. 6430 (1886).

Articles

HARDING, ARTHUR LEON, "Matrimonial Domicile and Marital Rights in Movables," 30 Mich. L. Rev. 859–77 (1932).
LEFLAR, ROBERT A., "Community Property and Conflict of Laws," 21 Calif. L. Rev. 221–38 (1933).

Notes

"Community Property—Effect of Removal of Personal Property Acquired in Common-Law State to Community-Property State with Change of Domicile," *In re Bruggemeyer's Estate,* 115 Cal. App. 525; 2 P. (2d) 534 (1931)—20 Calif. L. Rev. 201–3 (1932); 5 So. Calif. L. Rev. 309–12 (1932).

"Conflict of Laws: Matrimonial Property: Effect on Movables of Change of Domicile from a Common-Law State to a Community-Property State," 10 Calif. L. Rev. 154–58 (1922); 15 Calif. L. Rev. 399–407 (1927).

"Marital Property Rights and the Conflict of Laws," 43 Harv. L. Rev. 1286–89 (1930).

§ 177]

Section 178. Community Property

CROSS REFERENCES: Effect of divorce on community property, **Sec. 101**; Separation agreements, **Sec. 138**; Marriage contracts, **Sec. 155**; Transactions between spouses, **Secs. 156, 182**; Wife's separate property, **Secs. 167** *et seq.;* Recording of wife's separate property, **Secs. 174, 175**; Conflict of laws, **Sec. 177**; Suits by wife, **Sec. 179**; Wife as a sole trader, **Sec. 187**; Community homestead, **Sec. 228**

I. Introduction

II. Statutory division between separate and community property
  A. Property acquired before marriage
  B. Property acquired after marriage
    1. By "gift, devise, or descent"
    2. Rents, issues, and profits of separate property
    3. By exchange, purchase, etc.
    4. Earnings of husband and wife
    5. Compensation for injury to person or property
    6. Miscellaneous

III. Statutory presumptions as to the character of property

IV. Management, control, and disposition of community property

V. Liability of community property

VI. Survivor's rights: descent, succession, administration, etc.

VII. Modifying the community by antenuptial and postnuptial contracts, etc.

VIII. Nature of community ownership, etc.

I. INTRODUCTION

That scheme of marital rights known as the "community property" system is incorporated into the statutes of eight American states (**Arizona, California, Idaho, Louisiana, Nevada, New Mexico, Texas, Washington**). It is significant that most of the territory now included within these jurisdictions was at one time a part of the Spanish possessions in America. The community-property system is fundamentally an institution of the civil law, quite foreign to anything known to the English common law. The system had its origin in Germanic or Gothic customary law. Following the Gothic invasion of Europe, it became the statutory law of Spain at an early date, and later it was made the law of France by incorporation into the Code Napoléon. As to its inception and retention in the United States, McKay says:

[§ 178

The Spaniards established the system in their possessions which included the territory now comprising the states of Arizona, California, Louisiana, Nevada, New Mexico, and Texas. The law of community was displaced in Nevada, and later restored by statute. . . . . The community property system established by the first Code of Louisiana was composite in character, combining French and Spanish elements. . . . . The Code of Louisiana furnished the material largely for the first Code of California, and in turn this became the model of the first codes in Arizona, Idaho, Nevada, and Washington. A later form of the Code of California became the basis of the present law in New Mexico. The first Code of Texas shows traces of its Louisiana origin. In Idaho and Washington, the system is an exotic one and the first statutes were copied from California.[1]

Comprehensive discussions of the origin and development of the community-property idea will be found among the references at the end of this section.

Under the common law, the legal personality of the wife for most practical purposes was suspended during coverture. The husband was the unit upon which the attention of the law was centered. Initiated by equity and matured by statute, in all of the American jurisdictions the wife has been made secure in the ownership of her property. In the so-called common-law states, as differentiated from the community-property states, all of the property of the spouses is owned separately by either the husband or the wife, or perhaps by both as tenants in common, joint tenants, or tenants by the entirety. In the eight community-property states, the property of the spouses is either the separate property of the husband, the separate property of the wife, or a part of "the common fund of matrimonial gains" called the community property. It is this third classification which formally differentiates these states from neighboring jurisdictions. In a broad sense, the community property is owned by the community of husband and wife. The American jurisdictions, however, are in much dispute as to the exact nature of that ownership. The fundamental purpose of this odd creation of the civil law seems to have been to guarantee to the wife, at least upon dissolution of the marriage, her fair share of the marital gains.

In spite of the same ultimate origin, the community-property systems found in the eight American states today vary greatly. Each has to some extent taken its own individual course of statutory development. More significant, however, is the fact that with substantially similar statutes the courts of the several states have developed radically different conceptions of the systems established by those statutes. Perhaps the student

[1] George McKay, *The Law of Community Property*, Sec. 6, p. 4.

§ 178]

of the civil-law community would find in the children nothing in common with the parent but the name which the system carries. Of course, one of the reasons, except in **Louisiana,** is that the children were reared by courts educated in the common law. The purpose of this section is to compare the legislation of the community-property states as found in the statutes today. Such a comparison reveals interesting and significant facts. To adequately understand the law of any single jurisdiction, however, one must be familiar with both the legislative and judicial history of that jurisdiction. Such a study is not within the scope of this volume. For further enlightenment, the reader is referred to the several brilliant discussions among the references given at the end of this section.

II. STATUTORY DIVISION BETWEEN SEPARATE AND COMMUNITY PROPERTY

As one writer wittily remarks, "It is rather easier to define separate than community property, and one may thereafter say, to cover up his difficulty, that all other is community."[1] In fact, that is exactly the position which the statutes take. All of the jurisdictions have what McKay calls the "statutory formula,"[2] that is, a definition of separate property followed by a declaration that all other property owned by the spouses is community property. Whether particular property belongs to the community fund must be determined by a process of exclusion. **Idaho** and **Louisiana** present exceptions in that each partially and affirmatively defines community property.

A. PROPERTY ACQUIRED BEFORE MARRIAGE

Property acquired before marriage remains separate property. This is written into the statutes of all of the jurisdictions. Occasionally, it may be difficult to determine whether particular property is, in a legal sense, acquired before or after marriage.

B. PROPERTY ACQUIRED AFTER MARRIAGE

1. *By "gift, devise, or descent."*—This is the commonest expression found in the statutes. In all of the jurisdictions, a "gift" (or "donation,"

---

[1] Alvin E. Evans, "The Ownership of Community Property," 35 Harv. L. Rev. 47 (1921).
[2] McKay, *op. cit.,* chap. 9, p. 146.

[§ 178

in **Louisiana**) made to one of the spouses is his or her separate property. **Louisiana,** however, expressly provides that the donation must be made to the spouse "particularly," and that a donation made to both spouses "jointly" belongs to the community. In the other jurisdictions, a gift made to the husband and wife jointly would presumably vest each with a separate interest as owner in common, joint owner, or possibly as owner by the entireties. The statutes do not define the term "gift." Difficulty is encountered when one enters the realm of onerous and conditional "gifts." The determination of the character of property acquired from the government under homestead and pre-emption statutes has occasioned considerable litigation in past years. Property acquired by succession, or descent and distribution, is made separate property in all jurisdictions. It may be observed that the term "descent," used by the statutes of all of the states except **Louisiana** (and **Washington,** in connection with the definition of the wife's separate property), technically applies to the acquisition of real property only. Property acquired by either spouse under a will or testament is his or her separate property in all jurisdictions. Acquisitions of this character would be included within the term "gift," but all of the statutes except that in **Louisiana** employ the term "devise," and five of these the term "bequest" in addition. Technically, the latter is necessary to cover testamentary devolutions of personal property. All property acquired by the testamentary route, however, may not be separate property. Thus, a devise made under an agreement in consideration of support may be community property because of the community character of the consideration (*Andrews* v. *Andrews,* 116 Wash. 513; 199 P. 981 [1921]).

2. *Rents, issues, and profits of separate property.*—The Spanish law which sent the fruits of separate property into the community has been retained by **Texas,** modified by **Idaho** and **Louisiana,** and completely discarded by the other five jurisdictions. The statutes of **Arizona, California, Nevada, New Mexico,** and **Washington** make the rents, issues, and profits of separate property likewise separate property.

The **Idaho** statute expressly retains the Spanish formula except when the instrument conveying separate property to the wife provides that the fruits thereof be applied to her separate use. No similar exception is made in favor of the husband.

In **Louisiana,** the "profits of all the effects of which the husband has administration and enjoyment, either of right or in fact," and the fruits of the wife's paraphernal property administered by the husband or by both spouses "indifferently" belong to the community. Accord-

§ 178]

ingly, the rents, profits, and issues of the husband's separate property, of the wife's dotal property, and of the wife's paraphernal property unless she manages it herself are community property (see Table LXXXIX, footnote 5, p. 246). But there is apt to be no dotal property, and the wife may assume complete management of her paraphernal property if she so desires. Obviously, **Louisiana** allows the wife a considerable advantage in this respect.

In **Texas,** the rents, profits, and issues of separate property are not included within the definition of separate property, and hence are community property. One apparent exception is made by the ambiguous statutory expression, "the increase" of separate lands, which increase remains separate in character. That the exception is more apparent than real may be gathered from the declaration of the **Texas** court that the expression comprehends no more than "profit as may arise from the land's own enhancement in value, or such profit as may accrue from exchange of the lands for other more valuable property" (*Arnold* v. *Leonard,* 114 Tex. 535, 541; 273 S. W. 799, 802 [1925]).

The development of the law in **California** and **Texas** in respect to the fruits of separate property presents an interesting and rather amusing comparison. The **California** Constitution formerly provided that "all property, both real and personal, of the wife, owned or claimed by her before marriage, and that acquired afterward by gift, devise, or descent, shall be her separate property . . . ." (Const. 1849, Art. XI, Sec. 14). By an early statute, the rents and profits of the separate property of both husband and wife were made community property (St. 1850, Ch. 103, Sec. 9). This statute was held unconstitutional so far as it affected the fruits of the wife's separate property (*George* v. *Ransom,* 15 Cal. 322; 76 Amer. Dec. 490 [1860]). It was said that otherwise the rights intended to be secured to the wife by the Constitution would be barren indeed. In refusing to divorce the fruits from the corpus itself, the court was frankly influenced by common-law conceptions of property. The **Texas** Constitution contains a provision identical with that of the early **California** Constitution quoted above (Art. XVI, Sec. 15). The **Texas** legislature recently moved in a direction exactly opposite to that attempted in **California,** and declared the "rents and revenues" of separate property to be separate property (Sess. L. 1917, Ch. 194, p. 436; Sess. L. 1921, Ch. 130, p. 251; Baldwin's Complete St. 1925, Civ. St., Art. 4614). The **Texas** court held the statute unconstitutional so far as it affected the fruits of the wife's separate property, on the theory that the constitutional definition of the wife's separate property is exclusive

[§ 178

and prevents the legislature from prescribing additional modes by which she may acquire such property (*Arnold* v. *Leonard,* 114 Tex. 535; 273 S. W. 799 [1925]). The only exceptions which could be tolerated were stated to be in respect to "the increase" of the wife's separate lands, defined as noted above, and the increase of the wife's separate female slaves. The latter exception is a historical one, based upon sentiment and directed against the otherwise probable separation of the female slave from her offspring. The statute was upheld so far as it determined the character of the fruits of the husband's separate property in as much as the Constitution does not define his separate property (*Stephens* v. *Stephens* [Tex. Civ. App.]; 292 S. W. 290 [1927]). By Act of 1929, the **Texas** statute under discussion was amended so as to put both spouses back on an equal footing (Sess. L. 1929, Ch. 32, p. 66).

Numerous writers have suggested that the rents, profits, and issues of separate property ought to be left in the community as under the Spanish law. Certainly that more accurately reflects the fundamental purpose of the community-property system. The majority rule may lead to a very unfair result. The husband wealthy with separate property may devote his entire energy to managing the same, and leave no community property for the surviving wife to share in. The majority rule also creates the difficult problem of drawing a line between the fruits of separate property and the product of the spouse's labor devoted to separate property. The latter is fundamentally in the nature of earnings and should belong to the community.

3. *Property acquired by exchange, purchase, etc., with separate consideration.*—The general rule in all of the community-property states, except **Louisiana,** is that the character of property acquired by exchange or purchase follows the character of the consideration. None of the jurisdictions, except **Idaho** (in respect to the wife's separate property), have express statutes to that effect, unless it be in the employment of the term "issues" of separate property in the statutes of five states. The general rule is based upon the principle that the character of property should not change with a change of form. Thus, if particular property can be traced to a separate consideration, it is separate property. Considerable difficulty may be encountered in tracing it to its source. The consideration may have been part separate and part community in character. In that case, the courts recognize a proportionate ownership between the community and the spouse furnishing the separate consideration.

§ 178]

The **Louisiana** Code (Art. 2402) provides that property acquired during marriage "by purchase or in any other similar way" belongs to the community "even although the purchase be only in the name of one of the two and not of both, because in that case the period of time when the purchase is made is alone attended to, and not the person who made the purchase." In 1912, Article 2334, defining separate property, was amended so as to add property acquired "with separate funds" to the list of separate property (Sess. L. 1912, Act 170, p. 310). McKay[1] makes the following observations from an examination of the cases arising under the **Louisiana** Code prior to the 1912 amendment. In spite of the broad language of the Code, exchanges and purchases do not necessarily fall into the community. A sharp distinction is made between "exchanges" and "purchases," and between purchases by the husband and purchases by the wife. Property acquired by either spouse in exchange for separate property or pursuant to a separate right is separate. In the case of purchases by the wife, she may establish the same to be her separate property by parol proof that she purchased the property as her separate property with paraphernal funds administered by herself alone. Property purchased by the husband, however, is community property unless he recite in his act of purchase that the consideration paid is his separate property, and that his intention is to acquire the property for the benefit of his separate estate (see *Sharp* v. *Zeller,* 110 La. 61; 34 So. 129 [1902]). This discrimination is said to be justified on the theory that the public has notice of the wife's separate interests when she purchases property in her own name. The **Louisiana** courts apparently do not recognize any sort of proportional ownership between the community and one of the spouses. Thus, if property is purchased with part separate and part community consideration, the property belongs to the community. The spouse furnishing separate consideration, however, is in any event entitled to be reimbursed upon the dissolution of the community. McKay suggests that the 1912 amendment did not change the law of **Louisiana** except possibly in respect to purchases by the husband. No cases discussing the question were found, but from recent decisions one gathers that the amendment does not excuse the husband from making the foregoing double declaration if his purchase is to be his separate property (*Succession of Watkins,* 156 La. 1000; 101 So. 395 [1924]; *Schoeffner* v. *Schoeffner,* 163 La. 146; 111 So. 655 [1927]; see also *Kittredge* v. *Grau,* 158 La. 154; 103 So. 723 [1925]).

---

[1] *Op. cit.,* chap. 24, p. 276.

[§ 178

4. *Earnings of husband and wife.*—It is fundamental in the community-property system that the product of the earning capacity of both spouses belongs to the community fund. When the spouses are living together, this is true in all jurisdictions, except **Louisiana,** by reason of the fact that such earnings are not included within the statutory definition of separate property. The earnings of children not emancipated are likewise community property (*Messimer* v. *Echols* [Tex. Civ. App.] ; 194 S. W. 1171 [1917]). The **Louisiana** Code departs considerably from the general rule. The wife's earnings when she is living apart from the husband are her separate property. "The produce of the reciprocal industry and labor" of the spouses is designated as community property, but the wife's earnings "when carrying on a business, trade, occupation or industry separate from her husband" belong to her separately. One gathers that in **Louisiana** the wife's earnings are her separate property, even though she is living with the husband, unless such earnings are the product of the "reciprocal industry and labor" of both spouses. The husband's earnings must inevitably fall into the community. Obviously, this is a significant discrimination in favor of the wife. **Louisiana,** however, is not the only jurisdiction which gives the wife an advantage in this respect not enjoyed by the husband. The statutes of **Arizona, California, Idaho, Nevada, New Mexico,** and **Washington** give to the wife as her separate property the earnings and "accumulations" of herself and minor children living with her or in her custody while she is living separate from the husband. Literally read, these statutes do not require the separation to be by reason of the husband's fault. Finally, a **Nevada** statute makes the wife's earnings her separate property when the husband allows her to appropriate the same to her separate use.

5. *Compensation for injury to person or property.*—Only two jurisdictions have attempted to designate by statute the character of damages recovered for personal injury to either or both of the spouses. By a recent statute in **Texas,** compensation for personal injury sustained by the wife was made the wife's separate property (Sess. L. 1915, Ch. 54, p. 103 ; Complete St. 1928, Civ. St., Art. 4615). This statute was held unconstitutional, following the reasoning advanced in *Arnold* v. *Leonard, supra,* that the constitutional definition of the wife's separate property is exclusive (*Northern Texas Traction Company* v. *Hill* [Tex. Civ. App.] ; 297 S. W. 778 [1927] ; *Teague* v. *Fairchild* [Tex. Comm. of App.] ; 15 S. W. [2d] 585 [1929]). **Louisiana** provides that damages resulting from personal injury to the wife are her separate property and recoverable by her alone, that damages resulting from "offenses and

§ 178]

quasi-offenses" against her are her separate property, but that damages for "offenses and quasi-offenses" suffered by the husband are his separate property only if he is living apart from the wife by reason of her fault sufficient for separation or divorce. Here again the wife is given an advantage over the husband.

The general rule elsewhere seems well established that injury to either spouse during marriage gives rise to a community cause of action because the same is property not acquired from one of the statutory sources of separate property. In spite of the fact that the damages recovered are community property, **California** allows the wife to sue alone without the husband's joinder for injuries to her person (C. C. P. 1933 [Lake], Sec. 370). One of the necessary results of the general rule would seem to be that the contributory negligence of one spouse will bar a recovery for a negligent injury to the other. Thus, under the **Washington** conception of the community as an entity, it is said that the husband's contributory negligence is the negligence of the community (*Ostheller* v. *Spokane and Inland Empire Railroad Company,* 107 Wash. 678; 182 P. 630 [1919]) ; and in **California** it is said that the husband's contributory negligence must bar recovery for the wife's injury or the husband will be enabled to benefit by his own wrong (*Basler* v. *Sacramento Gas and Electric Company,* 158 Cal. 514; 111 P. 530 [1910]). The latter line of reasoning cannot be advanced if the husband dies subsequent to the injury. It is held, however, that the right to recover is determined as of the time of the injury and not by subsequent events (*Solko* v. *Jones,* 117 Cal. App. 372; 3 P. [2d] 1028 [1931]). The general rule above also leads to another dilemma. Suppose, for instance, that the wife wishes to recover from Madame X for the alienation of her husband's affections. Ordinarily the husband must be at least a passive partner in the intrigue. The wife should not be denied relief ; but it seems absurd and like rewarding the husband for his unfaithfulness to throw the proceeds of the suit into his control as a part of the community personal property. The **Texas** court, in a case in which the wife sought recovery for an injury in which the husband was a joint tort feasor, held the recovery to be the wife's separate property (*Nickerson* v. *Nickerson,* 65 Tex. 281 [1886]). While this decision is consonant with common sense, yet the **Texas** court thereby did the very thing which later in *Arnold* v. *Leonard, supra,* it forbade the legislature to do. The whole doctrine that a cause of action for personal injury to one of the spouses, and the proceeds thereof, are necessarily community property, has been fairly and severely criti-

[§ 178

cized as not only illogical but extremely inequitable.[1] There seems no escape, however, from the conclusion that recovery for loss of earning capacity sustained by one of the spouses should belong to the community.

Whether damages recovered for an invasion of property are community or separate depends upon the character of the property invaded. There are no statutes codifying this rule.

6. *Miscellaneous.*—In **California** and **Nevada,** the wife may become a sole trader under certain conditions and by meeting certain prerequisites, and thereby acquire, as her own, property which normally would belong to the community. These statutes are discussed in **Section 187.** The character of personal property acquired while domiciled in one of the so-called common-law states is not changed by the establishment of a domicile in one of the community-property states. **California** has recently attempted to effect such a metamorphosis. This statute, which is reproduced in Table LXXXIX, column three, and briefly discussed in **Section 177,** has recently been declared unconstitutional (*In re Thornton's Estate,* 221 Cal. 1; 33 P. [2d] 1 [1934]).

The discussion above takes into account all of the statutes defining separate and community property. The numerous instances in which the wife is placed at an advantage in the acquisition of separate property are perhaps more significant than the difference between states in the respective definitions of separate property. The statutory definition of community property by the process of exclusion may at first blush seem simple of application. Its application to concrete situations, however, is often difficult, and its literal application may not always lead to sensible results. Property may be acquired by many complex routes, routes which themselves are neither separate nor community in character.

One of the interesting problems, for the solution of which the statutes are of little assistance, arises when separate property is improved with community property, or vice versa. The general rule seems to be that the character of property is determined at the time of its acquisition; hence, improvements follow the title. Fairness demands that reimbursement be made. **Louisiana,** however, is the only jurisdiction which has an express statute providing for reimbursement and the measure thereof, and it refers only to the improvement of separate property by the use of community funds (see Table LXXXIX, footnote 21 *j,* p. 251).

---

[1] McKay, *op. cit.,* Sec. 398, p. 268.

§ 178]

The powers of the wife in relation to her separate property are discussed in other sections of this volume. The common-law incapacities of the wife were of course never recognized by **Louisiana,** and it is said that "the common law is not, and never has been, in force with respect to marital rights in **Texas**" (*Crim* v. *Austin* [Tex. Comm. of App.]; 6 S. W. [2d] 348, 350 [1928]). But even in these jurisdictions, as in the others, the same general evolution of the wife's legal personality has taken place. With the exception of **Texas,** the wife in all the community-property states may be regarded as a feme sole in relation to her separate property.

III. Statutory Presumptions as to the Character of Property

All property acquired during coverture by either of the spouses is presumed to be community property. This rebuttable presumption in favor of the community is said to be fundamental in the community-property system, but it is reduced to statute in none of the jurisdictions. Both **Louisiana** and **Texas,** however, have a statutory presumption that property possessed by either spouse at the dissolution of the marriage is community property.

The general presumption, instead of being reduced to statute, has been considerably modified by statute in **California** and **New Mexico,** and to a lesser extent in **Texas.** In **California** and **New Mexico,** when property is conveyed to the wife by written instrument, the presumption is that she gets title thereto as her separate property. If conveyed to the wife and husband, or to the wife and a third party, the presumption is that she takes her part as tenant in common unless the instrument expresses a different intention. The **California** statute expressly covers acquisitions of both real and personal property and of mortgages. Both statutes make the presumption conclusive in favor of the wife's bona fide purchaser. The advantage which the wife derives by means of this presumption is by no means insignificant. Thus, when property is conveyed to husband and wife, the presumption is that the spouses are tenants in common, the wife holding her interest in her separate right and the husband holding the remaining interest as community property (*Dunn* v. *Mullan,* 211 Cal. 583; 269 P. 604 [1931]). Even though the husband establishes that community consideration was given for the conveyance, he must then rebut the presumption that the wife holds her part in her separate right by reason of a gift from him. For a recent and

[§ 178

interesting **California** case in which property was deeded to husband and wife as joint tenants for a community consideration, and in which each spouse was finally held to hold his interest as separate property, the statutory presumption being inapplicable, see *Siberell* v. *Siberell,* 214 Cal. 767; 7 P. (2d) 1003 (1932).

By the **Texas** statute, bank deposits are presumed to be the separate property of the spouse in whose name they stand regardless of which spouse made the deposit. The presumption is apparently conclusive as to the bank in absence of notice to the contrary. A **Nevada** statute provides that when the husband allows the wife to appropriate her earnings to her own use the same are "deemed" a gift to her. A rebuttable presumption to that effect would arise in all jurisdictions, but the **Nevada** presumption appears to be conclusive.

Four of the community-property states have statutes enabling the wife to record an inventory or schedule of her separate personal property (**California, Idaho**), or of both her real and separate property (**Nevada, Texas**), and thus give notice that the same belongs to her separately. These statutes are summarized in **Sections 174** and **175.** The **Texas** statute goes so far as to make the registration of such schedule conclusive as against subsequent creditors of and purchasers from the husband. The mere fact that record title to property stands in the wife's name ought to be notice of her separate interest. The **Texas** court, however, reached the strange result that the presumption that property acquired during coverture is community property cannot be disputed as against the husband's bona fide purchaser, even though the record title stands in the wife's name (*Cooke* v. *Bremond,* 27 Tex. 457 [1864]).

IV. Management, Control, and Disposition of
Community Property

Although the community of husband and wife owns community property, the rights and powers of ownership are not equally divided between the spouses. Indeed, that the husband should be the dominant figure is fundamental in the system. According to the Spanish law, for all practical purposes he is regarded as the owner of community property while the marriage lasts. The wife is very much of a silent partner until the dissolution of the community. While none of the states, except possibly **California,** recognize the husband as the owner of community property, in all jurisdictions he is the recipient of most of the

§ 178]

powers incident to ownership. With minor exceptions found in several jurisdictions, the wife is without statutory power to manage or dispose of community property during coverture. In an effort to give greater protection to the wife, however, there has been a marked tendency to place a statutory check upon the husband's powers, especially in the disposition of real property.

In the words of the **Louisiana** Code, the husband is the "head and master" of the community. That he is the active manager of the community is written into the statutes of all jurisdictions. This is true to the extent that for most purposes the wife is not a proper party in a suit by or against the community. His exclusive power to manage has been invaded, however, in two jurisdictions. In **Idaho,** the wife is given the management and control of that part of the community property which she directly contributes, and, in **Nevada,** of the earnings and accumulations of herself and minor children when used for family support.

If the husband is to be an efficient manager of the community, he necessarily must have considerable freedom in disposing of community personal property. His power in this respect is practically complete, as is evidenced by the broad statements in the several statutes that he may dispose of community personalty during coverture as though it were his separate property. According to the statutes of **California** and **Louisiana** he is limited in his power to give it away, but the practical force of this restriction as a security to the wife is not certain. Of course, even in the absence of statute, the courts will protect the wife in cases of flagrant fraud. In **California,** the husband cannot sell certain articles such as household furniture without the wife's written consent, and statutes of general application commonly require the joinder of both spouses in a mortgage of exempt property. **Nevada** (in the case of earnings and accumulations of wife and children when used for family maintenance) gives the wife some affirmative power to dispose of a particular part of the community personal property. This seems to be true also in **Idaho,** by reason of the general control which the wife has over her earnings and the fruits of her separate property, and in **Texas** when the wife becomes a sole trader (**Sec. 187**) and by reason of the statutory presumption in respect to bank deposits. In 1913, **Texas** empowered the wife to manage, control, and dispose of her earnings, the rents from her lands, and the interest and dividends from her securities (Sess. L. 1913, Ch. 32, p. 61). Following the legislative attempt to take the rents and revenues of her separate property out of the community, this provision was removed, perhaps inadvertently, from the statutes (Sess. L.

[§ 178

1927, Ch. 148, p. 219; Complete St. 1928, Civ. St., Art. 4619). As a matter of domestic routine, the normal wife without the aid of statute probably assumes the power to control that part of the community property which she directly contributes.

A more stringent check is placed upon the husband's power to dispose of community real property. So far as the statutes are concerned, his power in this respect is still complete in three jurisdictions, except as to the disposal, etc., of the community homestead (**Nevada, Texas**) and conveyances by a gratuitous title (**Louisiana**). Also, a recent **Louisiana** statute requires him to secure the wife's written consent when she holds record title to the property. The remaining jurisdictions (**Arizona, California, Idaho, New Mexico, Washington**) all have statutes, most of them of fairly recent origin, requiring the wife's joinder in a conveyance or encumbrance of community real property. This legislation is reproduced in the table following, in the phraseology of the statutes so far as practicable. According to the literal wording of the **New Mexico** statute, the husband's sole conveyance is void (*Terry* v. *Humphrey,* 27 N. M. 564; 203 P. 539 [1922]); and the same result seems to be reached under the **Idaho** statute (*McKinney* v. *Merritt,* 35 Idaho 600; 208 P. 244 [1922]). In **California,** the husband's sole conveyance is said to be voidable only, at the instance of the wife when she has not estopped herself by her subsequent conduct (*Schelling* v. *Thomas,* 96 Cal. App. 682; 274 P. 755 [1929]). The **California** cases contain statements that the husband's conveyance is voidable only to the extent of the wife's interest in the community (*Pretzer* v. *Pretzer,* 215 Cal. 659; 12 P. [2d] 429 [1932]). Probably this is true only when the community has since been dissolved by death or divorce. The very short statute of limitations set up by the **California** statute must as a practical matter render the wife's protection rather insufficient even as against the husband's donee.

These statutes which require the joinder of both spouses in the disposition of community real property are designed for a worthy purpose. They do not in themselves, however, prevent the husband with record title from selling such property to a bona fide purchaser and then dissipating the consideration. This situation presents two equally worthy interests. A bona fide purchaser who deals with the husband on the strength of his record title deserves as much sympathy as the neglected wife. Only two states (**California, Washington**) have specific legislation dealing with this problem. Of course, if the sole conveyance of the husband is actually void, further legislation is unnecessary, but a

§ 178]

harsh result is reached. The **California** statute provides that the sole deed, etc., of the husband with record title to a bona fide purchaser without knowledge of the marriage is "presumed" to be valid. Until recently it was thought that this so-called presumption was conclusive (*Rice* v. *McCarthy,* 73 Cal. App. 655; 239 P. 56 [1925]). A late decision, however, holds that it is disputable and that the wife if not estopped may have the instrument set aside, but only upon the condition that the innocent purchaser has his consideration returned (consideration which passed into the husband's control and which we may assume has been improvidently squandered) (*Mark* v. *Title Guarantee and Trust Company,* 122 Cal. App. 301; 9 P. [2d] 839 [1932]). Obviously, relief upon such a condition will ordinarily avail the wife nothing. But a choice must be made between the bona fide purchaser and the wife. One of them is bound to suffer. **Washington** seems to have reached an admirable statutory solution to this perplexing problem by providing that the spouse holding the record title may convey full legal and equitable title to an actual bona fide purchaser, but that the other spouse may protect his or her community interest by recording a written notice of such interest.

Under the **California** and **New Mexico** statutes, to which reference has already been made, if the wife holds record title to real property, her conveyance to a bona fide purchaser is conclusively presumed to be a conveyance of her separate property.

Any general powers which the wife has to dispose of community property mature only upon dissolution of the community by reason of her death. In the matter of testamentary control, both spouses stand upon an equal footing in six jurisdictions. In **Arizona, California, Idaho, Louisiana, Texas,** and **Washington** each may dispose of his or her one-half interest in the community property, subject of course to its share of the community debts. **Idaho,** however, limits the direction which such testamentary disposition may take (see Table LXXXIX); and in **Louisiana,** the testamentary control of the spouses is limited by the rights of forced heirs (lineal descendants and parents). **Nevada** and **New Mexico** alone discriminate against the wife. In these two jurisdictions, the husband may dispose of one-half of the community property by will; but so long as the marital ship sails upon smooth waters, the wife has no testamentary control and the husband is entitled to all of the community property upon her death. The **Nevada** and **New Mexico** statutes were copied from **California,** where the same situation existed prior to a 1923 amendment (Sess. L. 1923, Ch. 18, p. 29). This discrimination rests upon the supposed desirability of allowing the hus-

[§ 178

band's possession and control to remain undisturbed by the death of
the wife.

It is somewhat of a surprise to find that only four jurisdictions
(**California, Idaho, New Mexico, Texas**) have any special legislation
anticipating the emergency which arises when the husband becomes incapacitated to act as the managing head of the community, or when the
wife becomes incapacitated to join in conveyances. These statutes are
briefly summarized in footnote 12 of Table LXXXIX (pp. 247–48). The
statutes of **New Mexico** and **Texas** under which the wife may be
substituted as managing head of the community when the husband for
any reason becomes incapacitated (**New Mexico**) or when he deserts
the wife or is adjudged insane (**Texas**) are of special significance.

Even in the absence of special statute, the wife may perhaps acquire
the power to dispose of community property in circumstances creating
an emergency. In a most interesting **Washington** case, the wife in the
husband's absence took possession of a community automobile which
the unfaithful spouse had given his mistress, and sold and passed good
title to the same (*Marston* v. *Rue,* 92 Wash. 129; 159 P. 111 [1916]).
The court thought that the automobile should be properly classed with
perishable goods!

V. LIABILITY OF COMMUNITY PROPERTY

An examination of the statutes does not reveal either the limits or
the substance of the liability of community property. The reader is directed to those ambiguous statements of community liability in general,
found in the statutes of **Arizona, Louisiana, Texas,** and **Washington.**
Then also in connection with testate and intestate administration, the
community property is said to be subject to "community debts" (**Idaho,
Washington**) or the "husband's debts" (**California, Nevada, New
Mexico**). This field of community-property law has been largely developed in the cases. In fact, the statutes are in the main concerned with
exempting particular community property from liability.

With but few exceptions, the husband as community manager necessarily has the exclusive power to bind the community property. If the
wife may charge the community property by her contracts, it must be
upon some theory of agency or quasi contract. The general inability of
the wife in this respect is written into the statutes of **Arizona, California, New Mexico,** and **Texas.** There are some exceptions, however,
and the most significant of these is found in **Texas.** Under the **Texas**
statute, that part of the community property directly contributed by the

§ 178]

wife (her earnings, and the rents and revenues of her separate property) is placed outside the general rule. The wife may, then, indirectly dispose of that part of the community property. Further exceptions seem to exist in **Louisiana** under an old provision which enables the wife to bind the husband when she acts as a "public merchant," and in **Idaho** and **Nevada** by reason of the wife's statutory power to manage and control a particular part of the community property. In all the jurisdictions the community property is liable for necessaries furnished to the wife. Express statutes to that effect are found in **Arizona** and **Texas.** This liability may be said to grow out of the husband's duty to support rather than out of any special power which the wife has to bind the community property. The statutes are silent as to the liability of the community property for the torts of the wife. **Texas** expressly provides that the separate property of the husband is not liable for the wife's torts; and **California** and **Washington** provide that damages therefor may be recovered from the wife alone, the husband being liable only as a joint tort feasor (**Sec. 157**). Neither of these latter statutes expressly precludes holding the community property liable. Having regard for the nature and structure of the system, the community property ought not to be charged with the wife's civil wrongs unless upon some theory of agency or unless the husband himself is liable therefor. A **Texas** court has held that the husband's liability remains undisturbed except to the extent of the statute above, and that the community property may be subjected to a judgment against him for the wife's negligence (*Campbell* v. *Johnson* [Tex. Civ. App.]; 284 S. W. 261 [1926], affirmed in 290 S. W. 526 [1927]). A recent **Arizona** case holds the community property liable for the wife's negligence when as a matter of law she is acting as the agent of the community (*Selaster* v. *Simmons,* 39 Ariz. 432; 7 P. [2d] 258 [1932]).

Except in **Arizona** and **Washington,** the general rule seems to be that the husband's creditors may look to the community property for the satisfaction of liabilities incurred by the husband, whether before or after marriage, in tort or in contract, as manager of the community or in his individual separate capacity. This follows naturally from the **California** conception that the husband owns the community property, and perhaps in the other jurisdictions as a practical scheme to make the system function fairly. But the result is not always strictly logical. Though the joinder of both spouses may be required in a conveyance of community real property, the husband may indirectly dispose of the same by charging it with his separate obligations. Though the wife may be conceded to

[§ 178

have a present vested interest in community property, such interest may be seized and sold to satisfy obligations from which neither she nor the community derived any benefit. The **Louisiana** statute reproduced in Table LXXXIX seems to forbid the husband's premarital creditors attacking the community fund. An early decision, however, holds that the community property is liable for the husband's antenuptial debts, and that this provision applies only to a division of the property upon dissolution of the community, at which time the wife is entitled to reimbursement (*Guice* v. *Lawrence,* 2 La. Ann. 226 [1847]).

The **Washington** court, consistent with its entity theory of the community, holds that the community property is liable for "community" obligations only. These are, roughly, obligations incurred (ordinarily, of course, by the husband) in tort or contract for the benefit of the community or while managing the community (*Schramm* v. *Steele,* 97 Wash. 309; 166 P. 634 [1917]; *J. I. Case Threshing Machine Company* v. *Wiley,* 89 Wash. 597; 154 P. 437 [1916]; *Wimmer* v. *Nicholson,* 151 Wash. 199; 275 P. 699 [1929]). Thus, in the *Schramm* case, the community property was held not liable on a judgment against the husband for alienation of affections. **Arizona** now appears to have adopted in full the **Washington** view (*Cosper* v. *Valley Bank,* 28 Ariz. 373; 237 P. 175 [1925], overruling *Villescas* v. *Arizona Copper Company,* 20 Ariz. 268; 179 P. 963 [1919]). The result in **Arizona** is largely based upon the wording of the local statute under which community property is liable for "community debts" contracted by the husband. In these two jurisdictions, debts incurred by the husband during marriage are presumed to be community obligations. The **Arizona** and **Washington** rule goes a long way in the direction of equal rights, and is more consistent with the recognition that the wife has a present vested interest in community property. But it enables the husband without separate property to develop extensive community assets, yet to escape during marriage just contractual and tortious obligations.

Statutes commonly place that part of the community property which the wife accumulates outside the reach of the ordinary run of community creditors. Thus, in **Idaho,** the rents and profits of the wife's separate property, and, in **Texas,** the rents from the wife's lands and the interest and dividends from the wife's bonds, stocks, etc., are not liable for the husband's obligations, whether in tort or contract. The wife's earnings are protected from the husband's debts in **California, Nevada, New Mexico, Texas,** and **Washington.** The **Texas** statute expressly excludes liability for the husband's torts, and such is the probable effect

§ 178]

of the others. This protection probably continues so long as the wife's earnings can be identified. The exemption seems intended to cover obligations incurred by the husband for the benefit of the community. It has been so held under the **California** and **Texas** statutes (*Street* v. *Bertolone,* 193 Cal. 751; 226 P. 913 [1924]; *In re Gutierrez,* 33 F. [2d] 987 [1929]). In **Washington,** however, it is said that the wife's earnings are not exempt from a judgment against the community (*Fisher* v. *Marsh,* 69 Wash. 570; 125 P. 951 [1912]). Finally, an **Idaho** statute exempts compensation "due and owing" to the wife for personal services from execution against the husband. According to a recent decision, the exemption ceases when the earnings are converted into other property, and perhaps also when such earnings are collected and are no longer due and owing (*McM'illan* v. *United States Fire Insurance Company,* 48 Idaho 163; 280 P. 220 [1929]). One gathers that the **Idaho** statute comprehends all types of obligations incurred by the husband.

With the exception of **Louisiana,** the statutes are silent as to the liability of community property for the wife's antenuptial obligations, and the **Louisiana** provision apparently is not intended to define community liability during coverture. **Arizona, California, Idaho, Nevada, New Mexico,** and **Texas** provide that the husband's separate property is not liable for the debts of the wife "contracted" before marriage, and **Washington** provides that the husband is not liable for the debts of the wife incurred before marriage (**Sec. 151**). **California** and **Texas,** upon different lines of reasoning, have held the community property liable for the wife's antenuptial contracts (*Van Maren* v. *Johnson,* 15 Cal. 308 [1860]; *Johnson* v. *Taylor,* 120 Cal. App. 771; 4 P. [2d] 999 [1931]; *Taylor* v. *Murphy,* 50 Tex. 291 [1883]; *Crim* v. *Austin* [Tex. Comm. of App.]; 6 S. W. [2d] 348 [1928], affirming 299 S. W. 322 [1927]). **Arizona,** consistent with its general view of community liability, has reached a contrary result (*Forsythe* v. *Paschal,* 34 Ariz. 380; 271 P. 865 [1928]); and in accord with **Arizona** is the net effect of a 1905 **Washington** decision (*Anderson* v. *Hilker,* 38 Wash. 632; 80 P. 848 [1905]).

Finally, it needs to be mentioned that the husband's separate property is charged not only with those liabilities which he incurs for his own separate benefit, but with those he incurs as manager of the community as well. The separate property of the wife, on the other hand, is liable for neither type of obligation unless it be because of her own affirmative conduct. The statutes which protect the wife's separate property from the husband's debts are summarized in **Section 159.**

[§ 178

VI. Survivor's Rights: Descent, Succession, Administration, etc.

One of the fundamental features of the community-property system is that the surviving spouse comes into a several ownership of one-half of the community fund upon the dissolution of the community. It is at the husband's death that the wife assumes the role of an equal in the marital venture. Whatever may have been the exact nature of her interest during coverture, she now becomes owner of her share of the marital gains. Thus, in **Arizona, California, Idaho, Louisiana, Texas,** and **Washington,** upon the death of either spouse, one-half of the community property "goes" or "belongs," etc., to the survivor. In the two jurisdictions which discriminate, **Nevada** and **New Mexico,** one-half "goes" to the surviving wife upon the husband's death, while ordinarily the entire community property "belongs" to the surviving husband upon the wife's death. In no jurisdiction does either spouse have testamentary control over more than his moiety. If a greater control is attempted, the survivor may be put to an election. Under the **California** conception of community ownership, and contrary to the results reached in the other states, the surviving wife has been held to take her moiety as heir of the husband (*In re Burdick's Estate,* 112 Cal. 387; 44 P. 734 [1896]). Hence, her moiety is subject to inheritance tax (*In re Moffitt's Estate,* 153 Cal. 359; 95 P. 653 [1908]; *Moffitt* v. *Kelly,* 218 U. S. 400; 31 Sup. Ct. 79; 54 L. Ed. 1086 [1910]). In 1917, however, she was expressly exempt from such tax (Sess. L. 1917, Ch. 589, p. 880). For the other pertinent provisions of the present inheritance tax law of **California,** see footnote 21 *e* of Table LXXXIX (p. 250).

If either husband or wife dies intestate, **California** and **Idaho** give his or her moiety to the survivor, while **Arizona, Louisiana, Texas,** and **Washington** prefer decedent's descendants. If no descendants (**Arizona, Texas, Washington**) or no forced heirs (**Louisiana**) survive, then the surviving wife takes the whole of decedent's moiety. **Louisiana** also gives the survivor a usufruct for life, or until remarriage, of the share inherited by issue of the marriage. In **Nevada** and **New Mexico,** if the wife dies intestate having testamentary power over a part of the community property because of the husband's misconduct, the husband for obvious reasons is not made her heir; and if the husband dies intestate, **Nevada** prefers his descendants, while in **New Mexico** the surviving wife shares with his descendants.

Attention is directed to the odd course of devolution prescribed by

§ 178]

California and **New Mexico** in the case of an intestate without issue leaving property which was formerly the community property of himself and a previously deceased spouse (see Table LXXXIX, footnote 21 *c*, p. 250). It is also of interest that **Louisiana** is the only jurisdiction with legislation on the effect of an invalid or putative marriage upon property rights (see table, footnote 21 *l*, p. 251).

The statutes dealing with the administration of community-property estates are peculiarly few and fragmentary. If the surviving husband takes the deceased wife's moiety, there seems to be no practical necessity for administration inasmuch as the community property is not liable for the wife's debts. That administration in this situation is unnecessary is written into the statutes of **Nevada, New Mexico,** and **Texas** and is implied by the statute of **California.** If, however, the husband dies, or the wife dies and the husband's control is broken by reason of her will or the laws of descent, it is evident that some type of administration is necessary in order to give creditors convenient access to the entire community estate. In the absence of special statute, there seems to be some logical difficulty in justifying the jurisdiction of a probate court over the survivor's moiety, if the survivor holds his moiety by some right more secure than that of an heir. Strangely enough, **California,** in which the wife has been held to take her moiety as an heir, appears to be the only jurisdiction to provide in direct terms for the administration of community-property estates. The other statutes are more concerned with withdrawing the community estate from administration in certain situations, or in establishing a substitute for administration (see Table LXXXIX, and footnote 16, pp. 248–49).

One of the serious disadvantages incident to the community-property system is the disruption of the husband's business activities caused by the wife's death. The husband may have spent years in building a successful enterprise and find it suddenly broken up by the untimely death of his spouse and the interference of her heirs or devisees. **Nevada** and **New Mexico** avoid this situation by giving the entire community property to the surviving husband. In the same general direction are the statutes found in three jurisdictions (**California, Texas, Washington**) giving the surviving husband some special control over the dissolved community (see footnote 17, p. 249, of Table LXXXIX). Both the **Texas** and **Washington** statutes, however, give an equal advantage to the surviving wife. The rights enjoyed by the surviving spouse in **Texas** seem a complete substitute for any ordinary probate administration.

[§ 178

The statutes contain only vague statements as to the rights of creditors against the dissolved community. Upon the death of either spouse, the entire community property must bear the debts chargeable against it. But in those jurisdictions in which the husband's separate creditors may pursue the community property, some kind of an equitable distribution of the burden of the husband's debts between the community property and his separate property ought to be, but is not, provided for. From a literal reading of several of the statutes, one might gather that the deceased wife's moiety must bear all of the debts chargeable against the community property. The statutes are also silent as to whether the deceased wife's separate creditors may intercept her moiety on its way to her heirs or devisees after the primary charges against the community property have been met. To allow her creditors this advantage seems only fair, and not repugnant to the reasons for excluding the wife from active participation in the community during coverture. An analogous situation arises in **Arizona** and **Washington** when the husband's separate creditors seek to intercept the deceased husband's moiety of the community property. The statutes of both states are silent on the matter, but in both it has been held that his moiety is liable for his separate debts after the community obligations have been satisfied (*Jackson* v. *Griffen,* 39 Ariz. 183; 4 P. [2d] 900 [1931] ; *In re McHugh's Estate,* 165 Wash. 123; 4 P. [2d] 834 [1931]).

The civil law of **Louisiana** is quite different from the law of any other jurisdiction. An heir is offered his succession. If he accepts without reservation, he becomes liable for a proportionate share of decedent's debts. If he renounces, he loses his rights but escapes liability. He may, however, pursue a middle course and accept "under benefit of inventory," in which case his liability is limited to the value of his succession. Upon the husband's death, the same alternatives are open to the surviving wife in respect to her moiety of the community property. A similar choice is of course not open to the surviving husband. Certain further provisions in **Louisiana** relating to the division of property, etc., upon dissolution of the community are collected in footnote 20 of Table LXXXIX (pp. 249–50).

VII. MODIFYING THE COMMUNITY BY ANTENUPTIAL AND POSTNUPTIAL CONTRACTS, ETC.

One of the incidents of marriage and domicile in the eight states under discussion is the community system of property ownership. Like

§ 178]

dower and curtesy, it exists by operation of law, quite independent of any express agreement between the parties entering matrimony. Probably in all jurisdictions except **Texas,** however, a betrothed couple has extensive capacity to create a modified or conventional community or even obtain a complete separation of property by antenuptial agreement. **Louisiana** is the only jurisdiction with express statute to that effect (see Table LXXXIX, footnote 21 *g,* p. 251). In addition, **Arizona, Louisiana,** and **Texas** have almost identical legislation containing a broad general authority for the making of marriage contracts not contrary to good morals or rule of law, with certain specified limitations, among which is a limitation upon the power of the parties to change the legal order of descent (**Sec. 155**). This statute apparently had its origin in **Louisiana.** The prohibition against altering the legal order of descent is consistent with the general civil-law inability of the spouses to defeat the rights of forced heirs by transactions inter se. With this broad statute in mind, a **Texas** court recently said: "No contract that has for its effect the denying of the wife of her interest in the future earnings of the community is valid and enforceable" (*Gorman* v. *Gause* [Tex. Civ. App.] ; 36 S. W. [2d] 279 [1931]). The court had before it an agreement whereby the separate property of the parties, and the anticipated acquisitions during coverture, were to be pooled and split one-third to the wife and two-thirds to the husband. Such an agreement was thought to undermine the status accorded to the wife by the constitution and statutes of the state, to subvert the laws of descent, and in general to be contrary to public policy. This seems to be a very narrow interpretation and to practically obliterate the operative force of the statute. **California, Idaho, Nevada,** and **New Mexico** impliedly authorize the making of marriage contracts by prescribing certain formalities which such contracts must meet to be legally effective (**Sec. 155**). In addition, the statutes of these four jurisdictions contain in substance the statement that the property rights of the spouses are governed by the provisions in respect to separate and community property unless there is a marriage contract containing stipulations to the contrary (see Table LXXXIX, footnote 21 *g,* p. 251), thus recognizing the legal capacity of the parties themselves to define their future property relationship. **Washington** is the only community-property state without specific legislation on the subject of marriage contracts. It is not probable, however, that the parties there have less freedom to enter into such agreements.

The community is of course dissolved upon dissolution of the marriage, whether by death or divorce. The division of community property

upon divorce is discussed in Volume II, **Section 101** of this study. The
Louisiana Code is also specific to the effect that a limited divorce dis-
solves the community (C. C., Art. 155). In both **California** and **New
Mexico,** either spouse may in a proper case obtain a judicial division
of the community property without divorce (see Table LXXXIX, footnote 21 *k,* p. 251). The wife in **California** and **Nevada** may obtain a
partial separation of property by acquiring the status of a feme sole
trader (**Sec. 187**). With the exception of **Louisiana** and **Washington,**
however, the statutes are silent as to the ability of the spouses to modify
or dissolve the community by postnuptial contract.

The general scheme of the **Louisiana** civil law in respect to family
property is necessarily opposed to postnuptial modifications of property
rights by contract between husband and wife. Thus, the Code expressly
provides that a voluntary separation of property is of no effect, even as
between the spouses. One exclusive mode by which a postnuptial separation of property may be obtained without death or divorce is established. The wife is authorized to sue for a separation of property when
her separate property is endangered by the husband's financial mismanagement (see Table LXXXIX, footnote 21 *i,* p. 251). This she
may do even though for the purpose of protecting her future anticipatory
earnings only (*Pfaff* v. *Bender,* 38 F. [2d] 642 [1929]). If the separation is decreed, her rights in the community are the same as when the
marriage is dissolved by death. She may renounce or accept under benefit of inventory and thus escape or limit her liability for community
obligations. It is of interest that the wife after a separation of property
is under a duty to contribute to the family expenses "in proportion to her
fortune and to that of her husband."

Washington provides that the spouses may contract concerning the
status or disposition of community property, present or expectant, "to
take effect upon the death of either" (**Sec. 156**). This statute is not
construed as exclusive. Thus, a postnuptial agreement that the property
each acquires thereafter shall be his or her separate property is valid
if mutually observed (*Union Securities Company* v. *Smith,* 93 Wash.
115; 160 P. 304 [1916]); and present separate property may be changed
to community property by a properly executed agreement (*Volz* v. *Zang,*
113 Wash. 378; 194 P. 409 [1920]). **California, Nevada,** and **New
Mexico** have almost identical statutes clothing the spouses with a broad
power to alter their legal relations as to property by contract subject to
the rules respecting fiduciary relationships (**Sec. 156**). In these states,
as in **Washington,** the husband and wife may undoubtedly contract so

§ 178]

as to obtain for all practical purposes a complete separation of property, subject of course to the legally protected rights of creditors. Thus, the husband may effectively agree to relinquish his interest in community property, both present and expectant (*Perkins* v. *Sunset Telephone and Telegraph Company,* 155 Cal. 712; 103 P. 190 [1909]; see also *Gray* v. *Perlis,* 76 Cal. App. 511; 245 P. 221 [1926]). Referring to the **California** statute, the **California** court has said: "Under this plenary authority, the separate property of each may be converted into community property, and the community property of both may likewise be converted into separate property of both or either" (*Siberell* v. *Siberell,* 214 Cal. 767; 7 P. [2d] 1003, 1004 [1932]); and this may apparently be accomplished by a mere oral understanding (*In re Sill's Estate,* 121 Cal. App. 202; 9 P. [2d] 243 [1932]). The remaining jurisdictions (**Arizona, Idaho, Texas**) do not expressly authorize the spouses to contract inter se, and recourse must be had to those statutes defining generally the wife's contractual capacity (**Sec. 152**) and to the general jurisprudence of the state. **Texas** seems to allow the spouses little freedom to alter the community relationship. It is said that the "husband and wife have no power to change, by mere agreement made in advance, the status of community property yet to come into existence, to that of wife's separate property" (*Frame* v. *Frame,* 120 Tex. 61; 36 S. W. [2d] 152, 155 [1931]); and that "any division of community property made by husband and wife during marriage, except in contemplation of separation, is void and unenforceable" (*Gorman* v. *Gause* [Tex. Civ. App.]; 36 S. W. [2d] 279, 280 [1931]). Contrary to **California, Texas** does not allow the spouses to convert community property to separate property or vice versa except by a contract which in law has the effect of an actual conveyance (*Blair* v. *Stewart,* 49 F. [2d] 257 [1931], and cases there cited). Finally, it seems probable that a separation of property may be obtained as incident to a separation agreement in all jurisdictions except **Louisiana.**

If the husband or wife may pass his or her interest in present community property to the other by legally recognized modes of transfer and conveyance, subject to the rights of creditors, it is obvious that they may effect a partial or complete separation of property at any particular time. That this may be done is no doubt the general rule in all jurisdictions but **Louisiana. New Mexico** and **Washington,** however, are the only states with express statutes to that effect, and they refer to the conveyance of community interest in real property only. **Louisiana** prescribes a narrow boundary within which the spouses may engage in property

[§ 178

transactions together (see **Secs. 156, 182**). Generally speaking, neither can convey directly or indirectly to the other his or her interest in community property (see *Dummir* v. *Davis Bros. Lumber Company, Ltd.,* 17 La. App. 309; 135 So. 684 [1931]). In **Arizona,** it was thought until recently that the statute requiring the joinder of both spouses in a conveyance of community real property would preclude a conveyance from wife to husband, but such a conveyance is now recognized as possible (*Schofield* v. *Gold,* 26 Ariz. 296; 225 P. 71 [1924], reversing on rehearing same case, 25 Ariz. 213; 215 P. 169 [1923]). The statutes requiring the wife's joinder in conveyances of community lands are designed to protect the wife in the husband's transactions with third parties, and obviously should not be applied so as to prevent conveyances between the spouses.

VIII. Nature of Community Ownership, etc.

The nature of community ownership and of the wife's interest in community property has occasioned much discussion and controversy. The statutes allocate various powers ordinarily thought by the common-law lawyer to be the incidents of ownership, but they do not otherwise define or describe the ownership of community property. Tiffany, in the recent edition of his *Law of Real Property* (Sec. 195), finds two theories of community ownership in the United States. Mr. Evans, writing in 35 Harvard Law Review 46, finds four distinct theories: (*a*) the **California** or single-ownership theory, which makes the husband the owner of community property, and gives the wife only an expectancy during marriage; (*b*) the **Washington** or entity theory, which ostensibly recognizes ownership in the "community," a distinct entity composed of husband and wife and in which each spouse has an equal interest; (*c*) the **Idaho** or double-ownership theory (followed by **Arizona, Nevada, New Mexico**), which recognizes a sort of co-ownership in which each spouse has legal title equal to that of the other; (*d*) the **Texas** or trust theory, under which the beneficial interest of the spouses is equal, but the legal title is in the husband or the spouse with record title. Mr. Evans indicates that **Louisiana** has followed the **Texas** theory more nearly than any other but perhaps cannot be placed in any of the categories above. McKay (*Community Property,* Sec. 1182) agrees with this classification, except as to some minor differences, and except as to **Louisiana,** which he places in the same general category as **California.** Mrs. Daggett (19 Calif. L. Rev. 567), familiar with **Louisiana** jurisprudence, agrees that the **Louisiana** system contemplates the husband as owner of

§ 178]

the community property during marriage, but confesses that the courts have at times found a vested interest of some kind in the wife. Finally, we have it from the **Arizona** court itself that "the community law of this state, as construed by our decisions, is more like that of the State of **Washington** than any other of the community-property states" (*Selaster* v. *Simmons,* 39 Ariz. 432; 7 P. [2d] 258 [1932]).

The nature of the wife's interest in community property has recently been given a close scrutiny in connection with federal income tax returns. The contention is that the wife may make a separate return of one-half of the community income if she has a vested interest therein. Justice Holmes's decision in *United States* v. *Robbins* (269 U. S. 315; 46 Sup. Ct. 148; 70 L. Ed. 285 [1926]), holding that under the **California** system the husband must return the entire community income, raised doubt as to the practice of split returns followed in some of the other community-property states. In a series of 1930 decisions, the United States Supreme Court affirmed the right of the husband and wife in **Arizona, Louisiana, Texas,** and **Washington** to return one-half of the community income each (*Goodell* v. *Kock* [Ariz.], 282 U.S. 118; 51 Sup. Ct. 62; 75 L. Ed. 247 [1930]; *Bender* v. *Pfaff* [La.], 282 U. S. 127; 51 Sup. Ct. 64; 75 L. Ed. 252 [1930]; *Hopkins* v. *Bacon* [Tex.], 282 U. S. 122; 51 Sup. Ct. 62; 75 L. Ed. 249 [1930]; *Poe* v. *Seaborn* [Wash.], 282 U. S. 101; 51 Sup. Ct. 58; 75 L. Ed. 239 [1930]). These cases go on the ground that in the foregoing jurisdictions the wife has an equal vested interest of some kind in community property. It seems evident that the same results must be reached in respect to the systems in **Idaho, New Mexico,** and **Nevada.** This of course means that the spouses may effect a considerable saving in taxes, with a corresponding loss in revenue to the federal government as long as the income tax statutes remain in their present form.

The **California** situation is interesting. The cases have consistently held that the ownership of community property lies in the husband, the wife having only an expectancy during coverture; and this conception of community ownership has not changed as new limitations upon the husband's control of community property have been written into the statutes (*Van Maren* v. *Johnson,* 15 Cal. 308 [1860]; *In re Burdick's Estate,* 112 Cal. 387; 44 P. 734 [1896]; *Stewart* v. *Stewart,* 199 Cal. 318; 249 P. 197 [1926]; 204 Cal. 546; 269 P. 439 [1928]). From this primary premise, the cases have as consistently held that the various legislative attempts to lessen the husband's control and increase the wife's control of community property cannot be effective upon property already

[§ 178

acquired without disturbing the husband's vested rights of ownership (*Spreckels* v. *Spreckels,* 116 Cal. 339; 48 P. 228 [1898]; *McKay* v. *Lauriston,* 204 Cal. 557; 269 P. 519 [1928]). In 1927, following the decision in *United States* v. *Robbins, supra,* the **California** legislature enacted the much-discussed Section 161a of the Civil Code, defining the wife's interest in community property as a "present, existing and equal" interest (see footnote 21 *d* of Table LXXXIX, p. 250). It will be observed that this legislation does not employ the term "vested," or in any way alter the statutory allocation of the powers of management and control. Nevertheless, it proved sufficient for immediate purposes. In a recent decision, the United States Supreme Court finds that the wife now has such a present interest in community property that she may make an income tax return upon one-half of the husband's current salary (*United States* v. *Malcolm,* 282 U. S. 792; 51 Sup. Ct. 184; 75 L. Ed. 714 [1931]). Section 161a does not enlarge the wife's interest in community property acquired before 1927 (*Stewart* v. *Stewart,* 204 Cal. 546; 269 P. 439 [1928]; *Levell* v. *Metropolitan Life Insurance Company,* 118 Cal. App. 426; 5 P. [2d] 430 [1931]). No other word has come from the **California** Supreme Court indicating what effect it will give to this strange bit of legislation. Only one conclusion seems reasonable, namely, that the wife now has an equal beneficial interest of some kind in community property acquired since 1927. Furthermore, it may well be argued that the **California** statute passed in 1923 (Prob. C. 1933 [Lake], Sec. 201) giving the wife the right of testamentary disposition of one-half of the community property should be construed as recognizing in her a present, vested right during marriage. (See an article by M. R. Kirkwood in 7 So. Calif. L. Rev. 1, at p. 10 [1933].)

It is remarkable that so many different conceptions of the fundamental nature of the community - property system should have been developed under substantially similar statutes. The courts have undoubtedly been influenced by the nation-wide clamor for equal rights. The recent statutory changes in respect to management and control have also been in that same direction. In conceding that the wife has a vested interest in community property, the courts have given her a status which the parent system apparently never intended her to have. Although differing as to the exact nature of her interest, they have made her a co-owner of a sort. In certain isolated instances, as in respect to inheritance and income taxation, whether the wife has a vested interest or only an expectancy may be thought extremely important. But in the ordinary points of contact between the husband and wife and third parties it seems

§ 178]

to make little difference. By and large, the husband exercises the rights of ownership. Whether he exercises those rights because he is owner, as in **California,** or because he is the statutory manager of the community, as in other jurisdictions, seems relatively unimportant. The wife finds herself with a "vested interest" in property which she cannot bind by contract, and which (except in **Arizona** and **Washington**) may be taken from her by the husband's separate creditors.

That the community-property system as it developed in the civil law was an eminent advance over the grotesque common law of marital rights cannot be questioned. Whether it or its offspring in the eight American states is to be preferred over the modern statutory systems found in the more enlightened of the so-called common-law states may well admit of doubt. One thing is certain: the community system has added its share to the perplexities of the law.

The table and notes follow.

[§ 178

Jurisdiction and Citation[2]	Husband's Separate Property	Wife's Separate Property	Community Property	Statutory Presumptions	Husband's Debts
Arizona .... R. C. 1928, Secs. 955, 985, 2172–76, 4175	All property, both real and personal, owned or claimed by husband before marriage, and that acquired afterward by gift, devise, or descent, together with increase, rents, issues, and profits of same (2173)	All property, both real and personal, owned or claimed by wife before marriage, and that acquired afterward by gift, devise or descent, together with increase, rents, issues and profits of same. Earnings and accumulations of wife and her minor children in her custody while living separate and apart from husband (2173)	All property acquired by either spouse during marriage, except that acquired by gift, devise or descent, or earned by wife and her minor children while living separate and apart from husband (2172)		Liable for "community debts" contracted by husband during marriage unless specifically excepted by law (2175)
California ...... Const., Art. XX, Sec. 8; C. C. 1933 (Lake), Secs. 137, 161–64, 167–69, 172, 172a–172d, 177, 687; Prob. C. 1933 (Lake), Secs. 21, 201–3, 228	All property owned by husband before marriage, and that acquired afterwards by gift, bequest, devise, or descent, with rents, issues, and profits thereof (163)[3]	All property owned by wife before marriage, and that acquired afterward by gift, bequest, devise, or descent, with rents, issues, and profits thereof (162).[3] Earnings and accumulations of wife and her minor children living with her or in her custody, while she is living separate from husband (169). See also **Sec. 187**	All property acquired by husband and wife, or either, during marriage, when not acquired as separate property of either (687),[4] including real property situated in California, and personal property wherever situated heretofore or hereafter acquired by spouses while domiciled elsewhere which would not have been separate property of either if acquired while domiciled in California (164)	When real or personal property or interest therein, or encumbrance thereon, is acquired by wife by instrument in writing, presumption is that same is her separate property; if acquired by wife and husband, or by wife and other person, presumption is that she takes her part as tenant in common unless instrument expresses different intention. Above presumptions are conclusive in favor of bona fide purchaser of wife (164)[8]	Earnings of wife are not liable for debt of husband

* See pages 246–51 for all numbered footnotes to this table.

§ 178]

XXXIX*

USBAND AND WIFE[1]

...nity Property	Control of Community Property				Survivor's Rights, Descent, Succession, Administration, etc.
Wife's Debts	Management	Disposition of Real Property during Marriage	Disposition of Personal Property during Marriage	Testamentary Control	
ife of 21 years s same rights adult male, cept right to ke contracts ding common operty (2174). case of dgment for bts contracted wife for cessaries upon edit of hus- nd, execution ied first upon nmon prop- ty (2176)		"A conveyance or encumbrance of the community property shall not be valid" unless executed and acknowledged by both spouses, except unpatented mining claims which may be conveyed, etc., by spouse having title or right of possession without other's joinder (955)	Personal property may be disposed of by husband only (2172)	Upon death of spouse, one half goes to survivor, and other half is subject to testamentary disposition of decedent (985)	One half goes to survivor. If testamentary power over other half not exercised, it goes to decedent's descendants equally if of same degree of kindred; otherwise, by right of representation. If no descendants survive, other half goes to surviving spouse. Community estate passes charged with the debts against it (985)[16]
t liable for tracts of e made after rriage unless ured by dge or mort- e thereof ecuted by sband (167)	Husband has management and control of both real and personal property (172–172a)	Wife, personally or by agent, must join in execution of any instrument by which real property or interest therein is leased for more than a year, or is sold, conveyed or encumbered, except in conveyances, etc., between spouses (172a)[9, 12]	Husband has absolute power of disposition, except testamentary, as of his separate property, except that he cannot make gift of it, or dispose of it without valuable consideration, or sell or encumber household furniture and furnishings or wearing apparel of wife or minor children without written consent of wife (172)	Upon death of spouse, one half belongs to survivor, and other half is subject to testamentary disposition of decedent (Prob. C., 201)	One half belongs to survivor. If testamentary power over other half not exercised, it goes to survivor (Prob. C., 201). Community property passing from control of husband by reason of his death or testamentary disposition of wife is subject to his debts and to administration (Prob. C., 202)[16, 17]

TABLE LXXXIX

Liability of Co

Jurisdiction and Citation[2]	Husband's Separate Property	Wife's Separate Property	Community Property	Statutory Presumptions	Husband's Debts
Idaho .... Comp. St. 1919, Secs. 4656, 4659–60, 4663, 4666–67, 4670, 6919; Sec. 7803, amd. by Sess. L. 1927, Ch. 165, p. 219; Sec. 7803(A), added by Sess. L. 1927, Ch. 72, p. 90; Secs. 7901(A)– 7901(K), added by Sess. L. 1927, Ch. 216, p. 307	All property owned by husband before marriage, and that acquired afterward by gift, bequest, devise or descent (4659)	All property owned by wife before marriage and that acquired afterward by gift, bequest, devise or descent, or that which she acquires with proceeds of her separate property (4656). Earnings and accumulations of wife and her minor children living with her or in her custody while she is living separate from husband (4663). Rents and profits of her separate property if instrument by which same is acquired so provides (4660)	All other property acquired after marriage by either spouse, including rents and profits of separate property of both spouses, unless instrument by which wife acquires separate property provides that rents and profits thereof be applied to her sole and separate use (4660)		Rents, issues, and profits of wife's separate property, and all compensation due and owing for her personal services, are exempt from execution against husband (6919

§ 178]

(Continued)

munity Property		Control of Community Property			
Wife's Debts	Management	Disposition of Real Property during Marriage	Disposition of Personal Property during Marriage	Testamentary Control	Survivor's Rights, Descent, Succession, Administration, etc.
	Husband has management and control of community property (4666),[12] except that wife has management and control of her earnings for personal services and rents and profits of her separate estate (4667)	Husband cannot sell, convey or encumber community real estate unless wife joins in executing and acknowledging deed or other instrument of conveyance, etc. (4666)[12]	See footnote 12	Upon death of spouse, one half goes to survivor, and other half is subject to testamentary disposition of decedent in favor only of survivor, children, grandchildren, or parents of either spouse. Not more than one-half of decedent's half may be left to parent or parents unless limited to estate for life or less. Any part of decedent's share in excess of unencumbered appraised value of $25,000 may be disposed of as testator sees fit (7803)	One half goes to survivor subject to community debts. If testamentary power over other half not exercised, it goes to surviving spouse, subject to community debts, family allowance, and expenses of administration (7803)[16]

[§ 178

TABLE LXXXIX

Liability of Co...

Jurisdiction and Citation[2]	Husband's Separate Property	Wife's Separate Property	Community Property	Statutory Presumptions	Husband's Debts
Louisiana ...... C. C., Arts. 64, 117–18, 131; Art. 915, amd. by Sess. L. 1920, Act 160, p. 250; Arts. 916, 2334–35, 2350, 2384–86, 2399–2403; Art. 2404, amd. by Sess. L. 1926, Act 96, p. 138; Arts. 2405–19, 2422–37, 2807; Marr, Ann. R. S. 1915, Art. 4452	Property which husband brings into the marriage, or thereafter acquires with separate funds, or by inheritance, or by donation made to him "particularly." Actions for damages resulting from offenses and quasi-offenses suffered by husband living separate and apart from wife by reason of her fault sufficient for separation or divorce (2334)	Property which wife brings into the marriage, or thereafter acquires with separate funds, or by inheritance, or by donation made to her "particularly"; earnings of wife when living apart from husband although not separated by judgment. Earnings of wife when carrying on a business, trade, occupation, or industry separate from husband; actions for damages resulting from offenses and quasi-offenses; and property purchased with all funds thus derived (2334). Damages resulting from personal injury to wife (2402)	Property acquired by spouses during marriage in any different manner (2334). Profits of all the effects of which husband has administration and enjoyment either of right or in fact;[5] produce of reciprocal industry and labor of both spouses; property acquired by donation made "jointly" to both spouses, or by purchase, "or in any other similar way," even though purchase be in name of one spouse only "because in that case the period of time when the purchase is made is alone attended to, and not the person who made the purchase" (2402). Fruits of wife's paraphernal property if administered by husband or by both spouses indifferently (2386)	At dissolution of marriage, all effects which both spouses possess are presumed common effects or gains, unless it be satisfactorily proved which of such effects they brought in marriage, were given them separately, or were inherited (2405)	"The debts contracted during the marriage enter into the partnership or community of gains, and must be acquitted out of the common fund." Antenuptial debts of husband must be acquitted out of his own personal and individual effects (2403)

Continued)

| nunity Property | Control of Community Property | | | | |
Wife's Debts	Management	Disposition of Real Property during Marriage	Disposition of Personal Property during Marriage	Testamentary Control	Survivor's Rights, Descent, Succession, Administration, etc.
ntenuptial ebts of wife ust be ac- uitted out of er own per- nal and indi- idual effects 2403). If the ife is a "pub- c merchant," er obligations herein bind usband if a ommunity ex- sts between hem (131)	Husband is "head and master" of the commu- nity. "He administers its effects" (2404)	Husband may alienate commu- nity effects by onerous title without consent of wife, and may dispose of reve- nues of such effects (2404). But when title to community property stands in name of wife, it cannot be mortgaged or sold without her writ- ten authority or consent (2334). Husband can make no convey- ance inter vivos of immovables by gratuitous title[10] unless it be for establishment of children of the marriage (2404)[9]	Husband may alienate commu- nity effects by onerous title with- out consent of wife, and may dis- pose of revenues of such effects (2404). But when title to community property stands in name of wife, it cannot be mort- gaged or sold without her writ- ten authority or consent (2334). Husband can make no convey- ance inter vivos "of the whole or of a quota of the movables" by gratuitous title[10] unless for estab- lishment of chil- dren of the mar- riage, but he may dispose of mov- able effects by "a gratuitous and particular title" to the benefit of all persons (2404)	See last column; also footnote 13	If either spouse die in- testate leaving neither father, mother, or descendants,[8] dece- dent's share is inheri- ted by surviving spouse in full owner- ship. If descendants survive, decedent's share is inherited by them in manner pro- vided by law.[18] If no descendants survive, but father or mother survive, decedent's share goes one half to father and mother or survivor, and one half to surviving spouse (915)[20]

[§ 178

TABLE LXXXI

Liability of Co

Jurisdiction and Citation[2]	Husband's Separate Property	Wife's Separate Property	Community Property	Statutory Presumptions	Husband's Debts
Nevada .... Const., Sec. 82; Comp. L. 1929 (Hillyer), Secs. 3355–56, 3360, 3362, 3364–65, 3367–69, 3380	All property owned by husband before marriage, and that acquired by him afterward by gift, devise, bequest, or descent, with rents, issues and profits thereof (3355)	All property owned by wife before marriage, and that acquired by her afterward by gift, bequest, devise, or descent, with rents, issues, and profits thereof (3355). Earnings and accumulations of wife and her minor children living with her or in her custody while she is living separate from husband (3368). When husband allows wife to appropriate her earnings to her own use, the same with issues and profits thereof is deemed a gift to her and is her separate property (3369). See also Sec. 187	All other property acquired after marriage by husband or wife, or both (3356)	When husband allows wife to appropriate her earnings to her own use, same with issues and profits thereof is deemed a gift from him to her and is her separate property (3369)	Earnings of wi are not liable for debts of husband (3367
New Mexico .... St. Ann. 1929, Secs. 38(104)– 38(105), 38(109), 68(301)– 68(305), 68(401)– 68(410), 68(502)	All property owned by husband before marriage, and that acquired afterward by gift, bequest, devise, or descent, with rents, issues, and profits thereof (68[303])	All property owned by wife before marriage, and that acquired afterward by gift, bequest, devise, or descent, with rents, issues and profits thereof (68[302]).[3] Earnings and accumulations of wife and her minor children living with her or in her custody while she is living separate from husband (68[305])	All other property acquired after marriage by husband or wife or both (68[401])	If property is conveyed to wife by instrument in writing, presumption is that title is thereby vested in her as her separate property; if conveyance be to wife and husband or to wife and other person, presumption is that she takes her part as tenant in common unless instrument expresses different intention. Above presumptions are conclusive in favor of bona fide purchaser of wife (68[401])[8]	Earnings of wi are not liable for debts of husband (68[304]

§ 178]

(Continued)

munity Property Wife's Debts	Management	Control of Community Property			Survivor's Rights, Descent, Succession, Administration, etc.
		Disposition of Real Property during Marriage	Disposition of Personal Property during Marriage	Testamentary Control	
	Husband has management and control, except that wife has management and control of earnings and accumulations of herself and minor children living with her when used for family maintenance (3360)	Husband has like absolute power of disposition as of his separate estate, but no deed or mortgage of homestead is valid for any purpose unless both spouses execute and acknowledge same as provided for conveyance of real estate (3360)	Husband has like absolute power of disposition as of his separate estate, except that wife has like power of disposition of earnings and accumulations of herself and minor children living with her when same are used for care and maintenance of family (3360)	Upon death of husband, one half goes to surviving wife, and other half is subject to his testamentary disposition (3365). Upon death of wife, entire community property belongs to surviving husband without administration, except that if husband has abandoned wife and lived separate without cause entitling him to divorce, half of community property subject to its share of community debts is subject to wife's testamentary disposition (3364)	Upon death of husband, one half goes to surviving wife. If he dies intestate, other half goes to his surviving children equally, and, if no children, entire community property belongs to surviving wife, subject to husband's debts (3365).[16, 19] Upon death of wife, entire community property belongs to surviving husband without administration; except that if by reason of husband's misconduct wife has testamentary control over one-half, and dies intestate, her moiety goes to her descendants, and, if no descendants, to her heirs at law exclusive of husband (3364)
Not liable for contracts of wife made after marriage, unless secured by pledge or mortgage thereof executed by husband (68[402])	Husband has management and control of personal property (and real property) (68[403])[12]	Both spouses must join in all deeds and mortgages affecting community real estate.[12] Transfer or conveyance of same by either spouse alone "shall be void and of no effect," except conveyances between spouses, which may be made without other's joinder (68[403])	Husband has sole power of disposition, other than testamentary, as he has of his separate estate (68[403])[12]	Upon death of husband, one half goes to surviving wife, and other half is subject to his testamentary disposition (38[105]). Upon death of wife, entire community property belongs to surviving husband without administration, except such portion as may have been set apart to wife by judicial decree for support and maintenance, which portion is subject to her testamentary disposition (38[104])	Upon death of husband, one half goes to surviving wife. If he dies intestate, one-fourth of his moiety goes to surviving wife, and remainder to his children equally and further as provided by law (38[105]).[19] Upon death of wife, entire community property belongs to surviving husband without administration; except that if a portion thereof has been set apart by judicial decree for wife's support, and she dies intestate, such portion goes to her descendants or heirs exclusive of husband (38[104])

[§ 178

TABLE LXXXI>

Liability of Co:

Jurisdiction and Citation[2]	Husband's Separate Property	Wife's Separate Property	Community Property	Statutory Presumptions	Husband's Debts
Texas .... Const., Art. XVI, Sec. 15; Complete St. 1928, Civ. St., Arts. 2578–79, 3627–30, 3661–83; Arts. 4613–14, amd. by Supp. 1931, p. 381; Arts. 4615–16, 4618–24	All property, both real and personal, owned or claimed by husband before marriage, and that acquired afterward by gift, devise, or descent, "as also the increase of all lands thus acquired . . . ." (4613)	All property, both real and personal, owned or claimed by wife before marriage, and that acquired afterward by gift, devise, or descent, "as also the increase of all lands thus acquired . . . ." (4614).[3] Property or monies received as compensation for personal injuries sustained by wife, except actual and necessary expenses accumulated against husband for hospital fees, medical bills, etc. (4615)[6]	"All property acquired by either the husband or wife during marriage, except that which is the separate property of either, shall be deemed the common property of the husband and wife" (4619)	All effects which husband and wife possess at time marriage is dissolved shall be regarded as common effects or gains unless contrary be satisfactorily proved (4619). Funds on deposit in bank are presumed to be separate property of spouse in whose name they stand regardless of who made deposit (4622)	Rents from wife's separate real estate, interest on wife's bonds and note: dividends on wife's stocks, and wife's personal earnings are not subjec: to payment of husband's debts or torts (4616)
Washington .... Remington, Comp. St. 1922, Secs. 570, 1145, 1342, 1370, 1419, 6890–96, 6898, 10572, 10575, 10577–79	Property and pecuniary rights owned by husband before marriage and that acquired by him afterward by gift, bequest, devise, or descent, with rents, issues, and profits thereof (6890)	Property and pecuniary rights of wife at marriage or afterward acquired by gift, devise, or inheritance, with rents, issues, and profits thereof (6891). Earnings and accumulations of wife and her minor children living with her or in her custody while she is living separate from husband (6896)[7]	Property otherwise acquired after marriage by husband or wife, or both (6892)		Wife's persona earnings exempt from attachment and execution upor any liability o: judgment against husban so long as she or any minor heir of her bo be living (570)

(Continued)

unity Property		Control of Community Property			
Wife's Debts	Management	Disposition of Real Property during Marriage	Disposition of Personal Property during Marriage	Testamentary Control	Survivor's Rights, Descent, Succession, Administration, etc.
ommunity roperty, other aan wife's per- nal earnings nd rents and evenues of her eparate prop- rty, is not sub- ect to payment f debts con- acted by wife nless husband ins in execu- on of contract, xcept debts ontracted by ife for neces- aries for her- elf and children 4621, 4623)[14]		During coverture, community prop- erty may be dis- posed of by husband only (4619),[12] except that community homestead may not be disposed of except by joint conveyance of both spouses (4618)	During cover- ture, community property may be disposed of by husband only (4619),[12] but funds on deposit in any bank are presumed to be separate property of spouse in whose name they stand, and, unless noti- fied to contrary, such bank shall be governed ac- cordingly in honoring checks, etc. (4622)	See footnote 13	Upon dissolution of marriage by death, entire community property goes to sur- vivor if decedent leaves no descend- ants.[16] If issue sur- vive, surviving spouse is entitled to one half and other half passes to children, or their descendants by right of representation (2578).[17] Community estate passes charged with the debts against it (2579)
ee footnote 15	Husband has management and control of real and per- sonal property (6892, 6893)	Husband shall not sell, convey, or encumber real property unless wife join in executing and acknowledging deed or other in- strument of con- veyance (6893),[9] except that con- veyances between spouses of com- munity interest are authorized and may be made without joinder of grantee spouse (10572)[11]	Husband has like power of dispo- sition, except testamentary, as of his separate personal prop- erty (6892)	Upon death of spouse, one half goes to survivor, and other half is subject to testa- mentary disposi- tion of decedent, charged with community debts (1342)	One half goes to sur- vivor subject to com- munity debts. If testa- mentary power over other half not exer- cised, it descends equally to decedent's legitimate issue; if no issue or representa- tives thereof survive, entire community property passes to surviving spouse to exclusion of collateral heirs, subject to community debts, family allowance and expenses of adminis- tration (1342)[17]

[§ 178

TABLE LXXXIX (*Continued*)

[1] The reader must bear in mind that Table LXXXIX contains only the statutory provisions which expressly deal with the subject of this section. Certain miscellaneous provisions not outlined elsewhere will be found in footnote 21 following. See also the cross references at the beginning of the section.

[2] As a more specific reference to the statutes, the exact article or section number is inserted in parentheses at appropriate points in the body of the table. The statutory compilation or session law in which the material is found may be determined by reference to the citations appearing in the citation column of the table.

[3] The separate property of the wife is defined by the constitutions of three jurisdictions, and the separate property of the husband in one jurisdiction, as follows: "All property, real and personal, owned by either husband or wife, before marriage, and that acquired by either of them afterward by gift, devise, or descent shall be their separate property" (**California**, Const., Art. XX, Sec. 8); "All property, both real and personal, of the wife, owned or claimed by her before marriage, and that afterward acquired by gift, devise, or descent, shall be her separate property; and laws shall be passed more clearly defining the rights of the wife in relation, as well to her separate property as to that held in common with her husband. Laws shall be passed providing for the registration of the wife's separate property" (**Nevada**, Const., Sec. 82; **Texas**, Const., Art. XV, Sec. 15).

[4] The **California** Civil Code (Sec. 2419e) provides: "A partner's right in specific partnership property is not subject to dower, curtesy, or allowances to widows, heirs, or next of kin, and is not community property."

[5] In **Louisiana**, the wife's separate property is divided into dotal and extradotal, or paraphernal, property. The dotal property is that which the wife brings to the husband to assist him in bearing the expenses of the marriage establishment. The wife's other separate property is paraphernal. It is said that dotal property is now rare in **Louisiana** owing to the decline of the custom of settling a dowry by marriage contract. The wife may administer her paraphernal property personally without assistance from the husband, but the husband has the sole administration of the dotal property. If the husband mismanages it, the wife may petition for a separation of property. The income and proceeds of the dotal property belong to the husband and are intended to assist him in supporting the charges of the marriage. No attempt will be made here to summarize the many provisions found in the **Louisiana** Civil Code on this subject. The reader is directed in particular to Articles 2335, 2337–91, 2425–39, and 3319.

[6] The attempt in **Texas** to make damages for personal injury to the wife her separate property is unconstitutional (*Northern Texas Traction Company* v. *Hill* [Tex. Civ. App.]; 297 S. W. 778 [1927]; *Teague* v. *Fairchild* [Tex. Comm. of App.]; 15 S. W. [2d] 585 [1929]).

[7] **Washington** also provides that "a wife may receive the wages of her personal labor, and maintain an action therefor in her own name, and hold the same in her own right . . . ." (Remington, Comp. St. 1922, Sec. 6895). It is held that this provision and the one given in the table must be read together, and that the former refers only to the earnings of the wife while living separate from the husband (*Abbott* v. *Wetherby, Administrator,* 6 Wash. 507; 33 P. 1070 [1893]).

[8] **California** provides that when the wife conveys real property which she acquired prior to May 19, 1889, the husband (or his heirs, etc.) is barred from bringing an action to recover the same, or to show that it was community property from and after one year from the filing for record of such conveyance (C. C. 1933 [Lake], Sec. 164). The **New Mexico** statute is the same except that it refers to property acquired prior to March 18, 1907 (St. Ann. 1929, Sec. 68[401]).

[9] In **California**, the sole lease, contract, mortgage, or deed of the husband holding the record title to community real property to a purchaser, etc., in good faith without knowledge of the marriage is presumed to be valid; and an action to avoid the husband's sole deed, etc., must be commenced within one year from the filing of the same for record (C. C. 1933 [Lake], Sec. 172a). In **Louisiana**, "if it should be proved that the husband has sold the common property, or otherwise disposed of the same by fraud, to injure his wife, she may have her action against the heirs of her husband, in support of her claim in one-half of the property, on her satisfactorily proving the fraud" (C. C., Art. 2404). **Washington** lays down the flat rule that the spouse holding the record legal title to real property may convey full legal and equitable title to an actual bona fide purchaser, free of all claims not appearing of record (Remington, Comp. St. 1922, Sec. 10577). The other spouse, however, may protect his or her community interest

§ 178]

TABLE LXXXIX (*Continued*)

by recording, in the proper county within ninety days from the recording of the legal title, a written instrument setting forth such interest (Sec. 10578). When recorded, the instrument has the same effect as a deed as regards notice. It is a cloud upon the title, and may be removed by release, or by judicial action when it appears that the property is the separate property of the spouse holding the record title (Sec. 10579).

[10] A 1926 amendment to the **Louisiana** Code (Art. 2404) provides that "a gratuitous title within the contemplation of this article embraces all titles wherein there is no direct, material advantage to the donor" (Sess. L. 1926, Act 96, p. 138). Prior to this amendment, it was held that a conveyance by the husband of a community immovable in consideration of his interest in education, conditioned that it be utilized for educational uses, etc., was not a conveyance by gratuitous title under the Code (*Thompson* v. *Société Catholique d'Éducation Religieuse et Littéraire,* 157 La. 875; 103 So. 247 [1925]).

[11] The **Washington** statute provides that a conveyance between the spouses of the grantor's community interest in real property operates to divest such property from its community character, and to vest the same in the grantee as separate property, but that such conveyance shall not affect any existing equity in favor of the grantor's subsisting creditors (Remington, Comp. St. 1922, Sec. 10572). **Washington** also expressly authorizes a power of attorney between the spouses for the sale, etc., of his or her interest in community real property, a power of attorney between either spouse and a third party to join with the other spouse in a conveyance of community realty, and a power of attorney between both spouses and a third party for the sale, etc., of community realty (Sec. 10575).

[12] Four states have special statutes relative to the control of community property when one spouse is insane, etc., as follows:

In **California,** when either spouse has been adjudged insane or incompetent, the other spouse may make a verified petition to the superior court of the county in which community real property is situated to sell, mortgage, lease, or execute a deed of trust upon such property in order to provide for the support of either spouse or minor children, to preserve the community estate, or whenever it appears for the best interests of the spouses, their dependents, or the community estate. Notice of the application must be given by publication, and in addition personal notice must be served on the nearest resident relative of the insane or incompetent spouse, and, if none is known, on the public administrator, whose duty it then is to represent the interests of the insane or incompetent spouse at the hearing. A sale, etc., made pursuant to the order of the court must be reported to and confirmed by the court (C. C. 1933 [Lake], Secs. 172[b]–172[d]).

In **Idaho,** if the husband is adjudged insane, the wife is given the management and control of the community personal property with power to dispose of the same (Comp. St. 1919, Sec. 7901[K]). **Idaho** also provides that if either spouse has been adjudged insane and a guardian has been appointed, the other spouse may petition the probate court of the county in which community real property is situated for an order authorizing the sale, lease, or mortgage of such property, including the community homestead. It must appear that the same is necessary to satisfy an encumbrance on community property, or to provide for the support of either spouse or education of minor children, or for reinvestment if such reinvestment appears advantageous. Order to show cause must be published, and personal service had upon the insane spouse, his or her guardian, the nearest male resident relative of the insane spouse, and the prosecuting attorney in the same manner as a civil suit summons. The prosecuting attorney must protect the interests of the insane spouse if no one else appears in his behalf at the hearing. If the court grants the petition, it may order either a private or a public sale. The order must specify the reasons why the petition is granted, and designate for what purpose the money obtained shall be used. Bond must be given conditioned to account for the proceeds and apply them as the court directs. Appeal from the order of the court for or against petitioner may be had. The sale, notice, return, confirmation, etc., not otherwise provided for are governed by the general statutes relative to the sale of estates of decedents (Secs. 7901[A]–7901[J]).

New Mexico has the broadest statute of this type. When the husband is non compos mentis, or has been convicted of a felony and sentenced to imprisonment for more than a year, or has abandoned the wife or wife and family without support, or is a habitual drunkard, or is for any other reason incapacitated to manage the community property, the wife may present a verified petition to the district court of the county in which any of the community property is situated, praying that she be substituted as head of the community with the same powers as are vested in the husband. Service is had as in civil actions in all cases except when the husband is

TABLE LXXXIX (*Continued*)

alleged to be non compos mentis, in which case a guardian ad litem must be appointed before the action proceeds. The court may adjudge the wife the head of the community with full power of administration and disposition of both real and personal community property, with such limitation as the court sees fit. Judgment, when recorded in the county in which any property affected is situated, is notice of the facts therein set out (St. Ann. 1929, Secs. 68[404]–68[408]).

In **Texas**, if the husband disappears and his whereabouts remain unknown continuously for more than a year, the wife, by following the procedure outlined by the statute, may obtain authorization to manage, control, and dispose of the community property with the same powers as are conferred upon the husband. Notice by publication is required. The wife may retain her control until the husband returns and until either of them records an affidavit of such return (Complete St. 1928, Civ. St., Art. 4619). **Texas** also provides that if either spouse becomes insane, having no children and no separate property, the administration of the community property passes to the sane spouse, charged with the debts of the community, and no guardianship is necessary (Art. 3662). And if either spouse becomes insane, having children, the other may obtain administration of the community property under the same conditions as govern the rights of the survivor to administer the community property (Arts. 3663–81). See footnote 17 following.

[13] Neither **Louisiana** nor **Texas** has legislation which in direct terms authorizes the husband and wife to dispose of his or her moiety of the community property by will. In **Louisiana**, such testamentary power is clearly implied by the Civil Code, Articles 915 and 916 (see table, last column, and footnote 18), which provide that if either spouse die without having disposed "by last will and testament of his or her share of the community property . . . ." etc. In **Texas**, resort must be had to the general legislation authorizing the testamentary disposition of property, and to the local concept of the system. The wife may dispose of her moiety by will (*Brown* v. *Pridgen*, 56 Tex. 124 [1882]; *Sutton* v. *Harvey*, 24 Tex. Civ. App. 26; 57 S. W. 879 [1900]). The **Texas** reports abound with decisions involving the doctrine of election in which the husband's testamentary control of one-half of the community property is silently assumed without question.

[14] The **Texas** statutes contain the following provisions which when read together are not entirely free from ambiguity. The community property of the husband and wife is liable for their debts contracted during marriage except as specifically excepted by law (Complete St. 1928, Civ. St., Art. 4620). The community property is not liable for debts or damages resulting from contracts of the wife, except for necessaries, unless the husband joins in the execution of the contract (Art. 4621). The community property "other than the personal earnings of the wife, and the income, rents and revenues from the separate property," is not subject to the payment of debts contracted by the wife, except for necessaries (Art. 4623). In case of judgment in suit on wife's contracts for necessaries, "the court shall decree that execution may be levied upon either the common property or the separate property of the wife at the discretion of the plaintiff" (Art. 4624).

[15] The only other provision found in **Washington** relative to the liability of the community property is to the effect that the community real estate is subject to the liens of mechanics, etc., for labor and materials in erecting structures and improvements thereon, to liens of judgments recovered for "community debts," and to sale on execution issued thereon (Remington, Comp. St. 1922, Sec. 6893). Filing of lien is notice to the spouse of the one with record title, and subjects all the community interest of both spouses to the lien (Sec. 1145).

[16] Certain further provisions obviating the necessity of putting the community estate through administration follow. An **Arizona** statute provides that, if the wife dies owning community property which passed upon her death to the surviving husband, the husband may obtain a decree determining such facts, a certified copy of which when recorded has the same effect as a final decree of distribution (R. C. 1928, Sec. 4175). Inasmuch as **Arizona** does not make the husband the favored heir of the wife, this statute is not of much significance. In **Idaho**, if the wife dies intestate, the surviving husband may obtain a similar decree with like effect (Comp. St. 1919, Sec. 7803[*A*]). **California** has a somewhat analogous statute providing for a judicial determination of death, etc., but it does not specifically refer to community-property estates (C. C. P. 1933 [Lake], Sec. 1723). In **Nevada**, if the husband dies intestate, and the surviving wife, or the surviving wife and children, pay or secure all the debts due from the community, the community property is not subject to administration (Comp. L. 1929 [Hillyer], Sec. 3365). In **Texas**, when either spouse dies intestate without children or separate property, the community

§ 178]

TABLE LXXXIX (*Continued*)

property passes to the survivor charged with the debts of the community and no administration is necessary (Complete St. 1928, Civ. St., Art. 3662). **Texas** also provides that after letters are granted, inventory and appraisal made, and claims filed the survivor may obtain a partition upon executing bond for the value of his or her interest, conditioned upon payment of one-half of the debts owed by the community (Arts. 3627–30).

[17] Statutes giving one or either of the spouses as survivor some control over the dissolved community were found in three jurisdictions, as follows:

In **California**, the statute provides that when the wife disposes of her moiety by will the husband's possession and control shall be transferred to her personal representative only to the extent necessary to carry her will into effect; pending administration, the husband retains the same power to sell, manage, and deal with community personal property as he had in her lifetime (Prob. C. 1933 [Lake], Sec. 202). After forty days from the wife's death, the husband has full power to sell, lease, mortgage, or otherwise dispose of the community real property unless notice is recorded in the county where such property is situated to the effect that a specified interest therein is claimed by another under the wife's will (Sec. 203).

In **Texas**, if either spouse dies leaving issue, the survivor is given an extensive control over the dissolved community (Complete St. 1928, Civ. St., Arts. 3663–81). The survivor within four years may make application to be put in control of the community estate, setting forth certain facts enumerated by the statute. Appraisers may be appointed without citation, who with the survivor must make a complete and verified inventory, including all claims against the community. The survivor must give bond with sureties equal to the whole value of the community estate, conditioned that he or she will faithfully administer the estate and pay over one-half of the same to the persons entitled thereto after payment of the debts owed by the community. The survivor may obtain practically complete power to manage, control, and dispose of the community property, subject to the duty to account to the court and to the heirs upon final partition. Creditors not paid within a year may cause the survivor to be cited to appear and render explanation. One year after the filing of survivor's bond, the persons entitled to deceased's moiety may obtain a partition and distribution. If the surviving wife marries, her rights as survivor cease, and the estate then becomes subject to administration. The provisions outlined above apparently refer to intestate estates only.

Washington has a peculiar statute which entitles the surviving spouse, if otherwise qualified, to administer upon the community property notwithstanding contrary provisions in decedent's will (Remington, Comp. St. 1922, Sec. 1419). Application for such appointment must be made within forty days or the right is waived. If a person other than the survivor apply for letters prior to the expiration of the forty days, notice must be given to the survivor unless applicant produces survivor's written waiver of the right.

[18] In **Louisiana**, lineal descendants and parents are forced heirs (C. C., Arts. 1493–95). Testator's disposition of his property cannot exceed the following fractions: two-thirds if one child survives, one-half if two children survive, one-third if three or more children survive, two-thirds if a parent or parents but no children survive. Issue of deceased children represent such deceased children. When the husband or wife dies intestate leaving issue of the marriage with the survivor, the survivor holds a usufruct for life of so much of the share of the deceased spouse in the community property as may be inherited by such issue, such usufruct to cease, however, when the survivor contracts a second marriage (Art. 916).

[19] Both **Nevada** (Comp. L. 1929 [Hillyer], Sec. 3365) and **New Mexico** (St. Ann. 1929, Sec. 38[105]) expressly provide that in case the marriage is dissolved by the husband's death the entire community property is equally subject to the husband's debts, the family allowance, and the expenses of administration.

[20] The **Louisiana** Code contains a number of provisions relative to the division of property, etc., upon dissolution of the marriage (see C. C., Arts. 2406–23). The community property is divided "into two equal portions" including the profits arising from the effects which both spouses brought reciprocally in marriage and which have been administered by the husband or both spouses jointly, "although what has been thus brought in marriage, by either the husband or wife, be more considerable than what has been brought by the other, or even although one of the two did not bring anything at all" (Art. 2406). "The fruits hanging by the roots" on separate lands, and the young of separate cattle "yet in gestation," are also equally divided; but the fruits of the wife's paraphernal property which she administered herself are excepted from this rule (Art. 2407). Upon partition, each is equally liable for his share of the community

[§ 178

TABLE LXXXIX (Continued)

debts (Art. 2409). The surviving wife may, however, exonerate herself by renouncing the community (Art. 2410), or limit her liability by accepting the community "under the benefit of inventory" in the same manner that heirs are allowed to accept a succession under benefit of inventory (Marr, Ann. R. S. 1915, Art. 4452). She has a limited time in which to make the election (C. C., Arts. 2413, 2414), and loses her right to renounce after taking an "active concern" in the effects of the community (Art. 2412), or allowing judgment to pass against her as a community partner (Art. 2417), or if she "has concealed or made away" with any of the community effects (Art. 2418). The renunciation must be made before a notary or parish recorder, and two witnesses (Art. 2415). If the wife renounces, she loses all rights in the community, but gets back her dotal and paraphernal property which the husband has administered (Art. 2411). The wife's creditors may attack a renunciation made to defraud them, and accept the community in their own names (Art. 2421). Pending her election, the wife is entitled to maintenance out of community funds (Art. 2422). Upon the wife's death, her heirs may renounce the community in the same manner and form as prescribed for the surviving wife (Art. 2423).

[21] Certain miscellaneous statutory provisions follow:

a) The husband and wife may hold property as joint tenants, tenants in common, or as community property (**California**, C. C. 1933 [Lake], Sec. 161; **Nevada**, Comp. L. 1929 [Hillyer], Sec. 3362; **New Mexico**, St. Ann. 1929, Sec. 68[301]).

b) Four states provide in substance that the property rights of the spouses are governed by the provisions dealing with separate and community property, unless there is a marriage contract containing stipulations to the contrary (**California**, C. C. 1933 [Lake], Sec. 177; **Idaho**, Comp. St. 1919, Sec. 4670; **Nevada**, Comp. L. 1929 [Hillyer], Sec. 3380; **New Mexico**, St. Ann. 1929, Sec. 68[409]).

c) Two states establish a peculiar course of descent when decedent leaves neither spouse nor issue surviving and his estate or part thereof was the community property of decedent and a previously deceased spouse. Instead of descending to the kin of decedent, it goes to the children of the deceased spouse and their descendants, and, if neither, one-half goes to the parent or parents of decedent, and one-half to the parent or parents of the deceased spouse, or to the brothers and sisters of decedent and deceased spouse if the parents of either do not survive (**California**, Prob. C. 1933 [Lake], Sec. 228; **New Mexico**, St. Ann. 1929, Sec. 68[410]).

d) By a recent statute, **California** has attempted to define the wife's interest in the community property by the following provisions: "The respective interests of the husband and wife in community property during continuance of the marriage relation are present, existing and equal interests under the management and control of the husband as is provided in Sections 172 and 172*a* of the Civil Code. This section shall be construed as defining the respective interests and rights of husband and wife in community property" (C. C., Sec. 161*a*; Sess. L. 1927, Ch. 264, p. 484).

e) The **California** inheritance act contains the following pertinent provisions. Upon the death of the husband, one-half of the community property is taxable. If the husband attempts to devise or bequeath more than his moiety of the community property and forces the wife to elect, the one-half or less of the community property which she takes under his will in lieu of her statutory share is not taxable. The moiety belonging to either spouse upon the death of the other is not deemed to go to such spouse as heir and is not taxable. If the wife dies intestate, her moiety then passing to the surviving husband is not deemed to pass to him as an heir and is not taxable. For the purposes of the act, personal property wherever situated heretofore or hereafter acquired by the spouses while domiciled elsewhere which would not have been the separate property of either if acquired while domiciled in California is deemed to be community property. For the purposes of the act, the presumption that property acquired during coverture is community property does not apply, but the burden of proof is upon the one claiming the property to be community property (Sess. L. 1921, Ch. 821, p. 1500, Sec. 1, as amended by Sess. L. 1923, Ch. 337, p. 693, and Sess. L. 1925, Ch. 284, p. 471). That part of the act which discriminates in favor of the husband when the wife dies intestate seems of doubtful legality if the wife now has an equal beneficial interest in community property during coverture (see footnote 21 *d* above).

f) **Washington** expressly provides that the title to community real property vests imme-

TABLE LXXXIX (*Concluded*)

diately upon death in the person or persons to whom the same descends or is devised (Remington, Comp. St. 1922, Sec. 1370).

g) **Louisiana** is the only jurisdiction which expressly provides that the parties may create a modified community or obtain a complete separation of property by marriage contract. "The partnership, or community of acquets or gains, needs not to be stipulated; it exists by operation of law, in all cases where there is no stipulation to the contrary. But the parties may modify or limit it; they may even agree that it shall not exist" (C. C., Art. 2332). "Every marriage contracted in this state superinduces of right partnership or community of acquets or gains, if there be no stipulation to the contrary" (Art. 2399). "Married persons may, by their marriage contract, modify the legal community, as they think fit, either by agreeing that the portions shall be unequal, or by specifying the property, belonging to either of them, of which the fruits shall not enter into the partnership" (Art. 2424).

h) While the **Louisiana** Code in numerous instances speaks of the community as a partnership, in the chapter on partnerships proper it is provided that "the community of property, created by marriage, is not a partnership; it is the effect of a contract governed by rules prescribed for that purpose in this code" (C. C., Art. 2807).

i) The **Louisiana** Code seems to establish one exclusive mode by which the community may be dissolved while the normal marital status of the parties continues. "Every voluntary separation of property is null, both as respects third persons and the husband and wife between themselves" (C. C., Art. 2427). The wife, however, may petition for a separation of property "whenever her dowry is in danger, owing to the mismanagement of her husband, or otherwise, or when the disorder of his affairs induces her to believe that her estate may not be sufficient to meet her rights and claims" (Art. 2425). The husband's neglect to reinvest the wife's dotal effects in cases where the law directs the same is also sufficient cause (Art. 2426). The separation can be made by judicial decree only, after hearing all parties, including the husband's creditors (Arts. 2427, 2434). The decree must be published and promptly executed (Arts. 2428, 2429). If the wife accepts the community to the date of separation, she must pay her share of the community obligations (Art. 2430). She may, however, limit her liability by accepting under the benefit of inventory (Marr, Ann. R. S., Art. 4452). After obtaining a separation of property, the wife "must contribute, in proportion to her fortune and to that of her husband, both to the household expenses and to those of the education of their children. She is bound to support those expenses alone, if there remains nothing to her husband" (C. C., Art. 2435). If the parties were married in the state but removed to a foreign country where the husband so acted as to entitle the wife to a separation of property, the wife may institute such suit upon returning to the domicile where her marriage was contracted (Art. 2437). The husband and wife of an absentee may choose to dissolve the community, or to continue the same (Art. 64).

j) In **Louisiana**, when the separate property of either the husband or wife has been increased or improved during marriage, the other spouse, or his or her heirs, are entitled to one-half of the value created "if it be proved that the increase or ameliorations be the result of the common labor, expenses or industry"; but there is no reward due if it be proved that the same is due only to the "ordinary course of things, to the rise in the value of property, or to the chances of trade" (C. C., Art. 2408).

k) **California** authorizes a division of the community property incident to granting either spouse permanent support and maintenance without divorce (C. C. 1933 [Lake], Sec. 137); and in **New Mexico**, when the husband and wife are permanently separated, either may institute suit for a division of property without divorce (St. Ann. 1929, Sec. 68[502]).

l) **Louisiana** is the only jurisdiction in which statutory material was found prescribing the effect upon property rights of an invalid marriage. The Civil Code there provides that "the marriage, which has been declared null, produces nevertheless its civil effects as it relates to the parties and their children, if it has been contracted in good faith" (C. C., Art. 117). "If only one of the parties acted in good faith, the marriage produces its civil effects only in his or her favor, and in favor of the children born of the marriage" (Art. 118). One of the "civil effects" is the community of acquets and gains which results from a lawful marriage (*McCaffrey* v. *Benson,* 40 La. Ann. 10; 3 So. 393 [1888]).

REFERENCES

Books

BALLINGER, RICHARD A. *A Treatise on the Property Rights of Husband and Wife, under the Community or Ganancial System* (1895).

DAGGETT, HARRIET S. *The Community Property System of Louisiana* (1931).

McKAY, GEORGE. *The Law of Community Property*, 2d ed. (1925).

STIMSON, F. J. *American Statute Law*, Secs. 6433–34 (1886).

TIFFANY, HERBERT THORNDIKE. *Law of Real Property and Other Interests in Land*, 2d ed., Vol. 1, Sec. 195 (1920).

Articles

BOBBITT, FRANK. "Is There More than One Class of Community Property in Texas?" 4 Tex. L. Rev. 154–69 (1926).

BRUTON, PAUL W. "The Taxation of Family Income," 41 Yale L. Jour. 1172–94 (1932).

COOPER, JOSEPH D. "Community Property: Status of Property Conveyed to Husband and Wife as Co-grantees," 20 Calif. L. Rev. 546–52 (1932).

DAGGETT, HARRIET S. "A Comparison of the German Community Property System with That of Louisiana," 4 Tulane L. Rev. 27–57 (1929).

——. "The Modern Problem of the Nature of the Wife's Interest in Community Property—A Comparative Study," 19 Calif. L. Rev. 567–601 (1931).

EVANS, ALVIN E. "Community Obligations," 10 Calif. L. Rev. 120–44 (1922).

——. "Community Property in Public Lands," 9 Calif. L. Rev. 267–75 (1921).

——. "Primary Sources of Acquisition of Community Property," 10 Calif. L. Rev. 271–99 (1922).

——. "The Ownership of Community Property," 35 Harv. L. Rev. 47–67 (1921).

HOOKER, ROBERT G. "Nature of Wife's Interest in Community Property in California," 15 Calif. L. Rev. 302–12 (1927).

INBAU, F. E. "An Interpretation of the Phrase 'Upon the Net Income of Every Individual' of the Income Tax Act as It Concerns Husband and Wife in Community-Property States," 5 Tulane L. Rev. 301–7 (1931).

JACOB, F. W. "Law of Community Property in Idaho," 1 Idaho L. Jour. 1–55, 118–71 (1931).

KIRKWOOD, M. R. "Equality of Property Interests between Husband and Wife," 8 Minn. L. Rev. 579–94 (1924).

——. "Ownership of Community Property in California," 7 So. Calif. L. Rev. 1–17 (1933).

LEFLAR, ROBERT A. "Community Property and Conflict of Laws," 21 Calif. L. Rev. 221–38 (1933).

LOBINGIER, CHARLES S. "The Marital Community: Its Origin and Diffusion," 14 Amer. Bar Assoc. Jour. 211–18 (1928).

MAGGS, DOUGLAS B. "Community Property and the Federal Income Tax," 14 Calif. L. Rev. 351–78, 441–60 (1926).

MECHEM, FRANK L. "Progress of the Law in Washington Community Property," 7 Wash. L. Rev. 367–76; 8 *ibid.* 1–19 (1933).

MERRILL, A. L. "Power of a Deserted Wife to Deal with Community Real Estate," 2 Idaho L. Jour. 120–26 (1932).

§ 178]

Sebree, J. Emmett. "Federal Taxation of Community Property," 12 Tex. L. Rev. 273–302 (1934).

Simkins, W. S. "Some Phases of the Law of Community Property in Texas," 3 Tex. L. Rev. 362–83 (1925).

Simmons, William M. "Interest of a Wife in California Community Property," 22 Calif. L. Rev. 404–18 (1934).

Stumberg, G. W. "Marital Property and the Conflict of Laws," 11 Tex. L. Rev. 53–66 (1932).

Notes

"Compensation for Wife's Injuries as Community Property—Gift from Husband to Wife—Nature of Funds on Deposit in Wife's Name," *Teague* v. *Fairchild* (Tex. Comm. of App.); 15 S. W. (2d) 585 (1929)—8 Tex. L. Rev. 398–408 (1930).

"Community Property—Agency—Liability of Husband for Debt Incurred by Wife," *Hulsman* v. *Ireland,* 205 Cal. 345; 270 P. 498 (1928)—17 Calif. L. Rev. 265–70 (1929) ; 2 So. Calif. L. Rev. 375–83 (1929).

"Community Property—Conveyances between Husband and Wife—Presumptions," 1 So. Calif. L. Rev. 388–90 (1928).

"Community Property—Effect of Removal of Personal Property Acquired in Common-Law State to Community-Property State with Change of Domicile," *Estate of Bruggemeyer,* 115 Cal. App. 525; 2 P. (2d) 534 (1931)—20 Calif. L. Rev. 201–3 (1932).

"Community Property—Power of Husband to Convey or Encumber—Effect of Husband's Sole Conveyance or Encumbrance," 1 So. Calif. L. Rev. 467–74 (1928).

"Conflict of Laws—Matrimonial Property—Effect on Movables of Change of Domicile from a Common-Law State to a Community-Property State," *Estate of Frees,* 187 Cal. 150; 201 P. 112 (1921)—10 Calif. L. Rev. 154–57 (1922); *Estate of Drishaus,* 199 Cal. 369; 249 P. 515 (1926)—15 Calif. L. Rev. 399–407 (1927).

"Community Property, Sole Conveyance by Husband Holding Record Title to Property," *Mark* v. *Title Guarantee and Trust Company,* 122 Cal. App. 301; 9 P. (2d) 839 (1932)—7 So. Calif. L. Rev. 106–7 (1933) ; 21 Calif. L. Rev. 170–72 (1933).

"Community Property, Status of Property Conveyed to Husband and Wife as Co-grantees," *Siberell* v. *Siberell* (Cal.) ; 295 P. 385 (1931)—20 Calif. L. Rev. 546–52 (1932)

"Community Property, Wife's Interest as an Expectancy and as Vested," 5 So. Calif. L. Rev. 144–50 (1931).

"Community Property, Wife's Liability on Contracts," *Leffin* v. *Jeffers* (Tex. Comm. of App.) ; 52 S. W. (2d) 81 (1932)—11 Tex. L. Rev. 81–89 (1932).

"Descent and Distribution, Community Property, Construction of Word 'Widow' under Civil Code, Section 1386," *Estate of McArthur,* 210 Cal. 439; 292 P. 469 (1930)—19 Calif. L. Rev. 313–23 (1931).

"Income Taxes on Wife's Share of Community Property, Effect of California Code Amendments of 1917, 1923, 1927," *United States* v. *Malcolm,* 282 U. S. 792; 51 Sup. Ct. 184 (1931)—4 So. Calif. L. Rev. 395–400 (1931).

[§ 178

"Liability of Community and Separate Property for Contracts of Husband and Wife," 22 Calif. L. Rev. 554–64 (1934).

"Status for Federal Income Tax Purposes of Income from Community Property Acquired before 1927," *Hirsch* v. *United States,* 62 F. (2d) 128 (1932)—22 Calif. L. Rev. 106–11 (1933).

"Community Property," *Hawkins* v. *Britton State Bank* (Tex. Comm. of App.) ; 52 S. W. (2d) 243 (1932)—11 Tex. L. Rev. 391–92 (1933).

"Community Property, Federal Estate Tax," *Hernandez* v. *Becker,* 54 F. (2d) 542 (1931)—6 So. Calif. L. Rev. 151–57 (1933).

"Community Property, Internal Revenue, Income Tax Returns," *Poe* v. *Seaborn,* 282 U. S. 101 ; 51 Sup. Ct. 58 (1930)—6 Wash. L. Rev. 90–91 (1931).

"Community Property, Life Insurance Policy Payable to a Beneficiary Outside the Community," *Shields* v. *Barton,* 60 F. (2d) 351 (1932)—13 B. U. L. Rev. 81–87 (1933).

"Community Property, Power of Independent Executor to Convey Wife's Interest to Pay Community Debts," *Lovejoy* v. *Cockrell* (Tex. Comm. of App.) ; 63 S. W. (2d) 1009 (1933)—12 Tex. L. Rev. 348–51 (1934).

Annotations

"Cause of Action for Assault and Battery upon the Wife as Community Property," 6 A. L. R. 1059–61 (1920).

"Community Character of Interest of a Partner in Partnership Real Property," 20 A. L. R. 374 (1922).

"Conveyance of Interest in Community Property by One Spouse to Other," 37 A. L. R. 282–308 (1925).

"Effect on Joint Estate, Community Estate, or Estate by Entireties of Death of Both Tenants in Same Disaster," 18 A. L. R. 105–6 (1922).

"Profits Accruing during Marriage in Connection with Property Belonging to Separate Estate of Either Spouse as Community Property," 31 L. R. A. (N.S.) 1092–98 (1911).

"Property Acquired during Marriage in Exchange for Separate Property of One of the Spouses as Community," 64 A. L. R. 246–51 (1929).

"Purchase-Money Mortgage Executed by Husband Alone on Property Purchased for or Subject to Community," 47 A. L. R. 1025 (1927).

"Right of Community to Reimbursement for Community Funds, Applied to Improvement of, or Discharge of Liens on, Separate Property of One of the Spouses," 77 A. L. R. 1021–25 (1932).

"Change of Domicil as Affecting Character of Property Previously Acquired as Separate or Community Property," 92 A. L. R. 1347–55 (1934).

"Husband's Gift of Community Property as Fraud on Wife," 64 A. L. R. 495–96 (1929).

"Stockholders' Statutory Added Liability as Enforceable against Community Property," 90 A. L. R. 1296–99 (1934).

"Survival against Community of Right of Action for a Tort of the Deceased Member of the Community," 67 A. L. R. 1159–60 (1930).

Section 179. Suits by and against the Wife

CROSS REFERENCES: Suits by abandoned and separated wives, **Sec. 143**; Equal-rights statutes, **Sec. 150**; Suits by one spouse against the other, **Sec. 180**; Wife as a sole trader, **Sec. 187**; Suits by and against the child, **Secs. 237, 272**; Suits by and against insane persons, **Sec. 303**

At common law the suspension of the wife's legal existence made it necessary to join the husband as a party in any suit by or against her. In equity, however, she was permitted to sue and be sued alone in actions relating to her separate equitable estate, and early statutes often adopted this equitable rule.

The emancipation of the wife in most jurisdictions has now reached the point where her procedural disabilities have been completely abolished. Much of this legislation is of comparatively recent origin. Stimson, writing in 1886, found only nineteen jurisdictions with express statutes broadly permitting the wife to sue and be sued alone, while today there are thirty-seven jurisdictions with explicit provisions to that effect, and at least six others which have probably accomplished the same result. Some of these broad statutes expressly state that a husband is not a proper party merely because of the marriage relation. An implication that the wife may sue alone may also be drawn from statutes, discussed elsewhere in this volume, which confer certain substantive rights on her.

The forty-three jurisdictions mentioned above may be classified as follows: (1) The great majority, thirty-one in all, have legislation similar to that found in **Kansas**: "A woman may, while married, sue and be sued, in the same manner as if she were unmarried." (2) **Oregon** and **Wisconsin** give the wife the same procedural freedom that the husband has. (3) Four jurisdictions combine the two preceding types of statutes and place the wife upon a procedural equality with both her husband and a single woman. (4) Six jurisdictions (**Alabama, Connecticut, District of Columbia, Maine, Maryland, New Hampshire**) have ambiguous legislation which authorizes the wife to prosecute and defend certain enumerated types of actions. These statutes probably are designed to free her of all procedural disability, but some of them do not seem broad enough in terms to reach that result.

The eight remaining jurisdictions are less progressive than those already discussed. **Arizona** and **Nevada,** both community-property states, provide that the husband must be joined except in actions relating to the wife's separate property. **Florida, Georgia, Indiana,** and **Vermont** enumerate a few actions in which a wife may be a party alone.

In **North Carolina** it is specifically provided that the husband must be joined except in certain limited cases. **Texas** is even more restrictive. The wife may sue alone only for the recovery of her separate property, it also being necessary in such a case that the husband have failed to sue or to join with her; and also that she have the authority of the court.

Other common but less important statutes provide that if husband and wife are sued together the wife may defend for her own right and also his if he neglects to.

Certain miscellaneous statutes relevant to actions in which a wife is a party are collected in the table following, together with citations to all statutes discussed.

TABLE XC*

SUITS BY AND AGAINST A WIFE

Jurisdiction and Citation	In General	Specific Suits	Miscellaneous
Alabama C. 1923, Secs. 5714, 8265–66, 8268	Wife must sue alone on all her contracts; for the recovery, or income of her separate property, or injuries to such property; and for all injuries to her person or reputation. She must be sued as if sole on contracts made by her; and for all torts committed by her	Wife is liable and suable as if sole, for her antenuptial or postnuptial debts, engagements or torts	Action by or against single woman does not abate on her marriage, but proceeds in her new name[1]
Alaska Comp. L. 1913, Secs. 494–95, 860	Wife has the same right to appeal in her own name alone to all courts for unjust usurpation of her property or natural rights as husband has. She may prosecute and defend all actions for the preservation and protection of her rights and property as if unmarried	Contracts and liabilities of wife may be enforced by and against her in the same manner as if she were unmarried. She may maintain an action in her own name for wages of her personal labor	
Arizona R. C. 1928, Secs. 3715, 3729	When wife is a party, her husband shall be joined except in actions concerning her separate property, or between herself and husband, in which she may sue or be sued alone		If spouses are sued together, wife may defend in her own right. Spouses shall be sued jointly for debts contracted by wife for necessaries furnished herself or children. Wife may be sued in the county in which husband resides, unless she is living separate from him

* See page 267 for numbered footnotes to this table.

§ 179]

TABLE XC (*Continued*)

Jurisdiction and Citation	In General	Specific Suits	Miscellaneous
Arkansas .... Crawf. and Moses, Dig. 1921, Secs. 1108, 1332, 5577, 5581, 5586–87	Wife shall have all the rights to sue and be sued as if sole. All statutory and common-law disabilities of wife are expressly removed[2]	Wife may sue or be sued alone on account of her separate personal property, trade or business, or her services performed on her separate account	If spouses are sued together, wife may defend for her own right, and for husband's if he neglects to. Where spouses unite in an action, service of notice on husband is deemed service on wife. Judgment against wife may be enforced by execution against her separate property as if she were sole
California ...... C. C. P. 1933 (Lake), Secs. 370–71	Wife may sue and be sued without her husband being joined, in all actions, including those for injury to her person, libel, slander, false imprisonment, or malicious prosecution, or for the recovery of her earnings, or concerning her right or claim to homestead property		If spouses are sued together, wife may defend for her own right, and for husband if he neglects to
Colorado .... Comp. L. 1921, C. C. P., Sec. 6; G. S., Secs. 5577–78, 5586, 6308	Wife may sue and be sued in all matters as if sole	Wife may sue and be sued as if sole, in all matters relating to her property, person, reputation; and to her trade, business, labor, services or earnings. She may sue in her own name for damages caused by intoxication of her husband	Judgment against wife may be enforced by execution or other process as if she were sole
Connecticut .... G. S. 1930, Secs. 5154, 5170, 5493, 5539	Wife may bring suit in her own name upon contracts or for torts; and may be sued for a breach of contract or for a tort	Wife married on or before April 20, 1877, may sue and be sued as if unmarried, in relation to her separate estate	In any civil action by or against wife, husband may be joined; but costs shall be taxed only for or against the one, in favor of or against whom a cause of action is found. Marriage by female plaintiff does not abate the action
Delaware ...... R. C. 1915, Sec. 3048, amd. by Sess. L. 1919, Ch. 197, p. 524	Wife may sue and be sued and exercise all other rights and powers which a feme sole may do		See footnote 2

[§ 179

TABLE XC (*Continued*)

Jurisdiction and Citation	In General	Specific Suits	Miscellaneous
District of Columbia ... C. 1929, T. 14, Sec. 43; T. 25, Sec. 323	Wife has power to sue separately on her contracts, for the recovery or protection of her property, and for torts against her, as fully and freely as if unmarried. She may be sued separately as if unmarried, on her contracts or for wrongs independent of contracts	Wife, a tenant of real estate, who is in default, may be ejected as if sole	Execution against wife on a judgment may be issued as if she were unmarried
Florida .... R. G. S. 1920, Secs. 1867, 2563, 2578, 2937, 3951–52	Wife may sue alone as if single on a claim to her personal property levied on under legal process; in actions concerning her land and rights therein; and for her earnings acquired in employment separate from her husband	Liens of a municipality on land of wife may be enforced in equity, and the court shall appoint a guardian ad litem	Marriage of a female party shall not abate an action; judgment shall be rendered for or against her alone, and execution issue on her property alone
Georgia .... C. 1926, C. C., Secs. 2994, 3945	For torts upon the person or reputation of wife, either spouse may sue and recover. Wife may enforce contracts made in reference to her own acquisitions	Wife acting as executrix or administratrix may sue and be sued as a feme sole, touching the estate; and her separate estate is bound for all judgments as though she were sole	
Hawaii .... R. L. 1925, Secs. 2130, 2998	Wife may sue and be sued in the same manner as if sole, but this does not authorize suits between spouses	Wife may sue in own name for damages caused by intoxication of husband	
Idaho .... Comp. St. 1919, Secs. 6637–38, 7327	Wife may sue and be sued in same manner as if single	Coverture is not a defense in action against wife for unlawful detainer; but if husband is not joined or if the wife is not a free trader, execution on a judgment in such action can only be enforced against property on premises at commencement of action	If spouses are sued together, wife may defend her own right and also husband's if he neglects to

§ 179]

TABLE XC (*Continued*)

Jurisdiction and Citation	In General	Specific Suits	Miscellaneous
Illinois .... Cahill, R. S. 1931, Ch. 1, Sec. 9; Ch. 68, Secs. 1, 2, 6, 7	Wife may, in all cases, sue and be sued without joining husband, to same extent as if unmarried	Contracts and liabilities of wife may be enforced against her as if she were single. She may sue for own earnings in her own name, free from interference of husband or his creditors	Marriage of female party does not abate action, but she may continue as if sole. Attachment or judgment against wife may be enforced by or against her as if she were single. If spouses are sued together, wife may defend for own right, and, if either neglect to defend, other may do so for such one
Indiana .... Burns, Ann. St. 1926, Secs. 262, 8742, 8751; Supp. 1929, Sec. 8751.1	Wife may sue alone in actions: (*a*) concerning her separate property, except that actions relative to her lands must be prosecuted by or against husband and wife if they are living together; (*b*) between herself and husband; (*c*) for injury to her person or character. She may be sued as if single for her torts. In no case need she sue or defend by guardian or next friend unless she is under the age of twenty-one years		
Iowa .... C. 1927, Secs. 2056, 10461– 62, 10466, 10992–93	Wife in all cases may sue and be sued without joining husband. She may prosecute and defend all actions for the preservation and protection of her rights and property as if unmarried	Wife may sue as if single for damage caused by intoxication of husband. She may sue in her own name for wages of her personal labor; and contracts or liabilities of wife may be enforced by or against her as if she were single	Attachment or judgment shall be enforced by or against wife as if she were single. If spouses are sued together, wife may defend for own right and, if either neglects to defend, other may do so for both. Any woman in an action for her wrongful injury may recover for loss of time, medical attendance, and other expenses incurred, in addition to elements of damage recoverable by common law

[§ 179

TABLE XC (*Continued*)

Jurisdiction and Citation	In General	Specific Suits	Miscellaneous
Kansas .... R. S. 1923, Secs. 21(2150)– 21(2151), 21(2155), 23(203), 23(205), 60(404)– 60(405)	Wife may sue and be sued in same manner as if she were unmarried	Wife may sue as if unmarried for damages caused by intoxication of husband (see next column)	If spouses are sued together, wife may defend for own right, and also for husband if he neglects to. Wife has the sole right of action for wrongful personal injury to her, except that recovery based on impairment of her ability to perform household services and domestic duties is for husband's benefit so far as he is entitled thereto
Kentucky ...... Carroll, St. 1922, Sec. 2128; C. C. of Prac. 1906, Secs. 34, 629	Wife may sue and be sued as a single woman[2]		If spouses are sued together, wife may defend for herself and also for husband if he fails to do so. When sued together, service on husband is deemed service on wife
Louisiana ...... Marr, Ann. R. S., Supp. 1926, Act 219, p. 1739, Sec. 2; Sess. L. 1928, Act 283, p. 583	Wife shall have capacity to institute or defend suits, or otherwise appear in judicial proceedings, and to stand in judgment, without the authority of her husband or of the judge. Wife is competent to appear in court, and to sue and be sued in same manner as though she were a feme sole		
Maine .... R. S. 1930, Ch. 74, Secs. 3–5; Ch. 105, Sec. 29; Ch. 137, Sec. 19	Wife may prosecute and defend suits at law or in equity, of tort or contract, in her own name, without joinder of husband, for the protection of her property and personal rights or the redress of her injuries, as if unmarried, although she may prosecute such suits jointly with husband	Wife may sue in own name for wages of her personal labor, and for damages caused by intoxication of husband. She may be sued as if sole for her antenuptial debts; for her postnuptial debts in her own name; and for her torts in which her husband takes no part	Wife's property may be attached and taken on execution in action for her debts or torts, but she cannot be arrested. In action to enforce a lien for labor or materials, coverture is not a defense

§ 179]

TABLE XC (*Continued*)

Jurisdiction and Citation	In General	Specific Suits	Miscellaneous
Maryland ...... Bagby, Ann. C. 1924, Art. 26, Sec. 20; Art. 45, Secs. 5, 17, 20; Art. 88, Sec. 2	Wife may sue on her contracts, for the recovery or protection of her property, and for torts against her, as if unmarried. She may be sued separately on her contracts, and for her wrongs independent of contract, as if unmarried	Landlord may levy rent by distress or sue for unlawful detainer against wife as if she were sole. Wife may sue in her own name in action of slander for defamation as to her chastity. She may sue and be sued as if sole on her contracts of partnership	Female plaintiff who marries after judgment may have execution in her new name; and on marriage of a female defendant, plaintiff may obtain writ of scire facias. Execution may issue against wife as if she were unmarried
Massachusetts .. G. L. 1932, Ch. 138, Sec. 49; Ch. 209, Sec. 6	Wife may sue and be sued in same manner as if sole; but this does not authorize suits between spouses	Wife may sue in own name for the intoxication of husband	
Michigan . .... Comp. L. 1929, Secs. 9193, 12733, 13059, 14013–14	Whenever a cause of action accrues to or arises against wife, she may sue or be sued in the same manner as if she were sole	A bill for divorce may be exhibited by wife in her own name. She may be sued on her contracts made in relation to her sole property; she may sue and be sued in relation to her sole property in the same manner as if unmarried; and she may sue alone where husband's property cannot be sold or encumbered without her consent, or when his property is exempt by law from sale on execution. She may sue in her name for damages from intoxication of husband	
Minnesota ...... G. S. 1923, Secs. 3239, 8616, 9168	Wife may sue and be sued as if unmarried, without joining husband. She also has the same right to appeal to the courts in her own name alone for protection or redress that the husband has	Wife may sue in own name for damages from intoxication of husband	If a woman marry while a party to a pending action, she is thereafter to be designated by her married name

[§ 179

TABLE XC (*Continued*)

Jurisdiction and Citation	In General	Specific Suits	Miscellaneous
Mississippi C. 1930, Sec. 1940	Wife is fully emancipated from all disability of coverture, and may sue and be sued, with all the rights and liabilities incident thereto, as if she were not married		
Missouri R. S. 1929, Secs. 704, 1340, 2998, 3003, 4487, 6264	Wife may, in her own name, with or without joining husband as a party, sue and be sued as if sole	Wife may sue in her own name for the recovery of her personal property, including rights in action, as if she were sole. She may sue in her name for damages from intoxication of husband. In condemnation proceedings against lands of wife, husband must be joined	A judgment in an action where wife is a party has the same force and effect as if she were single. Wife may invoke all exemption and homestead laws available to head of a family, except where husband has claimed such rights for protection of his own property
Montana R. C. 1921, Secs. 5791, 5809, 9069–70, 9319	Wife may sue and be sued in the same manner as if she were sole	Wife may sue in her own name for injuries to her person, property, and character	If spouses are sued together, wife may defend for her own right and also for husband's if he neglects to. A judgment for or against wife may be rendered and enforced as if she were single
Nebraska Comp. St. 1929, Secs. 20(305)– 20(306), 53(147)– 53(148)	Wife may sue and be sued in the same manner as if she were unmarried	Wife may sue in her own name for damage sustained by an unlawful sale of liquor to husband	If spouses are sued together, wife may defend for her own right and also for husband's if he neglects to
Nevada Comp. L. 1929 (Hillyer), Secs. 8546–47	Husband must be joined when wife is a party except: In actions concerning her separate property or her right or claim to homestead property, she may sue alone; and in actions between herself and husband, she may sue or be sued alone		If spouses are sued together, wife may defend of her own right, and either may defend for both, if the other neglects to
New Hampshire. Pub. L. 1926, Ch. 144, Secs. 52, 53; Ch. 288, Sec. 2	Wife may sue and be sued in all matters in law and equity, upon her contracts, or for any wrong by her, as if she were unmarried	Wife may sue in her own name for damage caused by intoxication of husband	

§ 179]

TABLE XC (*Continued*)

Jurisdiction and Citation	In General	Specific Suits	Miscellaneous
New Jersey .... Comp. St. 1910, pp. 3235–37, Secs. 10–12*B*; p. 4058, Sec. 22; Cum. Supp. 1911–24, Sec. 124(17); Supp. 1925–30, Sec. 124(5)	Wife may sue or be sued without joining husband, in any case where he would not be a necessary party if he were not her husband	Wife may sue in her own name alone for torts committed against her or her separate property; for breaches of contract; for recovery of earnings, (debts), and her separate property, and for the protection of such property, as if single. She may be sued in her own name alone for her debts; and on her contracts	Judgment and execution against wife are as valid and effectual as if she were unmarried. Marriage of a female party does not abate the action, but action proceeds to final judgment, in name of such female, as case may be notwithstanding such marriage[2]
New Mexico .... St. Ann. 1929, Sec. 105(109)	Wife shall sue and be sued as if she were unmarried		
New York ...... Cahill, Consol. L. 1930, Ch. 14, Secs. 51, 57, 60; Cahill, Civ. Prac. Act 1931, Secs. 28, 200, 276	Wife may be a party in the same manner as if single, and husband is not a necessary or proper party solely because of his relationship	Wife has a right of action as if unmarried for injury to her person, property, character, or injury arising out of the marital relation; for all remuneration from her services or business; she is liable on her contracts respecting property as if unmarried	Judgment for or against wife may be rendered and enforced as if she were single
North Carolina.. C. 1927, Secs. 454, 603, 665, 2513, 2520–21	When wife is a party, her husband must be joined except: She may sue alone where action concerns her separate property; for her earnings derived from her personal service; for any tort she sustains. She may sue or be sued alone in an action between herself and husband, but in no case need she prosecute or defend by guardian or next friend		Judgment and execution against wife may be levied and collected solely out of her separate estate. In all actions against wife, who is not a free trader, summons shall be served on husband also; and on motion he may be allowed, with her consent, to defend in her name; but he may be discharged from such defense if it is not bona fide in wife's interest

[§ 179

TABLE XC (*Continued*)

Jurisdiction and Citation	In General	Specific Suits	Miscellaneous
North Dakota... Comp. L. 1913, Secs. 4411, 7398, 7679, 7716, 10121	In all actions by or against wife she shall sue and be sued in her own name. When she is a party, her appearance, prosecution or defense, or joinder of another party must be governed by the same rules as if she were single	She may sue in her own name for damages caused by intoxication of husband	Judgment and execution against wife may be levied on and collected only from her separate estate
Ohio .... Complete G. C. 1931 (Page), Secs. 6203, 11245–46, 11591	Wife shall sue and be sued as if unmarried, and husband joined only when cause of action is in favor of or against both	Wife may sue in her own name for damages caused by intoxication of husband	When spouses are sued together, wife may defend for own right and also husband's if he neglects to. When wife is a party, judgment may be had and enforced as if she were single. She is entitled to benefits of exemptions to heads of families
Oklahoma ...... St. 1931, Secs. 145–46, 1665, 2652	Wife may sue and be sued in same manner as if unmarried; and shall have the same right to appeal in her own name alone to the courts that husband has, for injury to her reputation, person, property, character or any natural right	Wife may sue in her own name for damages caused by intoxication of husband	If spouses are sued together, wife may defend for her own right and also for husband's if he neglects to
Oregon .... C. 1930, Sec. 33(215)	All laws imposing civil disabilities on wife not imposed on husband are repealed. She has the same right to appeal in own name alone to the courts for redress that husband has, for unjust usurpation of her property or natural rights		
Pennsylvania ... St. 1920 (West), Sec. 14602	Wife may sue and be sued civilly in all respects, in any form of action and with same effect and results, as an unmarried person except as to suits between spouses	See footnote 2	Wife may not be arrested or imprisoned for her torts
Rhode Island.... G. L. 1923, Sec. 4206	In all actions, suits and proceedings, in law or equity, wife shall sue and be sued alone		

§ 179]

TABLE XC (*Continued*)

Jurisdiction and Citation	In General	Specific Suits	Miscellaneous
South Carolina .. C. of L. 1922, C. C. P., Sec. 357, amd. by Sess. L. 1925, No. 171, p. 263; Sec. 597; C. C., Sec. 5540	Wife may sue and be sued as if she were unmarried	Contracts of wife may be enforced in law or equity, by or against her in her own name apart from husband	Judgment may be enforced by execution against her separate estate in the same manner as if she were sole
South Dakota ... Comp. L. 1929, Secs. 178, 2309, 10309	When wife is a party, her appearance, the prosecution or defense of the action, and joinder of any other person must be governed by the same rules as if she were single	Wife may sue in her own name without her husband for injury to her reputation, person or property and for damages caused by intoxication of husband. She may be sued without her husband on her separate contracts, for her torts, or in actions relating to her individual property	
Tennessee ...... C. 1932, Sec. 8460	Wife is fully emancipated from all disability on account of coverture; and has same capacity to sue and be sued as if she were not married		
Texas .... Complete St. 1928, Civ. St., Arts. 1983–85, 1995(1), 2084	See next column	Husband and wife shall be jointly sued on debts incurred by wife including those for necessaries furnished herself or children and for expenses incurred by wife for benefit of her separate property. He may sue alone or jointly with her for recovery of her separate property, but, if he neglects to do so, she may, by court's authority, sue alone	Wife may be sued in county where husband has domicile. Marriage of a female party shall not abate action, but husband may make himself a party plaintiff; or if she is a defendant, a scire facias may be issued on husband, and the suit proceed

[§ 179

TABLE XC (*Continued*)

Jurisdiction and Citation	In General	Specific Suits	Miscellaneous
Utah .... R. S. 1933, 40-2-4, 104-3-3, 104-3-4, 104-30-6	Wife may sue and be sued in same manner as if she were unmarried	Wife may sue in her own name for wages of her personal labor. She may recover against third person as if unmarried, for any personal injury or wrong to her, and such recovery shall include expenses paid or assumed by the husband in connection with such injury	Judgment for or against wife may be rendered and enforced as if she were single. If spouses are sued together, wife may defend for her own right and, if either neglect to defend, other may do so for both
Vermont .... G. L. 1917, Secs. 3521, 3530, 6579	Wife may sue and be sued without husband, on all contracts made by her	Wife may sue in own name for damages caused by intoxication of husband	In actions by or against wife on her contracts, execution may issue against her and be levied on her separate property. Action is not abated by marriage of a female party
Virginia .... C. 1930, Secs. 4675(26); 5134, amd. by Sess. L. 1932, Ch. 25, p. 21	Wife may sue and be sued in the same manner as if she were unmarried	Wife may sue in own name for damages caused by intoxication of husband, as if unmarried (see next column)	Wife may recover entire damage sustained from personal injury to her, including expenses incurred therefrom (whether chargeable to her or her husband)
Washington .... Remington, Comp. St. 1922, Secs. 182, 1713, 6900–6901, 7348	Every married person has the same right to sue and be sued as if he or she were unmarried. All laws imposing civil disabilities on wife, not imposed on husband, are abolished, and she has the same right to appeal in her own name to the courts that he has	Wife may sue in her own name for damages caused by intoxication of husband	If spouses are sued together, wife may defend for her own right, and also for husband's if he neglects to
West Virginia .. C. 1931, Ch. 48, Art. 3, Secs. 14, 19, 21	Wife may sue or be sued alone as if she were a single woman, and her husband shall not be joined unless it is proper for reasons other than the marital relation	Antenuptial debts of wife may be enforced against her and her property as if she were single	Judgment against wife is enforceable against her and her property in the same manner as if she were single

§ 179]

TABLE XC (*Concluded*)

Jurisdiction and Citation	In General	Specific Suits	Miscellaneous
Wisconsin ..... St. 1931, Secs. 6.015, 246.07	Women shall have the same rights and privileges under the law as men, in all respects	Wife may sue in her own name in regard to her separate property, business, or earnings; for injury to her person or character; for alienation of husband's affections. She may be sued as if unmarried in respect to her separate property or business	Judgment may be rendered and enforced against wife and her separate property in all respects as if she were unmarried
Wyoming ...... R. S. 1931, Secs. 69(103), 69(105), 89(504)– 89(505), 89(2212)	In any civil action when wife is a party, it shall not be necessary to join her husband except where such joinder would be necessary without reference to fact of marriage	Wife may sue and be sued as if sole in regard to her property, person or reputation; and her trade, business, services, earnings	When spouses are sued together, wife may defend for her own right and also his if he neglects to. When wife is a party alone, judgment may be rendered and enforced as if she were unmarried, but she is entitled to benefit of all exemptions to heads of families

[1] In Alabama (C. 1923, Sec. 6138), a wife may appeal from any judgment subjecting to sale any property of, or for payment of money, or the doing of any act by wife, without giving security for costs of appeal; on making affidavit that she is unable to give such security; and the appeal stays proceedings under such judgment.

[2] Five states have provisions inconsistent with those outlined in the table, which, although not expressly repealed, presumably have been rendered obsolete by the later broad statutes: **Arkansas,** Crawford and Moses, Digest, 1921, Sections 1107, 1110, 2155–56; **Delaware,** Revised Code, 1915, Section 4195; **Kentucky,** Civil Code of Practice, 1906, Section 34; **New Jersey,** Compiled Statutes, 1910, page 1525, Section 5; **Pennsylvania,** Statutes, 1920 (West), Section 14607.

REFERENCES

Books

MADDEN, JOSEPH W. *Handbook of the Law of Persons and Domestic Relations,* pp. 156–58 (1931).

STIMSON, F. J. *American Statute Law,* Secs. 6453–55 (1886).

Article

TURNER, JENNIE McMULLIN. "Women's Rights by Blanket Legislation," 2 Wis. L. Rev. 103–9 (1922).

Note

"Joinder of Husband in Wife's Actions," *Shore* v. *Holt,* 185 N. C. 212; 117 S. E. 165 (1923)—2 N. C. L. Rev. 56–59 (1923).

Annotation

"Civil Action for Assault and Battery on Female Parties," 6 A. L. R. 1023–25 (1920).

[§ 179

Section 180. Suits between Spouses

CROSS REFERENCES: Contracts between husband and wife, **Secs. 155, 156**; Crimes between spouses, **Sec. 166**; Wife's property, **Sec. 167**; Husband's property, **Sec. 176**; Suits by and against the wife, **Sec. 179**; Conveyances between husband and wife, **Sec. 182**; Husband and wife as witnesses for and against each other, **Sec. 226**

It was fundamental at common law that no action could be maintained between husband and wife. However, divorce from bed and board was allowed in the ecclesiastical courts; and equity recognized litigation between spouses to enforce equitable rights and obligations relating to the wife's separate equitable estate.

The law today is in a state of confusion. Little express legislation exists. The more definite rules developed by implication from statutes not express on the subject are as follows: (1) Statutes permitting contracts and property transactions between spouses (**Secs. 155, 156, 182**) must necessarily give the right to enforce the same by legal action. **Maryland** is express to that effect respecting contracts. (2) Statutes giving separate property rights to the wife (**Sec. 167**) have generally been held to allow her to enforce them against the husband, with divided authority as to whether she may sue at law or only in equity. (3) The broad statutes allowing the wife to sue and be sued as if sole (**Sec. 179**) in many cases have provided authority for suits by her against the husband, even to the extent of allowing actions for his personal torts. (4) The Married Women's Acts have been interpreted by many courts as so completely destroying the unity of husband and wife in property matters that the husband may sue in equity or at law for the protection of his property. However, some courts maintain that such acts were not intended to increase the husband's rights and consequently that he is still subject to the old common-law and equitable rules.

Upon some one of the views discussed above, it is generally held that even in the absence of express statutes property actions may be brought between spouses. There is more conflict of authority as to personal torts. The majority of jurisdictions have denied such actions, although several late cases have strengthened the minority view. No jurisdiction has been found which, by statute, adopts either rule relative to personal torts.

Fragmentary legislation found in twenty-one jurisdictions may be broadly classified as follows: statutes permitting, to some extent, actions relating to property (**Alaska, Illinois, Iowa, Louisiana, Maine, Missouri, Oregon, Pennsylvania, Utah, Washington**); ambiguous statutes which may only define the wife's procedural rights, but which, in some cases, have been construed as a rather broad sanction for suits between spouses (**Arizona, Arkansas, Indiana, Mississippi, Nevada, North Carolina, South Carolina, Washington**) ; statutes expressly restricting, in some degree, actions between spouses (**Hawaii, Louisiana, Massachusetts, Pennsylvania**) ; and a few miscellaneous statutes permitting or denying specific suits (**Florida, Maryland, North Carolina, Pennsylvania, South Dakota**).

It is the writer's opinion that property actions and even personal-tort actions within some limitations should be permitted. It is argued that by denying actions between spouses domestic tranquillity will be protected, but at the stage in which a spouse wishes to sue there is usually little tranquillity left. It is also argued that if such actions are permitted the courts will be filled with trivial suits. It is submitted that this may be answered by recognizing, as to unimportant acts technically torts, an implied consent and license arising from the marriage relation. In cases of more serious injury where there is no license, grave injustice is often worked by denial of a legal remedy. Many negligence actions might be denied on the ground that there is an assumption of risk where there is a common enterprise by husband and wife. Where this is not true an action should be allowed. At any rate, it is unfortunate that the legislatures have been loath to decide which policies are controlling.

Summary of Relevant Statutes

Alaska (Comp. L. 1913, Sec. 440) : If either spouse obtains possession or control of property belonging to the other, the owner of such property may maintain an action therefor, or for any right growing out of the same, as if unmarried.

Arizona (R. C. 1928, Sec. 3729) : When a wife is a party, her husband must be joined except when . . . . the action is between herself and husband, in which she may sue or be sued alone.

Arkansas (Crawf. and Moses, Dig. 1921, Sec. 1107) : Substantially like the **Arizona** statute. (See also Table XC, **Sec. 179.**)

Florida (R. G. S. 1920, Sec. 3948) : The wife may not sue her husband for rent, issues, or profits of her property managed by him.

Hawaii (R. L. 1925, Sec. 2998) : A married woman may sue and be sued as if sole, but this does not authorize suits between husband and wife.

Illinois (Cahill, R. S. 1931, Ch. 68, Sec. 10) : Same as the **Alaska** statute.

[§ 180

Indiana (Burns, Ann. St. 1926, Sec. 262) : A wife may sue alone
. . . . when the action is between herself and husband.

Iowa (C. 1927, Sec. 10448) : Same as the **Alaska** statute.

Louisiana (Marr, R. C. of Prac. 1927, Art. 105, p. 42; C. C., Art.
2391) : A wife cannot sue her husband except: For separation from
bed and board or for divorce; for the separation of property; for the
restitution and enjoyment of her paraphernal property; or in case she
holds her property separate by the marriage contract; but in no case
may she sue him without authorization of the court. (But see Sess. L.
1928, Act 283, p. 583.) Married women have capacity to prosecute or
defend suits . . . . without the authority of their husbands, or of the
judge.

Maine (R. S. 1930, Ch. 74, Sec. 6; Ch. 91, Sec. 36) : Either spouse
may sue in equity against the other for the recovery, conveyance, or
transfer of any property exceeding one hundred dollars in value, in the
possession or control of the other, or to which he or she has legal title.

Maryland (Bagby, Ann. C. 1924) : A husband may obtain a court
order in equity preventing his wife from pledging his credit (Art. 16,
Sec. 49) ; a wife may sue and be sued as if sole on her contracts with
her husband (Art. 45, Sec. 20).

Massachusetts (G. L. 1932, Ch. 209, Sec. 6) : Substantially like the
Hawaii statute.

Mississippi (C. 1930, Sec. 1941) : Husband and wife may sue each
other.

Missouri (R. S. 1929, Sec. 1518) : Wife may petition circuit court
for injunction to restrain husband from squandering or wasting or
fraudulently converting to his own use property to which she is entitled
in her own right. Court may allow such injunction and may appoint a
receiver to manage such property for her benefit. Husband shall be made
a party defendant to said petition.

Nevada (Comp. L. 1929 [Hillyer], Sec. 8546) : Substantially like
the **Arizona** statute.

North Carolina (C. 1927) : Substantially like the **Arizona** statute
(Sec. 454) ; no husband, having received without objection the income
from the wife's separate estate, shall be liable to account for any greater
time than the year next preceding the date of a summons issued against
him in such action, or next preceding her death (Sec. 2514).

Oregon (C. 1930, Sec. 33[202]) : Same as the **Alaska** statute.

Pennsylvania (St. 1920 [West]) : Neither spouse may sue the
other except for divorce or to protect or recover his or her separate

§ 180]

property (Sec. 14602) ; a wife may sue her husband in ejectment for land purchased with her money (Sec. 21339).

South Carolina (C. of L. 1922, C. C. P., Sec. 357, as amended by Sess. L. 1925, No. 171, p. 263) : When the action is between herself and husband, a wife may sue or be sued alone.

South Dakota (Comp. L. 1929, Sec. 2978) : A wife may sue for her seduction although the seducer is her husband, if he abandons her, or entered into the marriage to avoid prosecution.

Utah (R. S. 1933, 40-2-6) : Same as the **Alaska** statute.

Washington (Remington, Comp. St. 1922) : Substantially like the **Arizona** statute (Sec. 181) (but see Table XC, **Sec. 179**) ; same as the **Alaska** statute (Sec. 6903).

REFERENCES

Articles

ALBERTSWORTH, E. F. "Tort Actions by Wife against Husband," 10 Calif. L. Rev. 471–80 (1922).

FARAGE, D. J. "Recovery for Torts between Spouses," 10 Ind. L. Jour. 290–303 (1935).

LIPPMAN, JACOB. "The Breakdown of Consortium," 30 Col. L. Rev. 651–73 (1930).

McCURDY, WILLIAM E. "Torts between Persons in Domestic Relation," 43 Harv. L. Rev. 1030–82 (1930).

Notes

"Action by Wife against Husband for Defamation, Whether Maintainable," *Ralston* v. *Ralston,* (1930) 2 K. B. 238 ; 99 L. J. K. B. 266—4 Aust. L. Jour. 151–52 (1930) ; 4 Camb. L. Jour. 224 (1931) ; 9 Can. B. Rev. 41–44 (1931) ; 6 Ind. L. Jour. 276–77 (1931) ; 30 Mich. L. Rev. 142–49 (1931).

"Action by Wife for Tort of Husband Committed before Marriage," *Gotliffe* v. *Edelston,* (1930) 2 K. B. 378 ; 46 T. L. R. 544—4 Camb. L. Jour. 222 (1931) ; 9 Can. B. Rev. 41–44 (1931) ; 31 Col. L. Rev. 323 (1931) ; 26 Ill. L. Rev. 88–90 (1931) ; 47 L. Quar. Rev. 163–64 (1931) ; 37 W. Va. L. Quar. 224–26 (1931).

"Conflict of Laws, Constitutional Law, Full Faith and Credit, Action between Spouses on Foreign Judgment," *Weidman* v. *Weidman,* 274 Mass. 118 ; 174 N. E. 206 (1931)—31 Col. L. Rev. 702–4 (1931).

"Discharge of Obligation in Tort by Subsequent Marriage of Parties," *Buckeye* v. *Buckeye,* 203 Wis. 248 ; 234 N. W. 342 (1931)—6 Wis. L. Rev. 103–5 (1931) ; 79 Univ. of Pa. L. Rev. 804–6 (1931) ; 44 Harv. L. Rev. 1138–39 (1931) ; 31 Col. L. Rev. 884–85 (1931) ; 35 Law Notes 74–75 (1931) ; 29 Mich. L. Rev. 937–38, 1072–73 (1931).

"Effect of Subsequent Marriage of a Negligent Employee to the Injured Party on the Latter's Right of Action against the Employer," *Webster* v. *Snyder,* 103 Fla. 1131 ; 138 So. 755 (1932)—80 Univ. of Pa. L. Rev. 1027–28 (1932).

[§ 180

"Right of Wife to Sue Husband for Personal Injuries," *Katzenberg* v. *Katzenberg,* 183 Ark. 626; 37 S. W. (2d) 696 (1931)—12 B. U. L. Rev. 134–39 (1932) ; 10 Tex. L. Rev. 242–43 (1932) ; 35 Law Notes 213–14 (1932).

"Right of Wife to Sue Husband's Principal in Tort for Husband's Negligence," *Sacknoff* v. *Sacknoff,* 131 Me. 280; 161 A. 669 (1932)—12 B. U. L. Rev. 701–6 (1932) ; 17 Minn. L. Rev. 450–51 (1933).

"Tort Action by Wife of Partner against Partnership," *Wadsworth* v. *Webster,* 257 N. Y. S. 386 (1932)—18 Cor. L. Quar. 101–7 (1932).

"Recovery for Negligent Injury of One Spouse by the Other," *Wait* v. *Pierce,* 191 Wis. 202; 209 N. W. 475 (1926)—21 Ill. L. Rev. 515–17 (1929) ; 4 Wis. L. Rev. 37–40 (1926).

"Right of Wife to Sue Her Husband for Personal Injuries, Interpretation of Statutes," 37 W. Va. L. Quar. 92–96 (1930).

"Rights of Wife against Husband—Wife's Right to Sue Husband for Personal Torts," *Fiedler* v. *Fiedler,* 42 Okla. 124; 140 P. 1022 (1914)—28 Harv. L. Rev. 109–10 (1914).

"Tort as between Husband and Wife," *Gowin* v. *Gowin* (Tex. Civ. App.) ; 264 S. W. 529 (1924)—10 Cor. L. Quar. 61–64 (1924).

Annotations

"Husband's Right to Sue Wife for Personal Tort," 23 L. R. A. (N.S.) 699–700 (1910).

"Right of One Spouse to Maintain an Action against the Other for Assault and Battery, under the Married Women's Acts," 6 A. L. R. 1038–48 (1920).

"Right of One Spouse to Maintain Action against Other for Personal Injury," 29 A. L. R. 1482–84 (1924) ; 33 A. L. R. 1406 (1924) ; 44 A. L. R. 794–95 (1926) ; 48 A. L. R. 293–94 (1927).

"Right of One Spouse to Maintain Civil Action at Law against the Other," 21 Ann. Cas. 924–25 (1911).

"Right of Wife to Sue Husband for Personal Tort," 30 L. R. A. (N.S.) 1153 (1911).

"Liability of Employer for Injury to Wife of Employee through Latter's Negligence," 64 A. L. R. 296–97 (1929).

"Marital Relation between Plaintiff and Member of Partnership as Affecting Right to Maintain Action in Tort against Partnership or Partners," 81 A. L. R. 1106–7 (1932).

"Right of One Spouse to Maintain Action against Other for Personal Injury," 89 A. L. R. 118–26 (1934).

Cases

Brown v. *Brown,* 88 Conn. 42; 89 A. 889 (1914).
Fitzmaurice v. *Fitzmaurice,* 62 N. D. 191; 242 N. W. 526 (1932).
Thompson v. *Thompson,* 218 U. S. 611; 31 Sup. Ct. 111; 54 L. Ed. 1180 (1910).

Section 181. Wife's Power to Make a Will

CROSS REFERENCES: Effect of marriage on wife's will, **Sec. 61**; Powers and rights of abandoned wife, **Sec. 143**; Wife's conveyances, etc., **Secs. 182–85**; Curtesy, abolished or modified, **Sec. 216**; Curtesy election, **Sec. 219**; Descent and distribution, **Sec. 227**

The ecclesiastical law recognized the right of the wife to make a testamentary disposition of her personal property, but only with the particular consent of the husband. Indeed, as has already been seen, the question of the wife's power to bequeath her personalty was not likely to arise if the husband fully exercised his marital rights in her property. By the first Statute of Wills (32 Hen. VIII, c. 1), it was enacted that "all and every person and persons" having lands, etc., might devise them. Whether the unity theory of the spouses, and the wife's attendant incapacities, precluded a construction of the statute which would bring married women within its operation appears never to have been judicially determined before the statute (34 Hen. VIII, c. 5) was enacted expressly excluding married women from the class authorized to devise real property. That the wife's will was void, and her testament effective only with the husband's particular consent, was accepted by the early American courts as the common law. The wife could, however, make a valid will in the exercise of a power, and equity might enforce her testamentary disposition of property recognized as her separate estate in equity. Also, presumably in those extreme situations in which the husband was regarded as civilly dead, the wife had the testamentary capacity of a feme sole.

Early American statutes often codified the common law. Others gave the wife testamentary power, but required the husband's written consent annexed to the will, or a separate examination of the wife, or excepted the husband from those whom the wife could make the object of her bounty. **Georgia** formerly provided that "married women are incapable of making wills for want of perfect liberty of action, being presumed to be under the control of their husbands" (C. 1882, Sec. 2410), and in the present Compiled Statutes of **Kentucky** and **New Jersey** are found provisions (since superseded by later enactments) expressly denying the power of the wife to make a will. Most jurisdictions, however, gave the wife full testamentary capacity as one of the first steps in the statutory evolution of her economic emancipation.

Undoubtedly the wife today may make a valid will and testament

in all of the fifty-one jurisdictions examined. Statutes expressly authorizing her to make a testamentary disposition of property without special
formality were found in thirty-six jurisdictions (**Alabama, Alaska,
Arizona, Arkansas, Delaware, District of Columbia, Hawaii,
Idaho, Indiana, Iowa, Kentucky, Louisiana, Maine, Maryland,
Massachusetts, Michigan, Minnesota, Missouri, Montana, Nebraska, Nevada, New Jersey, North Carolina, North Dakota, Oklahoma, Oregon, Rhode Island, South Carolina, South Dakota,
Tennessee, Utah, Vermont, Washington, West Virginia, Wisconsin, Wyoming**). Five of these (**Alabama, Arkansas, Michigan,
North Carolina, Utah**) have constitutional provisions to that effect.
In five jurisdictions (**Florida, Mississippi, New Hampshire, Pennsylvania, Texas**), the wife is not specifically mentioned, but "married
persons" are expressly included within the class having testamentary
capacity. In three more jurisdictions (**New York, Ohio, Virginia**),
the wife may "dispose" of property as if single, which obviously authorizes her to make a testamentary disposition of property. In the remaining seven jurisdictions (**California, Colorado, Connecticut, Georgia,
Illinois, Kansas, New Mexico**), while no specific statutory authority
was found, it seems clear that married women fall into the general class
of "persons" capable of making a valid will and testament. The early
American decisions proceed upon the theory that statutes such as the
first Statute of Wills were not intended to confer capacity on the wife,
surrounded as she was with all the disabilities of coverture (*Marston* v.
Norton, 5 N. H. 205 [1830] ; *Osgood* v. *Breed,* 12 Mass. 525 [1815]).
In view of the independent status, both as to ownership and disposition
of property, now accorded to the wife in all jurisdictions, no court could
with propriety insist that the wife is without testamentary capacity even
though the same is not expressly conferred upon her. Too, in a majority
of the jurisdictions last mentioned, statutes tacitly recognize the testamentary capacity of the wife by controlling the exercise thereof when
the husband survives.

Though the wife has testamentary capacity, her testamentary power
is limited in the sense that she cannot dispose of her property in derogation of the rights accorded by law to the surviving husband. Thus,
she cannot defeat the husband's right as tenant by the curtesy consummate where the same is recognized, or defeat that statutory share in her
estate accorded to the surviving spouse in most jurisdictions (**Sec. 216**).
This limitation on her testamentary power is written into many of the
statutes collected in this section. She may, however, put the surviving

husband to an election between his rights under the law and his rights under her will (**Sec. 219**). The wife also has a very limited testamentary control over the community assets in those jurisdictions where the community-property system prevails (**Sec. 178**).

A comparison of the general statutes defining those persons having testamentary capacity is not within the scope of this section. Suffice it to say that perhaps a majority of jurisdictions require the testator or testatrix to be twenty-one years of age or "of full age." A number of jurisdictions, however, set a lower age requirement for the disposition of personal property than for the disposition of real property; and in some, the age minimum is lower for females than for males. The wife, like other persons, must satisfy the general statutory requirements. In four jurisdictions (**Arizona, Maine, New Hampshire, Texas**), however, a married woman of any age may apparently make an effective testamentary disposition of her property; and in **Wisconsin,** a married woman of eighteen years of age may make a will and testament, while other persons must be "of full age." Also, in some jurisdictions, a female becomes "of age" upon marriage (**Sec. 282**).

When the wife was incapable of making a valid will, the will of a feme sole was quite naturally regarded as revoked by her subsequent marriage. Present statutes in many jurisdictions so provide, but for a totally different reason (**Sec. 61**).

A summary of the statutory material on the subject of this section follows. General statutes are referred to only when nothing expressly referring to married women was found. It will be observed that most legislatures have little regard for the technical use of the terms "devise," "bequeath," etc.

Alabama (Const., Sec. 209; C. 1923, Sec. 8276): Married women may, by last will and testament, dispose of their separate estates as if single.

Alaska (Comp. L. 1913, Secs. 489, 563): The wife, if twenty-one years of age, etc., may "devise" her real and personal property, except as to any rights the husband may have as tenant by the curtesy.

Arizona (R. C. 1928, Secs. 2174, 3636): The wife's separate property may be "bequeathed" by her as if single. Every person of sound mind, aged twenty-one or more, "or who may be or has been lawfully married," may make a last will and testament.

Arkansas (Const., Art. IX, Sec. 7; Crawf. and Moses, Dig. 1921, Sec. 5574): The wife may devise or bequeath her separate property the same as if sole.

[§ 181

California (Prob. C. 1933 [Lake], Sec. 20): "Every person" of sound mind, over age of eighteen years, may dispose of his or "her" separate property by will. (Before the adoption of the recent Probate Code, **California** expressly authorized the wife to make a will by a statute similar to that of **North Dakota** [C. C. 1929 (Ragland), Sec. 1273].)

Colorado (Comp. L. 1921, G. S., Secs. 5184–85): "Every person," aged twenty-one years, etc., may devise all the rights, etc., which he or "she" has in real property, etc., or goods, chattels and personal estate; "all persons" of seventeen years, etc., may dispose of their personal estate by will; provided, that no "married man or woman" shall devise or bequeath away from the other more than one-half of his or her property, without the consent in writing of the other executed after death of testator or testatrix. In *Deutsch* v. *Rohlfing,* 22 Colo. App. 534; 126 P. 1123 (1912), the **Colorado** court affirmed the right of the wife to make a will with or without the consent of the husband.

Connecticut (G. S. 1930, Secs. 4875, 5156, 5165): "Any person" of eighteen years of age, etc., may dispose of "his" estate by will. Wife cannot defeat surviving husband's statutory share by will. The wife may bequeath personal property held by husband as her statutory trustee (in case of marriages before April 20, 1877).

Delaware (R. C. 1915, Sec. 3048, as amended by Sess. L. 1919, Ch. 197, p. 524): The wife may devise or bequeath her separate property and may make a will as if single, subject to the husband's curtesy.

District of Columbia (C. 1929, T. 14, Sec. 21; T. 29, Sec. 21): The wife may dispose of her property by will as fully as if single.

Florida (Sess. L. 1933, Ch. 16103, p. 545, Sec. 5): Every person, male or female, married or single, who is at least eighteen years of age and who is of sound mind may make a will.

Georgia (C. 1926, C. C., Sec. 3838): "Every person" is entitled to make a will unless laboring under some disability of law. Held, in *Urquhart* v. *Oliver,* 56 Ga. 345 (1876), that the wife may dispose of her separate property by will without the husband's consent.

Hawaii (R. L. 1925, Sec. 3318): "Any" married woman may dispose of her property by will in like manner as a person under no disability might do.

Idaho (Comp. St. 1919, Sec. 7809): The wife may dispose of all her separate estate by will, without the consent of her husband, and may alter or revoke the same as if single. Her will must be attested, witnessed, and proved in like manner as all other wills.

§ 181]

Illinois (Cahill, R. S. 1931, Ch. 148, Sec. 1): "Every female" of the age of eighteen years, etc., may devise her real and personal property.

Indiana (Burns, Ann. St. 1926, Sec. 3450): Adult married women may devise and bequeath, by last will and testament, their real and personal estate to any person or corporation capable of holding the same.

Iowa (C. 1927, Secs. 10446, 11846): The wife may dispose of real and personal property by will to the same extent and in the same manner that the husband may dispose of property belonging to him (i.e., subject to surviving husband's distributive share).

Kansas (R. S. 1923, Secs. 22[201], 22[238]–22[239]): "Any person" of full age, etc., may dispose of property by will. No married woman shall bequeath away from her husband more than one-half of her property, except by his consent in writing executed in the presence of two witnesses. "Any married person" having no children may devise one-half of his or her property to other persons than the spouse.

Kentucky (Carroll, St. 1922, Sec. 2147): A married woman of twenty-one years of age, etc., may dispose of her estate by last will and testament subject to the survivor's rights. (For former law, see Secs. 4825, 4827 [now repealed].)

Louisiana (C. C., Art. 135): The wife may make her last will without the authority of the husband.

Maine (R. S. 1930, Ch. 74, Sec. 1; Ch. 88, Sec. 1): A married woman "of any age" may dispose of her real and personal property by will.

Maryland (Bagby, Ann. C. 1924, Art. 45, Sec. 4): The wife has the same power to dispose of her property of every description by will that the husband has to dispose of his property.

Massachusetts (G. L. 1932, Ch. 191, Sec. 1): The wife may make a will in the same manner and with the same effect as any other person (subject to rights of surviving husband).

Michigan (Const., Art. XVI, Sec. 8; Comp. L. 1929, Sec. 13057): The wife may devise or bequeath her real and personal property as if single.

Minnesota (G. S. 1923, Sec. 8735): The words "every person" in Wills Act shall include married women.

Mississippi (C. 1930, Sec. 3550): Every person aged twenty-one years, male or female, married or unmarried, etc., may make a will.

Missouri (R. S. 1929, Sec. 518): Any married woman of twenty-one years of age, etc., may devise her realty and bequeath her personalty (subject to rights of surviving husband).

[§ 181

Montana (R. C. 1921, Sec. 6975) : The wife may make a will in the same manner and with the same effect as if she were single, except that she cannot, without the written consent of her husband, deprive him of more than two-thirds of her real or personal estate.

Nebraska (Comp. St. 1929, Sec. 30[201]) : "Any married woman" may devise and dispose of her real and personal property by her last will and testament in writing, and may alter or revoke the same in like manner that a person under no disability may do.

Nevada (Comp. L. 1929 [Hillyer], Sec. 9906) : "Any married woman" may dispose of all her separate estate by will without the consent of her husband, and may alter or revoke the same in like manner as a person under no disability may do. Her will must be attested, etc., as other wills.

New Hampshire (Pub. L. 1926, Ch. 297, Sec. 1) : Every person of twenty-one years of age, and "married persons" under that age, may devise or dispose of their real and personal property by their last will in writing.

New Jersey (Comp. St. 1910, p. 3235, Sec. 9) : The wife may make a well and testament as if single, but she cannot dispose of any interest or estate in real property to which her husband is at death entitled by law. (For former law, see p. 5862, Sec. 3, now repealed.)

New Mexico (St. Ann. 1929, Sec. 154[101]) : "Any person" of twenty-one years of age, etc., may dispose by will of all "his" property except . . . . what is given by law as privileged property to "his wife or family." Section 38(104) recognizes the wife's testamentary control over a part of the community property. While Section 154(101) seems to refer to the husband only, the wife's control over her separate property must include the power to dispose thereof by will and testament.

New York (Cahill, Consol. L. 1930, Ch. 13, Secs. 10, 15; Ch. 14, Sec. 51) : The wife has all the rights in respect to property and the "disposition" thereof, as if she were unmarried. "All persons," except infants, etc., may devise their real estate by last will and testament. "Every person" of eighteen years, etc., may bequeath his or her personal estate by will in writing.

North Carolina (Const., Art. X, Sec. 6; C. 1927, Secs. 2506, 2511, 4129–30) : A married woman may devise and bequeath her real and personal property as if single. Devises and bequests made by the wife to the husband are void if wife becomes insane, and if a decree of limited or absolute divorce is obtained by either (applies to Gaston County only).

§ 181]

North Dakota (Comp. L. 1913, Sec. 5641) : A married woman may dispose of all her separate estate by will without the consent of her husband, and may alter or revoke the same as if single. Her will must be executed and proved in like manner as other wills.

Ohio (Complete G. C. 1931 [Page], Secs. 8001, 10503) : A "married person" may "dispose" of real or personal property as if single. A "person" of full age, etc., may dispose of property by will.

Oklahoma (St. 1931, Secs. 1537, 1539) : A married woman may dispose of all her separate estate by will without the consent of her husband, except that she shall not "bequeath" away from the husband so much of her estate that he would receive less in value than would be obtained through succession by law.

Oregon (C. 1930, Secs. 10[501]–10[502], 33[211]) : The wife may "devise" her property in the same manner that the husband may devise his property. The wife may by will "dispose" of her real estate subject to the husband's rights as tenant by the curtesy.

Pennsylvania (St. 1920 [West], Secs. 8307, 14569) : Every person of twenty-one years of age, etc., "whether married or single" may dispose of his or her real or personal property by will. The wife may "dispose" of property in the same manner and to the same extent as a single person.

Rhode Island (G. L. 1923, Secs. 4199, 4302) : Any married woman of sane mind and not less than twenty-one years of age may dispose of real estate, and of sane mind and not less than eighteen years of age may dispose of personal estate, by last will and testament executed as other wills are required to be executed, subject to the husband's curtesy.

South Carolina (C. of L. 1922, C. C., Secs. 5350, 5539) : A married woman has the power to bequeath or devise her separate property as if unmarried. The probate of any last will of a married woman made in the execution of a power, and a devise or bequest thereunder, is as effectual in law as if she were single.

South Dakota (Comp. L. 1929, Sec. 605) : Subject to right of occupancy of a homestead, a married woman may dispose of all her separate estate by will, without the consent of her husband, and may alter or revoke the same as if single. Her will must be proved and executed in like manner as other wills.

Tennessee (C. 1932, Sec. 8098) : Married women twenty-one years of age, or over, may dispose of their realty or personalty, legal or equitable, by will in as complete manner as if single, but such disposition shall not operate to defeat any husband's right of curtesy in the property so disposed.

[§ 181

Texas (Complete St. 1928, Civ. St., Art. 8281) : Every person aged twenty-one years or upward, "or who may be or may have been lawfully married," being of sound mind, may make a last will and testament under the rules, etc., prescribed by law.

Utah (R. S. 1933, 101-1-3) : Same as **North Dakota** (see also Const., Art. XXII, Sec. 2; R. S. 1933, 40-2-1).

Vermont (G. L. 1917, Sec. 3200) : The words "every person" in the Wills Act shall include married women.

Virginia (C. 1930, Secs. 5134, 5227, 5228) : The wife may "dispose" of property acquired since April 4, 1877, as if single, but cannot defeat husband's right to curtesy by her sole act. Section 5227 provides that "every person" not prohibited by Section 5228 may dispose of property by will. Section 5228 enumerates persons of unsound mind or under twenty-one years of age, except that minors of eighteen years of age or more may dispose of personal property by will.

Washington (Remington, Comp. St. 1922, Sec. 6891) : The wife may "devise" by will her separate property to the same extent and in the same manner that her husband may devise property belonging to him.

West Virginia (C. 1931, Ch. 48, Art. 3, Sec. 2) : Any married woman may devise or bequeath real and personal property in the same manner and with like effect as if she were single, but she cannot affect the husband's right to dower in her real estate.

Wisconsin (St. 1931, Secs. 238.01, 238.05, 246.03) : Every person of full age, and any married woman of eighteen years of age or more, of sound mind, may devise or bequeath his or her real or personal property by last will and testament in writing.

Wyoming (R. S. 1931, Secs. 69[104], 88[101]) : Any woman may, while married, make a will the same as though she were single, subject to surviving husband's rights.

REFERENCES

Books

PAGE, WILLIAM HERBERT. *The Law of Wills,* 2d ed., Vol. 1, Secs. 131–35 (1926).

STIMSON, F. J. *American Statute Law,* Secs. 3305, 6460 (1886).

TIFFANY, HERBERT THORNDIKE. *The Law of Real Property and Other Interests in Land,* 2d ed., Vol. 3, Sec. 593 (1920).

Section 182. Conveyances and Transfers between Husband and Wife

CROSS REFERENCES: Wife's contracts, in general, **Sec. 152**; Wife's contracts with husband, **Sec. 156**; Wife's property, **Sec. 167**; Conveyance of community interest between husband and wife, **Sec. 178**; Wife's transfers and conveyances to third persons, **Secs. 183–85**; Power of attorney between husband and wife, **Sec. 186**

At early common law, a transfer of personal property between the spouses was an utter impossibility. The wife had none to transfer, and any attempt of the husband in that direction was bound to fail if for no other reason than that title would immediately revert to him. The unity theory likewise precluded a conveyance of real property from the husband directly to the wife. According to Blackstone, ". . . . a man cannot grant anything to his wife . . . . for the grant would be to suppose her separate existence . . . ." (1 Black. 442). For the same reason, and also because the husband was required to join in her deed, the wife was powerless to convey the fee to her lands directly to the husband. The common law did, however, recognize an indirect conveyance between the spouses through the medium of a third party. Also, the husband might make a settlement on the wife through the intervention of a trustee, and equity might enforce the equities involved in direct transactions inter se. But transactions between the spouses have always been closely scrutinized, both because of the confidential relationship in which the parties stand, and because of the peculiar opportunity afforded them to work fraud upon subsisting creditors.

Statutes containing some express authority for transfers and conveyances between the spouses were found in twenty-seven jurisdictions. Eight (**California, Montana, Nevada, New Mexico, North Dakota, Ohio, Oklahoma, South Dakota**) vest husband and wife with a broad power to enter into any "transaction" with the other respecting property. In six (**Alaska, Iowa, Oregon, Utah, West Virginia, Wisconsin**), a "conveyance," or "transfer," between them is as valid as between other persons. Of the latter, the statutes of all except **West Virginia** also expressly include "liens." Seven (**Connecticut, Hawaii, Massachusetts, New Hampshire, New Jersey, New York, Rhode Island**) authorize direct conveyances of real property between the spouses. **Massachusetts,** however, by implication forbids mortgages between husband and wife. Perhaps mortgages are thought to be too likely vehicles of fraud. **Florida** legalizes direct conveyances of real property from husband to wife; and **Pennsylvania,** direct conveyances of real property

[§ 182

from wife to husband. **Connecticut, Rhode Island,** and **New York** authorize conveyances of personal property between the spouses; and **Massachusetts,** "gifts" of personal property. **Washington** expressly empowers either spouse to convey his or her interest in community real property to the other, but is silent on the matter of conveyances of separate property. Additional statutes of limited application are found in **Michigan, Oregon,** and **New Jersey,** for reference to which the reader is directed to the table following. A few other jurisdictions impliedly recognize transactions between the spouses by codifying special rules respecting fraudulent conveyances between them.

In addition, the statutes of three jurisdictions (**Georgia, Louisiana, Minnesota**) are so peculiar as to necessitate special mention. In **Georgia,** a sale by the wife to the husband of her separate property is valid only if with judicial sanction; yet she may by express statute give property to him, although such gifts will not be presumed (see *Glover* v. *Summerour,* 165 Ga. 513; 141 S. E. 211 [1928]). The civil law discouraged dealings between husband and wife, not however because of any unity conception of the spouses, but apparently as a practical rule of conduct. Thus, in **Louisiana,** donations between married persons, although expressly authorized, are made revocable; and a "contract of sale" between the spouses is limited to certain specified situations. The right of the husband to convey or transfer either community property or his separate property to the wife in satisfaction of her claims against him for paraphernal funds has long been recognized. This is termed a "dation en paiement," and in this respect the wife appears much preferred over other creditors (see *Pons* v. *Yazoo and M.V.R. Company,* 122 La. 156; 47 So. 449 [1908]; *Hart* v. *Stinger,* 46 F. [2d] 321 [1930]). **Minnesota** has the most archaic provision to be found in a progressive state. The statute there provides that "no contract between the husband and wife relative to the real estate of either, or any interest therein," is valid. This statute seems like the common law codified. It precludes conveyances directly between the spouses (*Luse* v. *Reed,* 63 Minn. 5; 65 N. W. 91 [1895]; *Snortium* v. *Snortium,* 155 Minn. 230; 193 N. W. 304 [1923]); but an indirect conveyance through the medium of a third party is effectual even though the same is in pursuance of an invalid agreement between the spouses (*Jorgenson* v. *Minneapolis Threshing Company,* 64 Minn. 489; 67 N. W. 364 [1896]).

Certain statutes elsewhere considered in this volume require additional examination at this time. Three jurisdictions (**Hawaii, Massachusetts, Vermont**) expressly forbid contracts between spouses (**Sec.**

§ 182]

156). Of these, **Massachusetts** expressly authorizes conveyances of real property and "gifts" of personal property between husband and wife; and **Hawaii,** deeds executed by either spouse to the other. The statutes of five jurisdictions (**Colorado, Kansas, Nebraska, New Hampshire, Vermont**) enabling the wife to hold in her own right, etc., property acquired after marriage expressly except "gifts" from the husband from the operation of the statute (**Sec. 167**). The effect of this provision is not clear. In net result, however, the wife in this respect seems to be left about as she was at common law. The equitable rule that gifts from husband to wife will prevail if not in prejudice of the rights of subsisting creditors is not abrogated by a statute which is intended to strengthen the wife's position rather than to restrict her rights as to property (*First National Bank of Wahoo* v. *Havlik,* 51 Neb. 668; 71 N. W. 291 [1897]; *Dayton Spice Mills Company* v. *Sloan, 49* Neb. 662; 68 N. W. 1040 [1896]; *Walston* v. *Allen,* 82 Vt. 549; 74 A. 225 [1909]; *Fletcher* v. *Wakefield,* 75 Vt. 257; 54 A. 1012 [1903]). If this be true, then the wife in these jurisdictions is in substantially as good a position as elsewhere.

Statutes which require the husband's joinder in the wife's conveyance or general act of transfer present some difficulty. One of the reasons given in the older cases holding that the wife cannot convey directly to the husband is that the husband cannot at the same time be both grantee and grantor nor "contract with himself." Of the eight jurisdictions (**Alabama, Florida, Indiana, Kentucky, New Jersey, North Carolina, Pennsylvania, Texas**) which require the husband's co-operation for the validity or effectiveness of the wife's deed (**Sec. 183**), two (**New Jersey, Pennsylvania**) expressly authorize the wife to convey directly to the husband. In **Alabama,** under the statute authorizing the spouses to contract (**Sec. 156**), it is very sensibly held that the wife may convey directly to the husband, the necessity of his joinder being confined to conveyances to third parties (*Crosby* v. *Turner,* 200 Ala. 189; 75 So. 937 [1917]; *Osborne* v. *Cooper,* 113 Ala. 405; 21 So. 320 [1896]). In **North Carolina,** it seems to be assumed that she can convey directly to the husband by reason of her constitutional authority to convey with the husband's consent (**Sec. 183**), and her statutory authority to contract with the husband concerning her separate real property (**Sec. 156**), but the statutory requirement of privy examination and certificate thereof must be closely followed (*Caldwell* v. *Blount,* 193 N. C. 560; 137 S. E. 578 [1928]). On the other hand, in **Indiana, Kentucky,** and **Texas,** it seems that an effective conveyance from the wife directly to the hus-

[§ 182

band is still an utter impossibility in law [*Price* v. *Brittain,* 80 Ind. App. 294; 137 N. E. 620 [1923] ; *McCord* v. *Bright,* 44 Ind. App. 275; 87 N. E. 654 [1909] ; *Hall* v. *Hall,* 236 Ky. 42; 32 S. W. [2d] 536 [1930] ; *Ray* v. *Bushakra,* 237 Ky. 178; 35 S. W. [2d] 19 [1931] ; *Minchew* v. *Hankins* [Tex. Civ. App.] ; 278 S. W. 306 [1925] ; *Riley* v. *Wilson,* 86 Tex. 240; 24 S. W. 394 [1893]).

A few jurisdictions have statutes dealing with the effect of inter-spouse transactions as between the parties. Such transactions are of course subject to those rules of law controlling persons standing in a confidential relationship. Seven jurisdictions (**California, Montana, Nevada, New Mexico, Ohio, Oklahoma, South Dakota**) so provide by statute. **West Virginia** stands alone in requiring all such trans-actions to be evidenced by a memorandum signed by the party to be charged, or the same are not enforceable at law. **West Virginia** also throws the burden of proof upon the spouse in whose favor the transfer or conveyance is made when attacked by the spouse making the same. **Massachusetts** strangely provides that no conveyance of real property has any effect until recorded.

In spite of the facility with which husband and wife may engage in fraudulent practices, only a few jurisdictions have special statutory rules governing transfers and conveyances between them. For the most part, the ordinary statutory or common-law rules govern. Three jurisdictions (**Illinois, Kentucky, Mississippi**) handle the troublesome problem respecting change of possession by providing that transfers of personal property between the spouses are not valid as against third parties unless in writing, acknowledged and recorded. In **Mississippi,** this recording statute was very sensibly held not to apply to gifts of wearing apparel and personal ornament from husband to wife (*Kennington* v. *Hemming-way,* 101 Miss. 259; 57 So. 809 [1912]). Three other jurisdictions (**District of Columbia, Maryland, Maine**) have some statement as to the rights of subsisting creditors in certain instances ; and three juris-dictions (**Georgia, Washington, West Virginia**) allocate the burden of proof when transactions between husband and wife are challenged by creditors.

In most jurisdictions the wife may deal with third parties as if sole. There is no reason why the husband and wife should not be allowed complete freedom to deal with each other respecting property, subject of course to those rules of confidence surrounding the marital relation-ship and to those rules of law protecting the rights of creditors. If the wife is in danger of being "over-reached" by the husband, the courts

§ 182]

will be alert to that fact and quick to aid her. In the absence of special statutory limitation, as a general proposition the husband and wife may now do directly in law what formerly they could do only indirectly, and may now do in law what formerly they could do only in equity. It is interesting to note, however, that as late as 1920 the **Arkansas** court said that a conveyance from husband to wife passes only the beneficial title, the husband retaining the legal title as trustee (*Phillips* v. *Phillips,* 141 Ark. 583; 217 S. W. 794 [1920]). With the unity conception universally discarded, and with the wife sui juris as to the acquisition and disposition of property (**Secs. 167, 183, 185**), and as to contracts (**Sec. 152**), the capacity of the wife to deal with the husband ought to follow in most jurisdictions without express statutory authority. Perhaps that may explain why the statutes found on the subject of this section are fragmentary, incomplete, and far from symmetrical. As a matter of clarity, however, and in order to put the matter beyond the reach of archaic and prejudiced judicial reasoning, all jurisdictions might well copy the broad statute adopted by **California** and the seven other jurisdictions noted above. As a convenient protection to both wife and creditor, a recording statute similar to the one in **Illinois** seems advisable, if for no other reason than to avoid the application of that troublesome rule respecting change of possession in transfers of personal property from husband to wife.

The table and citations follow.

TABLE XCI*

Conveyances and Transfers between Spouses

Jurisdiction and Citation	Conveyances between Spouses	Transfers between Spouses	Protection to Creditors, Miscellaneous
Alaska .... Comp. L. 1913, Sec. 441; Sec. 488, amd. by Sess. L. 1929, Ch. 66, p. 147	A conveyance or lien executed by either spouse to or in favor of the other is valid to the same extent as between other persons	A transfer or lien executed by either spouse to or in favor of the other is valid to the same extent as between other persons	Tenancy by the entireties may be created by conveyance between spouses
California ...... C. C. 1933 (Lake), Sec. 158	Either spouse may enter into any "transaction" with the other respecting property which either might if unmarried, subject to the general rules respecting persons occupying a confidential relationship (as defined by the title on trusts)	See preceding column	

* See page 292 for all numbered footnotes to this table.

TABLE XCI (*Continued*)

Jurisdiction and Citation	Conveyances between Spouses	Transfers between Spouses	Protection to Creditors, Miscellaneous
Connecticut .... G. S. 1930, Sec. 5154	The wife may convey her real property to the husband, and receive conveyances of real property from the husband, as if unmarried[1]	The wife may convey personal property to the husband, and receive conveyances of personal property from the husband, as if unmarried[1]	
District of Columbia ... C. 1929, T. 14, Secs. 25, 27			No acquisition of property passing from husband to wife after coverture is valid if made or granted to her in prejudice of the rights of subsisting creditors[2]
Florida .... R. G. S. 1920, Sec. 3797	A conveyance of real estate by the husband direct to the wife is effectual to convey the legal title to the wife in all cases in which it would be effectual if the parties were single		
Georgia .... C. 1926, C. C., Secs. 3009–11, 3740	A sale by the wife to the husband of her separate property is not valid unless allowed by court order. The wife may give property to her husband	See preceding column	A gift from the wife to husband will not be presumed. The evidence to support the same must be clear, and the intention of the parties free from doubt. When a transaction between the husband and wife is attacked for fraud by creditors of either, the onus is upon the spouses to show that the transaction was fair[3]
Hawaii .... R. L. 1925, Sec. 2994, amd. by Sess. L. 1931, Act 146, p. 142	Any deed executed by either husband or wife to or in favor of the other is valid to the same extent as between other persons		
Illinois .... Cahill, R. S. 1931, Ch. 68, Sec. 9			When the spouses are living together, no transfer or conveyance of goods and chattels between them is valid as against third parties unless the same is in writing, acknowledged and recorded as required for chattel mortgages when possession remains with mortgagor

§ 182]

TABLE XCI (*Continued*)

Jurisdiction and Citation	Conveyances between Spouses	Transfers between Spouses	Protection to Creditors, Miscellaneous
Iowa .... C. 1927, Sec. 10449	A conveyance or lien executed by either spouse to or in favor of the other is valid to the same extent as between other persons	A transfer or lien executed by either spouse to or in favor of the other is valid to the same extent as between other persons	
Kentucky .... Carroll, St. 1922, Sec. 2128			A gift, transfer or assignment of personal property between the spouses is not valid as to third persons unless the same is in writing, acknowledged and recorded as required for chattel mortgages. The recording will not validate a gift, etc., which is fraudulent or voidable as to creditors or purchasers
Louisiana ...... C. C., Arts. 1749, 1751; Art. 1752, amd. by Marr, Ann. R. S., Supp. 1926, p. 243; Art. 2446	A contract of sale between husband and wife can take place in three situations only.[4] A man or woman contracting a second marriage and having issue of the former marriage may give to his or her spouse by donation inter vivos in full property or in usufruct all of his or her estate that he or she could legally give to a stranger	See preceding column	All donations between married persons during marriage, though termed inter vivos, shall always be revocable. Married persons cannot during marriage make to each other by an act, either inter vivos or mortis causa, any mutual or reciprocal donation by one and the same act
Maine .... R. S. 1930, Ch. 74, Sec. 1			Real estate directly conveyed by husband to wife cannot be conveyed by her without husband's joinder, excepting real estate conveyed to her as security or in payment of a bona fide debt actually due to her from him. When payment is made for property conveyed to wife from property of husband or when property is conveyed to her by husband without a valuable consideration, it may be taken as the husband's property to pay his prior debts

[§ 182

TABLE XCI (*Continued*)

Jurisdiction and Citation	Conveyances between Spouses	Transfers between Spouses	Protection to Creditors, Miscellaneous
Maryland ...... Bagby, Ann. C. 1924, Art. 45, Sec. 1, amd. by Sess. L. 1929, Ch. 398, p. 1054; Art. 45, Sec. 2			No acquisition of property passing from one spouse to the other is valid if the same has been made or granted in prejudice of the rights of subsisting creditors. Such creditors must assert their claims within three years after the acquisition or be absolutely barred. For the purpose of this statute, claims not yet due and matured are considered as due and matured[2]
Massachusetts .. G. L. 1932, Ch. 209, Sec. 3	Conveyances of real estate, other than mortgages, between husband and wife, are valid to the same extent as if they were single, except .... (see last column)	"Gifts" of personal property between husband and wife are valid to the same extent as if they were single	No conveyance of real estate between the spouses has any effect in passing title or otherwise, until the deed is duly acknowledged and recorded
Michigan ...... Comp. L. 1929, Sec. 13069	When the spouses own any interest in land as tenants by the entirety, such tenancy may be terminated by a conveyance from either one to the other of his or her interest therein. (Deemed to be declaratory of the common law as existing in the state)		
Minnesota ...... G. S. 1923, Sec. 8621	No contract between husband and wife relative to the real estate of either, or any interest therein, is valid		
Mississippi .... C. 1930, Sec. 1944			A transfer or conveyance of goods and chattels or lands, or any lease of lands, between the spouses is not valid against third persons unless the same is in writing, acknowledged and recorded as required for a mortgage or deed of trust. Possession of the property is not a substitute for recording

TABLE XCI (*Continued*)

Jurisdiction and Citation	Conveyances between Spouses	Transfers between Spouses	Protection to Creditors, Miscellaneous
Montana .... R. C. 1921, Sec. 5786	Either spouse may enter into any "transaction" with the other respecting property which either might if unmarried, subject to the general rules respecting persons occupying a confidential relationship (as defined in provisions relative to trusts)	See preceding column	
Nevada .... Comp. L. 1929 (Hillyer), Sec. 3373	Either spouse may enter into any "transaction" with the other respecting property which either might if unmarried, subject to the general rules respecting persons occupying a confidential relationship	See preceding column	
New Hampshire . Pub. L. 1926, Ch. 288, Sec. 5	Real estate may be conveyed directly by husband to wife, or wife to husband, in all cases where the same thing might be lawfully done through the intervention of a third person		
New Jersey ..... Comp. St. 1910, p. 2850, Sec. 37; Supp. 1925–30, Secs. 44(140), 44(140*a*)	Either husband or wife may convey real estate or interest therein directly to the other. Such conveyance is effective in law and equity to convey grantor's title and interest regardless of whether grantor and grantee are both non-residents. The grantee need not join in or acknowledge the conveyance	A wife holding an insurance policy on the life of the husband or other person may transfer and assign the same to the husband as if she were unmarried	
New Mexico.... St. Ann. 1929, Secs. 68(201), 68(403)	Either spouse may enter into any "transaction" with the other respecting property which either might if unmarried, subject to the general rules of common law respecting persons occupying a confidential relationship. Either spouse may convey his or her interest in the community real property directly to the other without such other joining in the conveyance	See preceding column	

[§ 182

TABLE XCI (*Continued*)

Jurisdiction and Citation	Conveyances between Spouses	Transfers between Spouses	Protection to Creditors, Miscellaneous
New York ...... Cahill, Consol. L. 1930, Ch. 14, Sec. 56	Husband or wife may convey real property directly to the other without the intervention of a third party, and may make partition or division of any real property held by them in common, jointly or as tenants by the entireties	Husband or wife may transfer personal property directly to the other without the intervention of a third person	
North Dakota... Comp. L. 1913, Sec. 4411	Either spouse may enter into any "transaction" with the other respecting property which either might if unmarried	See preceding column	
Ohio .... Complete G. C. 1931 (Page), Sec. 7999	Either spouse may enter into any "transaction" with the other respecting property which either might if unmarried, subject to the general rules respecting persons occupying a confidential relationship	See preceding column	
Oklahoma ...... St. 1931, Sec. 1655	Either spouse may enter into any "transaction" with the other respecting property which either might if unmarried, subject to the general rules respecting persons occupying a confidential relationship (as defined by the title on trusts)	See preceding column	
Oregon .... C. 1930, Sec. 33(203)	A conveyance or lien executed by either spouse to or in favor of the other is valid to the same extent as between other persons	A transfer or lien executed by either spouse to or in favor of the other is valid to the same extent as between other persons	An estate in entirety is created when one spouse conveys to the other an undivided one-half of his or her real property and the conveyance uses words indicating an intention to create such an estate
Pennsylvania ... St. 1920 (West), Sec. 14598	The wife may make a conveyance of real estate to her husband as if she were a feme sole		
Rhode Island.... G. L. 1923, Secs. 4196, 4286	The wife may sell and convey directly to, or may take directly from, her husband any estate or interest in any real property as if single. Either spouse may convey to the other alone or jointly with another person	The wife may sell and convey directly to or may take directly from her husband any estate or interest in personal property as if unmarried. A thing in action may be conveyed by one spouse to the other	The statutory authority for conveyances and transfers between spouses shall not be construed to support any transfer in fraud of creditors

§ 182]

TABLE XCI (*Continued*)

Jurisdiction and Citation	Conveyances between Spouses	Transfers between Spouses	Protection to Creditors, Miscellaneous
South Dakota... Comp. L. 1929, Sec. 171	Either spouse may enter into any "transaction" with the other respecting property which either might if unmarried, subject to the general rules respecting persons occupying a confidential relationship (as defined by the chapter on trusts)	See preceding column	
Utah .... R. S. 1933, 40-2-3	A conveyance or lien executed by either husband or wife to or in favor of the other is valid to the same extent as between other persons	A transfer or lien executed by either husband or wife to or in favor of the other is valid to the same extent as between other persons	
Washington .... Remington, Comp. St. 1922, Secs. 5828, 10572	Either spouse may give, grant, sell, or convey directly to the other his or her community interest in the community real property, vesting the same in the grantee as separate property. The grantee need not join therein		Conveyances between the spouses of community property shall not affect any existing equity in favor of creditors of the grantor at the time. When question arises as to good faith of any transaction between husband and wife, the burden of proof is upon the party asserting the good faith
West Virginia .. C. 1931, Ch. 48, Art. 3, Sec. 7	Any conveyance of property or interest therein executed by either spouse to or in favor of the other, directly or indirectly, is valid to the same extent as between other persons	Any transfer of property or interest therein executed by either spouse to or in favor of the other, directly or indirectly, is valid to the same extent as between other persons	A note or memorandum of transactions between spouses must be made and signed by the party to be charged or the same is not enforceable at law. When a conveyance or transfer between the spouses is directly attacked by the one making the same, or his or her heir, devisee or creditor, the party in whose favor it was made has the burden of showing that the same was in all respects lawful and valid
Wisconsin ...... St. 1931, Sec. 246.03	A conveyance or lien executed by either spouse to or in favor of the other is valid to the same extent as between other persons	A transfer or lien executed by either spouse to or in favor of the other is valid to the same extent as between other persons	

[§ 182

TABLE XCI (*Concluded*)

Jurisdiction and Citation	Conveyances between Spouses	Transfers between Spouses	Protection to Creditors, Miscellaneous
Wyoming ...... R. S. 1931, Sec. 69(101)			The statute securing to the wife her separate property (see **Sec. 167**) contains the following proviso: "provided, that the same shall not have been conveyed to her by her husband in fraud of his creditors"

[1] The **Connecticut** provision applies to marriages contracted after April 20, 1877.

[2] In the case of real or personal property passing from the husband directly or indirectly to the wife, and thence to a third party, a subsisting creditor of the husband has no greater right or lien against the property of the third person than he would have if the property had been passed directly or indirectly to the third party by the husband; and the fact of a previous conveyance, transfer, etc., by the husband to the wife, or the recital thereof in any instrument, shall not be deemed at law or equity to give notice to third persons of the existence of subsisting creditors of the husband (**District of Columbia, Maryland**).

[3] **Georgia** further provides that, as between husband and wife, payment of purchase money by one and causing the conveyance to be made to the other will be presumed to be a gift, but that a resulting trust in favor of the one paying the money may be shown and the presumption rebutted.

[4] A contract of sale between husband and wife can take place only (1) when one spouse makes a transfer of property to the other who is judicially separated from him or her, in payment of his or her rights; (2) when the transfer made by husband to wife, even though not separated, has a legitimate cause, as the replacing of her dotal or other effects alienated; (3) when the wife makes a transfer of property to the husband in payment of a sum promised to him as a dowry (**Louisiana**).

REFERENCES

Books

BUMP, ORLANDO FRANKLIN. *Conveyances Made to Defraud Creditors,* 4th ed. (1896).

GLENN, GARRARD. *The Law of Fraudulent Conveyances* (1931).

MAY, HENRY WILLIAM. *The Statutes of Elizabeth against Fraudulent Conveyances,* 2d Eng. ed. (1887).

MOORE, DEWITT CLINTON. *Fraudulent Conveyances and Creditors' Remedies,* 2 vols. (1908).

STIMSON, F. J. *American Statute Law,* Secs. 6471, 6476 (1886).

TIFFANY, HERBERT THORNDIKE. *The Law of Real Property and Other Interests in Land,* 2d ed., Vol. 3, Sec. 593 (1920).

WAIT, FREDERICK SCOTT. *Fraudulent Conveyances and Creditors' Bills,* 3d ed. (1897).

Notes

"Conveyance by Wife Directly to Husband and Wife," *In re Vandegrift's Estate,* 105 Pa. Super. Ct. 293; 161 A. 898 (1932)—37 Dick. L. Rev. 56–58 (1932).

"Parol Gifts of Land by Husband to Wife," *Mann* v. *Nies,* 213 Ia. 121; 238 N. W. 601 (1932)—20 Geo. L. Jour. 533–34 (1932).

§ 182]

"Presumptions, Transfer of Property from Wife to Husband," *Brunswick Bank and Trust Company* v. *Valentine,* 158 Va. 512; 164 S. E. 569 (1932)—11 N. C. L. Rev. 84–88 (1932).

Annotations

"Attacks by Creditors on Conveyances Made by Husbands to Wives," 90 Amer. St. Rep. 497–555 (1901).

"Effect of Conveyance by Husband to Wife," 69 L. R. A. 353–80 (1903).

"Conveyance of Interest in Community Property by One Spouse to Other," 37 A. L. R. 282–308 (1925).

"Marriage Settlement or Gift from One Spouse to Other as Affected by Misconduct," 29 A. L. R. 198–220 (1924).

"Grantee's Oral Promise to Grantor as Giving Rise to Trust Where Parties Are Husband and Wife," 80 A. L. R. 205–6 (1932).

"Presumption as to Whether Payments between Husband and Wife Were Intended as Gratuities or as Credits on Debt," 71 A. L. R. 1025 (1931).

Section 183. Wife's Conveyances of Her Real Property to Third Persons

CROSS REFERENCES: Conveyance of deserted or abandoned wife, **Sec. 143;** Wife's contracts, **Sec. 152;** Wife's property, in general, **Sec. 167;** Wife's control over community property, **Sec. 178;** Conveyances between spouses, **Sec. 182;** Wife's acknowledgments, **Sec. 184;** Wife's power of attorney, **Sec. 186;** Barring dower by deed, **Sec. 200;** Barring curtesy by deed, **Sec. 220;** Conveyance of homestead, **Sec. 225;** Contracts and conveyances of infants, **Secs. 273, 274;** Wife's conveyance when husband insane, **Sec. 311**

While the common law allowed the wife to retain the fee to her lands, the loss of her legal personality rendered her unable to make a binding and effective conveyance of the same. Custom, however, developed in England a method by which the husband and wife could pass title to the wife's lands by joining in a distorted use of a fictitious action to levy a fine or suffer a common recovery. This grotesque method of conveyancing was never much utilized in this country. At an early date, however, a married woman in the Colonies was permitted by local custom or local statute to bar herself and her heirs by deed in which the husband joined and which she acknowledged in privy examination. Equity recognized her sole conveyance in connection with her equitable separate property, although in some jurisdictions this was true only when the instrument creating her estate granted her such power.

[§ 183

The necessity of the husband's joinder in the wife's conveyance, and of the wife's separate examination, was almost universally retained years after the creation of the wife's separate statutory estate. Stimson lists only eighteen jurisdictions which in 1886 authorized the wife to convey her own interest in her real property by her sole transfer. Though the wife was empowered to acquire and hold real property, her capacity to dispose of the same was hemmed and embarrassed by these inane limitations. That the husband must join in the wife's conveyance is in itself inconsistent with the traditional implications of the term "separate property." The philosophy of our legislatures in this respect has been rather intricate. To protect the wife from unconscionable third parties, the law forced upon her the husband's counsel and consent. For fear that the husband's counsel might in fact amount to coercion, her separate examination upon that point was required. The latter formality has been discarded by most jurisdictions for all purposes (**Sec. 184**). It is not surprising to find that the necessity of the husband's joinder in the wife's conveyance has likewise been generally abandoned.

The constitutions of three jurisdictions (**Arkansas, North Carolina, Utah**), and the statutes of all of the jurisdictions with one exception (**Georgia**), contain specific statements respecting the wife's power to dispose of her real property. It seems that in only eight jurisdictions (**Alabama, Florida, Indiana, Kentucky, New Jersey, North Carolina, Pennsylvania, Texas**) is there any general requirement which compels the wife to seek the husband's counsel and consent when she wishes to convey her real property. The statutory situation in these jurisdictions is given in some detail later in this section. In the balance of the fifty-one jurisdictions (except possibly **Oregon** and **Virginia** [see Table XCII, footnotes 12 and 14, p. 316], and except that both spouses must commonly unite in conveying the wife's homestead property [**Sec. 225**]), it seems clear that the wife's sole conveyance is effective to pass her interest in her lands. Twelve jurisdictions have express statutory statements to the effect that the husband's joinder or consent is not necessary; and twenty-nine jurisdictions provide that she may convey or dispose of her property as though she were unmarried, or to the same extent as the husband may dispose of his property. In a handful of jurisdictions, she is expressly authorized to convey directly to the husband (**Sec. 182**). Of course, in many jurisdictions the husband has a contingent interest in the wife's lands, by way of curtesy or a statutory substitute therefor, which the wife cannot defeat by her sole act (**Sec. 216**). To bar such interest, it may be necessary for the husband

§ 183]

either to join in her conveyance or otherwise to release the same (**Sec. 220**).

Of the eight jurisdictions already mentioned, six (**Alabama, Florida, Indiana, North Carolina, Pennsylvania, Texas**) require the husband's joinder in the wife's conveyance or mortgage of her real property. In **Kentucky,** the wife may convey by separate instrument, but the husband must have first conveyed. A recent **New Jersey** statute allows the wife to convey her interest in her real property by a separate instrument providing the husband conveys his interest therein by a separate deed. This concession to the wife is apparently intended to eliminate the necessity of the husband's joinder in the same instrument, but not to eliminate the necessity of his joinder in the same general act of transfer. This statute is held to have no application to the execution of mortgages. The husband must join therein as before (*Dreier* v. *Pomeroy,* 104 N. J. Eq. 504; 146 A. 178 [1929]). In three other jurisdictions the husband's joinder is expressly required in certain special instances, as follows: **Connecticut** (in the case of marriages before April 20, 1877), **Maine** (in the case of real estate conveyed to the wife by the husband unless the same was as security for or in payment of a bona fide debt due from him), **Vermont** (in the case of property seized jointly with the husband, and property acquired by the wife before February 13, 1919, not seized to her "sole and separate use"). In **Texas,** if the husband refuses to co-operate, the wife may obtain a judicial order authorizing her sole conveyance or encumbrance upon a satisfactory showing that the same is "advantageous" to her. In the other jurisdictions she apparently must await his pleasure (see, however, Table XCII, footnote 4, pp. 314–15). Whether the wife in the jurisdictions above may lease her lands by her sole act depends in general upon the construction given to the phraseology of the statutes considered in this section, and upon the wife's general contractual capacity, etc. **North Carolina**, however, expressly requires the husband's joinder except in the case of certain leases (see table) ; while in **Pennsylvania** she may lease her lands (St. 1920 [West], Sec. 14569) and in **Kentucky** she may rent her lands (Carroll, St. 1922, Sec. 2128) as if unmarried. **New Jersey** has held that an assignment of a lease for ninety-nine years is not a conveyance within the meaning of the statute (*De Kyne* v. *Lewis,* 5 N. J. Misc. 948; 139 A. 434 [1927]). The statutes of many jurisdictions expressly recognize the wife's sole conveyance when the husband has deserted or abandoned her (**Sec. 143**) or when the husband is insane (**Sec. 311**). In most jurisdictions these statutes are of course mere surplusage.

[§ 183

In those jurisdictions in which the wife's sole conveyance is without effect, one may wonder what effect will be given to her sole contract to convey. The statutes of **Indiana** and **Kentucky** expressly negative any suggestion that she may bind herself by an executory contract to convey or mortgage her lands in which the husband does not unite (**Sec. 152**). The other statutes are silent on the point, and resort must be had to the cases. Granting that her sole contract to convey cannot ordinarily be specifically enforced without doing violence to that inane policy of the statutes which allows the validity of the wife's conveyance to depend upon the husband's pleasure, will a bona fide failure to secure the proper manifestation of the husband's consent excuse her from damages in law for a breach of her contract to convey? In **Alabama,** her sole contract to convey does not bind her (*Cooper* v. *Pearce,* 222 Ala. 540; 133 So. 583 [1931]). In **Texas,** while the wife may convey with the husband's joinder, she cannot contract to convey even with his joinder because of a lack of general capacity to bind herself by executory engagement (*Blakely* v. *Kanaman,* 107 Tex. 206; 175 S. W. 674 [1915]; *Hammett* v. *Farrar* [Tex. Civ. App.]; 8 S. W. [2d] 236 [1928]). In **Florida,** her sole contract to convey probably does not bind her for the same reason (**Sec. 152**). In **Pennsylvania,** she is apparently liable to the vendee for any loss he has sustained by reason of his reliance upon the contract (*McCoy* v. *Niblick,* 228 Pa. 342; 77 A. 551 [1910]); and in **New Jersey** and **North Carolina,** by reason of her broad statutory capacity to bind herself by contract, she may be held in damages for a breach of her agreement to convey (*Wolff* v. *Meyer,* 75 N. J. L. 181; 66 A. 959 [1907]; *Warren* v. *Dail,* 170 N. C. 406; 87 S. E. 126 [1915]; *Everett* v. *Ballard,* 174 N. C. 16; 93 S. E. 385 [1917]). In short, while she cannot convey by her sole act, she can by her sole act lay herself open to damages and her property open to execution for a failure to convey. The result seems incongruous. It is an illustration of the frequent patchwork evolution of the law. A dissenting **North Carolina** justice likens it to "whipping the devil around the stump." Our criticism in this instance, however, must be directed at the statute lawmaker and not at the judicial lawmaker.

While the power to convey includes the lesser power to encumber, many of the statutes expressly authorize the wife to mortgage her property by her sole act. Nine of the statutes considered in this section contain specific reference to the matter of the wife's infancy. Thus, a wife of twenty-one years (**Arizona, District of Columbia, New Jersey**), or of eighteen years (**Louisiana**), or of "full age" (**New Hampshire,**

§ 183]

Wisconsin), or of any age (**Florida, Maine, Minnesota**) may make an effective conveyance. A statute authorizing married women to convey does not, of course, of itself authorize an infant wife to convey. A review of the statutes dealing in general with the conveyances of infants will be found in **Section 274.** Six jurisdictions (**Arkansas, Colorado, Indiana, Missouri, North Carolina, Pennsylvania**) have taken special precaution to negative the husband's control of the wife's property by providing that he cannot alienate the same by his sole act. Even at common law, however, he was powerless to convey the fee to the wife's lands. While as a general proposition the wife may dispose of her property to whom and in the manner she pleases, she may be unable to convey to certain persons under the peculiar statutes of some jurisdictions. Thus, in a few states, she cannot convey directly to the husband (**Sec. 182**). In **Georgia,** a sale to her trustee is valid only with a court order. **Georgia** also provides that a sale to a creditor of the husband in extinguishment of his debt is void; and in **New Hampshire,** a conveyance as surety or guarantor of the husband is not binding. The latter may be true in a few other jurisdictions which still restrict the wife's undertakings for her husband or for third parties (**Sec. 152**).

Even at common law a married woman might be the donee of a power, and exercise the same without the husband's concurrence. Nine jurisdictions, which have set up a statutory system of powers, have some legislation specifically dealing with the wife as a donee (Table XCII, footnote 6, p. 315).

The wife was empowered to convey by deed in which the husband joined long before she could contract to convey and long before her general disability to bind herself by promise was removed. The covenants in her deed continued to have no binding effect on her personally, and by weight of authority were not effectual to pass title to after-acquired property by way of estoppel. Statutes dealing specifically with the wife's covenants were found in only nine jurisdictions (**Colorado, Delaware, Florida, Indiana, Missouri, Nebraska, New Jersey, Nevada, West Virginia**). In only four of these (**Indiana, Missouri, New Jersey, West Virginia**) is there any express or implied statement that the wife is liable thereon as if single. With the exception of **Florida,** the statutes of the others are inconsistent with the general contractual capacity enjoyed by the wife in those jurisdictions (**Sec. 152**). If the wife is given a general power to bind herself by contract, there is no reason why her covenant should not bind her personally as well as by way of estoppel. A number of other jurisdictions expressly

[§ 183

limit the effect upon the wife of covenants in a deed in which the wife joins only for the purpose of releasing her dower (**Sec. 200**).

With the exception of a small minority of jurisdictions, it is apparent that there has been a rather consistent attempt on the part of American legislatures to allow the wife complete independence not only in respect to the ownership and acquisition of property, but in respect to the disposition thereof as well. To require that the husband must join in the wife's deed is a superficial gesture of the past and out of harmony with her general advanced position. This is all the more true in view of the widespread abolition of the husband's common-law curtesy (**Sec. 216**). In cutting away the limitations which embarrassed the wife in the disposition of her real property, the lawmaker has also realized that the modern wife is very often her own breadwinner, and perhaps too often the breadwinner for her husband as well.

For an outline of the statutes which were found concerning the subject of this section, together with citations for the same, the reader is directed to the table and notes following. It must be observed that in the community-property states the statutes here considered refer to the wife's separate property only (and in **Louisiana,** to her paraphernal property only). The wife's control over the community real property is discussed in **Section 178.**

TABLE XCII*

WIFE'S CONVEYANCES OF HER REAL PROPERTY TO THIRD PERSONS

Jurisdiction and Citation	In General	Necessity of Husband Joining	Separate Examination, Acknowledgment, etc.[1] (See **Sec. 184**)	Covenants, Miscellaneous[2]
Alabama .... C. 1923, Sec. 8269		The wife cannot alienate or mortgage her lands without assent and concurrence of husband manifested by his joining in the alienation	Such alienation shall be in the ordinary mode prescribed by law for execution of conveyances of land	

* See pages 314–16 for all numbered footnotes to this table.

§ 183]

TABLE XCII (*Continued*)

Jurisdiction and Citation	In General	Necessity of Husband Joining	Separate Examination, Acknowledgment, etc.[1] (See Sec. 184)	Covenants, Miscellaneous[2]
Alaska Comp. L. 1913, Sec. 482, amd. by Sess. L. 1923, Ch. 40, p. 51; Sec. 489; Sec. 512, amd. by Sess. L. 1933, Ch. 10, p. 44; Sec. 513	The wife may sell and convey her property and pecuniary rights to the same extent and in the same manner that her husband can property belonging to him	The wife may sell or convey any estate of inheritance in lands without husband's joining in conveyances, and bar his claim to curtesy therein	Acknowledgment of wife to conveyance of real property shall be taken in the same manner as if she were unmarried	When non-resident wife joins husband in conveyance of real estate in the District, the conveyance has the same effect as if she were sole, and the acknowledgment or proof of execution may be the same as if she were sole[3]
Arizona R. C. 1928, Secs. 955, 962, 2174	The wife has exclusive control of her separate property and may sell, mortgage or convey the same as if single	Married persons of 21 years of age may convey their separate property without being joined by the spouse	Acknowledgment of wife may be taken in same form as if she were single. Separate examination or separate certificate of acknowledgment is not required	
Arkansas Const., Art. IX, Sec. 7; Crawf. and Moses, Dig. 1921, Secs. 1505, 1524, 5574	The wife may convey her real estate by deed of conveyance executed by herself the same as if she were a feme sole		The wife's conveyances may be executed the same as if she were single	
California C. C. 1933 (Lake), Secs. 162, 1093, 1187	The wife's conveyance has the same effect as if she were single	The wife may convey her separate property without the consent of her husband	The wife's conveyance may be made, executed, and acknowledged in the same manner as if she were single	
Colorado Comp. L. 1921, G. S., Secs. 4911, 5583, 5585	Any woman while married may bargain, sell, and convey her real property as if she were sole			Express or implied covenant in wife's deed does not bind her or her heirs except to pass to purchaser all her present estate thereby conveyed. The separate deed of the husband conveys no interest in wife's lands

[§ 183

TABLE XCII (*Continued*)

Jurisdiction and Citation	In General	Necessity of Husband Joining	Separate Examination, Acknowledgment, etc.[1] (See Sec. 184)	Covenants, Miscellaneous[2]
Connecticut .... G. S. 1930, Secs. 5009, 5154	In case of marriages after April 20, 1877, the wife may convey her real estate as if single	Conveyance of wife married prior to April 20, 1877, executed jointly with husband, duly acknowledged and recorded, shall be valid and effectual to transfer her real estate; conveyance thereof by husband alone does not convey wife's interest		In conveying property acquired prior to her marriage, the wife shall state in instrument the name under which she acquired such property
Delaware .... R. C. 1915, Sec. 3047; Sec. 3048, amd. by Sess. L. 1919, Ch. 197, p. 524; Sec. 3052, amd. by Sess. L. 1919, Ch. 197, p. 526; Secs. 3200, 3206–7	The wife may sell, convey, encumber or otherwise dispose of her separate real property as if single (subject to husband's curtesy, if any, and to requirement of separate examination). She may secure the purchase price of real estate by mortgage as if single	The husband need not be a party or consent to wife's mortgage to secure purchase price of real estate	The wife's deed concerning lands is valid and effectual if, upon private examination apart from husband, she acknowledges that she executed the same willingly and without compulsion from husband. Examination may be taken before chancellor, or any judge, a notary, or two justices of peace for same county, but need not be taken in county where land lies. Certificate of examination shall be endorsed upon or annexed to the deed	The wife's deed concerning lands shall not bind her to any warranty except a special warranty against herself, her heirs, and persons claiming by or under her. No covenant on her part of a more extensive or different effect shall be valid against her
District of Columbia ... C. 1929, T. 14, Sec. 21	Married women shall hold all their property of every description for their separate use, and shall have power to dispose of the same by deed, mortgage, lease, gift, or otherwise, as fully as if single			No disposition of real property by deed, mortgage or other conveyance is valid if made by a married woman under 21 years of age

§ 183]

TABLE XCII (*Continued*)

Jurisdiction and Citation	In General	Necessity of Husband Joining	Separate Examination, Acknowledgment, etc.[1] (See Sec. 184)	Covenants, Miscellaneous[2]
Florida .... R. G. S. 1920, Secs. 3801, 3803, 3805; Sec. 3813, amd. by Sess. L. 1927, Ch. 12083, p. 811; Sec. 3949, amd. by Sess. L. 1927, Ch. 12255, p. 1137; Sec. 3953	The wife may sell, convey, or mortgage her real property, but the husband must join therein.[4] Her deed, duly acknowledged, is valid notwithstanding her minority at time of execution and acknowledgment	To render her conveyance or mortgage effectual to pass her estate, she must acknowledge before an authorized officer, separately and apart from the husband, that she executed the same freely, voluntarily, and without compulsion from or fear of the husband.[4] The officer's certificate shall set forth the foregoing requirements	The wife who joins with husband in executing a conveyance or mortgage may enter into any covenants as to title or against encumbrances or of warranty, but such covenants have no other effect than to estop her and all persons claiming as her heirs or by or through her, in same manner as if she were single; except that her covenants and warranties made with respect to her separate statutory property bind her to the amount of purchase price received by her for such property
Georgia .... C. 1926, C. C., Secs. 3007, 3009	The wife is a feme sole as to her separate estate, unless controlled by settlement	See footnote 5	See footnote 5	The wife's contract of sale of her separate estate with her husband or trustee is not valid unless the same is allowed by order of superior court of county of her domicile. The wife's sale of her separate estate to a creditor of the husband in extinguishment of his debts is absolutely void
Hawaii .... R. L. 1925, Sec. 2993, amd. by Sess. L. 1925, Act 274, p. 392; Sec. 3150	The wife may dispose of real property in the same manner as if she were sole		The acknowledgment of the wife may be taken in the same form as if she were sole, and without any examination separate and apart from her husband	

[§ 183

TABLE XCII (*Continued*)

Jurisdiction and Citation	In General	Necessity of Husband Joining	Separate Examination, Acknowledgment, etc.[1] (See **Sec. 184**)	Covenants, Miscellaneous[2]
Idaho .... Comp. St. 1919, Secs. 4657, 5393	The wife has the absolute power of disposition of her separate property. She may bargain, sell and convey her real property in the same manner, to the same extent, and with like effect as the husband may in relation to his real property		The acknowledgment of the wife may be taken and certified to in the same manner and form as that of a single person	
Illinois .... Cahill, R. S. 1931, Ch. 30, Secs. 19, 20; Ch. 68, Sec. 9	The wife may sell and convey her real property to the same extent and in the same manner that the husband can property belonging to him		The acknowledgment or proof of the wife's deed, mortgage, conveyance, etc., may be made and certified the same as if she were a feme sole, and shall have the same effect	Any wife above the age of 18 years, joining with husband in execution of any deed, mortgage, or conveyance of her lands, is bound and concluded by the same, in respect to her right, title, claim or interest therein as if she were sole
Indiana .... Burns, Ann. St. 1926, Secs. 8739, 8741, 8750, 13382, 13401	The joint deed of the husband and wife shall be sufficient to convey and pass the lands of the wife	The wife cannot convey or mortgage her real estate unless the husband join therein; but she is bound by an estoppel in pais, like any other person	The wife's acknowledgment to her deeds may be taken in the same form as required for single persons	The separate deed of the husband conveys no interest in the wife's lands. The wife is bound by her covenants of title in conveyances of her separate estate as if sole

TABLE XCII (*Continued*)

Jurisdiction and Citation	In General	Necessity of Husband Joining	Separate Examination, Acknowledgment, etc.[1] (See Sec. 184)	Covenants, Miscellaneous[2]
Iowa C. 1927, Secs. 10050–51, 10099, 10446	The wife may convey or encumber her real estate or interest therein to the same extent and in the same manner as other persons		The acknowledgment of the wife may be taken in the same form as if she were sole, and without any examination separate and apart from her husband	Every conveyance made by husband and wife is sufficient to pass any and all right of either in the property conveyed, unless the contrary appears on the face of the conveyance
Kansas R. S. 1923, Secs. 23(202), 67(416)	The wife may bargain, sell and convey her real property in the same manner, to the same extent and with like effect as the husband may in relation to his real property			See footnote 6
Kentucky Carroll, St. 1922, Secs. 505–6, 2128–29	The wife may convey any real estate which she owns or in which she has an interest, legal or equitable, in possession, reversion or remainder	The wife's conveyance may be by the joint deed of husband and wife, or by separate instrument, but in the latter case the husband must first convey or have theretofore conveyed	The wife's conveyance must be acknowledged and recorded in the manner required by the chapter on conveyances (no special form required)	
Louisiana Sess. L. 1926, Act 132, p. 208; Sess. L. 1928, Act 283, p. 583; Marr, Ann. R. S., Supp. 1926, Act 226, p. 2, Sec. 2	Married women of 18 years of age may make contracts of all kinds, and may sell, alienate, mortgage or otherwise dispose of or encumber their separate and paraphernal property	The wife does not need the authorization of the husband to alienate, mortgage, etc., her separate and paraphernal property[7]	The wife's acknowledgment may be taken in the same form as if she were sole and without any examination separate and apart from her husband	

[§ 183

TABLE XCII (*Continued*)

Jurisdiction and Citation	In General	Necessity of Husband Joining	Separate Examination, Acknowledgment, etc.[1] (See Sec. 184)	Covenants, Miscellaneous[2]
Maine .... R. S. 1930, Ch. 74, Sec. 1; Ch. 87, Sec. 20	A married woman of any age may sell and convey her real estate without the joinder or assent of her husband	The wife's conveyance without the joinder or assent of her husband does not bar his right and interest by descent in the estate conveyed. Real estate directly conveyed by husband to wife cannot be conveyed by her without joinder of husband, unless it was conveyed to her as security or in payment of a bona fide debt actually due to her from him		
Maryland .... Bagby, Ann. C. 1924, Art. 45, Sec. 4	Married women hold all their property of every description for their separate use, and have all the power to dispose of the same by deed, mortgage, lease or other instrument that husbands have to dispose of their property, and no more			
Massachusetts .. G. L. 1932, Ch. 183, Sec. 31; Ch. 209, Sec. 1	The wife may dispose of her real property in the same manner as if sole	The wife's conveyance does not (except as otherwise provided) extinguish or impair the husband's right to curtesy unless he joins therein, or otherwise releases the same	The wife's acknowledgment may be taken in the same form as if she were sole, and without any examination separate and apart from her husband	

§ 183]

TABLE XCII (*Continued*)

Jurisdiction and Citation	In General	Necessity of Husband Joining	Separate Examination, Acknowledgment, etc.[1] (See Sec. 184)	Covenants, Miscellaneous[2]
Michigan .... Comp. L. 1929, Secs. 13002, 13009, 13012–13, 13051, 13057, 13288, 13331, 13337	The wife may sell, transfer, mortgage and convey her real property as if single		The wife's acknowledgment may be taken in the same form as if she were sole, and without any examination separate and apart from her husband (see footnote 1)	When a non-resident wife joins with husband in conveyance of real estate situated in this state, the conveyance has the same effect as if she were sole[3] and the acknowledgment or proof of execution thereof may be the same as if she were sole[6]
Minnesota ...... G. S. 1923, Secs. 6972, 8114, 8121, 8124–25, 8144, 8162, 8196, 8618	Wife may convey by separate deed any real estate owned by her (except homestead) subject to rights of husband therein	The husband and wife by their joint deed may convey the real estate of either	No separate examination of wife is required. If both spouses join in the execution and acknowledgment of any instrument, the certificate shall describe them as husband and wife. If they make acknowledgment separately before different officers or at different times, each shall be described as the spouse of the other	The minority of the wife shall not invalidate any conveyance executed by her[6]
Mississippi ..... C. 1930, Secs. 1780, 1940, 2137	Marriage shall impose no disability or incapacity on a woman as to the disposition of property. The wife has the same capacity to dispose of real property (except her homestead) as if she were single		When wife executes any instrument affecting her separate real property, her acknowledgment may be taken and certified as if she were sole. A separate examination is not required. If she unites with husband in the execution of an instrument, she should be described in acknowledgment as his wife, but failure to so describe her does not affect the acknowledgment	

[§ 183

TABLE XCII (*Continued*)

Jurisdiction and Citation	In General	Necessity of Husband Joining	Separate Examination, Acknowledgment, etc.[1] (See Sec. 184)	Covenants, Miscellaneous[2]
Missouri .... R. S. 1929, Secs. 2998, 3002, 3015, 3029	The wife is deemed a feme sole so as to enable her to transact business on her own account, to contract and be contracted with, etc. Her separate property is "under her sole control"[8]	A husband and wife may convey the real estate of the wife[8]	No separate examination of the wife is required. Her acknowledgment may be taken and certified as if she were sole. If the wife unites with the husband in execution of instrument, she shall be described in the acknowledgment as his wife	No conveyance by the husband during coverture of the wife's real estate is valid unless the same be by deed executed by the wife jointly with husband and acknowledged by her as provided by law.[8] Any covenant, express or implied in deed, conveying wife's property binds the wife and her heirs as if she were single
Montana .... R. C. 1921, Sec. 5792, amd. by Sess. L. 1933, Ch. 63, p. 119; Secs. 6800–6801, 6861, 6911–12, 6916, 6950	The wife's conveyance has the same effect as if she were single	The wife may convey her separate property (except her homestead) without the consent, agreement, or signature of her husband	The wife's acknowledgment must be taken the same as that of any other person	See footnote 6
Nebraska .... Comp. St. 1929, Secs. 42(202), 42(207)	The wife may bargain, sell and convey her real property in the same manner, to the same extent, and with like effect as the husband may in relation to his real property			The wife is not bound by any covenant in a joint deed of herself and husband[9]
Nevada .... Comp. L. 1929 (Hillyer), Secs. 1476, 1494–95, 3363, 3386, 3388	The wife's conveyance has the same effect as if she were single	The wife may, without the consent of her husband, convey, charge, encumber, or otherwise in any manner dispose of her separate property	The wife's conveyance may be acknowledged in the same manner as if she were single. Any officer authorized to take acknowledgments of deeds may take and certify her acknowledgment	No covenant, express or implied in "any such conveyance,"[10] shall bind the wife or her heirs except so far as necessary to convey from her and her heirs all her right and interest expressed to be conveyed thereby

§ 183]

TABLE XCII (*Continued*)

Jurisdiction and Citation	In General	Necessity of Husband Joining	Separate Examination, Acknowledgment, etc.[1] (See Sec. 184)	Covenants, Miscellaneous[2]
New Hampshire. Pub. L. 1926, Ch. 288, Secs. 1, 2, 4	A married woman of full age may convey her real estate. She has the same rights and liabilities in relation to her property as a single woman	The wife shall hold her property to her own use free from the interference or control of the husband		The wife's conveyance as surety or guarantor for the husband is not binding on her, except a mortgage releasing her right of dower and homestead
New Jersey .... Comp. St. 1910, p. 3229, Sec. 7; p. 3232, Sec. 8(*k*); Cum. Supp. 1911–24, Secs. 44(21*a*), 44(39); Supp. 1925–30, Secs. 124(3*a*), 124(8*w*-1); Sess. L. 1931, Ch. 281, p. 710	The wife, if above 21 years of age, may execute and deliver any conveyance of real estate or interest therein separate and apart from husband, provided her husband has conveyed or does convey his interest in such real estate by separate deed, and provided her conveyance is duly acknowledged and her acknowledgment certified according to law[11]	No estate or interest of wife in lands in state shall pass by her deed or conveyance without a previous acknowledgment made by her before a proper officer that she signed, etc., the same as her voluntary act, such officer being satisfied that she is the person named in the deed and having first made known to her the contents thereof. Officer's certificate must be annexed to deed (Cum. Supp. 1911–24, Sec. 44[39]; Sess. L. 1918, Ch. 37, p. 119). Wife's conveyance, etc., may be executed without a private examination apart from husband, and it is sufficient if she acknowledges the same as if she were single (Cum. Supp. 1911–24, Sec. 44[21*a*]; Sess. L. 1916, Ch. 157, p. 321)	The wife, who joins with the husband in the execution of deed, may enter into any covenant as to title of lands conveyed, or against encumbrances, or warranting the same, provided, that such covenants, except so far as they relate to land, or some interest therein, owned by her in her own right, have no greater effect than to estop her and those claiming as her heirs or by or through her[11]

[§ 183

TABLE XCII (*Continued*)

Jurisdiction and Citation	In General	Necessity of Husband Joining	Separate Examination, Acknowledgment, etc.[1] (See Sec. 184)	Covenants, Miscellaneous[2]
New Mexico .... St. Ann. 1929, Secs. 1(113), 68(202), 68(302), 68(403)	The wife may enter into any transaction respecting property which she might if single	The wife may convey or mortgage her separate property without the husband joining	No separate examination of wife is required. Her acknowledgment may be taken and certified as if sole. If she joins with husband in execution of instrument, she shall be described in the acknowledgment as his wife	
New York ...... Cahill, Consol. L. 1930, Ch. 14, Secs. 50, 51, 56; Ch. 51, Secs. 142–43, 302	The wife has all rights in respect to real property and the disposition thereof, as if she were unmarried	The wife's separate property shall not be subject to the husband's control	The acknowledgment or proof of a conveyance of real property within the state may be made by a married woman the same as if unmarried	The husband and wife may make a partition or division of any real property held by them as tenants in common, joint tenants, or tenants by the entireties[6]
North Carolina .. Const., Art. X, Sec. 6; C. 1927, Secs. 997–1001, 2506–7, 2509–10, 3295, 3299, 3301, 3324–25, 3346	The wife's separate estate may, with the written consent of the husband, be conveyed by her as if she were unmarried (Constitution). No conveyance of her real estate is valid unless made with the written assent of the husband	Every conveyance or other instrument affecting the wife's estate in lands (except lease, sublease, etc., to run not more than three years, and to begin in possession less than six months after execution) must be executed by the wife and her husband[4]	Acknowledgment must be made by both husband and wife. A private examination of wife, separate and apart from husband, must be made touching her voluntary assent to the instrument.[4] No instrument is the act or deed of the wife unless her private examination is taken. Officers authorized to take proofs and acknowledgments of the execution of any instrument may take such examination. Husband and wife may acknowledge, etc., before different officers, and the order thereof is immaterial	The husband cannot sell or lease the wife's lands except with her consent manifested by deed and private examination. No deed executed by husband and wife with private examination by wife properly certified is invalid because its acknowledgment or execution was procured by fraud or duress, etc., unless grantee participates therein or had notice thereof. Bona fide purchaser of grantee not affected even though grantee participated in fraud, etc., or had notice

TABLE XCII (*Continued*)

Jurisdiction and Citation	In General	Necessity of Husband Joining	Separate Examination, Acknowledgment, etc.[1] (See Sec. 184)	Covenants, Miscellaneous[2]
North Dakota ... Comp. L. 1913, Secs. 4411, 5400–5401, 5417, 5420, 5427, 5431–32, 5568	The wife may enter into any engagement or transaction respecting property which she might if unmarried. The wife's conveyance has the same effect as if she were unmarried		The wife's conveyance may be acknowledged in the same manner as if she were unmarried	See footnote 6
Ohio .... Complete G. C. 1931 (Page), Secs. 7999, 8001, 8511	The wife may enter into any transaction respecting property which she might if unmarried. A married person may dispose of real property as if unmarried		A deed, mortgage or lease of any estate or interest of a married person in real property must be signed, attested, acknowledged and certified in the manner prescribed (for deeds, etc., of other persons)	
Oklahoma ...... St. 1931, Secs. 1655, 1658, 11856–57, 11873, 11876, 11883, 11887–88	The wife may enter into any engagement or transaction respecting property which she might if unmarried	The wife may convey or mortgage her real estate (except the homestead) without the husband's joinder or consent		See footnote 6
Oregon .... C. 1930, Secs. 33(211), 33(215), 63(103), 63(116), 63(119)	The wife may sell and convey her property and pecuniary rights to the same extent and in the same manner that her husband may property belonging to him. All laws which recognize or impose civil disabilities upon the wife not imposed or recognized as existing as to the husband are repealed	A husband and wife may by their joint deed convey the real estate of the wife in like manner as she might do by her separate deed if she were unmarried[12]	The wife's acknowledgment to conveyances of real property may be taken in the same manner as if she were unmarried	When a non-resident wife joins with husband in conveyance of real estate situated in this state, the conveyance has the same effect as if she were sole, and the acknowledgment or proof of execution thereof may be the same as if she were sole[3]

[§ 183

TABLE XCII (*Continued*)

Jurisdiction and Citation	In General	Necessity of Husband Joining	Separate Examination, Acknowledgment, etc.[1] (See Sec. 184)	Covenants, Miscellaneous[2]
Pennsylvania ... St. 1920 (West), Secs. 8687–90, 14569–70, 14586, 14614, 21315		The wife may not mortgage or convey her real property unless her husband join in such mortgage or conveyance[4]	The wife's acknowledgment may be taken before any person authorized by law to take acknowledgments of deeds in the same manner and form as though she were a feme sole. Such acknowledgment has the same force and effect as if taken separate and apart from the husband	The wife's separate property shall not be conveyed, mortgaged, etc., without the wife's written consent duly acknowledged. The wife as a joint or sole trustee may convey lands as if sole. Non-resident wife may make acknowledgment before judge of any court of record of other state, or minister, ambassador, etc., of United States in a foreign country
Rhode Island ... G. L. 1923, Secs. 4196–97, 4200, 4271	The wife may sell and convey to any person any interest or estate in real property in the same manner and with the same effect as if she were single, subject to husband's curtesy		The wife's acknowledgment of her deeds may be taken in the same manner as if she were single	
South Carolina.. C. of L. 1922, C. C., Sec. 5539	The wife may convey her separate property in the same manner and to the same extent as if she were single. Her deeds, mortgages, etc., have the same legal effect as if she were single		The wife's deeds, mortgages, etc., may be executed by her in the same manner as if she were single	

§ 183]

TABLE XCII (*Continued*)

Jurisdiction and Citation	In General	Necessity of Husband Joining	Separate Examination, Acknowledgment, etc.[1] (See Sec. 184)	Covenants, Miscellaneous[2]
South Dakota ... Comp. L. 1929, Secs. 174, 178, 407, 423, 451, 581	The wife's conveyance has the same effect as if she were unmarried	The wife may convey her real estate (except the homestead) without joining the husband and without his consent	The wife's conveyance may be acknowledged in the same manner as if she were single	See footnote 6
Tennessee ...... C. 1932, Secs. 7635, 8460–61	Marriage shall impose no disability on a woman as to the disposition of property. The wife has the same capacity to dispose of real property in possession as if she were single (subject to husband's curtesy)		The wife's acknowledgment may be taken in the same form as if she were sole, and without any examination separate and apart from her husband	
Texas .... Complete St. 1928, Civ. St., Art. 1299; Art. 4614, amd. in Supp. 1931, p. 381; Arts. 4617, 6605		The joinder of the husband is necessary for the wife's conveyance or encumbrance of her separate real property[4]	The wife's conveyance is not effective without acknowledgment after an examination privily and apart from the husband before an officer authorized to take acknowledgments to deeds. Such officer must explain the instrument to her, and shall not certify to the same unless she acknowledges to him that it is her act and deed, that she has willingly signed the same, and that she does not wish to retract it	If the husband refuses to join, the wife may obtain a judicial order authorizing her sole conveyance or encumbrance upon a satisfactory showing that such conveyance, etc., would be advantageous to her
Utah .... Const., Art. XX, Sec. 2; R. S. 1933, 40-2-1	The wife may convey her real property as if she were unmarried			

TABLE XCII (*Continued*)

Jurisdiction and Citation	In General	Necessity of Husband Joining	Separate Examination, Acknowledgment, etc.[1] (See Sec. 184)	Covenants, Miscellaneous[2]
Vermont .... G. L. 1917, Sec. 3523, amd. by Sess. L. 1919, No. 90, p. 98, and further amd. by Sess. L. 1929, No. 48, p. 63	The wife may by her separate deed convey or mortgage the real estate of which she is seized in her own right "to her sole and separate use," as she might if single. The wife may by her sole deed convey or mortgage any other real estate "hereafter" acquired by her[13]	A homestead interest in the wife's real estate and real estate of which the wife is seized jointly with her husband may be conveyed or mortgaged only by the joint deed of herself and husband		
Virginia .... C. 1930, Secs. 5134, 5137, 5211	The wife may "dispose" of property acquired since April 4, 1877, as if she were unmarried, but she cannot deprive the husband of his curtesy by her sole act	A conveyance by husband and wife operates to pass from the wife and her representative all right, title and interest which the wife may have in any estate conveyed thereby, as effectually as if she were single[14]		A married woman who is a minor may bring a bill in equity by her next friend for an order, etc., to sell her real estate
Washington .... Remington, Comp. St. 1922, Secs. 6891, 6900	The wife may lease, sell, convey, or encumber her separate property to the same extent and in the same manner that her husband can property belonging to him. Married persons have the same right and liberty to dispose of every species of property as if unmarried			

§ 183]

TABLE XCII (*Continued*)

Jurisdiction and Citation	In General	Necessity of Husband Joining	Separate Examination, Acknowledgment, etc.[1] (See **Sec. 184**)	Covenants, Miscellaneous[2]
West Virginia... C. 1931, Ch. 39, Art. 1, Sec. 5; Ch. 48, Art. 3, Secs. 2, 3, 13	The wife may lease, sell, dispose, and convey her real property in the same manner and with like effect as if she were single except that her sole act shall not affect the husband's right to dower therein. The wife's deed, or other writing selling or conveying her own real estate, signed and delivered, operates to convey her rights in the property conveyed as effectually as if she were single (except that it does not affect the husband's dower)	The wife's deed does not affect the husband's dower in the property conveyed if he does not join therein	If the husband and wife join in a conveyance, the wife may acknowledge the same together with, or separately from, the husband. Either may sign and acknowledge before the other	The wife is liable as if unmarried on any covenant contained in her deed conveying her own real estate. Property to which wife is entitled in law or equity may not be subjected to any restraints on alienation that may not lawfully be imposed upon property of other persons
Wisconsin ...... St. 1931, Secs. 6.015, 232.42, 235.26, 235.29, 246.03	Women have the same rights and privileges under the law as men in holding and conveying property. A wife of full age, residing in this state or elsewhere, may by joint or separate deed convey her lands in this state, including that held in joint tenancy with the husband, in the same manner and with like effect as if she were single		The wife's conveyance, whether executed alone or in conjunction with her husband, may be acknowledged, or proof of execution thereof may be taken and certified the same as if she were single. The acknowledgment of a married woman when required by law may be taken in the same form as if she were sole	The wife's grant in the execution of a power must be acknowledged by her in the manner prescribed for conveyances by married women

TABLE XCII (*Continued*)

Jurisdiction and Citation	In General	Necessity of Husband Joining	Separate Examination, Acknowledgment, etc.[1] (See Sec. 184)	Covenants, Miscellaneous[2]
Wyoming ...... R. S. 1931, Secs. 69(102), 97(105), 97(120)	The wife may, by her deed or mortgage, convey her real estate in like manner as she might if she were single			When a non-resident wife joins with husband in conveyance of real estate situated in this state, the conveyance has the same effect as if she were sole, and the acknowledgment or proof of execution thereof may be the same as if she were sole[3]

[1] Unless otherwise designated in the table, the statutes outlined above apply in express terms to the wife's acknowledgment of any instrument (**Arizona, Hawaii, Idaho, Iowa, Louisiana, Massachusetts, Minnesota, Michigan, Montana, New Jersey, New Mexico, New York, North Dakota, Pennsylvania, South Dakota, Tennessee, Texas**), of any instrument relating to the sale or disposition of real estate (**Illinois, Missouri**), of any instrument affecting lands (**Delaware, North Carolina**). Where the statutes are silent on the matter in whole or in part, the wife's acknowledgment may presumably be made and taken as if she were single. Although the **North Carolina** statute in express terms covers the matter of the wife's contracts to convey to third persons, it is said that she may make such contracts without privy examination by reason of her statutory capacity to contract "as if unmarried" (*Everett* v. *Ballard,* 174 N. C. 16; 93 S. E. 385 [1917]). **Michigan** has an old provision not consistent with subsequent legislation but apparently not intended to be repealed. Section 13038 (Comp. St. 1929) requires the wife's grant in the execution of a power to be acknowledged by her on a private examination in the manner prescribed for her conveyances (which prescription has been repealed for fifty years).

[2] Statutes validating deeds, etc., in which the wife's execution, acknowledgment, separate examination, etc., have been defective in some particular, or which for some other reason were not regular when made, are passed with some frequency. A comparative analysis of these statutes is hardly worth while. As a matter of completeness, however, the citations for those found are given, as follows: **Delaware,** Sess. L. 1927, Ch. 195, p. 575; R. C. 1915, Sec. 3049, as amended by Sess. L. 1919, Ch. 197, p. 525; **District of Columbia,** C. 1929, T. 25, Secs. 157–59, 174; **Florida,** R. G. S. 1920, Secs. 3816–18; **Hawaii,** R. L. 1925, Sec. 3026; **Michigan,** Comp. L. 1929, Sec. 13338; **Minnesota,** G. S. 1923, Secs. 8197, 8199–8200; **New Jersey,** Comp. St. 1910, p. 3232, Sec. 8(*j*); Cum. Supp. 1911–24, Sec. 44(406); Supp. 1925–30, Secs. 44(216*b*), 44(119*f*), 124(8*x*), 124(8*w*-1); **New Mexico,** St. Ann. 1929, Sec. 1(115); **North Carolina,** C. 1927, Secs. 3346, 3348, 3351; **North Dakota,** Comp. L. 1913, Sec. 5517; **Oregon,** C. 1930, Secs. 63(117), 63(154)–63(155); **Pennsylvania,** St. 1920 (West), Secs. 8747–52, 8755, 8769–70, 14609, 14611, 14616–17, 21316; Cum. Supp. 1928 (West), Secs. 8769(*a*), 8770(*a*); **Washington,** Remington, Comp. St. 1922, Secs. 10572–76; **Wisconsin,** St. 1931, Sec. 246.04. Similar enactments, not incorporated into the various compiled codes and statutes, may be found in the session laws of the different jurisdictions.

[3] The provision above is found in **Alaska, Michigan, Oregon,** and **Wyoming.** In all of these jurisdictions, with the possible exception of **Oregon,** the wife may apparently convey her property without the husband's joinder. It is not probable that a different rule is intended for non-resident wives.

[4] If the wife is decreed a free dealer as authorized by the **Florida** statutes (**Secs. 152, 167, 187,** this volume), she may convey her real property by her sole conveyance as if single (*Lerch* v. *Barnes,* 61 Fla. 672; 54 So. 763 [1911]). In **North Carolina,** however, the fact that the wife

§ 183]

TABLE XCII (*Continued*)

becomes a free trader by registered writing (Sec. 187, this volume) does not abrogate the necessity of the husband's joinder and the wife's separate examination (*Council* v. *Pridgen,* 153 N. C. 443; 69 S. E. 404 [1910]). In Pennsylvania, the real property of a woman decreed a feme sole trader is subject to her "free and absolute disposal" (**Sec. 187,** this volume). The **Texas** statute enabling the wife to be decreed a feme sole for "mercantile or trading" purposes (**Sec. 187,** this volume) seems hardly broad enough to authorize her to convey her real property by her separate deed.

⁵ Section 4204 of the **Georgia** Code providing for the wife's joinder with the husband in a deed of conveyance, and giving a special form for the wife's acknowledgment (**Sec. 200,** this volume), does not apply to the wife's conveyance of her own property (*Haines* v. *Fort,* 93 Ga. 24; 18 S. E. 994 [1893]).

⁶ The following provisions were found which specifically deal with the subject of powers given to a married woman. A general and beneficial power may be given to the wife to dispose of lands conveyed or devised to her in fee, without the concurrence of her husband (**Kansas, Michigan, Minnesota, New York, North Dakota, Oklahoma**). A special and beneficial power may be granted to the wife to dispose during marriage without the consent of the husband of any estate less than a fee, belonging to her in lands to which the power relates (**Michigan, Minnesota, New York, North Dakota, Oklahoma**). A mortgage executed by the wife by virtue of a beneficial power does not extinguish or suspend the power, but the power is bound by the mortgage (**Michigan, Minnesota, North Dakota, Oklahoma**). The effect of such a lien on the power is that the mortgagee is entitled in equity to an execution of the power so far as the satisfaction of his debt may require, and that a subsequent estate created in execution of the power becomes subject to the mortgage as if in terms embraced therein (**Michigan, Minnesota, North Dakota, Oklahoma**). The wife may execute a power during marriage without the consent of the husband, unless otherwise prescribed by the terms of the power; but no power may be exercised by the wife until she attains her majority (**Michigan, Minnesota, Montana, North Dakota, Oklahoma, South Dakota**); when the wife is entitled to an estate in fee and is authorized by a power to dispose of the same during marriage, she may create any estate which she might if single (**Michigan, Minnesota, North Dakota, Oklahoma, South Dakota**). Wisconsin provides that the wife's grant in execution of a power must be acknowledged by her in the manner prescribed for conveyances of married women. **Michigan** apparently still requires the wife's acknowledgment on private examination for her grants in the execution of a power, although conveyances of her separate property may be acknowledged as if she were single (see footnote 1).

⁷ The **Louisiana** Act of 1928, cited above, purports to remove completely the disabilities of coverture, at least so far as the wife's separate paraphernal property is concerned. It is difficult to ascertain what authority this gives her over her dotal property (which is said to be rare in **Louisiana** at the present time). The Civil Code provides that dotal immovables may not be alienated unless declared alienable by the marriage contract, in which case they may be alienated with the wife's consent (Arts. 2360, 2364); but that the wife may mortgage such property with the authorization of the judge and husband (Arts. 126–28).

⁸ Under the broad statute securing to the wife her separate real and personal property "under her sole control" and deeming the wife a feme sole so as to enable her to contract, etc., the **Missouri** court has held that the wife may convey her lands without the necessity of the husband joining in her conveyance (*Farmers' Exchange Bank* v. *Hageluken,* 165 Mo. 443; 65 S. W. 728 [1901]; *Evans* v. *Morris,* 234 Mo. 177; 136 S. W. 408 [1911]).

⁹ The wife is liable upon her covenants in her conveyance of her separate property, even though the husband joins therein, the provision above being abrogated to that extent by subsequent legislation broadening the powers and liabilities of the wife (*Real* v. *Hollister,* 17 Neb. 661; 24 N. W. 333 [1885]). The provision above is effective, however, to protect her when she joins with the husband for the sole purpose of relinquishing her contingent interest in his property (*Pauley* v. *Knouse,* 109 Neb. 716; 192 N. W. 195 [1923]).

¹⁰ This section refers to Section 2588, **Nevada** General Statutes, 1885, since repealed, requiring the joinder of the husband in the wife's deeds.

¹¹ Section 124(3a), Supplement of 1925–30, authorizing the wife to convey by her separate deed providing the husband conveys his interest by separate deed was enacted in 1926 (Sess. L., Ch. 186, p. 310). Formerly **New Jersey** required the husband's joinder in the same instrument; and until 1916, the wife's separate acknowledgment was essential (p. 3237, Sec. 14; p. 3238, Sec. 16; p. 1547, Sec. 39). The 1926 Act does not apply to the wife's mortgages, but

TABLE XCII (*Concluded*)

the husband's joinder therein is necessary as before (*Dreier* v. *Pomeroy,* 104 N. J. Eq. 504; 146 A. 178 [1929]). The wife may convey by her sole deed in the execution of a written contract to which the husband is a party or to which he assents in writing, provided the contract is acknowledged in the manner required for deeds, and is recorded before or at the time the conveyance is recorded (p. 3231, Secs. 8*f*, 8*g*). The husband may join in the wife's deed by duly authorized attorney (p. 1548, Sec. 39*a*). The statutory citations given in this note refer to Compiled Statutes, 1910.

   12 In *Ellis* v. *Abbott,* 69 Ore. 234; 138 P. 488 (1914), the section above was held to be impliedly repealed by Section 9758, **Oregon** Laws, 1920, passed in 1878 (Sess. L., p. 94, Sec. 9), which authorized the wife to contract and incur liabilities as if sole. Section 9758 was expressly repealed in 1927 during the course of a general statutory revision (Sess. L., Ch. 144, p. 161). In 1926, however, the section outlined in the table above was treated as still being in force (*Dutton* v. *Buckley,* 116 Ore. 661; 242 P. 626 [1926]). It will be observed that the husband's joinder is not in terms made mandatory. The broad powers given to the wife in respect to property by the **Oregon** statutes seem clearly to authorize her to convey her property without the necessity of the husband's joinder.

   13 Prior to the amendment of February 13, 1919, to Section 3523, **Vermont** General Laws, the wife could mortgage or convey by her sole act only that property secured to her "sole and separate use." Her other real estate could be conveyed or mortgaged only by instrument executed by both of the spouses (Secs. 2735, 3523), which requirement it seems she must now meet in respect to her conveyances of such property acquired before February 13, 1919.

   14 Section 5211 of the **Virginia** Code, outlined above, refers more particularly to the wife's relinquishment of her dower in the husband's property, but its operation is not in terms confined to the same. In view of the wife's right to "dispose" of her property as if unmarried, Section 5211, which is not mandatory in form, does not seem to necessitate the husband's joinder in her conveyance.

REFERENCES

Books

PECK, EPAPHRODITUS. *The Law of Persons and of Domestic Relations,* Sec. 83 (1930).

STIMSON, F. J. *American Statute Law,* Secs. 6500, 6507–11 (1886).

Article

CARLIN, LEO. "Conveyances by Husband and Wife under the Revised Code," 40 W. Va. L. Quar. 1–23 (1933).

Notes

"Necessity of Privy Examination of Wife," *Jefferson County Bank* v. *Hale,* 152 Tenn. 648; 280 S. W. 408 (1925)—9 Tenn. L. Rev. 109–10 (1931).

"What Constitutes Joinder of Husband in Deed of Wife's Separate Estate," *Foust* v. *Hill,* 215 Ky. 364; 285 S. W. 235 (1926)—11 Minn. L. Rev. 377–78 (1927).

Annotation

"What Constitutes Cloud on Title Removable in Equity—Conveyance by Married Person without Joinder of Spouse," 78 A. L. R. 280–82 (1932).

§ 183]

Section 184. Separate Examination of the Wife

CROSS REFERENCES: Wife's conveyances of her real property, **Sec. 183;** Barring dower by deed, **Sec. 200;** Conveyance of homestead, **Sec. 225**

Early legislatures were consistent in the belief that the wife needed protection from the sinister influence of the husband. Practically all of the American jurisdictions required the wife to acknowledge, on examination separate and apart from the husband, that she executed her conveyance without fear or coercion. Stimson, writing in 1886, lists eighteen states as then requiring a separate examination of the wife. The theoretical utility of this artificial formality was probably far greater than its practical utility. At any rate, such an antiquated and discriminatory practice is highly inconsistent with the independent status now given to the wife, and with the modern philosophy that the wife can stand on her own feet in the exercise of her property rights without the need of special protection from her spouse. It is small wonder that the separate examination and other formalities appended to the wife's acknowledgment have been almost completely dropped from the statutes.

Only four jurisdictions (**Delaware, Florida, North Carolina, Texas**) require the wife's conveyance of her real property to be acknowledged by her on separate examination. A very few other jurisdictions prescribe this special formality when the wife relinquishes her dower or other contingent interest in the husband's property (**Sec. 200**), or when she joins with the husband in a conveyance of the homestead (**Sec. 225**). Apparently in **Michigan** the wife's acknowledgment to her grant in the execution of a power must be taken on separate examination. With the exceptions already noted, none of the jurisdictions prescribe any special formality which the wife must follow in acknowledging the execution of her conveyances. Fourteen jurisdictions, however, expressly provide that her separate examination is not necessary, and twenty-seven jurisdictions provide that her acknowledgment may be taken as if she were single. In four jurisdictions (**Minnesota, Mississippi, Missouri, New Mexico**), if the spouses join in the execution of an instrument, the acknowledgment shall describe them as husband and wife. Finally, four jurisdictions (**Alaska, Michigan, Oregon, Wyoming**) expressly authorize a simple acknowledgment in the case of a non-resident wife. This latter provision is of course mere surplusage.

The statutory material found on the subject matter of this section is outlined in Table XCII, **Section 183.** It will be observed that most of the statutes refer to the wife's acknowledgments generally, and are not

[§ 184

confined in application to conveyances. The Uniform Acknowledgments Act, approved by the National Conference on Uniform State Laws in 1892, provides that "the acknowledgment of a married woman, when required by law, may be taken in the same form as if she were sole and without any examination separate and apart from her husband." This Act has been adopted in whole or in part by but nine jurisdictions (**Iowa, Louisiana, Massachusetts, Michigan, Minnesota, Montana, New Mexico, North Dakota, Tennessee**). It is apparent, however, that the provision respecting the wife's acknowledgment has been substantially adopted in more than half of the jurisdictions.

REFERENCES
Book
STIMSON, F. J. *American Statute Law,* Sec. 6501 (1886).

Article
GREER, D. EDWARD. "A Legal Anachronism: The Married Woman's Separate Acknowledgment to Deeds," 1 Tex. L. Rev. 407–22 (1923).

Note
"Necessity of Privy Examination of Wife," *Jefferson County Bank* v. *Hale,* 152 Tenn. 648; 280 S. W. 408 (1925)—9 Tenn. L. Rev. 109–10 (1930).

Annotations
"Acknowledgment—Necessity of Privy Examination of Married Women," 1 A. L. R. 1080–1103 (1919).
"Duress Exercised by Third Person as Affecting Certificates of Acknowledgment by Married Woman," 4 A. L. R. 869 (1919).

Section 185. Wife's Transfers of Personal Property to Third Persons

CROSS REFERENCES: Wife's real and personal property, **Sec. 167;** Registration of wife's separate personal property, **Secs. 174, 175;** Transfers between spouses, **Sec. 182;** Wife's conveyances, **Secs. 183, 184;** Wife as a sole trader, **Sec. 187;** Transfer of household goods, **Sec. 230;** Contracts and conveyances of infants, **Secs. 273, 274**

At common law, the wife could not make an effectual transfer of personal property in possession, except as the husband's agent, because of a sheer want of title (**Sec. 167**). She was likewise powerless to assign her choses in action so as to defeat the husband's right to reduce the same to possession, or her chattels real so as to defeat his right to the enjoy-

§ 185]

ment thereof. The early statutes which established the right of the wife to own and enjoy the personal property which she brought to the altar, or thereafter acquired, usually gave her express authority to dispose of the same. The requirement that the husband must consent to her transfers, as a matter of protection to her, was not uncommon. A recognition of the basic difference between real and personal property, and the practical necessity of allowing the wife greater freedom in the control of the latter, led most jurisdictions, however, at an early date to authorize the wife to dispose of her personal property without the intermeddling of the husband and without that extra formality insisted upon in respect to her conveyances of real property (**Secs. 183, 184**). The early cases also recognized this practical distinction. While the statutory right to hold and acquire real property was thought to carry no implied right to dispose of the same, a number of courts saw the right to transfer personal property as a necessary incident to the ownership thereof.

In all of the fifty-one jurisdictions except seven (**Alabama, Georgia, Minnesota, Missouri, New Hampshire, North Dakota, Vermont**) statutes were found which expressly empower the wife to dispose of her personal property. The constitutions of three of these (**Arkansas, North Carolina, Utah**) so provide. In the seven jurisdictions above named, the wife unquestionably has an equally extensive power of disposition derived by implication from the less specific statutory capacity given her to hold, acquire, and control property, and to contract freely concerning it.

The statutes considered in this section are phrased in a variety of ways. Some employ the generic term "property." Many use the term "convey" to signify the transfer of personalty as well as of realty. In some (**Alaska, Idaho, Illinois, Iowa, Kansas, Maryland, Nebraska, Oregon, Washington**), it is provided that the wife has capacity to dispose of her personalty equal to the husband's capacity to dispose of his property. Despite the differences in phraseology, however, it is clear that all of them, with the few exceptions noted below, give the wife the exclusive control of her separate personalty, to deal with the same as she pleases. The power to transfer includes, of course, the lesser power to encumber. Nine jurisdictions (**Arizona, Delaware, District of Columbia, Louisiana, Maryland, Michigan, Nevada, New Mexico, Washington**), however, expressly authorize the wife to encumber her personal property. Perhaps as a vestige of our industrial revolution and the extension of corporate enterprise, special statutory capacity is given the wife to transfer by her sole act corporation stock in general (**Cali-**

fornia, **Idaho, Montana, Nevada, Oklahoma, Pennsylvania, South Dakota, Washington**), stock of building and loan associations and similar organizations (**Idaho, Illinois, Louisiana, Michigan, New Mexico, North Carolina, Oklahoma, South Dakota**), stock of railroad corporations (**New Mexico, Pennsylvania**), municipal and state bonds (**Pennsylvania**). All of these statutes are probably no more than mere surplusage at the present time.

In a number of jurisdictions, the spouses must join in a transfer or mortgage of household goods, whether owned by husband or wife (**Sec. 225**). **Texas**, however, is the only jurisdiction which appears to allow the husband any substantial control over the wife's transfers. The joint signature of husband and wife is made essential to the transfer of stocks and bonds owned by the wife. If the husband refuses to join, and upon a proper showing that such transfer would be advantageous to her, the wife may obtain a court order allowing her to make the transfer by her sole act. Why **Texas** should subject the wife to this embarrassment is not clear. It may be said that **Texas** is backward in its family laws in many respects. Until 1927, **Florida** required the husband's joinder in the wife's transfers. The right of the wife to dispose of her personalty under the present statute is inconsistent with and derogatory to the husband's management of her property (**Sec. 167**). The statutory situation in **North Carolina** is unique. The Constitution secures to the wife her real and personal property and provides that such property may "with the written assent of her husband" be "conveyed by her as if she were unmarried." This provision was intelligently construed as requiring the husband's assent to the wife's conveyances of real property only, and as in no way disparaging her right to dispose of her personal property as if sole (*Vann* v. *Edwards,* 135 N. C. 661; 47 S. E. 784 [1904]).

In **Georgia**, the wife's sale to a creditor of the husband in extinguishment of the latter's debt is void. The same result may follow in the few other jurisdictions which restrict the wife's undertakings for the husband (**Sec. 152**). **Georgia** also provides that a sale to her trustee is valid only if allowed by judicial order. A few jurisdictions by express statute limit the effect of transfers between spouses (**Sec. 182**). In **Louisiana**, the statute does not apply to married women under eighteen years of age; and in the **District of Columbia**, a bill of sale is not valid if executed by a married woman under twenty-one years of age; while in **Maine**, a wife "of any age" may dispose of her personal property (see also **Secs. 273, 274**).

The statutes of the community-property states discussed in this sec-

§ 185]

tion refer to the wife's separate personal property only, and, in **Louisiana,** to the wife's paraphernal property only. The wife ordinarily has no control of the community personal property. It must also be mentioned that the **Connecticut** statute is expressly confined to the case of marriages after April 20, 1877, and the **Virginia** statute to property acquired by the wife after April 4, 1877.

The citations for the statutes dealing with the subject of this section follow:

Alaska, Comp. L. 1913, Secs. 489–90; **Arizona,** R. C. 1928, Sec. 2174; **Arkansas,** Const., Art. IX, Sec. 7; Crawf. and Moses, Dig. 1921, Secs. 5574, 5581; **California,** C. C. 1933 (Lake), Secs. 162, 328(c); **Colorado,** Comp. L. 1921, G. S., Sec. 5585; **Connecticut,** G. S. 1930, Sec. 5154; **Delaware,** R. C. 1915, Sec. 3048, as amended by Sess. L. 1919, Ch. 197, p. 524; **District of Columbia,** C. 1929, T. 14, Sec. 21; **Florida,** R. G. S. 1920, Sec. 3949, as amended by Sess. L. 1927, Ch. 12255, p. 1137; **Georgia,** C. 1926, C. C., Secs. 3007, 3009; **Hawaii,** R. L. 1925, Sec. 2993, as amended by Sess. L. 1925, Act 274, p. 392; **Idaho,** Comp. St. 1919, Secs. 4657, 4731, 4915; **Illinois,** Cahill, R. S. 1931, Ch. 32, Sec. 392; Ch. 68, Sec. 9; **Indiana,** Burns, Ann. St. 1926, Sec. 8739; **Iowa,** C. 1927, Sec. 10446; **Kansas,** R. S. 1923, Sec. 23(202); **Kentucky,** Carroll, St. 1922, Secs. 505, 2128; **Louisiana,** Sess. L. 1926, Act. 132, p. 208; Sess. L. 1928, Act 283, p. 583; Marr, Ann. R. S. 1915, Secs. 772, 4467; **Maine,** R. S. 1930, Ch. 74, Sec. 1; **Maryland,** Bagby, Ann. C. 1924, Art. 45, Sec. 4; **Massachusetts,** G. L. 1932, Ch. 209, Sec. 1; **Michigan,** Comp. L. 1929, Sec. 12140, as amended by Sess. L. 1931, p. 210; Secs. 13057, 13061; **Mississippi,** C. 1930, Sec. 1940; **Montana,** R. C. 1921, Sec. 5792, as amended by Sess. L. 1933, Ch. 63, p. 119; Sec. 5955; **Nebraska,** Comp. St. 1929, Sec. 42(202); **Nevada,** Comp. L. 1929 (Hillyer), Secs. 1683, 1722, 1826, 3363; **New Hampshire,** Pub. L. 1926, Ch. 288, Sec. 8; **New Jersey,** Comp. St. 1910, p. 3232, Sec. 8(m); p. 3238, Sec. 16; **New Mexico,** St. Ann. 1929, Secs. 18(104), 68(302), 116(141); **New York,** Cahill, Consol. L. 1930, Ch. 14, Sec. 51; **North Carolina,** Const., Art. X, Sec. 6; C. 1927, Secs. 2506, 5181; **Ohio,** Complete G. C. 1931 (Page), Sec. 8001; **Oklahoma,** St. 1931, Secs. 1658, 9741, 9824; **Oregon,** C. 1930, Sec. 33(211); **Pennsylvania,** St. 1920 (West), Secs. 2443, 14569, 14572, 14576; **Rhode Island,** G. L. 1923, Sec. 4196; **South Carolina,** C. of L. 1922, C. C., Sec. 5539; **South Dakota,** Comp. L. 1929, Secs. 174, 178, 249, 9065(o); **Tennessee,** C. 1932, Sec. 8460; **Texas,** Complete St. 1928, Civ. St., Art. 4614, as amended by Supp. 1931, p. 381; Art. 4617; **Utah,** Const., Art. XXII, Sec. 2; R. S. 1933, 40-2-1; **Virginia,** C. 1930, Sec. 5134; **Washington,** Remington, Comp. St. 1922, Secs. 6891, 6900; Sec. 3819(1), added by Supp. 1927, p. 446; **West Virginia,** C. 1931, Ch. 48, Art. 3, Sec. 2; **Wisconsin,** St. 1931, Secs. 6.015, 246.03; **Wyoming,** R. S. 1931, Sec. 69(102).

REFERENCES
Book

STIMSON, F. J. *American Statute Law,* Sec. 6501 (1886).

[§ 185

Section 186. Power of Attorney of Husband and Wife

CROSS REFERENCES: Wife's contracts, **Sec. 152**; Wife's conveyances and transfers, **Secs. 183, 184, 185, 200, 225**

At common law, the basic incapacity of the wife obviously rendered her as completely unable to act through an agent as she was unable to act personally. Indeed, so great was her incapacity to act as a principal that even in the event of an action or suit in which the spouses were joined she could not effectively name an attorney to represent her. In spite of the unity conception of the spouses, however, she could act as the agent of her husband or a third party; though, of course, no true contract of agency could exist between them. We have seen that most jurisdictions now treat the wife in most respects as a feme sole in property matters. As a general proposition, what one may do himself by reason of rights which inhere in him he may do through a duly appointed agent or attorney. As a general proposition, then, the wife may act through an agent where she can act herself.

The statutes considered in this section are fragmentary and do not present a complete or symmetrical picture. Most of them are in their very nature mere surplusage in that they vest the wife with a particular authority where by implication of law she is vested with a general authority. The most significant of these statutes are those which expressly authorize an agency relationship between the spouses.

Thirty-four jurisdictions have legislation of some kind dealing with the wife as a principal, and two others impliedly recognize her ability to act through an agent in certain cases by prescribing the manner in which she shall acknowledge her power of attorney. In eleven of these jurisdictions, the husband is authorized to act as the agent of the wife for the purposes specified. Twelve jurisdictions have some statutory treatment of the wife as an agent, and in all but two of these the subject matter of the statute concerns the wife as the agent of the husband only. It will be observed that most of the statutes which expressly authorize the wife to act through a third-party agent are in express terms limited in application to the disposition of real property or an interest therein. Eight Western jurisdictions, however, have statutes substantially alike in phraseology particularly empowering the wife to control and transfer her corporation stock through an agent or proxy (see Table XCIII, footnote 1, p. 332).

Twenty-three jurisdictions have express statutes which enable the wife to dispose of her real property, or to release her rights in the hus-

§ 186]

band's property, or both, by an agent acting under a duly executed power of attorney. Five of these statutes refer only to the wife's release of dower, etc. In this general connection, three jurisdictions expressly but superfluously authorize the husband to join in the wife's conveyance by attorney. The wife's power of attorney to convey real estate, or an interest therein, must be executed and acknowledged in the manner prescribed for her conveyances. Most of the statutes here considered expressly so provide. Thus, it may be necessary for the husband to join in the power of attorney, and for the wife to undergo a separate examination (**Secs. 183, 184, 200, 225**).

It is apparent that more than half of the jurisdictions have either no legislation or only fragmentary legislation respecting the wife's general capacity to convey real property by attorney. In the absence of express legislation, many of the older cases arising under statutes which required the husband to join in the wife's conveyance and the wife to be separately examined refused to allow the wife to convey by attorney even though her power of attorney followed all of the formalities prescribed for her deeds (*Matt* v. *Smith,* 16 Cal. 533, 556 [1860] ; *Holland* v. *Moon,* 39 Ark. 120, 124 [1882] ; *Sumner* v. *Conant,* 10 Vt. 9 [1836]). These decisions are based upon the theory that the statutes authorizing the wife to convey must be strictly followed and that those formalities designed to protect the wife in the execution of her conveyances must be literally complied with. A privy acknowledgment by an agent was said to involve a contradiction. Later cases influenced by the general extension of the wife's property rights (and perhaps by the decision of the United States Supreme Court in *Williams* v. *Paine,* 169 U. S. 55 [1897], affirming 7 App. D. C. 116 [1895]) with sound reason take the position that the spirit and form of the statute is sufficiently followed if the wife executes and acknowledges the power of attorney in the manner prescribed for her conveyances. As a matter of fact, the problem here considered is not as significant now as formerly. The formality of a separate examination for any purpose has been almost completely dropped from the statutes. Of those four jurisdictions which still require the wife's conveyance of her real property to be privily acknowledged, three (**Delaware, Florida, North Carolina**) expressly authorize her to convey by attorney, and the fourth (**Texas**) reaches the same result by judicial decision (*Nolan* v. *Moore,* 96 Tex. 341 ; 72 S. W. 583 [1903]). Also, all but three (**Alabama, Pennsylvania, Texas**) of those jurisdictions which require the husband to join in the wife's deed of her real property expressly authorize her to convey by attorney. We have seen that in most jurisdic-

[§ 186

tions the wife may convey as if sole. In those jurisdictions, there can be little doubt of her ability to convey by a properly authorized agent. It may be safely said that in all jurisdictions today the wife may dispose of her property by attorney. The same observation is probably equally applicable to her conveyances in release of her dower or other rights in the property of the husband.

With but two exceptions (**Minnesota, Rhode Island**), the statutes of the eleven jurisdictions which authorize the husband to act as the agent of the wife refer in express terms to the control or disposition of property. In **Minnesota,** a power of attorney between the spouses to convey real estate, or interest therein, is not valid. This strange statute cannot be explained or justified on the basis of modern standards. **Hawaii** seems to provide impliedly that the wife cannot release her dower through the agency of her husband, while **Oregon** and **Wyoming** expressly recognize her ability to do so. In the absence of special limitation respecting engagements between the spouses, the wife undoubtedly may in all jurisdictions make the husband her agent for most if not all purposes. Where the wife may convey by her sole deed, a conveyance executed by her husband as her agent under a duly executed power of attorney ought unquestionably to be valid and effective. This may not follow, however, in those jurisdictions in which the husband must join in the wife's deed. It will be observed that none of the statutes which authorize the husband to act as the wife's agent in the disposition of property are of jurisdictions which require his joinder in her conveyances.

Eleven jurisdictions also expressly authorize the wife to act as the agent or attorney in fact of the husband. In all but three (**Georgia, Minnesota, Rhode Island**), the statutes in express terms refer to the control and disposition of property. The freak **Minnesota** statute prevents the wife from effectively executing a conveyance of real estate as the attorney of the husband. **Georgia** provides that proof of the wife's authority must be made as in other cases. In the absence of express statutory authority or special limitation, the wife at least for most purposes may bind the husband as his agent in fact. The common-law right of the wife to bind the husband in the purchase of necessaries as his "agent of necessity" remains substantially untouched in all jurisdictions (**Secs. 153, 160**).

Only two jurisdictions have express statutes respecting the wife's capacity to act as an agent of third parties. **Louisiana** provides that she may be appointed an attorney; and **Georgia,** clinging to the unity conception of the spouses in this particular, archaically provides that she

§ 186]

cannot be an agent for a third person without the husband's consent, in which case he is bound by her acts.

The table with an outline of the statutes discussed in this section, together with the citations therefor, follows.

TABLE XCIII*

POWER OF ATTORNEY OF HUSBAND AND WIFE

Jurisdiction and Citation	In General[1]	Between Spouses
Alabama .... C. 1923, Sec. 7433	The wife may relinquish her dower by joining with the husband in a power of attorney authorizing the conveyance of husband's lands. Her signature must be witnessed or acknowledged in the manner prescribed for other conveyances	
Alaska .... Comp. L. 1913, Sec. 442		The husband or wife may constitute the other his or her attorney in fact to control or dispose of his or her property, and may revoke the same to the same extent and in the same manner as other persons
Arizona .... R. C. 1928, Sec. 957		Either husband or wife may authorize the other, by power of attorney executed and acknowledged as prescribed for conveyances, to execute, etc., any conveyance, mortgage, or other instrument affecting his or her separate or community property

* See page 332 for numbered footnotes to this table.

[§ 186

TABLE XCIII (*Continued*)

Jurisdiction and Citation	In General[1]	Between Spouses
Arkansas .... Crawf. and Moses, Dig. 1921, Sec. 5576	The wife's conveyance executed by her through an agent duly appointed by power of attorney, recorded in the county wherein the land is situated, is as valid and binding as though executed by herself	
California ...... C. C. 1933 (Lake), Sec. 1094	The wife may make, execute and revoke powers of attorney for the sale, conveyance, and encumbrance of her real and personal property with the same effect as if she were single. Such powers may be acknowledged in the manner prescribed for deeds[1]	
Delaware .... R. C. 1915, Sec. 3212	The wife may make a letter of attorney as though she were a feme sole[2]	
Florida .... R. G. S. 1920, Sec. 3814	The wife's deed, mortgage, lease or other transfer of her separate real property or relinquishment of her dower executed by virtue of a power of attorney has the same effect as if executed by her in person. The husband must join in the execution of the power of attorney, and the same must be executed and acknowledged by her in the manner prescribed for her deeds or her relinquishments of dower, as the case may be	
Georgia .... C. 1926, C. C., Secs. 2998, 3573		The wife may act as attorney and agent for the husband, but proof of such authority must be made as in other cases (except in her purchase of necessaries). She cannot be an agent for another than her husband except with the husband's consent, in which case he is bound by her acts

TABLE XCIII (*Continued*)

Jurisdiction and Citation	In General[1]	Between Spouses
Hawaii R. L. 1925, Sec. 3026	The wife may delegate to an attorney in fact, other than her husband, the power to execute a conveyance releasing her dower, by either general or special power of attorney which may be executed and acknowledged by her as if she were sole	
Illinois Cahill, R. S. 1931, Ch. 30, Secs. 18–20; Ch. 68, Sec. 14	Any wife above the age of 18 years who joins with the husband in the execution of a power of attorney relating to the sale, conveyance or other disposition of her lands is bound thereby in respect to her right and interest in such lands as if she were sole.[3] Wife may relinquish dower by joining with husband in a power of attorney. The acknowledgment or proof of such power of attorney may be made and certified as if she were sole	The husband or wife may constitute the other his or her attorney in fact to control and dispose of his or her property for their mutual benefit, and may revoke the same to the same extent and in the same manner as other persons
Indiana Burns, Ann. St. 1926, Sec. 13379	The wife may join in a power of attorney with her husband for the conveyance or mortgage of lands, or of any interest therein	
Iowa C. 1927, Sec. 10450		The husband or wife may constitute the other his or her attorney in fact to control or dispose of his or her property for their mutual benefit, and may revoke the appointment, the same as other persons
Kentucky Carroll, St. 1922, Sec. 508	A resident or non-resident wife may by agent convey any interest in real or personal estate in **Kentucky** which she could convey in person. Such conveyance must be made by virtue of a power of attorney, executed, acknowledged or proven as is prescribed for the wife's deeds	

[§ 186

TABLE XCIII (*Continued*)

Jurisdiction and Citation	In General[1]	Between Spouses
Louisiana ...... C. C., Arts. 130, 3001	The wife may appoint one or more agents with power, during her temporary or permanent absence from the state, to sign a renunciation of her mortgage or privilege on the property of the husband, as she herself might do if personally present. Such power may be general or special. Women (including married women) may be appointed attorneys	
Maine .... R. S. 1930, Ch. 74, Sec. 2		The wife may release to the husband the right to control her property, and to dispose of the income thereof for their mutual benefit, and may in writing revoke the same
Maryland .... Bagby, Ann. C. 1924, Art. 45, Sec. 12	A wife of any age may authorize an agent by power of attorney, executed jointly with her husband or separately, to relinquish her dower rights. The husband may similarly relinquish his rights in the wife's lands	
Michigan .... Comp. L. 1929, Sec. 13384	The husband and wife may effectually convey the legal title to lands in this state by their attorney in fact under a joint power of attorney, executed, acknowledged and recorded as is required for the joint deed of the spouses[3]	
Minnesota ...... G. S. 1923, Secs. 8196, 8621	Either husband or wife may separately appoint an attorney to sell or convey any real estate owned by such husband or wife, or to join in any conveyance made by or for the other	No power of attorney or other authority between the spouses to convey real estate, or interest therein, is valid. In relation to all other subjects, either spouse may be constituted the agent of the other

§ 186]

TABLE XCIII (*Continued*)

Jurisdiction and Citation	In General[1]	Between Spouses
Missouri .... R. S. 1929, Sec. 3016	The wife may convey her real estate or relinquish her dower by a power of attorney authorizing its conveyance, executed and acknowledged by her jointly with the husband as is prescribed for their deed conveying such estate[3]	
Montana .... R. C. 1921, Sec. 5792, amd. by Sess. L. 1933, Ch. 63, p. 119; Secs. 5811, 6862	The wife may without the husband's consent, agreement and signature execute a power of attorney for the conveyance or transfer of her real or personal property. She may contract, and may waive or relinquish any right or interest in real estate by attorney, as if single[1]	
Nevada .... Comp. L. 1929 (Hillyer), Sec. 3387	The wife's power of attorney authorizing the execution of an instrument conveying or affecting her real property shall be acknowledged in the manner prescribed for her conveyances[1]	
New Jersey ..... Comp. St. 1910, p. 1547, Sec. 39(*a*); p. 1549, Sec. 40	Any conveyance made by virtue of a letter of attorney for the conveyance, etc., of any lands or other property, or interests therein, executed by the wife and husband is as effectual to pass the wife's dower or other estate as if she were sole, provided her acknowledgment is made and certified in the manner prescribed for her deeds. The husband may join in the wife's deed by duly authorized attorney	
New Mexico .... St. Ann. 1929, Secs. 1(115), 68(202)	The husband need not join when the wife executes a power of attorney for herself.[1] The wife need not join when the husband executes a power of attorney for himself. The wife may make, sign and acknowledge any deed or conveyance by an attorney authorized by a written power of attorney, executed and acknowledged by herself and husband	

[§ 186

TABLE XCIII (*Continued*)

Jurisdiction and Citation	In General[1]	Between Spouses
New York ...... Cahill, Consol. L. 1930, Ch. 51, Sec. 207	A wife of any age may release her inchoate right of dower by attorney in fact in any case where she can personally release the same	
North Carolina.. C. 1927, Secs. 997, 1002	The wife's power of attorney relating to her estate or interest in land is valid and effective if the husband joins therein, and if the same is executed and acknowledged in the manner prescribed for her conveyances	
Oregon .... C. 1930, Sec. 33(204)		The husband or wife may constitute the other his or her attorney in fact to control, convey, mortgage, or bar dower or curtesy in his or her property, and may revoke the same in the same manner as other persons
Pennsylvania ... St. 1920 (West), Secs. 14613–14, 14619	(No express authorization was found, but provision is made for the wife's acknowledgment of powers of attorney taken in another state or another country, and for the recording of those letters of attorney which the wife is authorized to make without the husband's joinder)	. . .
Rhode Island ... G. L. 1923, Secs. 4197, 4203	If deed affecting wife's dower right in husband's lands during his life be executed by attorney of the wife, the letter of attorney shall be acknowledged in same manner as if she were single	The wife may act as agent or attorney of her husband. The husband may act as agent or attorney of his wife
Utah .... R. S. 1933, 40-2-8		A husband or wife may constitute the other his or her attorney in fact to control and dispose of his or her property for their mutual benefit or otherwise, and may revoke the appointment the same as other persons

§ 186]

TABLE XCIII (*Continued*)

Jurisdiction and Citation	In General[1]	Between Spouses
Virginia .... C. 1930, Sec. 5215	A resident or non-resident wife may, in conjunction with the husband by power of attorney duly executed, acknowledged and certified, appoint an attorney in fact for her. Such attorney may execute and acknowledge for record any deed or other writing which the wife might execute and acknowledge in conjunction with the husband. Such deed, etc., is effectual to convey the wife's title to real estate and to bar her dower	
Washington .... Remington, Comp. St. 1922, Secs. 10573–76	The husband or wife may make and execute a power of attorney, acknowledged and certified as prescribed for conveyances, for the sale, conveyance, transfer or encumbrance of his or her separate property, without the joinder of the other spouse.[1] A conveyance, etc., executed under such power shall be executed, acknowledged and certified as if the person making the power had been unmarried. Either husband or wife may execute a letter of attorney to a third person to join with the other in conveyance of any interest either in the separate real estate of either or in the community real estate. The spouses may jointly execute a power of attorney to a third person authorizing the sale, encumbrance or other disposition of community real property	The husband or wife may appoint the other his attorney in fact to sell, convey, transfer or encumber his or her separate property. The husband or wife may make and execute a letter of attorney to the other, authorizing the sale or other disposition of his or her community interest in the community property
West Virginia .. C. 1931, Ch. 48, Art. 3, Sec. 6	The wife may, by power of attorney duly executed, without the husband joining, appoint an attorney in fact to execute any deed or other writing which she might execute in person. Such deed, etc., executed in pursuance thereof is effectual to convey her title or interest in the lands so conveyed, and to bar her right of dower therein, as if she had in person executed the same	

[§ 186

TABLE XCIII (*Concluded*)

Jurisdiction and Citation	In General[1]	Between Spouses
Wisconsin ...... St. 1931, Secs. 235.28, 235.29	The wife may by letter of attorney authorize her attorney to bar her dower or to convey any other interest in real estate in the same manner, and in the same cases as she might personally do. Her letter of attorney, whether executed alone or in conjunction with the husband, may be acknowledged and certified as if she were sole	
Wyoming ...... R. S. 1931, Sec. 97(111)		A husband or wife may constitute the other his or her attorney in fact to control or dispose of his or her property or any inchoate or other interest therein, and may revoke the same in the same manner and to the same extent as other persons

[1] The eight jurisdictions named below provide that the wife may transfer corporation stock standing in her name, or owned by her, by agent or attorney, as if unmarried. All but **Oklahoma** and **South Dakota** specify that dividends from such stock may be paid to her agent or attorney; and all but **California** specify that the wife's power or proxy touching such stock is as valid and binding as though she were single. The citations for these provisions are: **California**, C. C. 1933 (Lake), Sec. 328(*c*); **Idaho**, Comp. St. 1919, Sec. 4731; **Montana**, R. C. 1921, Sec. 5955; **Nevada**, Comp. L. 1929 (Hillyer), Secs. 1722, 1826; **New Mexico**, St. Ann. 1929, Sec. 116(114); **Oklahoma**, St. 1931, Sec. 1658; **South Dakota**, Comp. L. 1929, Sec. 249; **Washington**, Remington, Comp. St., Supp. 1927, Sec. 3819(1).

[2] The **Delaware** provision above probably does not mean that the wife may authorize the conveyance of her property with less formality than is required in her own conveyance.

[3] Some of the statutes outlined above seem inconsistent with the freedom with which the wife may herself execute conveyances of her own real property. This is true in **Illinois**, **Michigan**, and **Missouri** if the statutes in those jurisdictions are construed as requiring the husband's joinder in the wife's power of attorney.

REFERENCES

Book

STIMSON, F. J. *American Statute Law,* Sec. 6506 (1886).

§ 186]

Section 187. Wife as a Sole Trader

CROSS REFERENCES : Powers of abandoned and separated wives, **Sec. 143**; Wife's power to contract, **Secs. 152** *et seq.;* Wife's property, **Secs. 167** *et seq.;* Wife's earnings, **Sec. 173**; Suits by and against the wife, **Sec. 179**; Wife as a stockholder, etc., **Sec. 230**

The term "feme sole trader" has been used to designate a wife who for some reason was allowed to carry on a trade with the powers and liabilities of a single woman. At least in the absence of an antenuptial or postnuptial agreement with the husband or in the absence of those extreme circumstances in which the husband was regarded as civilly dead, the common law did not permit the wife to conduct a business on her separate account and for her separate gain. Quite to the contrary, her contracts were void, and her earnings and services together with her personal property belonged to the husband. The common law did, however, make an exception under the so-called "Custom of London," by which "where a feme, covert of the husband, useth any craft in the said city on her sole account, whereof the husband meddleth nothing, such a woman shall be charged as a feme sole concerning everything that toucheth the craft."[1] This unusual exception to the general rule was apparently recognized in none of the American jurisdictions except **South Carolina.** Early legislators and courts looked with some disfavor upon the wife entering the role of a sole trader while living with the husband unless her stock in trade became liable for the husband's debts, and the husband liable for her debts.

From an early date, however, legislatures have allowed the wife in certain extreme situations (as when deserted by husband) to become a sole trader. As the common-law incapacities of the wife were removed, legislation giving her a special capacity to engage in business became less necessary. With the extension of equal-rights legislation, many of these early statutes have disappeared from the books. There is, however, a lingering sentiment in some jurisdictions that to allow the wife to engage in business involves inherent dangers and demands special legislative attention.

The table following will reveal that twenty-three jurisdictions give the matter here discussed a present statutory consideration. Of these, twelve (**Arkansas, Colorado, District of Columbia, Indiana, Kansas, Maryland, Missouri, Nebraska, New York, Rhode Island, West Virginia, Wyoming**) vest the wife with broad authority to con-

---

[1] Joel P. Bishop, *The Law of Married Women,* II, 418 (1875).

[§ 187

duct a business on her separate account without the necessity of formal or special prerequisites. **Louisiana** recognizes the right which the wife had under the civil law to bind herself as a "public merchant," and did so even before the wife was given a general contractual capacity. In the remaining jurisdictions, the statutes are difficult to classify and in some instances are no more than antiquated relics. They differ in scope, in purpose, and in the formalities prerequisite to the wife obtaining the status of a sole trader. In general, they appear to be inspired by the desire to enable the wife to secure a livelihood when the husband fails her, or to surround the sole trader with certain formalities to protect the husband's creditors and to prevent collusion between the spouses to the detriment of the husband's creditors.

Two jurisdictions (**Hawaii, Massachusetts**), while tacitly recognizing the right of the wife to conduct a business on her own account, require a recorded notice of the enterprise to save the wife's stock in trade from the husband's debts and to save the husband from liability on the wife's business contracts. Literally read, these statutes do not require good faith on the part of third-party creditors. **Florida** and **Texas** are two of the very few jurisdictions in which the wife has no general contractual capacity (see **Sec. 152**) ; but by complying with the statute, she may by judicial decree acquire the status of a free dealer (**Florida**), or a feme sole for mercantile and trading purposes (**Texas**). In three jurisdictions (**North Carolina, Pennsylvania, Wisconsin**), a wife in certain extreme circumstances is deemed a sole trader without formality. **Pennsylvania** still has on the statute books an act of this type, respecting wives of absent mariners, adopted in 1718. By a subsequent **Pennsylvania** statute, in certain cases of non-support, the wife may become a sole trader by judicial decree. In **North Carolina,** any wife of twenty-one years may become a "free trader" with the husband's consent evidenced by either an antenuptial agreement or a writing signed by the spouses, proved and registered. Also, for the purpose of enforcing liability upon the wife in **North Carolina,** she is deemed a free trader when she is the undisclosed principal of the husband.

The statutes of **California, Montana,** and **Nevada** are the most detailed. They are designed to offer the wife relief from an improvident spouse, and at the same time to prevent her from defrauding his creditors. In **California** at least, it appears that the statute is seldom utilized. In all of these jurisdictions, the formalities required include notice by publication of intention to make application to become a sole trader, trial or hearing, affidavit of good faith, and recording of the judgment

§ 187]

or order. Any creditor of the husband may contest the application. In **Montana** and **Nevada,** the wife must not allow the husband to manage or superintend her business.

The statutes in the community-property states call for a few additional observations. In **California** and **Nevada,** the statutes contemplate that the wife may use not exceeding five hundred dollars of the husband's separate funds or of the community funds in the prosecution of her business. This amounts to a considerable concession if the husband is near insolvency. In **Texas,** the statute merely confers capacity upon the wife and does not purport to separate her from the community; while in **California** and **Nevada,** she may conduct her business on her separate account and for her separate profit, and not for the purpose of increasing the community productivity. This, also, is obviously a considerable concession. In **Louisiana** the wife's earnings while carrying on a trade "separate" from the husband are her separate property.

If the sole trader follows the formalities prescribed by the various statutes, the husband is not liable for her engagements; though, of course, the statutes do not protect a husband who is in fact the wife's principal. In **California, Montana,** and **Nevada,** the husband is liable only for debts contracted with or upon his written consent. Under the peculiar **Louisiana** system, however, the husband is liable if a community exists between the spouses.

The fact that the wife is a sole trader does not relieve the husband of his duty of support, but by the statutes of **California, Montana,** and **Nevada** a sole trader is made responsible for the support of her minor children.

Most of the statutes are silent as to whether the wife may form a partnership with the husband. **Rhode Island** stands alone in expressly forbidding a trading partnership between the spouses. In **West Virginia,** on the other hand, she may carry on a business separately or with "any other person"; and as before observed, **West Virginia** and **Maryland** expressly authorize the wife to form a partnership with the husband, and in **Colorado** and **New Mexico** she may be his special partner (**Sec. 156**).

Presumably, in at least most of those jurisdictions without express statute on the subject here under discussion, the wife may engage in business on her separate account, deriving such authority from her broad capacity to contract, to sue and be sued, to acquire, hold, and dispose of property, etc. (see cross references above). Thus, even under the older type of statute authorizing the wife to contract in reference to her sepa-

[§ 187

rate property only, she could use her property in carrying on a trade or business. Where the wife's common-law disabilities are now entirely removed, or nearly so, it seems quite unnecessary to give her special authority to engage in business, unless the wife in business presents dangers which as a matter of policy require the prescription of special formalities. Many of the statutes considered in this section are of ancient origin. Some of them (as in **Pennsylvania, North Carolina,** and **Wisconsin**), which purport only to create a limited capacity and not to protect third parties, seem mere misleading surplusage in view of the general capacity of the wife in those jurisdictions.

It remains to observe that, although the wife may have the capacity to embark on a business career, the husband's authority as head of the family and his right to her services and society in the household may enable him to prevent her assuming such a role if he is properly supporting her. In an unusual case in which the wife was permanently enjoined from conducting a business in competition with the husband, the **Michigan** court said: "that the wife may, with the husband's consent, conduct a business upon her own account, is not open to question . . . . but we are unable to find any decision . . . . which affirms this right in the wife, where her husband is able and willing to support her and withholds his consent" (*Root* v. *Root,* 164 Mich. 638; 130 N. W. 194 [1911]).

For a more complete picture of the statutory material discussed in this section, the reader is directed to the table following.

TABLE XCIV*

Wife as a Sole Trader

Jurisdiction and Citation	In General	Process, Decree, etc.	Effect of Order, or Decree, etc.
Arkansas . . . . Crawf. and Moses, Dig. 1921, Secs. 5580–81	A married woman may carry on any trade or business on her sole and separate account, and the earnings therefrom shall be her sole and separate property. She may alone sue or be sued on account of said business		

* See pages 344–45 for all numbered footnotes to this table.

§ 187]

TABLE XCIV (*Continued*)

Jurisdiction and Citation	In General	Process, Decree, etc.	Effect of Order, or Decree, etc.
California ...... C. C. P. 1933 (Lake), Secs. 1811–21	A married woman may become a sole trader by judgment of superior court of the county in which she has resided for six months next preceding her application	Applicant must give notice by publication of intention to make application,[1] and file verified petition setting forth that application is made in good faith to enable her to support herself, the fact of insufficient support from husband and causes thereof if known, other grounds which are causes for divorce with reason why divorce not sought, nature of business proposed, capital to be invested therein, and sources from which derived. Any creditor of husband may oppose application.[2] After trial or hearing, if facts found sustain application, the court must render judgment, authorizing applicant to carry on, in her own name and on her own account, the business specified[3]	The wife may invest a sum derived from community property or separate property of husband not exceeding $500. She is entitled to carry on the business specified in her own name. The property, etc., invested, and profits thereof, belong exclusively to her, and are not liable for husband's debts. She thereafter has all the privileges of, and is liable to all the legal processes provided for, debtors and creditors, and may sue and be sued alone. A sole trader is liable for the maintenance of her minor children. The husband is not liable for any debts contracted by her in her business, unless contracted upon his written consent
Colorado .... Comp. L. 1921, G. S., Sec. 5578	A married woman may carry on any trade or business on her sole and separate account, and the earnings therefrom shall be her sole and separate property, and may be used and invested by her in her own name. She may sue and be sued in regard to her trade, etc., as if sole. Her property acquired by her trade, etc., may be taken on execution against her		

TABLE XCIV (*Continued*)

Jurisdiction and Citation	In General	Process, Decree, etc.	Effect of Order, or Decree, etc.
District of Columbia ... C. 1929, T. 14, Sec. 43	Married women shall have the power to engage in any business, and to contract, whether engaged in business or not, as fully as if unmarried		
Florida .... R. G. S. 1920, Secs. 3218–22	Resident married woman may apply by petition in chancery to circuit court, circuit of residence, for a license to take charge of and manage her own estate and property, and to become a free dealer	The wife shall give notice by publication (once a week for four successive weeks) of her intention to apply for such license. The petition is referred by judge to a master with directions to take testimony and make inquiry as to capacity, etc., of applicant. If the judge, upon the filing of master's report and hearing thereof, is satisfied as to capacity, etc., of applicant, he may grant the license prayed for. All costs are a lien upon estate of applicant, and taxed as costs in other cases	After publishing copy of order or decree granting license once a week for four successive weeks, the wife shall be authorized to take charge of and control her estate, to contract and be contracted with, to sue and be sued, and to bind herself in all respects as fully as if unmarried
Hawaii .... R. L. 1925, Secs. 2994, 3003	Married women may contract with third parties as if unmarried (except personal service contracts)	When a married woman does or proposes to do business on her separate account, she or her husband shall file with Territory treasurer a certificate stating name and residence of herself and of husband, nature and location of the business. A new certificate is necessary when changes are made. Certificate is recorded in public record	If certificate not filed, personal property employed in such business is liable to attachment as property of husband and to be taken on execution against him; and husband is liable upon all contracts lawfully made in prosecution of said business in the same manner as if the contracts had been made by himself

§ 187]

TABLE XCIV (*Continued*)

Jurisdiction and Citation	In General	Process, Decree, etc.	Effect of Order, or Decree, etc.
Indiana .... Burns, Ann. St. 1926, Sec. 8740	A married woman may carry on any trade or business on her sole and separate account, and the earnings therefrom shall be her sole and separate property		
Kansas .... R. S. 1923, Sec. 23(204)	Any married woman may carry on any trade or business on her sole and separate account, and the earnings therefrom shall be her sole and separate property, and may be used and invested by her in her own name		
Louisiana ...... C. C., Arts. 131, 1786, 2334	The earnings of the wife while carrying on a business, trade, occupation, or industry separate from her husband, and property purchased therewith, are her separate property. If the wife is a "public merchant" she may obligate herself in anything relating to her trade, and in such case the husband is bound also, if there exists a community between them[4]		
Maryland ...... Bagby, Ann. C. 1924, Art. 45, Sec. 5; Art. 47, Sec. 35	Married women shall have the power to engage in any business, and to contract whether engaged in business or not, as fully as if unmarried. The general insolvency statutes apply to a married woman engaged in business as a feme sole		

TABLE XCIV (*Continued*)

Jurisdiction and Citation	In General	Process, Decree, etc.	Effect of Order, or Decree, etc.
Massachusetts .. G. L. 1932, Ch. 209, Secs. 2, 9–11	A married woman may contract with third parties as if unmarried	If a married woman does or proposes to do business on her separate account, she or her husband shall record with town clerk of town where business located certificate stating name of herself and husband, nature and location of business, and name (which shall not be her husband's) under which she proposes to carry on business. A new certificate necessary when changes are made	If certificate not recorded, the personal property employed in such business is liable to attachment as property of husband and to be taken on execution against him; and husband is liable upon all contracts lawfully made in prosecution of such business in the same manner as if such contracts had been made by him
Missouri .... R. S. 1929, Sec. 2998	A married woman shall be deemed a feme sole so far as to enable her to carry on and transact business on her own account		
Montana .... R. C. 1921, Secs. 9982–89	A married woman may become a sole trader by the judgment of district court of the county in which she has resided for six months next preceding her application	Applicant must give notice by publication of intention to make application,[1] and file verified petition setting forth that application is made in good faith to enable her to support herself, the fact of insufficient support from husband and cause thereof if known, other grounds which are causes for divorce with reason why divorce not sought, nature of business proposed, capital to be invested therein, and sources from which derived. Any creditor of husband may oppose application.[2] After trial or hearing, if facts found sustain application, the court must render judgment authorizing applicant to carry on, in her own name and on her own account, the business specified[3]	The sole trader is entitled to carry on the business specified in her own name. The property, etc., invested, and the profits thereof, belong exclusively to her, and are not liable for the husband's debts. She thereafter has all the privileges of, and is liable to all the legal processes provided for, debtors and creditors, and may sue and be sued alone. A sole trader is liable for the maintenance of her minor children. The husband is not liable for any debts contracted by her in her business, unless contracted upon his written consent. The husband must not manage or superintend the wife's business for her or act as her agent therein; if he does so act, the property of the sole trader is liable for his debts

TABLE XCIV· (*Continued*)

Jurisdiction and Citation	In General	Process, Decree, etc.	Effect of Order, or Decree, etc.
Nebraska .... Comp. St. 1929, Sec. 42(203)	A married woman may carry on a trade or business on her sole and separate account, and the earnings thereof shall be her sole and separate property, and may be used and invested by her in her own name		
Nevada .... Comp. L. 1929 (Hillyer), Secs. 3390–92	Married women shall have the right to carry on and transact business under their own names, and on their own account, by complying with the regulations prescribed (see next column)	Applicant must give notice by publication of intention to make application.[1] On hearing, if it appears to the court after examination of applicant on oath that a proper case exists, an order may be entered authorizing applicant to carry on in her own name and on her own account the business, etc., named in her notice. Insolvency of husband, apart from other cause tending to prevent his supporting the family, is not sufficient cause for granting application. Any creditor of the husband may oppose the application, and if it appears that application is made for purpose of defrauding such creditor or preventing him from collecting his debt, or will occasion such result, application shall be denied[3]	The sole trader is entitled to carry on the business specified in her own name. The property so invested shall belong exclusively to her, and is not liable for the husband's debts. She shall be allowed all the privileges and be liable to all legal process provided by law against debtors and creditors. She may sue and be sued alone. She is not authorized to carry on business in her own name when the same is managed or superintended by her husband. A sole trader is responsible for the maintenance of her children. The husband is not responsible for any debts contracted by her in her business without his special consent given in writing, nor may his separate property be taken on execution for her debts
New York ...... Cahill, Consol. L. 1930, Ch. 14, Sec. 51	A married woman has all the rights to carry on any business, trade or occupation, and to exercise all powers and enjoy all rights in respect thereto, as if she were unmarried		

[§ 187

TABLE XCIV (*Continued*)

Jurisdiction and Citation	In General	Process, Decree, etc.	Effect of Order, or Decree, etc.
North Carolina.. C. 1927, Secs. 2525–30, 3202	Every woman living separate from husband under judgment of divorce or registered deed of separation, or whose husband has been declared an idiot or lunatic, shall be deemed a free trader. An abandoned wife shall be deemed a free trader so far as to be competent to contract and bind her separate property. (See next column)	A married woman, 21 years of age or upwards, with consent of husband may become a free trader by antenuptial contract, proved and registered as prescribed, or by a writing, signed by the spouses, stating that the wife enters herself as a free trader with husband's consent. Such writing may be proved by subscribing witness or acknowledged before proper officer, and shall be registered in county where wife proposes to have principal or only place of business. Certified copy of such writing is admissible in evidence in same manner as certified copy of registered deed	After registration of writing, the wife shall be a free trader and authorized to contract and deal as if she were a feme sole. Revocation of right to act as free trader may be made by entry on record to effect that thereafter she ceases so to act and by publication to that effect weekly for three weeks in county wherein she had her principal or sole place of business. Such revocation impairs no liabilities previously incurred, nor subsequent liability to one fraudulently induced to deal with her as a sole trader[5]
Pennsylvania ... St. 1920 (West), Secs. 14579–81; Sec. 14582, amd. by Cum. Supp. 1928 (West), p. 621	The wife may petition the court of common pleas, county of her residence, to be decreed a sole trader wherever husband, though living with wife under same roof, has failed to support wife or family for five years or more, or whenever the spouses live separate and apart for one year or more with no marital relations, and the husband for that time has not supported wife or children and the latter are maintained by efforts of wife and/or children, or from income of wife's separate property[6]	If upon proof presented, it appears that husband has failed to support wife or family for five years or more, or that spouses have been living separate and apart for one year or more and that husband has not supported or contributed toward support of wife and that wife by her own industry or joint industry of herself and children or by reason of income of her separate estate has maintained herself or been maintained by her children, she shall be declared a feme sole trader[6]	A feme sole trader's real and personal property is subject to her free and absolute disposal during life or by will without interference of husband, and, in case of intestacy, it goes to her next of kin as if he were previously dead

§ 187]

TABLE XCIV (*Continued*)

Jurisdiction and Citation	In General	Process, Decree, etc.	Effect of Order, or Decree, etc.
Rhode Island ... G. L. 1923, Sec. 4201	A married woman may carry on any trade or business as if she were single, but her husband shall not be liable for her debts, contracts or torts therein. Nothing herein shall be construed to allow husband and wife to enter into any trading partnership together		
Texas .... Complete St. 1928, Civ. St., Art. 4626	Any married woman within the state may, with the consent of and joined by her husband, apply by written petition to district court, county of residence, for judgment removing her disabilities of coverture and declaring her feme sole for mercantile and trading purposes	Petition shall set out the causes making it advantageous to wife to be declared a feme sole. If upon a hearing of petition and evidence relating thereto, it appears to court that it would be to advantage of applicant, a decree may be entered declaring her a feme sole for mercantile or trading purposes	A feme sole trader may in her own name contract and be contracted with, sue and be sued. Her contracts and obligations are binding upon her, and all of her separate property not exempt from execution is subject to her debts and liable under execution therefor
West Virginia... C. 1931, Ch. 48, Art. 3, Sec. 17	A married woman, separately or with any other person, may carry on any profession, trade, occupation or business. The equipment, stock, etc., used therein, and the issues and profits thereof, together with her earnings realized from such profession, trade, etc., shall be her own property not subject to the control or disposal of the husband nor liable for his debts		

[§ 187

TABLE XCIV (*Continued*)

Jurisdiction and Citation	In General	Process, Decree, etc.	Effect of Order, or Decree, etc.
Wisconsin ...... St. 1931, Secs. 246.06, 246.07	When the husband deserts her, or from drunkenness, profligacy, or any cause neglects or refuses to provide for her support or support, etc., of children, the wife shall have the right to transact business in her own name, collect and receive the profits of such business and the earnings of herself and minor children, and apply the same for the support of herself and children. Such business and earnings are not subject to husband's control or liable for his debts. The wife has all the remedies of a single woman in regard to her business		
Wyoming .... R. S. 1931, Sec. 69(105)	A married woman may carry on any trade or business on her sole and separate account, and the earnings thereof shall be her "whole" and separate property and may be used and invested by her in her own name. She may sue and be sued in regard to her trade, etc., as if sole. Her property acquired by her trade, etc., may be taken on execution against her (except when otherwise exempt)		

[1] In **California** and **Montana**, the notice must specify the day upon which application will be made, the nature and place of business proposed, and the name of the husband. In **Nevada**, only the date of the intended application and the nature of the proposed business must be set forth.

[2] In **California** and **Montana**, the husband's creditor may oppose the application by filing a written opposition, verified, either containing a specific denial of the truth of any material allegation of the petition or setting forth that the application is made for the purpose of defrauding him, or to prevent him, or that it will prevent him, from collecting his debt.

[3] The sole trader (**California, Montana**) or the applicant, before order is made (**Nevada**), must make an affidavit to the effect that her application was made in good faith to enable her to

§ 187]

TABLE XCIV (*Concluded*)

support herself and not with intent to defraud, etc., the husband's creditors, and (in **California** and **Nevada**) that, of the moneys to be used in her business, not more than $500 have come directly or indirectly from the husband. In all three jurisdictions, the judgment or order, together with the affidavit or oath, must be duly recorded in the county, or counties, in which the sole trader carries on business.

4 The wife in **Louisiana** is considered a "public merchant" if she carries on a separate trade, but not if she retails only the merchandise belonging to the commerce carried on by her husband (C. C., Art. 131). Even before the wife had any general contractual capacity, and could contract only with the authorization of the husband or the judge, the authorization of the husband to her commercial contracts was presumed by law, if he permitted her to trade in her own name (C. C., Art. 1786).

5 In **North Carolina**, a wife who is the undisclosed principal of her husband or other agent conducting a business as trader or merchant is deemed a free trader as to all debts contracted in the course of such business; and the stock of goods used therein is liable for the debts contracted by the person in charge of the business (C. 1927, Sec. 3292).

6 A **Pennsylvania** statute adopted in 1718 provides that wives of absent mariners left "at shop-keeping or to work for their livelihood at any other trade" are deemed feme sole traders (St. 1920 [West], Sec. 14579). By a later law, procedure is outlined whereby such a wife may be judicially decreed a feme sole trader (Sec. 14580). Section 14581, adopted in 1855, provides that the wife may have all the rights, etc., granted by the 1718 act, when the husband neglects or refuses to provide for her or deserts her. This latter section appears broader in scope than Section 14582, adopted in 1915, amended in 1927, and outlined in the table above.

REFERENCES

Book

STIMSON, F. J. *American Statute Law,* Secs. 6520–23 (1886).

Note

"Wife as a Public Merchant, Art. 131 of the Louisiana Civil Code," *Lob's Sons* v. *Karnofsky* (La. App.); 144 So. 164 (1932)—7 Tulane L. Rev. 446–47 (1933). (Reversed, 177 La. 229; 148 So. 34 [1933].)

Section 188. Dower—In General

CROSS REFERENCES: Dower, abolition and statutory substitutes, **Sec. 189**; Curtesy, in general, **Sec. 215**; Curtesy, abolition and statutory substitutes, **Sec. 216**

At common law the widow was entitled as her dower estate to the use for life of a one-third part of the lands and tenements of which the husband was seized at any time during coverture in fee simple or fee tail, provided that her issue, if any, could have inherited such property. It was not necessary, however, that issue actually be born. Until his death she had a protected expectancy known as "inchoate dower"—an interest which constituted an encumbrance upon his lands, and which

[§ 188

could not be defeated by his sole act. Upon his death, her interest became "consummate" or "vested"; although, before assignment, it still was not regarded as an estate (see **Sec. 208**). The purpose of dower was to provide for the widow's support after the husband's death; and dower was, in effect, an extension of his inter vivos duty of support. The doctrine that "life, liberty and dower are dear to the law" developed at a time when the wife was almost completely shorn of her property rights by coverture; dower was then necessary and proper for her protection. Dower differed from the husband's curtesy interest in three main respects: (*a*) the size of the interest; (*b*) the necessity of birth of issue; (*c*) the nature of the interest during coverture (see **Sec. 215**). Dower was adopted in the United States as a part of the common law, and early statutes often codified the common-law rules.

The common law, however, has been changed in England. By the Dower Act of 1833 (3 and 4 Wm. IV, c. 105, ss. 4, 6, 7, 9) the husband was given power to defeat dower by conveying or devising his property, or by declaring in his deed or will that the wife was not to be entitled to dower. Furthermore, the Administration of Estates Act of 1925 (15 Geo. V, c. 23, s. 45[*c*]) abolished dower completely. Compare the English legislation with the tendency in the United States to increase the provisions for the widow's support by dower legislation and by homestead, exempt property, and allowance statutes (see **Sec. 228**).

The present section and the sections on dower which follow (**Secs. 189–214**) are concerned primarily with the share which the widow is entitled to receive from the real or personal estate of the husband whether he dies testate or intestate, i.e., the share which he cannot defeat by his will. Such interest of the widow is included, although it may not be called "dower" and although it may differ materially from common-law dower. A complete picture of the widow's property rights on the husband's death has been attempted (see especially **Sec. 189**), with three exceptions. The eight community-property states (**Arizona, California, Idaho, Louisiana, Nevada, New Mexico, Texas, Washington**) are not included in the present group of sections. They have been discussed in **Section 178** because of their peculiar system of marital property. The right of the widow to share in intestate property of the husband as a true statutory heir or distributee is considered in **Section 227**. Her rights in the homestead and other exempt property, and to an allowance for support, are dealt with in **Section 228**.

The most pronounced reaction of the writer after having examined the statutes in this field is a feeling of disgust for the slipshod methods

§ 188]

of lawmakers. Many statutes are practically incomprehensible without a knowledge of local practice and of the legislative and case history in the particular jurisdiction. The statutes are filled with ancient matter which, coupled with piecemeal innovations, forms an inconsistent, ambiguous hodgepodge. In no field is there more evidence of haphazard, fragmentary legislation; and, in most jurisdictions, no field is more deserving of a complete renovation. As in other fields of property law, the inertia of legislatures is apparent; it is difficult to obtain an abandonment of such a venerable institution as dower. Many jurisdictions have declared that dower is abolished, but have failed to do away with it completely; the result is a new system couched in dower terms and confused by dower rules.

In spite of the lack of uniformity in legislation relating to dower, the following tendencies have been noted: (*a*) to treat husband and wife alike as to the rights of the surviving spouse (see **Secs. 189, 216**); (*b*) to abolish the inchoate interest of the wife during coverture, and to confine her dower or statutory substitute to property owned by the husband at his death (**Secs. 189, 191**); (*c*) to increase the amount of the share given to the widow (**Sec. 190**); (*d*) to give the wife a protected interest of some sort in the personal property of the husband, as well as in his realty (**Secs. 189, 191**). The advisability of these tendencies will be considered later, in connection with criticisms of the statutory situation.

It is interesting to note the types of statutory schemes that have been evolved. They are considered in detail in **Section 189,** but may be summarized briefly as follows: (1) Fifteen jurisdictions have substantially retained common-law dower. (2) Eight jurisdictions have retained common-law dower in general, but have added other more generous rights, e.g., a fee interest in realty which the widow may elect to take in lieu of dower. (3) Ten jurisdictions have abolished common-law dower in name or in effect, and have substituted a statutory system in which the wife has a protected inchoate interest during coverture which the husband cannot defeat by his sole act. (4) Seven jurisdictions have abolished dower and have substituted a statutory scheme whereby the widow is, in reality, a forced heir. Her inchoate interest during coverture is abolished, and she takes an absolute share in the property owned by the husband at his death. (5) Two jurisdictions have done away with any protected interest of the wife (except as to her homestead rights [see **Sec. 228**]); she is entitled to share only in intestate property (**North Dakota, South Dakota**). (6) The remaining one of the forty-three jurisdictions (**Ohio**) has an odd system unlike those described above (see **Sec. 189**). The statutes of **North Dakota** and **South Dakota** stand out because they are completely at variance with the general tendency in the United States to increase the wife's protected share. There are many qualifications and limitations in the foregoing systems, as to which later sections must be consulted.

A survey of the legislation in the field of dower reveals certain other defects subject to criticism, in addition to the uncertainty and inconsistency already referred to. These defects are pointed out in subsequent sections, but it is felt that the general picture will be clearer if the criticisms are summarized briefly, and the recommendations noted.

First and foremost, is the question of dower itself. The writer has already indicated his distaste for such a law-given right. It is no longer applicable to modern property conditions or to the present status of husband and wife; and the widespread statutory changes evidence the fact that legislatures have recognized its inappropriateness. The mistake of the majority of jurisdictions has been the building of new statutory schemes upon the foundation of dower. The result is an anomalous situation where ancient rules supplement statutory rights of a different character, and where many objectionable features of dower are retained because they have been overlooked. The desirable remedy, found in a few jurisdictions, is the complete abolition of dower and the adoption of a new system free of dower formulae and dogma. Such a system should recognize three general principles: first, husband and wife should be treated alike; second, the survivor's share should attach to both real and personal property of the deceased spouse; third, the legitimate rights of creditors should not be disregarded. For an example of a statutory scheme which includes the principles above, the reader is referred to the **New York** provisions adopted in 1930, as set forth in Table XCV of **Section 189.**

There are three main factors in the present lack of uniformity as to the amount of property to which the widow is entitled in the various jurisdictions. First, the proportion of the husband's property given to her, and the nature of the estate which she takes therein, vary considerably (**Secs. 189, 190**). For example, some jurisdictions give her a one-third part for life, whereas others give her one-half in fee. In several jurisdictions, she is entitled to dissent from the husband's will and take a share equal to that which she would have taken if the husband had died intestate. Where there are no next of kin, these statutes enable the widow to take all of the estate as against the husband's will—a result

§ 188]

that is unjustified. In the second place, there is a great variation as to the property subject to the widow's interest (**Secs. 189, 191**). Thus, in some jurisdictions she shares in both real and personal property; in others, she shares only in realty. Some have retained a protected inchoate interest which attaches to any realty during coverture; others confine her share to property owned by the husband at his death. Third, the jurisdictions are not agreed as to whether her interest is subject to the husband's debts, or whether it is given only from his surplus estate (**Secs. 189, 190**).

It is difficult to formulate a method of determining the widow's share which will be simple in its operation and yet which will include certain factors believed by the writer to be advisable. The share should depend, in part, upon the amount of the widow's own property and upon the size of the husband's estate. Subject to such limitations, an absolute one-third part of all of the real and personal property does not seem excessive. However, it is submitted that her share should be limited to property owned by the husband at his death; there should be no protected interest during coverture. The theoretical protection of the wife from such an interest is outweighed by the disadvantage of the restriction upon the alienation of the husband's property, together with the controversies and litigation arising therefrom. Finally, since the widow is to be given an absolute share, her interest should not be entirely exempt from the husband's debts. An exemption up to a small stated value might be advisable depending upon the amount of protection she is entitled to receive under the homestead and allowance statutes (see **Sec. 228**).

The question of barring dower presents another source of confusion and uncertainty at the present time (see **Sec. 195**). The situation could be materially clarified in three respects. (1) The method of barring dower by jointure is inconsistent with the modern freedom of husband and wife to contract; and the antiquated jointure statutes should be abolished (**Sec. 196**). (2) To remove any uncertainty on the question, it should be provided expressly that husband and wife can, by antenuptial or postnuptial contract, control the right of the surviving spouse to a protected share in the decedent's property, such contracts to be subject to rules respecting persons in confidential relations (**Secs. 197, 198**). (3) It has already been suggested that the wife should have no protected interest during coverture. If it were so provided, barring dower by deed, a source of litigation at present (**Sec. 200**), would be obsolete.

The husband's inability to defeat the wife's interest by his will is a fundamental and proper part of the dower legislation. However, she

[§ 188

should not be entitled to her law-given share and also to a testamentary provision; consequently, the husband may require her to elect between the two rights (**Sec. 199**). Statutes requiring election and prescribing the necessary formalities have been widely adopted (see **Secs. 199, 205–7**). In general, they are comprehensive and definite, and, with minor changes (see **Sec. 205**), should form a part of any system which gives the wife a protected interest.

The question of forfeiture of dower and statutory substitutes for the misconduct of the wife has received relatively little attention from the legislatures. The few statutes which have been passed are, in the writer's opinion, too lenient (see **Secs. 202–3**). Serious misconduct such as desertion or adultery should work a forfeiture of the widow's protected interest. Stringent rules would not be unfair if they applied in like manner to both spouses. A careful revision of the legislation on this subject is needed.

It is pointed out in **Sections 208** and **210–13** that statutes in many jurisdictions have materially simplified the technical common-law rules regarding assignment of dower. Such remedial legislation is necessary if dower or a similar interest is retained. But under the suggested statutory scheme whereby the widow would be, in reality, a forced heir, the admeasurement of her interest by an independent proceeding would seem to be unnecessary. Her share could properly be set off as part of the settlement and distribution of the estate in like manner as the share of an heir or devisee. Also, if she is looked upon as an heir, although a forced one, many of the difficulties concerning her rights in the interim between the husband's death and assignment (see **Secs. 208, 214**) would be obviated.

The widow's right to share in the husband's property at his death constitutes an important phase of the marital relation; and the writer feels justified in the extended criticism above. The recommendations made have been motivated by a desire for certainty, simplicity, uniformity, and equal rights of husband and wife. The fact that several jurisdictions have adopted entirely new statutory schemes in place of dower is encouraging. The writer regretfully adds, however, that not all of the recent legislation has been satisfactory. **Florida** materially changed the nature of dower in 1933 but retained the name and certain of the dower incidents. The tendency to carry dower into a new system is not easily overcome.

For the reader's convenience, it is suggested that **Sections 189, 215,** and **216** be read immediately in conjunction with the present section.

§ 188]

REFERENCES

Books

BISHOP, JOEL P. *Commentaries on the Law of Married Women,* Vol. I, Secs. 239–470 (1873).

POLLOCK, SIR FREDERICK, and FREDERICK WILLIAM MAITLAND, *The History of English Law,* 2d ed., II, 147, 374, 390, 394, 404, 420–28 (1899).

SCRIBNER, CHARLES H. *A Treatise on the Law of Dower,* 2d ed. (1883).

TIFFANY, HERBERT T. *The Law of Real Property and Other Interests in Land,* 2d ed., Vol. 1, Secs. 208–36 (1920).

Articles

EAGLETON, WILLIAM L. "Introduction to the Intestacy Act and the Dower Rights Act," 20 Ia. L. Rev. 241–43 (1935).

———. "The Dower Rights Act," 20 Ia. L. Rev. 261–65 (1935).

SAYRE, PAUL L. "Husband and Wife as Statutory Heirs," 42 Harv. L. Rev. 330–64 (1929).

SULLIVAN, JOSEPH D. "Passing of Dower and Curtesy," 19 Geo. L. Jour. 306–15 (1931).

Annotation

"Constitutionality of Statutes in Relation to Dower," 20 A. L. R. 1330–34 (1922).

Section 189. Dower—Abolition and Statutory Substitutes

CROSS REFERENCES: Dower, in general, **Sec. 188**; Extent of dower and property subject to, **Secs. 190, 191**; Curtesy, abolished, modified, etc., **Secs. 216** *et seq.;* Widow's share of real and personal property of intestate husband, **Sec. 227**; Dower and homestead, exempt property, widow's allowance, **Sec. 228**

In the eight community-property states (**Arizona, California, Idaho, Louisiana, Nevada, New Mexico, Texas, Washington**), the common-law institution of dower either was never recognized or has been expressly or impliedly abolished. Dower and curtesy, whether as at common law or as modified by statute, are inconsistent with the fundamental concepts and purpose of the community-property system. These jurisdictions give the surviving spouse no general right to share in the separate property of the deceased spouse except as heir in case of intestacy, and hence are excluded from consideration in the discussion of this and following sections. The survivor's interest in the marital gains upon dissolution of the community is discussed in **Section 178.**

[§ 189

In the table at the end of this section an attempt is made to present a tabular picture of the property rights (exclusive of homestead and provisions for temporary support) which the other forty-three jurisdictions accord to the surviving wife and which are protected from the husband's testamentary disposition. That picture is necessarily incomplete unless viewed in connection with the matters developed in subsequent sections also dealing with dower and substitutions therefor. The statutes collected in the table vary so widely in detail that only a general summary of them seems worth while.

DOWER AND STATUTORY SHARE IN REAL PROPERTY

The statutes of sixteen states purport to expressly abolish dower (**Colorado, Connecticut, Indiana, Kansas, Maine, Minnesota, Mississippi, Nebraska, New York, North Dakota, Oklahoma, Pennsylvania, South Dakota, Utah, Vermont, Wyoming**); and in most of the other jurisdictions it has been sheared of some of its common-law attributes. The American legislator, however, has been reluctant to banish this venerable institution from the law; and even in those jurisdictions which have abolished dower the substitute systems established often incorporate many of the features of the common law. The statutes considered in this section are hardly susceptible of any measured classification, but for purposes of convenience they may be grouped as follows:

1. **North Dakota, South Dakota.** The statutes of these two states stand out as striking exceptions to the general trend of legislative thought in this country. Dower has been abolished, and apparently nothing of a substantial nature has been substituted. Aside from limitations as to homestead, exempt property, etc., the husband has complete testamentary control of his property.

2. **Alabama, Alaska, Arkansas, Delaware, District of Columbia, Georgia, Hawaii, Illinois, Kentucky, Maryland, Massachusetts, Michigan, Missouri, Montana, New Hampshire, New Jersey, North Carolina, Ohio, Oregon, Rhode Island, South Carolina, Tennessee, Virginia, West Virginia.** In these twenty-four jurisdictions, common-law dower is more or less substantially retained. The widow is entitled to an estate for life in one-third part, except in **New Jersey** and **Oregon** (and, in certain situations, in **Alabama** and **Arkansas**), where her dower has been raised to a life estate in one-half part. Inchoate dower during marriage is preserved in all but four jurisdictions, in which the widow's estate attaches to lands of which the husband died "seized," etc. (**Alaska, Georgia, New Hampshire, Ten-**

nessee) or to lands to which he obtained title "in right of his wife" (**Georgia**). Apparently in these four jurisdictions, the husband may defeat the widow's dower by his sole conveyance, unless fraudulently made for that purpose.

a) In fifteen of the jurisdictions above (**Alabama, Alaska, Delaware, District of Columbia, Georgia, Hawaii, Kentucky, New Jersey, North Carolina, Oregon, Rhode Island, South Carolina, Tennessee, Virginia, West Virginia**), the widow may demand her dower if not barred thereof, but, as against the husband's will, she is not privileged to elect a distributive share of his lands in lieu of her dower.

b) In eight of the jurisdictions above, the widow is entitled to other and more generous rights. **Illinois, Michigan, Missouri,** and **New Hampshire** permit her to elect to take an absolute share of the estate of which the husband dies seized or owning, the amount thereof depending upon the existence, absence, or number of lineal descendants. In **Montana,** she has a similar choice when the husband leaves no lineal descendants. It is difficult, however, to determine from some of these statutes whether the right to dower is a prerequisite to the right of election. **Illinois, Missouri,** and **Montana** are express to the effect that the distributive share is in lieu of dower in the estate of which the husband "died seized." In **Maryland** and **Massachusetts,** dower is deemed waived in favor of rights under the statute of descent unless an affirmative election to take the same is made; and if the husband dies testate, the widow may dissent from his will and demand a distributive share of his estate. Finally, **Arkansas** allows the widow an absolute share of the real property of which the husband died seized if the property is not ancestral and he leaves no children.

c) While retaining inchoate dower, **Ohio** has virtually abolished vested dower by a rather unique statute passed in 1931. Under it the widow's dower is deemed barred upon the husband's death except as to property conveyed or encumbered by him; and in lieu of the estate thus barred, she is entitled to a distributive share of his property under the statute of descent and distribution.

3. **Colorado, Connecticut, Mississippi, New York, Oklahoma, Vermont, Wyoming.** With the possible exception of **Vermont,** dower has been completely abolished in these seven jurisdictions. The wife has no inchoate interest which is protected from destruction during coverture. As a substitute for dower, she is entitled to an absolute share of his estate in fee (except in **Connecticut,** where her interest endures for

[§ 189

life only), which the husband cannot defeat by his will without her consent. The **Vermont** statute refers to real estate of which the husband dies "seized" and perhaps retains much of the dower formula in respect to the property subject to the widow's claim.

4. **Florida, Indiana, Iowa, Kansas, Maine, Minnesota, Nebraska, Pennsylvania, Utah, Wisconsin.** In these ten jurisdictions, the widow is entitled to an absolute share of the husband's real property in fee simple, fixed at one-third or one-half or based upon the intestate table. Statutes expressly abolishing dower were found in all except **Florida, Iowa,** and **Wisconsin,** where the distributive share is called "dower." In all of them, however, the wife has an inchoate interest during marriage which in varying degrees is as substantial as inchoate dower at common law. Her statutory share, with some exceptions, attaches to all lands of which the husband was seized or possessed, etc., during coverture (**Iowa, Kansas, Maine, Minnesota, Nebraska, Utah, Wisconsin**), or to lands conveyed by the husband without the wife's joinder as well as to lands of which he died seized or owning (**Florida, Indiana, Pennsylvania**). In spite of the substantial nature of the wife's interest during coverture and the protection which it receives, the statutes of **Indiana, Maine, Minnesota,** and **Nebraska** are express to the effect that she takes by descent or by inheritance. Obviously, these terms are not used in their ordinary technical sense.

"Dower" and Statutory Share in Personal Property

In ten jurisdictions, no statutes were found which secure to the widow a distributive share of the husband's personal estate, except as his heir in case of intestacy (**Alaska, Delaware, Georgia, New Jersey, North Dakota, Oregon, Rhode Island, South Carolina, South Dakota, Utah**). By way of comparison, sixteen jurisdictions give the surviving husband no greater rights in the wife's personal estate (**Sec. 216**). In the remaining thirty-three jurisdictions, the widow is entitled to a statutory share of the personalty, free from the testamentary control of the husband. This share is called "dower" in **Arkansas** and **Florida**; and in **Hawaii** it is said to be "by way of dower." It will be observed that, in general, the wife has no protected inchoate interest in the husband's personal property similar to her inchoate dower in his lands. She shares only in such property as he may die owning. However, a statute recently adopted in **Florida** (1933) apparently provides that the widow is entitled to "dower" in personal property conveyed by the husband without her relinquishment, as well as in the personalty owned by him

§ 189]

at death. Although the terms of the statute seem clear, the writer hesitates to be dogmatic, for, if such interpretation is correct, the statute is definitely out of line with legislation in other jurisdictions. The practical disadvantages of such a provision are obvious. The share which the widow takes is an absolute one in all but **Connecticut,** where it endures for life only. In some, it is fixed at one-third or one-half, while in others it is based upon the table of distribution. Almost universally, it is subject to estate creditors (see table following). The recent **Florida** statute, however, exempts the dower in personalty from the decedent's debts, estate and inheritance taxes, and expenses of administration, except that the lien of a person in possession of personal property is not thereby impaired.

In the table which follows, the statutory wording has been reproduced so far as is practicable.

TABLE XCV*

Dower and Statutory Substitutes Therefor

Jurisdiction[1] and Citation	Dower Expressly Abolished	Extent	Property Subject to (See Also Sec. 191)	Share in Personal Property	Election between Will or Dower and Distributive Share; Miscellaneous (See Also **Secs.** 199, 205-7)
	Share in Real Property				
Alabama .... C. 1923, Secs. 7427-30; Sec. 10593, amd. by Sess. L. 1932, No. 304, p. 307		Dower in one-half if husband leaves no lineal descendants and his estate is solvent; but if insolvent, dower in one-third part. Dower in one-third part if husband leaves lineal descendants whether his estate be solvent or not. But extent of widow's dower depends also on extent of her separate property[2]	All lands of which husband was seized in fee during marriage, or of which another was seized in fee to his use; or to which at death he had a perfect equity, having paid all the purchase money therefor	See next column	If widow dissents from provision made for her in husband's will, or if no provisions made for her, she may claim her dower and intestate share of personal estate,[3] except that if there are no children or their descendants, and the personal estate exceeds $50,000 in value at time of the return of the appraisement, she shall take the first $50,000 of the personal estate. But extent of dower and share of personalty depends on extent of her separate property[2]
Alaska .... Comp. L. 1913, Secs. 462, 595		Dower: use during life of one-third part in value	All lands of which husband dies seized of an estate of inheritance	Widow is distributee in case of intestacy[3]	

* See pages 368-71 for all numbered footnotes to this table.

TABLE XCV (*Continued*)

| Jurisdiction[1] and Citation | Share in Real Property | | | Share in Personal Property | Election between Will or Dower and Distributive Share; Miscellaneous (See Also Secs. 199, 205–7) |
	Dower Expressly Abolished	Extent	Property Subject to (See Also Sec. 191)		
Arkansas .... Crawf. and Moses, Dig. 1921, Secs. 3514, 3535–36, 3543		Widow is endowed of a third part (but see also footnote 4)	All lands of which husband was seized of an estate of inheritance during marriage	As a part of her dower, widow is entitled absolutely to one-third of the personal estate, including choses in action, of which husband died seized or possessed (but see also footnote 4)	
Colorado .... Comp. L. 1921, G. S., Secs. 5151, 5184	Yes	See last column	See last column	See next column	Husband cannot devise or bequeath away from widow more than one-half of his property without her written consent executed after his death
Connecticut .... G. S. 1930, Secs. 5154, 5156	Yes[5]	The use for life of one-third in value	All the real property legally or equitably owned by husband at death, after payment of debts and estate charges	The use for life of one-third in value of all personal property legally or equitably owned by husband at death, after payment of debts and estate charges	Wife has no interest in husband's property except as to her share as survivor
Delaware .... R. C. 1915, Secs. 3303, 3382		A third part for life to hold as tenant in dower, free from debts of husband	All lands and tenements of which the husband was seized of an estate of inheritance during marriage	Widow is distributee in case of intestacy[3]	
District of Columbia ... C. 1929, T. 14, Secs. 28, 29, 38–41		Dower (as at common law)	All lands of husband held by equitable or legal title during marriage, whether held by him at death or not	See next column	If widow renounces provision made for her in husband's will, or if no provision made for her, she is entitled, in addition to dower, to her intestate share of personal property[3]

TABLE XCV (*Continued*)

Jurisdiction[1] and Citation	Share in Real Property			Share in Personal Property	Election between Will or Dower and Distributive Share; Miscellaneous (See Also **Secs.** 199, 205–7)
	Dower Expressly Abolished	Extent	Property Subject to (See Also **Sec. 191**)		
Florida .... Sess. L. 1933, Ch. 16103, Sec. 35, p. 553		One-third in fee (called dower), free from decedent's debts, all estate and inheritance taxes, and expenses of administration (mortgage lien is not impaired)	The real property owned by husband at his death or that conveyed by him without relinquishment by wife	Dower: one-third part absolutely of personal property owned by husband at his death or that conveyed by him without relinquishment by wife, free from debts, etc., in like manner as the real property (lien of person in possession of personalty is not impaired)[6]	Whenever widow is not satisfied with her intestate share or share under the will, or both, she may elect (in manner provided for) to take dower in real and personal property
Georgia .... C. 1926, C. C., Sec. 3832; C. of Prac., Sec. 5247		Dower: estate for life in one-third according to valuation (to include dwelling house, which is not to be valued unless in a town or city)	Lands of which husband was seized and possessed at death, or in which he obtained title in right of his wife	Widow is distributee in case of intestacy[3]	Husband may "bequeath his entire estate to strangers, to the exclusion of his wife . . . ." (except her dower)[7]
Hawaii .... R. L. 1925, Sec. 3017		Widow is endowed of one-third part	All lands owned by husband during marriage in fee simple	Widow is entitled "by way of dower" to an absolute property in one-third part of husband's movable effects in possession or reducible to possession at time of his death, after payment of his debts	

[§ 189

TABLE XCV (*Continued*)

Jurisdiction[1] and Citation	Share in Real Property			Share in Personal Property	Election between Will or Dower and Distributive Share; Miscellaneous (See Also Secs. 199, 205–7)
	Dower Expressly Abolished	Extent	Property Subject to (See Also Sec. 191)		
Illinois .... Cahill, R. S. 1931, Ch. 41, Secs. 1, 10, 12		Widow is endowed of a third part	All lands of which husband was seized of an estate of inheritance during marriage, including equitable estates	If husband leaves lineal descendants, widow is entitled to one-third of all personal property owned by him at death, after debts and estate charges are paid; and to one-half thereof if no lineal descendants survive	After renouncing will, widow may waive dower in lands of which husband dies seized in favor of absolute estate of one-third of each parcel of real estate which husband owns at death, after payment of debts. If husband dies testate, widow may elect, in lieu of dower in estate of which husband dies seized and of statutory share in personal property, an absolute estate as follows: one-half of the real and personal estate after payment of debts and estate charges if husband leaves no lineal descendants, and one-third thereof if husband leaves lineal descendants
Indiana .... Burns, Ann. St. 1926, Secs. 3337, 3343, 3349, 3377	Yes	One-third descends to widow in fee simple free from demands of creditors; but when value of husband's real estate (a) exceeds $10,000, or (b) exceeds $20,000, she takes (a) one-fourth only, or (b) one-fifth only as against creditors	Real estate which husband owns at death, including equitable interests. Real estate of which husband was seized in fee simple during marriage and in the conveyance of which the wife did not join	If husband dies testate, one-third of his personal estate descends to widow, subject to its proportion of decedent's debts	

§ 189]

TABLE XCV (*Continued*)

Jurisdiction[1] and Citation	Share in Real Property			Share in Personal Property	Election between Will or Dower and Distributive Share; Miscellaneous (See Also **Secs.** 199, 205–7)
	Dower Expressly Abolished	Extent	Property Subject to (See Also Sec. 191)		
Iowa .... C. 1927, Secs. 11846, 11986, 11990, 11992		One-third in value in fee, called dower (to include homestead)	All the legal or equitable estates in real property possessed by husband during marriage, which have not been sold on execution or other judicial sale	Personal property "not necessary for the payment of debts, nor otherwise disposed of," is distributed to the same persons and in the same proportions as real estate[8]	Husband may dispose of his property by will, subject to "the distributive share of his estate given by law" to the surviving wife[8]
Kansas .... R. S. 1923, Secs. 22(101), 22(108), 22(127), 22(130), 22(238)	Yes	One-half in value in fee simple	All the real estate in which husband during marriage had a legal or equitable interest, which has not been sold on execution or other judicial sale, and which is not necessary for payment of debts	Personal property after payment of debts, not otherwise disposed of according to law, is distributed in same proportions as real estate	Husband cannot "bequeath" away from wife more than one-half of his property without her consent
Kentucky .... Carroll, St. 1922, Secs. 2132, 2134		Life estate in one-third	All the real estate of which husband or anyone for his use was seized of an estate in fee simple during coverture. Seisin in law is sufficient	An absolute estate in one-half of the surplus personalty left by husband	

[§ 189

TABLE XCV (*Continued*)

Jurisdiction[1] and Citation	Share in Real Property			Share in Personal Property	Election between Will or Dower and Distributive Share; Miscellaneous (See Also Secs. 199, 205–7)
	Dower Expressly Abolished	Extent	Property Subject to (See Also Sec. 191)		
Maine .... R. S. 1930, Ch. 89, Secs. 1, 8, 13, 14, 20	Yes	Widow is heir of husband in case of intestacy.[3] In any event, one-third descends to her free from payment of debts (see last column)	Real estate of deceased husband, including all of which he was seized during coverture	Widow is distributee in case of intestacy.[3] Surplus personalty of intestate is distributed in same manner as real estate (see next column)	If widow waives provision for her in husband's will, or if no provision is made for her, she is entitled to the same share of real estate, and the same distributive share of personal estate, as if husband died intestate[3, 9]
Maryland ...... Bagby, Ann. C. 1924, Ch. 45, Sec. 6; Ch. 46, Secs. 3, 4; Ch. 93, Secs. 311–14		Dower (as at common law)	Lands held by husband at any time during coverture by equitable as well as legal title	Widow's "legal share" is one-third of surplus personalty if husband left descendants; otherwise, one-half thereof	Unless affirmative election to take dower is made, the same is presumed to have been waived in favor of share of lands under statute of descent. If widow renounces testamentary provision in her favor, or if no provision is made for her, she may take dower and legal share of personalty, or legal share of both real and personal property. Legal share of lands is one-third as heir if husband left descendants; otherwise, one-half as heir
Massachusetts .. G. L. 1932, Ch. 189, Sec. 1; Ch. 190, Sec. 1; Ch. 191, Sec. 15		Dower (as at common law)	Widow is entitled to "dower at common law" in her deceased husband's land	See next column	Unless affirmative election to take dower is made, the same is presumed to have been waived in favor of share of lands under statute of descent. Widow may waive any provisions in husband's will for her, and claim her intestate share of real and personal property[3] (with certain exceptions)[10]

§ 189]

TABLE XCV (*Continued*)

Jurisdiction[1] and Citation	Share in Real Property			Share in Personal Property	Election between Will or Dower and Distributive Share; Miscellaneous (See Also Secs. 199, 205–7)
	Dower Expressly Abolished	Extent	Property Subject to (See Also Sec. 191)		
Michigan .... Comp. L. 1929, Sec. 13072; Sec. 13085, amd. by Sess. L. 1931, No. 243, p. 422; Sec. 15564		Dower: the use for life of one-third part	All lands of which husband was seized of an estate of inheritance during marriage	Husband's testamentary disposition of his personal property is subject to election of widow to take her intestate share up to $5,000 and, of the residue, one-half of her intestate share[3]	If lands devised to wife or other provision made for her in husband's will, she may elect to take such lands or other provision, to take her dower, or to take her intestate share of real estate[3] left by husband. If election to take intestate share enables her to take all of husband's real estate, then such election is limited so as to enable her to take one half thereof absolutely, and other half goes to her subject to any devise or legacy in husband's will
Minnesota ...... G. S. 1923, Secs. 8720, 8726	Yes[11]	Undivided one-third by inheritance subject to proportional share of decedent's debts not paid out of personal estate, and to all judgment liens	Lands of which husband was seized or possessed during marriage to the disposition of which by will or otherwise the wife has not consented in writing except such as has been sold by judicial partition proceedings or appropriated to payment of husband's debts by execution or judicial sale, by general assignment for benefit of creditors or by insolvency proceedings	One-third of surplus personal estate by inheritance, free from any testamentary disposition to which wife has not consented in writing	

[§ 189

TABLE XCV (*Continued*)

| Jurisdiction[1] and Citation | Share in Real Property | | | Share in Personal Property | Election between Will or Dower and Distributive Share; Miscellaneous (See Also Secs. 199, 205–7) |
	Dower Expressly Abolished	Extent	Property Subject to (See Also Sec. 191)		
Mississippi ..... C. 1930, Secs. 1404, 1942, 3560–63	Yes	See last column	See last column	See next column	If husband's will does not make "satisfactory" provision for widow, she may renounce the same, with certain limitations,[12] and elect to take her intestate share[3] in both real and personal property (but in no event is she entitled to more than one-half thereof). She is entitled to same share if will makes no provision for her
Missouri .... R. S. 1929, Secs. 318, 323, 325–28	Widow is endowed of a third part to hold during life	All lands of which husband or any other to his use was seized of an estate of inheritance during marriage	If husband leaves descendants, an absolute share in personal estate belonging to husband at death equal to a child's share. If husband dies without any child or other descendants in being capable of inheriting, one-half of the personal estate subject to payment of debts	If husband leaves descendants, and a child of the marriage[14] is living, the widow may, in lieu of dower in lands of which husband died seized, elect to be endowed absolutely in a child's share of such lands, subject to payment of debts. If husband leaves no descendant capable of inheriting, widow may, in lieu of dower, elect to take absolutely one-half of the real and personal estate belonging to husband at death, subject to payment of debts[13]	
Montana .... R. C. 1921, Secs. 5813, 5821	Widow is endowed of a third part	All lands of which husband was seized of an estate of inheritance during marriage. Equitable estates are subject to dower	See footnote 15	If husband dies leaving no children or descendants thereof, the widow may, in lieu of dower in estate of which husband died seized, elect to take absolutely one-half of all real estate remaining after payment of all debts and claims against husband	

§ 189]

TABLE XCV (*Continued*)

Jurisdiction[1] and Citation	Share in Real Property			Share in Personal Property	Election between Will or Dower and Distributive Share; Miscellaneous (See Also Secs. 199, 205–7)
	Dower Expressly Abolished	Extent	Property Subject to (See Also Sec. 191)		
Nebraska .... Comp. St. 1929, Secs. 30(101), 30(103)– 30(104), 30(107)	Yes	Widow shares under statute of descent[3] (see last column)	All real estate of which husband was seized of an estate of inheritance during marriage, or in which he was possessed of an equitable or legal interest at death, and which has not been sold under execution or judicial sale or "lawfully devised" descends to widow, subject to debts and right of homestead	Widow shares in personal estate not "lawfully disposed of" by will, under the statute of distribution[3] (see next column)	If husband makes testamentary provision for widow, she may elect to take under the will, or "by inheritance, descent and distribution the interest in the estate of the deceased, provided by law"[3]
New Hampshire. Pub. L. 1926, Ch. 306, Secs. 3, 5; Secs. 10, 11, amd. by Sess. L. 1933, Ch. 118, p. 171		Widow is endowed of so much of husband's real estate as will produce a yearly income equal to one-third of the yearly income thereof at the time husband died, "or parted with his title"	Widow is entitled to dower "in the real estate of which her husband died seized"	Widow of testate or intestate, by waiving provision of will in her favor, if any, is in addition to dower and homestead rights entitled to the following distributive share of personal estate after payment of debts and expenses of administration: one-third, if husband leaves issue; $5,000 of the value thereof and one-half of the remainder if he leaves no issue and dies testate; $7,500 of the value and one-half the remainder if he leaves no issue and dies intestate	Widow of testate or intestate, by waiving testamentary provision in her favor, if any, and releasing her dower and homestead right, is entitled instead thereof to the following portion of all the real estate of which husband died seized, after payment of debts and expenses of administration: one-third part in fee if husband leaves issue surviving; $5,000 of value thereof and one-half of the remainder if he leaves no issue and dies testate; $7,500 of value and one-half the remainder if he leaves no issue and dies intestate

[§ 189

TABLE XCV (*Continued*)

Jurisdiction[1] and Citation	Share in Real Property			Share in Personal Property	Election between Will or Dower and Distributive Share; Miscellaneous (See Also Secs. 199, 205–7)
	Dower Expressly Abolished	Extent	Property Subject to (See Also Sec. 191)		
New Jersey .... Comp. St. 1930, Supp. 1925–30, Sec. 63(1)		Widow of husband dying testate or intestate is endowed for life of the one full and equal half part	All lands, tenements, and other real estate whereof the husband, or any other to his use, was seized of an estate of inheritance during marriage	Widow is distributee in case of intestacy[3]	
New York ...... Cahill, Consol. L. 1930, Ch. 13, Sec. 18, amd. by Sess. L. 1933, Vol. 2, Ch. 650, p. 1346; Secs. 83, 98; Ch. 51, Sec. 190	Yes[16]	See last column	See last column	See next column	If husband dies testate, widow has a personal right of election to take her intestate share of real and personal property,[3] subject to certain limitations and exceptions,[17] and in no event to exceed more than one-half of the net estate after deduction of debts, administration and funeral expenses, and estate tax
North Carolina.. C. 1927, Secs. 4096–4100		If husband dies intestate or if she dissents from his will, widow is entitled to a dower estate in one-third in value (which includes dwelling house) not subject to payment of estate charges	All lands, tenements and hereditaments of which husband was seized or possessed during coverture, including equitable estates	See next column	If widow dissents from husband's will, she is entitled to the same rights and estates in his real and personal property as if he had died intestate (i.e., dower, year's support, and distributive share of personalty)[3]
North Dakota... Comp. L. 1913, Sec. 4414, amd. by Supp. 1913–25, p. 928; Sec. 5643; Sec. 5743, amd. by Supp. 1913–25, p. 1143; Sec. 5744	Yes	Widow is heir of husband in case of intestacy[3]	See preceding column	Widow is distributee in case of intestacy[3]	"Every estate or interest in real or personal property to which heirs, husband, widow or next of kin might succeed may be disposed of by will"

TABLE XCV (*Continued*)

Jurisdiction[1] and Citation	Share in Real Property			Share in Personal Property	Election between Will or Dower and Distributive Share; Miscellaneous (See Also Secs. 199, 205–7)
	Dower Expressly Abolished	Extent	Property Subject to (See Also Sec. 191)		
Ohio .... Complete G. C. 1931 (Page), Supp. 1932, Secs. 10502(1), 10504(55)		*a*) Life estate in one-third, called dower *b*) In lieu of such dower interest as terminates and is barred by husband's death (see next column), widow is entitled to distributive share provided by statute of descent and distribution[3]	*a*) All real property of which husband was seized of an estate of inheritance during marriage, but such dower interest terminates and is barred upon death of husband, except to the extent that such property was conveyed by husband during marriage, or encumbered by him by mortgage, judgment, lien (except tax lien) or otherwise,[18] the wife not having relinquished or been barred of dower therein	See next column	If husband dies testate, widow may elect to take under the statute of descent and distribution,[3] but in the event of such election, she can take not to exceed one-half of the estate
Oklahoma ...... St. 1931, Secs. 1539, 1618, 1659	Yes	See last column	See last column	See next column	The husband may not "bequeath" away from surviving wife so much of his estate that she would receive less in value than would be obtained through succession by law[3]
Oregon .... C. 1930, Secs. 10(102), 10(301), 10(501)		Dower: use during life of one-half part	All lands of which husband was seized of an estate of inheritance during marriage	Widow is distributee in case of intestacy[3]	Every male person .... may devise and bequeath all of his real and personal estate, saving to the widow her dower
Pennsylvania ... St. 1920 (West), Secs. 8335, 8342–44, 8352	Yes	Widow is entitled to her intestate share with modification (see last column)	Statutory share is in lieu of dower at common law in land of which husband died seized. Widow's share in lands aliened by husband without her joinder is the same as in lands of which the husband died seized	See next column	If husband dies testate, widow may elect to take against his will and to share in his real and personal estate as if he had died intestate, except that, even if there is no issue, she is entitled to no more than one-half

[§ 189

TABLE XCV (*Continued*)

Jurisdiction[1] and Citation	Share in Real Property			Share in Personal Property	Election between Will or Dower and Distributive Share; Miscellaneous (See Also Secs. 199, 205–7)
	Dower Expressly Abolished	Extent	Property Subject to (See Also Sec. 191)		
Rhode Island ... G. L. 1923, Secs. 5554, 5781		Widow is endowed of one full and equal third part	All lands, tenements and hereditaments of which husband or any other to his use was seized of an estate of inheritance during marriage	Widow is distributee in case of intestacy[3]	
South Carolina.. C. of L. 1922, C. C., Secs. 5239, 5255, 5327		Dower (as at common law)	Widow has "her dower, after the due course and order of the common law"	Widow is distributee in case of intestacy[3]	
South Dakota ... Comp. L. 1929, Secs. 175, 607, 701–2	Yes	Widow is heir of husband in case of intestacy[3]	See preceding column	Widow is distributee in case of intestacy[3]	"Every estate or interest in real or personal property to which heirs, husband, widow, or next of kin might succeed may be disposed of by will"
Tennessee ...... C. 1932, Secs. 8351–54, 8358, 8360, 8366		Dower: life estate in one-third part (which includes dwelling house)	All lands of which husband died seized and possessed or of which he was at death equitable owner	One-third part of husband's personal estate if husband leaves not more than two children. A child's part thereof if husband leaves more than two children	Widow may dissent from husband's will when a satisfactory provision in real or personal estate is not made for her; in which case, she is entitled to her dower, and her distributive share (as outlined in preceding column)
Utah .... R. S. 1933, 101-1-1, 101-4-3, 101-4-4, 101-4-5, 101-4-9	Yes	One-third in value in fee simple (after deducting value of homestead set apart), free from husband's debts except those secured by mechanic's or laborer's liens for work, etc., thereon, those created for purchase thereof or for taxes levied thereon	All the legal or equitable estates in real property possessed by husband at any time during marriage	Widow is distributee in case of intestacy[3]	Husband may not devise away from wife more than two-thirds in value of his legal or equitable estates in real property without her consent in writing

TABLE XCV (*Continued*)

Jurisdiction[1] and Citation	Share in Real Property			Share in Personal Property	Election between Will or Dower and Distributive Share; Miscellaneous (See Also Secs. 199, 205–7)
	Dower Expressly Abolished	Extent	Property Subject to (See Also Sec. 191)		
Vermont .... G. L. 1917, Secs. 3278–79; Sec. 3401, amd. by Sess. L. 1929, No. 46, p. 62; Sec. 3413; Sec. 3416, amd. by Sess. L. 1929, No. 46, p. 62	Yes	One-third in value in fee; but one-half in value in fee if husband left surviving only one heir, and such heir is issue of widow or heir by adoption of both	Real estate of which husband died seized	Widow may waive provision for her in husband's will, and receive one-third of his personal estate, after payment of debts and administration expenses[19]	If husband leaves no issue and widow does not elect to take a third in value of real estate, or waives provisions of husband's will, she is entitled to all of husband's estate if not over $4,000, or to $4,000 and half the remainder
Virginia .... C. 1930, Secs. 5117, 5276		Widow is endowed of one-third. Dower in residue, subject to husband's creditors, if he dies wholly intestate and without issue of this or a former marriage. Dower in residue, subject to rights of creditors and devisees, if he dies partially intestate and without such issue	All the real estate of which husband or any other to his use was seized of an estate of inheritance during coverture	If widow renounces provision for her in husband's will, or if no provision is made for her, she is entitled to one-third of husband's surplus personal estate if he leaves issue of this or a former marriage, and one-half thereof if he leaves no such issue	
West Virginia... C. 1931, Ch. 42, Art. 2, Sec. 1; Art. 3, Secs. 1, 2; Ch. 43, Art. 1, Sec. 1		Widow is endowed of one-third	All the real estate of which the husband or any other to his use or in trust for him was seized of or entitled to an estate of inheritance during coverture, either in possession, reversion, remainder, or otherwise	See next column	If widow renounces provision for her in husband's will, or if no provision be made for her, she is entitled to such share in his real and personal estate as she would have taken had he died intestate leaving children[3] (dower, and one-third of surplus personalty)

[§ 189

TABLE XCV (Continued)

Jurisdiction[1] and Citation	Share in Real Property			Share in Personal Property	Election between Will or Dower and Distributive Share; Miscellaneous (See Also Secs. 199, 205–7)
	Dower Expressly Abolished	Extent	Property Subject to (See Also Sec. 191)		
Wisconsin ...... St. 1931, Secs. 233.01, 233.13, 233.14		Dower: defined to be a one-third part	All lands of which husband was seized of an estate of inheritance during marriage (except homestead)	See next column	If widow dissents from provisions made for her in husband's will, or if no provision is made for her, she is entitled to dower and the same share of his personal estate as if he had died intestate[3] (but not to exceed one-third part of his net personal estate)
Wyoming .... R. S. 1931, Secs. 88(101), 88(4001)	Yes	See last column	See last column	See next column	If husband's will deprives widow of more than one-half of his surplus estate, she may accept the conditions of his will, or elect to take one-half of his real and personal estate; but if husband leaves issue of former marriage and no issue of last marriage, he may will to others than widow not exceeding three-fourths of his property, after payment of debts

[1] The eight community-property states (**Arizona, California, Idaho, Louisiana, Nevada, New Mexico, Texas, Washington**) are not included in the table above for the reason that the surviving spouse has no general rights in the separate property of the deceased spouse except under the law of intestate descent and distribution. The present statutory compilations of five of these jurisdictions contain an express abolition of dower and curtesy (**California**, C. C. 1933 [Lake], Sec. 173; **Idaho**, Comp. St. 1919, Sec. 4668; **Nevada**, Comp. L. 1929 [Hillyer], Sec. 3361; **New Mexico**, St. Ann. 1929, Sec. 68[308]; **Washington**, Remington, Comp. St. 1922, Secs. 1343, 6897). A qualification, however, must be noted in the case of **Louisiana**, which provides that "when the wife has not brought any dowry or when what she brought as a dowry is inconsiderable with respect to the condition of the husband, if either the husband or wife dies rich, leaving the survivor in necessitous circumstances, the latter has a right to take out of the succession of the deceased what is called the marital portion," that is, one-fourth in full property if there be no children, one-fourth in usufruct only when there are three or a smaller number of children, a child's share in usufruct when there are more than three children, less what has been left as a legacy to the survivor by the deceased spouse (C. C., Art. 2382, as amended by Act 113, p. 176, of Sess. L. 1926).

[2] In **Alabama** (C. 1923, Secs. 7429–30), if the widow's separate estate, exclusive of rents, incomes and profits, is equal to or greater in value than her dower interest and distributive share

§ 189]

TABLE XCV (*Continued*)

(estimating her dower interest at seven years' rent thereof), she is not entitled to either. But if her separate estate is less in value, she is allowed so much as with her separate estate would be equal to her dower and distributive share.

[3] The reader is directed to **Section 227** for the share of real and personal property which the widow takes under the statutes of descent and distribution.

[4] In **Arkansas** (Crawf. and Moses, Dig. 1921, Sec. 3536), the following further provisions apply when the husband leaves no children: The widow is endowed to one-half of the real estate in fee simple of which husband died seized and which is a new acquisition, and one-half of the personal estate absolutely, as against collateral heirs; but as against creditors, one-third of such real estate and personal estate. If the real estate is ancestral, she is given a life estate in one-half as against collateral heirs, and one-third as against creditors.

[5] The **Connecticut** provisions given in the table are applicable in the case of persons married on or after April 20, 1877, or persons married before that date who have agreed by written contract to abandon property rights under the former law. Otherwise, a widow married before April 20, 1877, is entitled to dower in one-third part of the real estate of which the husband died possessed in his own right (except in certain situations in which the spouses were separated) and a life use of one-third in value of the personal property (G. S. 1930, Secs. 5157–58, 5171).

[6] The **Florida** statute, in terms giving the wife a protected inchoate interest in the husband's personal property, is unique, and, in the writer's opinion, ill-advised. No judicial construction of the enactment has been found, but, unless violence is done to the language, the result of the provision is as set forth in the table.

[7] See, in this connection, *Falligant* v. *Barrow*, 133 Ga. 87; 65 S. E. 149 (1909).

[8] The **Iowa** statute is construed so as to secure to the widow the same share of the personal estate (after payment of debts) as of real estate. See *In re Noble's Estate*, 194 Ia. 733; 190 N. W. 511 (1922); *Nick* v. *Nick*, 195 Ia. 351; 189 N. W. 829 (1922); *Ward* v. *Wolf*, 56 Ia. 465; 9 N. W. 350 (1881).

[9] **Maine** (R. S. 1930, Ch. 89, Sec. 21) provides that life insurance of decedent, deducting premiums paid within three years with interest, may be disposed of by will, but, if the estate is insolvent, such disposition is limited to a distribution among the widow or widower and issue as decedent designates. In this connection, see *Berman* v. *Beaudry*, 118 Me. 248; 107 A. 708 (1920).

[10] In **Massachusetts** (G. L. 1932, Ch. 191, Sec. 15), if the surviving spouse waives the provision of the will, he or she is entitled to share in the real and personal property as if the deceased had died intestate, subject to the following exceptions: If the intestate share exceeds $10,000 in value, the survivor receives in addition to that amount only the income for life of the excess, the personal property to be held in trust and the real property vested in him or her for life. If the deceased leaves no kindred, the survivor is entitled to such interest as he or she would take if the deceased had died leaving kindred but no issue ($5,000 in value plus one-half of the remainder).

[11] Common-law dower was abolished in **Minnesota** by the Session Laws of 1875, Chapter 40, Section 5.

[12] In **Mississippi** (C. 1930, Secs. 3561, 3563), even though the deceased spouse left no descendant, the survivor is entitled to one-half of the estate only. If the surviving spouse has separate property, further limitations are as follows: if such separate property does not amount in value to one-fifth of the survivor's legal share, he may renounce the will as above; if such separate property is equal in value to his legal share, he cannot dissent from the will or elect to take his legal share; if such separate property is not equal in value to his legal share (but amounts in value to one-fifth or more thereof), he may dissent from the will and have the deficiency made up.

[13] The **Missouri** statutes are needlessly confused and complex; it is difficult for one not familiar with local practice to interpret them. If the husband leaves no descendants capable of inheriting, and the widow has no dower, she is apparently entitled without election to one-half of the real and personal estate belonging to husband at death, subject to payment of debts; and also to all the real and personal property "which came to the husband in right of the marriage, and to all personal property of the husband which came to his possession with the written assent of the wife," remaining undisposed of, not subject to debts (R. S. 1929, Sec. 325). **Missouri** also provides that, when the husband dies leaving issue of a former marriage only, the widow

[§ 189

TABLE XCV (*Continued*)

"may in lieu of dower elect to take, in addition to her real estate, the personal property in posses-sion of her husband that came to him in right of the wife by means of the marriage, or by her consent in writing, subject to the payment of the husband's debts" (Sec. 326). Why such archaic provisions remain in the statutes is difficult of explanation.

14 The **Missouri** statute is construed so as to allow the widow to make the election referred to in the table if "descendants" of such child be living, although the child may not be living (*Keeney* v. *McVoy,* 206 Mo. 42; 103 S. W. 946 [1907]).

15 Whether the wife is in the nature of a forced heir as to personal property is not clear from the **Montana** statutes. Section 5819 of the Revised Code, 1921, provides that every devise or bequest bars a widow's dower in lands "or her share in personal estate" unless otherwise expressed in the will, but that she may elect whether she will take such devise or bequest or whether she will renounce the same "and take her dower in the lands and her share in the per-sonal estate." Presumably, the share in the personal estate referred to is her intestate share. Section 5820 provides that after renunciation the widow is entitled to "dower in the lands or share in the personal estate of her husband."

16 **New York** has preserved inchoate dower to the following extent: In case of marriages prior to September 1, 1930, the widow is "endowed of the third part of all the lands whereof her husband was," prior to September 1, 1930, "seized of an estate of inheritance at any time during marriage" (Cahill, Consol. L. 1930, Ch. 51, Sec. 190).

17 In **New York**, the right of election referred to in the table accrues to the surviving spouse of a testator dying after August 31, 1930, leaving a will thereafter executed, and is subject to the following limitations, with the reservation that the term "intestate share," wher-ever used below, is not to be construed as meaning more than one-half of such net estate: (1) in no event is the surviving spouse entitled to more than one-half of the net estate; (2) if the intestate share exceeds $2,500 and the deceased spouse has devised or bequeathed in trust an amount equal to or greater than the intestate share, with income thereof payable to the survivor for life, the surviving spouse has the limited right to elect to take $2,500 absolutely, which sum is then deducted from the principal of the trust and the terms of the will otherwise remain effective; (3) if the intestate share does not exceed $2,500, the surviving spouse may elect to take the intestate share absolutely in lieu of any provision for his benefit in the will; (4) if the will contains an absolute legacy or devise to the surviving spouse amounting to $2,500 or more and also contains a provision for a trust for his benefit for life of a principal equal to or more than the excess between the legacy or devise and the intestate share, the survivor has no right of election whatever; (5) if the will contains an absolute legacy or devise to the survivor amounting to less than $2,500 and also contains a provision for a trust for his benefit for life of a principal equal to or more than the excess between the legacy or devise and the intestate share, such sur-viving spouse has the limited right to elect to take not more than the sum of $2,500, inclusive of the legacy or devise, and the difference between the legacy or devise and the sum of $2,500 is deducted from the principal of the trust fund, and the terms of the will otherwise remain effective; (6) if the aggregate of the testamentary provisions made for the survivor, including the principal of a trust or a legacy or devise or other form of testamentary provision, is less than the intestate share, the surviving spouse has a limited right to elect to take the difference between such aggregate and the amount of the intestate share, and the will otherwise remains effective; (7) the provision with regard to the creation of a trust with income payable to the survivor for life likewise applies to a legal life estate or to an annuity for life or any other form of income for life created by the will for the benefit of the survivor. In computing the value of the provisions under the will, the capital value of the fund producing the income is taken and not the value of the life estate.

18 In the event that any of the real property of which the deceased spouse was seized of an estate of inheritance at death was so encumbered, the dower interest therein is computed on the basis of the amount of the encumbrance at the death of such spouse (Complete G. C. 1931 [Page], Supp. 1932, Sec. 10502[1]).

19 In **Vermont** (G. L. 1917, Sec. 3278), the surviving spouse receives such part of the personal estate as the probate court may assign, according to his or her circumstances and the estate and degree of the deceased, which shall not be less than a third of the surplus. The fore-going applies when the survivor waives the provisions of the will, except in case the deceased dies without issue, "when the husband or widow may take estate as is provided in like cases of

TABLE XCV (*Concluded*)

intestate estates, or when the widow waives the jointure or pecuniary provision made for her in lieu of her interest (in real estate), or when either waives the provisions of the law in case the deceased dies without issue, and shall be in lieu of his or her claim to the personal estate. If the widow was not the first wife of the deceased, and he does not leave issue by her, and an agreement was entered into between them previous to their marriage, this provision shall not be subject to the exception in relation to the allowance of such third interest to the widow in such case."

REFERENCES
Books

STIMSON, F. J. *American Statute Law,* Secs. 3105(a), 3109, 3201, 3202B (1886).
TIFFANY, HERBERT THORNDIKE. *The Law of Real Property and Other Interests in Land,* 2d ed., Vol. 1, Sec. 236 (1920).
WOERNER, J. G. *The American Law of Administration,* 3d ed., Sec. 106 (1923).

Articles

EAGLETON, WILLIAM L. "The Illinois Dower Act as Applied to Estates Consisting of Personal Property," 26 Ill. L. Rev. 164–67 (1931).
FOX, SAMUEL. "The Illinois Dower Act," 26 Ill. L. Rev. 145–64 (1931).
SAYRE, PAUL L. "Husband and Wife as Statutory Heirs," 42 Harv. L. Rev. 330–64 (1929).

Section 190. Dower—Extent

CROSS REFERENCES: Dower, abolition and statutory substitutes, **Sec. 189**; Dower, property subject to, **Sec. 191**; Curtesy, extent, **Sec. 217**; Widow's share of real and personal property when husband dies intestate, **Sec. 227**; Homestead and exempt property, **Sec. 228**

The statutes fixing the size of the widow's estate evidence little uniformity. Approaching extreme generosity are those of several jurisdictions under which the widow is entitled to a flat one-half of the husband's real and personal property. On the other extreme are **North** and **South Dakota,** which leave the husband's testamentary control of his property completely unfettered (aside from homestead, exempt property, etc.). Between the two extremes is found an odd assortment of combinations (**Sec. 189**). The obvious tendency has been to increase the widow's bounty, occasionally with a severe loss to creditors, and to place additional limitations upon the testamentary control which the husband may exercise over his property. We may assume that ordinarily

[§ 190

the husband, if he dies testate, has made adequate provision for his spouse, and that she will respect his last wishes as expressed in his will. The extent to which she can upset his will in many jurisdictions, however, seems extreme. It is evident that modern legislation which secures to the widow a generous distributive share of the husband's real and personal property has a much broader purpose than dower at common law. There seems to be a rather well defined sentiment that the surviving wife is entitled not only to support, but also to a "partner's" share of the husband's fortune when the marital venture is ended by his death. Quite unlike the situation in the community-property states (**Sec. 178**), her share is not confined to property acquired during the union. While the statutes reflect an admirable consciousness of the family unit, one may well wonder whether the process has not been carried to an extreme. Certainly, the statutes as a whole do not reflect any very reasoned philosophy.

In those twenty-five jurisdictions which give the widow her dower or other life estate in lands, the common-law measure is retained in all but **New Jersey** and **Oregon** (and, in certain circumstances, in **Alabama** and **Arkansas**), where it is raised to a life estate in one-half part. **Connecticut** is the least generous in respect to personalty, likewise allowing the widow a life use only of one-third part thereof. We have seen that most jurisdictions entitle her to an absolute share of the personalty, and that a majority of them give her an absolute share of the realty as an extended dower, a substitute for dower, or which she may take in lieu of dower (**Sec. 189**). The size of this statutory share is variously fixed at one-third (realty, six; personalty, seven) or at one-half (realty, three; personalty, four) ; or depends upon the existence, absence, or number of lineal descendants (realty, five; personalty, seven) ; or is her intestate share, generally subject to a set maximum (realty, nine; personalty, fourteen). In some of these latter jurisdictions her share may under some circumstances be less than one-third. **Missouri** and **Wyoming** discriminate against a childless second wife when issue of a former union survive; and the same is true in several other jurisdictions when her rights are measured by the intestate table (**Sec. 227**). Ordinarily, her share of lands is inclusive of the homestead (**Sec. 228**). The more recent statutes evidence a tendency to give the widow the same share of the husband's estate as she would take in case of intestacy, subject to a maximum limitation, or to otherwise increase her bounty when no lineal descendants survive. In view of the husband's power to disinherit his children, one may wonder why her statutory share should

§ 190]

be made to vary with the presence, absence, or number of issue. Quite absurd is the situation in several jurisdictions in which the surviving wife may apparently demand her intestate share of lands or personalty, or both, without limitation. It must follow that the husband has been completely shorn of his testamentary control of his property when he dies without next of kin.

The statutes of four jurisdictions merit special consideration. In **Alabama** and **Mississippi** the extent of the widow's statutory rights varies with the size of her separate estate. If the latter is equal in value to the former, she cannot upset the husband's will. The motivating theory behind legislation of this kind seems eminently sound and fair if not carried to an extreme. The operation of the rule in **Alabama** and **Mississippi,** however, is perhaps far too severe when the husband's estate is not large. In **Massachusetts,** the statutory share which the widow may take in lieu of dower is drastically reduced in the case of large estates. If her share exceeds $10,000, she is entitled to the income only of the balance. **New York,** which is the most recent jurisdiction to abolish dower and curtesy and establish a substitute system, has a desirable type of statute. Under it, the extent to which the widow can upset the husband's will is severely limited if he has made suitable provision for her by way of testamentary trust, etc. It is of course a difficult matter to draft a statute which will be simple of application and yet operate reasonably under all circumstances. It does seem, however, that the size of the husband's estate and the personal fortune of the surviving wife should be of influence in fixing the extent of her rights. There is little reason to allow her to demand a third or a half of a million-dollar estate against contrary provisions in the husband's will. Especially is this true when she is wealthy in her own right. Also, to discourage and take the profit out of a popular type of second marriage, scant consideration should be accorded a childless second wife when issue of a former union survive.

At common law, inchoate dower was protected from destruction by the husband's creditors. With but few exceptions, this is true today in those jurisdictions which retain inchoate dower or a similar estate during coverture (**Secs. 195, 201**). Likewise, the widow took her vested dower free from estate creditors. Of those jurisdictions which substantially retain common-law dower, three (**Alabama, Delaware, North Carolina**) have codified the common law in this respect; and the same result is obtained in the rest by reason of an absence of legislative expression to the contrary. If, however, the creditor has a lien on the land which

[§ 190

is superior to dower by reason of the fact that it was secured before the marriage, or after marriage with the wife's release, the widow is postponed. **Georgia,** which permits the husband to convey free of dower (**Sec. 189**), has a rather unusual statute which provides that "no lien created by the husband in his lifetime, though assented to by the wife, shall in any manner interfere with her right to dower" (C. 1926, C. of Prac., Sec. 5254). When the widow is given a generous share of real and personal property in lieu of dower or as a substitute for dower, it becomes a rather serious matter if she may take the same free from the demands of estate creditors. A considerable number of statutes, especially in respect to personalty, are express to the effect that she shares in surplus property only; and such seems the obvious intent of most of the others which are silent on the matter. In a few, however, her share in lands actually appears to be a mere enlargement of common-law dower. The widow's enlarged estate is protected from creditors by express statute in five jurisdictions. Thus, in **Florida** and **Maine** (and in **Indiana** and **Utah** with certain qualifications), she takes her third of the lands free of creditors. The same is true in **Arkansas** when the husband dies without issue and the property is not ancestral. In **Florida,** her "dower" in personalty (one-third) is not liable for the husband's debts. Under the **Arkansas** statute a similar result is reached by decision; and if the personal representative uses the personalty to pay debts, she may be subrogated to creditors and paid out of the realty (*Crouch* v. *Edwards,* 52 Ark. 499; 12 S. W. 1070 [1890]; *Thompson* v. *Union and Mercantile Trust Company,* 164 Ark. 411; 262 S. W. 324 [1924]). Statutes which increase the widow's bounty many fold at the expense of honest creditors can hardly be justified. It should be observed, however, that, in those jurisdictions where the surviving wife shares in surplus property only, her enlarged estate actually means less to her when the husband dies insolvent than did her common-law dower.

The statutory material discussed in this section is collected in Table XCV at the end of **Section 189** (p. 355).

REFERENCES

Book

STIMSON, F. J. *American Statute Law,* Sec. 3202 (1886).

§ 190]

Section 191. Dower—Real Property Subject to

CROSS REFERENCES: Dower, abolition and statutory substitutes, **Sec. 189;** Dower, extent of share, **Sec. 190;** Barring dower, **Secs. 195** *et seq.;* Dower in lands aliened by husband, or mortgaged by husband and wife, **Sec. 200;** Property in which husband is entitled to curtesy, etc., **Sec. 218**

Scope of section.—In this section and Table XCVI those statutes are collected which define the real property in which the widow is entitled to dower or statutory share. Only those jurisdictions, however, which substantially retain common-law dower or which give the wife an inchoate interest during coverture similar to inchoate dower are considered. This excludes six jurisdictions (**Colorado, Connecticut, Mississippi, New York, Oklahoma, Wyoming**) which appear to have completely abolished dower, and which as a substitution therefor give the widow a statutory share of all the property which the husband dies owning (**Sec. 189**). Included in this section, however, are the statutes of a number of jurisdictions (**Kansas, Minnesota, Utah,** etc.) which have formally abolished dower and substituted an enlarged estate which is protected during coverture (**Sec. 189**). Whether the technical law of dower remains in these jurisdictions depends upon whether the substitute systems created are to be regarded as a mere enlargement of common-law dower. In three states (**Indiana, Maine, Nebraska**), the statutes seem to give the widow her statutory share in all the real property which the husband dies owning but leave the law of dower to govern her rights in lands disposed of by the husband during coverture without her relinquishment. One must go to the reports of the courts to be certain of the situation in most jurisdictions.

In general.—According to the common law, the widow is entitled to dower in all of the lands and tenements of which the husband is seized of an estate of inheritance during coverture, excluding fee tails which her issue could not inherit. In general, the statutes considered in this section are little more than declaratory of fundamental common-law principles, with occasional legislative innovations. In three jurisdictions (**Maryland, Massachusetts, South Carolina**), no statutory definition of dower is found. In five, the widow's dower or statutory share attaches to land of which the husband died seized only (**Alaska, Georgia, New Hampshire, Tennessee, Vermont**) or to which he obtained title in right of his wife (**Georgia**). Similarly, in many jurisdictions dower of a non-resident wife is not an encumbrance on the husband's lands during coverture (**Sec. 200**). In others, the widow has dower or statutory share in lands of which the husband dies seized or owning, and in

[§ 191

lands which he conveys during the marriage without her joinder (**Flor-ida, Indiana, Pennsylvania**). Under the **Pennsylvania** statute she is given a distributive share in lieu of dower in the lands of which the husband dies seized; and in **Ohio,** vested dower is virtually abolished and a distributive portion substituted therefor (**Sec. 189**).

Seisin of the husband.—This essential element of common-law dower is expressly required by most of the statutes. In twenty-seven juris-dictions, the term "seized" has been incorporated into the legislative definition of property subject to dower or statutory share, as follows: "seized" (twenty-one), "seized and possessed" (three), "seized or pos-sessed" (two), "seized of or entitled to" (one). A few others use the term "possessed" (three), or "owned" (one). Seisin in law, as distin-guished from seisin in fact or deed, has always been regarded as sufficient to support dower. **Kentucky** is the only jurisdiction which has an express statute to that effect. The present import of the term "seisin," which had such great significance in the early law, is uncertain. For dower purposes, it is probably sufficient if the husband has legal title coupled with an unobstructed right to immediate possession. The re-quirement of seisin, however, remains of considerable importance in at least two situations. In the absence of legislation to the contrary, it probably operates to deprive the widow of dower in estates in reversion or remainder upon a particular freehold estate in another which does not terminate before the husband's death, and also in cases where the husband is disseised before marriage and does not exercise his right of entry before death. By express statute in several jurisdictions, the widow has dower or statutory share in reversions (**West Virginia**), in remain-ders (**Pennsylvania, West Virginia**), and in rights of entry (**Mis-souri, Virginia, West Virginia**). A similar result may be reached in other jurisdictions in which her statutory interest is not regarded as a mere enlargement of her common-law estate.

Equitable estates.—Until changed by the Dower Act of 1833 (3 and 4 Wm. IV, c. 105), the English courts required seisin of the legal estate, thus precluding dower in equitable estates. In this country, however, a contrary rule has usually been followed and dower allowed in equitable estates of inheritance, some jurisdictions confining the same to equitable interests which the husband owns at death. About half the jurisdictions have statutes which govern the matter in full or in part. Rather broad provisions to the effect that the widow is entitled to dower or statutory share in equitable estates generally are found in eleven jurisdictions (**District of Columbia, Illinois, Indiana, Iowa, Kansas, Maryland,**

§ 191]

Montana, **Nebraska, North Carolina, Tennessee, Utah**). In three
(**Indiana, Nebraska, Tennessee**), the statute refers to equitable interests owned at death. The statutes of seven additional jurisdictions
appear to sanction dower in the estate of a cestui que use or cestui que
trust (**Alabama, Kentucky, Missouri, New Jersey, Rhode Island,
Virginia, West Virginia**). In the absence of statute, the authorities
differ as to whether the widow has dower in equitable estates arising
under executory contracts of purchase. Some deny the same altogether,
while others require that the equity be complete, and others that it be
owned at death. Six of the states above (**Alabama, Illinois, Indiana,
Kentucky, Missouri, Montana**) and **Georgia** have legislation permitting dower in equitable estates of that nature. In **Alabama** the equity
must be complete, and in **Alabama, Georgia, Indiana**, and **Kentucky**
it must be owned at death. If the contract is completed after the husband's death and the balance of the purchase money paid from the assets
of his estate, **Indiana** and **Missouri** give the widow the same share as
if the legal estate had vested during coverture; and the same is implied
by the statutes of **Illinois** and **Montana**. That seems to be the fair rule
to follow when she is entitled to a distributive share of the personalty
in addition to dower.

Lands mortgaged before marriage or to secure purchase money.—
Contrary to the English view, but in harmony with the general American
view that equitable estates are subject to dower, the courts of most states
have allowed dower in the husband's redemption interest under a mortgage which is superior to the widow's dower claim. In those jurisdictions
in which the mortgagor is regarded as seized of the legal estate, her right
to dower as against all but the mortgagee would seem to follow without
question. With but few exceptions, the statutes do little more than codify
the case law on the subject. Thus, twelve jurisdictions have express
legislation to the effect that the widow is entitled to dower or statutory
share in lands mortgaged before marriage as against all but the holder
of the mortgage lien. Some of them state the general rule that dower is
subject to all liens created before marriage. When the husband buys land
during coverture and secures the purchase money with a mortgage on
the same in which the wife does not join, the mortgage lien is nevertheless held to be superior to her dower on the theory that the husband's
seisin is only transitory and insufficient to support dower, or for the
better reason that the vendor's equity is greater. This rule is expressly
recognized by the statutes of sixteen jurisdictions. Several of them give
the same priority to the implied vendor's lien. Statutes governing dower

[§ 191

in lands mortgaged by the husband and wife are collected in **Section 200**. In those jurisdictions in which the widow shares in lands of which the husband dies seized only, her estate is of course subject to all liens created by the husband unless in fraud of her dower. Three such jurisdictions (**Georgia, Tennessee, Vermont**) have some legislation governing her right to share in his redemption estates.

If the land is sold during marriage to satisfy a mortgage lien paramount to dower, the authorities differ as to whether her inchoate interest is thereby extinguished. Interesting statutes are found in **Virginia** and **West Virginia**, giving the wife a protected right to share in the surplus. The **West Virginia** legislation is especially significant in that she is entitled to so much of the surplus as represents the present value of her inchoate dower in the whole of the premises. That the widow is entitled to dower in the surplus when the land is sold after the husband's death to satisfy the lien is recognized by the statutes of ten jurisdictions. The **West Virginia** statute applies the same generous measure to which reference has already been made. Certain other legislation dealing with the subject of this subsection will be found in Table XCVI and the notes following.

Exchanges.—If the husband exchanges one tract of land for another, a literal application of the common-law definition of dower would give the widow dower in both tracts. For obvious reasons, however, the common law denied dower in both, and required an election. This rule is incorporated into the statutes of seven jurisdictions, with the further provision that, if her election is not made as required, she is deemed to have elected dower in the lands received in exchange (**Arkansas, Hawaii, Illinois, Michigan, Montana, Oregon, Wisconsin**).

Leasehold interests.—An estate for a term of years, being regarded as a chattel interest, is not subject to dower. By express statute in **Hawaii, Massachusetts,** and **Missouri** the common-law rule is abrogated and dower is allowed in leaseholds of a certain duration. In those jurisdictions in which the widow is entitled to a distributive share of personalty, the matter is not of great importance except as it affects creditors.

Partnership lands.—In the United States, most courts have taken the position that partnership lands are to be treated in equity as personal property so far as necessary to satisfy creditors and adjust the equities of partners, but that the residue retains its original character and is subject to dower. The Uniform Partnership Act, which incorporates the English view that partnership realty is to be treated as personalty for all purposes, has been adopted in nineteen jurisdictions (twelve of

§ 191]

which are treated in this section). The matter is of importance in those jurisdictions in which the widow shares in the husband's lands but not in his personal property.

Unimproved lands.—Several New England decisions deny dower in wild lands on the theory that the widow could not beneficially enjoy them without committing waste and suffering a forfeiture. These decisions probably do not represent the general law on the subject. By express provision in **Massachusetts** and **New Hampshire,** the widow is not entitled to dower in wild lands, except wood lot in connection with dwelling, etc.; while in **Maine** (where her interest has been raised to a fee), the statute is express to the contrary; but in neither **Maine** nor **Massachusetts** does she share in wild lands conveyed by the husband although afterward cleared.

Non-beneficial title, etc.—Statutes merely declaratory of the unwritten law were found in several jurisdictions to the effect that dower does not exist in the estate of a trustee (**New Jersey**), or the estate of a mortgagee (**Arkansas, Hawaii, Illinois, Montana**), or in lands sold but not conveyed by the husband before marriage (**Kentucky**).

The foregoing completes a brief résumé of the statutes found on the subject of this section. The common law of dower, with all of its technical and subtle distinctions, seems strangely out of harmony with modern efforts to simplify our statutory law. It stands as one of those relics of antiquity which we retain, partly because of our reverence for institutions of the past, but mainly because of inertia. Regardless of the nature of the estate which we may secure to the surviving wife, whether it involve a protected inchoate interest during coverture or not, there seems little reason why her estate should not attach to all interests in real property. We have seen that there is a very definite tendency to widen the widow's rights, and that in most jurisdictions she is entitled to a distributive share of the personalty in addition to dower or other share in lands. In a number of jurisdictions an absurd situation must exist which deprives the widow of a share in certain of the husband's property because the same is neither personalty nor the type of realty subject to dower. The reversion, the remainder, the right of entry, or the equitable estate in which the widow does not share may well happen to be the most valuable part of the estate.

The table follows.

[§ 191

Jurisdiction and Citation	In General	Equitable Estates, in General	Mortgage before Marriage
Alabama .... C. 1923, Sec. 7427	All lands of which husband was seized in fee during marriage	All lands of which another was seized in fee to husband's use, or to which at death husband had a perfect equity, having paid all the purchase money therefor	
Alaska .... Comp. L. 1913, Sec. 462; Sess. L. 1917, Ch. 69, p. 169	All lands whereof husband died seized of an estate of inheritance		
Arkansas .... Crawf. and Moses, Dig. 1921, Secs. 3514, 3516–20, 3543	All lands whereof husband was seized of an estate of inheritance during marriage. Lands sold by husband without wife's consent		Dower as against every person except mortgagee and those claiming under him[a]
Delaware ...... R. C. 1915, Sec. 3303	All lands and tenements whereof husband was seized of an estate of inheritance during marriage		
District of Columbia ... C. 1929, T. 14, Secs. 28, 29	All lands of husband which were his during coverture	Lands held by equitable title during marriage, whether held at death or not	
Florida .... Sess. L. 1933, Ch. 16103, p. 553, Sec. 35	Real property owned by husband at death or that which he had conveyed without wife's relinquishment		

* See pages 392–93 for all numbered footnotes to this table

§ 191]

XCVI*

SUBJECT TO DOWER

Purchase-Money Mortgage, etc.	Exchanges	Partnership Lands, Leaseholds, Remainders; Miscellaneous
		A partner's right in specific partnership property is not subject to dower[1]
No dower as against mortgagee or those claiming under him although wife did not join, but dower as against all others[2]	Widow must elect between lands given or those taken in exchange[3]	No dower in lands conveyed to husband by way of mortgage unless he acquires absolute estate during marriage
Widow's dower shall not operate to prejudice claim for purchase money of lands or other lien on same		

[§ 191

TABLE XCVI

Jurisdiction and Citation	In General	Equitable Estates, in General	Mortgage before Marriage
Georgia .... C. 1926, C. of Prac., Secs. 5247–48	Lands of which husband was seized or possessed at death or to which he obtained title in right of his wife	Dower may be assigned in lands held under bond for title or other writing having like effect, when a portion of the purchase money has been paid; but estate in dower is liable for the unpaid balance	
Hawaii .... R. L. 1925, Secs. 3017–22	All lands owned by husband during marriage in fee simple or freehold		Dower as against every person except mortgagee and those claiming under him
Illinois .... Cahill, R. S. 1931, Ch. 41, Secs. 1, 3–6, 17; Ch. 106a, Sec. 25	All lands whereof husband was seized of an estate of inheritance during marriage	Equitable estates are subject to dower, including all real estate of every description contracted for by husband, title to which may be completed after his death	Dower as against every person except mortgagee and those claiming under him[2]
Indiana .... Burns, Ann. St. 1926, Secs. 3337, 3349–52	Real estate which husband owns at death. Real estate of which husband was seized in fee simple during marriage, in the conveyance of which wife did not join	All lands in which husband had an equitable interest at death. If husband made contract for purchase of lands and unpaid purchase money shall be paid after his death out of the proceeds of his estate, widow has same share as if legal estate had vested during coverture[4]	
Iowa .... C. 1927, Sec. 11990	All the legal estates in real property possessed by husband during marriage	All the equitable estates in real property possessed by husband during marriage	

§ 191]

(Continued)

Purchase-Money Mortgage, etc.	Exchanges	Partnership Lands, Leaseholds, Remainders; Miscellaneous
Dower may be assigned when portion of purchase money has been paid, but estate in dower is liable for the unpaid balance		
No dower as against mortgagee or those claiming under him, although wife did not join, but dower as against all others[2]	Widow must elect between lands given or those taken in exchange[3]	Dower in estates for 50 years or more so long as 25 years of term remains unexpired. No dower in lands conveyed to husband by way of mortgage unless he acquires absolute estate during marriage
No dower as against mortgagee or those claiming under him, although wife did not join, but dower as against all others[2]	Widow must elect between lands given or those taken in exchange[3]	A partner's right in specific partnership property is not subject to dower.[1] No dower in lands conveyed to husband by way of mortgage unless he acquires absolute estate during marriage
Widow is not entitled to statutory share as against mortgagee or those claiming under him, although she did not unite in mortgage, but she is entitled to the same as against all others		

[§ 191

TABLE XCVI

Jurisdiction and Citation	In General	Equitable Estates, in General	Mortgage before Marriage
Kansas .... R. S. 1923, Sec. 22(108)	All the real estate in which husband had a legal interest during marriage	All the real estate in which husband had an equitable interest during marriage	
Kentucky .... Carroll, St. 1922, Secs. 2132, 2134–35, 2142–43	All the real estate of which husband was seized of an estate in fee simple during marriage. Seisin in law is sufficient	All the real estate of which another was seized for husband's use of an estate in fee simple during the marriage. Equitable right in lands held by executory contract if owned at death	No dower in lands sold in good faith after marriage to satisfy lien or encumbrance created before marriage; but dower in surplus unless received or disposed of by husband in his lifetime
Maine .... R. S. 1930, Ch. 89, Secs. 1, 17	Real estate of deceased husband including all of which he was seized during coverture		Widow is entitled to statutory share as against every person except mortgagee and those claiming under him[2]
Maryland ...... Bagby, Ann. C. 1924, Art. 45, Sec. 6; Art. 73A, Sec. 25(e)	As at common law (see next column)	Lands held by equitable as well as legal title in husband during coverture	
Massachusetts .. G. L. 1932, Ch. 108A, Sec. 25(e); Ch. 186, Secs. 1, 2; Ch. 189, Secs. 1, 3, 4	Widow entitled to "her dower at common law in her deceased husband's land"		If husband is seized of land subject to mortgage "which is valid and effectual against his wife," she is nevertheless entitled to dower therein as against every person except mortgagee and those claiming under him[2]
Michigan .... Comp. L. 1929, Secs. 9865, 13072–77	All lands whereof husband was seized of an estate of inheritance during marriage		Dower as against every person except mortgagee and those claiming under him[2]

§ 191]

(Continued)

Purchase-Money Mortgage, etc.	Exchanges	Partnership Lands, Leaseholds, Remainders; Miscellaneous
No dower in lands sold in good faith to satisfy lien for purchase money; but dower in surplus unless received or disposed of by husband in his lifetime		No dower in lands sold but not conveyed before marriage. Dower in husband's moiety of lands held by spouses as tenants in common
		If husband is seized of land mortgaged by another, wife is entitled to statutory share as against every person except mortgagee and those claiming under him[2, 5]
Widow's dower shall not operate to prejudice claim for purchase money of lands or other lien on same		A partner's right in specific partnership property is not subject to dower[1]
See preceding column		Dower in estates for 100 years or more so long as 50 years remain unexpired, but, if dower is assigned therein, widow must pay one-third of rent to owner of the term. A partner's right in specific partnership property is not subject to dower[1, 5]
No dower as against mortgagee or those claiming under him, although wife did not join, but dower as against all others[2]	Widow must elect between lands given or those taken in exchange[3]	A partner's right in specific partnership property is not subject to dower[1]

[§ 191

TABLE XCVI

Jurisdiction and Citation	In General	Equitable Estates, in General	Mortgage before Marriage
Minnesota ...... G. S. 1923, Secs. 7408, 8198, 8720	Lands of which husband was seized or possessed during coverture		
Missouri .... R. S. 1929, Secs. 318, 321–22, 340, 14057	All lands whereof husband was seized of an estate of inheritance during marriage	All lands of which another was seized to the husband's use of an estate of inheritance during the marriage. If husband made contract for purchase of lands and unpaid purchase money shall be paid after his death out of assets of his estate, widow is endowed as if he had been seized during coverture[6]	
Montana .... R. C. 1921, Secs. 5813–17, 5822	All lands whereof husband was seized of an estate of inheritance during marriage	Equitable estates are subject to dower, including real estate of every description contracted for by husband, title to which may be completed after his death	Dower as against every person except mortgagee and those claiming under him[2]
Nebraska .... Comp. St. 1929, Secs. 13(509), 30(101)	All the real estate of which husband was seized of an estate of inheritance during marriage or in which he was possessed of a legal interest at death	All the real estate in which husband was possessed of an equitable interest at death	
New Hampshire. Pub. L. 1926, Ch. 306, Secs. 2, 4	Real estate of which husband died seized		

(Continued)

Purchase-Money Mortgage, etc.	Exchanges	Partnership Lands, Leaseholds, Remainders; Miscellaneous
Widow is not entitled to any inchoate or contingent right in such land as against mortgagee or those claiming under him even though she did not join		A partner's right in specific partnership property is not subject to widow's statutory interest[1]
See footnote 6		Widow has dower, although there may have been no actual possession or recovery of possession by husband in lifetime, and although held by him as tenant in common or coparcener. No dower in cemetery lands. Dower in leasehold estate for term of 20 years or more is granted and assigned as in real estate; for a term less than 20 years, as in personal property
No dower as against mortgagee or those claiming under him, although wife did not join, but dower as against all others[2]	Widow must elect between lands given or those taken in exchange[3]	No dower in lands conveyed to husband by way of mortgage unless he acquires absolute estate during marriage
		No dower in cemetery lands
		See footnote 5

[§ 191

TABLE XCVI

Jurisdiction and Citation	In General	Equitable Estates, in General	Mortgage before Marriage
New Jersey..... Comp. St. 1910, p. 2044, Sec. 1a; Cum. Supp. 1911–24, Sec. 150(106); Supp. 1925–30, Sec. 63(1)	All lands, tenements and other real estate whereof husband was seized of an estate of inheritance d u r i n g marriage	All lands, tenements and other real estate whereof another was seized to the husband's use of an estate of inheritance during the marriage	
North Carolina.. C. 1927, Secs. 4100–4101	All lands, tenements and hereditaments whereof husband was seized and possessed during marriage	Equitable estates in lands, tenements and hereditaments whereof husband was seized in fee during marriage	Dower in legal and equitable rights of redemption subject to all valid encumbrances existing before marriage
Ohio .... Complete G. C. 1931 (Page), Supp. 1932, Sec. 10502(1)	All real property of which husband was seized of an estate of inheritance d u r i n g marriage		
Oregon .... C. 1930, Secs. 10(301)–10(306)	All lands whereof husband was seized of an estate of inheritance during marriage		Dower as against every person except mortgagee and those claiming under him[2]
Pennsylvania ... St. 1920 (West), Secs. 8352, 16620	Statutory share is in lieu of dower in lands of which husband dies seized. Widow entitled to same share in lands aliened by husband in lifetime without her joinder		
Rhode Island.... G. L. 1923, Sec. 5781	All lands, tenements and hereditaments whereof husband was seized of an estate of inheritance d u r i n g marriage	All lands, tenements and hereditaments whereof another was seized to husband's use of an estate of inheritance during the marriage	

§ 191]

(*Continued*)

Purchase-Money Mortgage, etc.	Exchanges	Partnership Lands, Leaseholds, Remainders; Miscellaneous
		A partner's right in specific partnership property is not subject to dower.[1] No dower in estate of trustee when provision of trust appears on face of deed, etc.
Mortgage or trust deed to secure purchase money is effectual to pass whole interest without wife's joinder		
No dower as against mortgagee or those claiming under him, although wife did not join, but dower as against all others[2]	Widow must elect between lands given or those taken in exchange[3]	
		A partner's right in specific partnership property is not subject to dower.[1] Widow is entitled to statutory share in estate in remainder vested in interest during husband's lifetime, although particular estate shall not terminate before his death

TABLE XCVI

Jurisdiction and Citation	In General	Equitable Estates, in General	Mortgage before Marriage
South Carolina C. of L. 1922, C. C., Sec. 5239	If no jointure, widow "shall be admitted and enabled to pursue, have, and demand her dower, after the due course and order of the common law"		
Tennessee C. 1932, Secs. 7864, 8351–52	All lands of which husband died seized and possessed	All lands of which husband was equitable owner at death (see also last column)	
Utah R. S. 1933, 69-1-22e, 101-4-3	All the legal estates in real property possessed by husband during marriage	All the equitable estates in real property possessed by husband during marriage	
Vermont G. L. 1917, Sec. 3401, amd. by Sess. L. 1929, No. 46, p. 62; Secs. 3402–4	Real estate of which husband died seized	See last column	
Virginia C. 1930, Secs. 4359(25), 5117–19, 5158	All real estate whereof husband was seized of an estate of inheritance during marriage	All the real estate whereof any person was seized of an estate of inheritance to husband's use or in trust for him during the marriage	When land is bona fide sold in lifetime of husband to satisfy lien or encumbrance thereon created before marriage or otherwise paramount to wife, she is not entitled to dower therein; but she is entitled to dower in surplus, and court of equity may make such order as is proper to secure such right

§ 191]

(Continued)

Purchase-Money Mortgage, etc.	Exchanges	Partnership Lands, Leaseholds, Remainders; Miscellaneous
		Dower in lands mortgaged or conveyed in trust after marriage as security when husband dies before foreclosure or sale. A partner's right in specific partnership property is not subject to dower[1]
Widow's statutory share is subject to liens created for purchase		A partner's right in specific partnership property is not subject to dower[1]
		Widow entitled to statutory share in equity of redemption of lands mortgaged by husband or held by him at his death under mortgagor. She may pay a proportionate share of amount due, and have her statutory share of the lands[2]
See preceding column		Dower when husband or another to his use has right of entry or action if she would be entitled to same if possession recovered. A partner's right in specific partnership property is not subject to dower[1]

[§ 191

TABLE XCVI

Jurisdiction and Citation	In General	Equitable Estates, in General	Mortgage before Marriage
West Virginia C. 1931, Ch. 43, Art. 1, Secs. 1–4	All real estate whereof husband was seized of or entitled to estate of inheritance during marriage	All real estate whereof another was seized of or entitled to an estate of inheritance to the husband's use or in trust for him during the marriage	When land is subject to lien or encumbrance created before marriage, widow is not entitled to dower therein as against the holder of such lien, etc., but is entitled to dower in the whole thereof as against all others.[2] If such land is bona fide sold in lifetime of husband to satisfy such lien, etc., she is entitled to dower in surplus and shall be paid out of surplus an amount equal to present value of inchoate dower in the whole of such land
Wisconsin St. 1931, Secs. 123.21, 233.01, 233.03–233.07	All lands whereof husband was seized of an estate of inheritance during marriage (except homestead of which husband dies seized)		Dower as against every person except mortgagee and those claiming under him[2]

[1] The Uniform Partnership Act contains the following provision: "A partner's right in specific (Sec. 25[e]). In addition to the twelve jurisdictions listed above, the Act has been adopted in the Ch. 129, p. 658, Sec. 25); **Idaho** (Comp. St. 1919, Sec. 5837); **New York** (Cahill, Consol. L. 1930, 1294Y); **Wyoming** (R. S. 1931, Sec. 81[502]).

[2] If the land is sold on foreclosure, etc., after the death of the husband, the widow is entitled to such part of the surplus as shall represent the present value of her dower right in the whole of such the widow is entitled to dower or statutory share in the lands after the amount paid is deducted (**Maine**, the mortgage and the administrator does so, the probate court may in its discretion decree that she take band's death, the widow may pay her proportionate share of the debt, and take dower in the whole of the

[3] The widow is deemed to have elected to take dower in the lands received in exchange unless she husband's death (**Arkansas, Illinois, Michigan, Montana, Oregon, Wisconsin**). Hawaii provides dower in the lands received in exchange.

[4] And if such contract subsists at time of his death, and the real estate is sold thereafter under any statutory share thereof in proportion to the amount paid under the contract by the husband (**Indiana**).

[5] No dower in wild lands of which husband dies seized except wood lot, etc., in connection with (**Maine**); no dower in wild lands conveyed by husband though afterward cleared (**Massachusetts**,

[6] And if such contract subsists at the time of his death, and the real estate is sold thereafter under the widow is entitled to dower therein as against every person except such as may hold a lien thereon

§ 191]

(Concluded)

Purchase-Money Mortgage, etc.	Exchanges	Partnership Lands, Leaseholds, Remainders; Miscellaneous
When land is subject to lien or encumbrance created for purchase money thereof or otherwise paramount to claim of widow, she is not entitled to dower therein as against the holder of such lien, etc., but is entitled to dower in the whole thereof as against all others.[2] If such land is bona fide sold in lifetime of husband to satisfy such lien, etc., she is entitled to dower in surplus and shall be paid out of surplus an amount equal to present value of inchoate dower in the whole of such land		Dower in estate of inheritance in possession, reversion, remainder or otherwise. Dower when husband or another to his use has right of entry or action if she would be entitled to same if possession recovered
No dower as against mortgagee or those claiming under him, although wife did not join, but dower as against all others[2]	Widow must elect between lands given or those taken in exchange[3]	A partner's right in specific partnership property is not subject to dower[1]

partnership property is not subject to dower, curtesy, or allowance to widows, heirs or next of kin" following seven jurisdictions: **California** (C. C. 1933 [Lake], Sec. 2419); **Colorado** (Sess. L. 1931, Ch. 40, Sec. 51); **Nevada** (Sess. L. 1931, Ch. 74, p. 119, Sec. 25); **South Dakota** (Comp. L. 1929, Sec.

dower in the surplus (**Arkansas, Hawaii, Illinois, Michigan, Montana, Oregon, Wisconsin**) or to land (**West Virginia**). If the heir or other person claiming under the husband satisfies the mortgage, **Massachusetts, Michigan, Oregon, Vermont, Wisconsin**). If there is sufficient personal estate to pay her statutory share in the whole of the lands (**Vermont**). If the mortgage is redeemed after the husbands (**Maine, Massachusetts**).

commences proceedings to recover dower in the lands given in exchange within one year after the merely that if her election is not made within six months after the husband's death she shall take her

decree or by virtue of any power or devise in the will of the husband, the widow is entitled to her

farm or dwelling (**Massachusetts, New Hampshire**); dower in wild lands of which husband dies seized **Maine**).

order or judgment of court, by virtue of power in contract, or by any power or devise in will of husband, for purchase money (**Missouri**).

[§ 191

REFERENCES

Books

Scribner, Charles Harvey. *A Treatise on the Law of Dower,* 2d ed., I, 197–602 (1883).

Stimson, F. J. *American Statute Law,* Secs. 3202(*b*), 3210–19 (1886).

Tiffany, Herbert Thorndike. *The Law of Real Property and Other Interests in Land,* 2d ed., Vol. 1, Secs. 210–18 (1920).

Woerner, J. G. *The American Law of Administration,* 3d ed., Secs. 110–11 (1923).

Article

Herriott, Maxwell H. "Dower in Trust Estates in Wisconsin," 4 Wis. L. Rev. 92–100 (1927).

Notes

"Dower—Right of Widow to Dower in Improvements Made by Husband's Alienee after Husband's Death," 18 Va. L. Rev. 83–84 (1931).

"Real Property—Dower—Wife's Right to Dower in Equitable Estates of the Husband," 12 Cor. L. Quar. 104–8 (1927).

"Real Property—Dower in Equitable Estates—Executory Contract for Purchase of Land," 38 Yale L. Jour. 996–97 (1929).

"Right of Dower in Unopened Mines," *Trimble* v. *Kentucky River Coal Corporation,* 235 Ky. 301; 31 S. W. (2d) 367 (1930)—19 Geo. L. Jour. 243–45 (1931); 44 Harv. L. Rev. 647–48 (1931).

Annotations

"Dower in Permanent Leaseholds," 39 A. L. R. 340–41 (1925).

"Dower in Reversion or Remainder Interest of Husband," 21 A. L. R. 1073–80 (1922).

"Dower Rights of Widow of Deceased Partner in Partnership Real Estate," 25 A. L. R. 411–14 (1923).

"Dower Rights of Wife of Purchaser under Executory Contract," 66 A. L. R. 65–77 (1930).

"Dower Rights of Wife in Real Property Which Was Subject to Executory Agreement for Sale by Husband at Time of Marriage," 63 A. L. R. 136–39 (1929).

"Dower or Marital Rights of Husband or Wife in Respect of Improvements Made by Spouse's Alienee or His Successor after Death of Spouse," 74 A. L. R. 1168–72 (1931).

Section 192. Dower—Waste

Cross References: Widow's duty to make repairs, **Sec. 193**; Liability of tenant by the curtesy for waste, **Sec. 222**

At common law, a tenant in dower, as any other tenant for life, is liable for waste committed on the dower premises. Indeed, under the very early law, the action of waste could be maintained only against a

§ 192]

tenant of an estate created by operation of law. Most jurisdictions have
statutes providing in some detail for the relief which a reversioner or
remainderman may obtain against tenants generally who commit or
suffer waste. A number of them have adopted in substance the provisions
of the early Statute of Gloucester (6 Edw. I, c. 5) which made the tenant
liable to forfeiture of the premises wasted and treble damages. Tenants
in dower are of course subject to the provisions of these general statutes.
Legislation expressly providing that the widow as tenant in dower is
liable for waste was found in twelve jurisdictions (**Delaware, District
of Columbia, Illinois, Maryland, Massachusetts, Michigan, Montana, New Hampshire, New Jersey, Ohio, Oregon, Rhode Island**).
Under these statutes she is subject to treble damages in two (**District
of Columbia, New Jersey**), double damages in two (**Delaware,
Michigan**), and forfeiture of the premises wasted in seven (**Delaware,
District of Columbia, Illinois, Massachusetts, New Jersey, Ohio,
Rhode Island**). The statutes are silent as to what constitutes waste.
New Hampshire, however, provides that the widow may take the neces-
sary fuel for use at her residence even though she does not reside on the
dower land.

The widow is under a duty to pay the taxes assessed on the premises
assigned to her as her dower, and in some jurisdictions her failure to do
so has been regarded as waste. **Ohio** is apparently the only jurisdiction
which has a statute on the subject. Under it, she not only is liable for
damages sustained by such neglect, but is subject to a forfeiture of her
estate to the next person entitled to the same if the lands are sold for the
payment of back taxes and she does not redeem within one year after
such sale.

Citations for the foregoing statutes are as follows:

Delaware, R. C. 1915, Secs. 3323–33; **District of Columbia,** C. 1929, T. 25,
Sec. 491; **Illinois,** Cahill, R. S. 1931, Ch. 41, Sec. 45; **Maryland,** Bagby, Ann. C.
1924, Art. 93, Sec. 316; **Massachusetts,** G. L. 1932, Ch. 242, Sec. 1; **Michigan,**
Comp. L. 1929, Secs. 13089, 15115–20; **Montana,** R. C. 1921, Sec. 5827; **New
Hampshire,** Pub. L. 1926, Ch. 306, Sec. 7; **New Jersey,** Comp. St. 1910, p. 5790,
Sec. 3; **Ohio,** Complete G. C. 1931 (Page), Sec. 5688; Supp. 1932, Sec. 10502(7);
Oregon, C. 1930, Sec. 10(322); **Rhode Island,** G. L. 1923, Sec. 5806.

REFERENCES

Books

SCRIBNER, CHARLES H. *A Treatise on the Law of Dower,* 2d ed., II, 795–810
    (1883).
STIMSON, F. J. *American Statute Law,* Sec. 3231 (1886).

[§ 192

"Protection of Inchoate Dower against Exploitation of Mineral Resources or Other Act in Nature of Waste or Which Impairs Value of Land," 53 A. L. R. 309–11 (1928).

Section 193. Dower—Repairs

CROSS REFERENCE: Liability of tenant by the curtesy for repairs, **Sec. 222**

A tenant in dower is probably liable for permissive waste to the same extent as any other life tenant. Of the statutes expressly providing that the widow is impeachable for waste (**Sec. 192**), those of **Illinois, Massachusetts, Michigan, Montana, New Hampshire, Ohio, Oregon,** and **Rhode Island** forbid her to commit or "suffer" waste. It is generally said that a tenant in dower is bound to make the ordinary repairs necessary to prevent deterioration of the improvements on the dower land. The statutes of six jurisdictions expressly charge the widow with that duty (**Illinois, Michigan, Montana, New Hampshire, Oregon, Rhode Island**). In five of these (all except **New Hampshire**), the statute requires her to "maintain the houses and tenements, with fences and appurtenances, in good repair." In **Maryland,** the Orphans' Court is authorized to determine what part of the expenses for repairs and improvements shall be borne by the widow, when such repairs and improvements have first been sanctioned by the court and the interests of minors are concerned. Under a **Rhode Island** statute, the widow's personal representative may enter within six months after her death and remove any buildings or fences which she has erected during her tenancy.

The following are the citations for the statutes discussed above:

Illinois, Cahill, R. S. 1931, Ch. 41, Sec. 45; **Maryland,** Bagby, Ann. C. 1924, Art. 93, Secs. 320–23; **Michigan,** Comp. L. 1929, Sec. 13089; **Montana,** R. C. 1921, Sec. 5827; **New Hampshire,** Pub. L. 1926, Ch. 306, Sec. 7; **Oregon,** C. 1930, Sec. 10(322); **Rhode Island,** G. L. 1923, Secs. 5806, 5810.

REFERENCES

Book

STIMSON, F. J. *American Statute Law,* Sec. 3232 (1886).

§ 193]

Section 194. Dower—Emblements

CROSS REFERENCE: Widow's right to growing crops before assignment, **Sec. 214**

The usual doctrine of emblements operates in favor of a tenant in dower in the same manner as in the case of any other life tenant. The law on the subject in England was clarified by the early Statute of Merton (20 Hen. III, c. 2), which is said to be generally recognized as a part of the common law in the United States.[1] This statute has been substantially re-enacted in several American jurisdictions. Thus, the widow may bequeath the crops growing on the dower land at the time of her death in the same manner as crops growing on other lands held by her for life (**Arkansas, New Jersey, Rhode Island, South Carolina, Virginia, West Virginia**) and, if she dies intestate, the same goes to her personal representative (**Arkansas, Virginia, West Virginia**).

The citations for the foregoing statutes are as follows:

Arkansas, Crawf. and Moses, Dig. 1921, Sec. 3559; **New Jersey,** Comp. St. 1910, p. 5864, Sec. 12; **Rhode Island,** G. L. 1923, Sec. 5810; **South Carolina,** C. of L. 1922, C. C., Sec. 5338; **Virginia,** C. 1930, Scc. 5130; **West Virginia,** C. 1931, Ch. 43, Art. 1, Sec. 17.

REFERENCES

Books

SCRIBNER, CHARLES H. *A Treatise on the Law of Dower,* 2d ed., II, 778–80 (1883).
STIMSON, F. J. *American Statute Law,* Sec. 3233 (1886).

Section 195. Dower—Methods of Barring in General

CROSS REFERENCES: Dower, abolition and statutory substitutes, **Sec. 189**; Barring dower by jointure, contract, deed, will, partition, execution, sale, etc., **Secs. 196–201**; Forfeiture of dower, **Sec. 202**; Barring curtesy, **Sec. 220**; Forfeiture of curtesy, **Sec. 221**

Consistent with the underlying purpose of dower, the common law has always been extremely solicitous in protecting the dower estate from destruction by placing it outside the husband's control and improvidence. Also, because of the wife's basic incapacity, she herself was permitted

---

[1] See Charles H. Scribner, *On the Law of Dower,* 2d ed., II, 778–80.

to exercise little control over it. In general, the law of the cases and of the statutes still favors the widow's estate. We have seen, however, that common-law dower has been widely modified by legislation (**Sec. 189**). Going to the extreme are the growing number of jurisdictions which have abolished dower and given the husband the same control of his lands as of his personal property, limiting him only in his testamentary control of the same. And, consistent with the general recognition of married women, the wife has been given a more extensive authority to deal with her dower or statutory share.

In this section and the six sections which follow, the statutes prescribing the methods by which the widow's dower or statutory share of real and personal property may be barred are collected. Only a general comment is intended in this section. The legislation on the subject is far from satisfactory. Much of it is of ancient origin and ill suited to meet the needs of the present day. In many jurisdictions, the statutes are not in harmony with the modified scheme of marital rights established. There is a need both for the revision of existing legislation and for additional legislation.

The earliest method of barring dower seems to have been by the creation of a substitute known as *dower ad ostium ecclesiae,* consisting of a grant of lands to the bride made with her assent at the church door as a part of the marriage ceremony. It is interesting to note that the Code of the **District of Columbia** carries forward an ancient English statute which recognizes this mode of barring dower (C. 1929, T. 14, Sec. 28). *Dower ad ostium ecclesiae* was supplanted by the common-law and equitable jointures, which form the background for the statutory jointure found in twenty-five jurisdictions today (**Sec. 196**). The statutes which permit the barring of dower or statutory share by jointure or settlement of property before or after marriage are archaic in design and probably are seldom utilized. Most of them do not in express terms offer a means whereby the widow's statutory share of personal property may be barred. A few of them do not seem to require the intended wife's assent when the settlement is made before marriage; and none of them are in harmony with the modern freedom of the spouses to contract inter se. While it is now generally recognized that the parties may freely contract before or after marriage in respect to the rights of each in the property of the other, there is little express legislative recognition of this fact (**Secs. 197, 198**). To clarify the law and to remove useless and confusing material from the statutes, the jointure legislation should be discarded and replaced by an express recognition of the right of the

§ 195]

spouses to bar dower and similar interests by simple antenuptial or post-nuptial contracts. The position of a few states which expressly forbid the spouses to contract inter se, generally or particularly in reference to dower, etc., seems indefensible (**Sec. 198**).

In all jurisdictions with the exception, apparently, of **Florida** (see **Sec. 189,** Table XCV, p. 369), the husband may freely dispose of his personal property by his sole transfer inter vivos. In most of those jurisdictions which retain inchoate dower or a similar interest in lands, the common practice of barring the same by joint deed of the spouses is sanctioned by express statute. Consistent with the trend of legislation in respect to the wife's conveyances of her own real property, the separate examination has been almost universally abolished, and a majority of states permit her to release her inchoate interest by her sole deed to the husband's grantee or one holding under him (**Sec. 200**). Express legislation of this latter type is desirable and is worthy of adoption in all jurisdictions.

The husband, of course, cannot defeat the widow's dower or statutory share by his will. The most that he can do is to force her to an election by offering her a substitute provision. Statutes commonly define in some detail the manner and time in which the election shall be made (**Secs. 205–7**). The common-law rule of construction in respect to the effect of a devise or bequest not expressly in lieu of dower has been widely abolished by express legislation; and the prevailing rule now is that the widow is put to an election unless it clearly appears from the will that she is intended to have both the testamentary provision and dower or statutory share (**Sec. 199**). A few jurisdictions, however, retain the common-law rule generally or in respect to bequests of personalty.

While at common law absolute divorce bars dower and statutory share, statutes often save the same when the divorce is decreed because of the husband's misconduct. In the absence of divorce, however, the lawmakers do not seem to have arrived at any well-defined or uniform policy of forfeiting the wife's rights in the husband's property because of her misconduct during the marriage. Statutes working a forfeiture, generally for adultery or desertion, were found in twenty-four jurisdictions; but most of them are fragmentary and narrow in character (**Sec. 202**). Many of them purport to bar dower or statutory share of lands only. The writer believes that the forfeiture principle should be extended, and that the widow should be barred of her dower or statutory share of real and personal property, and all right to elect against the husband's will, when she has deserted him or when he has lived apart

[§ 195

with cause sufficient for divorce a substantial period immediately preceding his death. While the penalty may seem drastic, it is merited, and entirely justified if applied to both spouses with equal force. There is also a real need for legislation permitting the husband to convey his lands free of dower when he has been deserted or is living apart for any cause.

In those jurisdictions which retain inchoate dower or a similarly protected estate during coverture, there is little legislation modifying the common-law rule that, when lands are sold to satisfy an obligation subordinate to dower, the purchaser takes subject to the wife's inchoate interest (**Sec. 201**). A few jurisdictions which give the widow an enlarged estate protected from the husband's sole conveyance expressly permit his creditors to defeat the same during marriage or after his death. Generally, however, not only are his creditors powerless to defeat the wife's inchoate interest, but the court is powerless to order the lands sold free of the same. Legislation similar to that found in **West Virginia** (**Sec. 201**) permitting the court to order the sale free of the dower estate and protecting the wife in the proceeds is highly desirable and merits adoption elsewhere. It represents a convenient and practical solution to the problem, and does not work an undue hardship on the wife.

Especial attention is also directed to another admirable statute found in **West Virginia** enabling the husband or his promisee under a contract for the sale of his real property to bring suit to consummate the same and bar dower with compensation (**Sec. 201**).

REFERENCES

[See also references on jointure, **Sec. 196**]

Books

STIMSON, F. J. *American Statute Law,* Sec. 3240 (1886).

TIFFANY, HERBERT THORNDIKE. *The Law of Real Property and Other Interests in Land,* 2d ed., Vol. 1, Sec. 224 (1920).

WOERNER, J. G. *The American Law of Administration,* 3d ed., Sec. 114 (1923).

Article

HARPER, FOWLER V. "Effect of Foreign Divorce upon Dower and Similar Property Interests," 26 Ill. L. Rev. 397–422 (1931).

Notes

"The Relinquishment of Dower and Curtesy between Husband and Wife in Virginia," 13 Va. L. Rev. 418–25 (1927).

"Real Property—Husband and Wife—Dower—Protection of the Inchoate Right of Dower," 11 Minn. L. Rev. 354–66 (1927).

§ 195]

Section 196. Dower—Barring by Jointure or Settlement

CROSS REFERENCES: Barring dower, in general, **Sec. 195**; Barring dower by settlement or contract before or after marriage, **Secs. 197, 198**; Forfeiture or failure of provision in lieu of dower, **Secs. 203, 204**; Election and waiver, **Secs. 205–7**

The jointure as a legal method of barring dower was introduced by the Statute of Uses. Because of the prevalence of use estates, of which the wife was not endowed under the English law, it became a common practice to require the intended husband to make other provision for the wife by way of a conveyance of lands before marriage. When the Statute of Uses fastened the legal estate to the use estate, in order to prevent the widow having both dower in the husband's legal estates and also the substitute provisions made for her, the statute expressly provided that a woman having a jointure should not be endowed (27 Hen. VIII, c. 10, s. 6). As the statute was construed, the following requisites were said to be necessary for a conveyance before marriage to operate as a bar: "1. The jointure must take effect immediately on the death of the husband. 2. It must be for her own life at least . . . . 3. It must be made to herself, and to no other in trust for her. 4. It must be made, and so in the deed particularly expressed to be, in satisfaction of her whole dower, and not of any particular part of it."[1] The assent of the intended wife was held to be unnecessary and hence her infancy immaterial, for the operative force of the legal jointure as a substitute for dower rested in the sufficiency of its provisions. If a jointure meeting the foregoing requisites was settled after marriage, it did not operate as an absolute bar, but the statute required the widow to elect between the same and her dower (27 Hen. VIII, c. 10, s. 9). An antenuptial settlement in lieu of dower which did not meet the technical requirements of a legal jointure was enforced in equity if assented to by the wife before marriage, or by her parent or guardian if she were an infant. The equitable jointure as a bar to dower rests primarily on a contract basis.[2]

Statutes which provide for the barring of dower or statutory share in lands by "jointure" were found in twenty-two jurisdictions (**Alaska, Arkansas, Delaware, District of Columbia, Hawaii, Illinois, Indiana, Kentucky, Maine, Maryland, Massachusetts, Michigan, Missouri, Montana, New Jersey, Oregon, Rhode Island, South Carolina, Vermont, Virginia, West Virginia, Wisconsin**). Legislation of a similar import is found in three others (**Georgia, New**

[1] Sir William Blackstone, *Commentaries on the Laws of England,* II, 138.

[2] Herbert Thorndike Tiffany, *Law of Real Property,* 2d ed., Vol. 1, Sec. 226.

Hampshire, Ohio). With but few exceptions, these jurisdictions belong to that class which retain dower substantially as at common law
(**Sec. 189**). In general, the statutory jointure represents an admixture
of the features of both the old legal and the equitable jointure, with
emphasis upon the latter. By the terms of most of the statutes, a settlement of personal property is as effective as a conveyance of lands, and
the assent of the wife before marriage is usually required for either. The
most common type of statute, found in a number of jurisdictions in
almost identical form, provides that dower in lands may be barred by
a jointure of lands or by pecuniary provision settled on the intended
wife before marriage with her assent; if settled before marriage without
her assent, or after marriage, she may elect between the same and dower,
but is not entitled to both. By way of summary, the terms of the statutes
comprehend settlements in lieu of dower by conveyance of lands before
marriage (twenty-five), by pecuniary provision before marriage (eighteen), by conveyance of lands after marriage (twenty-one), by pecuniary
provision after marriage (sixteen). Except in **Kentucky, New Hampshire, Vermont,** and **Wisconsin,** the subject matter of the legislation
is apparently confined to the barring of dower or other interest in lands
only.

As under the Statute of Uses, a jointure of lands must commonly
consist of an estate for the life of the wife at least (thirteen jurisdictions) and take effect before or immediately on the death of the husband
(sixteen jurisdictions). In others, a charge upon real estate (**Delaware**)
or any estate (**Maryland, Ohio, Virginia, West Virginia**) seems sufficient. A jointure originally was created by a conveyance to both of the
parties to the intended marriage jointly or "in jointure." The statutes
of six states expressly recognize that form of jointure. Three (**Arkansas, Illinois, Indiana**) are express to the effect that the conveyance
may be made in trust for the intended wife, and the same is probably
true in other jurisdictions. The statute of **Maryland** is confined to
settlements made by the husband himself, but that limitation is not
usual. While the provision made for the widow must be clearly intended to be in lieu of dower in order to operate as a bar thereof or to
force an election, an express statement of such intention in the instrument is not ordinarily required. A few of the statutes, however, seem
to establish that requirement. The **Virginia** statute goes to the other
extreme in presuming that a provision made for the wife by deed is
intended in lieu of dower unless a contrary intention appears therein or
in some other writing signed by the party making the provision.

§ 196]

The assent of the intended wife to the jointure or pecuniary provision is expressly required in fourteen jurisdictions. If the same is made before marriage without her assent, she is not entitled to dower in addition, but is put to an election (thirteen jurisdictions). Some of the statutes requiring her assent are not clear as to the effect of a settlement made without it. It is commonly provided that her assent shall be expressed by becoming a party to the instrument if of age, or by joining therein with her father or guardian if a minor (ten jurisdictions). Other states, however, do not permit a minor absolutely to bar her dower in this manner, but allow her to elect between the provisions and dower (**Kentucky, Ohio, Virginia, West Virginia**).

The legislation of six jurisdictions (**District of Columbia, Maryland, Missouri, New Jersey, Rhode Island, South Carolina**) does not seem to require the assent of the intended wife for the jointure to operate as a bar to her dower. The statutes of the **District of Columbia** and **New Jersey** are taken directly from the Statute of Uses. If the legal jointure is perpetuated in these jurisdictions, the provision found in three of them (**Missouri, New Jersey, Rhode Island**) permitting the widow to waive the jointure and demand dower if the same was settled on her before marriage and during her infancy seems strangely inconsistent and illogical. The **Vermont** statute is unlike any of the others. Regardless of whether the settlement be made before marriage with or without her concurrence, or after marriage with her consent, the widow may waive the same and take her statutory share of lands.

All of the statutes which refer to a jointure or pecuniary provision settled on the wife during the marriage in lieu of dower carry forward the provision of the Statute of Uses that the widow may elect between the same and her dower, but is not entitled to both. That the wife consents to the provision when it is made is apparently immaterial. These statutes seem to be founded upon the principle that the wife even by agreement cannot create an absolute bar to her dower claim; and as such are out of harmony with the modern law in many of the same jurisdictions. When the widow is put to an election because the settlement was made after marriage, or before marriage without her assent or during her infancy, the statutes generally require her to waive the same within a limited time after the husband's death or lose her right to demand dower.

Most of the statutes considered in this section are of rather ancient origin, and are probably little utilized today. They were designed to offer a means of barring dower when other means were very limited.

[§ 196

As such, they are not in harmony with the greater freedom now allowed the husband and wife to contract before or after marriage concerning the rights of each in both real and personal property of the other (**Secs. 197, 198**).

The statutes discussed above will be found outlined in the table which follows.

TABLE XCVII

BARRING DOWER BY JOINTURE OR SETTLEMENT

Jurisdiction and Citation	In General	Assent of Intended Wife; How Expressed	Election (See Also Secs. 205-7)
Alaska .... Comp. L. 1913, Secs. 468-71, 473	Dower in all lands of husband may be barred by jointure settled on intended wife with her assent or by any pecuniary provision made for her benefit in lieu of dower with her assent. Jointure must consist of a freehold estate in lands for life of wife at least, to take effect in possession or profit immediately on death of husband	If of full age, by joining in conveyance by which jointure or pecuniary provision is settled; if under that age, by joining in conveyance with father or guardian	If jointure or pecuniary provision be made before marriage without assent of intended wife, or if made after marriage, she may elect after death of husband to take the same or be endowed. She is deemed to have elected to take jointure, etc., unless within one year after death of husband she files her written election to relinquish her rights under same
Arkansas .... Crawf. and Moses, Dig. 1921, Secs. 3522-25, 3527	Dower in all lands of husband may be barred by jointure settled on intended wife with her assent or by any pecuniary provision made for her benefit in lieu of dower with her assent. Jointure may be by conveyance to person and intended wife or in trust for them, or to intended wife alone or in trust for her	If of full age, by becoming a party to conveyance by which jointure or pecuniary provision is settled; if she be an infant, by joining with father or guardian in conveyance	If jointure or pecuniary provision be made before marriage without assent of intended wife, or if made after marriage, she may elect to take the same or be endowed. She is deemed to have elected to take jointure, etc., unless within one year after death of husband she enters on lands to be assigned for her dower or commences proceedings for recovery or assignment of dower
Delaware ...... R. C. 1915, Sec. 3305	Dower is barred if woman of 21 years or more prior to and in contemplation of marriage, by agreement, accepts an estate in or charge upon real estate to take effect at or before death of intended husband and to continue during her life as a provision for her support in lieu of dower in lands (termed a jointure by statute)	See preceding column	

§ 196]

TABLE XCVII (*Continued*)

Jurisdiction and Citation	In General	Assent of Intended Wife; How Expressed	Election (See Also Secs. 205-7)
District of Columbia .. C. 1929, T. 14, Secs. 32, 33	Statute provides for legal jointure, which is a bar to claim of dower[1]		If jointure settled on wife during marriage, she may after death of husband refuse the same and demand her dower
Georgia .... C. 1926, C. of Prac., Sec. 5249	Dower may be barred "by provisions made prior to the marriage and accepted by the wife in lieu of dower"; and by provision made by deed and accepted by wife after husband's death, expressly in lieu of dower or with that manifest intention	See preceding column	See first column
Hawaii .... R. L. 1925, Secs. 3027-29	Dower in lands of husband may be barred by jointure settled on intended wife with her assent or by any pecuniary provision made for her benefit in lieu of dower with her assent. Jointure must consist of an estate in lands for life of wife at least, to take effect immediately on death of husband	If of full age, by becoming a party to conveyance by which jointure or pecuniary provision is settled; if under age, by joining with father or guardian in conveyance	If jointure or pecuniary provision be made before marriage without assent of intended wife, or if after marriage, dower is barred unless within six months after notice of death of husband and of such jointure, etc., she elects to waive the same and to be endowed
Illinois .... Cahill, R. S. 1931, Ch. 41, Secs. 7-9, 11, 13	Dower in all lands of husband may be barred by jointure settled on intended wife with her assent. Jointure may be by conveyance of an estate in land to intended husband and wife or in trust for them or to intended wife or in trust for her	If of full age, by becoming a party to conveyance by which jointure is settled; if a minor, by joining with father or guardian in conveyance	If jointure settled before marriage without assent of intended wife, or if settled after marriage, she may elect to take the same or be endowed. She is deemed to have elected to take the jointure unless, within one year after letters testamentary or of administration are issued, she transmits to county court a written renunciation thereof (statute gives form for renunciation)

[1] The statutes of the **District of Columbia** and **New Jersey** are taken directly from the Statute of Uses (27 Hen. VIII, c. 10, s. 6).

[§ 196

TABLE XCVII (*Continued*)

Jurisdiction and Citation	In General	Assent of Intended Wife; How Expressed	Election (See Also Secs. 205–7)
Indiana .... Burns, Ann. St. 1926, Secs. 3367–70	Statutory share in lands of husband may be barred by jointure with assent of intended wife. Jointure may be by conveyance of estate in lands to intended husband and wife or to the latter alone or to any person in trust for her; or by pecuniary provision made for benefit of intended wife in lieu of statutory share. Jointure consisting of real estate must not be less than a freehold estate to take effect in possession or profit immediately on death of husband	Her assent to receive the same in lieu of statutory share must be at time of creation of jointure by writing endorsed upon or attached to deed creating jointure. If she be an infant, her assent is not valid unless her father, or mother (if father dead), or guardian (if both dead), joins therein	If jointure or pecuniary provision be made before marriage without assent of intended wife, or if made after marriage, she may elect within one year after death of husband to take the same or her statutory share
Kentucky ...... Carroll, St. 1922, Sec. 2136	Wife's interest in the property and estate of husband may be barred by a conveyance or devise of real or personal property by way of jointure		If jointure be made before marriage without consent of intended wife or during her infancy or after marriage, she may within 12 months after death of husband waive the same by written relinquishment and claim her dower or share of husband's estate
Maine .... R. S. 1930, Ch. 89, Secs. 10–12	Right and interest by descent in husband's lands may be barred by jointure settled on intended wife with her assent, or by pecuniary provision made for her benefit with her consent in lieu of statutory rights in husband's lands. Jointure shall consist of freehold estate in lands for life of wife at least, to take effect immediately on husband's death	If of full age, by becoming a party to the conveyance by which jointure or pecuniary provision is settled; if under age, by joining with her father or guardian	If jointure or pecuniary provision be made before marriage without consent of intended wife, or if made after marriage, it bars her right and interest by descent in husband's lands unless within six months after husband's death she makes written election to waive the same, filed in registry of probate
Maryland ...... Bagby, Ann. C. 1924, Art. 93, Sec. 315	If married woman has any estate settled on her by her husband by jointure or other settlement before marriage, such jointure or settlement bars her of dower in husband's lands; but she may accept what husband gives her in his will		

§ 196]

TABLE XCVII (*Continued*)

Jurisdiction and Citation	In General	Assent of Intended Wife; How Expressed	Election (See Also Secs. 205–7)
Massachusetts .. G. L. 1932, Ch. 189, Secs. 7–9	Dower in all lands of husband may be barred by jointure settled on intended wife with her assent before marriage, or by pecuniary provision made for her benefit in lieu of dower with her assent. Jointure must consist of a freehold estate in land for life of wife at least, to take effect in possession or profit immediately upon death of husband	If of full age, by becoming a party to conveyance by which jointure or pecuniary provision is made; if a minor, by joining with father or guardian in conveyance	Jointure or pecuniary provision made after marriage, or before marriage without assent of intended wife, bars her dower unless within six months after death of husband or notice of his death (if husband absent) she elects to waive the same. She also has six months after notice of existence of jointure, etc., in which to make election
Michigan ...... Comp. L. 1929, Secs. 13081– 84, 13086	Dower in all lands of husband may be barred by jointure settled on intended wife with her assent before marriage, or by any pecuniary provision made for her benefit in lieu of dower with her assent. Jointure must consist of a freehold estate in lands for life of wife at least, to take effect in possession or profit immediately on death of husband	If of full age, by becoming a party to conveyance by which jointure or pecuniary provision is settled; if under age, by joining with father or guardian in conveyance	If jointure or pecuniary provision be made before marriage without assent of intended wife, or if made after marriage, she may after death of husband elect to take the same or be endowed. She is deemed to have elected to take jointure, etc., unless within one year after death of husband she commences proceedings for assignment or recovery of dower
Missouri .... R. S. 1929, Secs. 334–35	If intended wife, prior to and in contemplation of marriage, in agreement or marriage contract with intended husband or other person, receives any estate of real or personal property to take effect after death of husband by way of jointure and expressed to be in full discharge of her dower claim, the same is a bar thereto. When lands are conveyed to husband and wife, or to other person to use of husband and wife or to use of wife for the jointure of the wife, her dower in residue is barred		If conveyance, assurance, agreement or contract for jointure be made after marriage, or if made before marriage during infancy of intended wife, the widow may at her election renounce the jointure and take dower

[§ 196

TABLE XCVII (*Continued*)

Jurisdiction and Citation	In General	Assent of Intended Wife; How Expressed	Election (See Also Secs. 205–7)
Montana .... R. C. 1921, Secs. 5824–25	Dower may be barred in all lands of husband by jointure settled on intended wife with her consent before marriage provided such jointure consists of a freehold estate in lands for the life of the wife at least, to take effect in possession or profit immediately on death of husband	If of full age, by her becoming a party to conveyance by which jointure is settled; if under age, by joining with father or guardian in conveyance	
New Hampshire. Pub. L. 1926, Ch. 306, Sec. 15	If settlement is made upon wife before marriage, stipulated to be in lieu of her right of dower, homestead, distributive share, or either of them, in husband's estate, widow is not entitled to any right or rights in lieu of which settlement is made		
New Jersey .... Comp. St. 1910, p. 2047, Secs. 10, 12	Statute provides for legal jointure, which is a bar to claim of dower[1]		If jointure be made before marriage and during infancy of intended wife, or after marriage, the widow may at her election waive the same and demand her dower
Ohio .... Complete G. C. 1931 (Page), Supp. 1932, Sec. 10502(2)	Conveyance of an estate or interest in real property to woman in lieu of dower to take effect on death of grantor, if accepted by grantee, will bar her right of dower in real property of grantor		If conveyance in lieu of dower was made during intended wife's minority or during marriage, she may waive the same and demand dower
Oregon .... C. 1930, Secs. 10(314)– 10(317), 10(319)	Dower may be barred in all lands of husband by jointure settled on intended wife with her assent before marriage, or by any pecuniary provision made for her benefit in lieu of dower with her assent. Jointure must consist of a freehold estate in lands for life of wife at least, to take effect in possession or profit immediately on death of husband	If of full age, by becoming a party to conveyance by which jointure or pecuniary provision is settled; if under age, by joining with father or guardian in conveyance	If jointure or pecuniary provision made before marriage, without assent of intended wife, or if made after marriage, she may after death of husband elect to take the same or be endowed. She is deemed to have elected to take the jointure, etc., unless within one year after death of husband she executes, acknowledges and records in deed records of county where estate administered her election to accept dower

[1] The statutes of the **District of Columbia** and **New Jersey** are taken directly from the Statute of Uses (27 Hen. VIII, c. 10, s. 6).

§ 196]

TABLE XCVII (*Continued*)

Jurisdiction and Citation	In General	Assent of Intended Wife; How Expressed	Election (See Also Secs. 205–7)
Rhode Island.... G. L. 1923, Sec. 5807	If any real or personal estate be conveyed by deed for jointure of wife in lieu of dower to take effect in her own possession immediately on death of husband and to continue during her life or in fee, determinable by such acts only as would forfeit dower at common law, such conveyance bars her dower in the residue of husband's lands		If conveyance in lieu of dower is made before marriage and during infancy of woman, or after marriage, widow may at her election waive jointure and demand her dower providing she make a written election within twelve months after probate of will or granting of letters of administration
South Carolina.. C. of L. 1922, C. C., Secs. 5238, 5241–42	Wife having jointure is barred of dower in residue of lands of husband by whom she has the jointure		If wife has jointure of lands given or assured during marriage for term of her life, she may after death of husband refuse the same and demand her dower
Vermont .... G. L. 1917, Sec. 3405	Statutory share of lands may be barred by jointure settled on widow by husband or other person, or pecuniary provision made for her before marriage with or without her agreement or consent, or after marriage with her consent, to have effect after death of husband, and expressed to be in lieu or discharge of statutory share		Within eight months after will probated or letters of administration granted or in such further time as court allows, widow may by written election waive jointure or pecuniary provision and take her statutory share of lands[2]
Virginia .... C. 1930, Secs. 5120–21	If any real or personal estate, intended to be in lieu of dower, is conveyed or devised for jointure of wife, her dower in lands is barred. Every such provision by deed or will is taken to be intended in lieu of dower unless a contrary intention plainly appears in deed or will or in some other writing signed by party making the provision	See next column	If jointure made before marriage without assent of intended wife in writing or during her infancy, or if made after marriage, widow may elect to waive the same and demand her dower. Such election shall be made within one year after death of husband, but if suit brought within the year to construe conveyance, time may be extended to not exceeding six months after the final order made

[2] If the widow was not the first wife of husband and he leaves no issue by her, and an agreement before or after marriage was entered into between them, the court may deny her statutory share of lands or any provision other than that provided for by the agreement, if in the opinion of the court she has sufficient provision for comfortable support during life (**Vermont**). By Section 3279, General Laws, 1917, apparently the widow is not entitled to share in the husband's personal estate unless she waives the jointure or pecuniary provision made for her in lieu of statutory share in the husband's lands.

[§ 196

TABLE XCVII (*Concluded*)

Jurisdiction and Citation	In General	Assent of Intended Wife; How Expressed	Election (See Also Secs. 205–7)
West Virginia... C. 1931, Ch. 43, Art. 1, Secs. 7, 8	If any real or personal estate, intended to be in lieu of dower, is conveyed or devised for jointure of wife, her dower in lands is barred	See next column	If jointure made before marriage without assent of intended wife or during her infancy, or if made after marriage, widow may elect to waive the same and demand her dower. If jointure be created by conveyance of husband, widow's election shall be made within eight months after his death by a writing acknowledged and proved as required for deeds and recorded with clerk of county court of county where instrument creating jointure is recorded
Wisconsin ..... St. 1931, Secs. 233.09–233.12, 233.14, 233.15	Dower in all lands of husband may be barred by jointure settled on intended wife with her assent before marriage, or by any pecuniary provision made for her benefit in lieu of dower with her assent. Jointure must consist of a freehold estate in lands for life of wife at least, to take effect in possession or profit before or immediately on death of husband	If of full age, by becoming a party to conveyance by which jointure or pecuniary provision is made; if under age, by joining with father or guardian in conveyance	If jointure or pecuniary provision be made before marriage and without assent of intended wife, or if made after marriage, she may elect to take the same or to take her dower in lands and share of personalty. She is deemed to have elected to take jointure, etc., unless within one year after petition for administration or probate of will, she files with proper court her written election to take provisions made for her by law[3]

[3] Provisions relative to election do not apply when husband dies intestate without issue. Election may be made by guardian of insane widow, or personal representative of deceased widow leaving issue by the deceased husband, within two years from filing petition for administration, etc. Time consumed in action brought to contest jointure, etc., does not constitute any part of the period within which election may be made.

REFERENCES

Books

SCRIBNER, CHARLES H. *A Treatise on the Law of Dower,* 2d ed., Vol. II, ch. xv, pp. 389–437 (1883).

STIMSON, F. J. *American Statute Law,* Secs. 3241–43 (1886).

TIFFANY, HERBERT THORNDIKE. *The Law of Real Property and Other Interests in Land,* 2d ed., Vol. 1, Sec. 226 (1920).

§ 196]

Section 197. Dower—Barring by Contract or Settlement before Marriage

CROSS REFERENCES: Antenuptial contracts, **Sec. 155**; Barring dower by jointure, **Sec. 196**; Barring dower by postnuptial contract, **Sec. 198**

In the preceding section, an outline was made of the legislation which provides for the barring of dower or statutory share in lands by jointure or other settlement of property created in lieu thereof. As was there indicated, most of this legislation does not in express terms purport to offer a means of barring the widow's statutory share in personalty. While the jointure presents a method of barring dower, the statutes considered in **Section 196** are not generally regarded as exclusive in nature. Hence they do not operate to prevent the wife from releasing her dower by any other recognized form of antenuptial contract.

The early common law did not tolerate the release of dower by antenuptial agreement. Now, however, it is generally recognized in law as well as in equity that parties intending marriage may define the rights of each in the property of the other by a contract which is fair and without imposition. Thus dower and other rights in the real and personal property of the husband may be relinquished by contract before marriage not subject to the limitations, and for a totally different consideration than is prescribed, in the jointure statutes. Such contracts are obviously not against public policy; but because of the relationship of the parties involved, and the traditional judicial attitude of affording extensive protection to the dower estate, they will be closely scrutinized for evidence of overreaching.

As has already been observed (**Sec. 155**), there is little direct legislative recognition of antenuptial contracts. Statutes were found in six jurisdictions permitting the wife by agreement before marriage to waive her statutory right to take against the husband's will (**New York**); to release her dower and other rights which she may acquire by marriage in the property of the husband (**North Carolina**); to bar her statutory share in the husband's real and personal estate (**Connecticut**), or in his lands (**Nebraska**); to determine what rights she shall have in the property of the husband during marriage and after its dissolution by death (**Delaware, Maine**). The **Connecticut** and **Maine** statutes seem to contemplate a property settlement of some kind. This seems like a rather fragmentary bit of legislation to be found upon so important a matter. Further legislative recognition of the power of the husband

[§ 197

and wife to release dower and other rights in the property of the other by contract before marriage seems advisable.

The details of the statutes above will be found in **Section 155.** Citations for the same follow:

Connecticut, G. S. 1930, Sec. 5156; **Delaware,** R. C. 1915, Sec. 3050, as amended by Sess. L. 1919, Ch. 197, p. 525; **Maine,** R. S. 1930, Ch. 74, Sec. 8; **Nebraska,** Comp. St. 1929, Sec. 30(106); **New York,** Cahill, Consol. L. 1930, Ch. 13, Sec. 18(9); **North Carolina,** C. 1927, Sec. 2516.

REFERENCES

Annotations

"Antenuptial Contract, Consideration of Marriage, Contract a Bar to Dower," 2 L. R. A. 372–73 (1889).

"Validity of Antenuptial Agreement for Release of Dower and Like Interests in Property of Intended Spouse," Ann. Cas. 1914B 620.

"Validity of Contract Relinquishing Rights in Intended Husband's Estate, Signed by Intending Wife in Ignorance of Her Legal Rights," 9 L. R. A. (N.S.) 953–54 (1907).

"What Amounts to Laches or Delay on Part of Wife or Widow in Attacking Antenuptial Settlement Which Will Prevent Relief," 74 A. L. R. 559–61 (1931).

Section 198. Dower—Barring by Contract or Settlement after Marriage

CROSS REFERENCES: Contracts and conveyances between spouses, **Secs. 156, 182;** Barring dower by jointure, **Sec. 196;** Barring dower by contract before marriage, **Sec. 197**

The common law did not recognize the power of the spouses to contract inter se. Hence the wife could not release her dower to the husband during coverture, at least unless as part of a separation agreement. A postnuptial settlement of property in lieu of dower was likewise not binding as a bar, either in law or equity; but in equity the widow was put to an election, and the same was true at law under the Statute of Uses when the settlement met the requirements of a legal jointure. Legislation found on the subject of barring dower, etc., by jointure or other settlement of property after marriage is outlined in **Section 196.** Reference to that section will indicate that the statutes are generally concerned with the barring of dower or other interest in lands only,

§ 198]

and that all of them carry forward the provision of the Statute of Uses permitting the widow to waive the postnuptial settlement and demand her dower, etc. The statutes are of more or less ancient origin and are not generally regarded as exclusive in nature. They are obviously in discord with the general power which the wife now has to bind herself by contract with the husband.

In the majority of jurisdictions today, the wife may contract for most purposes as if sole (**Sec. 152**). In many, she is given express authority to contract with the husband (**Secs. 156, 182**). Under these statutes or others making the wife sui juris as to property, it is commonly held that she may execute a binding release of her dower or other interest in the husband's property by contract with him during coverture. As in the case of antenuptial agreements, the contract must be fair and without imposition. By express statute in three jurisdictions, the wife by contract with the husband may bar her statutory share in real and personal estate (**Connecticut**), waive her right of election to take against the husband's will (**New York**), and release her dower or other right which she may acquire by the marriage in his property (**North Carolina**). In addition, a **Kansas** statute enables the wife to permit the husband to dispose of more than one-half of his property by will, thereby waiving her right to take against his will.

The statutes of a few jurisdictions forbid contracts generally between husband and wife (**Sec. 156**). **Iowa** and **Oregon** have interesting legislation to the effect that when property is owned by husband or wife the other has no interest therein which can be made the subject of a contract between them. These statutes seem to preclude the release of dower, etc., by contract inter se. **Minnesota** reaches a similar result by providing that contracts between the spouses relative to the real estate of either or any interest therein are invalid.

There is no good reason why the husband and wife should not have complete freedom to contract inter se in reference to the rights of each in the property of the other, subject to the ordinary rules controlling parties standing in a confidential relationship. A further legislative recognition of this fact seems desirable.

The statutes of the foregoing seven jurisdictions are outlined in Table LXXX, **Section 156** (p. 67). Citations for the same follow:

Connecticut, G. S. 1930, Sec. 5156; **Iowa**, C. 1927, Sec. 10447; **Kansas**, R. S. 1923, Sec. 22(238); **Minnesota**, G. S. 1923, Sec. 8621; **New York**, Cahill, Consol. L. 1930, Ch. 13, Sec. 18(9); **North Carolina**, C. 1927, Sec. 2516; **Oregon**, C. 1930, Sec. 33(201).

[§ 198

REFERENCES

Annotation

"Validity of Postnuptial Agreement Releasing or Waiving Rights of Surviving Spouse on Death of Other Spouse," 49 A. L. R. 116–53 (1927).

Section 199. Dower—Barring by Will

CROSS REFERENCES: Dower and statutory share in real and personal estate, **Sec. 189**; Election and waiver, **Secs. 205–7**; Barring homestead by will, **Sec. 228**

Consistent with the general protection accorded to common-law dower, the husband cannot by his will defeat the widow's estate or force upon her a substitute provision. He may offer her a substitute by way of testamentary provision in lieu of dower, but she is free to refuse the same. By the English Dower Act of 1834 (3 and 4 Wm. IV, c. 105, s. 4), dower was made subject to destruction by the husband's will. It has been seen, however, that in this country the tendency has been in the direction of further limiting his testamentary control of his property. **North and South Dakota** are exceptions. In those two jurisdictions there is no general limitation upon the power of the husband to will his property to others than his spouse (**Sec. 189**). The other jurisdictions, exclusive of the community-property states, have preserved dower or have established a system of enlarged rights which insures the widow a share in the husband's lands or in both his real and personal estate (**Sec. 189**). This share cannot be defeated by his will if she pursues her rights as the statutes direct. The husband may, however, force her to choose between her rights under the law and what he offers her in his will in lieu thereof. Most of the statutes are express to that effect (see résumé at end of this section). In some jurisdictions, especially in those which have abolished dower, the right to dissent from the husband's will is the very basis of the widow's security. The statutes governing her election between the will and dower or statutory share are collected in **Sections 205–7**. Generally, she must affirmatively refuse the provisions of the will in order to save her legal rights.

This section, however, is primarily concerned with legislation determining when a provision for the widow in the husband's will puts her to an election, and when she may take what the will gives her in addition to her dower or statutory share. In the absence of statute, there is a strong presumption that the widow shall have both the testamentary provision and her dower in lands. The generally recognized rule is that a devise or bequest to the widow is deemed to be in addition to dower and not in lieu of dower, unless the will expresses a contrary intention or unless a contrary intention is manifestly implied by reason of terms therein inconsistent with her demand of dower. **Georgia** is the only jurisdiction which substantially codifies the common law in this respect (see *Speer* v. *Speer,* 67 Ga. 748 [1881]). In most of the jurisdictions which retain dower or an analogous substitute, and in several which have established a radically different system of statutory rights, the common-law rule is expressly abrogated in favor of a statutory rule reaching exactly the opposite result. Statutes of this tenor were found in twenty-nine jurisdictions. Under them, a testamentary provision for the widow is deemed to be in lieu of dower or statutory share, and not in addition thereto, unless a contrary intention appears or is expressed in the will. Of those jurisdictions without express legislation on the subject, it is probable that the common-law doctrine is generally abolished by implication.

By the express terms or obvious import of most of the statutes, it is immaterial whether the testamentary provision for the widow be of real or personal estate (**Alaska, Connecticut, Hawaii, Illinois, Indiana, Iowa, Kansas, Kentucky, Maine, Massachusetts, Michigan, Minnesota, Mississippi, Montana, Nebraska, New Hampshire, Ohio, Oregon, Utah, Vermont, Virginia, West Virginia, Wisconsin**). In a few states, however, the statutory rule is expressly confined to cases of a devise of real estate (**Arkansas, Delaware, Missouri, New Jersey**) ; and apparently the common-law rule still controls the effect of a bequest of personalty (see *Kollar* v. *Noble,* 184 Ark. 297 ; 42 S. W. [2d] 408 [1931] ; *Rice* v. *Rice,* 12 Del. Ch. 245 ; 111 A. 439 [1920] ; *In re Goessling's Estate,* 287 Mo. 663 ; 230 S. W. 613 [1921]). Ordinarily, the testamentary provision is made a bar to the widow's share in both real and personal property. In ten of the foregoing jurisdictions, however, the statutes in terms provide that the devise or bequest is deemed to be in lieu of dower or statutory share of lands only (**Alaska, Delaware, Massachusetts, Michigan, Missouri, New Jersey, Oregon, Utah, Vermont, Virginia**). Of these ten jurisdictions, the widow has no share of personal estate protected from the husband's will in **Alaska, Delaware, New Jersey, Oregon,** and **Utah** (Sec. 189). In the other five, with the exception of **Missouri,** the statutes imply that she is put to an election in the same manner as between the will and dower. The legislation found in the **District of Columbia** and **Mary-**

[§ 199

land represents a unique combination of the common-law and statutory rules. In those two jurisdictions a devise of lands or a bequest of personal estate is construed to be intended in lieu of dower in lands and statutory share of personal estate "respectively," unless otherwise expressed in the will.

If the widow is to escape the necessity of an election, most of the statutes require that the intention to give her the devise or bequest in addition to dower, etc., must be found in the will itself. It is commonly provided that such intention must "plainly" or "clearly" appear from the will (eleven jurisdictions); or be declared or expressed in the will (ten jurisdictions). In **Virginia,** it is sufficient if the intention be found in some other writing signed by the husband. In **Vermont,** the widow is put to an election when in the judgment of the probate court the testamentary provision was intended to be in lieu of her statutory share. A literal interpretation of the **Kansas** statute would require her to elect regardless of the husband's intention.

In the remaining eleven jurisdictions (**Alabama, Colorado, Florida, New York, North Carolina, Oklahoma, Rhode Island, Pennsylvania, South Carolina, Tennessee, Wyoming**) no express statutory statement was found establishing the effect of a devise or bequest to the wife when the will does not reveal testator's intention. In at least **South Carolina** and **Rhode Island,** the common-law rule persists (*Scott* v. *Vaughn,* 83 S. C. 362; 65 S. E. 269 [1909]; *Bomar* v. *Wilkins,* 154 S. C. 64; 151 S. E. 110 [1930]; *Rhode Island Hospital Trust Company* v. *Briggs,* 52 R. I. 254; 160 A. 197 [1932]). In the others, the common-law doctrine seems clearly abolished by reason of the radically different system of survivor's rights obtaining (**Colorado, New York, Oklahoma, Pennsylvania, Wyoming**) or by statutes establishing the widow's right to dissent from the husband's will (see *Sanders* v. *Wallace,* 118 Ala. 418; 24 So. 354 [1898]).

The statutory material found on the subject of this section is outlined below in the words of the statutes so far as is practicable. It should be read in connection with **Section 189,** and **Sections 205–7.** Also, the statutes of four jurisdictions (**Kentucky, Rhode Island, Virginia, West Virginia**) provide for the barring of dower in lands by jointure created by will, subject to the provisions of the jointure statutes referred to in **Section 196.**

Alabama (C. 1923, Sec. 10593): Widow may dissent from will of husband and, in lieu of provisions made for her therein, take her dower in lands and statutory share of personal estate.

§ 199]

Alaska (Comp. L. 1913, Sec. 472) : If lands be devised to wife or other provision made for her in husband's will, expressly in lieu of dower, she shall elect between the same and dower in lands of husband; but she is not entitled to both unless it plainly appears by the will to have been so intended.

Arkansas (Crawf. and Moses, Dig. 1921, Secs. 3526, 3538–39) : If land be devised to wife or other provision made for her by will in lieu of her dower, she shall elect between the same and dower in lands of husband (Sec. 3526). If husband devises and bequeaths to wife any portion of real estate of which he died seized, it shall be deemed in lieu of dower out of his estate unless he declares otherwise in his will (Sec. 3538). In case of provisions made by will for widow in lieu of dower she shall elect to accept the same or be endowed of the lands and personal property of which husband died seized (Sec. 3539).

Colorado (Comp. L. 1921, G. S., Secs. 5184–85) : If husband or wife wills away from survivor more than one-half of his or her real and personal property, the survivor may by timely election receive one-half of the deceased spouse's property notwithstanding the will.

Connecticut (G. S. 1930, Sec. 5156) : If husband or wife devises or bequeaths a portion of his or her property to the survivor, such provision shall be taken to be in lieu of survivor's statutory share of real and personal property unless the contrary is expressly stated in the will or clearly appears therein; but survivor may elect between the same and his or her statutory share.

Delaware (R. C. 1915, Sec. 3307) : If husband devises to wife any portion of his real estate, such devise shall be deemed and taken to be in lieu of dower out of his estate, unless he otherwise declares by his will; but widow may elect between devise and dower.

District of Columbia (C. 1929, T. 14, Secs. 37–41) : Every devise of land or estate therein, or bequest of personal estate, to wife of testator shall be construed to be intended in bar of dower in lands or share of personal estate respectively, unless it be otherwise expressed in the will; but she may renounce the same and take dower and distributive share of personalty. If husband wills both real and personal estate, she must renounce the whole or be barred of her right to both real and personal estate. If husband wills real estate only or personal estate only, the devise or bequest bars her of only real or personal estate, as the case may be; but if the devise or bequest or both are expressly in lieu of her legal share of real or personal estate or both she is barred accordingly unless she renounces the same.

[§ 199

Florida (Sess. L. 1933, Ch. 16103, p. 553, Sec. 35): Whenever widow is not satisfied with portion of the estate to which she is entitled under the law of descent and distribution or under the will, or both, she may elect to take dower in real and personal property.

Georgia (C. 1926, Prac. C., Secs. 5249–50): Dower may be barred by a provision made by will, expressly in lieu of dower or where that intention is plain and manifest, and accepted by wife after husband's death (Sec. 5249). If husband devises to wife an interest in his lands, her election of dower bars her of such devise, but does not deprive her of personalty bequeathed to her unless it is expressed to be in lieu of dower (Sec. 5250).

Hawaii (R. L. 1925, Sec. 3030): If husband makes provision for widow by will, she shall elect to take the same or be endowed of his real and personal estate; but she is not entitled to both unless it plainly appears by the will to have been his intention.

Illinois (Cahill, R. S. 1931, Ch. 41, Sec. 10): Any devise of land or estate therein, or any other provision made by deceased spouse's will for survivor, bars dower in lands and statutory share of personal estate, unless otherwise expressed in the will; but survivor may renounce testamentary provision, etc.

Indiana (Burns, Ann. St. 1926, Secs. 3356–57): When real or personal property is left to survivor, or other provision is made for survivor by deceased spouse's will, the survivor shall take under the will only, unless otherwise expressly provided therein, subject to right to elect to take his or her statutory share of the estate.

Iowa (C. 1927, Secs. 11847, 11860, 12006–10): When surviving spouse is named as devisee or legatee in will, it shall be presumed that such devise or legacy is in lieu of distributive share, homestead, and exemptions, unless the intention is clear and explicit to the contrary; subject to survivor's right of election.

Kansas (R. S. 1923, Secs. 22[117], 22[127], 22[238], 22[245]): If any provision is made for widow in husband's will, and she has not consented thereto in writing, she is put to an election between the same and her statutory share of his estate, but is not entitled to both. Widow's statutory share cannot be affected by husband's will if she objects thereto, and relinquishes all rights under the same. The provisions above also govern rights of widower.

Kentucky (Carroll, St. 1922, Secs. 1404, 2136): Widow claiming dower and distributive share of husband's estate is charged with the value of any devise or bequest to her in his will; or she may relinquish

§ 199]

the latter and receive the former; or she may receive both if such is the intention of the testator, plainly expressed in the will or necessarily inferable therefrom (Sec. 1404). The statute on jointures (Sec. 2136), outlined in Table XCVII, **Section 196** (p. 406), includes within its provisions a "conveyance or devise of real or personal estate, by way of jointure," etc.

Maine (R. S. 1930, Ch. 89, Sec. 13): When a specific provision for survivor is made in deceased spouse's will, survivor may elect between the same and his or her statutory share of the estate; but is not entitled to both unless it appears by the will that testator plainly so intended.

Maryland (Bagby, Ann. C. 1924, Art. 93, Secs. 310–14, 326): Substantially the same as the statute of the **District of Columbia.** The same provisions govern rights of widower.

Massachusetts (G. L. 1932, Ch. 191, Secs. 15, 17): Widow or widower is not entitled to dower or curtesy in addition to provisions of the deceased spouse's will, unless such plainly appears by the will to have been his or her intention (Sec. 17). Survivor may waive provisions made for him or her in deceased spouse's will, and claim his or her statutory share of real and personal property (Sec. 15).

Michigan (Comp. L. 1929, Sec. 13085, as amended by Sess. L. 1931, No. 242, p. 421; Sec. 15564): If any lands be devised to wife, or other provision be made for her in will of husband, she shall elect between the same and dower in lands of husband or statutory share of lands left by husband; but she is not entitled to more than one choice unless it plainly appears by the will to have been so intended (Sec. 13085). Husband's testamentary disposition of personal property is subject to election of widow to take any interest that may be given her by the will or her statutory share of personalty (Sec. 15564). If any special devise or bequest is made to wife in lieu of any particular thing or interest, to which she might be entitled in case of intestacy, election by her to take the special devise or bequest or the other particular thing or interest shall not deprive her, or any other person, of the right to leave the testamentary disposition of property in all other respects unaffected, and to have the benefit of any other provision therein (Sec. 15564).

Minnesota (G. S. 1923, Secs. 8720, 8722, 8726): Survivor is entitled to statutory share of lands and personal estate free from testamentary disposition of deceased spouse to which survivor has not consented in writing (Secs. 8720, 8726). If will of "deceased parent" makes provision for surviving spouse in lieu of statutory rights in his estate, such spouse is put to an election; "and no devise or bequest to a surviving

[§ 199

spouse" shall be treated as adding to his or her statutory rights unless it clearly appears from contents of will that such was testator's intention (Sec. 8722). The latter part of the preceding section is apparently not limited in application to cases in which the testator is a "deceased parent" (*In re Evan's Estate,* 145 Minn. 252; 177 N. W. 126 [1920]).

Mississippi (C. 1930, Secs. 3560–61): Any provision for survivor in deceased spouse's will shall be construed to bar any share of the real or personal estate of testator, unless it be otherwise expressed in the will; but survivor may renounce benefit of will when satisfactory provision is not made for him or her therein.

Missouri (R. S. 1929, Secs. 319, 332–33): If testator passes any real estate to wife by will, such devise shall be in lieu of dower out of the real estate of which husband died seized or in which he had an interest at time of death, unless his will declares otherwise; but widow may renounce benefit of will, etc. The provisions above also govern the surviving husband's dower.

Montana (R. C. 1921, Sec. 5819): Every devise or bequest shall bar a widow's dower in lands or her share in personal estate unless otherwise expressed in the will; but she may elect whether to take the same or her dower in lands and share in personal estate.

Nebraska (Comp. St. 1929, Sec. 30[107]): If any real estate be devised by husband or wife to the other, or other provision be made for survivor in his or her will, survivor is entitled to elect between the same and his or her statutory share of lands and personalty in testator's estate; but is not entitled to both unless it plainly appears by the will to have been so intended.

New Hampshire (Pub. L. 1926, Ch. 306, Secs. 10–13, 17): Every devise or bequest by husband or wife to survivor shall be held to be in lieu of the rights which either has by law in the estate of the other, unless it appears by the will that such was not the intention; but survivor may waive benefit of will, etc.

New Jersey (Comp. St. 1910, p. 2048, Sec. 16): If husband devises real estate to wife for life or otherwise, without expressing whether the same is intended to be in lieu of dower, she is not entitled to dower in any lands devised by husband unless she renounces the benefit of devise to her.

New York (Cahill, Consol. L. 1930, Ch. 13, Sec. 18): When husband or wife dies testate, the survivor has a personal right of election to take his or her statutory share of the estate, etc.

§ 199]

North Carolina (C. 1927, Secs. 4096–97): Widow may dissent from husband's will and take the same rights and estates in husband's real and personal property as if he had died intestate.

Ohio (Complete G. C. 1931 [Page], Supp. 1932, Sec. 10504[61]): If survivor elects to take under the will, he or she is barred of all right to statutory share of estate, and shall take under the will alone, unless it plainly appears from the will that the provision therein was intended to be in addition to his or her statutory share.

Oklahoma (St. 1931, Sec. 1539): Husband or wife shall not bequeath away from survivor so much of his or her estate that the survivor will receive less in value than would be obtained through succession by law.

Oregon (C. 1930, Secs. 10[318], 10[330]): If lands be devised to widow or other provision made for her in husband's will, she shall elect between the same and dower in lands of husband; but she is not entitled to both unless it plainly appears by the will to have been so intended. The provision above also governs the surviving husband's curtesy.

Pennsylvania (St. 1920 [West], Sec. 8335): When husband or wife dies testate, the survivor may elect to take against the will, and is thereupon entitled to his or her statutory share of real and personal estate.

Rhode Island (G. L. 1923, Secs. 4311, 5807): Widow of testator, in whose will provision is made in lieu of dower, shall, in case of her non-acceptance of the same, signify her dissent in writing to probate court within one year from probate of will (Sec. 4311). The statute on jointures (Sec. 5807), outlined in Table XCVII, **Section 196** (p. 409), includes within its provisions "any estate, real or personal," conveyed by deed, or "devised or bequeathed for the jointure of the wife in lieu of her dower," etc.

South Carolina (no relevant provision found).

Tennessee (C. 1932, Secs. 8358–60): Widow may dissent from husband's will when a satisfactory provision in real or personal estate is not made for her, etc., in which case she is entitled to her statutory share of personalty in addition to dower. Surviving husband may likewise dissent from wife's will, in which case he is entitled to his statutory share of personalty in addition to curtesy.

Utah (R. S. 1933, 101-4-4): If husband's will makes any provision for widow, such provision shall be construed to be in lieu of distributive share in lands, unless it appears from the will that it was intended to be

[§ 199

additional thereto, in which case she is presumed to have accepted both. Otherwise, widow is put to an election.

Vermont (G. L. 1917, Secs. 3279, 3405) : Widow's statutory share of lands of which the husband died seized is barred when provision is made for her in husband's will, which in judgment of probate court was intended to be in lieu thereof ; but widow may waive such provision, etc. (Sec. 3405). Widower's statutory share of lands is barred if he accepts provision made for him in wife's will, but he may waive provisions of her will as she may his (Secs. 3414, 3415). Survivor is entitled to statutory share of personal property when he or she waives provision made for him or her in deceased spouse's will (Sec. 3279).

Virginia (C. 1930, Secs. 5120, 5276) : If any real or personal estate, intended to be in lieu of dower, is devised for jointure of wife, such provision bars dower in lands, subject to her right of election ; and every such provision by will shall be taken to be intended in lieu of dower unless a contrary intention plainly appears in will or in some other writing signed by party making the provision (Sec. 5120). The preceding provision is a part of the jointure statute outlined in Table XCVII, **Section 196** (p. 409). When any provision for survivor is made in deceased spouse's will, the survivor may renounce the same and claim his or her statutory share of personal estate (Sec. 5276).

West Virginia (C. 1931, Ch. 42, Art. 3, Sec. 2 ; Ch. 43, Art. 1, Secs. 7, 8) : Provision for survivor in deceased spouse's will shall be construed to be in lieu and bar of dower and statutory share of personalty in his or her estate, and if not renounced is all the survivor shall take of estate of deceased spouse, unless it clearly appears from a construction of the will, and attendant facts proper to be considered in connection with it, that testator intended the provision to be in addition thereto (Ch. 42, Art. 3, Sec. 2). The statute on jointures (Ch. 43, Art. 1, Secs. 7, 8) includes within its provisions "any estate, real or personal," conveyed or "devised for jointure of husband or wife," etc.

Wisconsin (St. 1931, Secs. 233.13, 233.14) : If lands be devised to widow or other provision made for her by will of husband, she shall elect between the same and her dower and statutory share of personal property ; but she is not entitled to both unless it plainly appears by the will to have been so intended.

Wyoming (R. S. 1931, Sec. 88[101]) : The survivor may dissent from provisions of deceased spouse's will and take his or her statutory share of real and personal property.

§ 199]

REFERENCES

Books

POMEROY, JOHN N. *A Treatise on Equity Jurisprudence,* 4th ed., Vol. 1, Secs. 492–502 (1918).

SCRIBNER, CHARLES H. *A Treatise on the Law of Dower,* 2d ed., Vol. II, ch. xvi, pp. 437–95 (1883).

STIMSON, F. J. *American Statute Law,* Sec. 3244 (1886).

WOERNER, J. G. *The American Law of Administration,* 3d ed., Sec. 119 (1923).

Annotation

"When Is Widow Put to Her Election between Provisions Made for Her by Husband's Will, and Her Dower, Homestead or Community Right," 22 A. L. R. 437–524 (1923) ; 68 A. L. R. 507–20 (1930).

Section 200. Dower—Barring by Deed

CROSS REFERENCES: Wife's conveyances of real property, **Secs. 182–84**; Barring dower by power of attorney, **Sec. 186**; Methods of barring dower, **Sec. 195**; Conveyance of homestead, **Sec. 225**; Conveyance of infant wife, **Sec. 274**; Barring dower of insane wife, **Sec. 311**

One of the distinctive features of inchoate dower at common law is the absolute protection it enjoys from destruction at the husband's hand. Thus, he cannot by sole conveyance transfer his title free from the encumbrance of the wife's contingent interest. This is true today in most of those jurisdictions which retain the institution of dower or which have a statutory substitute therefor. We have seen, however, that in a number of jurisdictions the widow's dower or statutory share is confined to such real property as the husband owns or is seized of at death (**Secs. 189, 191**). In these jurisdictions he can bar the wife's interest therein by his sole conveyance, at least unless in fraud of her rights as survivor. In this latter connection **Tennessee** provides that the widow is entitled to dower in lands fraudulently conveyed with an intent to defeat her estate (C. 1932, Sec. 8365) ; and **Vermont** provides that a voluntary conveyance by the husband to take effect after his death, and made with intent to defeat the widow's statutory share, does not operate to bar her claim (G. L. 1917, Sec. 3413). Likewise, dower in equitable estates is often limited to such as the husband owns at death (**Sec. 191**). Also, some jurisdictions permit the husband to convey full title by his sole conveyance when the wife is a non-resident. Statutes of varying

[§ 200

breadth, affirmatively or inferentially to this effect, were found in eight
jurisdictions (see Table XCVIII following). Finally, the husband in
some states may alienate his lands as if single when the wife deserts or
abandons him (**Sec. 144**).

While the purpose of the law required that great protection be given
to inchoate dower, commerce in lands would have been seriously impeded
without some method whereby the wife could voluntarily release her
contingent interest to the husband's purchaser. Apparently at early common law the only method by which this result could be obtained was for
both spouses to join in levying a fine or suffering a common recovery.
This strange manner of conveyancing was never much employed in this
country. Sanctioned by local custom or statute at an early date, the wife
was permitted to release her dower right by joining in the husband's
conveyance. As a theoretical protection from the husband's coercion,
her acknowledgment on separate examination was generally required.
Barring dower or statutory share by joint conveyance of the spouses
is in universal practice today, and is sanctioned by express statute in
most jurisdictions. Just as the necessity of the husband's joinder in the
wife's conveyance of her own lands has been generally abolished (**Sec.
183**), so today express statutes in a majority of jurisdictions permit the
wife to release her dower right by her sole deed. The requirement of a
separate examination for this, as for most purposes, has almost completely disappeared from the statutes.

Of the thirty jurisdictions which retain inchoate dower or a similarly
protected interest during coverture (**Secs. 189, 191**), legislation affirmatively or by negation sanctioning the wife's joinder in the husband's
conveyance for the purpose of releasing her dower right is found in all
but **Delaware, Kansas, Kentucky, New Jersey, Ohio, South Carolina,** and **Utah.** Of these seven latter jurisdictions, a general statutory
authority to bar dower by deed is found in **Delaware, Kansas,** and
New Jersey. In **South Carolina,** a special formal renunciation is employed, which may be by separate instrument or endorsed upon the husband's deed. Probably in all jurisdictions the wife with the husband's
concurrence may execute a release subsequent to his sole deed; and a
few of the statutes so provide. By express legislation in eighteen jurisdictions the wife may release her dower or other interest by an instrument executed without the husband's concurrence therein. The same
result is probably reached in other states by reason of the general
married women's legislation. In a few, however, the wording of the
statutes seems to require the joint act of both spouses. The requirement

§ 200]

of acknowledgment on separate examination is apparently retained by five states only (**Arkansas, Delaware, Florida, North Carolina, South Carolina**). A number of the statutes considered in this section permit a minor wife to release her dower with the same freedom as if adult (see Table XCVIII, and **Sec. 274**). Seven jurisdictions have legislation limiting the effect upon the wife of covenants in the husband's deed in which she joins.

While most of the statutes refer to the wife's joinder in the husband's deed, she may bar her dower by joining in the execution of a mortgage in the same manner as in a deed absolute. In at least one state, however, it seems that she cannot execute her sole release to the husband's mortgagee as she can to his grantee (**Virginia**). When the wife joins in the mortgage or otherwise releases her interest to the mortgagee, she is nevertheless entitled to dower as against all others. She retains sufficient interest to permit her to redeem, and in some states she can compel exoneration. Little legislation is found defining her rights (footnote 1 of Table XCVIII, p. 434). If the mortgage is foreclosed during the marriage, the cases differ as to whether her inchoate right is completely extinguished. The statutes of **Virginia** and **West Virginia** permit her to share in the surplus, while **Kentucky** takes a contrary view. The statutes of five jurisdictions recognize the general rule that she is entitled to share in the surplus if the mortgage is foreclosed after the husband's death. In either event, the **West Virginia** statute allows her so much of the surplus as represents the present value of her dower right in the whole rather than in the surplus proceeds only.

Inchoate dower cannot ordinarily be released to a stranger to the title. Most of the legislation expressly or impliedly imposes that limitation but does not define the estate which the releasee must possess. None of the statutes considered in this section expressly permit the wife to make a binding relinquishment to her husband, except for a limited purpose. The language of most of them does not comprehend such a release and a few seem to forbid the same. A release to the husband can be supported in many jurisdictions, however, by reason of the broad statutory authority sanctioning transactions between the spouses (**Secs. 156, 182, 198**).

Express legislation permitting the wife to release her dower by attorney under a power executed by herself alone or by both spouses is collected in **Section 186**. Barring the dower of an insane wife is discussed in **Section 311**. In this section, no attempt has been made to cite or make reference to the numerous statutes validating improperly executed or acknowledged releases, or limiting or denying the right of the widow to recover dower in lands alienated by the husband alone by certain past conveyances. Further details of the statutes discussed above, together with other relevant legislation, will be found in the table which follows.

TABLE XCVIII*

BARRING DOWER BY DEED

Jurisdiction and Citation	In General	Separate Examination, etc.	Non-resident Wives; Covenants in Joint Deed; Miscellaneous
Alabama .... C. 1923, Secs. 7433–34, 7436	If 18 years of age, wife may relinquish dower by joining with husband in conveyance of lands, or by her separate instrument executed by her alone subsequent to husband's conveyance	Wife's signature must be witnessed or acknowledged in manner prescribed for other conveyances. "The form of the separate and apart acknowledgment of homestead by the wife shall be sufficient to relinquish or pass dower right"	Wife residing or living beyond the state may release dower in like manner (as resident wife), the conveyance being acknowledged as other conveyances beyond the state. Neither wife nor her separate estate is bound by covenants in joint deed unless there be a special covenant of wife expressing her intention to bind her separate estate
Arkansas .... Crawf. and Moses, Dig. 1921, Secs. 1506, 1524, 3529, 3543	Wife may relinquish her dower by joining with husband in deed of lands, or by a separate instrument to husband's grantee or one claiming title under him	Wife must voluntarily appear before proper court or officer and in absence of husband declare that she signed the relinquishment for the purpose therein contained of her own free will and without compulsion or undue influence of husband	No deed of husband without assent of wife evinced by acknowledgment in manner required by law shall bar her dower estate. Widow is endowed of lands sold by husband without her consent in legal form against all creditors of the estate
Delaware ...... R. C. 1915, Secs. 3201, 3321	Wife "may bar her dower by deed duly acknowledged"	(Presumably, wife's separate examination is required; see preceding column and Table XCII, Sec. 183, p. 300)	In case of sales of lands under judgment, or by trustee of insane husband, wife may bar her dower by a separate release

* See page 434 for numbered footnotes to this table.

TABLE XCVIII (*Continued*)

Jurisdiction and Citation	In General	Separate Examination, etc.	Non-resident Wives; Covenants in Joint Deed; Miscellaneous
District of Columbia ... C. 1929, T. 14, Secs. 31, 51	If 18 years of age, wife may release her dower by joining in husband's conveyance, or by her separate deed	Wife's deed releasing dower shall be signed, sealed, and acknowledged, and her acknowledgment certified in the manner prescribed for other conveyances	When wife has been absent or unheard of for seven years, the husband may convey or encumber by separate deed as if unmarried any real estate which he acquires since the beginning of such absence
Florida .... R. G. S. 1920, Secs. 3802–4; Sec. 3813, amd. by Sess. L. 1927, Ch. 12083, p. 811	Wife may relinquish her dower by joining in husband's conveyance or mortgage, or by a separate deed executed in like manner as other conveyances. Relinquishment executed and acknowledged by a minor wife is valid	To render relinquishment effectual, wife must acknowledge before proper officer, separate and apart from husband, that she executed the same freely and voluntarily without fear, etc. Officer's certificate shall set forth the statutory requirements	Wife who joins in conveyance with husband may enter into covenants of warranty or against encumbrances, but such covenants have no other effect than to estop her and those claiming by or through her
Georgia .... C. 1926, C. C., Secs. 4204, 5249	Wife may bar her dower (in such lands the title to which came through her) by joining with husband in deed thereof (see **Secs. 189, 191**)	Wife must sign and seal deed before authorized officer and declare that she joined therein of her own free will without compulsion of husband	
Hawaii .... R. L. 1925, Secs. 2882, 3026, 3150	Wife may bar her dower in estate conveyed by husband by joining in deed, or by a separate deed releasing the same made at the time or subsequently	Acknowledgment of wife when required by law may be taken in the same form as if she were single	See footnote 1
Illinois .... Cahill, R. S. 1931, Ch. 30, Secs. 18, 20; Ch. 41, Sec. 16	Wife may relinquish dower by joining with husband in deed, mortgage, release or other writing relating to the sale or disposition of his lands. When husband's interest has been divested by process of law or otherwise, wife may release her dower by separate deed, duly executed and acknowledged, to purchaser or grantee	Acknowledgment of wife's deed, release of dower, or other writing relating to disposition of lands or interest therein may be made and certified the same as if she were a feme sole	No deed of husband without assent of wife evinced by acknowledgment as required by law shall prejudice her dower or jointure

[§ 200

TABLE XCVIII (*Continued*)

Jurisdiction and Citation	In General	Separate Examination, etc.	Non-resident Wives; Covenants in Joint Deed; Miscellaneous
Indiana .... Burns, Ann. St. 1926, Secs. 3349, 3365, 13401	Widow is entitled to statutory share in real estate of husband, etc., "in the conveyance of which she may not have joined in due form of law." No act or conveyance of husband without assent of wife evidenced by acknowledgment thereof in manner required by law, nor any disposition, transfer or encumbrance by virtue of any decree, execution or mortgage to which wife is not a party, shall prejudice or extinguish her right to statutory share (except as otherwise provided)	It is not necessary for the wife to acknowledge "her deed" in any form other than that required of single persons	
Iowa .... C. 1927, Secs. 10043, 10050–52, 10099, 11993	Conveyance of husband and wife is sufficient to pass any and all right of either in property conveyed unless the contrary appears on face of instrument. Wife may convey any interest in real estate belonging to her as if single	Acknowledgment of wife when required by law may be taken in the same form as if she were single	As against purchaser from non-resident alien, widow is not entitled to statutory share if, at time of purchase, she was also a non-resident alien. When wife joins in husband's conveyance, she is not bound by covenants therein unless it is expressly so stated on the face thereof. When she joins in such conveyance to relinquish her dower only and she subsequently acquires an interest in the property, such after-acquired interest does not inure to benefit of grantee
Kansas .... R. S. 1923, Sec. 22(108)	Widow is entitled to statutory share of husband's real estate of which she "has made no conveyance"		Widow is not entitled to statutory share in lands conveyed by husband when wife at time of conveyance is not and never has been a resident of the state

§ 200]

TABLE XCVIII (*Continued*)

Jurisdiction and Citation	In General	Separate Examination, etc.	Non-resident Wives; Covenants in Joint Deed; Miscellaneous
Kentucky ...... Carroll, St. 1922, Secs. 2135, 2146	(For general statute, see Table XCII, **Sec. 183,** p. 303)		Widow is not endowed of land sold in good faith after marriage to satisfy lien created before marriage or by deed in which she joined or to satisfy a lien for purchase money, but is entitled to dower in surplus of land or proceeds unless received or disposed of by husband in his lifetime.[1] Wife of infant, idiot or imbecile husband may unite with guardian, etc., in conveyance of his lands to release her dower if 21 years of age or with approval of court. Court may permit infant wife to unite with adult husband in conveyance of his lands
Maine .... R. S. 1930, Ch. 89, Sec. 9	Wife of any age may bar her right to statutory share in estate conveyed by husband by joining in the same or a subsequent deed, or in a deed with his guardian, or by her sole deed		Wife shall not be deprived of her interest by sale of husband's lands on execution, but, after right of redemption has expired, she may release such interest by her sole deed
Maryland .... Bagby, Ann. C. 1924, Art. 45, Sec. 12; Art. 46, Sec. 3	Wife of any age may relinquish her dower by joining in deed with husband or by her separate deed		Husband cannot convey his land free of wife's dower without her joinder
Massachusetts .. G. L. 1932, Ch. 183, Sec. 31; Ch. 189, Secs. 1A, 4–6; Ch. 209, Secs. 14, 16; Ch. 244, Sec. 16	Wife may bar her dower in land conveyed by husband or by operation of law by joining in deed, or by subsequent deed executed separately or jointly with husband. Signature of wife under 21 years of age to instrument relating to conveyance of husband's lands has same effect as if she were over that age	Wife's acknowledgment may be taken in the same form as if she were single	Deed signed by wife of grantor releases dower if she is competent so to act, unless such right is expressly reserved in deed. Wife may release her dower by joining in deed with guardian or conservator of husband, and the proceeds of the sale may be so invested as to secure to her her rights therein[1]

[§ 200

TABLE XCVIII (*Continued*)

Jurisdiction and Citation	In General	Separate Examination, etc.	Non-resident Wives; Covenants in Joint Deed; Miscellaneous
Michigan Comp. L. 1929, Secs. 13076–77, 13080, 13088, 13098, 13331, 13337	Resident wife of 18 years of age may bar her dower by joining in deed with husband or his guardian, properly acknowledged, or by joining in subsequent deed with husband, or by her separate deed to one who holds the husband's title if the intent to bar her dower is therein expressed	Acknowledgment of wife when required by law may be taken in the same form as if she were single	Non-resident wife is entitled to dower in lands of which husband died seized[1]
Minnesota G. S. 1923, Secs. 8196, 9551	Husband and wife by joint deed may convey the real estate of either. Wife may relinquish by separate conveyance her rights in husband's real estate conveyed by him. Minority of wife does not invalidate any conveyance executed by her	(For general statute, see Table XCII, **Sec. 183**, p. 305)	Wife may release to husband her contingent interest in his real estate by writing executed and acknowledged in same manner as a conveyance, and whole proceeds shall be paid to husband (partition sale)
Missouri R. S. 1929, Secs. 330, 3015, 3026, 3029	Wife may relinquish her dower by joining with husband in deed acknowledged and certified as required by law	Separate examination in respect to execution of release of dower is not required. When wife unites with husband in execution of deed, she shall be described in acknowledgment as his wife	No deed of husband without assent of wife evidenced by her acknowledgment in manner required by law shall prejudice her dower. Covenant in deed conveying property of husband shall not bind wife except so far as necessary to effectually convey all her interest expressed to be conveyed
Montana R. C. 1921, Secs. 5811, 5813–14, 5816, 5818, 5828, 6911–12, 6916, 9569	When wife joins with husband in execution of conveyance, she thereby relinquishes her inchoate dower. Wife may waive or relinquish any interests in real estate in person or by attorney as if single	The acknowledgment of wife to instrument purporting to be executed by her must be taken and certified the same as if single	Husband residing and owning land in state, whose wife has never been in the state, can convey full title by his sole deed or mortgage. No deed of husband without assent of wife evidenced by her acknowledgment thereby in manner required by law shall prejudice her dower or jointure. Wife may release to husband or purchaser her right of dower in property directed to be sold in partition action, by written instrument duly acknowledged and certified[1]

TABLE XCVIII (*Continued*)

Jurisdiction and Citation	In General	Separate Examination, etc.	Non-resident Wives; Covenants in Joint Deed; Miscellaneous
Nebraska .... Comp. St. 1929, Secs. 30(101), 30(105), 42(207)	Wife's right to statutory share may be barred by a conveyance executed by both spouses while residents of the state		Wife's right to statutory share may be barred, if either husband or wife be a non-resident, by conveyance executed by both spouses or by conveyance of husband. Wife is not bound by any covenant in joint deed of herself and husband
New Hampshire. Pub. L. 1926, Ch. 288, Sec. 4	Wife, though not of full age, may join with husband in release of dower (but see **Secs. 189, 191** as to property subject to dower)		
New Jersey .... Comp. St. 1910, p. 2790, Sec. 14*c*; p. 2805, Sec. 7; p. 3229, Sec. 7; p. 3230, Sec. 8*c*; p. 3231, Sec. 8*e*; Cum. Supp. 1911–24, Secs. 44(21*a*), 44(39), 44(40*a*); Supp. 1925–30, Secs. 55(12), 55(66*a*), 63(1)	Widow is endowed by lands of husband "to which she shall not have relinquished or released her right of dower by deed executed and acknowledged in the manner prescribed by law." (For general statute, see Table XCII, Sec. 183, p. 307.) Wife's deed executed, acknowledged and certified as required shall release and bar her right of dower	(See Table XCII, Sec. 183, p. 307, for applicable statutes)	Wife may release her dower by separate instrument in case of certain sales of lands of lunatic or infant husband or when husband's lands have been sold under judgment or decree. When living in state of separation and entitled by decree to alimony or separate maintenance, she may by separate deed release her dower to husband or any other person. She may release dower by joining in deed with husband's attorney. Covenants of title, etc., in joint deed of spouses have no greater or other effect than to estop her and those privy to her. When wife has been judicially declared dead by reason of seven years' absence, husband may dispose of lands free of dower

[§ 200

TABLE XCVIII (*Continued*)

Jurisdiction and Citation	In General	Separate Examination, etc.	Non-resident Wives; Covenants in Joint Deed; Miscellaneous
North Carolina.. C. 1927, Secs. 997, 2523, 4101–2, 4103(*b*)	Wife, even though under 21 years of age, may bar her dower right by joining with husband in conveyance. Every conveyance or other instrument affecting the estate, right or title of wife in lands must be executed by wife and husband	When wife joins in conveyance to release dower she must be privately examined as to her consent thereto	No alienation of husband alone has any other effect than to pass his interest subject to wife's dower right. If wife elopes with adulterer or abandons husband, he may convey his lands as if single
Oregon .... C. 1930, Secs. 10(305)– 10(306), 10(313), 10(321), 63(116)	Wife may bar her right of dower by joining in deed of property with husband or his guardian if he be a minor, or by her separate deed, with or without mentioning the barring of dower, provided her separate deed shall not be executed to a stranger to the title but to husband's grantee or his heirs or assigns	Acknowledgment of wife to conveyances of real property shall be taken in same manner as if she were single	If wife resides out of state, she is entitled to dower in lands in the state of which husband died seized[1]
Pennsylvania ... St. 1920 (West), Secs. 8352, 8687, 8690; Secs. 9298–99, amd. by Cum. Supp. 1928 (West), p. 396	Widow is entitled to same share in lands aliened by husband "without her joining in the conveyance" as in lands of which he died seized. Deed of husband's lands executed and acknowledged by wife jointly with him is valid and effectual notwithstanding the minority of the wife	Wife's acknowledgment when required by law shall be taken in the same manner and form as if she were single	When deed is executed under order of court by committee in lunacy, etc., or by guardian of insane husband, etc., the wife may release or divest her dower right, or claim in the nature thereof, in the property conveyed in the same manner as if she were a widow, provided that such release is executed prior to a decree declaring husband restored of his sanity, etc.
Rhode Island ... G. L. 1923, Secs. 4197–98, 4271, 5781	Widow is entitled to dower in lands "to which she shall not have relinquished her right of dower by deed" (subject to certain exceptions). Wife may bar her dower right by joining with husband in conveyance of lands, and therein releasing same, or by her separate deed	Wife's deed releasing her dower right shall be acknowledged by her in the same manner as if she were single	

§ 200]

TABLE XCVIII (*Continued*)

Jurisdiction and Citation	In General	Separate Examination, etc.	Non-resident Wives; Covenants in Joint Deed; Miscellaneous
South Carolina.. C. of L. 1922, C. C., Sec. 5233, amd. by Sess. L. 1922, No. 524, p. 936; Secs. 5234–35, 5312; Sess. L. 1924, No. 674, p. 111	Wife, whether she be of age or a minor, may release her dower right by renunciation of dower in favor of person or persons who shall have succeeded the husband in title either immediately or mediately, irrespective of the method whereby title passed out of the husband. Certificate of renunciation may be endorsed on husband's deed or by separate instrument, and when recorded is effectual to bar her dower although she has not executed or acknowledged any deed of conveyance for that purpose	Wife's renunciation of her dower right must be made before certain designated officers upon a private and separate examination (statute gives form for the certificate)	
Utah .... R. S. 1933, 101-4-3			Wife is not entitled to statutory share in estate of which husband has made a conveyance when she is not, or never has been, a resident of the state at the time of the conveyance
Virginia .... C. 1930, Secs. 5119, 5135, 5211, 5338a, 5344–45	Wife, whether she be of age or a minor, may dispose of her contingent dower right by uniting with husband in deed or contract; if husband has previously disposed of his interest, she may thereafter, but not before, release her dower by her sole act as if single. Joint deed of husband and wife, whether admitted to record or not, operates to convey from wife her dower right in the real estate embraced therein		When wife joins in conveyance of husband's lands, no covenant or warranty therein operates to bind her further than to convey her interest therein, unless there is an express stipulation binding herself personally. When order is made for the sale of real estate of insane or infant husband, wife if 21 years of age may join in conveyance to release her dower and is entitled to be secured in the proceeds[1]

[§ 200

TABLE XCVIII (*Concluded*)

Jurisdiction and Citation	In General	Separate Examination, etc.	Non-resident Wives; Covenants in Joint Deed; Miscellaneous
West Virginia C. 1931, Ch. 37, Art. 1, Sec. 8; Ch. 39, Art. 1, Sec. 5; Ch. 43, Art. 1, Secs. 3, 4; Ch. 48, Art. 3, Secs. 4, 5	Wife may convey her dower right by joining with husband in deed or other writing conveying his real estate. If husband has conveyed his interest, she may relinquish her dower thereafter, but not before, by her separate deed. Wife may bind herself to release her dower by joining with husband in contract to convey, or by her separate agreement after husband has contracted to convey	When both spouses join in a conveyance, the wife may acknowledge the same together with or separately from husband. Either may sign and acknowledge before the other	When order is made for conveyance of real estate of insane, infant, or convict husband, wife may join in conveyance and release her dower right, and is entitled to receive the value of her inchoate dower out of the proceeds[1]
Wisconsin St. 1931, Secs. 233.02, 233.06, 233.07, 235.26– 235.29	Wife of 18 years or upwards may bar her dower by joining with husband or guardian in conveyance of the lands, duly executed and acknowledged by her, and the joinder of her name as grantor with husband is sufficient to bar her dower without any other words therein. When husband's title has been lawfully conveyed to another, she may bar her dower either before or after husband's death by quitclaim deed to such other person, properly executed and acknowledged[2]	Wife's conveyance, whether executed alone or in conjunction with husband, may be acknowledged or proof of execution taken and certified the same as if she were single	Non-resident wife is entitled to dower in lands of her husband, being in this state, of which he died seized only[1]

[1] The following fragmentary provisions were found expressly dealing with the effect of the wife's joinder in the husband's mortgage: The wife is entitled to dower in the mortgaged lands as against all but the mortgagee and those claiming under him (**Massachusetts, Montana, West Virginia**). If the land is sold on foreclosure, etc., after the death of husband, she is entitled to dower in the surplus (**Michigan, Montana, Oregon, Wisconsin**), or to such part of the surplus as represents the present value of her dower right in the whole of the land (**West Virginia**). If the heir or other person claiming under husband satisfies the mortgage debt, she is entitled to dower in the lands after the amount paid is deducted (**Massachusetts, Michigan, Oregon, Wisconsin**), or she may contribute her proportionate share of debt and take dower in the whole of the lands (**Massachusetts**). Foreclosure by sale under a power is effectual to bar all claim of dower (**Hawaii, Massachusetts**). Both **Virginia** and **West Virginia** give the wife a dower right in surplus proceeds when the land is sold in good faith during the lifetime of the husband. In the latter, she is entitled to such part of the surplus as represents the present value of her inchoate dower in the whole of the lands. See also the **Kentucky** provision in the last column of the table above.

[2] Section 235.26 of the **Wisconsin** Statutes also provides that a wife "of full age" may by joint or separate deed of conveyance release her dower in lands which have been conveyed voluntarily by husband or upon execution, judgment of foreclosure or decree of court.

§ 200]

REFERENCES

Books

SCRIBNER, CHARLES H. *A Treatise on the Law of Dower,* 2d ed., Vol. II, chs. xii–xiv, pp. 283–388 (1883).

STIMSON, F. J. *American Statute Law,* Secs. 3245, 6504 (1886).

TIFFANY, HERBERT THORNDIKE. *The Law of Real Property and Other Interests in Land,* 2d ed., Vol. 1, Sec. 224 (1920).

WOERNER, J. G. *The American Law of Administration,* 3d ed., Sec. 114 (1923).

Article

NELMS, W. J. "Disinheriting the Consort," 18 Va. L. Rev. 334–38 (1932).

Note

"Dower Rights, Necessity of Joinder of Husband in a Deed of Conveyance," *Scott* v. *Scott,* 324 Mo. 1055; 26 S. W. (2d) 598 (1930)—17 St. Louis L. Rev. 90–91 (1931).

Annotations

"Barring Dower by Conveyance to Trustee," 7 A. L. R. 243–45 (1920).

"Dower Rights of Wife Who Unites with Husband in Mortgage," 12 A. L. R. 1347–61 (1921); 65 A. L. R. 963–67 (1930).

"Rights or Interests Covered by Quitclaim Deed—Dower Right," 44 A. L. R. 1275 (1926).

Section 201. Dower—Barring by Other Means

CROSS REFERENCES: Barring dower, in general, **Sec. 195**; Partition sales and executor's sales after husband's death, **Sec. 214**; Barring curtesy, **Sec. 220**

Certain statutes relative to the barring of inchoate dower, not discussed elsewhere, are collected in this section. For purposes of convenience, they are grouped as follows:

1. *Barring inchoate dower by appropriation for payment of husband's debts.*—If the husband's lands are sold under a lien or encumbrance paramount to the wife's dower, her inchoate right therein is barred and she must find her security in the proceeds, if at all. The fragmentary bits of legislation defining her rights in such case are collected in **Sections 191** and **200**. The statutes of **Kentucky, Virginia,** and **West Virginia** permit the husband himself to bar the wife's dower by a sale made in good faith to satisfy a paramount lien. If, however, the land is sold by execution or otherwise to satisfy a lien subordinate to dower, the wife's inchoate

dower is not barred and the purchaser takes subject thereto. This is generally true today in those jurisdictions which retain inchoate dower or a similarly protected estate during coverture. The statutes of two states are express to that effect (**Maine, Massachusetts**). In a number of jurisdictions, however, a sale of the husband's lands under execution, etc., during the marriage defeats the widow's estate for the reason that her dower or statutory share is confined to real estate of which he dies seized or owning (**Sec. 189**). The statutes of six states which retain an inchoate estate protected from the husband's sole conveyance are of especial interest in that they permit the husband's lands to be appropriated for the payment of his debts, free and clear of the wife's contingent interest, as follows: The widow is not entitled to statutory share in lands sold on execution or "judicial" sale (**Iowa, Kansas, Minnesota, Nebraska**), or appropriated by general assignment for benefit of creditors, or by insolvency or bankruptcy proceedings (**Minnesota**); the wife's inchoate interest is divested by sale by trustee or assignee under federal bankruptcy or state insolvency statutes (**Pennsylvania**), and by sale under execution if wife is a party (**Delaware**). In **Illinois,** a mechanic's lien is superior to dower, if the wife has knowledge of the improvements and does not give written notice of her objection before the making thereof.

Attention is called to the unusual legislation existing in **Indiana,** as follows: In case of "judicial sales" of the husband's lands when the wife's inchoate interest is not directed by the judgment to be sold, her interest becomes absolute and vests in the same manner as upon the husband's death. If she dies during the marriage holding lands which vested as above, the same descend to the surviving husband. If she contracts a second marriage, she cannot alienate such real estate during the marriage, and if she dies during such marriage, it descends to her children by the first marriage. The statute applies to sales of real estate of the value of $20,000 or less, or to so much as does not exceed that figure.

Several other pertinent statutes were found to the following effect: In the case of judicial sales for the purpose of subjecting lands to the satisfaction of the husband's debts or liens subordinate to dower, the court may order the same sold free of her inchoate right if she is made a party, but she is entitled to such part of the proceeds as represents the present value of her inchoate dower (**West Virginia**). Legislation of this kind seems eminently sensible and worthy of adoption elsewhere. A somewhat similar **Maine** statute provides for procedure whereby an

§ 201]

assignee for benefit of creditors, trustee in bankruptcy, or any person holding title by levy or sale on execution may have the wife's inchoate interest divested with compensation to her for the same. In **New Jersey,** when real estate is sold at judicial sale subject to dower, the purchaser may have the dower portion admeasured and set off pending perfection of the dower right, and thereupon hold the remainder free of the wife's inchoate estate.

2. *Barring inchoate dower by partition.*—While the doctrine of survivorship precludes dower in the interest of a joint tenant, the wife is entitled to dower in lands held by the husband in common. Her dower right, however, is generally said to be subordinate to the paramount right of a co-tenant to compel partition; hence her inchoate interest may be defeated by partition, whether voluntary or involuntary. If the land is partitioned in kind, she becomes endowed of the part set off to the husband in severalty. If the land is sold under partition proceedings, her inchoate dower is barred, and this is generally held to be true even though she is not made a party to the action. In the absence of statute, she is usually given no right to share in the proceeds.

Judicial partition is regulated in detail by statutes in most states. Only those which refer in express terms to the barring of the wife's inchoate interest are collected here. That her inchoate interest may be barred by partition sale is true in all jurisdictions. The statutes of ten jurisdictions are express to that effect (**Alabama, Delaware, District of Columbia, Kentucky, Maryland, Michigan, Minnesota, New Jersey, Virginia, West Virginia**), if the wife is a party (**Delaware, Kentucky, West Virginia**), or regardless of whether she is made a party (**District of Columbia, Virginia**). The prevailing rule under the statutes probably is that the wife is not a necessary party. The statutes of twelve jurisdictions provide that the wife is entitled to be secured in the husband's share of the proceeds, either by way of compensation for the present value of her inchoate interest or by investment of the proceeds, etc. (**Alaska, Delaware, Hawaii, Iowa, Kentucky, Michigan, Minnesota, Nebraska, New Jersey, Oregon, West Virginia, Wisconsin**), unless the husband's share be less than $1,000 or unless she has abandoned him (**Iowa**). The same result is probably reached in other jurisdictions under provisions of the partition statutes protecting contingent interests generally.

3. *Barring inchoate dower when husband is under contract to sell.*—**West Virginia** has legislation permitting a husband who has contracted to sell real estate and whose wife refuses to release her dower, or the

party contracting to purchase, to bring suit in equity to have the contract consummated and her dower interest barred with compensation. A somewhat similar but perhaps less useful statute is found in **Maine** whereby a husband under contract to sell may have the wife's inchoate interest released with compensation. It seems strange that more states have not adopted legislation of this kind. In the normal household, the wife is undoubtedly willing to assist the husband in an advantageous disposition of his lands. If the spouses are not in accord, however, the dower encumbrance practically precludes the husband selling his real property at a fair price unless his purchaser be assured of title free from the wife's claim. To meet that situation a statute similar to that of **West Virginia** seems reasonable and highly desirable.

4. *Miscellaneous.*—A number of the statutes contain general statements of common-law principles to the effect that no act of the husband without the properly expressed assent of the wife, no judgment or decree confessed or recovered against him, no laches, default or covin of the husband (**Arkansas, Illinois, Indiana, Missouri, Montana**), nor any recovery obtained by default or collusion (**District of Columbia, Kentucky, New Jersey, Ohio, Virginia, West Virginia**) shall prejudice the widow's dower (or jointure: **Arkansas, Illinois, Indiana, Montana**). By the early common law, dower was barred by the husband's attainder for treason or felony. Forfeiture for crime is of course universally abolished. It is interesting to note that the statutes of four states (**Arkansas, Illinois, Missouri, Montana**) expressly protect dower from the effects of the husband's crime.

The citations for the statutory material of this section follow, grouped according to the subsections used above:

1. **Delaware,** R. C. 1915, Sec. 4320; Sec. 4373, as amended by Sess. L. 1929, Ch. 269, p. 793; **Illinois,** Cahill, R. S. 1931, Ch. 82, Sec. 1; **Indiana,** Burns, Ann. St. 1926, Secs. 3361–64; **Iowa,** C. 1927, Sec. 11190; **Kansas,** R. S. 1923, Sec. 22(108); **Kentucky,** Carroll, St. 1922, Sec. 2135; **Maine,** R. S. 1930, Ch. 89, Secs. 9, 19; **Massachusetts,** G. L. 1932, Ch. 236, Sec. 55; **Minnesota,** G. S. 1923, Sec. 8720; **Nebraska,** Comp. St. 1929, Secs. 30(101), 30(105); **New Jersey,** Comp. St. 1910, p. 2051, Sec. 25; **Pennsylvania,** St. 1920 (West), Sec. 9300, as amended by Cum. Supp. 1928 (West), p. 396; **Virginia,** C. 1930, Sec. 5119; **West Virginia,** C. 1931, Ch. 43, Art. 1, Secs. 3, 5.

2. **Alabama,** C. 1923, Sec. 7432; **Alaska,** Comp. L. 1913, Sec. 1262; **Delaware,** R. C. 1915, Sec. 3286; **District of Columbia,** C. 1929, T. 25, Secs. 384, 386; **Hawaii,** R. L. 1925, Sec. 2772, as amended by Sess. L. 1929, Act 83, p. 89; **Iowa,** C. 1927, Sec. 12347; **Kentucky,** Carroll, Civ. C. of Prac. 1906, Sec. 495; **Maryland,** Bagby, Ann. C. 1924, Art. 16, Sec. 46; **Michigan,** Comp. L. 1929, Secs. 15079–81; **Minnesota,** G. S. 1923, Secs. 8720, 9550; **Nebraska,** Comp. St. 1929, Sec.

§ 201]

20(2198); **New Jersey,** Comp. St. 1910, p. 3909, Sec. 39; p. 3914, Sec. 66; **Oregon,** C. 1930, Sec. 6(628); **Virginia,** C. 1930, Sec. 5281; **West Virginia,** C. 1931, Ch. 43, Art. 1, Sec. 5; **Wisconsin,** St. 1931, Sec. 276.36.

3. **Maine,** R. S. 1930, Ch. 89, Sec. 19; **West Virginia,** C. 1931, Ch. 43, Art. 1, Sec. 6.

4. **Arkansas,** Crawf. and Moses, Dig. 1921, Sec. 3529; **District of Columbia,** C. 1929, T. 14, Sec. 34; **Illinois,** Cahill, R. S. 1931, Ch. 41, Sec. 16; **Indiana,** Burns, Ann. St. 1926, Sec. 3365; **Kentucky,** Carroll, St. 1922, Sec. 2140; **Missouri,** R. S. 1929, Sec. 330; **Montana,** R. C. 1921, Sec. 5828; **New Jersey,** Comp. St. 1910, p. 2046, Sec. 5; **Ohio,** Complete G. C. 1931 (Page), Supp. 1932, Sec. 10502(6); **Virginia,** C. 1930, Sec. 5129; **West Virginia,** C. 1931, Ch. 43, Art. 1, Sec. 16.

REFERENCES

Book

Stimson, F. J. *American Statute Law,* Secs. 3249–50 (1886).

Notes

"Husband and Wife—Dower—Right to Share in Proceeds of Land Taken by Eminent Domain," 80 Univ. of Pa. L. Rev. 749–50 (1932).

"Forcing Release of Inchoate Dower under Statutory Scheme," *Ruby* v. *Ruby,* 112 W. Va. 62; 163 S. E. 717 (1932)—39 W. Va. L. Quar. 163–70 (1933).

"Liability in Iowa of a Married Woman Who, to Release Her Dower Interest, Casually Signs a Note with Her Husband," 17 Ia. L. Rev. 245–49 (1932).

Annotation

"Tax Sale of Property as Extinguishing Right of Dower or Curtesy," 75 A. L. R. 430–33 (1931).

Section 202. Dower—Forfeiture of

Cross References: Effect of absolute divorce upon husband's property, **Secs. 96, 99, 100;** Effect of limited divorce upon husband's property, **Sec. 129;** Conveyances of husband when wife deserts, **Sec. 144;** Barring dower, **Secs. 195** *et seq.;* Forfeiture of curtesy, etc., **Sec. 221**

In the absence of affirmative legislation, the fact that the widow has been guilty of serious misconduct during the marriage does not generally operate to deprive her of dower and other rights in her deceased husband's property. The majority of jurisdictions have not seen fit to make substantial changes in the common-law rule in this respect. This may possibly be explained upon the theory that the divorce court offers the aggrieved husband adequate means of protection. Statutes establishing one or more grounds of forfeiture were found in twenty-four jurisdic-

[§ 202

tions, but many of them are fragmentary and narrow in character. As will be seen from the topical analysis which follows, adultery and desertion are the most common forms of misconduct penalized by a forfeiture of dower, etc.

1. *Divorce for wife's misconduct.*—At common law, the general rule is that an absolute divorce bars all contingent rights dependent upon a continuation of the marriage. Thus the wife loses her dower and other rights in the husband's property; and this is so even though the decree may be granted for his misconduct. Legislation dealing with the effect of absolute divorce upon the husband's property is collected in Volume II of this work, **Sections 96, 99,** and **100.** Reference to those sections will indicate that statutes commonly make it a matter of forfeiture, preserving dower or statutory substitute when the wife obtains the decree because of the husband's misconduct, and barring the same when she is the guilty spouse. In a few states the vesting of dower is accelerated by divorce for the husband's fault. **South Carolina,** the only American jurisdiction which does not grant absolute divorce, provides that the wife forfeits her dower right if she goes to another jurisdiction and obtains a decree (see résumé at end of this section). Since the marriage is not terminated by a limited divorce, dower and similar interests are not affected by the decree unless by force of legislation to the contrary. The few statutes changing the common-law rule are collected in **Section 129.** A handful of jurisdictions treat the matter the same as in the case of absolute divorce.

2. *Adultery of wife.*—By the early common law, even elopement and adultery did not work a forfeiture of dower; but by the Statute of Westminster II (13 Edw. I, c. 34), it was provided that if the wife willingly left the husband and continued with an adulterer she should forfeit her dower unless the husband became reconciled to her and suffered her to dwell with him. Although there is a difference of opinion on the point, a number of courts have regarded this early statute as a part of the American common law. By express statute in thirteen jurisdictions, adultery is penalized by a forfeiture of dower or statutory share of lands; and in six of these, the rule is extended so as to bar the wife's distributive share of personalty. Most of these statutes are substantial re-enactments of the Statute of Westminster II, and in terms require a voluntary separation by the wife, followed by a continuing adultery of some sort. **Georgia,** however, merely provides that dower is barred by the adultery of the wife, unpardoned by the husband; and the statutes of **Illinois** and **North Carolina** seem to require no more than a single

§ 202]

act of adultery. Going to the other extreme is **South Carolina,** which requires that the separation and adultery continue for five years. The same state, however, also provides that a conviction of adultery bars dower, unless condoned by the husband.

3. *Desertion or abandonment by wife.*—In the absence of statute to the contrary, desertion or abandonment without cause, unaccompanied by adultery, does not affect the widow's rights in the husband's estate. In addition to the adultery statutes, legislation which penalizes a deserting wife by barring her rights as widow was found in eleven jurisdictions. In four, the husband may obtain a decree, when the wife deserts him, which operates to deprive her of dower, etc. In the other seven jurisdictions, the statute is concerned with desertion existing at the time of the husband's death; and only two of these require the desertion to have continued for any specified time before his death. In all but three of the eleven jurisdictions, desertion is equally effective to bar the widow's share of personalty. In addition, a few states have legislation permitting a deserted husband to convey his real property as if unmarried (see **Sec. 144**).

4. *Bigamy.*—The fact that the wife contracts a bigamous marriage will not ordinarily affect her right to dower, etc., in her first husband's estate, unless her misconduct falls within the desertion or adultery statutes noted above. Four states, however, make bigamy a separate ground for forfeiture (**Kentucky, Maryland, Michigan, South Carolina**). In two (**Kentucky, Maryland**), the wife must be convicted of the crime; and in one (**Michigan**), she must be living in bigamy at the husband's death. If the husband is convicted of bigamy, the wife in **Kentucky** and **Maryland** is entitled to dower and statutory share of personalty as if he were dead.

5. *Felonious killing of husband.*—By the sounder view, the fact that the wife murders her husband does not operate to bar her of dower and similar rights in his estate, unless the legislative body so directs. Express statutes creating a forfeiture when the wife feloniously kills the husband were found in only three states (**Arkansas, Iowa, North Carolina**). Two of them require a conviction. Perhaps the majority of jurisdictions now have general statutes which deprive a murderer of all rights in the estate of his victim. Many of these statutes contain language broad enough to deprive the widow of dower and other rights in the property of a husband whom she has criminally killed.

6. *Miscellaneous.*—One of the broadest statutes found on the subject of this section is that of **New Hampshire** which provides that the

[§ 202

wife loses all her interest in the husband's estate, except such as the will gives her, if at the time of his death he is living separate because of her misconduct constituting cause for divorce. In three states, if the husband lives apart for cause (**Maine, Massachusetts**) or has cause for divorce (**Minnesota**), he may obtain a decree barring the wife's statutory share. Finally, in two states (**Missouri, New Jersey**), the wife forfeits her dower if after being ravished she consents to the ravisher, unless there is a subsequent reconciliation and cohabitation with the husband.

From the fragmentary character of the foregoing legislation it is apparent that the majority of jurisdictions have not seen fit to penalize an unfaithful wife except when her misconduct is followed by a divorce. The fact that the husband may bar the wife's dower, etc., by obtaining a divorce, but fails to do so, is no reason for allowing her to participate in benefits to which she is not morally entitled. To punish her for her serious misconduct by depriving her of valuable property rights in his estate may seem drastic, but is entirely justified if an unfaithful husband is given the same measure of punishment (see **Sec. 221**). A woman who wilfully deserts her husband and continues such desertion for a substantial period immediately preceding his death deserves no share of his property, except such as may be given her in his will. That she is not also an adulteress does not strengthen her position. Further legislation to that effect seems desirable. Indeed, the rule might well be extended to all cases in which the husband at death is living apart for cause sufficient for divorce. In those jurisdictions in which the wife has an inchoate interest in the husband's lands, there is also a real need for legislation enabling him to convey free thereof when she has deserted him or he is living apart for cause.

A summary by jurisdiction of the statutes discussed above follows:

Arkansas (Crawf. and Moses, Dig., Supp. 1927, Sec. 3514a) : If wife kills husband and is convicted of murder in first or second degree, she forfeits dower in real and personal estate of husband.

Connecticut (G. S. 1930, Sec. 5156) : Wife forfeits statutory share of real and personal property when, without sufficient cause, she abandons husband and continues such abandonment to the time of his death.

Delaware (R. C. 1915, Sec. 3311) : If wife willingly leaves husband and goes with an adulterer, or willingly lives in adultery in a state of separation not occasioned by husband's fault, she forfeits dower and all demands as widow upon his real or personal estate, unless husband is reconciled to her and suffers her to dwell with him.

§ 202]

District of Columbia (C. 1929, T. 14, Sec. 30) : If wife willingly leaves husband, goes away and continues with her advoutrer, she forfeits dower in lands "if she be convict thereupon," unless husband willingly reconcile her and suffer her to dwell with him.

Georgia (C. 1926, C. of Prac., Sec. 5249) : Dower is barred by adultery of wife unpardoned by husband.

Illinois (Cahill, R. S. 1931, Ch. 41, Sec. 15) : If wife voluntarily leaves husband and commits adultery, she is barred of dower unless she and husband are reconciled and dwell together.

Indiana (Burns, Ann. St. 1926, Sec. 3353) : If wife leaves husband and is living at time of his death in adultery, she shall take no part of his estate.

Iowa (C. 1927, Sec. 12032) : If wife feloniously takes, or causes or procures another to take, husband's life, she loses all her interest in his estate as surviving wife or under his will.

Kentucky (Carroll, St. 1922, Secs. 1217, 1405, 2133) : If wife is convicted of bigamy, she forfeits her claim to dower in first husband's estate; but if husband is convicted of bigamy, she shall on his conviction be endowed of his lands and receive one-third of his other estate in fee. If wife voluntarily leaves husband and lives in adultery, she forfeits all right and interest in the property and estate of husband, unless they afterward become reconciled and live together as man and wife.

Maine (R. S. 1930, Ch. 74, Sec. 11) : If wife deserts husband for one year or husband lives apart for cause for one year, probate court may decree that husband is deserted, etc., and wife is not entitled to any share of his estate or to waive provision in his will.

Maryland (Bagby, Ann. C. 1924, Art. 27, Sec. 23) : Wife, on husband's conviction for bigamy, shall be forthwith endowed of his lands, and receive one-third of his personal estate as if he had died intestate; if wife is convicted of bigamy, she forfeits dower and distributive share of personal estate.

Massachusetts (G. L. 1932, Ch. 209, Sec. 36) : Probate court may decree that husband has been deserted by wife or that he is living apart for cause, and wife thereupon loses right to waive provision of his will, or to claim such part of his estate as she would take if he died intestate, and she forfeits dower if he leaves a will.

Michigan (Comp. L. 1929, Sec. 13510) : If wife at time of death of husband is living with another person pursuant to a bigamous marriage, she forfeits dower and all other right or interest in the real and personal property of the husband.

[§ 202

Minnesota (G. S. 1923, Sec. 8622) : When husband is deserted by wife for one year, or has cause for divorce, he may bring action for a decree which shall bar wife of statutory share in his lands.

Missouri (R. S. 1929, Sec. 337) : If the wife voluntarily leaves husband and goes away and continues with an adulterer, or abandons him without cause and continues to live separate for one year next preceding his death, or after being ravished consents to the ravisher, she forfeits dower, homestead or statutory allowances unless the husband is reconciled voluntarily to her and suffers her to dwell with him.

New Hampshire (Pub. L. 1926, Ch. 306, Sec. 19) : If husband at his death is living apart because of wife's misconduct constituting cause for divorce, wife is not entitled to any interest or portion in the real or personal estate of husband, except such as his will gives her.

New Jersey (Comp. L. 1910, p. 2048, Secs. 14, 15) : If wife voluntarily leaves husband and goes away and continues with her adulterer, or after being ravished consents to the ravisher, she forfeits dower unless husband be voluntarily reconciled to her and suffers her to dwell with him.

New York (Cahill, Consol. L. 1930, Ch. 13, Sec. 18) : Wife who has abandoned husband loses right to elect to take against husband's will.

North Carolina (C. 1927, Secs. 10, 11, 2522–23, 4099) : Dower, year's support and distributive share of personal property is forfeited if wife is convicted of felonious slaying of husband or of being accessory before the fact of such slaying, or if she elopes with an adulterer, or wilfully and without cause abandons husband and refuses to live with him and is not living with him at his death. Dower is barred if wife commits adultery and is not living with husband at death.

Ohio (Complete G. C. 1931 [Page], Supp. 1932, Sec. 10502[5]) : Wife who leaves husband and dwells in adultery is barred of dower in lands, unless the offense is condoned by husband.

Pennsylvania (St. 1920 [West], Sec. 8355) : Widow's interest in husband's real and personal estate is forfeited if, for one year previous to his death, she wilfully and maliciously deserts him.

South Carolina (C. of L. 1922, C. C., Secs. 5237, 5243–48, 5333; Sess. L. 1928, No. 669, p. 1243) : Dower is forfeited if wife willingly leaves husband, and goes away and continues with her advoutrer, and so continues uninterruptedly for five consecutive years, or if she leaves the state and obtains a divorce under the laws of any state, or if she is convicted of adultery, unless husband willingly reconciles her after the elopement, or condones the conviction and lives with her afterward. Dower is forfeited if wife marries another man during lifetime of husband

§ 202]

whether she be divorced or not, or whether divorce decree rendered in another state be regarded in this state as valid or invalid. Distributive share of intestate husband's real estate is forfeited if dower is forfeited. If resident wife voluntarily and without cause leaves husband and remains continuously absent from his bed and board for one year, he may bring action for decree forfeiting her dower and authorizing him to convey free thereof.

Virginia (C. 1930, Secs. 5123, 5277) : If wife wilfully deserts or abandons husband and such desertion or abandonment continues until his death, she is barred of all interest in his estate as tenant by dower, distributee or otherwise. If wife leaves husband and lives in adultery she forfeits her distributive share of personal estate and right to renounce provision of husband's will, unless before his death they were reconciled and lived together.

West Virginia (C. 1931, Ch. 42, Art. 3, Sec. 3 ; Ch. 43, Art. 1, Sec. 19) : Wife forfeits dower if she voluntarily leaves husband and lives in adultery and they are not afterward reconciled and live together, or if she voluntarily leaves or abandons husband without cause sufficient for absolute or limited divorce and is so living apart from husband at time of his death. If dower is barred, widow cannot renounce provisions of husband's will, and is not entitled to any part of his estate except such as is given to her by his will.

REFERENCES

[See also references at end of Secs. 96, 99, 100]

Books

Scribner, Charles H. *A Treatise on the Law of Dower,* 2d ed., Vol. II, chs. xviii–xix, pp. 531–57 (1883).

Stimson, F. J. *American Statute Law,* Sec. 3246 (1886).

Tiffany, Herbert Thorndike. *Real Property and Other Interests in Land,* 2d ed., Vol. 1, Sec. 227 (1920).

Woerner, J. G. *A Treatise on the American Law of Administration,* 3d ed., Vol. I, Sec. 109 (1923).

Note

"Effect on Dower Right of Prohibition against Remarriage by Guilty Party," *Loughran* v. *Loughran,* 66 F. (2d) 567 (1933)—34 Col. L. Rev. 563–65 (1934) ; 14 B. U. L. Rev. 392–96 (1934) ; 32 Mich. L. Rev. 999–1001 (1934).

Annotation

"Misconduct of Surviving Spouse as Affecting Marital Rights in Other's Estate," 71 A. L. R. 277–90 (1931).

[§ 202

Section 203. Dower—Forfeiture of Provision in Lieu of Dower

CROSS REFERENCES: Barring dower by jointure, etc., **Secs. 196–99;** Forfeiture of dower, **Sec. 202**

Legislation expressly defining the effect of the wife's misconduct upon settlements made in lieu of dower was found in only five states, as follows: jointure (**Arkansas, Illinois, Missouri, New Jersey**), devise, or pecuniary provision made in lieu of dower (**Arkansas**) ; any estate or charge settled upon wife or in trust for her in lieu of dower is forfeited when dower is forfeited (**Arkansas**), by adultery when dower is forfeited (**Delaware, Illinois, Missouri, New Jersey**), by consenting to her ravisher when dower is forfeited (**Missouri, New Jersey**), by abandonment when dower is forfeited (**Missouri**), by divorce for the wife's adultery (**Delaware**), by divorce for the wife's fault (**Illinois**). Some of the statutes outlined in **Section 202** on forfeiture of dower are broad enough to cover settlements or other provision made in lieu of dower. Somewhat analogous legislation is found in four states (**Missouri, New Jersey, Ohio, Rhode Island**) to the effect that if the widow's jointure fails to be a legal bar to dower because of some defect, and she avails herself of such defect and demands dower, the estate conveyed as a jointure is determined.

Citations for the foregoing statutes are as follows:

Arkansas, Crawf. and Moses, Dig. 1921, Sec. 3528; **Delaware,** R. C. 1915, Secs. 3017, 3311 ; **Illinois,** Cahill, R. S. 1931, Ch. 41, Secs. 14, 15; **Missouri,** R. S. 1929, Secs. 336, 337; **New Jersey,** Comp. St. 1910, p. 2048, Secs. 13–15; **Ohio,** Complete G. C. 1931 (Page), Supp. 1932, Sec. 10502(3); **Rhode Island,** G. L. 1923, Sec. 5808.

REFERENCES

Book

STIMSON, F. J. *American Statute Law,* Sec. 3247 (1886).

§ 203]

Section 204. Dower—Failure of Provision in Lieu of Dower

CROSS REFERENCES: Barring dower by jointure or other settlement, **Sec. 196**; Barring dower by will, **Sec. 199**; Forfeiture of provision in lieu of dower, **Sec. 203**

By express provision of the Statute of Uses (27 Hen. VIII, c. 10, s. 7), if the widow was lawfully evicted from any part of her legal jointure, she was entitled to dower in the residue of the husband's lands to an amount equal to her loss. The provision was construed, however, so as to limit her recovery in any event to the amount of her dower.

Most of the jurisdictions having the jointure statutes outlined in **Section 196** have substantially re-enacted this provision of the Statute of Uses. Thus, if the widow is lawfully evicted from the lands settled on her by way of jointure (**Alaska, Delaware, District of Columbia, Indiana, Kentucky, Maine, Massachusetts, Michigan, Missouri, Montana, New Jersey, Ohio, Oregon, Rhode Island, South Carolina, Vermont, Virginia, West Virginia, Wisconsin**), or is lawfully evicted from a part thereof (**Delaware, District of Columbia, Kentucky, Missouri, New Jersey, Ohio, Rhode Island, South Carolina, Virginia, West Virginia**), or is deprived of provision made for her in lieu of dower, etc., by will or otherwise (**Alaska, Indiana, Kentucky, Maine, Massachusetts, Michigan, Missouri, Montana, Oregon, Rhode Island, Vermont, Virginia, West Virginia, Wisconsin**), she is entitled to dower or statutory share of lands as if such jointure or provision had not been made (**Alaska, Delaware, Indiana, Maine, Massachusetts, Michigan, Missouri, Montana, Oregon, Vermont, Wisconsin**), or to compensation by way of dower to an amount equal to her loss (**District of Columbia, New Jersey, Ohio, Rhode Island, South Carolina, Virginia, West Virginia**), or to indemnity out of the husband's estate (**Kentucky**), or to have the deficiency made up (**Delaware, Missouri**); but her recovery is limited to so much as together with what remains of her jointure shall equal the value of her dower (**Delaware**). In general, the effect of these statutes is to entitle the widow to dower pro tanto when she loses a part of the provision settled on her in lieu of dower.

The citations for the foregoing statutes are as follows:

Alaska, Comp. L. 1913, Sec. 474; **Delaware**, R. C. 1915, Sec. 3306; **District of Columbia**, C. 1929, T. 14, Sec. 36; **Indiana**, Burns, Ann. St. 1926, Sec. 3371; **Kentucky**, Carroll, St. 1922, Sec. 2137; **Maine**, R. S. 1930, Ch. 117, Sec. 12; **Massachusetts**, G. L. 1932, Ch. 189, Sec. 15; **Michigan**, Comp. L. 1929, Sec. 13087; **Missouri**, R. S. 1929, Sec. 335; **Montana**, R. C. 1921, Sec. 5826; **New Jer-**

sey, Comp. St. 1910, p. 2047, Sec. 11; **Ohio,** Complete G. C. 1931 (Page), Supp. 1932, Sec. 10502(4); **Oregon,** C. 1930, Sec. 10(320); **Rhode Island,** G. L. 1923, Sec. 5809; **South Carolina,** C. of L. 1922, C. C., Sec. 5240; **Vermont,** G. L. 1917, Sec. 3411; **Virginia,** C. 1930, Sec. 5122; **West Virginia,** C. 1931, Ch. 43, Art. 1, Sec. 9; **Wisconsin,** St. 1931, Sec. 233.17.

REFERENCES

Books

SCRIBNER, CHARLES H. *A Treatise on the Law of Dower,* 2d ed., II, 432–37, 525–27 (1883).

STIMSON, F. J. *American Statute Law,* Sec. 3248 (1886).

Section 205. Dower—Election and Waiver, in General

CROSS REFERENCES: Dower, abolition and statutory substitutes, **Sec. 189;** Election in case of lands exchanged, **Sec. 191;** Election between jointure or settlement and dower, **Sec. 196;** Failure of provision in lieu of dower, **Sec. 204;** Time limit for and manner of election and waiver, **Sec. 206;** Election when widow dies or is disabled; effect of a failure to elect; miscellaneous provisions, **Sec. 207;** Husband's election between curtesy and will, **Sec. 219;** Election between dower or statutory share and share as heir, **Sec. 227;** Election between homestead, etc., and will, **Sec. 228**

All of the so-called common-law jurisdictions, except **North and South Dakota,** give the widow dower or statutory share of the husband's property protected from a contrary disposition by his will (**Sec. 189**). In a few, as against his will, she is entitled to dower or statutory share in lands only (**Alaska, Delaware, Georgia, New Jersey, Oregon, Rhode Island, South Carolina, Utah**); but in the others she is entitled to a statutory share of his personal estate in addition. If these rights are barred by the husband's will, it is because he has offered her a substitute provision which, theoretically at least, she has accepted in satisfaction thereof. If the husband makes a devise or bequest to the widow expressly in lieu of her rights under the law, she is put to an election; and under the statutory presumption established in most jurisdictions, the same is true whenever the will does not express an intention that the testamentary provision be in addition to her rights under the law (see **Sec. 199** and statutes there collected). Of course, if the wife has effectively relinquished her dower or statutory share, or if she has

§ 205]

been barred thereof by her misconduct, she cannot upset the provisions of the will.

In most jurisdictions, the widow's right of election has been made a strictly statutory right, the exercise of which is usually governed by rather detailed legislation (**Secs. 206, 207**). Statutes of this type, differing in scope and completeness, were found in all jurisdictions except three (**Georgia, Oklahoma, South Carolina**), and are collected in tabular form at the end of this section. To the extent applicable in the particular case, these statutes supplant the old rules governing the widow's election in equity. The courts are inclined to go a long way in protecting the widow in the full enjoyment of the right which the statute gives her; but the right, being statutory, must be exercised substantially in the manner prescribed or it will be lost.

In establishing the right of election, varying terminology is employed by the statutes. Under many, the widow may "elect" between the will and her dower or statutory share, or "elect" to take her dower or statutory share (seventeen). Under others, she may "dissent" from the will (four), or "renounce" (ten), "waive" (four), "relinquish" (one), "refuse" (one), or "accept" (one) the provisions made for her therein. It will be observed that the phraseology employed generally suggests the rule expressly incorporated into many of the statutes that she may refuse to accept the conditions of the will, but that if she does not formally do so she is deemed to have accepted the same and to have waived her rights under the law (**Sec. 207**). It is the fact that the will offers her a substitute provision which necessitates an election. Thus, if the will gives her nothing, no action on her part is ordinarily required (**Sec. 207**). Some of the statutes, however, if literally applied would require an election whenever any provision is made for the widow, even though expressly in addition to her rights under the law. Such an election of course is an absurdity.

One is impressed with the looseness with which many of the statutes are drafted. A few are so ambiguous as to render an understanding of them difficult without a knowledge of local practice (for instance, in **Arkansas, Missouri, Vermont**). Three states have two sets of provisions governing the widow's election between the will and her rights under the law (**Arkansas, Michigan, Virginia**). Especial attention is directed to the unique and rather complex mechanics of the **Illinois** statute. In a number of jurisdictions, the statutes are incomplete in scope, and leave the widow's election in certain instances to be governed by the case law on the subject. Thus in **Delaware, Missouri,** and **New**

[§ 205

Jersey, the legislation is concerned with an election between a devise of lands and dower in lands only and has no application when the will leaves a legacy of personalty in lieu of dower. More remarkable, however, is the **Minnesota** statute, which in terms is confined to an election against the will of a "deceased parent." Why this eccentricity should persist in the statutes has not been explained (see *Hentges* v. *Hoye,* 158 Minn. 402; 197 N. W. 852 [1924]; *Radl* v. *Radl,* 72 Minn. 81; 75 N. W. 111 [1898]).

As has already been observed, a few jurisdictions give the widow a subsidiary right of election between dower in lands and a share in fee (**Sec. 189**). Statutes governing this election are included in Table XCIX, which follows, although most of them are as applicable when the husband dies intestate as when he dies testate.

A further discussion of the statutes governing the widow's election between her rights under the husband's will and under the law is found in **Sections 206** and **207**. For other instances in which the widow is put to an election, the reader is directed to the cross references at the beginning of this section.

The table follows.

TABLE XCIX

STATUTORY ELECTION BETWEEN WILL AND DOWER, ETC.

Jurisdiction[1] and Citation	Occasion for Election, etc. (See Secs. 189, 199)	Time Limit for Election	Manner of Election, etc.	Effect of Failure to Elect	Miscellaneous
Alabama .... C. 1923, Secs. 10593–94, amd. by Sess. L. 1931, No. 724, p. 840; Secs. 10595–96	Dissent from husband's will, in favor of dower in lands and statutory share of personalty	Six months from probate of will. Fifteen months from probate of will when title to property devised or bequeathed to widow is involved in pending litigation	By a writing deposited with judge of probate. Entry of record must be made specifying day on which dissent is made		Widow 18 years old when will admitted to probate has capacity to dissent. Dissent unnecessary when will makes no provision for widow If widow is insane, under 18 years, or has died before time for dissent expires, statute authorizes probate court, after petition and hearing, to make dissent

[1] No statutes were found in **Georgia, Oklahoma,** and **South Carolina** regulating the widow's election between the provisions of the husband's will and dower or statutory share. **Georgia** permits the widow to elect to take a child's part of the real estate in lieu of dower (C. 1926, C. of Prac., Secs. 5249[3], 5250), but this provision does not apply to testate property or confer additional rights as against the husband's will (*Falligant* v. *Barrow,* 133 Ga. 87; 65 S. E. 149 [1909]).

§ 205]

TABLE XCIX (*Continued*)

Jurisdiction and Citation	Occasion for Election, etc. (See Secs. 189, 199)	Time Limit for Election	Manner of Election, etc.	Effect of Failure to Elect	Miscellaneous
Alaska .... Comp. L. 1913, Secs. 472–73	Election between testamentary provision in lieu of dower and dower in lands of husband	One year after death of husband	By a writing filed in district court relinquishing rights under will	Widow is deemed to have elected to take under the will	
Arkansas .... Crawf. and Moses, Dig. 1921, Secs. 3526–27, 3539–42	a) Election between testamentary provision made for widow in lieu of dower, and dower in lands (Sec. 3526)[2]	a) One year after death of husband[2]	a) By entering on lands to be assigned as dower, or by beginning proceedings for recovery or assignment thereof[2]	a) Widow is deemed to have elected to take testamentary provision	
	b) Election between lands devised by husband to widow in lieu of dower, and dower in lands and personalty of which husband died seized (Sec. 3539)[2]	b) Eighteen months after death of husband[2]	b) By deed of release executed to heirs renouncing estate devised[2]	b) Widow is deemed to have elected to take testamentary provision	
Colorado .... Comp. L. 1921, G. S., Secs. 5185–86	Election to take one-half of husband's estate when he wills to others more than one-half thereof	Six months after will is admitted to probate	By written election to take one-half of husband's estate, filed in county court in which will probated	Conclusive evidence of consent to accept provisions of will	Upon filing of election, will is inoperative as to one-half of estate
Connecticut ..... G. S. 1930, Sec. 5156	Election between testamentary provision and statutory share of real and personal property	Two months after expiration of time limited for exhibition of claims against estate	By a writing signed by widow and lodged with probate court	Widow is deemed to have accepted provisions of will, and is barred of statutory share	

[2] As to the applicability of these two sets of provisions on election, see *Pumphrey* v. *Pumphrey,* 52 Ark. 193; 12 S. W. 390 (1889).

[§ 205

TABLE XCIX (*Continued*)

Jurisdiction and Citation	Occasion for Election, etc. (See Secs. 189, 199)	Time Limit for Election	Manner of Election, etc.	Effect of Failure to Elect	Miscellaneous
Delaware ...... R. C. 1915, Secs. 3307–10, 3944	Election between dower and devise of lands by husband's will in lieu of dower in lands	Thirty days' notice by citation to appear and make election	Before orphans' court of county where will recorded, by voluntary appearance of widow, or upon citation issued at request of interested party requiring her to appear and make election	Devise stands in lieu and in bar of dower in husband's lands	Upon satisfactory evidence of widow's inability to appear, election may be made by attorney duly constituted in writing
District of Columbia... C. 1929, T. 14, Secs. 38, 41	Renunciation of devise or bequest, in favor of dower in lands and statutory share of personal estate	Six months after administration granted. If before expiration thereof suit is instituted to construe will, the period begins from date when suit finally determined	By written renunciation filed in probate court (statute gives form)	Widow is barred of dower and statutory share of personal estate	Renunciation unnecessary when will makes no provision for widow or when in effect nothing passes. Widow accepting testamentary provision in lieu of legal right is considered a purchaser for value
Florida .... Sess. L. 1933, Ch. 16103, p. 553, Secs. 35, 36	Election to take dower (absolute share) in real and personal property when widow is not satisfied with share under law of descent and distribution or under will, or both	Nine months after the first publication of notice to creditors	By an instrument in writing, signed by widow and duly acknowledged or sworn to by her, filed with county judge in whose court the estate is being administered. Such election is recorded	Widow is not entitled to dower	
Hawaii .... R. L. 1925, Secs. 3030–31	Election between testamentary provision and dower in real and personal estate	Six months after probate of will. If widow fails to elect, executor shall immediately apply for citation requiring her to elect within time fixed by court	By written election filed in probate court	Widow is conclusively presumed to have reserved her dower if she fails to elect after citation issued; or if, whether cited or not, she fails to elect before administration closed and executor discharged	

TABLE XCIX (*Continued*)

Jurisdiction and Citation	Occasion for Election, etc. (See Secs. 189, 199)	Time Limit for Election	Manner of Election, etc.	Effect of Failure to Elect	Miscellaneous
Illinois .... Cahill, R. S. 1931, Ch. 41, Secs. 10–13	*a*) Renunciation of testamentary provision in favor of dower in lands and statutory share of personalty	*a*) One year after letters testamentary are issued	*a*) By transmitting to county court of proper county a written renunciation of benefits under the will (statute gives form)	*a*) Widow is deemed to have elected to take testamentary provision. Renunciation when filed and recorded bars all claim under will	Nothing in the act shall bar widow's right, after renunciation of will, to dower existing at husband's death in real estate not then owned by him
	b) After renunciation of testamentary provision, waiver of dower, in favor of absolute estate of one-third of each parcel of real estate which husband owns at death, after payment of debts, in lieu of dower in real estate of which he dies seized	*b*) One year after letters testamentary are issued	*b*) By written waiver duly signed and acknowledged, subsequent to renunciation of will, recorded in county in which real estate lies (see also next column)	*b*) Waiver of dower after renunciation of will is effected by failure to record within time specified an election to take dower in real estate instead of an absolute one-third	
	c) Election when husband dies testate to have in lieu of dower in estate of which husband died seized and statutory share of personalty, an absolute share of both real and personal estate after payment of debts (see table, **Sec. 189**)	*c*) Two months after notification of payment of debts, whether dower has been assigned or not			
Indiana .... Burns, Ann. St. 1926, Secs. 3356, 3358–59	Renunciation of testamentary provision and election to take statutory share of real and personal property	One year after will admitted to probate	By written renunciation and election duly signed and acknowledged, filed and recorded in office of clerk of circuit court in which will probated	Widow takes under will, and receives nothing from husband's estate by reason of law of dissent, unless otherwise expressly provided in will	Statute makes provision for election by guardian of insane widow after judicial hearing and determination as to which provision is most advantageous to widow

[§ 205

TABLE XCIX (Continued)

Jurisdiction and Citation	Occasion for Election, etc. (See Secs. 189, 199)	Time Limit for Election	Manner of Election, etc.	Effect of Failure to Elect	Miscellaneous
Iowa C. 1927, Secs. 12007–11	Election to take testamentary provision or to refuse same and claim distributive share of husband's real and personal estate	Six months after will admitted to probate if widow is executor; six months from date of completed service of notice upon widow by executor or other interested person (made when widow has not voluntarily elected within 60 days from admission of will to probate) requiring election within six months	By a writing filed with clerk of probate court, or by election in open court in obedience to citation. Election entered in records of court	Conclusively presumed that widow consents to provisions of will and elects to take thereunder	Statute makes provision for election by court after hearing when widow mentally incapable
Kansas R. S. 1923, Secs. 22(245)– 22(248)	Election to take testamentary provision or to take statutory share of real and personal estate	Thirty days after service of citation issued by probate court forthwith after probate of will, requiring widow to appear and make election	In person in probate court. Duty of court to explain to widow her rights under will and under law	Widow retains her statutory share of real and personal estate	If widow elects to take under will, she takes under will alone. When widow unable to appear because of ill health or is not a resident of county, court on application must issue commission to take her election. Statute authorizes court to make election for insane widow after investigation
Kentucky Carroll, St. 1922, Sec. 1404	Relinquishment of testamentary provision in order to receive dower in lands and distributive share of husband's personal estate	Twelve months after probate of will. If within said period, an appeal from judgment of probate court is taken, then twelve months after such appeal is disposed of	By a writing acknowledged before and left for record with clerk of probate court, or acknowledged before witnesses and proved before and left for record with clerk	If widow claims dower and distributive share, she is charged with value of testamentary provision[3]	Widow, though under full age, has capacity to relinquish rights under will

[3] The **Kentucky** statute provides that if the widow claims dower and distributive share of the husband's estate she shall be charged with the value of any devise or bequest to her by the will, or she may relinquish the testamentary provision and claim dower, etc. In construing this provision, the **Kentucky** court has held that the widow loses her right to dower and distributive share if she fails to renounce the testamentary provision and that she cannot claim the same subject to reduction by the amount of the devise or bequest; but that if she receives part of the property devised or bequeathed before her formal renunciation, she is to be charged with the same in the assignment of dower and the distribution of the personal estate (*Bayes* v. *Howes,* 113 Ky. 465; 68 S. W. 449 [1902]).

§ 205]

TABLE XCIX (*Continued*)

Jurisdiction and Citation	Occasion for Election, etc. (See Secs. 189, 199)	Time Limit for Election	Manner of Election, etc.	Effect of Failure to Elect	Miscellaneous
Maine .... R. S. 1930, Ch. 89, Secs. 13–15	Election whether to accept testamentary provision or claim statutory share	Six months after probate of will. If widow brings bill for construction within thirty days after probate of will, time extended to thirty days after certificate returned[4]	Notice of election to be filed in registry of probate for record. Register of probate to file copy of notice for record with registry of deeds for county where husband's lands are situated		Election may be made by general guardian or guardian ad litem for insane widow. If will makes no provision for widow, she is entitled to statutory share of estate if, within six months after probate of will, she files in registry of probate written notice that she claims same[5]
Maryland ...... Bagby, Ann. C. 1924, Art. 46, Secs. 3, 4; Art. 93, Sec. 311; Sec. 311*A*, added by Sess. L. 1933, Ch. 588, p. 1121; Sec. 314	*a*) Election to take dower in lieu of share of lands under statute of descent	*a*) Six months after death of husband	*a*) Written election filed with orphans' court or register of wills in county where lands situate	*a*) Widow is presumed to have waived dower and to have accepted provisions of statute of descent	*a*) Renunciation unnecessary when in effect nothing passes by will. Widow accepting testamentary provision in lieu of legal right is considered a purchaser for value
	b) Renunciation of devise or bequest in favor of dower in lands and statutory share of personalty or statutory share of both real and personal estate	*b*) Six months after first grant of letters testamentary. Time may be enlarged before its expiration by order of orphans' court for further period of not exceeding six months upon any one application, upon petition showing reasonable cause and on such notice as orphans' court may direct	*b*) By written renunciation transmitted to court or register of wills where administration granted (statute gives form)	*b*) Widow is barred of dower and statutory share of estate	*b*) Renunciation may be made by guardian of infant spouse, or on behalf of an incompetent, when authorized by the proper court

[4] If election is not made within the period specified, and estate is thereafter rendered insolvent and commissioners appointed, the widow may elect within six months thereafter.

[5] The widow's election does not affect title to real estate acquired from executor before the election, but she may demand one-third of sums received from real estate sold.

[§ 205

TABLE XCIX (*Continued*)

Jurisdiction and Citation	Occasion for Election, etc. (See Secs. 189, 199)	Time Limit for Election	Manner of Election, etc.	Effect of Failure to Elect	Miscellaneous
Massachusetts .. G. L. 1932, Ch. 189, Sec. 1; Ch. 191, Sec. 15	*a)* Election to take dower in lieu of share of lands under statute of descent	*a)* Six months after date of approval of bond of executor or administrator	*a)* By written election filed in registry of probate	*a)* Widow is held to have waived dower in lands	
	b) Waiver of testamentary provision, if any, and demand of statutory share of real and personal estate	*b)* Six months after probate of will. If proceedings instituted wherein validity or effect of will is drawn in question, probate court may, within said six months, on petition, extend time to six months after termination of proceedings	*b)* By a writing signed by widow, filed in registry of probate		
Michigan ...... Comp. L. 1929, Sec. 13085, amd. by Sess. L. 1931, No. 242, p. 421; Secs. 13086, 15564–65	*a)* Election between testamentary provision and dower in lands or statutory share of lands of husband	*a)* One year after death of husband	*a)* By commencing proceedings for assignment or recovery of dower	*a)* Widow is deemed to have elected to take testamentary provision	If will makes no provision for widow, she is entitled to elect to take statutory share of personal estate
	b) Election between testamentary provision and statutory share of personalty	*b)* One year from probate of will[6]	*b)* By written election filed in court in which will is probated	*b)* Widow is deemed to have elected to take under the will[6]	
Minnesota ...... G. S. 1923, Sec. 8722	Renunciation of testamentary provision for widow in will of "deceased parent," in favor of statutory share of real and personal estate	Six months after probate of will. If title to homestead be in litigation pending at expiration of such period, time extended to 30 days after litigation concluded	By a writing filed in probate court renouncing provisions of will	Widow is deemed to have elected to take under will	

[6] If widow fails to elect, and after principal administration is closed, administration de bonis non granted because of newly discovered assets, she may elect out of such assets only on good cause shown at any time before the new administration is closed.

§ 205]

TABLE XCIX (*Continued*)

Jurisdiction and Citation	Occasion for Election, etc. (See Secs. 189, 199)	Time Limit for Election	Manner of Election, etc.	Effect of Failure to Elect	Miscellaneous
Mississippi ..... C. 1930, Secs. 3561–62	Renunciation of testamentary provision when husband makes unsatisfactory provision for widow, in favor of statutory share of real and personal estate	Six months after probate of will	By a written renunciation filed in office where will probated (statute gives form)		Renunciation unnecessary if will makes no provision for widow
Missouri .... R. S. 1929, Secs. 326–29, 332–33	*a*) Renunciation of devise of lands in favor of dower in lands whereof husband died seized or in which he had an interest at death	*a*) Twelve months after proof of will. If will contested and set aside, widow may elect under (*b*) below within six months after will set aside as not the will of husband	*a*) By a writing duly executed and acknowledged as for deeds, filed in office of court in which will probated, and recorded	*a*) Widow shall not be endowed in lands whereof husband died seized or in which he had interest at death	If widow is of unsound mind or a minor, her guardian may elect for her in same manner as she might do if capable
	b) Election between dower and child's share of lands, etc. (see table, **Sec. 189**)	*b*) Twelve months after first publication of notice of granting of letters testamentary or of administration	*b*) By declaration in writing acknowledged and filed in office of clerk of court in which letters granted, and filed in recorder's office of county in which letters granted	*b*) Widow is endowed	
Montana .... R. C. 1921, Secs. 5820–21	*a*) Renunciation of testamentary provision, in favor of dower in lands and share of personal estate	*a*) One year after the authentication or probate of will	*a*) By written renunciation transmitted to district court of proper county and filed in office of clerk (statute gives form)	*a*) Widow is deemed to have taken testamentary provision	Renunciation operates as a complete bar to later claim of benefits under will
	b) Election to take absolutely one-half of real estate after payment of debts in lieu of dower in estate of which husband died seized, when husband leaves no descendants	*b*) If dower has been assigned, two months after being notified of payment of debts			

[§ 205

TABLE XCIX (*Continued*)

Jurisdiction and Citation	Occasion for Election, etc. (See Secs. 189, 199)	Time Limit for Election	Manner of Election, etc.	Effect of Failure to Elect	Miscellaneous
Nebraska ...... Comp. St. 1929, Sec. 30(108)	Election between testamentary provision and statutory share of real and personal estate	One year after issuance of letters testamentary	By written refusal to take testamentary provision and declaration of intention to take statutory share, filed in office of county court wherein estate is administered, and executed and acknowledged as for deeds	Widow is deemed to have elected to take under the will	
New Hampshire. Pub. L. 1926, Ch. 291, Sec. 3; Ch. 306, Secs. 10, 11, 14	a) A waiver of testamentary provision, if any, in favor of statutory share of personalty in addition to dower and homestead	a) One year after death of husband, and not afterwards unless by permission of judge of probate for good cause shown	a) By a writing, filed in probate office		Guardian of insane widow may execute waiver and release for ward
	b) Waiver of testamentary provision, if any, and release of dower and homestead in favor of statutory share of real estate	b) Same as above	b) Same as above, plus recording in registry of deeds of county in which real estate situated		
New Jersey .... Comp. St. 1910, p. 2048, Sec. 16	Dissent to receive lands devised by husband to widow in bar of dower in other lands disposed of by will	Six months after probate of will	By a writing, filed with surrogate of county where widow resides or in which lands devised to widow are situated	Widow is not entitled to dower in lands devised by husband	
New York ...... Cahill, Consol. L. 1930, Ch. 13, Sec. 18	Election to take statutory share of real and personal estate when husband dies testate	Six months from date of issuance of letters. Time may be enlarged before its expiration by order of court for further period of not exceeding six months upon any one application, upon petition showing reasonable cause and on such notice as surrogate directs. Certified copy of order to be recorded in each county wherein real estate situated	By serving written notice of election upon representative of estate personally or in manner as surrogate directs, and by filing and recording copy of notice with proof of service in court where will probated		Election may be made by general guardian of infant when authorized by surrogate having jurisdiction of estate, and by guardian of incompetent when authorized by supreme court. After election, will is valid as to residue and terms thereof remain effective so far as possible

TABLE XCIX (*Continued*)

Jurisdiction and Citation	Occasion for Election, etc. (See Secs. 189, 199)	Time Limit for Election	Manner of Election, etc.	Effect of Failure to Elect	Miscellaneous
North Carolina.. C. 1927, Secs. 4096–98, 4100	Dissent from husband's will in favor of same rights in real and personal property as if husband died intestate (dower, year's support, distributive share of personalty)	Six months after probate of will	Dissent in person or by attorney before clerk of superior court of county where will proved. Dissent filed as record of court		Guardian of infant or insane widow may dissent for ward. Dissent may be by attorney duly authorized in writing. Lands taken under husband's will, not exceeding quantity she would be entitled to as dower, are not subject to payment of husband's debts during widow's life
Ohio .... Complete G. C. 1931 (Page), Supp. 1932, Secs. 10504(55)– 10504(65)	Election to take under husband's will or under statute of descent and distribution	One month after service of citation to elect. After probate of will and filing of inventory, appraisement, and schedule of debts, probate court on motion of executor or on own motion shall issue citation to widow to elect. If proceedings for construction or to contest will are begun within period for election, time extended to three months after final disposition thereof	Whether or not citation issued, election may be made in person in probate court or by a writing, signed, duly acknowledged, and filed in probate court. Duty of court to explain to widow her rights under will and under law. Election shall be entered upon minutes of court when made in person	Widow is conclusively presumed to have elected to take under will. If widow dies within period for election without having elected, she is conclusively presumed to have elected to take under statute of descent and distribution	If widow elects to take under will, she is barred of all right to intestate share and takes under will alone unless contrary intention appears in will.[7] If widow unable to appear because of ill health or is not a resident of county, court on application shall issue a commission to take her election. Statute authorizes court, after investigation, to make election for widow under legal disability[8]
Oregon .... C. 1930, Secs. 10(318)– 10(319)	Election between testamentary provision and dower in lands of husband	One year after death of husband	Written statement, executed, acknowledged, and recorded in deed records of county where estate administered, that she elects to accept dower	Widow is deemed to have elected to take under will	

[7] Election to take under the will does not bar widow's right to remain in mansion or to year's allowance unless will otherwise directs.

[8] Election made after expiration of time limit for filing claims is not affected by claims subsequently filed.

TABLE XCIX (*Continued*)

Jurisdiction and Citation	Occasion for Election, etc. (See Secs. 189, 199)	Time Limit for Election	Manner of Election, etc.	Effect of Failure to Elect	Miscellaneous
Pennsylvania ... St. 1920 (West), Sec. 8335; Sec. 8336, amd. by Cum. Supp. 1928 (West), p. 361; Secs. 8337–39	Election to take under will, or against will in favor of statutory share of real and personal property	One year after issuance of letters. On application of interested party, court may issue citation at any time after six months from death of husband requiring widow to appear at a certain time, not less than one month thereafter, to make election	By a writing signed and duly acknowledged, delivered to executor or administrator (see also preceding column). Election, or certified copy of final decree when election or failure to elect under citation, shall be recorded by personal representative in office of recorder of deeds of county where will is probated, and may be recorded in any county	Failure to deliver writing is deemed an election to take under will. Failure to appear on citation is deemed election to take under will, and decree of court to that effect is conclusive	No payment from estate to widow, except widow's exemption, shall be required to be made unless her election is first executed, etc.
Rhode Island.... G. L. 1923, Sec. 4311	Non-acceptance of testamentary provision in lieu of dower	One year from probate of will	Widow shall signify her non-acceptance in writing to probate court		
Tennessee ...... C. 1932, Secs. 8358, 8360–64	Dissent from husband's will when satisfactory provision is not made for her, in favor of dower and statutory share of personal estate	One year after probate of will, when title of widow to property devised or bequeathed is involved in pending litigation so that election cannot be advisedly made. She shall have an additional year, upon application. Upon proper showing of litigation not concluded, court may further extend time	Widow shall signify her dissent in open court in writing, to be entered of record. Personal representative under duty to disclose to widow the condition of the estate upon application		Widow may sue for dower without formal dissent, when personal property is bequeathed to her, but whole of estate including bequest is taken for payment of debts. Statute authorizes court to declare dissent for infant or insane widow, upon petition of guardian, etc.; or on petition of personal representative of widow dying before time for dissent expires

§ 205]

TABLE XCIX (*Continued*)

Jurisdiction and Citation	Occasion for Election, etc. (See Secs. 189, 199)	Time Limit for Election	Manner of Election, etc.	Effect of Failure to Elect	Miscellaneous
Utah .... R. S. 1933, 101-4-4	Acceptance of testamentary provision in lieu of distributive share of lands	Four months after admission of will to probate, or within such additional time before distribution as court allows	By written instrument filed with clerk of court accepting testamentary provision, which acceptance is construed as renunciation of distributive share	Widow is conclusively presumed to have renounced testamentary provision and to have accepted distributive share of lands	If widow is insane, incompetent, or absent from state, general or special guardian shall make election for her
Vermont .... G. L. 1917, Secs. 3279, 3405	Waiver of testamentary provision (or provisions of the law in case husband dies without issue) in favor of statutory share of real and personal estate	Eight months after will of husband is proved or letters granted, or in such further time as court in its discretion allows	Widow shall notify probate court of her election in writing		
Virginia .... C. 1930, Secs. 5120–21, 5276	*a*) Waiver of testamentary provision in lieu of dower in lands, and election to take dower	*a*) One year after will admitted to probate. If suit brought within the year to construe will as to provisions for widow, court on application shall extend period a reasonable time, not exceeding six months after final order made	*a*) Election shall be made in any court of record in county where husband resided at death, or by a writing recorded therein or in clerk's office thereof, duly acknowledged or proved	*a*) Testamentary provision in lieu of dower in lands bars dower, subject to right of election	If will contains no provision for widow, no renunciation necessary to entitle widow to statutory share of personalty
	b) Renunciation of testamentary provision so as to entitle widow to statutory share of personalty	*b*) Same as above. Also, widow may, within six months after expiration of the year, institute suit for construction, and on application, court shall allow widow not exceeding one month after final decree entered	*b*) Renunciation may be made in person before court in which will recorded, or by a writing recorded therein or in clerk's office thereof, duly acknowledged or proved	*b*) Widow receives no more of surplus personalty than is given her by the will	

[§ 205

TABLE XCIX (*Concluded*)

Jurisdiction and Citation	Occasion for Election, etc. (See Secs. 189, 199)	Time Limit for Election	Manner of Election, etc.	Effect of Failure to Elect	Miscellaneous
West Virginia... C. 1931, Ch. 42, Art. 3, Secs. 1, 2; Ch. 43, Art. 1, Sec. 8	Renunciation of testamentary provision (or waiver of jointure created by will) in favor of dower, and distributive share of personalty	Eight months from admission of will to probate. If will contested or order admitting it to probate be appealed, renunciation may be made within two months of final decision	Renunciation may be made either in person before court by which will admitted to probate, or by a writing recorded in office of clerk thereof, duly acknowledged or proved	Widow shall have no more of estate than is given by will	If will contains no provision for widow, renunciation is unnecessary
Wisconsin ..... St. 1931, Secs. 233.14, 233.15	Election to take dower and statutory share of personal estate instead of testamentary provision	One year after filing of petition for probate of will. Two years after filing thereof when election made by guardian or personal representative of widow. Time consumed in action to contest will or for interpretation of will does not constitute any part of period within which election may be made	By notice in writing of election, filed in court having jurisdiction of settlement of estate	Widow is deemed to have elected to take under will	If will makes no provision for widow (and no jointure or pecuniary provision made for her), election is unnecessary. Election for incompetent may be made by her guardian. If widow dies within period for election, leaving issue by deceased husband, election may be made by her personal representative
Wyoming ...... R. S. 1931, Sec. 88(101)	Election to accept conditions of husband's will or statutory share of his real and personal estate	Six months after probate of will	By a writing signed and acknowledged, and filed in office of clerk of court in which will admitted to probate	The will shall govern and control in distribution of estate	

§ 205]

REFERENCES

Books

PAGE, WILLIAM HERBERT. *The Law of Wills,* 2d ed., Vol. II, Secs. 1187–1224 (1926).

SCRIBNER, CHARLES H. *A Treatise on the Law of Dower,* 2d ed., Vol. II, ch. xi, Secs. 48–55; ch. xvii (1883).

STIMSON, F. J. *American Statute Law,* Secs. 3260–64 (1886).

TIFFANY, HERBERT THORNDIKE. *The Law of Real Property and Other Interests in Land,* 2d ed., Vol. 1, Sec. 225 (1920).

WOERNER, J. G. *The American Law of Administration,* 3d ed., Sec. 119 (1923).

Articles

EAGLETON, WILLIAM L. "The Illinois Dower Act as Applied to Estates Consisting of Personal Property," 26 Ill. L. Rev. 164–67 (1931).

FOX, SAMUEL. "The Illinois Dower Act," 26 Ill. L. Rev. 145–64 (1931).

SAYRE, PAUL L. "Husband and Wife as Statutory Heirs," 42 Harv. L. Rev. 330–64 (1929).

Notes

"Acceptance by Wife of Distributive Share under Statute of Another State as Election Not to Take under Will," *McGehee* v. *McGehee,* 152 Md. 661; 136 A. 905 (1927)—28 Col. L. Rev. 252–53 (1928).

"Election to Take under Will as a Waiver of Curtesy Interest," *Austin* v. *Collins,* 317 Mo. 435; 297 S. W. 36 (1927)—28 Col. L. Rev. 388–89 (1928).

"Legacy in Lieu of Dower as a Charge on Land," *Davis* v. *Davis,* 138 Va. 682; 123 S. E. 538 (1924)—23 Mich. L. Rev. 197 (1924).

"Surviving Spouse Is Heir," *Hartford-Connecticut Trust Company* v. *Lawrence,* 106 Conn. 178; 138 A. 159 (1927)—37 Yale L. Jour. 272 (1927).

"Widow Is Not an Heir of Husband," *McCarthy* v. *Walsh,* 123 Me. 157; 122 A. 406 (1923)—22 Mich. L. Rev. 855–56 (1924).

"Wills, Effect on Rights of Husband or Wife, Election and Renunciation," *Suiter* v. *Suiter,* 323 Ill. 519; 154 N. E. 337 (1926)—22 Ill. L. Rev. 200–202 (1927).

Annotations

"Effect of Death of Widow within Time for Making Election between Dower and Other Interest," 5 Ann. Cas. 82–83 (1907).

"Election by Widow to Take under Will as Affecting Her Right to Intestate Property," Ann. Cas. 1918B, pp. 986–96 (1918).

"Election on Behalf of One under Disability of Coverture to Take under or against Will," 74 A. L. R. 465–67 (1931).

[§ 205

"Estoppel by Conduct during Testator's Life to Dissent from or Attack Validity of Will," 74 A. L. R. 659–64 (1931).

"When Is Widow Put to Her Election between Provision Made for Her by Her Husband's Will, and Her Dower, Homestead, or Community Right?" 22 A. L. R. 437–524 (1923) ; 68 A. L. R. 507–20 (1930).

Section 206. Dower—Time Limit for and Manner of Election and Waiver

CROSS REFERENCES: Election and waiver, in general, **Sec. 205**; Election when widow dies or is disabled; effect of a failure to elect, **Sec. 207** (see also cross references at beginning of **Sec. 205**)

1. *Time limit for election and waiver.*—Apart from legislation, there is no definite period of time within which the widow must make her election, but an unreasonable delay may bar her from exercising the right as against intervening equities. The statutes, however, invariably prescribe a fixed date after which her right of election is barred, and the law makes an election for her. While there is a great variation of detail, the statutes fall roughly into two classes. Under the first and most common type, found in thirty-two jurisdictions, a definite period within which the election must be made is set, and this period begins to run from the death of the husband or from a specified step in the administration of his estate. The length of the period varies, but it is more commonly a year (sixteen jurisdictions) or six months (twelve jurisdictions). The point at which the period commences is the death of the husband in five jurisdictions; but in the others, it is variously described as the filing of petition for probate, the admission of the will to probate, the issuance of letters testamentary, the expiration of the time for filing claims, etc. In the second class are the statutes of four jurisdictions, under which the widow need not elect until served with citation by the probate court or personal representative requiring her to elect. Finally, in two jurisdictions, a definite period is set, but she may be compelled to elect before the expiration thereof by the service of citation.

It is obviously expedient to place definite limitations on the time within which the widow may exercise her election, both to facilitate the orderly administration of the estate and to fix the rights of others interested in the estate. She should not, however, be hurried into an election when one cannot be advisedly made because of uncertainty concerning the condition of the estate or her rights under the will. The fact that an action is pending to construe the will or otherwise affecting the comparative rights of the widow under the will and under the law does not of itself extend the time for her election. While the statutory period in most jurisdictions is liberal, circumstances in a particular case may make an extension of time both necessary and proper. Less than half of the jurisdictions, however, appear to have given the matter statutory attention. Legislation expressly permitting an extension of time was found in only sixteen jurisdictions, but perhaps the same result is reached in others by reason of general legislation. In eleven states, the statute either itself grants a definite extension or permits the court to do so in the particular instances enumerated (i.e., when suit is pending to construe or contest the will, when property left to the widow is involved in litigation, etc.). Most of them are fragmentary and do not necessarily insure the widow of an opportunity to make an intelligent election. A much more desirable type of legislation is found in five jurisdictions (**Maryland, New Hampshire, New York, Utah, Vermont**) broadly permitting the court in its discretion to grant an extension of time for good cause.

2. *Method of election.*—In the absence of legislation, the widow's election may be by express declaration or by conduct amounting to an election. Practically all of the statutes, however, are explicit as to the manner in which the election shall be manifested. These statutes are generally regarded as exclusive in character, so that to be effective the election must be made substantially in the manner prescribed. The great majority of jurisdictions (twenty-nine) require a writing. In five, the election may be in writing, or made in person in open court in obedience to a citation or otherwise. In three, the statutes seem to require an election in person before the court. The writing signifying the widow's election must generally be filed or lodged with the probate court or judge or clerk thereof (twenty-nine jurisdictions) or served on the personal representative (two jurisdictions). Most of the statutes do not require the writing to be executed with any particular formalities, but under some it must be executed and acknowledged or proved in the manner required for deeds, or before an officer of the court. Occasionally, the election or a copy thereof must be filed by the widow, personal representative, or clerk of court with the recorder of the county where lands affected are situated.

[§ 206

The statutes discussed in this section, together with the citations therefor, are collected in Table XCIX, **Section 205** (pp. 450–62).

REFERENCES

[See also references at end of **Sec. 205**]

Book

STIMSON, F. J. *American Statute Law,* Secs. 3265, 3267 (1886).

Section 207. Dower—Election and Waiver, Miscellaneous

CROSS REFERENCES: Election and waiver, in general, **Sec. 205**; Time limit for and manner of election and waiver, **Sec. 206** (see also cross references at beginning of **Sec. 205**)

I. Effect of failure to exercise right of election
II. Election when widow dies or is disabled, etc.
III. Election when will contains no provision for widow
IV. Widow's share in lands aliened by husband and intestate property when she takes under the will
V. Liability of substitute provision for husband's debts

I. EFFECT OF FAILURE TO EXERCISE RIGHT OF ELECTION

If the husband offers the widow a substitute provision in his will, she may accept the same or claim her dower or statutory share. If she fails to exercise her right of election, the law will elect for her. Whether she then takes under the will or under the law depends upon the terms of the statute governing her election. The substantial question to be determined is whether inaction on her part is to be regarded as an acceptance of the substitute provision and a waiver of dower and statutory share, or vice versa. The statutes of twenty-seven jurisdictions contain an express statement as to the effect of a failure to make an effective election. In twenty-four of these, the widow takes under the will. If

§ 207]

she would retain her dower and statutory share, she must affirmatively act, for otherwise she is deemed to have waived the same and to have accepted the substitute provision. In the other three (**Hawaii, Kansas, Utah**), the statutory rule is to the contrary; and in the absence of an actual acceptance of the substitute provision, she is presumed to have reserved her dower or statutory share. **Ohio** also adopts the minority rule when the widow dies before the expiration of the statutory period without having made her election. The majority rule follows naturally from the mechanics of most of the statutes under which the widow may "dissent" from the will, or "renounce," "waive," etc., the benefits thereunder. This is likewise true in most if not all of the other twelve jurisdictions in which the statutes do not contain an express statement as to the effect of the widow's failure to elect within the time allowed (see Table XCIX, **Sec. 205,** and the statutes collected in **Sec. 199**).

II. Election When Widow Dies or Is Disabled, etc.

The statutory right of election is generally regarded as strictly personal with the widow. In the absence of legislative authority, it cannot be exercised by another for her, whether it be her attorney, guardian, or personal representative. Thus, if the widow dies before the expiration of the statutory period without having elected, the right is lost, and her beneficiaries take what she would have received had she lived and failed to elect (i.e., the testamentary provision, in most states). When a disabled party was put to an election, the English court of equity did not hesitate to grant relief by itself electing for the disabled one; and a considerable number of American courts have assumed the same power as a part of either their general equitable or probate jurisdiction. Other courts have denied the power in the absence of legislation conferring it.

The statutes found which preserve the right of election when the widow dies (three jurisdictions) or which authorize another to elect for her when she is disabled (thirteen jurisdictions) are collected in Table XCIX, **Section 205.** Some of the procedural detail is necessarily omitted. Perhaps similar relief is found in other jurisdictions by reason of general legislation respecting guardians, etc., or respecting the powers of the particular courts involved.

The three jurisdictions which expressly preserve the right of election when the widow dies are **Alabama, Tennessee,** and **Wisconsin.** In the first two, the probate court is authorized to declare her dissent to the will after petition by the personal representative and a hearing as to

[§ 207

what is most advantageous to her estate. In Wisconsin, the personal representative may elect but the right survives only when the widow leaves issue by the deceased husband. While the Ohio statute does not preserve the right of election, it does change the effect of a failure to elect in this particular instance so as to preserve the generous statutory share for the widow's beneficiaries.

We have seen that a failure to elect is generally deemed an acceptance of the substitute provision offered in the will. In those states in which the widow is entitled only to a life interest in the husband's property, it is obvious that what she takes under the will will ordinarily be more advantageous to her heirs. A majority of jurisdictions, however, have adopted the theory that the surviving wife is entitled to a partner's share of the husband's accumulations and give her a generous share of his property, the benefits of which are designed to extend beyond her life. It seems strangely inconsistent, and not in harmony with the policy of these statutes, to permit these generous rights to be lost when the widow dies before electing. The writer believes that there is a need for express legislation whereby her right of election survives in either the probate court or her personal representative.

The statutes of fourteen jurisdictions offer relief when the widow is insane, and seven of these are broad enough to cover the case of an infant widow. In this latter connection, two jurisdictions confer capacity to elect on an infant widow (Kentucky) or a widow of eighteen years (Alabama). Under the statutes above, election for the disabled widow is made by the probate court after hearing or after an independent investigation (Alabama, Iowa, Kansas, Ohio, Tennessee), or by the widow's guardian as she might do if she had capacity (Maine, Missouri, New Hampshire, North Carolina, Utah, Wisconsin), or when authorized by the court (Indiana, New York). And in Maryland election may be made by a guardian of an infant spouse or made on behalf of an incompetent, with the authorization of the proper court. Wisconsin doubles the statutory time limit when the election is made by the guardian; and in the others which require special proceedings, those proceedings must generally be begun within the statutory period.

It remains to add that Delaware and North Carolina expressly permit the widow to elect by a duly authorized attorney; and that in Kansas and Ohio, if the widow cannot appear to make her election because of ill health or if she is not a resident of the county, it is the duty of the probate court on application to issue a commission to take her election.

§ 207]

III. Election When Will Contains No Provision for Widow

No occasion or consideration for an election is present except when the husband in his will offers the widow a substitute for her dower or statutory share. If she must signify her dissent from his will when no provision is made for her therein, in order to save her rights under the law, it must be by force of the statutes governing her election. Most of the statutes are silent on the matter. Eight jurisdictions are express to the effect that no formal dissent or renunciation is necessary. On the other hand, **Maine** requires the widow to claim formally her statutory share when no provision is made for her in the will. In most of the other jurisdictions, by the terms of the statute itself, the statute is not called into operation except when provision is made in lieu of dower or statutory share expressly or by reason of the statutory presumption. In some jurisdictions, however, the terms of the statute seem to require a formal dissent from the will whenever the husband dies testate; but even under these statutes the prevailing rule is that no action is necessary to preserve her rights under the law when no provision is made for her in the will. With the exception of the **District of Columbia, Maryland,** and **Tennessee,** the statutes are not clear as to whether the widow is put to an election when property is bequeathed or devised to her but the same is subsequently taken to satisfy the husband's creditors.

IV. Widow's Share in Lands Aliened by Husband and Intestate Property When She Takes under the Will

If the widow takes under the will, either voluntarily or because she has failed to exercise her right of election, she is barred of dower or statutory share in the property covered by the will. An interesting question, however, is presented as to her rights in property not covered by the will when the will contains no express direction on the point. The problem arises in respect to lands aliened by the husband without the wife's release, and in cases where the husband dies partially intestate. While there is a difference of opinion, the prevailing view excludes the widow from dower or statutory share in lands conveyed by the husband without her release, and from participation in intestate property. The doctrine is logically and severely criticized by Professor Sayre in 42 Harvard Law Review 330. The difference of opinion in the cases is often made to rest on the peculiar wording of particular statutes establishing the effect of a devise or bequest to the wife (see statutory résumé,

[§ 207

Sec. 199). It is obvious that most of the statutes were not designed in anticipation of the problem. Of the statutes collected in Table XCIX, **Section 205,** those of **Indiana, Kansas, Ohio,** and **West Virginia** seem clearly to confine the widow to the will and bar her from sharing in intestate property. The **Missouri** statute on the other hand does not in terms bar her of dower in lands aliened without her consent.

V. Liability of Substitute Provision for Husband's Debts

In perhaps a majority of jurisdictions, the widow's dower or statutory share of lands, and in some her statutory share of personalty, is free from the husband's debts. Some courts have clothed her rights under the will with the same superiority up to the value of her dower or statutory interest; a few have given her a position of equality with creditors; but the prevailing view is that she takes subject to the same liabilities as other beneficiaries. The only express statute on the matter is found in **North Carolina,** which insures the widow of at least an equivalent of dower free from estate creditors. A number of states, however, have legislation offering relief to the widow when there is a failure of the provision made in lieu of dower or statutory share of lands (**Sec. 204**). These statutes would seem to apply when the property given to her by the will is used to pay estate creditors.

The statutory material discussed in this section, and the citations therefor, will be found in Table XCIX, **Section 205.**

REFERENCES

[See also references at end of **Sec. 205**]

Book

Stimson, F. J. *American Statute Law,* Secs. 3265–67 (1886).

Section 208. Assignment of Dower—In General

CROSS REFERENCES: Allowance pending assignment, **Sec. 209;** Assignment by non-judicial action, **Sec. 210;** Assignment by summary proceedings, **Sec. 211;** Action to compel assignment and damages for withholding dower, **Sec. 212;** Method of assignment, **Sec. 213;** Dower in judicial sales and partition actions, and collusive assignment, **Sec. 214;** Assignment of dower to the husband, **Sec. 223**

DOWER CONSUMMATE

On the husband's death, the widow's "inchoate" dower, at common law, became "consummate." Yet she did not have an estate in the property, only a right to have dower assigned. Consequently she had no right to enter on the lands, or sue in trespass or ejectment, with the exception of the privileges she obtained from her quarantine right (**Sec. 209**). She could not alien her interest or exercise other similar powers which were dependent on the ownership of an estate. Her right, however, was recognized in equity—it could be assigned or otherwise transferred (*Pollock* v. *Columbia Bank,* 193 Wis. 389; 214 N. W. 363 [1927]); it was subject to claims of her creditors (*McMahon* v. *Gray,* 150 Mass. 289; 22 N. E. 923 [1889]); and it could be protected by injunction against waste by other tenants.

No statute has been found which expressly changes the common-law nature of dower consummate, but five states (**Florida, Iowa, Kansas, Vermont, Wisconsin**), while retaining provisions analogous to assignment of dower, give the widow an absolute share in fee (**Sec. 189**). Her status is closely akin to that of an heir, and it has been held in **Iowa** and **Wisconsin** that on the husband's death and before her share is set off the widow has an undivided interest in fee as tenant in common with the heirs (*Van Veen* v. *Van Veen,* 213 Ia. 323; 238 N. W. 718 [1931]; *Estate of Johnson,* 175 Wis. 248; 185 N. W. 180 [1921]). It is probable that she has a similar interest in **Kansas** and **Vermont,** and perhaps in **Florida.** A statute in **Massachusetts** which provides that on the husband's death the widow is entitled to possession of an undivided one-third of his real estate, until assignment, seems to recognize that she has some interest in the land more than a mere right to an assignment. However, in the majority of jurisdictions which have retained dower to some extent, the widow has only a right to have dower assigned, and not an estate or undivided interest. A **Missouri** statute (R. S. 1929, Sec. 320) permits the widow to transfer her unassigned dower interest, but it is in the nature of a transfer or a right of action, not of an estate. In juris-

[§ 208

dictions such as **New York** where dower has been abolished and where the wife is in the nature of a forced heir (**Sec. 189**), she presumably does have an interest on the husband's death and before her share is set off.

ASSIGNMENT OF DOWER

The function of assignment is not to vest in the widow a right to dower, as she has that on the husband's death; nor is it analogous to voluntary or involuntary partition, for she has, in general, no undivided interest in the estate. Rather it is a ministerial act of dividing the husband's property in order that the right to dower in severalty is capable of ascertainment.

In the group of states where dower has been abolished and the widow, in reality, is a forced heir (see **Sec. 189**; an example is **Colorado** or **New York**), her share is set off in the same manner as that of other heirs, and assignment of dower is obsolete. On the other hand, all of the twenty-four jurisdictions which have substantially retained dower have statutes on assignment, and they form the basis for the subsequent discussion. A third group of jurisdictions has made sweeping changes in the common-law theory of dower. Of this group, five (**Florida, Iowa, Kansas, Vermont, Wisconsin**) have been included in the following sections on assignment because in their provisions for setting out the widow's share they have retained some of the dower formula. Hereafter, for the sake of brevity, they will be treated as "true dower" states, but it must be remembered that they are distinguishable from such states.

The most important and satisfactory conclusion to be derived from an analysis of assignment of dower is that legislation has greatly improved the common law by its simplification and relaxation of the older rules. The statutes are far from uniform or complete and may be criticized in those respects; but their advantages, in the writer's opinion, far outweigh their faults.

Statutes were found in nineteen jurisdictions providing for a period after the husband's death during which the widow may remain in the dwelling house while waiting for her assignment. These are based on the common-law right of quarantine, but their general trend has been toward greater generosity to the widow (**Sec. 209**). The ministerial nature of assignment made judicial proceedings unnecessary at common law. Eighteen jurisdictions have statutes which expressly or impliedly recognize assignment by non-judicial action; in so doing, some have extended the common law, while others have merely codified it (**Sec. 210**).

§ 208]

The outstanding example of legislative progress is the widespread adoption of summary proceedings for assignment (**Sec. 211**). Twenty-eight jurisdictions have that method of judicial assignment in varying forms, and the remaining state, **Montana,** has a very similar proceeding, although it is considered as an action to compel assignment. Fourteen jurisdictions provide for actions at law to compel assignment, and here again the common law has been greatly modified. Eight jurisdictions recognize the jurisdiction of equity over assignment (see **Sec. 212** for both types of action). It seems fair that a person who withholds the widow's dower should be liable in damages to her, and sixteen jurisdictions have statutes to that effect (**Sec. 212**). **Florida** has a similar provision.

The actual mechanics of admeasuring dower, viz., valuation of the lands, actual division, etc., have been provided for to some extent in all twenty-nine jurisdictions, although the legislation is fragmentary (**Sec. 213**).

Table C following contains details and citations of the statutes referred to in this section and in **Sections 210–12,** inclusive. The material in **Sections 209** and **213** is presented in tabular form in each of those sections. References are collected at the end of each section of the group on assignment.

Jurisdiction and Citation	Assignment by Non-judicial Action	Court with Jurisdiction and Type of Action (Where Specified)	Person Who May Petition or Bring Action
Alabama .... C. 1923, Secs. 7438, 7444, 7446–48, 7450, 9579		*a*) Probate court of county in which land or any part of it lies. But if probate judge is incompetent, or if land aliened by husband is out of county, or assignment by metes and bounds is unjust, circuit court of such county	Widow, heir or personal representative of husband
Alaska .... Comp. L. 1913, Secs. 463, 465, 477–80, 1144, 1148		*a*) District court if husband died seized *b*) Action to recover possession of real property if widow's right is denied. But if, in such action, assignment would prejudice other owners, widow must continue as in action of partition	*a*) Widow or any person interested in lands *b*) Widow or her successor in interest
Arkansas .... Crawf. and Moses, Dig. 1921, Secs. 3544–47, 3555	Duty of heir-at-law to assign dower as soon as practicable after husband's death. Written specification of assignment, endorsed by widow, is filed with probate clerk. Minor heir acts by his guardian	*a*) Probate court (if dower not assigned as in preceding column) within one year from husband's death; or within three months after demand by widow	Widow
Delaware ...... R. C. 1915, Secs. 3312, 3315–16, 3318		*a*) Orphans' court of county in which land lies *b*) Action by writ of dower	*a*) Widow or any person interested *b*) Widow
District of Columbia... C. 1929, T. 25, Sec. 382; T. 29, Sec. 240		*a*) Probate court in executor's sale proceedings *c*) Equity division of supreme court of district	*c*) Widow or any person entitled to property subject to dower, or an undivided share in it

* In this table, *a* indicates summary proceedings; *b* indicates actions at law to compel assignment;

§ 208]

C*

OF DOWER

Assignment of Dower[1]

Effect of Commissioners' Report of Their Assignment	Damages for Withholding of Dower	Miscellaneous Provisions[2]
Written, signed return of commissioners, confirmed by court, is recorded, and vests life estate in widow		Proceedings or suit for dower must be brought within three years after husband's death, if rights of husband's alienee are involved; and in all other cases, within ten years after husband's death
a) When written return of commissioners is confirmed by court, recorded, and copy filed in precinct where lands lie, dower is fixed unless confirmation is set aside or reversed	In any action to recover dower in lands of which husband died seized, widow may recover damages equal to one-third of annual value of mesne profits, estimated against heirs—from husband's death; and against other persons—from demand; but not for use of permanent improvements made after husband's death by heirs or other persons claiming title to lands. If lands aliened by heir, widow may recover damages from him for withholding from husband's death to alienation, not exceeding six years, and less amount recovered from grantee. Amount she is entitled to recover from heir is deducted from amount she is entitled to recover from grantee	
If commissioners' return is confirmed by court, it is recorded and is conclusive on the parties		
a) Proceedings had in same manner as in partition actions b) On judgment for widow, commissioners appointed. After their return is approved by court, writ of possession issues to widow c) Commissioners' report to be ratified by court	b) Widow may recover reasonable damages which are in satisfaction of any demand by her for rents and profits. Damages are assessed by commissioners unless previously assessed by jury	

c indicates suits in equity. See pages 486–87 for all numbered footnotes to the table.

[§ 208

TABLE C

Judicial Proceedings for

Jurisdiction and Citation	Assignment by Non-judicial Action	Court with Jurisdiction and Type of Action (Where Specified)	Person Who May Petition or Bring Action
Florida[3] Sess. L. 1933, Ch. 16103, pp. 583–84, Secs. 113–16, 118	Duty of personal representative to assign dower immediately after widow has elected to take dower[4]	a) County judge's court in which administration of the estate is pending	a) Personal representative. If he fails to do so, widow may petition
Georgia C. 1926, Secs. 5249, 5257–58, 5264		a) Superior court at term time or judges at chambers	Any person entitled to dower. Application cannot be made until after three months from husband's death
Hawaii R. L. 1925, Secs. 2248–49, 3085, 3273	Guardian of infant may set out dower, from infant's estate	a) Judges of circuit court at chambers, in circuit where husband last domiciled; except that if domicile was outside Territory, then in any circuit where estate is b) Writ of dower implied (see last column)	
Illinois Cahill, R. S. 1931, Ch. 41, Secs. 18–20, 38, 41, 43, 44	Duty of heir-at-law or other person having next estate of inheritance or freehold in lands subject to dower, to assign as soon as practicable after husband's death	a) County court in executor's sales proceedings c) Petition in chancery in any court of record of competent jurisdiction in county where estate or part of it lies, if dower not assigned (as in preceding column) after one month from husband's death	a) Legal representative, guardian, conservator, or person entitled to dower c) Widow, heirs or others interested in estate
Iowa[3] C. 1927, Secs. 11994, 11999	Widow's share may be set off by mutual consent of all parties interested	a) Probate court or judge, administering estate, on application which must be made after twenty days and within ten years from husband's death	
Kansas[3] R. S. 1923, Secs. 22(109)–22(110), 22(115)	Widow's share may be set off by mutual consent of all parties interested	a) Probate court, on application which must be made after twenty days and within five years from husband's death	

§ 208]

(Continued)

Assignment of Dower[1]

Effect of Commissioners' Report of Their Assignment	Damages for Withholding of Dower	Miscellaneous Provisions[2]
a) Court shall confirm, reject, or modify commissioners' allotment. Judgment vests in widow, fee simple in lands and absolute ownership of personalty allotted. She is entitled to writ of possession if necessary	a) Mesne profits from the death of the decedent are included in judgment. All matters of mesne profits are decided by the court	a) Proceedings on petition shall be informal and summary. Right of dower as well as admeasurement shall be determined; provided that question of such right of dower is submitted to a jury upon written demand of any party
When commissioners' return is made final judgment of court, it is conclusive on all parties interested, and writs of possession issue to widow		Dower is barred by failure to apply for it within seven years from husband's death
		Judgment in writ of dower may be registered as an encumbrance on lands
c) Written report of commissioners, if approved by court, vests life estate in widow, who is given possession by writ to sheriff	In any action brought for purpose, if widow recovers dower, she may also recover reasonable damages from time of demand and refusal to assign. Damages may be assessed by court or jury	a) Proceedings similar to assignment in chancery court
Confirmation of referee's report is conclusive after thirty days unless appealed from, and thereafter widow may bring action for possession of land		
Confirmation of commissioners' report is conclusive after thirty days unless appealed from, and widow may thereafter bring suit for possession of land set apart		

[§ 208

TABLE C

Jurisdiction and Citation	Assignment by Non-judicial Action	Court with Jurisdiction and Type of Action (Where Specified)	Judicial Proceedings for Person Who May Petition or Bring Action
Kentucky ...... Carroll, St. 1922, Sec. 2139; Civ. C. of Prac. 1906, Sec. 499		*a*) Circuit or county court of county in which land or greater part thereof lies. Action in county court, if petition is controverted, may be removed to circuit court on motion of either party (above does not affect jurisdiction of equity to allot dower)	Person desiring allotment of dower
Maryland .... Bagby, Ann. C. 1924, Art. 16, Secs. 43, 47; Art. 46, Sec. 37		*a*) Circuit court in proceeding for partition of intestate's estate *b*), (*c*) The several courts of equity have full concurrent jurisdiction with courts of law	*c*) Any person holding land by descent, devise or purchase subject to dower (presumably widow may also do so)
Massachusetts .. G. L. 1932, Ch. 185, Sec. 90; Ch. 189, Secs. 1, 10, 14; Ch. 201, Sec. 39; Ch. 238, Secs. 1–4, 7, 9–10	Heir or other tenant of freehold may assign dower according to widow's satisfaction. Guardian or conservator may assign dower in his ward's estate to widow entitled	*a*) Probate court of county in which estate is settled *b*) If dower not assigned as in preceding column, or by probate court, writ of dower available after one month and within one year from written demand on person then seized of freehold. If demand expires, new one may be made	*a*) Widow. If she does not petition within one year after husband's death, heir, devisee, other person having estate subject to dower (or their guardians), or legal representative of husband if it appears to court that personal property is probably insufficient to pay debts *b*) Widow
Michigan .... Comp. L. 1929, Secs. 13091–95, 14904, 14954, 15111, 15395, 15755, 15785	If widow accepts assignment in satisfaction of claim for dower, her further claim is barred unless she is lawfully evicted of lands. Guardian may assign dower from ward's estate	*a*) Judge of probate for county in which estate is settled, if right to dower undisputed by heirs, devisees or persons claiming under them, and if husband died seized *b*) Ejectment after six months from time her right accrued	*a*) Widow or any person interested in lands *b*) Widow, or widow and her husband

§ 208]

(Continued)

Assignment of Dower[1]

Effect of Commissioners' Report of Their Assignment	Damages for Withholding of Dower	Miscellaneous Provisions[2]
If commissioners' report is confirmed by court, commissioner, by deed, conveys land set off. Report and deed are recorded	Widow may claim rent as follows: Against heir or devisee or his alienee—claim not to exceed five years before action; against purchaser from husband—claim only from commencement of action; and, in either case, continues up to final recovery. After action brought, claim does not abate by death of widow, or tenant, or both	
a), (*c*) Commissioners' return is confirmed or rejected by court as in other cases		
b) When commissioners' report is confirmed, and judgment fixing dower and damages is rendered, execution for possession and damages issues	*b*) If widow gets judgment, she may recover damages for detention of dower, assessed by jury unless parties agree that commissioners assess them. If demand (see column two) was not made as specified, defendant, tenant of freehold, is liable for damages only for time he held land. In such case, widow may, in tort action, recover rents and profits from prior tenant on whom demand made, for time he held land after such demand	Judgment in writ of dower may be registered as an encumbrance on lands. Claim for dower must be made within twenty years after husband's death or after widow has ceased to occupy her share, or receive profits from it
a) When commissioners' report is accepted by court and copy recorded in county where lands lie, dower is fixed unless confirmation is set aside or reversed *b*) When commissioners' report is confirmed, writ of possession issues to widow	In any action to recover dower in lands of which husband died seized, widow may recover damages equal to one-third annual value of mesne profits, estimated against heirs—from husband's death; and against other persons—from demand; but in either case, not to include use of permanent improvements made after husband's death by heirs or any person claiming title to lands. If lands aliened by heir, widow may recover from him, in action on the case, damages for withholding from husband's death to alienation, not to exceed six years, and less amount recovered from his grantee. Amount she is entitled to recover from heir is to be deducted from amount she is entitled to recover from grantee	

[§ 208

TABLE C

Jurisdiction and Citation	Assignment by Non-judicial Action	Judicial Proceedings for	
		Court with Jurisdiction and Type of Action (Where Specified)	Person Who May Petition or Bring Action
Missouri .... R. S. 1929, Secs. 339, 341–42, 347, 351, 354, 361, 363–66		Circuit court of county where real estate lies; if land divided by county line, in either county. If lands in several counties not severally held by different devisees or purchasers, then in county of principal messuage; or if none, in any county where lands lie. Court has complete jurisdiction[5]	Widow (see last column), heir, legatee, legal representative of husband, or any person having an interest in lands. Person not a party to proceedings, and having no notice, may petition for a reassignment which may be had in same manner as original proceedings
Montana .... R. C. 1921, Secs. 5829, 9015, 10158–60, 10165, 10168–69	Duty of heir-at-law, person in possession, or person having next estate of freehold or inheritance to assign dower to widow's satisfaction as soon as practicable after husband's death	b) District court of proper county, if dower not assigned (as in preceding column) within one month after husband's death	Widow
New Hampshire[6]. Pub. L. 1926, Ch. 293, Sec. 5; Ch. 308, Sec. 1; Ch. 317, Sec. 1; Ch. 353, Secs. 1, 2, 4, 5, 7	Heir or tenant of freehold may assign dower to widow's satisfaction	a) Judge of probate b) If not assigned as in preceding column, or by probate judge, action of dower available one month after written demand for dower (see last column) c) Superior court has equity powers in assignment of dower	b) Widow
New Jersey ..... Comp. St. 1910, p. 2045, Sec. 3; p. 2046, Sec. 4; p. 2047, Sec. 9; p. 2049, Sec. 17, amd. by Supp. 1925–30, Sec. 63(17); p. 2050, Secs. 19–21		a) If husband died seized, orphans' court of county where lands lie; if they lie in two or more counties, ordinary or surrogate-general b) Writ of dower in supreme court, or circuit court of proper county (see last column)	a) Widow, heir, devisee, or purchaser of lands b) Widow (see last column)

§ 208]

(Continued)

Assignment of Dower[1]

Effect of Commissioners' Report of Their Assignment	Damages for Withholding of Dower	Miscellaneous Provisions[2]
When report of assignment is approved, court gives judgment, awards writ of possession and execution for damages	In widow's action for dower, she may recover, as damages, value of dower from husband's death if he died seized, or from demand if not seized, until recovery. But if against alienee of heir, who, at purchase, had no actual notice of her claim, damages only from demand, estimated according to value of dower at time of recovery, exclusive of improvements made after alienation by heir or person claiming title to lands. If jury is demanded, one must be impaneled to assess damages. Execution issues only against estate from which dower was assigned. Action for damages, though not brought before widow's death, does not abate on her death	Widow may petition if deforced of dower, or if she cannot have it without suit, or unfair assignment made, or none made within two years after husband's death. Action for dower in real estate must be brought within ten years after husband's death
If commissioners' report is accepted, recorded, and copy filed in county where lands lie, dower fixed and certain unless confirmation of court is set aside, or reversed on appeal. Writ of possession then issues	In action to recover dower in lands of which husband died seized, widow may recover damages equal to one-third annual value of mesne profits, estimated against heirs—from husband's death; against other persons—from demand on them; in either case not to include use of permanent improvements made after husband's death by heirs or any person claiming title to lands	Action for dower must be brought within ten years after husband's death
	Widow in action of dower may recover reasonable damages for detention of dower by tenant in such action, after demand made	Demand shall be made in writing on person seized of freehold if in state; otherwise on tenant in possession
		b) Mode of setting out dower is same as in similar cases before probate judge
a) Confirmation of commissioners' report by court is conclusive on all parties concerned, unless set aside or reversed	In writ of dower, widow may recover damages equal to value of dower as follows: If husband died seized—from his death; if not seized—from demand; in either case till she recovers seisin by judgment	*b)* Widow may sue if deforced of dower, or cannot have it without suit, or unfairly assigned, or not assigned within forty days after husband's death

[§ 208

TABLE C

Judicial Proceedings for

Jurisdiction and Citation	Assignment by Non-judicial Action	Court with Jurisdiction and Type of Action (Where Specified)	Person Who May Petition or Bring Action
North Carolina.. C. 1927, Secs. 4104–5	If personal property of estate is sufficient to pay debts, heir or devisee and widow, by deed, may agree to assignment of dower	*a)* If no agreement (as in preceding column) is made, superior court	Widow; or on her default to petition within three months after husband's death, any heir or devisee may do so
Ohio[7] Complete G. C. 1931 (Page), Secs. 10493, 11398, 12005, 12007–8, 12010, 12014–15		*a)* Probate court on petition for sale of lands by legal representative, or guardian *b)* Common pleas court. If lands lie in several counties, such court of any of counties has complete jurisdiction	*b)* Widow
Oregon C. 1930, Secs. 5(113), 5(116), 10(308), 10(310), 10(324)– 10(328), 10(331), 28(1003), 63(378)	If widow accepts assignment in satisfaction of her claim for dower, any further claim is barred unless she is lawfully evicted of lands so set off	*a)* If husband died seized, and widow's right is undisputed, county court of county in which estate lies. If right disputed, proceedings transferred to circuit court *b)* Action to recover possession of real property if widow's right denied. But if in such action assignment would prejudice other owners, she must continue as in partition action	*a)* Widow or any person interested in lands *b)* Widow or her successor in interest
Rhode Island.... G. L. 1923, Secs. 5325, 5784–85, 5787, 5792–96, 5799– 5801, 5804	Heir or person having next immediate estate of freehold in all or any of estate may, in writing, set off dower. If tenant in possession, though only for years, gives notice inviting him to join in assignment, and then acts fairly and honestly, assignment by him is binding	*a)* Court of probate with jurisdiction over estate *b)* After one month from demand, or if assignment is unfair, writ of dower is available *c)* If lands are in several parcels, suit in equity available against all owners. Suit at law or in equity may be brought in any county where lands lie	*a)* Widow or owner of fee in estate *b)* Widow *c)* Widow or any owner of a parcel

§ 208]

(Continued)

Assignment of Dower[1]

Effect of Commissioners' Report of Their Assignment	Damages for Withholding of Dower	Miscellaneous Provisions[2]
		a) Court hears and passes on petition as in other cases of special proceedings
b) If court approves commissioners' report, it is recorded in court, is valid and effective in law, and execution for possession issues	*b*) Widow is entitled to one-third net yearly value of real estate estimated from filing of petition to assignment, exclusive of permanent or valuable improvements made after husband ceased to own lands. Such right of action may be revived by personal representative of widow if she dies before recovery	
a) If written commissioners' return is accepted, recorded, and copy filed in county where lands lie, dower is fixed and certain unless confirmation is set aside or reversed	In any action to recover dower in lands of which husband died seized, widow may recover damages equal to one-half annual value of mesne profits, estimated against heirs—from husband's death; and against other persons—from demand; but in either case not for use of permanent improvements made after husband's death by heir or person claiming title to lands. If lands aliened by heir, widow may recover damages from him for withholding from husband's death to alienation, not exceeding six years, and less amount recovered from grantee. Amount she is entitled to recover from heir is to be deducted from amount she is entitled to recover from grantee	Action to recover or reduce dower to possession must be brought within ten years after husband's death. County court may assign dower for purpose of final distribution of estate
b) When commissioners' report is confirmed and judgment recorded in town in which premises lie, writs of possession and execution for damages issue	Damages sustained by widow by detention after demand for dower may be recovered in law or equity actions, but not in probate court proceedings. If damages awarded against tenant from year to year and are paid, he may set them off against unpaid rent, or may recover from landlord, having a lien on landlord's interest in land from which dower was assigned. Appeal to superior court from probate court may be taken to obtain damages	Death of defendant, tenant of freehold, in action for dower does not abate it if property passes by descent or devise from him, his heir or devisee being substituted

[§ 208

TABLE C

Jurisdiction and Citation	Assignment by Non-judicial Action	Court with Jurisdiction and Type of Action (Where Specified)	Judicial Proceedings for Person Who May Petition or Bring Action
South Carolina.. Const., Art. V, Sec. 19; C. of L. 1922, C. C., Secs. 5239, 5255, 5257, 5263; C. C. P., Sec. 166	Widow, not having jointure, may pursue, have and demand dower according to due course of common law	a) Judge of probate of county in which lands are situate b) See column one	a) Widow
Tennessee ...... C. 1932, Secs. 8367, 8371, 8373, 10225, 10326, 10380		a) County, circuit and (c) chancery courts of county where husband last resided before death have concurrent jurisdiction	Widow
Vermont³ ...... G. L. 1917, Secs. 3406–8, 3412	If estate insolvent, widow and creditors with two-thirds of deceased's debts may agree on share assigned to her. This is binding if approved by probate court	a) Probate court	Widow, executor, administrator, heir, or other person entitled to estate
Virginia .... C. 1930, Secs. 5125–27, 5480	Dower may be assigned as at common law	a) Court in which husband's will recorded, administration of estate granted, or conveyance to alienee recorded b) Such remedy at law as would lie on behalf of life tenant with right of entry c) Suit in equity	a) Widow, heir, devisee, alienee b) Widow
West Virginia .. C. 1931, Ch. 43, Art. 1, Secs. 12–14; Ch. 55, Art. 4, Sec. 19	Dower may be assigned as at common law	a) Circuit court of county in which husband's estate is settled b) Such remedy at law as would lie on behalf of life tenant with right of entry c) Suit in equity	a) Widow, heirs, devisees b) Widow

§ 208]

(Continued)

Assignment of Dower[1]

Effect of Commissioners' Report of Their Assignment	Damages for Withholding of Dower	Miscellaneous Provisions[2]
a) Recorded return of commissioners is conclusive on all parties concerned	See column one	Allotment of dower in circuit court conforms to proceedings in probate court (apparently this applies to an appeal from probate court)
		Proceedings on application for assignment are summary unless applicant is personal representative
If written commissioners' return is accepted, recorded by court, and copy recorded where deed to such land is recorded, widow's share is fixed and certain		If real estate is held in common, widow's share is not set out until partition is made
a) Commissioners' return, if confirmed, has same effect as if made by heir at common law	*b*), (*c*) Damages recoverable by widow in these actions are as follows: Against heirs, devisees or their assigns—for withholding from husband's death, not exceeding five years; against one claiming under alienation from husband—from commencement of suit; and in either case till recovery of dower. After suit brought, it does not abate on widow's or tenant's death	
a) Commissioners' return, if confirmed, has same effect as if made by heir at common law	*b*), (*c*) Damages recoverable by widow in these actions are as follows: Against heirs, devisees, or their assigns—for withholding from husband's death, not exceeding five years; against one claiming under alienation from husband—from commencement of suit; and in either case, till recovery of dower. After suit brought, it does not abate on widow's or tenant's death	

[§ 208

TABLE C

Jurisdiction and Citation	Assignment by Non-judicial Action	Court with Jurisdiction and Type of Action (Where Specified)	Judicial Proceedings for Person Who May Petition or Bring Action
Wisconsin[3] ..... St. 1931, Secs. 233.18–233.21, 275.22, 314.01, 314.02	Acceptance by widow of assignment in satisfaction of claim for dower bars her further claim unless she is lawfully evicted of lands set off	a) County court of county proper for probate of estate, if husband died seized, and right to dower is undisputed b) Ejectment	a) Widow or any person interested in lands b) Widow

[1] The classification of the judicial proceedings for assignment of dower, as indicated in the table, not definite. Such a classification cannot be said to be entirely accurate without a knowledge of the

[2] There are many long and detailed statutes on procedure in the various proceedings for assign-bama, C. 1923, Secs. 7439–43; Alaska, Comp. L. 1913, Sec. 463; Arkansas, Crawf. and Moses, Dig. Sess. L. 1933, Ch. 16103, pp. 583–84, Secs. 115–18; Georgia, C. 1926, C. of Prac., Secs. 5259–63; Secs. 11995, 11997–98, 12000; Kansas, R. S. 1923, Secs. 22(110)–22(111), 22(113)–22(114), 22(116); Ch. 215, Secs. 35, 51; Ch. 238, Secs. 6, 8; Michigan, Comp. L. 1929, Secs. 14912–13, 14995, 15473, 1921, Secs. 10160–63; New Hampshire, Pub. L. 1926, Ch. 317, Sec. 1; Ch. 353, Secs. 3, 5–7; New Sec. 15; p. 2212, Sec. 17; North Carolina, C. 1927, Secs. 3901, 4107; Ohio, Complete G. C. 1931 Secs. 5369, 5581, 5788–89, 5791, 5798, 5800–5805; South Carolina, C. of L. 1922, C. C., Secs. 5256, St. 1931, Secs. 253.23, 314.01.

[3] Five jurisdictions included in the table have expressly abolished (Kansas, Vermont) or substan-visions analogous to those in true dower states as regards assignment of dower. Sections 189–91

[4] However, the Florida statute further provides that for the purpose of enabling the representative if satisfactory to the widow, would be valid does not appear.

[5] The legislation in Missouri appears to provide for a combination between an action at law to action to recover possession of real property in Kennedy v. Duncan, 224 Mo. 661; 123 S. W. 856 (1909).

[6] New Hampshire (Pub. L. 1926, Ch. 306, Sec. 11, as amended by Sess. L. 1933, Ch. 118, p. 171): Table XCV, Sec. 189, p. 363), is to be assigned in the same manner as dower; except that, if the entire interest petitions the probate court for assignment.

[7] Dower in Ohio is barred on the husband's death except as to property conveyed or encumbered dower therefore have relatively little importance today.

§ 208]

(Concluded)

Assignment of Dower[1]

Effect of Commissioners' Report of Their Assignment	Damages for Withholding of Dower	Miscellaneous Provisions[2]
a) If commissioners' return is confirmed, recorded by court, and copy recorded in county where lands lie, dower is fixed and certain unless confirmation is set aside or reversed on appeal *b*) If commissioners' report is confirmed, execution for possession issues	In any action to recover dower in lands of which husband died seized, widow may recover damages equal to one-third annual value of mesne profits, estimated against heirs—from husband's death; and against other persons —from demand; in either case not to exceed six years and not for use of permanent improvements made after husband's death by heirs or person claiming title to the lands. If lands aliened by heir, widow may recover damages from him for withholding from husband's death to alienation, not exceeding six years, and less amount recovered from grantee. Amount she is entitled to recover from heir is to be deducted from amount she otherwise would be entitled to recover from grantee	

has been made according to the writer's interpretation of the result of the statutes, many of which are cases and of the practice in each jurisdiction.

ment. Their importance does not justify setting them forth in detail, but citations are as follows: **Ala-** 1921, Secs. 3547–52, 3554, 3560; **Delaware,** R. C. 1915, Secs. 3312–14, 3317–18, 3781, 4468; **Florida,** **Hawaii,** R. L. 1925, Sec. 2544; **Illinois,** Cahill, R. S. 1931, Ch. 41, Secs. 21–33, 42; **Iowa,** C. 1927, **Kentucky,** Carroll, St. 1922, Secs. 950–51; Civ. C. of Prac. 1906, Sec. 499; **Massachusetts,** G. L. 1932, 15755–57; **Missouri,** R. S. 1929, Secs. 341, 343–44, 346, 350, 352, 354–58, 360, 367–68; **Montana,** R. C. **Jersey,** Comp. St. 1910, p. 2046, Sec. 4; p. 2047, Sec. 8; p. 2050, Secs. 18, 22; p. 2051, Sec. 23; p. 2211, (Page), Secs. 3006, 12006, 12008, 12017; **Oregon,** C. 1930, Sec. 11(102); **Rhode Island,** G. L. 1923, 5259; **Tennessee,** C. 1932, Secs. 8368–70, 8375, 8378–79; **Virginia,** C. 1930, Sec. 5216; **Wisconsin,**

tially changed (**Florida, Iowa, Wisconsin**) common-law dower; but they have retained certain pro-should be consulted as to the nature of the interest set apart to the widow.
to assign dower he "shall" file a petition, as set forth in the table. Whether the assignment by him,

compel assignment and a form of summary proceedings. A petition by the widow was considered as an

The widow's statutory share in lieu of dower, given when the husband leaves no issue surviving (see realty does not exceed the amount of her share, no assignment is necessary unless some party in

by him (Complete G. C. 1931 [Page], Supp. 1932, Sec. 10502[1]). The provisions on assignment of

[§ 208

REFERENCES

Annotation

"Liability of Unassigned Dower Right to Satisfaction of Widow's Debts," 81
A. L. R. 1110–17 (1932).

Section 209.   Assignment of Dower—Possession of Dwelling, etc., Pending Assignment

CROSS REFERENCES: Widow's paraphernalia, **Sec. 170**; Surviving husband's quarantine, **Sec. 223**; Homestead, widow's allowance, exempt property, etc., **Sec. 228**

In general, the common law gave the widow no right to take or remain in possession of dowable lands during the interim between the husband's death and the assignment of her dower. An exception to the general rule, however, was made by the Magna Charta, which established what came to be known as the widow's "quarantine,"[1] that is, the right "to tarry in the chief house of her husband," and to enjoy "her reasonable estovers of the common" for forty days after his death, or until her dower is assigned before the expiration thereof. The obvious purpose of this provision was to secure to the widow temporary shelter and sustenance pending the assignment of dower, although it has also been suggested that the provision was of incidental use in guarding against the danger of a supposititious child. The widow's quarantine as established under the early English law has generally been regarded as a part of the American common law.

Modern legislation is much more generous in this respect than the common law. The widow's statutory quarantine is usually more liberal in both extent and duration. Legislation patterned after the common law was found in sixteen of the jurisdictions which have retained dower. Similar statutes found in three states which have abolished dower (**Maine, Ohio, Vermont**) are also included in Table CI following.

---

[1] The **District of Columbia**, in the Code of 1929, Title 14, Section 28 (taken from 9 Hen. III, c. 7), adopts the widow's quarantine as defined by the Magna Charta as follows: ". . . . and she shall tarry in the chief house of her husband by forty days after the death of her husband, within which days her dower shall be assigned her (if it were not assigned her before) or that the house be a castle; and if she depart from the castle, then a competent house shall be forthwith provided for her, in which she may honestly dwell, until her dower be to her assigned, as it is aforesaid; and she shall have in the meantime her reasonable estovers of the common . . . ."

§ 209]

Under these statutes, the widow may remain in possession of the husband's "mansion house," "chief dwelling house," etc., rent free (eighteen), together with buildings appurtenant (one), messuage or curtilage (five), and farm or plantation adjoining (four). In **Massachusetts**, she is entitled to possession of one undivided third of the husband's real estate. The widow's right to estovers under the Magna Charta has been thought to include sustenance. Seven jurisdictions are express to the effect that she is entitled to "reasonable sustenance" as a part of her quarantine; while in six she may demand a third of the rents and profits of the husband's lands. In several others, support is assured by reason of her right to possess the farm or plantation adjoining the dwelling. There is considerable variation in the duration of her quarantine. In all but one jurisdiction (**District of Columbia**), it continues for a designated period, varying from forty days to a year, apparently regardless of whether dower is assigned before; and in ten, it continues until dower is assigned. Statutes of the latter type are not regarded as a hardship on the heir or devisee because of his right to compel assignment. Certain other miscellaneous legislation will be found in the table.

The statutes described above are only a fragmentary and often an antiquated part of the provisions made for the support and maintenance of the widow pending the settlement of the husband's estate. Legislation relative to homestead and exempt property, widow's allowance and selection, year's support, etc., is found in varying forms in most jurisdictions, and is collected in **Section 228**. In the dower states, these provisions usually exist independently of the widow's right to dower, and in addition to her quarantine.

The table follows.

TABLE CI

POSSESSION OF DWELLING, ETC., PENDING ASSIGNMENT OF DOWER

Jurisdiction and Citation	Widow Entitled to Possession of	Support, etc.	Duration	Other Provisions
Alabama C. 1923, Sec. 7437	Dwelling where husband most usually resided before death, with offices and buildings appurtenant and plantation connected therewith		Until dower is assigned	

[§ 209

TABLE CI (*Continued*)

Jurisdiction and Citation	Widow Entitled to Possession of	Support, etc.	Duration	Other Provisions
Alaska .... Comp. L. 1913, Secs. 467, 476	Husband's dwelling	Reasonable sustenance out of the estate	One year after husband's death	Widow may remain in possession of dowable lands of which husband died seized and enjoy rents, etc., with children and other heirs, or, if not residing thereon, receive one-third of rents, etc., without having dower assigned, so long as heirs and others interested do not object
Arkansas .... Crawf. and Moses, Dig. 1921, Secs. 89, 3530–31	Mansion or chief dwelling house of husband, and farm thereto attached	Reasonable sustenance out of the estate	Two months after husband's death; and thereafter until dower is assigned	Until dower is assigned, probate court shall order widow's proportionate share of rents of real estate paid to her
District of Columbia .... C. 1929, T. 14, Sec. 28	Chief house of husband (unless it be a castle)	Reasonable estovers of the common	Forty days after husband's death unless dower is assigned before	
Georgia .... C. 1926, C. of Prac., Sec. 5253	a) Dwelling house and b) Furniture therein		a) Until dower is assigned b) Until widow's portion of furniture is set apart	
Hawaii .... R. L. 1925, Secs. 3023–24	Husband's house	Reasonable sustenance out of the estate	Sixty days after husband's death	Widow may continue to occupy dowable lands of which husband died seized, with children or other heirs, or receive one-third part of rents, etc., thereof without having dower assigned, so long as heirs do not object
Kentucky ...... Carroll, St. 1922, Sec. 2138	Mansion house, yard, garden, stable, and orchard adjoining	One-third of rents and profits of husband's dowable real estate	Until dower is assigned	

TABLE CI (*Continued*)

Jurisdiction and Citation	Widow Entitled to Possession of	Support, etc.	Duration	Other Provisions
Maine .... R. S. 1930, Ch. 78, Sec. 17	Husband's house	Reasonable sustenance out of the estate	Ninety days after husband's death	
Massachusetts .. G. L. 1932, Ch. 189, Secs. 1, 13; Ch. 196, Sec. 1	a) One undivided third of the husband's real estate b) Husband's house	a) Profits of one undivided third of husband's real estate	a) Until assignment of dower b) Not more than six months after husband's death	Widow may continue to occupy dowable lands of which husband died seized, with heirs or devisees, or receive her share of rents, etc., thereof without having dower assigned so long as heirs or devisees do not object
Michigan .... Comp. L. 1929, Secs. 13079, 13090	Husband's dwelling house	Reasonable sustenance out of the estate	One year after husband's death	Widow may continue to occupy dowable lands of which husband died seized, with children or other heirs, or receive one-third part of rents, etc., thereof without having dower assigned so long as heirs or others interested do not object
Missouri .... R. S. 1929, Sec. 338	Husband's mansion house, and messuages or plantation thereto belonging		Until dower assigned	
New Hampshire . Pub. L. 1926, Ch. 306, Secs. 2, 8	Husband's house	Reasonable sustenance out of his estate	Forty days after husband's death	Widow is entitled to receive one undivided net third part of the rents and profits of estate of which husband died seized until dower is assigned
New Jersey ..... Comp. St. 1910, p. 2045, Sec. 2	Husband's mansion house and messuage or plantation thereto belonging		Until dower is assigned	

[§ 209

TABLE CI (*Continued*)

Jurisdiction and Citation	Widow Entitled to Possession of	Support, etc.	Duration	Other Provisions
Ohio .... Complete G. C. 1931 (Page), Supp. 1932, Sec. 10509(79)	Mansion house of deceased husband		One year	Mansion house may be sold within year for payment of husband's debts, with compensation to widow for unexpired term
Oregon .... C. 1930, Secs. 10(312), 10(323)	Husband's dwelling house	Reasonable sustenance out of the estate	One year after husband's death	Widow may continue to occupy dowable lands of which husband died seized with children or other heirs, or receive one-half part of rents, etc., thereof without having dower assigned so long as heirs or others interested do not object
Rhode Island ... G. L. 1923, Sec. 5786	Mansion house and messuage thereto belonging		Until dower is assigned, if widow brings writ of dower within twelve months after probate of will or granting of letters, or until she elects to take her jointure	
Vermont .... G. L. 1917, Sec. 3410	See last column			Until widow's statutory share of lands is set out, she may continue to occupy the same with children and family of husband, or receive a third of the rents, etc.
Virginia .... C. 1930, Sec. 5124	Mansion house and curtilage without charge for rent, repairs, taxes, or insurance	Widow is entitled to demand of heirs, devisees or alienees one-third of issues and profits of other dowable real estate after deducting necessary repairs, taxes, and insurance	Until dower is assigned	If deprived of mansion house, etc., widow may bring action to recover same with damages, but lien for taxes, and enforcement thereof, is not impaired

§ 209]

TABLE CI (*Concluded*)

Jurisdiction and Citation	Widow Entitled to Possession of	Support, etc.	Duration	Other Provisions
West Virginia C. 1931, Ch. 43, Art. 1, Secs. 10, 11	Mansion house and curtilage without charge for rent, repairs, taxes, or insurance[1]	Widow is entitled to demand of heirs, devisees, or alienees one-third of issues and profits of other dowable real estate after deducting necessary repairs, taxes, and insurance	Until dower is assigned[1]	If deprived of mansion house, etc., widow may bring action to recover same with damages[1]

[1] **West Virginia** further provides that if the husband leaves a widow and minor children they may occupy the mansion house and curtilage until the youngest child reaches the age of twenty-one years; and dower shall not be assigned until that time except with the consent of the widow, unless the mansion house, etc., is assigned to her as part of her dower or she elects to have dower assigned out of other real estate. Under this provision, the widow is liable for taxes, repairs, and insurance. The right ceases when the mansion house is no longer used as a home, and is subject to the right of the husband's creditors to resort to the mansion house and curtilage after exhausting the personal property and all other real estate.

REFERENCES

Books

SCRIBNER, CHARLES H. *A Treatise on the Law of Dower*, 2d ed., Vol. II, ch. iii, pp. 53–69 (1883).

STIMSON, F. J. *American Statute Law*, Secs. 3270 (note), 3278 (1886).

WOERNER, J. G. *A Treatise on the American Law of Administration*, 3d ed., Vol. I, Sec. 116, pp. 377–81 (1923).

Note

"Dower—The Widow's Right of Quarantine," *Tillotson* v. *Foster,* 310 Ill. 52; 141 N. E. 412 (1923)—6 Ill. L. Quar. 171 (1924).

Section 210. Assignment of Dower—By Non-judicial Action

CROSS REFERENCES: Assignment in general, **Sec. 208**; Assignment by judicial proceedings, **Sec. 212**; Method of assignment, **Sec. 213**; Collusive assignment by a guardian, **Sec. 214**; Admeasurement of surviving husband's share, **Sec. 223**

At common law the tenant of freehold in the estate subject to dower had the responsibility and duty of assignment. However, it was unnecessary that he be a lawful tenant if he were in possession, and if the admeasurement were properly made, the essential factor being a right or

[§ 210

claim to a freehold interest. A peculiar rule was developed by which a guardian in socage was not permitted to act for an infant tenant, assignment by the infant himself being necessary and binding. Such a situation was clearly undesirable, and has been changed in the United States by judicial decision and by legislation (see also **Sec. 214** for discussion of collusive assignment by a guardian). The widow's right to a fair admeasurement was safeguarded by the writ of dower that she might bring (**Sec. 212**), in which the tenant's action was subject to a judicial determination and decision; although the widow could become bound to accept a smaller portion than was due her, by agreement with the tenant (**Sec. 213**).

Statutory recognition of assignment without resort to court proceedings is neither extensive nor uniform, only eighteen jurisdictions having been found with legislation which to some extent has that effect. However, with the exception of assignment by a guardian mentioned above, the common law probably is still in force in the remaining jurisdictions which retain the theory of dower (**Sec. 189**), since they have not expressly made assignment by judicial action exclusive (*Sloss-Sheffield Steel and Iron Company* v. *Yancey*, 202 Ala. 458; 80 So. 842 [1919]). **South Carolina, Virginia,** and **West Virginia** specifically provide that dower may be assigned as at common law.

Six jurisdictions have express legislation providing that the following persons may assign the widow's dower: (1) heir-at-law (**Arkansas**); (2) heir or freehold tenant (**Illinois, Massachusetts, Montana, New Hampshire, Rhode Island**); (3) heir or person having the next estate of inheritance (**Illinois, Montana**); (4) person in possession (**Montana, Rhode Island**). Probably the personal representative can assign dower in **Florida** (see footnote 4 to Table C in **Sec. 208**, pp. 486–87). The statutes in **Montana** and **Rhode Island** allowing the person in possession to assign dower are worthy of special mention, for they definitely change the common-law rule which required the person admeasuring dower to be a freehold tenant. In **Rhode Island,** if such a person is a tenant for a term of years, he must first give notice to his freehold tenant inviting him to join in the assignment, after which the action of the tenant for years is valid and binding. In four of the jurisdictions above, it is also stated that the assignment is to be to the widow's "satisfaction" (**Massachusetts, Montana, New Hampshire**), or "accepted" by her (**Arkansas**).

Nine jurisdictions have less definite statutes, which, however, expressly or impliedly recognize non-judicial assignment (**Hawaii, Iowa,**

Kansas, Michigan, Oregon, South Carolina, Virginia, West Virginia, Wisconsin). Details concerning them are set forth in Table C in **Section 208**. The question of their extent and interpretation depends largely on the construction given them by the courts.

The remaining two jurisdictions have enactments which apply only to particular situations. Assignment by consent of the following persons is recognized: the heir or devisee and the widow may agree by deed, if the personal property is sufficient to pay the estate debts (**North Carolina**); the widow and creditors holding two-thirds of the debts against the estate may agree, if the estate is insolvent (**Vermont**). An implication that the heir may assign dower is presented in statutes relative to a collusive assignment by a guardian, discussed in **Section 214**.

Three miscellaneous changes in the common law have been effected by legislation. First, four jurisdictions (**Arkansas, Hawaii, Massachusetts, Michigan**) provide that the guardian of an infant shall make the assignment. Second, the common-law rule which permitted an oral assignment by the heir or tenant has been changed as follows: the assignment must be in writing (**Arkansas, Rhode Island**); endorsed by the widow and filed with the probate court (**Arkansas**). Third, it was usually considered at common law that it was the duty of the person admeasuring dower to do so within the quarantine period, but in **Arkansas, Illinois,** and **Montana** assignment is to be made "as soon as practicable after the husband's death," and in **Florida,** "immediately after the widow shall have exercised her election to take dower." Other statutes which state a time that must elapse before an action for dower can be brought (**Sec. 212**) imply that non-judicial assignment is to be made within that period.

Details of the statutes discussed above, and citations, are to be found in Table C in **Section 208**.

REFERENCES

Books

SCRIBNER, CHARLES H. *A Treatise on the Law of Dower,* 2d ed., Vol. II, ch. iv, pp. 71–89 (1883).

STIMSON, F. J. *American Statute Law,* Sec. 3271 (1886).

Annotations

"Assignment of Dower," 79 Amer. Dec. 600–602 (1862).

"Assignment of Dower," 39 Amer. St. Rep. 32–33 (1892).

Section 211. Assignment of Dower—By Summary Proceedings

CROSS REFERENCES : Assignment in general, **Sec. 208;** Action to compel assignment, **Sec. 212;** Method of assignment, **Sec. 213**

Assignment of dower by the heir or freehold tenant (**Sec. 210**) was often unsatisfactory to the widow and to the heir or tenant himself, because neither could be certain that the admeasurement was lawful and fair. On the other hand, the common-law action by writ of dower (**Sec. 212**) was cumbrous and inconvenient. To remedy such a situation, statutes have therefore been widely adopted which provide for assignment by summary proceedings. These enactments are in derogation of the common law, hence must be followed strictly ; but they are generally simple in operation and their requirements easily met. It is not surprising that, in practice where available, they have supplanted other forms of assignment to a great extent. This remedial legislation has been of inestimable benefit because of its simplification of the common law.

Twenty-eight jurisdictions have statutes which provide that petition for summary proceedings may be made to the following courts : the court (probate, county, orphans', etc.) which has probate jurisdiction (twenty) ; a court separate from the probate court (four) ; the probate court in executor's sale proceedings (four). The jurisdictions in the last group do not provide for assignment in general by summary proceedings ; the action of the probate or similar court is incidental to the executor's sale. It has been said that the probate court in making the assignment does so as a part of the administration of the estate. In the writer's opinion that result would be desirable and is implied in a few statutes ; but it is difficult, without a thorough knowledge of judicial decisions and legislative history in a particular jurisdiction, to say that assignment is a part of the settlement of the estate. Rather, it seems from the terms of a majority of statutes that the two are separate ; assignment is initiated by a separate petition and is not an addition to the court's probate jurisdiction (see *King* v. *Merritt,* 67 Mich. 194; 34 N. W. 689 [1887]).

In six of the jurisdictions above, the probate or corresponding court has no jurisdiction : (1) unless the husband died seized of the property (**Alaska, Michigan, New Jersey, Oregon, Wisconsin**) ; (2) if the right to dower is disputed (**Michigan, Oregon, Wisconsin**) ; (3) if the lands were aliened by the husband and are out of the county or assignment by metes and bounds would be unjust (**Alabama**). In **Kentucky,** proceedings in the county (similar to the probate) court may be removed to the circuit court on motion of either party if the widow's

§ 211]

right is disputed. In **Alabama** and **Oregon,** the circuit court has jurisdiction over the petition instead of the probate court under certain conditions (see Table C in **Sec. 208**) ; but in the remaining four jurisdictions apparently summary proceedings must be had in the probate court
or not at all.

It has been held that even in the absence of an express statute the
probate court has no jurisdiction unless the husband died seized, and the
widow's right is undisputed. However, there are cases to the contrary ;
the question depends on the terms of particular statutes and the judicial
construction given them.

The statutes are not uniform in their enumeration of the person or
persons who may petition for summary proceedings. It is clear that the
widow may do so; and the jurisdictions permitting other persons to
petition may be numerically classified as follows : (1) the heir or devisee
(six) ; (2) any person interested (six) ; (3) the husband's personal
representative (four) ; (4) a purchaser of the land (two) ; (5) any
person entitled to the land subject to dower (two) ; (6) a person desiring
the allotment of dower (one). These enactments are commendable. No
longer need the person who has the duty of assignment be uncertain as
to his admeasurement—he may obtain a judicial assignment by a convenient method.

In two states the widow has the first right to petition, and if she
fails to do so within three months (**North Carolina**) or within one year
(**Massachusetts**) after the husband's death other named persons may
do so (see Table C). In **Florida,** the opposite is true: the personal
representative may first petition, and if he fails to do so the widow may
petition. Three jurisdictions specify periods after the husband's death
which must elapse before petition to the probate court may be made
(**Arkansas, Iowa, Kansas**).

Provisions on venue, form and effect of judgment, recording of the
assignment, are detailed in Table C in **Section 208.** Citations to miscellaneous statutes on other procedural matters are collected in footnote 2
(pp. 486–87) of that table. They are too numerous and diverse to justify
their inclusion in tabular form. Citations and details of the statutes discussed above are to be found in the same table.

REFERENCES
Books

Scribner, Charles H. *A Treatise on the Law of Dower,* 2d ed., Vol. II, ch. viii,
    pp. 175–204 (1883).

[§ 211

STIMSON, F. J. *American Statute Law,* Secs. 3272–73 (1886).

WOERNER, J. G. *The American Law of Administration,* 3d ed., Vol. I, Sec. 117 (1923).

Case

Cole v. *Marvin,* 98 Ore. 175; 193 P. 828 (1920).

Section 212. Assignment of Dower—Action to Compel, and Damages for Withholding

CROSS REFERENCES: Assignment in general, **Sec. 208**; Assignment by summary proceedings, **Sec. 211**; Method of assignment, **Sec. 213**; Dower in partition actions, **Sec. 214**

ACTION TO COMPEL

A detailed discussion of the common-law writ of dower is not worth while because, as a practical matter, summary proceedings are generally used (**Sec. 211**); in the code states such action no longer exists; and even where retained in name, it has been greatly modified. Suffice it to say that the action was brought against the person who had the duty of assignment, and was extremely technical, with special rules of pleading and procedure. If judgment were given for the widow, the lands were admeasured by the sheriff, and possession recovered by ejectment. Demand for dower was not a prerequisite to the action but was important in obtaining maximum damages.

Equity jurisdiction over assignment was originally limited to proceedings ancillary to the common-law action; but it was gradually extended until it has generally been held that law and equity have concurrent jurisdiction. Furthermore, where the widow is entitled to dower in equitable estates (**Sec. 191**), and where law and equity are separate, equity has exclusive jurisdiction over assignment from such estates.

Statutes providing for actions to compel assignment may be divided into three classifications: (1) statutes retaining the common-law action in a modified form; (2) statutes introducing forms of action which were unavailable at common law; and (3) statutes recognizing equity jurisdiction.

In five states, action to compel assignment by writ of dower is expressly made available (**Delaware, Massachusetts, New Hampshire, New Jersey, Rhode Island**), subject to the following limitations: it

§ 212]

may be brought after the expiration of one month from a written demand (**Massachusetts, New Hampshire**); or after one month from demand (**Rhode Island**); or after forty days from the husband's death (**New Jersey**). In **Massachusetts,** if suit is not brought within one year from the written demand, the demand expires and a new one must be made. These actions may also be maintained as at common law, if dower has been unfairly assigned, or if the widow has been deforced of her share (see Table C, **Sec. 208,** for details). In addition to the simplification of pleading and procedure accomplished in all five states, all of them except **New Jersey** have replaced admeasurement by the sheriff after judgment by admeasurement by statutory commissioners, appointed by the court (see **Sec. 213**). **Hawaii** apparently has no express statute recognizing a writ of dower, but such action is clearly implied in a provision to the effect that judgment in a writ of dower may be registered as an encumbrance on the lands.

The nature of dower consummate at common law (**Sec. 208**) precluded an action of ejectment by the widow before assignment. However, in six jurisdictions, actions in the nature of ejectment have been substituted for the common-law writ of dower, and the widow may recover dower as follows: by ejectment (**Michigan, Wisconsin**); by an action to recover possession of real property if the widow's right is denied (**Alaska, Oregon**); and by such remedy at law as would lie on behalf of a life tenant with a right of entry (**Virginia, West Virginia**). In **Alaska** and **Oregon,** if it appears in the action that assignment by metes and bounds will prejudice other owners of the estate, the widow must thereafter proceed as in an action for partition (see **Sec. 214** for a discussion of dower in general in partition actions).

Three states have statutes which are difficult to classify. The widow may sue for dower in the district court if dower is not assigned within one month from the husband's death (**Montana**); and in the common pleas court (**Ohio**). These remedies, although analogous to summary proceedings, are apparently, in theory, actions at law to compel assignment, which have taken the place of the writ of dower. In **Missouri,** the widow may sue in the circuit court if she has been deforced of dower, if an unfair assignment has been made, or if no assignment has been made within two years after the husband's death. Thus far, the statutory remedy is really an action to compel assignment, but a further provision enables other persons—heir, legatee, etc.—to likewise sue. In this latter respect, the statute recognizes a form of summary proceedings because an action to compel assignment cannot be brought by the person who has

[§ 212

the duty of assignment. **Missouri** has therefore been included in this section and also in **Section 211.**

Eight jurisdictions expressly recognize the jurisdiction of equity over assignment of dower (**District of Columbia, Illinois, Maryland, New Hampshire, Rhode Island, Tennessee, Virginia, West Virginia**). The majority of such statutes are vague in terms (see Table C, **Sec. 208**); and two are limited as follows: suit may be brought if dower is not assigned within one month after the husband's death (**Illinois**); it may be brought if the lands are in several parcels (**Rhode Island**). Other states permit suits in equity without express statutory authority; but the question is unimportant in many jurisdictions where law and equity are no longer separate.

Only eight jurisdictions (**Alabama, Georgia, Iowa, Kansas, Massachusetts, Missouri, Montana, Oregon**) have been found with statutes of limitations which expressly apply to actions or claims for dower, as follows: they must be brought or made within five years after the husband's death (**Kansas**); seven years (**Georgia**); ten years (**Iowa, Missouri, Montana, Oregon**); twenty years (**Massachusetts**); or within twenty years after the widow has ceased to occupy or receive the profits of her share (**Massachusetts**). In **Alabama,** if the rights of the husband's alienee are involved, claim must be made within three years after the husband's death; but in other cases, within ten years after his death. In the jurisdictions without express statutes on the subject there has been a division of authority on the question whether or not the general statutes of limitations apply to actions for dower. The cases have proceeded largely on a consideration of the words of the statute, and the judicial decisions of the particular jurisdictions must be consulted. However, even where statutes of limitations are inapplicable, the widow may be guilty of such delay that on ordinary principles of laches equitable relief will be denied her.

DAMAGES FOR WITHHOLDING DOWER

At common law, damages could be recovered only from judgment for the widow in the writ of dower, and not for profits of the land during the interim between the husband's death and such judgment. The early English Statute of Merton (20 Hen. VIII, c. 1), however, allowed damages to be recovered against a person who would not assign dower, or who deforced the widow of dower, in lands of which the husband died seized. These damages included the rents and profits from a third part of the lands estimated from the husband's death to recovery of

§ 212]

dower if the widow had demanded her dower. If no demand had been made and the defendant did not dispute the widow's right, he could by a plea of willingness to assign (tout temps prist) limit recovery to damages from the commencement of the action.

In equity it has been universally recognized that, as against an heir or devisee, the widow has a right to an accounting and share of the mesne profits of the land from the husband's death; but as against the husband's alienee, the authorities are not agreed. The view of what seems to be the weight of authority is that mesne profits can be recovered from the alienee but only from the time of the widow's demand and his refusal to assign (*Roan* v. *Holmes,* 32 Fla. 295; 13 So. 339; 21 L. R. A. 180 [1893]). However, in **Florida** it is now expressly provided that mesne profits from the death of the husband are to be included in the judgment of the county judge's court (the proceeding for dower in such court is a summary one—see **Sec. 211**). Apparently the judgment is given against an alienee of the husband.

Sixteen jurisdictions have statutes which permit recovery of damages for withholding dower. The discussion of these provisions may be segregated for convenience and clarity into the following topics: (1) damages against alienee of husband; (2) damages against alienee of heir; (3) damages from demand of dower; (4) measure of damages; (5) survival of claim for damages.

1. *Damages against alienee of husband.*—In six states apparently no distinction is drawn between the husband's alienee and his heir or devisee (**Delaware, Illinois, Massachusetts, New Hampshire, Ohio, Rhode Island**). In five jurisdictions the opposite is true, and damages may be recovered "if the widow recovers dower in lands of which the husband died seized" (**Alaska, Michigan, Montana, Oregon, Wisconsin**). In the remaining five jurisdictions an intermediate position is taken: damages against the alienee are estimated from the commencement of the action (**Kentucky, Virginia, West Virginia**), or from demand on the alienee (**Missouri, New Jersey**); whereas, against an heir, devisee, etc., damages are estimated from the husband's death.

2. *Damages against alienee of heir.*—In the five jurisdictions named above in which damages may be recovered only if the husband died seized, a further distinction is made. Damages are estimated against an heir from the husband's death; but against "other persons," from demand, the provisions presumably being designed to protect the alienee of the heir. And in four of the jurisdictions (**Montana** not included) a separate action against the heir who aliened the lands is provided (see

[§ 212

Table C in **Sec. 208**). In **Missouri,** as against an heir, damages are estimated from the husband's death; but against the heir's alienee who at the time of alienation had no actual notice of the dower claim, only from demand.

3. *Damages from demand of dower.*—Statutes have been discussed in the two preceding topics which limit recovery of damages to time of demand when dower is recovered against an alienee of the husband or of the heir. Three jurisdictions have broader provisions allowing damages against any person to be estimated only from demand (**New Hampshire, Rhode Island**), or demand and refusal (**Illinois**). In **Massachusetts,** damages are recoverable only in a writ of dower, and, since written demand is a prerequisite of the action, it is an essential for damages. If demand has been made on a prior tenant of freehold, and not on the defendant in the action, the defendant is liable for damages only for the time he has held the land; but in a separate tort action, the widow may recover from the prior tenant a share of the rents and profits for the time he held the land after demand on him.

4. *Measure of damages.*—Subject to the foregoing rules as to the time of estimating them, damages are stated to be: (*a*) one-third of the annual value of mesne profits from the land (**Alaska, Michigan, Montana, Oregon, Wisconsin**); (*b*) reasonable damages (**Delaware, Illinois, New Hampshire**); (*c*) value of dower (**Missouri, New Jersey**); (*d*) rent (**Kentucky**); (*e*) one-third of the net yearly value of the real estate (**Ohio**); (*f*) damage sustained (**Rhode Island**); (*g*) and simply "damages" (**Massachusetts, Virginia, West Virginia**). In seven jurisdictions damages do not include the use of permanent improvements made, as follows: after the husband's death by the heir or person claiming title to the lands (**Alaska, Michigan, Montana, Oregon, Wisconsin**); after alienation by the heir (**Missouri**); after the husband has ceased to own the lands (**Ohio**). The general rule is that the widow is not entitled to dower in improvements made by the husband's alienee (**Sec. 213**); therefore, damages would not include the use of them, even in the absence of statutes.

5. *Survival of claim for damages.*—In five jurisdictions the common law has been changed by statutes; and after suit has been brought for damages (**Kentucky, Ohio, Virginia, West Virginia**), or regardless of its being brought (**Missouri**), the action or claim does not abate on the widow's death.

Details and citations of the statutes discussed in this section are set forth in Table C in **Section 208.**

§ 212]

REFERENCES

Books

POMEROY, JOHN N. *A Treatise on Equity Jurisprudence,* 4th ed., Vol. 4, Secs. 1380–83 (1919).

SCRIBNER, CHARLES H. *A Treatise on the Law of Dower,* 2d ed., Vol. II, chs. vi–vii, pp. 109–73; ch. xx, pp. 559–80; chs. xxv–xxvi, pp. 699–745 (1883).

STIMSON, F. J. *American Statute Law,* Secs. 3274, 3278 (1886).

Annotation

"The Right of a Doweress to Mesne Profits or Damages for the Detention of Dower," 21 L. R. A. 180–87 (1893).

Section 213. Assignment of Dower—Method of

CROSS REFERENCES: Assignment by non-judicial action, **Sec. 210**; Assignment by summary proceedings, **Sec. 211**; Action to compel assignment, **Sec. 212**; Dower in partition actions and judicial sales, annuity tables, **Sec. 214**; Homestead as affected by dower, **Sec. 228**

If the widow's right to dower is admitted or has been found by the court, the first step in assignment is the determination of the value of the estate subject to dower. At common law the value was estimated as of the time of assignment, thereby giving the widow the benefit of natural increments and of improvements made on the property between the husband's death and assignment, but subjecting her to depreciation of the property during the same interval. If the heir committed waste, the widow could recover damages from him, but it did not affect the manner of assignment. If, however, the husband's alienee wasted the property, the rule seems to have been that he was not liable to the widow. The older common-law rule has been qualified in the United States, where it has generally been held that the value of improvements made by the husband's alienee is not to be included in the total valuation of the property (*Sanders* v. *McMillan,* 98 Ala. 144; 11 So. 750; 18 L. R. A. 425 [1892]).

The second step in assignment, viz., the actual division of the estate, was usually done by setting out by metes and bounds a share which would bring the widow rents, issues, and profits equal to one-third the income to be derived from the entire estate. If such division in kind were impossible or would injure the estate, she was given a proportionate right to share in the rents and profits; or, in some cases, an alternate use and occupation with other interested persons. Dower from separate parcels of land was assigned from each tract rather than in an entire piece; and the heir or other tenant could not be compelled to give her the husband's dwelling house. If a dower claim existed against proceeds of a sale of property, a share of such proceeds was set apart and the interest paid the widow for life; she was not, as a matter of right, entitled to a gross sum in lieu of dower (*Herbert* v. *Wren,* 7 Cranch 369 [1813]).

However, the foregoing rules were limited to the assignment that both the widow and the tenant had a right to demand; and they could be abrogated by agreement between them. Such agreement was called "assignment contrary to common right," and was binding only on the parties who entered into it. By use of it the widow could be given as dower a single tract, or a share in the income, or the dwelling house, or a gross sum, or other compensation.

At common law, when dower was recovered by writ, the actual admeasuring was done by the sheriff. In most modern judicial proceedings, statutory commissioners have been substituted for the sheriff, three commissioners in nineteen jurisdictions; five commissioners in five jurisdictions (see Table CII following). They are usually appointed by the court, and the return of their assignment is subject to the court's approval or rejection (see Table C in **Sec. 208**).

Much of the legislation on this subject is fragmentary, supplemented by the common law; but the general situation has been improved by statutory relaxation of many of the common-law rules in order to accomplish greater justice.

The value of the estate presumably is estimated as of the time of assignment in the great majority of jurisdictions, since in them no express change in the common law has been found. In **South Carolina,** however, the estate is valued as follows: against the husband's purchaser— as of the time of alienation; but if the husband died seized—as of his death; in both cases with interest from the accrual of the right to dower. A **Kentucky** statute places the valuation as of the time the lands were received by an heir, devisee, or purchaser "so as not to include" permanent improvements; but in *Fritz* v. *Tudor,* 64 Ky. (1 Bush) 28 (1866), it was held that a strict interpretation of the statute would be absurd and that it meant only to exclude improvements by the purchaser and not to change the common-law rule as to time of valuation. The construction seems strained, but was reaffirmed in a later case. Four states in addition to **Kentucky** and **South Carolina** have codified the recognized

§ 213]

rule in the United States which permits the husband's alienee to retain the benefit of his improvements (**Michigan, Montana, Oregon, Wisconsin**). The same result is reached in **Virginia** and **West Virginia** by statutes which relieve the alienee against having the lands taken, on his payment to the widow as the statute directs, which excludes his improvements (see Table CII).

Nineteen jurisdictions provide for assignment in general to be made by metes and bounds. Where such actual division is inequitable or impossible, other methods have been adopted by the following numbers of jurisdictions: (1) the widow may share in the rents, issues, and profits (twelve); (2) the yearly value of dower or a fixed rental value may be ordered paid her annually (seven); (3) under certain conditions a gross sum may be paid in lieu of dower (eight) (see Table CII). It is apparent that in some jurisdictions the methods above are available in the alternative.

In addition to the more fundamental legislation discussed above, statutory changes in the common law have been made as follows: (1) In eight states dower may be set out in an entire parcel even though the husband's property is in separate tracts (**Georgia, Illinois, Kentucky, Missouri, New Hampshire, North Carolina, Rhode Island, Tennessee**). The usual limitation is that it be done only when no injustice is thereby worked, and it is probable that it could not be done if the separate tracts were held by different persons (expressly so in **Kentucky**). (2) Seven jurisdictions provide that the widow may have, as her right, the usual dwelling house, ordinarily if she so desires and if others' interests are not prejudiced (**Alabama, Arkansas, Georgia, Illinois, Iowa, North Carolina, Tennessee**). (See **Sec. 228** for a discussion of homestead rights as affected by dower.) (3) In two states the widow may select the tract to be given her, if her selection is without essential injury to the estate (**Arkansas**), or if there are distinct tracts of property in the same county (**Georgia**). In two states a gross sum may be paid in lieu of dower whether assignment by metes and bounds is unjust or not: with the assent of the executor or administrator and the widow (**Georgia**); with the widow's consent (**Missouri**). And in **New Jersey,** the widow and the guardian of a minor or insane person may agree, with the approval of the chancellor, on a gross sum in lieu of dower from the ward's estate. These provisions, although restricted to a gross sum, are analogous to assignment at common law "contrary to common right." Other statutes recognizing assignment by consent, which are broader in scope, are collected in Table C in **Section 208.**

[§ 213

Citations to the statutes mentioned in this section have been placed
in Table CII below, together with miscellaneous and less frequent provisions relative to method of assignment.

TABLE CII
METHOD OF ASSIGNMENT OF DOWER

Jurisdiction and Citation	Commissioners to Assign Dower	Dwelling House Included	Set Off by Metes and Bounds	Admeasurement if Division by Metes and Bounds Is Unjust or Impracticable	Miscellaneous Provisions
Alabama .... C. 1923, Secs. 7443–46, 7448– 49, 7451	Five freeholders not connected with parties by consanguinity or affinity, who act under oath	Yes, if estate solvent and heirs are not prejudiced thereby	Yes	If lands were aliened by the husband, and division by metes and bounds is unjust, widow is dowable of value at time of alienation, interest on one-third part thereof, to be paid her annually, secured if necessary by lien on land, unless parties agree to compensation in gross to which court must give effect	Decree of court describes lands and from what portion dower is to be set off. Homestead already allotted to widow or to widow and minor children is not charged to her in allotting dower in other lands. Lands not aliened, lying in different counties, may be set off by five freeholders from each county
Alaska .... Comp. L. 1913, Secs. 464–66	Three discreet and disinterested persons who act under oath		Yes	If division by metes and bounds is inequitable, assignment may be of rents, issues, and profits to be had by widow as tenant in common with other owners	
Arkansas .... Crawf. and Moses, Dig. 1921, Secs. 3532–34, 3553, 3556	Three commissioners of the vicinity	Yes, if without essential injury to estate	Yes	If lands or tenements will not admit of division, they may be rented, and one-third part of proceeds paid widow (see next column)	Widow may select lands if without essential injury to estate. In proceedings in circuit court for allotment, if assignment will greatly prejudice widow or heirs, sale may be made free of dower, and equitable portion of proceeds paid widow, or her interest otherwise secured
Delaware .... R. C. 1915, Secs. 3288–89, 3316, 3318	In action for dower by writ, five judicious and impartial freeholders of county, who act under oath		Yes	Dower may be assigned by the orphans' court in like proceedings as are provided for partition actions	Settlement, gift or advancement to child or issue of child of intestate is not considered in assigning dower

§ 213]

TABLE CII (*Continued*)

Jurisdiction and Citation	Commissioners to Assign Dower	Dwelling House Included	Set Off by Metes and Bounds	Admeasurement if Division by Metes and Bounds Is Unjust or Impracticable	Miscellaneous Provisions
District of Columbia... C. 1929, T. 25, Secs. 382–83; T. 29, Sec. 240	Three commissioners		Yes	If estate is entire and dower cannot be set off by metes and bounds, it may be assigned as of a third part of the net rents, issues, and profits	If husband was tenant in common, and partition is had, dower claim attaches to share assigned heirs in severalty
Florida .... Sess. L. 1933, Ch. 16103, p. 553, Sec. 35; p. 584, Secs. 116–17	Three suitable, disinterested persons, not connected with parties by consanguinity or affinity, who act under oath	Homestead is not included in property subject to dower			County judge may assign dower in real and personal property located in other counties, but such judgment is not effective until a certified copy thereof is recorded in such other county
Georgia .... C. 1926, C. of Prac., Secs. 5247, 5252, 5255–57	Five fit and discreet freeholders of county in which application for assignment is made	Yes			Value of dwelling house not to be included in dower value unless in town or city. If distinct tracts of land in same county, widow may elect entire dower in one body, and may select tract. If single tract divided by county lines, dower may be laid off in either county; but if several tracts in different counties, dower must be applied for and set out in each county. With assent of executor or administrator, widow may elect life estate in one-third part of proceeds of sale of lands; or an absolute sum estimated by commissioners. Amount awarded has preference over all other claims on proceeds of sale. If lands are outside city, town, village, or place of public business, assignment made according to quantity and valuation as commissioners think just and equitable; if other lands, according to their shape and valuation

[§ 213

TABLE CII (*Continued*)

Jurisdiction and Citation	Commissioners to Assign Dower	Dwelling House Included	Set Off by Metes and Bounds	Admeasurement if Division by Metes and Bounds Is Unjust or Impracticable	Miscellaneous Provisions
Hawaii .... R. L. 1925, Sec. 2248, amd. by Sess. L. 1929, Act 18, p. 14; Act 19, p. 15				If dower cannot be set apart without great injury to owners of estate, value of dower according to mortality and annuity tables may be ordered paid widow on reasonable terms	
Illinois .... Cahill, R. S. 1931, Ch. 41, Secs. 34–37, 39–40	Three disinterested commissioners, not connected with parties by consanguinity or affinity, who act under oath	Yes, if widow desires	Yes	If estate cannot be divided without damage or great injury to whole, dower may be assigned of rents, issues, and profits to be had by widow as tenant in common; or jury may assess yearly value of dower to be paid widow annually for life, and made a lien on real estate of person who is to make payments, or otherwise secured	Assignment made according to quality and quantity of estate. May be made in a body out of one or more tracts, if possible without prejudice to any person interested in premises
Iowa .... C. 1927, Secs. 11992, 11996, 12001–5	Referees	Yes, if widow desires, and estate solvent	Yes	If property or any part cannot be readily divided, court may order whole sold, and one-third proceeds paid widow, but no sale made if anyone interested gives security to pay share to widow or if widow does likewise to pay claims of persons interested, or if those in interest agree on mode of sharing rents, profits, or use	
Kansas .... R. S. 1923, Secs. 22(109), 22(112)	Commissioners		Yes		

§ 213]

TABLE CII (*Continued*)

Jurisdiction and Citation	Commissioners to Assign Dower	Dwelling House Included	Set Off by Metes and Bounds	Admeasurement if Division by Metes and Bounds Is Unjust or Impracticable	Miscellaneous Provisions
Kentucky .... Carroll, St. 1922, Secs. 2139, 2141	Three competent persons who act under oath. Two may act if one fails to do so				Assignment, whether against heir, devisee or purchaser from husband, is according to value of estate when received by such person so as not to include permanent improvements made by him. Where lands are not severally held by different devisees or purchasers, dower need not be out of each separate portion but may be out of one or more parcels
Maryland ...... Bagby, Ann. C. 1924, Art. 16, Sec. 47	Five commissioners				
Massachusetts .. G. L. 1932, Ch. 189, Secs. 11, 12	Three disinterested persons who act under oath	Yes	If estate cannot be divided without damage to the whole, assignment may be of the rents or profits, to be had by widow as tenant in common with other owners		If husband was tenant in common, land may be partitioned first by order of probate court, and dower assigned in part set off to husband's estate
Michigan ...... Comp. L. 1929, Secs. 13078, 14419, 14954, 15756–58	Three discreet, disinterested freeholders, who act under oath	Yes	If estate cannot be divided without damage to the whole, assignment may be of rents, issues, and profits to be had by widow as tenant in common with other owners. If lands aliened by husband in his lifetime, and above is true, sum of money may be paid widow in lieu of dower or in place of above described rents, issues, and profits		Lands aliened by husband in his lifetime which have been enhanced in value are estimated for assignment, at value when aliened

[§ 213

TABLE CII (*Continued*)

Jurisdiction and Citation	Commissioners to Assign Dower	Dwelling House Included	Set Off by Metes and Bounds	Admeasurement if Division by Metes and Bounds Is Unjust or Impracticable	Miscellaneous Provisions
Missouri .... R. S. 1929, Secs. 342, 344, 348–49, 361, 1570, 3132–34	Three competent persons who act under oath		Yes	If estate cannot be divided without great injury, widow is paid yearly value of dower as assessed by jury	Execution for yearly allowance (preceding column), given only against estate from which dower would have been set off. If lands are in different counties, not held by different devisees or purchasers, dower may be assigned out of any one or more tracts, if without prejudice to persons interested. Lump sum according to mortality tables may be given if widow willing to accept it in lieu of dower. In partition action, dower set apart in one body as near as practicable
Montana .... R. C. 1921, Secs. 5823, 10164–67	Three disinterested commissioners not connected with parties by consanguinity or affinity, who act under oath		Yes	If estate cannot be divided without great injury to it, widow is paid yearly value of dower as assessed by a jury. In lieu of such allowance, widow may consent to, or court order, gross sum paid her	Lands aliened by husband in his lifetime, which have been enhanced in value, are estimated for assignment at value when aliened. Dower estimated according to quantity and quality of all lands subject to it
New Hampshire. Pub. L. 1926, Ch. 306, Secs. 3, 5, 6; Ch. 353, Secs. 5–7	In action of dower, three discreet and disinterested men of neighborhood		Yes	If division by metes and bounds is inconvenient and inequitable, assignment shall be of third part of rents and profits	Assignment may be made in one or more parcels, as may be convenient. Assignment is made by giving such part of estate as will produce a yearly income equal to one-third of yearly income of estate. Method of setting out dower in action of dower is same as in similar cases before a judge of probate
New Jersey..... Comp. St. 1910, p. 2050, Sec. 21; p. 2633, Sec. 18; p. 4682, Sec. 19e; Supp. 1925–30, Sec. 63(17)	Three discreet, disinterested residents in county where lands are situated, in proceedings in probate court or before surrogate-general			If dower cannot be set off without great prejudice to owners of lands, orphans' court, after hearing, may order land sold free of dower, making compensation for its value	With approval of chancellor, widow and guardian of minor or insane person may agree on gross sum to be paid to her in lieu of dower from ward's estate

§ 213]

TABLE CII (*Continued*)

Jurisdiction and Citation	Commissioners to Assign Dower	Dwelling House Included	Set Off by Metes and Bounds	Admeasurement if Division by Metes and Bounds Is Unjust or Impracticable	Miscellaneous Provisions
North Carolina.. C. 1927, Sec. 4100; Sec. 4106, amd. by Sess. L. 1931, Ch. 393, pp. 477–78	Jury of three persons qualified to act as jurors, except if party demands greater number not exceeding twelve to be summoned by sheriff; except on demand of party, may be appointed by clerk of court	Yes, if widow desires			Jury need not assign dower in every separate tract of land but may allot it in one or more tracts with due regard to widow's and heirs' interest. If lands are in county other than that in which dower is to be assigned, clerk of superior court of county in which dower is to be assigned may commission sheriff of other county to summon jury to make assignment
Ohio[1] .... Complete G. C. 1931 (Page), Secs. 12009, 12011–13	Three judicious, disinterested men of county in which action pending, not of kin to either party, who act under oath		Yes	If estate is entire and cannot be divided by metes and bounds, assignment shall be of third part of rents, issues, and profits	If estate is timber or unimproved lands, or lots, and assignment by metes and bounds or of rents, issues, and profits would not give widow income commensurate to their value, lands may be sold for not less than two-thirds value appraised by commissioners, and value of dower paid widow; except that owners of lands may avoid sale by paying value of dower to widow. Relief as above may be given widow to whom dower has already been assigned
Oregon .... C. 1930, Secs. 10(307), 10(309)– 10(311)	Three discreet and disinterested persons, in proceedings in county court, who act under oath		Yes	If estate cannot be divided without damage to the whole, assignment may be of rents, issues, and profits, to be had by widow as tenant in common with other owners	Lands aliened by husband in his lifetime which have been enhanced in value after alienation are estimated for assignment at value when aliened

[1] Dower is barred in **Ohio** on the husband's death except as to property conveyed or encumbered by him (Complete G. C. 1931 [Page], Supp. 1932, Sec. 10502[1]).

[§ 213

TABLE CII (*Continued*)

Jurisdiction and Citation	Commissioners to Assign Dower	Dwelling House Included	Set Off by Metes and Bounds	Admeasurement if Division by Metes and Bounds Is Unjust or Impracticable	Miscellaneous Provisions
Rhode Island.... G. L. 1923, Secs. 5782–83, 5790, 5797	Three disinterested commissioners who act under oath		Yes	If estate is entire, where division cannot be made, or is of woodlands, assignment may be of third part of rents, issues, growth, or profits. In all actions at law or suits in equity for dower, court may substitute for metes and bounds an annual, fixed rental. Such rental is a charge on estate, and may be re-appraised every five years	Assignment need not be of each separate parcel, but may be of one lot according to interest and convenience of parties
South Carolina.. C. of L. 1922, C. C., Secs. 5257–58, 5260–62	Five persons, two nominated by each party, and fifth by court. Court may appoint for party if he refuses			If estate cannot fairly be divided without manifest disadvantage, commissioners or a majority of them may assess sum to be paid widow in lieu of dower by heir-at-law or person in possession of land	Value of lands as against a purchaser, taken as of time of alienation by husband; value of lands of which husband died seized, taken as of time of husband's death; in both cases, with interest from accrual of right of dower. Value against purchaser, whether alienation was before or after husband's death, is exclusive of improvements put on land
Tennessee ..... C. 1932, Secs. 8354–57, 8371–72, 8376–77	Two freeholders or householders of county, not connected with persons interested by affinity or consanguinity. County surveyor or deputy acts as third commissioner. They act under oath	Yes, if widow desires, and if no manifest injustice to children or other relations would result	Yes		Assignment need not be of each separate tract of land, but may be made according to quality and quantity so as to give her one-third in value of whole estate. Lands out of county, if court directs, may be taken into the estimate
Vermont .... G. L. 1917, Secs. 3406, 3408–9	Three disinterested freeholders who act under oath		Yes	If estate cannot be divided without injury, widow's third is set out to her as tenant in common with other owners, or court may direct estate to be sold, and a third of proceeds paid widow	

§ 213]

TABLE CII (*Concluded*)

Jurisdiction and Citation	Commissioners to Assign Dower	Dwelling House Included	Set Off by Metes and Bounds	Admeasurement if Division by Metes and Bounds Is Unjust or Impracticable	Miscellaneous Provisions
Virginia .... C. 1930, Secs. 5125, 5127–28, 5131–33	Commissioners			If in suit in equity assignment in kind cannot be made, court may order persons entitled to estate to pay widow the fair, net, annual value of her interest. Payment is a lien on estate and from time to time may be adjusted. Person who is to pay may turn estate over to receiver appointed by court, to be rented out, and payments thus made to widow—balance to owner	Assignment is of a third in kind of estate as it is on recovery, whether against alienee under court order or alienee of husband, or of his heirs, devisees, or their assigns. But alienee may prevent such recovery against him by paying widow, for life, lawful interest on one-third value of estate at husband's death, less value of permanent improvements made after alienation by alienee or his assigns. If widow entitled to such interest or to use of part of estate, and consents to accept, or party liable for interest has right to pay, or court decrees, gross sum in lieu thereof, sum is estimated by annuity table set forth
West Virginia.. C. 1931, Ch. 43, Art. 1, Secs. 14, 15; Art. 2, Secs. 1–3	Commissioners				Assignment is of a third part in kind of estate as it is when recovery is had. But alienee of husband, or under decree of court in lifetime of husband, may pay widow lawful interest from time of demand for dower on one-third value of estate at time of alienation; or he may pay gross sum computed by use of annuity tables as set forth
Wisconsin ...... St. 1931, Secs. 233.08, 275.22, 314.03	Three disinterested freeholders who act under oath	Yes		If estate cannot be divided without damage to the whole, assignment may be of rents, issues, and profits, to be had by widow as tenant in common with other owners	Lands aliened by husband in his lifetime, which have been enhanced in value after alienation, are estimated for assignment at value when aliened

[§ 213

REFERENCES

Books

SCRIBNER, CHARLES H. *A Treatise on the Law of Dower,* 2d ed., Vol. II, ch. iv, pp. 80–89; chs. xxi–xxiv, pp. 581–698 (1883).
STIMSON, F. J. *American Statute Law,* Secs. 3275–77, 3279 (1886).

Note

"Assignment of Dower in Improvements Made by Alienee of Husband after Husband's Death," *Gridley* v. *Wood,* 344 Ill. 153; 176 N. E. 356 (1931)—27 Ill. L. Rev. 82–84 (1932) ; 16 Minn. L. Rev. 315–16 (1932) ; 18 Va. L. Rev. 83–84 (1931).

Annotations

"Dower or Marital Rights of Husband or Wife in Respect of Improvements Made by Spouse's Alienee or His Successor after Death of Spouse," 74 A. L. R. 1168–72 (1931).
"Rights as between Surviving Spouse and Holder of Leasehold Interest under Lease from Deceased Spouse in Respect of Improvements Made Pursuant to Lease," 92 A. L. R. 1382–83 (1934).

Section 214. Dower—Miscellaneous Provisions

CROSS REFERENCES: Dower as subject to the husband's debts, **Secs. 190, 201;** Inchoate dower in partition actions; collusive or default judgment against husband as barring dower, **Sec. 201;** Miscellaneous provisions on curtesy, **Sec. 223;** Rights of alien doweress, **Sec. 293;** Barring dower of insane wife or widow, **Sec. 311**

Miscellaneous provisions relating to dower, found in twenty-five jurisdictions, may be conveniently classified under the following five heads: (1) vested dower in partition proceedings; (2) vested dower in executor's sales for the husband's debts; (3) collusive assignment of dower by a guardian; (4) computation of the present value of inchoate and vested dower; (5) other miscellaneous matters.

1. VESTED DOWER IN PARTITION PROCEEDINGS

A vested dower interest frequently exists in the whole of the lands sought to be partitioned or in an undivided share thereof. If so, three

§ 214]

principal questions are suggested. First, may dower be assigned in the proceedings? Second, if a sale of the property is necessary, is it free of dower? And third, if the sale is free of dower, what compensation does the widow receive? Express legislation on this subject has been found in sixteen jurisdictions and will be discussed briefly according to the questions just stated.

Legislation in nine jurisdictions recognizes to some extent and under varying conditions the duty of the court to have dower set off when suit is brought to compel partition of lands subject to dower (**Delaware, District of Columbia, Illinois, Maryland, Missouri, North Carolina, Ohio, Oregon, Tennessee**). The details of these statutes are set forth in Table CIII following. In **Illinois** and **Tennessee,** after assignment, the entire premises including the part set off as dower may be partitioned. The same is true in **Delaware** if the lands are subject to dower other than in an undivided share. In the majority of jurisdictions it is held that the unassigned dower right of the widow is not such an interest as will enable her to institute a partition action; but in the few jurisdictions where she is considered as a tenant in common with the heirs (**Sec. 208**), the contrary presumably is true.

Ten jurisdictions have legislation permitting a partition sale free of dower in general, under the following conditions: (1) if the widow is a party (**Kentucky, Michigan, Missouri, Montana, North Carolina**); (2) if the widow consents (**Illinois, Maryland, Tennessee**); (3) if prescribed notice has been given her (**New Jersey**); (4) on her application to the chancery court (**Virginia**). Five jurisdictions have statutes which distinguish between dower in an undivided share of the lands and dower in the whole of the lands (**Alaska, District of Columbia, Hawaii, Ohio, Oregon**). Details may be found in Table CIII. The remaining jurisdiction, **Delaware,** has legislation which brings it within the latter class of five jurisdictions; but in addition, **Delaware** has a general provision allowing a sale free of dower without specific limitations in all proceedings for a sale of real estate. A **Rhode Island** statute does not refer specifically to a partition action, but provides that any sale of real estate by court order may be free of dower upon the widow's petition and after notice (see Table CIII). In the absence of legislation specifically applicable to dower, on the one hand a partition sale is usually considered as binding on interested persons only if they are parties or have been given sufficient notice, and vested dower probably qualifies the widow as an interested person. On the other hand, the general statutes on partition often include a life tenant, and it would

[§ 214

seem that the widow may be considered as such and her interest disposed of by the sale (see *Bradford* v. *Stone,* 20 R. I. 53; 37 A. 532 [1897]).

Subject to the foregoing qualifications regarding a sale free of dower, statutes relating to methods of compensating the widow have likewise been found in seventeen jurisdictions, as follows: (1) a gross sum may be paid if the widow consents; or if there is no consent, a sum is invested for her benefit (**Alaska, Michigan, New Jersey, North Carolina, Oregon**); (2) a gross sum may be paid if the interested parties agree; or if there is no agreement, a sum may be invested for her benefit (**Hawaii**); (3) a gross sum is paid or a sum invested for her, apparently in the court's discretion (**Delaware, Illinois, Montana, Rhode Island, Tennessee**); (4) the present value of dower is paid her (**Missouri, Ohio, Virginia**); (5) other methods of payment (see Table CIII) are available (**Delaware, District of Columbia, Kentucky, Maryland**).

2. Vested Dower in Executor's Sales for the Husband's Debts

In jurisdictions where the widow's rights are superior to those of the husband's creditors (**Sec. 191**), it is the general rule, apart from statute, that the dower interest is not divested by an executor's or administrator's sale for the husband's debts.

Fifteen jurisdictions have statutes relating to this subject. Three (**District of Columbia, Illinois, Maryland**) provide for setting out dower in the proceedings. Statutes in ten jurisdictions provide that a sale for debts may be free of dower, as follows: (1) if the widow consents (**Alabama, Florida, District of Columbia, Illinois, New Hampshire, Ohio, Rhode Island**); (2) if prescribed notice has been given her (**Massachusetts, New Jersey**); (3) if she is a party (**North Carolina**). (See Table CIII for the form of consent necessary.) In **Delaware** and **Maryland**, general statutes covering all proceedings for a sale of real estate subject to dower apparently apply to executor's sales. The sale is free of dower if the widow consents (**Maryland**); whereas in **Delaware** there is no express limitation. The **North Carolina** statute is qualified by its provision that nothing contained in it prevents the widow from claiming dower by metes and bounds. In two jurisdictions, the executor or administrator may contract with the widow to give her one-third of the sale proceeds in lieu of dower (**Wisconsin**); and the widow claiming dower cannot be dispossessed of the mansion house after an executor's sale (**Georgia**). A statute in **Michigan** provides that in a proceeding in the probate court for a license to sell real estate of a decedent the widow may be required to elect whether she will take dower.

§ 214]

3. Collusive Assignment of Dower by a Guardian

A guardian may usually represent an infant heir or other freehold tenant in assigning dower (**Sec. 210**), or in an action against the infant to compel assignment. To protect the infant's rights, eleven jurisdictions have statutes to the effect that on his majority the infant may recover lands awarded the widow through the guardian's default or collusion, in so far as the widow cannot show herself entitled thereto (**Alaska, District of Columbia, Kentucky, Michigan, Missouri, New Jersey, Ohio, Oregon, Virginia, West Virginia, Wisconsin**). In **Missouri**, the infant's action to avoid a collusive assignment in proceedings instituted by the guardian must be brought within three years after the infant becomes of age.

4. Computation of the Present Value of Inchoate and Vested Dower

The valuation of inchoate dower includes the determination of the wife's expectancy of life as against the joint expectancy of husband and wife. The mathematics are too involved for discussion in this work, but the reader is referred to the case of *American Blower Company* v. *MacKenzie,* 197 N. C. 152; 147 S. E. 829 (1929), and to the **West Virginia** Code of 1931, Chapter 43, Article 2, Sections 4 and 5, for discussion and examples of the general method of valuation, viz., the use of annuity tables. **West Virginia** is the only jurisdiction found which provides for a definite statutory computation of inchoate dower.

Eight jurisdictions have legislation recognizing the use of annuity tables in valuing vested dower. In two, no specific tables are mentioned (**Alaska, Michigan**); in three, the American Experience Tables of Mortality are used (**Hawaii, Oregon, West Virginia**); in two, the Carlisle Tables are used (**Missouri, Virginia**); and in **North Carolina,** a special table is set forth in the statute. Five of the jurisdictions have statutory interest rates for dower—5 per cent (**Hawaii, West Virginia**); 6 per cent (**Missouri, North Carolina, Virginia**). Obviously, the actual calculation of the value of vested dower is simpler than that of inchoate dower, since, in the former, only the life expectancy of the widow need be considered.

If the reader is interested in the history of annuity tables, in their value as applied to dower, and in other details, the reference to Scribner's *Treatise on Dower* given at the end of this section should be consulted.

[§ 214

5. Other Miscellaneous Matters

A majority of cases have held that dower or the statutory share in lieu of dower is not subject to a general succession tax (*State* v. *Clayton,* 162 Tenn. 368; 38 S. W. [2d] 551 [1931]; *In re Bullen's Estate,* 47 Utah 96; 151 P. 533 [1915]). The theory is that the husband's death only vests the widow's contingent right which she acquired on the marriage, and does not transfer any property to her. However, in jurisdictions such as **Colorado** and **New York,** where the widow is really a forced heir (**Sec. 189**), a contrary result would be logical. The question is unimportant in many jurisdictions where dower and equivalent interests are expressly taxed, although such special statutes are outside the purview of this work.

The reader is referred to the miscellaneous column of Table CIII for a few minor details on dower. A unique statute in **Indiana** (Burns, Ann. St. 1926, Sec. 3342) provides that a widow who remarries cannot alienate her statutory share during the second marriage if there is a child, or children (or their descendants), alive by the prior marriage, and that, if she die, her share passes to such children of the previous marriage. In **Oregon** protection is afforded the widow by a statute prohibiting the registration of transfers of land or interests therein, unless it appears that dower in the lands has been released.

Citations and further details of the statutes discussed in this section are given in Table CIII following.

TABLE CIII

Dower—Miscellaneous Provisions

Jurisdiction and Citation	Vested Dower in Partition Proceedings	Vested Dower in Executor's Sale Proceedings[1]	Collusive Assignment by Guardian	Miscellaneous
Alabama .... C. 1923, Secs. 5877–78		On widow's written consent, sale may be free of dower, husband's personal representative paying her value of her interest according to her age and health, not to exceed one-sixth of purchase price		

[1] The term "executor's sale" indicates primarily the sales by the husband's executor or administrator for estate debts. However, some of the statutes have a broader scope, as Table CIII will show. The writer does not purport to define their extent in detail.

§ 214]

TABLE CIII (*Continued*)

Jurisdiction and Citation	Vested Dower in Partition Proceedings	Vested Dower in Executor's Sale Proceedings	Collusive Assignment by Guardian	Miscellaneous
Alaska .... Comp. L. 1913, Secs. 481, 1258–60	Necessary sale may be free of dower in an undivided share if widow is a party; she may receive a gross sum measured by law on annuities if she consents by instrument proved in same manner as a deed; if no consent, one-third of sale proceeds deposited in court, invested for her benefit		Infant entitled to lands assigned to widow not having a right of dower, by default or collusion of guardian, may recover them on his majority	
Delaware ...... R. C. 1915, Secs. 3286–87, 3289, 3292; Sec. 3318, amd. by Sess. L. 1927, Ch. 198, p. 580	Sale is free of dower in undivided share if widow is a party; share of proceeds is secured to her under court's direction. Partition of lands subject to dower other than in an undivided share is postponed until dower assigned; after assignment, residue and widow's part may be partitioned or other proceedings had concerning them[2] (see next column for more general provision)	In all proceedings for sale of real estate subject to any dower interest, on petition of widow or of other person interested, sale may be free of dower, and widow paid share of proceeds; paid interest on share by purchaser; or share paid into court and invested for her benefit[3]		
District of Columbia... C. 1929, T. 14, Secs. 34, 35; T. 25, Secs. 382–83, 385; T. 29, Sec. 240	On partition, dower in an undivided share of lands attaches solely to share set out to husband's heirs or devisees. If widow entitled to dower in whole of lands, sale, if ordered, is free of dower on her written consent; and portion of proceeds paid her according to her age, health and condition, not exceeding one-sixth or less than one-twentieth of proceeds. If no consent, court may assign dower before partition sale	Dower assigned before sale; but if that would injure property and if widow consents by answer to the petition, sale may be free of dower and widow paid share according to equity practice (see preceding column)	If widow having no right to dower is endowed by guardian by favor, or awarded it by his default or collusion, infant heir, on majority, may recover lands; but widow may show, if she can, a right to dower and so retain it	Widow may be aided in like manner as infant heir (see preceding column) if she is impleaded or lose dower by default

[2] **Delaware** (R. C. 1915, Sec. 3290): If there has been no partition of the residue after assignment of dower, the widow may, by petition, elect to take a share in the proceeds of sale in lieu of dower. The court may then set aside the assignment by metes and bounds and order the real estate sold, a share to be invested for the widow's benefit.

[3] In **Delaware**, according to Sections 3420–21 of the Revised Code of 1915, an executor's sale for debts may be free of dower ".... if the widow .... waive the assignment thereof by metes and

[§ 214

TABLE CIII (*Continued*)

Jurisdiction and Citation	Vested Dower in Partition Proceedings	Vested Dower in Executor's Sale Proceedings	Collusive Assignment by Guardian	Miscellaneous
Florida .... Sess. L. 1933, Ch. 16103, p. 589, Sec. 129	See next column	No sale or disposition of real property by proceeding in probate court shall be made until it appears that widow will not take dower, or until her dower has been assigned, unless she consents to sale and joins in deed		
Georgia .... C. 1926, C. of Prac., Sec. 6075		Widow claiming dower cannot be dispossessed of mansion house after executor's sale		
Hawaii .... R. L. 1925, Secs. 2762, 2772, 3273; Sess. L. 1929, Act 19, p. 15, Sec. 1	Widow shall be made a party. Dower attaches solely to share set off in severalty to heirs if it existed as to any part of property; and if property is sold and interested parties agree, gross sum may be paid in lieu of dower; if no agreement, a sum is invested for widow's benefit (see also last column)			Present value of dower in partition action or in admeasurement of dower is computed according to the American Experience Tables of Mortality, on interest at 5 per cent. Judgment in a writ of dower must be registered where lands are situated as an encumbrance on them
Illinois .... Cahill, R. S. 1931, Ch. 3, Sec. 102; Ch. 41, Secs. 44, 46; Ch. 106, Secs. 22, 32–34, 39	Dower may be assigned, and, if court directs, premises so set off may be partitioned among claimants, subject to dower. Necessary sale may be free of dower on written, signed assent of widow; and value of dower paid in gross or share of proceeds set aside, income therefrom paid widow	Court may have dower assigned. Sale may be free of dower on written, signed assent of widow; compensation being paid her (as in preceding column). No person who sells lands for debts by court order is deemed to have relinquished dower unless relinquishment is specified in conveyance		

bounds . . . ." etc.; but Section 3318, as amended by the Session Laws of 1927, Chapter 198, page 580, set out in the table above, apparently makes her consent or waiver immaterial. In Section 3422 it is provided that if a part only of the lands have been sold after the widow has waived assignment by metes and bounds the court may order the entire proceeds applied to the debts, dower being fully assigned from the remaining lands.

§ 214]

TABLE CIII (*Continued*)

Jurisdiction and Citation	Vested Dower in Partition Proceedings	Vested Dower in Executor's Sale Proceedings	Collusive Assignment by Guardian	Miscellaneous
Kentucky ...... Carroll, St. 1922, Sec. 2140; Civ. C. of Prac. 1906, Sec. 495	Widow shall be made a party in sale proceedings and court may, with or without her consent, order sale free of dower, reasonable compensation being paid her, or she may have dower in property purchased with proceeds		Infant heir is not bound by collusive or ex parte assignment except as doweress shows herself to have been entitled thereto	See footnote 4
Maryland .... Bagby, Ann. C. 1924, Art. 16, Secs. 45, 47; Art. 46, Secs. 37, 38; Art. 93, Secs. 324–25	In all cases where lands and tenements are sold under a decree, sale may be free of dower if widow consents in writing; she is then allowed portion of proceeds not exceeding one-seventh, nor less than one-tenth according to her age, health, and condition. If no consent, dower is assigned. Dower is assigned before division of lands among heirs; necessary sale may be free of dower (subject to rules above stated)	Sale under power of sale in will may be free of dower (subject to rules stated in preceding column)		
Massachusetts .. G. L. 1932, Ch. 202, Secs. 2, 3		Sale is subject to dower except that on executor's request, and after notice to widow, it may be free of dower; one-third of proceeds set apart and administered for her by trustee appointed by court, unless parties in interest agree on division of proceeds[5]		

⁴ In **Kentucky** (Civ. C. of Prac. 1906), certain sales of real estate of infants and persons of unsound mind (Sec. 489), or of reversions or remainders (Sec. 491), may be free of dower with the widow's consent, reasonable compensation being paid her, or she may have the same dower right in property purchased with the proceeds (Sec. 495).

⁵ **Massachusetts** (G. L. 1932, Ch. 236, Sec. 55): The widow is entitled to dower in land taken on execution against the husband's legal representative in like manner as if the land had been conveyed by the husband without release of dower.

[§ 214

TABLE CIII (*Continued*)

Jurisdiction and Citation	Vested Dower in Partition Proceedings	Vested Dower in Executor's Sale Proceedings	Collusive Assignment by Guardian	Miscellaneous
Michigan ...... Comp. L. 1929, Secs. 13096–97; Sec. 13440, amd. by Sess. L. 1931, No. 79, p. 127; Secs. 15022–23, 15036–41	Widow may be made a party; if so, partition decree is binding on her if dower is in an undivided share of premises. Necessary sale may be free of dower if widow is a party; gross sum paid her if she consents by instrument executed in same manner as a deed (sum estimated according to law on annuities); if no consent, one-third of sale proceeds invested for her benefit	In proceeding in probate court for license to sell real estate of decedent, widow may appear and waive dower and homestead. If she fails to do so, specified notice is served upon her to appear and elect whether she will take dower and homestead; if she then fails to elect, dower and homestead in such real estate are barred; provided that probate judge may give her additional time, if necessary	When a widow not having right to dower recovers dower by default or collusion of guardian of infant heir, such infant may reclaim the land so wrongfully awarded, when he comes of age	If dower is claimed by two or more widows, one whose husband was first seized is first entitled thereto. If such widow has received dower or her claim discharged, lands are not subject to further dower during her lifetime
Missouri .... R. S. 1929, Secs. 320, 353, 359, 1545, 1568–69, 1578, 1586, 1590, 3132–34	Dower may be assigned before partition if without great prejudice to parties in interest. If there would be prejudice, and if widow is a party, sale may be free of dower, and present value of her interest paid widow (see last column)		If widow having no right to dower is endowed by guardian from favor or awarded it by his default or collusion, minor has action on majority to demand seizin or to fairly admeasure dower[6]	Widow may transfer her unassigned dower interest. Gross sum paid in lieu of dower is computed according to Carlisle Tables of Mortality using 6 per cent interest. Widow may be aided in like manner as infant (see preceding column) if she is impleaded and lose dower by default
Montana .... R. C. 1921, Secs. 9567–68	If widow is a party and interests of all parties require it, sale may be free of dower, and widow paid gross sum, or one-third of proceeds paid into court and invested for her benefit			

[6] **Missouri** (R. S. 1929, Sec. 359): An action by an infant to avoid assignment of dower in proceedings instituted by a guardian in which dower was awarded through collusion must be brought within three years after the infant becomes of age.

§ 214]

TABLE CIII (*Continued*)

Jurisdiction and Citation	Vested Dower in Partition Proceedings	Vested Dower in Executor's Sale Proceedings	Collusive Assignment by Guardian	Miscellaneous
New Hampshire. Pub. L. 1926, Ch. 305, Secs. 5, 6		On administrator's application and with assent of widow, land may be sold free of dower; present value of dower being paid her, as estimated by judge according to her age		
New Jersey .... Comp. St. 1910, p. 1524, Secs. 1, 2; p. 2046, Sec. 6; p. 2047, Sec. 7; p. 3838, Sec. 81; p. 3912, Secs. 52, 53; p. 4680, Sec. 18; p. 4681, Sec. 19; p. 4682, Secs. 19*a*–19*d*; p. 4684, Secs. 24, 25	In all proceedings in orphans' court for partition or for sale by legal representative or by guardian, if interests of all persons interested, sale may be free of dower if prescribed notice is given widow. Gross sum may then be paid her if she consents in writing; if no consent, sum is invested for her benefit. Also, widow by sealed writing may request sale free of dower in above proceedings, and, if court approves, be compensated from proceeds (as above)	Sale of lands for decedent's debts does not affect any right of dower in said lands (but see preceding column)	If widow having no right to dower is endowed by guardian by favor, or awarded it by his default or collusion, infant heir on majority may recover lands if widow can show no right to dower	If tenant in dower is impleaded, reversioner or remainderman may defend his right. Nor is he prejudiced by default or surrender of widow. Widow may be aided in like manner as infant (see preceding column) if she is impleaded or lose dower by default. Sale for assessments may be free of dower if notice given widow; afterward she may share in surplus
North Carolina.. C. 1927, Secs. 74, 3226	Widow may join in petition for partition. Land may be allotted subject to dower, or dower may be assigned. On decree of sale, interest on one-third of proceeds paid her annually; or in lieu thereof, at her election, value of 6 per cent annuity paid absolutely	Widow shall be made a party and, on sale, is compensated (as in preceding column). Provided that this does not prevent widow from claiming dower by metes and bounds		

[§ 214

TABLE CIII (*Continued*)

Jurisdiction and Citation	Vested Dower in Partition Proceedings	Vested Dower in Executor's Sale Proceedings	Collusive Assignment by Guardian	Miscellaneous
Ohio[7] .... Complete G. C. 1931 (Page), Secs. 5680, 12016, 12018– 19, 12042–43	In all sales of real estate by court order, including partition and executors' sales, widow, being a party, may file answer, consent to sale free of dower, and receive dower value from proceeds. In partition action dower must be assigned except: (*a*) when it has already been done; (*b*) when widow consents to sale (as above); (*c*) when dower is in an undivided interest; in latter case, it may be assigned, or a sale may be made and widow paid value of dower	See preceding column	During minority of heir, if dower assigned to widow not entitled thereto, or if recovered by default, fraud, or collusion of guardian, heir on majority may recover lands	Tenant in dower is liable for taxes levied on the lands[8]
Oregon .... C. 1930, Secs. 6(603), 6(607), 6(623)–6(626), 10(329), 63(354)	Widow shall be made a party in action and her rights determined. Necessary sale may be free of dower in undivided share; and if widow consents by instrument acknowledged in same manner as a deed, she may receive gross sum measured by law on annuities; if no consent, one-third[9] of sale proceeds invested for her benefit		Infant entitled to lands assigned to widow not having a right of dower, by default or collusion of guardian, may recover them on majority	No transfer of title to land, estate, or interest therein, or mortgage, shall be registered until it appears that dower interest has been released or extinguished

[7] It must be remembered that the statutes on dower in **Ohio** apply only to real property conveyed or encumbered by the husband (Complete G. C. 1931 [Page], Supp. 1932, Sec. 10502[1]).

[8] **Ohio** (Complete G. C. 1931 [Page], Sec. 5688): A tenant in dower who neglects to pay taxes so that the lands are sold, and who does not redeem them, forfeits to the person next entitled to the lands in reversion or remainder all the estate in them, and is liable to such person for all damages sustained from the neglect.

[9] Apparently the statement that "one-third" of the proceeds are invested for the widow (C. 1930, Sec. 6[626]) is an oversight, for the widow in **Oregon** is now entitled to dower in one-half the property (C. 1930, Sec. 10[301]).

§ 214]

TABLE CIII (*Continued*)

Jurisdiction and Citation	Vested Dower in Partition Proceedings	Vested Dower in Executor's Sale Proceedings	Collusive Assignment by Guardian	Miscellaneous
Rhode Island ... G. L. 1923, Sec. 5360, amd. by Sess. L. 1929, Ch. 1370, p. 216; Sess. L. 1929, Ch. 1371, p. 216	In any sale of real estate by court order (except where specially provided otherwise) upon widow's petition and after notice, court may in its discretion: (*a*) order present value of dower paid her from sale proceeds, in lieu of dower; or (*b*) set apart for her life one-third of proceeds, annual income therefrom to be paid her until dower interest terminates	(See preceding column.) In proceedings for sale of real estate by executors, administrators, and guardians, probate court, with recorded consent of widow, may order sale free of dower; and, upon execution of a release by her, may order present value of her interest paid to her in lieu of dower		
South Carolina.. C. of L. 1922, C. C., Sec. 336				Widow who stands seized in dower is liable for taxes and assessments on real estate
Tennessee ...... C. 1932, Secs. 8374, 9166, 9193–96, 9209, 9211	Dower assigned before estate partitioned among heirs or devisees. Dower may be allotted in general partition action, but, after assignment, lands set off may also be partitioned. Partition decree is conclusive on widow with dower in individual share of premises, but not on widow with dower in whole of them. Dower may be sold with rest of land on widow's assent; gross sum may be paid her, or share invested for her benefit			

[§ 214

TABLE CIII (*Concluded*)

Jurisdiction and Citation	Vested Dower in Partition Proceedings	Vested Dower in Executor's Sale Proceedings	Collusive Assignment by Guardian	Miscellaneous
Virginia .... C. 1930, Secs. 5129, 5131–33a, 6266a	If there is dower in estate sold under partition or in estate which has been reduced to money, stocks, bonds, etc., susceptible of division, widow may apply to chancery court and, in court's discretion, have lump sum paid her according to annuity tables		Infant heir may recover lands assigned as dower by guardian, or awarded by his default or collusion, unless widow shows herself entitled thereto	Annuity tables as set forth with 6 per cent interest are used to calculate gross sum when payable in lieu of dower.[10] In suit to enforce lien, dower may be assigned and then sold; if that cannot be done, heirs or devisees may be requested to pay dower value, the surplus over liens paid widow (see also first column)
West Virginia.. C. 1931, Ch. 43, Art. 1, Sec. 16; Art. 2, Secs. 1–5			Infant heir may recover lands assigned as dower by guardian or given in judgment by default or collusion of guardian, unless widow shows herself entitled thereto	American Experience Tables of Mortality with interest at 5 per cent are used to calculate gross sum when payable in lieu of inchoate or vested dower
Wisconsin ...... St. 1931, Secs. 233.16, 233.22, 316.12		If any homestead is sold with widow's written consent, under power of sale in a will, she takes dower from proceeds of sale, as determined by court. In sale for debts, husband's legal representative may contract with widow to accept one-third of proceeds in lieu of dower[11]	Infant entitled to lands assigned to widow not having a right of dower, by default or collusion of guardian, may recover them with damages on his majority	

[10] See *Slater* v. *Slater*, 124 Va. 370; 98 S. E. 7 (1919), for a full discussion and interpretation of the statutes on annuity tables.

[11] In **Wisconsin** the contract to accept one-third of the proceeds in lieu of dower must be witnessed by two witnesses, acknowledged, filed with the county court, and approved by such court (St. 1931, Sec. 316.12).

§ 214]

REFERENCES

Books

SCRIBNER, CHARLES H. *A Treatise on the Law of Dower,* 2d ed., Vol. II, ch. xxiv, pp. 653–98 (1883).

STIMSON, F. H. *American Statute Law,* Sec. 3280 (1886).

Notes

"Method of Computing the Present Value of Wife's Dower Right during Husband's Life," *American Blower Company* v. *MacKenzie,* 197 N. C. 152; 147 S. E. 829 (1929)—33 Law Notes 91 (1929).

"Calculating Value of Dower," *Whitehead* v. *Brownsville Bank,* 166 Tenn. 249; 61 S. W. (2d) 975 (1933)—12 Tenn. L. Rev. 135–36 (1934).

Annotations

"Computation of the Value of an Inchoate Dower Right," 34 A. L. R. 1021–23 (1925); 64 A. L. R. 1053–54 (1929).

"Sale of Property by Widow as Executrix or Administratrix as Barring Her Right to Dower," 30 A. L. R. 944 48 (1924).

"Succession or Estate Tax in Its Application to Dower and Statutory Allowances," 37 A. L. R. 541–47 (1925).

Section 215. Curtesy—In General

CROSS REFERENCES: Wife's property, in general, **Sec. 167**; Wife's power to make a will, **Sec. 181**; Dower, in general, **Sec. 188**; Dower, abolition and statutory substitutes, **Sec. 189**; Curtesy, abolition and statutory substitutes, **Sec. 216**

At common law, the husband had two distinct types of rights in the real property of his wife: (*a*) his marital rights by virtue of the marriage, called "rights jure uxoris" or "tenancy by marital right"; and (*b*) his right as tenant by the curtesy. His marital rights entitled him to a present estate which existed during coverture and which could be aliened by him or levied upon for his debts. Husband and wife were considered to be jointly seized of the property, in the wife's right; but he had the sole right to the rents, issues, profits, and control.

[§ 215

It was not until issue was born of the marriage, capable of inheriting the property, that any right of curtesy existed. Upon birth of such issue, the husband became possessed of an estate by the "curtesy initiate" in all lands or tenements of which the wife was seized at any time during coverture in fee simple or fee tail. It is clear that after birth of issue the husband was entitled solely to the rents, issues, and profits of the property; his estate was alienable as a life estate and could be levied upon for his debts. Furthermore, it was generally held that the statute of limitations did not run against the wife, after birth of issue, while the husband was still alive. It has therefore usually been considered that curtesy initiate was an estate for the husband's life, held by him in his own right (*Foster* v. *Marshall,* 22 N. H. 491 [1851]; but see *Jones* v. *Davies,* 5 H. and N. 766 [1860]; 7 H. and N. 507 [1861]). It follows that if curtesy initiate was considered as such an estate the wife's death had no effect, although thereafter the husband was said to hold "curtesy consummate." Space does not permit a discussion of the question whether curtesy initiate was, theoretically, merely a life estate, or of the related question whether the wife's death did more than to change the term "initiate" to "consummate." The references at the end of this section should be consulted (and see *Foster* v. *Marshall* and *Jones* v. *Davies, supra*).

Curtesy differed from dower in three main respects: (*a*) in size; (*b*) in the necessity for birth of issue; (*c*) in the fact that before the wife's death curtesy was a present estate as distinguished from the mere protected expectancy of inchoate dower (**Sec. 188**).

Curtesy, in general, was abolished in England by the Administration of Estates Act of 1925 (15 Geo. V, c. 23, s. 45[1*b*]). It still exists, however, where the wife has an entailed interest of an equitable nature and dies without having disentailed by assurance and without having disposed of her interest by will (Administration of Estates Act, 1925 [15 Geo. V, c. 23, s. 45(2)]; Law of Property Act, 1925 [15 Geo. V, c. 20, s. 130(4)]).

In the United States, the Married Women's Acts which gave the wife the control and power of disposition over her property (see **Secs. 167** *et seq.*) had an important effect on the husband's rights. In the first place, they clearly abolished his marital rights *jure uxoris*. Secondly, some courts have held that common-law curtesy initiate was thereby impliedly abolished, and that the husband's curtesy interest upon the wife's death could be defeated by her conveyance or will (*Balster* v. *Cadick,* 29 App. D. C. 405 [1907]). Others, however, have held that

§ 215]

curtesy initiate as a present, vested estate was abolished, but that the husband was entitled during marriage to a protected expectancy similar to inchoate dower, which could not be defeated by the sole act of the wife (*Teckenbrock* v. *McLaughlin,* 246 Mo. 711; 152 S. W. 38 [1912]). The differing opinions may be explained by the differences in the language of the various statutes. Furthermore, common-law curtesy has been expressly abolished in the majority of jurisdictions and a variety of statutory schemes have been substituted (**Sec. 216**).

The present section and the following sections which deal with "curtesy" (**Secs. 216–23**) are concerned primarily with legislation respecting the right of a surviving husband to share in the wife's property as against her will. The fact that his interest is not termed "curtesy," or that it is dissimilar to common-law curtesy, does not prevent its inclusion. A general picture of the statutory situation has also been attempted, and if the husband has no protected right to share against the wife's will, that fact is pointed out in **Section 216.** The eight community-property states (**Arizona, California, Idaho, Louisiana, Nevada, New Mexico, Texas, Washington**) have been dealt with in **Section 178** and are not included in the discussion in the present group of sections. The rights of the husband as statutory heir and distributee of the intestate property of the wife are discussed in **Section 227,** and his rights in homestead and exempt property, in **Section 228.**

In general, the legislation concerning curtesy and related rights is subject to the same criticisms which were made of the dower statutes (see **Sec. 188**). Many of the provisions are haphazard, inconsistent, unintelligible, and do not evidence any general plan. In one respect, the confusion is less extensive than in the dower legislation, for more jurisdictions have entirely abolished curtesy without substituting any protected interest in its stead (**Sec. 216**). On the other hand, the confusion has been increased in some jurisdictions by the retention of the common-law inability of the wife to convey her lands without the husband's joinder. As in the dower legislation, the clarity of the statutes has suffered from the legislatures' failure to do away with common-law terms. There is a real need for revision of the legislation in accordance with a general plan embracing the rights of both husband and wife (see **Sec. 188**).

One of the outstanding features in the picture of marital property rights has been the willingness of legislatures to abolish the husband's protected interest in the wife's property, and yet to retain a similar interest for the wife—an interest that, in most jurisdictions, is greater than

her common-law dower (see **Sec. 216** for a comparative analysis of the
rights of husband and wife). Thus, only **North Dakota** and **South
Dakota** have failed to retain dower or a statutory substitute (**Sec. 189**) ;
whereas twelve jurisdictions have abolished any protected interest of the
husband in the wife's lands (**Sec. 216**). This discrimination, however,
was more extensive at a time when dower and curtesy were first under-
going statutory changes. Fortunately, the modern tendency is to treat
husband and wife alike. Other significant tendencies of the curtesy legislation include: (*a*) the abolition of any inchoate interest of the husband
during coverture, his share being thus confined to property owned by
the wife at her death (**Secs. 216, 218**) ; and (*b*) the giving of an absolute share in both real and personal property to the husband, as distinguished from his common-law curtesy of a life estate in all the realty
of the wife (**Sec. 217**).

The different types of statutory schemes that have been substituted
for curtesy are considered in detail in **Section 216.** They are somewhat
similar to those relating to dower (see **Secs. 188, 189**), but with an
important difference, viz., the number of jurisdictions which have
adopted the respective schemes varies considerably in the dower and
curtesy fields. Because of the many peculiarities and limitations in the
statutes relating to curtesy, it is impracticable to attempt to state in the
present section the number of jurisdictions which have adopted the
various systems; **Section 216** must be consulted.

The statutes of six states furnish interesting examples of the inconsistent legislation already referred to. In five, the effect of the legislation relating to the husband's rights is qualified by the retention of the
common-law inability of the wife to execute conveyances alone. Thus
in **Alabama, Florida,** and **North Carolina,** the wife may defeat the
husband's interest by her will, but cannot defeat it by her sole deed. In
Indiana and **Pennsylvania,** the husband is said to be entitled to a protected share only in lands of which the wife dies seized or owning, but he
receives an added protection during coverture because she cannot convey
without his joinder. Another peculiar statute is found in **Wisconsin.**
The husband is said to have an estate by the "curtesy," but the use of
that term is unjustified. His interest becomes consummate in intestate
lands only; it may be defeated by the wife's sole deed; it is extinguished
by his remarriage; and is extinguished if, by a former husband, the
deceased wife leaves issue to whom the lands might descend.

The recommendations concerning the dower legislation as set forth
in **Section 188** are, for the most part, applicable to the legislation re-

specting the husband's rights. Briefly, they may be recapitulated as follows: (1) curtesy and its attendant formulae should be completely abolished and a new statutory system evolved; (2) the husband's protected share should not be an arbitrary one; it should depend, in part, upon the size of the wife's estate and upon the amount of the husband's own property (**Sec. 217**); (3) his share should be an absolute part of the real and personal property of the wife (**Sec. 217**); (4) his interest should not be entirely exempt from the wife's creditors, although an exemption up to a small stated value might be advisable, especially if his own estate is small (**Sec. 217**); (5) the husband should not have a protected inchoate interest during coverture (**Sec. 217**); the wife should be able to convey her property without his joinder (see also **Sec. 183**); (6) the statute should definitely state when and how the husband is required to elect to take against the wife's will (**Sec. 219**); (7) the jointure statutes should be abolished; and antenuptial and postnuptial contracts barring the husband's interest should be expressly recognized by statute, subject to rules respecting persons in confidential relations (**Sec. 220**); (8) the few statutes which discriminate in favor of the husband as to forfeiture for misconduct should be changed; serious misconduct on the part of either spouse should work a forfeiture (**Sec. 221**).

At the risk of seeming repetitive, the writer again states his conviction that the protected rights of husband and wife in the property of the other should be the same. In most jurisdictions the widow is provided for by homestead, exempt property, and allowance statutes (**Sec. 228**). She should not be preferred in the present field of legislation. It is gratifying to note that in line with other legislation (see **Secs. 149–50**) the modern tendency is toward the equality recommended.

It is suggested that **Sections 188, 189,** and **216** be read in immediate conjunction with the present section.

REFERENCES

Books

BISHOP, JOEL P. *Commentaries on the Law of Married Women,* Vol. I, Secs. 471–585 (1873); Vol. II, Secs. 43, 141–50 (1875).

POLLOCK, SIR FREDERICK, and SIR FREDERICK WILLIAM MAITLAND. *The History of English Law,* 2d ed., II, 414–20 (1899).

STIMSON, F. J. *American Statute Law,* Sec. 3300 (1886).

[§ 215

TIFFANY, HERBERT T. *Real Property and Other Interests in Land,* 2d ed., Vol. 1, Secs. 238–42 (1920).

WOERNER, J. G. *The American Law of Administration,* 3d ed., Sec. 121 (1923).

Articles

EAGLETON, WILLIAM L. "Introduction to the Intestacy Act and the Dower Rights Act," 20 Ia. L. Rev. 241–43 (1935).

———. "The Dower Rights Act," 20 Ia. L. Rev. 261–65 (1935).

FARRER, FREDERICK E. "Tenant by the Curtesy of England," 43 Quar. Rev. 87–117 (1927).

SAYRE, PAUL L. "Husband and Wife as Statutory Heirs," 42 Harv. L. Rev. 330–64 (1929).

SULLIVAN, J. D. "Passing of Dower and Curtesy," 19 Geo. L. Jour. 306–15 (1931).

Annotation

"Extent and Effect of Exception in Married Women's Acts as to Husband's Right by the Curtesy," 29 A. L. R. 1338–43 (1924).

Section 216. Curtesy—Abolition and Statutory Substitutes

CROSS REFERENCES: Dower, abolition and statutory substitutes, **Sec. 189;** Curtesy, in general, **Sec. 215;** Extent of, and property subject to, curtesy, **Secs. 217, 218;** Husband's share of real and personal property when wife dies intestate, **Sec. 227;** Homestead, exempt property, etc., **Sec. 228**

In the eight community-property states, curtesy either was never recognized or has been expressly or impliedly abolished. The system of survivor's rights obtaining in those jurisdictions (see **Sec. 178**) is radically different from that found in any of the so-called common-law states, and hence is excluded from consideration in this and the following seven sections. In this section and in Table CV which follows at the end thereof, an attempt is made to present a general picture of the property rights (exclusive of homestead, exempt property, and provisions for temporary support) which the other forty-three jurisdictions accord to the surviving husband and which are protected from the wife's testamentary disposition. The writer is impressed with the fact that many

§ 216]

of the statutes are so needlessly confused and ambiguous as to render a certain understanding of them impossible without a knowledge of the legislative and case history of the matter in the particular jurisdiction, and that a danger of error lurks in positive statements.

The statutes of twenty-five jurisdictions expressly abolish tenancy by the curtesy as known to the common law, and that is the necessary effect of the substitute systems established in most of the other jurisdictions. While curtesy consummate persists in a few, most states either have reduced the surviving husband to the position of a mere heir of the wife, have diminished his curtesy to dower proportions, or have placed him in the position of a forced heir. At the time dower and curtesy first began to undergo radical statutory changes, the tendency was to abolish curtesy and substitute nothing in its place. The modern tendency, however, has been to treat widow and widower alike, and to give them both a generous share of both real and personal property which cannot be defeated by the will of the deceased spouse. That there is still much discrimination in favor of the widow is evident from the following table.

TABLE CIV

SHARE OF SURVIVOR AS AGAINST WILL OF DECEASED SPOUSE

Jurisdiction	Curtesy, Dower, or Share in Real Property		Share in Personal Property	
	Widow	Widower	Widow	Widower
Alabama	Yes	No	Yes	No
Alaska	Yes	Yes	No	No
Arkansas	Yes	No	Yes	No
Colorado	Yes	Yes	Yes	Yes
Connecticut	Yes	Yes	Yes	Yes
Delaware	Yes	Yes	No	No
District of Columbia	Yes	No	Yes	Yes
Florida	Yes	No	Yes	No
Georgia	Yes	No	No	No
Hawaii	Yes	Yes	Yes	Yes
Illinois	Yes	Yes	Yes	Yes
Indiana	Yes	Yes	Yes	Yes
Iowa	Yes	Yes	Yes	Yes
Kansas	Yes	Yes	Yes	Yes
Kentucky	Yes	Yes	Yes	Yes
Maine	Yes	Yes	Yes	Yes
Maryland	Yes	Yes	Yes	Yes
Massachusetts	Yes	Yes	Yes	Yes
Michigan	Yes	No	Yes	No

[§ 216

TABLE CIV (*Continued*)

Jurisdiction	Curtesy, Dower, or Share in Real Property		Share in Personal Property	
	Widow	Widower	Widow	Widower
Minnesota	Yes	Yes	Yes	Yes
Mississippi	Yes	Yes	Yes	Yes
Missouri	Yes	Yes	Yes	Yes
Montana	Yes	Yes	Yes	Yes
Nebraska	Yes	Yes	Yes	Yes
New Hampshire	Yes	Yes	Yes	Yes
New Jersey	Yes	Yes	No	No
New York	Yes	Yes	Yes	Yes
North Carolina	Yes	No	Yes	No
North Dakota	No	No	No	No
Ohio	Yes	Yes	Yes	Yes
Oklahoma	Yes	Yes	Yes	Yes
Oregon	Yes	Yes	No	No
Pennsylvania	Yes	Yes	Yes	Yes
Rhode Island	Yes	Yes	No	No
South Carolina	Yes	No	No	No
South Dakota	No	No	No	No
Tennessee	Yes	Yes	Yes	Yes
Utah	Yes	No	No	No
Vermont	Yes	Yes	Yes	Yes
Virginia	Yes	Yes	Yes	Yes
West Virginia	Yes	Yes	Yes	Yes
Wisconsin	Yes	No	Yes	No
Wyoming	Yes	Yes	Yes	Yes

Thus, while only two jurisdictions give the widow neither dower nor statutory share of real property (**Sec. 189**), in no less than twelve jurisdictions the surviving husband appears to have no interest in the wife's real property, either as heir or otherwise, which she may not defeat by will or by both will and conveyance. Of the thirty-one jurisdictions which give both spouses a survivor's share, widow and widower are treated alike in twenty-two (see Table CV following). A few discriminate in favor of the widower, but most of them are states which retain both dower and curtesy substantially as at common law. While ten jurisdictions do not secure the widow in a share of the husband's personal estate, these and six others do not permit the husband to share in her personal estate except as distributee in case of intestacy. In eleven, as against the wife's will, he shares in neither real nor personal estate. In twenty-six, however, he is substantially a forced heir and is entitled

§ 216]

to a statutory share of the wife's surplus personalty. With but one exception, his share is the same as that accorded to the widow (see Table CV).

The twelve jurisdictions in which no interest in the wife's lands is secured to the surviving husband may be classified as follows:

1. **Alabama, Arkansas, Florida, Georgia, Michigan, North Dakota, South Carolina, South Dakota, Utah.**—In these nine states, curtesy is either expressly or impliedly abolished. The husband is a mere heir of the wife and his expectancy as such may be defeated by her will. In four of them (**Alabama, Arkansas, Michigan, Utah**) the power of the wife to devise her property as if sole is written into the constitution. In all but **Alabama** and **Florida,** she likewise has complete power to alienate her lands without the husband's concurrence (see also **Sec. 183**).

2. **District of Columbia, North Carolina, Wisconsin.**—These three states give the husband what is labeled an estate by the "curtesy," but there is little to warrant the use of that term. In all of them, the estate becomes consummate in intestate lands only; and in the **District of Columbia** and **Wisconsin,** it may also be defeated by the wife's sole conveyance. The ridiculous **Wisconsin** statute further provides that the husband's right of curtesy is extinguished by his remarriage, and that if the widow leaves issue by a former husband to whom the lands might descend such issue take the same discharged of his estate.

The thirty-one jurisdictions which give the surviving husband an estate by the curtesy or some substitute which the wife may not defeat by her will are hardly susceptible of any measured classification, but for purposes of convenience may be grouped as follows:

1. **Alaska, Delaware, New Hampshire, Rhode Island, Tennessee.**—The husband has an estate as tenant by the curtesy in these five jurisdictions. In **Alaska,** the wife may defeat the same by her sole conveyance, and there need not be issue born alive; but in the other four, curtesy consummate apparently persists substantially as at common law (see *Shearin* v. *Shearin,* 161 Tenn. 172; 29 S. W. [2d] 254 [1930]; *Barlow* v. *Barlow,* 49 R. I. 117; 140 A. 467 [1928]). Of this group, **New Hampshire** stands alone in permitting the widower to release his curtesy and homestead right and claim an absolute share of the deceased wife's surplus estate.

2. **Connecticut, Hawaii, Illinois, Kentucky, Maryland, Massachusetts, Missouri, New Jersey, Ohio, Oregon, Virginia, West Virginia.**—In these twelve jurisdictions, the surviving husband has a

[§ 216

life estate in the wife's real property which is reduced to dower proportions (ten) or to a life estate in one-half (**New Jersey, Oregon**). His estate is labeled "curtesy" in four, and "dower" in six. In **Connecticut,** his interest attaches to surplus property owned at death, and is shorn of all the earmarks of common-law dower or curtesy. In the others, he has an inchoate estate during marriage similar to inchoate dower, but it may be defeated by the wife's sole conveyance in **Hawaii** and **Missouri.** In four of the foregoing jurisdictions (**Illinois, Massachusetts, Maryland, Missouri**), he may waive his dower or curtesy and take an absolute share of the wife's surplus lands in lieu thereof. Three of these states require him to affirmatively act or his waiver is presumed (**Sec. 219**). Finally, **Ohio** has virtually abolished vested dower by providing that the same is barred upon the wife's death except as to property conveyed or encumbered by her, and that in lieu of the estate thus barred he is entitled to a distributive share of her property under the statute of descent and distribution.

3. **Colorado, Indiana, Mississippi, Montana, New York, Oklahoma, Pennsylvania, Vermont, Wyoming.** — Curtesy is expressly abolished in the foregoing nine jurisdictions. The surviving husband is substantially a forced heir as to property owned by the wife at death. He may dissent from her will and demand an absolute share of her estate. During coverture, he has only an expectancy; but in **Indiana** and **Pennsylvania,** the interest which matures on the wife's death receives incidental protection during marriage by reason of the wife's incomplete capacity to dispose of her real property without the husband's concurrence (see also **Sec. 183**). Of the foregoing states, the only earmark of common-law curtesy is found in **Vermont,** which refers to real estate of which "a man and his wife are seized in her right in fee simple."

4. **Iowa, Kansas, Minnesota, Maine, Nebraska.**—These five jurisdictions also give the husband an interest in fee, which is either a specified share in undivided interest or value (**Iowa, Kansas, Minnesota**) or his intestate share (**Maine, Nebraska**). In all of them, however, he has an inchoate interest during marriage protected from destruction by the wife's sole conveyance. His share attaches, with some exceptions, to all the real property of which the wife is seized or possessed during marriage. In spite of the substantial nature of his estate, the statutes of **Maine, Minnesota,** and **Nebraska** are express to the effect that he takes by descent or inheritance. It seems obvious that these terms are not used in their ordinary technical sense.

§ 216]

Most of the statutes considered in this section are silent as to whether the common-law requisite of issue persists. The **District of Columbia, Delaware,** and **North Carolina** are express to the effect that the birth of issue is necessary, and the requirement probably persists also in **New Hampshire, Rhode Island,** and **Tennessee.** On the other hand, four jurisdictions (**Alaska, New Jersey, Oregon, Virginia**) expressly provide that the birth of issue is unnecessary, and the same result is undoubtedly reached in all other jurisdictions either by an express abolition of common-law curtesy or by the establishment of systems which are not mere modifications of common-law curtesy.

In Table CV, which follows, the words of the statute have been used wherever practicable.

[§ 216

TABLE

CURTESY AND STATUTORY

Jurisdiction[1] and Citation	Curtesy Expressly Abolished	Same Share as Widow	Extent	Property Subject to;[2] Necessity of Issue
Alabama .... Const., Sec. 209; C. 1923, Secs. 7376, 8269	....	No	The use during life	Separate realty of wife dying intestate
Alaska .... Comp. L. 1913, Sec. 482, amd. by Sess. L. 1923, Ch. 40, p. 51; Secs. 563, 595; Sess. L. 1917, Ch. 69, p. 169	....	No	Life estate as tenant by the curtesy	All lands not previously sold or conveyed by wife, whereof husband and his wife are seized in her right of any estate of inheritance, although they may not have had issue born alive[2]
Arkansas .... Const., Art. IX, Sec. 7; Crawf. and Moses, Dig. 1921, Sec. 5574; Supp. 1927, Sec. 3536a	....	No	Husband is heir in case of intestacy[3]	See preceding column
Colorado .... Comp. L. 1921, G. S., Secs. 5151, 5184	Yes	Yes	See last column	See last column
Connecticut .... G. S. 1930, Secs. 5154, 5156-57	Yes[4]	Yes	The use for life of one-third in value	All the real property legally or equitably owned by wife at death, after payment of debts and estate charges
Delaware .... R. C. 1915, Secs. 3048, 3052, amd. by Sess. L. 1919, Ch. 197, pp. 524, 526; Secs. 3267, 3382	....	No	Life estate as tenant by the curtesy[5]	Issue born alive during the marriage is necessary[5, 2]
District of Columbia C. 1929, T. 14, Secs. 21, 38, 42	....	No	Estate by the curtesy	"Real estate owned by wife in fee simple and intestate thereof" whether her estate be legal or equitable or her seisin in deed or in law, if a child has been born of the marriage capable of inheriting

* See pages 550-53 for all numbered footnotes to this table.

CV*

SUBSTITUTES THEREFOR

Share in Personal Property

Same Share as Widow	Amount, etc.	Wife May Defeat Share by Will or Deed; Election between Will or Curtesy and Distributive Share (See Also **Sec. 219**)
No	One-half of wife's separate personal estate if she dies intestate	Wife may devise and bequeath her real and personal estate the same as if single, but husband must join in her conveyance of lands
....	Husband is distributee in case of intestacy[3]	Wife may defeat husband's curtesy by conveyance, but not by will. Subject to husband's curtesy, wife may "devise" all her real and personal property
No	Husband is distributee in case of intestacy[3]	Wife may devise, bequeath or convey her real and personal estate the same as if she were single
Yes	See next column	Wife cannot devise or bequeath away from husband more than one-half of her property without his written consent executed after her death
Yes	The use for life of one-third in value of all personal property legally or equitably owned by wife at death, after payment of debts and estate charges	Wife cannot defeat surviving husband's statutory share by will
....	Husband is distributee in case of intestacy[3]	Wife's statutory power to dispose of her property by conveyance, devise, etc., as if unmarried, is subject to rights of husband as tenant by the curtesy in her lands
Yes	See next column	Wife has power to dispose of all her property by deed, will or otherwise as fully as if unmarried. If husband renounces provision made for him in wife's will, or if no provision is made for him, he is entitled to his intestate share of personal property[3]

[§ 216

TABLE CV

Share in Real Property

Jurisdiction[1] and Citation	Curtesy Expressly Abolished	Same Share as Widow	Extent	Property Subject to;[2] Necessity of Issue
Florida .... R. G. S. 1920, Sec. 3949, amd. by Sess. L. 1927, Ch. 12255, p. 1137; Sess. L. 1933, Ch. 16103, p. 545, Secs. 5, 6; p. 549, Sec. 24	....	No	Husband is heir in case of intestacy[3]	See preceding column
Georgia .... C. 1926, C. C., Secs. 3670, 3930	Yes	No	Husband is heir in case of intestacy[3]	See preceding column
Hawaii .... R. L. 1925, Sec. 2993, amd. by Sess. L. 1925, Act 274, p. 392; Sec. 3000, amd. by Sess. L. 1933, Act 68, p. 65; Sec. 3305	....	No[6]	Life interest in one-third, called curtesy	"Wife's real estate," whether she die testate or intestate[6]
Illinois .... Cahill, R. S. 1931, Ch. 41, Secs. 1, 3–6, 10–12, 17; Ch. 106a, Sec. 25	Yes	Yes	Husband is endowed of a third part	All lands of which wife was seized of an estate of inheritance during marriage, including equitable estates and all real estate contracted for by wife in her lifetime, title to which may be completed after her death[2]
Indiana .... Burns, Ann. St. 1926, Secs. 3345–46, 3377, 8739	Yes	No	One-third descends to husband, subject to its proportion of the wife's debts contracted before marriage	Wife's "real estate" when she dies testate or intestate ....
Iowa .... C. 1927, Secs. 11846, 11986, 11990–91, 12006	....	Yes	One-third in value in fee, called dower (to include homestead)	All the legal or equitable estates in real property possessed by wife during marriage which have not been sold on execution or other judicial sale
Kansas .... R. S. 1923, Secs. 22(101), 22(108), 22(127), 22(130), 22(238)	Yes	Yes	One-half in value in fee simple	All the real estate in which wife during marriage had a legal or equitable interest, which has not been sold on execution or other judicial sale, and which is not necessary for the payment of debts

§ 216]

(Continued)

Share in Personal Property

Same Share as Widow	Amount, etc.	Wife May Defeat Share by Will or Deed; Election between Will or Curtesy and Distributive Share (See Also Sec. 219)
No	Husband is distributee in case of intestacy[3]	Wife may dispose of her real and personal property by last will, but husband must join in her conveyances of real property
....	Husband is distributee in case of intestacy[3]	
No	Husband is entitled "by way of curtesy" to an absolute property in one-third part of wife's movable effects in possession or reducible to possession at time of her death, after payment of her debts	Wife may "dispose" of property, real and personal, "in the same manner" as if single[6]
Yes	If wife leaves lineal descendants, husband is entitled to one-third of all personal property owned by her at death, after debts and estate charges are paid; and to one-half thereof if no lineal descendants survive	After renouncing will, husband may waive dower in lands of which wife dies seized in favor of absolute estate of one-third of each parcel of real estate which wife owns at death, after payment of debts. If wife dies testate, husband may elect, in lieu of dower in estate of which wife dies seized and of statutory share in personal property, an absolute estate as follows: one-half of the real and personal estate after payment of debts and estate charges if wife leaves no lineal descendants, and one-third thereof if wife leaves lineal descendants
Yes	On wife's death, her personal property is "distributed in the same manner as her real estate descends" and is apportioned under the same circumstances	Wife cannot convey or mortgage her real estate without the husband's joinder
Yes	Personal property "not necessary for the payment of debts, nor otherwise disposed of," is distributed to the same persons and in the same proportions as real estate[7]	Wife may dispose of her property by will, subject to "the distributive share of her estate given by law" to the surviving husband[7]
Yes	Personal property after payment of debts, not otherwise disposed of according to law, is distributed to same persons and in same proportions as real estate	Wife cannot "bequeath" away from husband more than one-half of her property without his consent

[§ 216

TABLE CV

Share in Real Property

Jurisdiction[1] and Citation	Curtesy Expressly Abolished	Same Share as Widow	Extent	Property Subject to;[2] Necessity of Issue
Kentucky .... Carroll, St. 1922, Secs. 2132, 2134–35, 2142–43, 2147–48	....	Yes	Life estate in one-third	All the real estate of which wife or anyone for her use was seized in deed or law of an estate in fee simple during coverture; equitable right in lands under executory contract if owned by wife at death[2]
Maine .... R. S. 1930, Ch. 89, Secs. 1, 8, 13, 14, 20	Yes	Yes	Husband is heir of wife in case of intestacy.[3] In any event, one-third descends to him free from payment of debts (see last column)	Real estate of deceased wife, including all of which she was seized during coverture (wild lands conveyed, though afterward cleared, are excepted; wild lands of which wife dies seized are included)
Maryland .... Bagby, Ann. C. 1924, Art. 45, Sec. 7; Art. 46, Secs. 3, 4; Art. 73A, Sec. 25(e); Art. 93, Secs. 311–14, 326	....	Yes	Life estate in one-third, called dower	Lands held or owned by wife at any time during marriage, whether by legal or equitable title. Statute and common law as to wife's dower applicable to husband's estate unless such construction is unreasonable[2]
Massachusetts ..... G. L. 1932, Ch. 108A, Sec. 25(e); Ch. 186, Secs. 1, 2; Ch. 189, Secs. 1, 2; Ch. 190, Sec. 1; Ch. 191, Sec. 15	Yes	Yes	Life estate in one-third, as tenant by the curtesy	All lands owned by wife at any time during coverture. The law relative to dower shall be applicable to curtesy[2]
Michigan .... Const., Art. XVI, Sec. 8; Comp. L. 1929, Secs. 13057, 13440, 15726	....	No	Husband is heir in case of intestacy[3]	See preceding column
Minnesota .... G. S. 1923, Secs. 7408, 8198, 8720, 8726	Yes[10]	Yes	Undivided one-third by inheritance, subject to proportionate share of decedent's debts not paid out of personal estate, and to all judgment liens	Lands of which wife was seized or possessed during marriage to the disposition of which by will or otherwise the husband has not consented in writing, except such as has been sold by judicial partition proceedings or appropriated to payment of wife's debts by execution or judicial sale, by general assignment for benefit of creditors or by insolvency proceedings[2]

(Continued)

Share in Personal Property

Same Share as Widow	Amount, etc.	Wife May Defeat Share by Will or Deed; Election between Will or Curtesy and Distributive Share (See Also **Sec. 219**)
Yes	An absolute estate in one-half of the surplus personalty left by wife	Wife may dispose of her property by will subject to the rights of the surviving husband
Yes	Husband is distributee in case of intestacy.[3] Surplus personalty of intestate is distributed in same manner as real estate (see next column)	If husband waives provision for him in wife's will, or if no provision made for him, he is entitled to the same share of real estate and the same distributive share of personal estate as if wife died intestate[3, 8]
Yes	Husband's legal share is one-third of surplus personal estate if wife left descendants; otherwise, one-half thereof	Unless affirmative election to take dower is made, the same is presumed to have been waived in favor of share of lands under statute of descent. If husband renounces testamentary provision in his favor, or if no provision is made for him, he may take dower and legal share of personalty, or legal share of both real and personal property. Legal share of lands is one-third as heir if wife left descendants; otherwise, one-half as heir
Yes	See next column	Unless affirmative election to take dower is made, the same is presumed to have been waived in favor of share of lands under statute of descent. Husband may waive any provisions in wife's will for him, and claim his intestate share of real and personal property,[3] with certain exceptions[9]
No	Husband is distributee in case of intestacy[3]	Wife may convey, transfer, devise, or bequeath her real and personal property in the same manner and with like effect as if unmarried
Yes	One-third of surplus personal estate by inheritance free from any testamentary disposition to which husband has not consented in writing	

[§ 216

TABLE CV

Jurisdiction[1] and Citation	Share in Real Property			
	Curtesy Expressly Abolished	Same Share as Widow	Extent	Property Subject to;[2] Necessity of Issue
Mississippi .... C. 1930, Secs. 1404, 1942, 3560–63	Yes	Yes	See last column	See last column
Missouri .... R. S. 1929, Secs. 318, 319, 321–28, 340, 14057	Yes	No[12]	Husband is endowed of a third part to hold during life	All lands of which wife or any other to her use was seized of an estate of inheritance during marriage[12],[2]
Montana .... R. C. 1921, Secs. 5792, 5812, 6975	Yes	No	See last column	See last column
Nebraska .... Comp. St. 1929, Secs. 30(101), 30(103)–30(104), 30(107)	Yes	Yes	Husband shares under statute of descent[3] (see last column)	All real estate of which wife was seized of an estate of inheritance during marriage, or in which she was possessed of an equitable or legal interest at death, and which has not been sold under execution or judicial sale, or "lawfully devised," descends to husband, subject to debts and right of homestead
New Hampshire ... Pub. L. 1926, Ch. 306, Sec. 9; Secs. 12, 13, amd. by Sess. L. 1933, Ch. 118, p. 171	Expressly retained	No	Estate by the curtesy when he would be entitled to hold as tenant by the curtesy at common law[14]	All lands and tenements owned by wife[14]

§ 216]

(Continued)

Share in Personal Property

Same Share as Widow	Amount, etc.	Wife May Defeat Share by Will or Deed; Election between Will or Curtesy and Distributive Share (See Also **Sec. 219**)
Yes	See next column	If wife's will does not make "satisfactory" provision for husband, he may renounce the same, with certain limitations,[11] and elect to take his intestate share[3] in both real and personal property (but in no event is he entitled to more than one-half thereof). He is entitled to same share if will makes no provision for him
Yes	If wife leaves descendants, an absolute share in personal estate belonging to wife at death, equal to a child's share; if wife leaves no descendant in being capable of inheriting, one-half thereof absolutely, subject to payment of wife's debts	If wife leaves descendants and a child of the marriage is living,[13] husband may, in lieu of dower in lands of which wife died seized, elect to be endowed absolutely in a child's share of such lands, subject to payment of debts. If wife leaves no descendant capable of inheriting, husband may, in lieu of dower in lands, elect to take absolutely one-half of wife's lands belonging to her at death, subject to payment of debts
No	See next column	Wife may convey her separate property without consent of husband; but her will shall not, without his written consent, operate to deprive him of more than two-thirds of her real and personal estate
Yes	Husband shares in personal estate not "lawfully disposed of" by will, under statute of distribution (see next column)	If wife makes testamentary provision for husband, he may elect to take under the will, or "by inheritance, descent, and distribution, the interest in the estate of the deceased, provided by law"[3]
Yes	Husband of testate or intestate wife, by waiving testamentary provision in his favor, if any, is entitled in addition to curtesy and homestead rights to the following distributive share of wife's personal estate after payment of debts and expenses of administration: one-third if wife leaves issue; $5,000 of the value thereof and one-half of the remainder if wife leaves no issue and dies testate; $7,500 of the value and one-half the remainder if she leaves no issue and dies intestate	Husband of testate or intestate wife, by waiving testamentary provision in his favor, if any, and releasing his curtesy and homestead rights, is entitled instead thereof to the following portion of all the real estate of which wife died seized after payment of debts and expenses of administration: one-third in fee if she leaves issue by him surviving; one-third for life if she leaves issue but not by him and if he has no curtesy; $5,000 of the value thereof and one-half the remainder if she leaves no issue and dies testate; $7,500 of the value and one-half the remainder if she leaves no issue and dies intestate

[§ 216

TABLE CV

Share in Real Property

Jurisdiction[1] and Citation	Curtesy Expressly Abolished	Same Share as Widow	Extent	Property Subject to;[2] Necessity of Issue
New Jersey .... Comp. St. 1910, p. 3235, Sec. 9; Cum. Supp. 1911–24, Sec. 150(106); Supp. 1925–30, Secs. 63(34a[1]), 146(169)	....	Yes	Widower of wife dying testate or intestate is endowed for life of the one full and equal half part	All lands, tenements, and other real estate whereof the wife or any other to her use was seized of an estate of inheritance during coverture.[2] Issue need not be born
New York .... Cahill, Consol. L. 1930, Ch. 13, Secs. 18, 83, 98; Ch. 51, Sec. 189	Yes	Yes	See last column	See last column
North Carolina ..... Const., Art. X, Sec. 6; C. 1927, Secs. 137(8), 2511, 2519	....	No	Life estate as tenant by the curtesy after death of wife intestate	All the lands, tenements, and hereditaments whereof wife was beneficially seized in deed during coverture of legal or equitable estate. Issue capable of inheriting must be born alive
North Dakota ...... Comp. L. 1913, Sec. 4414, amd. by Supp. 1913–25, p. 928; Sec. 5641; Sec. 5743, amd. by Supp. 1913–25, p. 1143; Sec. 5744	Yes	....	Husband is heir in case of intestacy[3]	See preceding column
Ohio .... Complete G. C. 1931 (Page), Supp. 1932, Secs. 10502(1), 10502(8), 10504(55)	Yes	Yes	a) Life estate in one-third, called dower b) In lieu of such dower interest as terminates and is barred by wife's death (see next column), husband is entitled to distributive share provided by statute of descent and distribution[3]	a) All real property of which wife was seized of an estate of inheritance during marriage, but such dower interest terminates and is barred by death of wife, except to the extent that such property was conveyed by wife during marriage or encumbered by her by mortgage, judgment, lien (except tax lien) or otherwise,[16] the husband not having relinquished or been barred of dower therein
Oklahoma .... St. 1931, Secs. 1539, 1618, 1659	Yes	Yes	See last column	See last column

(*Continued*)

Share in Personal Property

Same Share as Widow	Amount, etc.	Wife May Defeat Share by Will or Deed; Election between Will or Curtesy and Distributive Share (See Also **Sec. 219**)
....	Husband is distributee in case of intestacy[2]	Wife may make a valid will as if single, but she cannot defeat the rights of surviving husband in her real property
Yes	See next column	If wife dies testate, husband has a personal right of election to take his intestate share of real and personal property,[3] subject to certain limitations and exceptions,[15] and in no event to exceed more than one-half of the net estate after deduction of debts, administration expenses and estate tax
No	Husband is distributee in case of intestacy[3]	Wife's real and personal estate may be devised and bequeathed by her as if single. Wife may convey her real estate with written assent of husband
....	Husband is distributee in case of intestacy[3]	Wife may dispose of all her separate estate by will without the consent of husband as if she were single
Yes	See next column	If wife dies testate, husband may elect to take under the statute of descent and distribution,[3] but in the event of such election he can take not to exceed one-half of the estate
Yes	See next column	Wife may not "bequeath" away from surviving husband so much of her estate that he would receive less in value than would be obtained through succession by law[3]

[§ 216

TABLE CV

Jurisdiction[1] and Citation	Curtesy Expressly Abolished	Same Share as Widow	Share in Real Property	
			Extent	Property Subject to;[2] Necessity of Issue
Oregon .... C. 1930, Secs. 5(203), 10(302), 10(306), 10(330), 10(501)–10(502)	Yes	Yes	The use during life of one-half part, as tenant by the curtesy	All lands of which wife was seized of an estate of inheritance during marriage.[2] There need not be issue born alive. So far as practicable, laws of state applicable to dower are applicable to curtesy
Pennsylvania ...... St. 1920 (West), Secs. 8335, 8342–44, 8353, 14570	Yes	Yes	Husband is entitled to his intestate share with modification (see last column)	Statutory share is in lieu and full satisfaction of curtesy at common law. Husband is entitled to same share in estate in remainder vested in interest in wife during her life as in property of which she dies seized, although particular estate does not terminate before her death
Rhode Island ...... G. L. 1923, Secs. 4200, 4302, 5553–54	....	No	See last column	See last column
South Carolina...... C. of L. 1922, C. C., Secs. 5327, 5539, 5542	Yes	No	Husband is heir in case of intestacy[3]	See preceding column
South Dakota....... Comp. L. 1929, Secs. 175, 605, 701–2	Yes	...	Husband is heir in case of intestacy[3]	See preceding column
Tennessee .... C. 1932, Secs. 7864, 8098, 8358–59, 8461	....	No	Nothing in the section removing the disabilities of coverture from married women "shall be construed as affecting the husband's right of curtesy consummate"	See preceding column[2]
Utah .... Const., Art. XXII, Sec. 2; R. S. 1933, 101-1-3, 101-4-5, 101-4-9	Yes	No	Husband is heir in case of intestacy[3]	See preceding column

§ 216]

(Continued)

Share in Personal Property

Same Share as Widow	Amount, etc.	Wife May Defeat Share by Will or Deed; Election between Will or Curtesy and Distributive Share (See Also Sec. 219)
....	Husband is distributee in case of intestacy[3]	Wife may dispose of her real and personal property by will subject to the husband's curtesy in her lands
Yes	See next column	If wife dies testate, husband may elect to take against her will, and to share in her real and personal estate as if she had died intestate,[3] except that, even if there is no issue, he is entitled to no more than one-half.[17] Wife cannot convey or mortgage her real property unless husband joins therein
....	Husband is distributee in case of intestacy[3]	Wife cannot defeat husband's curtesy by will. Right of husband as tenant by the curtesy is not impaired by married women's legislation, or by statute of descent
....	Husband is distributee in case of intestacy[3]	Wife has power to convey, devise, and bequeath her separate property to the same extent as if unmarried
....	Husband is distributee in case of intestacy[3]	Wife may dispose of all her separate estate (except homestead) by will without consent of husband
Yes	One-third part of wife's personal estate if she leaves not more than two children; a child's part thereof if she leaves more than two children	Husband may dissent from wife's will when a satisfactory provision in real or personal estate is not made for him; in which case, he is entitled to his curtesy, and his distributive share of personal property (as outlined in preceding column)
....	Husband is distributee in case of intestacy[3]	Wife may dispose of all of her separate property by will without consent of husband

[§ 216

TABLE CV

Share in Real Property

Jurisdiction[1] and Citation	Curtesy Expressly Abolished	Same Share as Widow	Extent	Property Subject to;[2] Necessity of Issue
Vermont .... G. L. 1917, Secs. 3278–79, 3414; Sec. 3416, amd. by Sess. L. 1929, No. 46, p. 62, Sec. 2	Yes	Yes	One-third in value in fee; but one-half in value in fee if wife left only one heir surviving and such heir is the issue of husband or the heir by adoption of both	Real estate of which a man and his wife are seized in her right in fee simple (at wife's death)
Virginia .... C. 1930, Secs. 4359(25), 5134, 5136, 5139a, 5158, 5276	....	Yes	Estate by the curtesy in one-third. Estate by the curtesy in residue, subject to wife's creditors, if wife dies wholly intestate and without issue. Estate by the curtesy in residue, subject to wife's creditors and devisees, if wife dies partially intestate and without issue	All the real estate whereof the wife or any other to her use was seized in fact or law of an estate of inheritance during coverture. Equitable estates of inheritance which if legal estates would support curtesy. It is not necessary that wife have a child born alive during coverture[2]
West Virginia...... C. 1931, Ch. 42, Art. 2, Sec. 1; Art. 3, Sec. 1; Ch. 43, Art. 1, Secs. 1–4, 18	Yes	Yes	Husband is endowed of one-third	All the real estate of which the wife or any other to her use or in trust for her was seized of or entitled to an estate of inheritance during coverture, either in possession, reversion, remainder, or otherwise[2]
Wisconsin .... St. 1931, Secs. 123.21, 233.23, 246.03	....	No	Life estate as tenant by the curtesy, but his right of curtesy is extinguished on his remarriage. If wife leaves issue by former husband, to whom estate might descend, such issue takes the same discharged of curtesy	The lands of which wife died seized and which were not disposed of by her will[2]
Wyoming .... R. S. 1931, Secs. 88(101), 88(4001)	Yes	Yes	See last column	See last column

[1] The eight community-property states are not included in the table above. See footnote 1 of
[2] Other legislation in respect to the real property subject to the husband's dower, curtesy, or
curtesy (Alaska, Illinois, Maryland, Massachusetts, New Jersey, Tennessee, Virginia, Wisconsin)
of the Uniform Partnership Act, see Table XCVI, Section 191, and footnote 1 (pp. 392–93) thereof.
during marriage (Illinois), or in lands sold but not conveyed before marriage (Kentucky), or in ceme-
curtesy is given in estates for 100 years or more so long as 50 years remain unexpired, but, if curtesy
given in wife's moiety of lands held in common (Kentucky, Missouri). Dower or curtesy is recognized
and in right of entry or action held by wife or another to her use if husband would have been entitled

§ 216]

(Continued)

Share in Personal Property

Same Share as Widow	Amount, etc.	Wife May Defeat Share by Will or Deed; Election between Will or Curtesy and Distributive Share (See Also **Sec. 219**)
Yes	Husband may waive provisions of wife's will and receive one-third of wife's personal estate, after payment of debts and administration expenses[18]	If wife leaves no issue and husband does not elect to take a third in value of real estate, or waives provision of wife's will, he is entitled to all of wife's estate if not over $4,000, or to $4,000 and half the remainder
Yes	If husband renounces provision for him in wife's will, or if no provision is made for him, he is entitled to one-third of her surplus personal estate if she leaves issue of this or a former marriage, and one-half thereof if she leaves no such issue	Wife cannot deprive husband of his curtesy by her sole act
Yes	See next column	If husband renounces provision for him in wife's will, or if no provision be made for him, he is entitled to such share in her real and personal estate as he would have taken had she died intestate leaving children[3] (dower, and one-third of surplus personalty)
No	Husband is distributee in case of intestacy[3]	Wife may devise real and personal property in the same manner and with like effect as if she were single
Yes	See next column	If wife's will deprives husband of more than one-half of her surplus estate, he may accept the conditions of her will or elect to take one-half of her real and personal estate; but if wife leaves issue of former marriage and no issue of last marriage, she may will to others than the husband not exceeding three-fourths of her property, after payment of debts

Table XCV, **Section 189** (p. 368), for citations to statutes in these states expressly abolishing curtesy. statutory share follows. A partner's right in specific partnership property is not subject to dower or or the widower's statutory interest (**Minnesota**). For other states which have adopted this provision There is no dower in lands conveyed to wife by way of mortgage unless she acquires an absolute estate tery lands (**Missouri**). Dower in leaseholds of 20 years or more is granted as in real estate (**Missouri**); is assigned therein, husband must pay one-third of rent to owner of term (**Massachusetts**). Dower is in real estate although no actual possession or recovery of possession by wife in lifetime (**Missouri**) to the same had possession been recovered (**Virginia, West Virginia**). The fact that husband conveyed

[§ 216

TABLE CV

or caused to be conveyed real estate to wife or to her use does not bar his curtesy therein (**Virginia**). could have been such seisin if real estate had not been committed (**Virginia**). In case of lands ex- in lands given in exchange within one year after death of wife, he is deemed to have elected to take mortgaged before marriage as against all but mortgagee and those claiming under him (**Illinois, Oregon**, husband did not join therein (**Delaware, Illinois, Maryland, Massachusetts, Minnesota, Oregon**, entitled to dower or curtesy share in surplus proceeds (**Illinois, Oregon**) or to such share thereof as in lifetime of wife for same purpose, husband is entitled to such share of surplus as represents present and disposed of by wife (**Kentucky**). If heir of wife or person claiming under her pays the mortgage was under contract to purchase, and part or all of consideration is paid out of assets of her estate, death, husband is endowed as against all but holders of purchase-money lien (**Missouri**).

³ The reader is directed to **Section 227** for the share of real and personal property which the
⁴ The **Connecticut** provisions above are applicable in the case of persons married on or after contract.
⁵ Curtesy prevails in **Delaware**. The foregoing provision, however, is found in the statute of curtesy.
⁶ In **Hawaii**, the Revised Laws of 1925, Section 2993, formerly provided that no sale or mortgage conflicting and ambiguous, apparently the wife may defeat the husband's curtesy by conveyance, but
⁷ The wife in **Iowa** cannot deprive the widower of his distributive share of personalty. See *Vos-* (p. 369).
⁸ See footnote 8 of Table XCV (p. 369).
⁹ In **Massachusetts**, the widower's share as outlined above is reduced in the case of large estates,
¹⁰ Common-law curtesy was abolished in **Minnesota** by the Session Laws of 1875, Chapter 40,
¹¹ In **Mississippi**, the extent to which the widower can upset the wife's will and claim his legal
¹² The Married Women's Act in **Missouri** is construed to permit the wife to defeat the husband's true in spite of the fact that the present dower act abolishes curtesy and gives the widower "the same
¹³ See footnote 13 of Table XCV (pp. 369–70).
¹⁴ The **New Hampshire** statute provides that "the husband of a person deceased, holding property her, when he would be entitled to hold as tenant by the curtesy at common law" (Pub. L. 1926, Ch.
¹⁵ The survivor's right of election in **New York** is subject to certain drastic limitations. See foot-
¹⁶ As to property held at death and so encumbered, see footnote 17 of Table XCV (p. 370).
¹⁷ The husband's right of election does not affect the power of the wife to devise or bequeath prop- appointment by deed or will (**Pennsylvania**, St. 1920 [West], Sec. 8335).
¹⁸ See also footnote 18 of Table XCV (p. 370) in respect to the survivor's share of personal estate

---

REFERENCES

Books

NORTHRUP, ELLIOT J. *Law of Real Property*, p. 336 (1919).

STIMSON, F. J. *American Statute Law*, Sec. 3301 (1886).

TIFFANY, HERBERT THORNDIKE. *Real Property and Other Interests in Land*, 2d ed., Vol. 1, Sec. 246 (1920).

WOERNER, J. G. *The American Law of Administration*, 3d ed., Vol. I, Sec. 121 (1923).

Articles

EAGLETON, WILLIAM L. "The Illinois Dower Act as Applied to Estates Consisting of Personal Property," 26 Ill. L. Rev. 164–67 (1931).

FOX, SAMUEL. "The Illinois Dower Act," 26 Ill. L. Rev. 145–64 (1931).

SAYRE, PAUL L. "Husband and Wife as Statutory Heirs," 42 Harv. L. Rev. 330–64 (1929).

§ 216]

(Concluded)

Seisin requisite for curtesy in minor wife's real estate committed to a receiver is presumed if there
changed by wife, widower must elect; if he does not commence proceedings to recover dower or curtesy
the same in the lands received in exchange (**Illinois, Oregon**). Dower or curtesy is given in lands
West Virginia); dower or curtesy is subordinate to purchase-money mortgage or lien even though
West Virginia). If lands are sold after wife's death to satisfy foregoing encumbrances, widower is
represents present value of dower right in the whole of the land (**West Virginia**); if sold bona fide
value of inchoate right in the whole of the land (**West Virginia**) or dower in surplus unless received
debt, the same is deducted from value of land and husband has curtesy in residue (**Oregon**). If wife
husband is endowed as though she were seized during coverture; if the lands are sold after wife's

widower takes under the statutes of descent and distribution.
April 22, 1877, or persons married before who have relinquished rights under the old law by written

descent, which provides that intestate realty descends subject to the widower's rights as tenant by the

of the wife's lands should be valid without the written consent of the husband. While the statutes are
not by will.
burg v. *Mallory,* 155 Ia. 165; 135 N. W. 577 (1912), and footnote 7 of Table XCV, **Section 189**

and when the wife leaves no kindred. See footnote 9 of Table XCV (p. 369).
Section 5.
share depends upon the amount of his separate property. See footnote 11 of Table XCV (p. 369).
inchoate dower by her sole deed (*Scott* v. *Scott,* 324 Mo. 1055; 26 S. W. [2d] 598 [1930]). This is
share" in the wife's lands as she has in his lands.

in her own right, shall be entitled to his estate by the curtesy in all lands and tenements owned by
306, Sec. 9).
note 16 of Table XCV (p. 370).

erty held in trust for her sole and separate use, which power she has by virtue of any authority or

in **Vermont**.

Annotation

"Extent and Effect of Exception in Married Women's Acts as to Husband's Right
by the Curtesy," 29 A. L. R. 1338–43 (1924).

Section 217. Curtesy—Extent

CROSS REFERENCES: Extent of dower and statutory share, **Sec. 190**; Curtesy, abolition and statutory substitutes, **Sec. 216**; Real property subject to curtesy or
statutory share, **Sec. 218**; Widower's share of real and personal property when
wife dies intestate, **Sec. 227**; Homestead, exempt property, etc., **Sec. 228**

As in the case of legislation fixing the size of the widow's share in
the deceased husband's property (**Sec. 190**), there is little uniformity

[§ 217

among the various jurisdictions as to what portion of the wife's estate should go to the surviving husband. Eleven jurisdictions impose no limitation upon the wife's testamentary control of her property (aside from exempt property, etc.). Going to the other extreme are several states which permit the husband to upset her will and claim a flat one-half of her estate. One of the fundamental differences between curtesy and dower at common law lies in the fact that, while the widower was entitled to a life estate in all of the wife's lands, dower extended to one-third part only of the husband's lands. Exclusive of those jurisdictions which have abolished common-law curtesy and established no substitute, the statutes evidence a very definite tendency to treat widow and widower alike (**Sec. 216**). One of the consequences of this tendency in some states has been to reduce the surviving husband's portion, but in most the net result has been in the opposite direction.

Of those jurisdictions which give the surviving husband a life estate in the wife's lands, the curtesy measure is retained in five, his share is reduced to dower proportions in ten, and in two he is entitled to a life estate in one-half. **Connecticut** is the only state which allows him a statutory share of personalty but limits him to a life use thereof. In twenty-six jurisdictions, the widower is entitled to an absolute share of personalty, and in twenty jurisdictions to an absolute share of real property as a substitute for curtesy or which he may take in lieu of his life estate. The size of this statutory share is variously fixed at one-third (realty, four; personalty, seven); at one-half (realty, three; personalty, four); or depends upon the existence, absence, or number of lineal descendants (realty, five; personalty, six); or is his intestate share, generally subject to a set maximum (realty, eight; personalty, nine). Since in most of these jurisdictions the surviving husband's share is identical with that of the widow, the same general remarks made in **Section 190** might be repeated here. Special mention was there made of the statutes in three jurisdictions whereby the extent to which the survivor can upset the deceased consort's will also depends upon the size of the survivor's separate estate (**Mississippi**), the size of decedent's estate (**Massachusetts**), and the benefits given to the survivor by the will (**New York**). The writer believes that these considerations should be of influence in fixing the size of the survivor's estate.

Many of the statutes do not explicitly state whether the husband's curtesy, dower, or statutory share comes to him free from the demands of the wife's creditors. The matter was relatively unimportant at common law because of the wife's general disability to contract obligations

§ 217]

during coverture. It is extremely important today not only because of the wife's capacity to incur debts, but also because of the enlarged estate which the surviving husband has in many jurisdictions. The husband of course has no interest in the wife's personal property which may not be defeated by execution against her during her lifetime; and the same is true of her real property in those states in which he shares in lands of which she dies seized or owning only. In the few jurisdictions which retain curtesy consummate substantially as at common law, on analogy to dower the husband's contingent estate probably cannot be defeated by the wife's creditors either during coverture or after her death. The same is true in most of the other jurisdictions in which he has an estate similar to inchoate dower during marriage. A few statutes which raise his interest to one in fee are, however, express to the contrary (see also **Sec. 220**). The husband's statutory share of personalty is universally subject to estate creditors. The distributive share of real property owned by the wife at death which he takes as a substitute for curtesy, or which he may take in lieu of his life estate as tenant by the curtesy or in dower, is likewise expressly or by clear implication subject to estate creditors in most jurisdictions. **Maine,** however, expressly provides that his one-third of the wife's lands goes to him free from the payment of her debts. **Indiana** has a ridiculous statute strangely out of harmony with modern concepts. It provides that the widower's one-third of the wife's real property descends to him "subject, however, to its proportion of the debts of the wife contracted before marriage." This provision has been construed to mean that his share is subject to her antenuptial debts only (*Kemph* v. *Belknap,* 15 Ind. App. 77; 43 N. E. 891 [1895]). Occasionally other courts have erred in interpreting modern statutes in the light of conditions long since removed. There is little justification in enlarging the survivor's share if it is done at the expense of deserving creditors.

The statutory material discussed in this section is collected in Table CV at the end of **Section 216.**

REFERENCES

Books

STIMSON, F. J. *American Statute Law,* Sec. 3301 (1886).
TIFFANY, HERBERT THORNDIKE. *Real Property and Other Interests in Land,* 2d ed., Vol. 1, Secs. 238–42 (1920).

Section 218. Curtesy—Real Property Subject to

CROSS REFERENCES: Real property subject to widow's dower, **Sec. 191**; Curtesy, abolition and statutory substitutes, **Sec. 216**; Extent of curtesy, **Sec. 217**; Barring curtesy, **Sec. 220**

The common law gave the husband curtesy in all the lands and tenements of which the wife is seized during coverture in fee simple or fee tail, provided there was issue born alive capable of inheriting the same. Contrary to the law of dower, the English courts required seisin in deed as distinguished from seisin in law. The American courts, however, have generally held seisin in law to be sufficient. Also contrary to the law of dower, the English courts at an early date allowed curtesy in equitable estates if other requisites were present. The American courts have generally allowed both dower and curtesy in such estates.

We have seen that little remains of technical common-law curtesy (**Sec. 216**). In nine jurisdictions which have expressly or impliedly abolished curtesy (**Alabama, Arkansas, Florida, Georgia, Michigan, North Dakota, South Carolina, South Dakota, Utah**), no analogous substitute is created, and the husband is a mere heir. In nine others (**Colorado, Connecticut, Indiana, Mississippi, Montana, New York, Oklahoma, Pennsylvania, Wyoming**), the surviving husband is in the position of a forced heir, and shares in all property (usually after payment of debts) which the wife dies owning. The subject of this section is obviously not significant in the jurisdictions above. Of the five states retaining curtesy substantially as at common law (**Alaska, Delaware, New Hampshire, Rhode Island, Tennessee**), three (**Delaware, Rhode Island, Tennessee**) do not even in a general way define the property subject to curtesy. Strangely, **North Carolina** (where curtesy may be defeated by will) requires seisin in deed. In most of the other jurisdictions which secure to the surviving husband a share of the wife's lands, the same or identical statutes govern the rights of both spouses. A detailed classification of the legislation defining the real property to which the husband's interest attaches would involve a repetition of much of what was said in **Section 191**. Citations to the statutes pertinent to the subject of this section are given below. The statutes themselves are outlined in the fourth column and footnote 2 of Table CV, **Section 216** (pp. 538–53), to which reference is made.

Alaska, Comp. L. 1913, Sec. 482, amd. by Sess. L. 1923, Ch. 40, p. 51; Sess. L. 1917, Ch. 69, p. 169; **Delaware,** R. C. 1915, Sec. 3052, amd. by Sess. L. 1919, Ch. 197, p. 526; **District of Columbia,** C. 1929, T. 14, Sec. 42; **Hawaii,** R. L. 1925,

Sec. 3000; **Illinois**, Cahill, R. S. 1931, Ch. 41, Secs. 1, 3–6, 17; Ch. 106*a*, Sec. 25; **Iowa**, C. 1927, Sec. 11990; **Kansas**, R. S. 1923, Secs. 22(108), 22(127); **Kentucky**, Carroll, St. 1922, Secs. 2132, 2134–35, 2142–43, 2148; **Maine**, R. S. 1930, Ch. 89, Sec. 1; **Maryland**, Bagby, Ann. C. 1924, Art. 45, Sec. 7; Art. 73*A*, Sec. 25(*e*); **Massachusetts**, G. L. 1932, Ch. 108*A*, Sec. 25(*e*); Ch. 186, Secs. 1, 2; Ch. 189, Secs. 1, 2; **Minnesota**, G. S. 1923, Secs. 7408, 8198, 8720; **Missouri**, R. S. 1929, Secs. 318–19, 321–22, 340, 14057; **Nebraska**, Comp. St. 1929, Sec. 30(101); **New Hampshire**, Pub. L. 1926, Ch. 306, Sec. 9; **New Jersey**, Comp. St. 1910, Cum. Supp. 1911–24, Sec. 150(106); Supp. 1925–30, Sec. 63(34*a*[1]); **North Carolina**, C. 1927, Sec. 2519; **Ohio**, Complete G. C. 1931 (Page), Supp. 1932, Sec. 10502(1); **Oregon**, C. 1930, Secs. 10(301)–10(306), 10(330); **Rhode Island**, G. L. 1923, Secs. 4200, 4302, 5553; **Tennessee**, C. 1932, Secs. 8460–61; **Vermont**, G. L. 1917, Sec. 3414; **Virginia**, C. 1930, Secs. 4359(25), 5136, 5139*a*, 5158; **West Virginia**, C. 1931, Ch. 43, Art. 1, Secs. 1–4; **Wisconsin**, St. 1931, Sec. 233.23.

REFERENCES

Books

STIMSON, F. J. *American Statute Law,* Sec. 3302 (1886).
TIFFANY, HERBERT THORNDIKE. *Real Property and Other Interests in Land,* 2d ed., Vol. 1, Secs. 241–42 (1920).

Annotations

"Curtesy in Equity of Redemption," 20 L. R. A. (N.S.) 454 (1909).
"Estate by the Curtesy in Land Settled on or Conveyed to Wife by Husband," 30 A. L. R. 1057–65 (1924).
"Right of Curtesy in Determinable Fee," 20 L. R. A. (N.S.) 858 (1909).

Section 219. Curtesy—Election

CROSS REFERENCES: Barring widow's dower, etc., by will, **Sec. 199**; Election of widow between will and dower or statutory share, **Secs. 205–7**; Curtesy, abolition and statutory substitutes, **Sec. 216**; Election between dower or curtesy and jointure, **Secs. 196, 220**; Election in case of lands exchanged, **Secs. 191, 218**; Election between curtesy, etc., and share as heir, **Sec. 227**; Election between homestead, etc., and will, **Sec. 228**

The wife now has testamentary capacity in all jurisdictions (**Sec. 181**). Aside from homestead, exempt property, etc., her testamentary power over her real property is complete in twelve jurisdictions, and over her personal property in sixteen jurisdictions (**Sec. 216**). A few jurisdictions give the surviving husband what is called an estate by the curtesy but the wife may defeat it by her will (**District of Columbia, North Carolina, Wisconsin**). In others, curtesy is abolished and he is reduced to the position of a mere heir who shares in case of intestacy only. In thirty-one jurisdictions, however, he has some interest in the wife's real property by way of curtesy, dower, or statutory share to which he is entitled notwithstanding the contrary provisions of her will if he pursues his rights as the statutes direct; and in twenty-seven jurisdictions, he likewise shares in her personal property (**Sec. 216**).

While the wife cannot deprive the husband of his curtesy, etc., by her will, he is put to an election if she makes provision for him in her will which is intended to be in lieu of his rights under the law. And in a majority of jurisdictions by statute, a devise or bequest to the surviving husband is deemed to be in lieu of his curtesy, dower, or statutory share unless a contrary intention appears or is expressed in her will. Legislation of that tenor was found in eighteen jurisdictions (**Connecticut, Hawaii, Illinois, Indiana, Iowa, Kansas, Maine, Maryland, Massachusetts, Minnesota, Mississippi, Missouri, Nebraska, New Hampshire, Ohio, Oregon, Vermont, West Virginia**). These statutes vary in terminology, effect, and scope. They are discussed in **Section 199**, where an outline of them together with others which govern only the widow, and citations for the same, may be found. That the surviving husband must elect between his rights under the will and under the law whenever provision is made for him and the will does not contain a contrary direction seems clear in several other jurisdictions by virtue of the statutes establishing his rights as survivor and enabling him to dissent from the wife's will (**Colorado, Montana, New York, Oklahoma, Pennsylvania, Tennessee, Wyoming**). (See statutory résumé, **Sec. 199**, and Table CV, **Sec. 216**.) In **Alaska, Delaware, Kentucky, New Jersey, Rhode Island**, and **Virginia**, the widower has an estate in lands substantially like or patterned after common-law curtesy or dower; but no legislation was found determining the effect of a devise or bequest to him when the will does not reveal the wife's intention. By analogy to the common law of dower, the presumption would be that the testamentary provision is in addition to his curtesy or dower, and no occasion for an election would arise (*Voss* v. *Stortz,* 177 Ky. 541; 197 S. W. 964 [1917]). There seem to be very few decisions which have considered the matter.

The surviving husband's election between the provisions made for him in the wife's will and his rights under the law is governed in most jurisdictions by rather detailed legislation which supplants the case law

§ 219]

on the subject. The contrary is true in six jurisdictions in which no statutory material on the problem was discovered (**Alaska, Delaware, Montana, New Jersey, Oklahoma, Rhode Island**). In the following twenty-three jurisdictions, however, the same statutes control the widower's election as control the widow's election: **Colorado, Connecticut, Hawaii, Illinois, Indiana, Iowa, Kansas, Maine, Maryland, Massachusetts, Minnesota, Mississippi, Missouri, Nebraska, New Hampshire, New York, Ohio, Oregon, Pennsylvania, Tennessee, Vermont, West Virginia, Wyoming**. The same is also true of his renunciation of benefits under the wife's will in favor of his statutory share of personalty (**Virginia**) and his election between dower or curtesy and a share of lands in fee (**Illinois, Maryland, Massachusetts, Missouri, New Hampshire**). These statutes and the citations therefor are outlined in Table XCIX, **Section 205,** to which reference is here made.[1] They should be read in connection with the legislation collected in **Section 199,** referred to above, and that collected in Table CV, **Section 216.** In addition to the jurisdictions above, fragmentary provisions are found in two others (**District of Columbia, Kentucky**), which are outlined below. A discussion of the legislation governing the surviving husband's election would be in the main but a repetition of what was said in **Sections 205–7** in respect to the widow's election. It is sufficient to say here that the prevailing rule under the statutes is that, if the surviving husband fails to exercise his right of election within the time fixed and in the manner prescribed, he is conclusively presumed to have accepted the benefits accruing to him under the wife's will and to have waived his claim to curtesy, dower, or statutory share.

The **District of Columbia** and **Kentucky** provisions, to which reference has been made above, are as follows:

District of Columbia (C. 1929, T. 14, Sec. 38): The surviving husband is entitled to his intestate share of personalty if the wife's will makes no provision for him, or if he renounces the benefits thereunder within six months after administration is granted on the wife's estate.

Kentucky (Carroll, St. 1922, Secs. 2136, 2148): A devise of real or personal property by way of jointure (i.e., intended in lieu of rights under the law) may bar the husband's interest in wife's estate, but he may waive the same within twelve months after her death by written

[1] For the purpose of this section, the following citations are added to those given in Table XCIX, **Section 205: Hawaii,** R. L. 1925, Sec. 3000, as amended by Sess. L. 1933, Act 68, p. 65; **Kansas,** R. S. 1923, Sec. 22(127); **Maryland,** Bagby, Ann. C. 1924, Art. 93, Sec. 326; **Missouri,** R. S. 1929, Sec. 319; **New Hampshire,** Pub. L. 1926, Ch. 306, Secs. 12, 13; **Oregon,** C. 1930, Sec. 10(330); **Tennessee,** C. 1932, Sec. 8359; **Vermont,** G. L. 1917, Sec. 3415.

[§ 219

relinquishment, acknowledged or proved before and left with the clerk of the county court, and take his statutory interest.

REFERENCES
Books

STIMSON, F. J. *American Statute Law,* Secs. 3303, 3305–6 (1886).
TIFFANY, HERBERT THORNDIKE. *Real Property and Other Interests in Land,* 2d ed., Vol. 1, Sec. 243 (1920).

Article

SAYRE, PAUL L. "Husband and Wife as Statutory Heirs," 42 Harv. L. Rev. 330–64 (1924).

Section 220. Curtesy—Methods of Barring

CROSS REFERENCES: Contracts between spouses before marriage, **Sec. 155;** Contracts between spouses after marriage, **Secs. 156, 182;** Barring the widow's dower or statutory share by contract, jointure, will, deed, etc., **Secs. 195–201;** Real property subject to curtesy or statutory share, **Sec. 218;** Executor's sales and partition sales after death of spouse, **Secs. 214, 223;** Election between will and curtesy or statutory share, **Sec. 219;** Barring curtesy of insane husband, **Sec. 311**

    I. Bar by contract, settlement, or jointure
   II. Bar by deed during marriage
 III. Bar by wife's will
 IV. Bar by appropriation for wife's debts during marriage
   V. Miscellaneous

I. BAR BY CONTRACT, SETTLEMENT, OR JOINTURE

Antenuptial agreements whereby parties intending marriage may effectively determine the rights which each is to have in the property of the other, and bar the rights of either as survivor, are now generally recognized in both law and equity. As a matter of public policy, such contracts should be encouraged. There is, however, little direct legislative sanction in the matter (**Sec. 155**). Statutes were found in six jurisdictions under which the husband by agreement before marriage may waive his statutory right of election to take against the wife's will (**New York**); release his curtesy or other rights which he acquired by marriage in the wife's property (**North Carolina**); determine what rights he

§ 220]

shall have in the property of the wife during marriage and after its dissolution by death (**Delaware, Maine**) ; and bar his statutory share of real and personal property (**Connecticut**), or his statutory share of lands (**Nebraska**). The husband may likewise effectively bar his curtesy or other rights as survivor by contract with the wife during marriage, unless contracts between spouses generally or that particular kind of agreement are not tolerated in the particular jurisdiction. By express statute in a number of jurisdictions, husband and wife may freely contract inter se (**Secs. 156, 182**) ; and in a majority of the others, the same is probably true by reason of the complete contractual capacity of the wife (**Sec. 152**) and the independent status as to property enjoyed by both spouses. Little legislation was found, however, expressly permitting a release of curtesy, etc., by postnuptial agreement. By statute in four jurisdictions, the husband may bar his statutory share of real and personal property (**Connecticut**), release his curtesy or other rights in the wife's property (**North Carolina**), waive his statutory right of election to take against the wife's will (**New York**), or consent in writing that the wife may dispose of more than one-half of her property by will (**Kansas**). The statutes of a few jurisdictions forbid contracts generally between husband and wife (**Sec. 156**) ; and three jurisdictions expressly forbid the particular kind of contract we are here concerned with. **Minnesota** provides that contracts between spouses relative to the real estate of either or any interest therein are invalid ; and in **Iowa** and **Oregon**, when property is owned by either spouse, the other has no interest therein which can be made the subject of a contract between them. It is difficult to justify legislation of that character.

The jointure statutes, offering a means whereby the widow's dower, etc., may be barred, are collected in Table XCVII, **Section 196.** In the following nine states, these same statutes may be used to bar the corresponding interest of the husband in the wife's property : **Illinois, Kentucky, Maryland, Massachusetts, Missouri, New Hampshire, Ohio, Oregon, West Virginia.** In addition, an **Indiana** statute provides that the husband's statutory share of lands may be barred by an antenuptial conveyance of lands or other property to him or to both spouses, if his assent is endorsed upon or attached to the conveyance. The jointure statutes are discussed in **Section 196.** They are fragmentary and antiquated in character and are probably seldom utilized. They are not generally regarded as exclusive in nature and hence do not preclude the release of curtesy, etc., by ordinary contract supported by a different consideration. The writer believes that there is a need for express legis-

[§ 220

lation recognizing the capacity of the spouses to fix the rights of each as survivor by contract before or during marriage, subject only to the ordinary limitations controlling parties standing in a confidential relationship.

II. Bar by Deed during Marriage

The husband has no interest in the wife's personal property which may not be defeated by a transfer made in good faith before or during the marriage. Likewise, the wife's conveyance before marriage defeats his prospective curtesy or other interest in the lands conveyed, unless made in fraud of his rights as survivor. In this connection, **Tennessee** provides that a conveyance fraudulently made with intent to defeat the husband's rights is voidable at his instance. Under the early law in this country, marriage incapacitated the wife to convey her lands without the husband's concurrence (**Sec. 183**). His joinder in her deed had a double effect. It operated to release his curtesy and also gave legal sanction to the wife's transfer of the fee. In most jurisdictions today, the wife has capacity to convey her lands as if sole, subject to any contingent interest which the husband may have therein (**Sec. 183**). In thirteen of the thirty-one jurisdictions which give the surviving husband curtesy, dower, or statutory share of lands protected from the wife's will, he shares in property of which she dies seized or owning only (**Sec. 216**) ; but in two of these (**Indiana, Pennsylvania**) his expectancy is preserved by reason of the wife's incomplete capacity to convey without his joinder. In the other eighteen jurisdictions, the husband has a contingent interest in the wife's lands generally, which she cannot defeat by her sole conveyance (**Sec. 216**). Of these, however, his interest in equitable estates is occasionally confined to such as the wife owns at death (**Sec. 216**). Also, the wife may occasionally convey full title by her sole deed when the husband has deserted or abandoned her (**Sec. 143**), when the husband has been judicially declared dead after seven years' absence (**New Jersey**), or when the husband is a non-resident. Legislation of this latter type, varying in breadth, was found in **Iowa, Kansas, Nebraska,** and **Oregon.** These statutes are the same as those governing the widow's share, outlined in the last column of Table XCVIII, **Section 200,** to which reference is here made.

In the eighteen jurisdictions in which the husband has a protected interest in the wife's lands during coverture, it is a matter of common practice for him to release the same by joining in the wife's conveyance. Probably in all jurisdictions he may accomplish the same result by his

§ 220]

separate release or quitclaim deed to the wife's grantee or successor in interest. Legislation on the subject was found in twelve jurisdictions, as follows: The wife's deed does not bar the husband's curtesy, etc., unless he joins therein or otherwise properly expresses his assent thereto (**Illinois, Maine, Maryland, Massachusetts, West Virginia**). The husband, though an infant (**Maine, Maryland, New Hampshire, Virginia**), may release his contingent interest by joining in the wife's conveyance (**Iowa, Kentucky, Maine, Maryland, Massachusetts, Minnesota, Nebraska, New Hampshire, Oregon, Virginia, West Virginia**), or by joining in a deed with the wife's guardian (**Maine, Oregon, West Virginia**), or by his separate release (**Kentucky, Maine, Maryland, Massachusetts, Minnesota, New Jersey, Oregon, Virginia, West Virginia**), subsequent to the wife's conveyance (**Massachusetts, Minnesota, Oregon, Virginia, West Virginia**). In **Kentucky,** if the spouses convey by separate instruments, the husband must apparently first convey for the wife's deed to be effective. The husband may of course bind himself to release his curtesy, etc., by joining in the wife's contract to convey or by his separate contract with the wife's promisee. Legislation to this effect was found in **Virginia** and **West Virginia. Massachusetts** provides that a deed signed by the husband of the grantor releases his curtesy unless the right is expressly reserved. In **Iowa,** a husband joining in the wife's conveyance is not bound by the covenants therein unless expressly so stated in the deed; and if he afterward acquires an interest in the property conveyed, such after-acquired interest does not inure to the benefit of the grantee. While the statutes above are primarily concerned with the wife's conveyances, the same principles control in the case of her mortgages. If the husband joins in her mortgage or otherwise releases his contingent interest to her mortgagee, his position thereafter is the same as that of the wife who has joined in his mortgage (**Sec. 200**). The matter has received little legislative attention. The statutes of **Kentucky, Massachusetts, Oregon,** and **West Virginia,** outlined in Table XCVIII, **Section 200** (and particularly in footnote 1 thereof [p. 434]), control the effect of the husband's joinder in the wife's mortgage, as well as the converse situation.

III. BAR BY WIFE'S WILL

The power of the wife to bar the husband's curtesy, dower, or statutory share by her will is discussed in **Section 219** in connection with his election between her will and his rights under the law.

[§ 220

IV. Bar by Appropriation for Wife's Debts during Marriage

The surviving husband's statutory share of personal property may be defeated in all jurisdictions by execution against the wife during the marriage, and in many jurisdictions the same is true of his interest in real property by reason of the fact that he shares in lands of which the wife dies seized or owning only (**Sec. 216**). But in those jurisdictions in which the husband has a contingent estate in the wife's real property, similar to inchoate dower, his interest cannot ordinarily be defeated by the wife's creditors. Thus, if her lands are sold on execution to satisfy a lien subordinate to his curtesy or statutory interest (i.e., unless the lien was created before marriage, or for purchase money, etc.), the purchaser takes subject to his estate as survivor. The statutes of **Maine** and **Massachusetts** are express to that effect. As a practical matter, the court should be empowered to order the lands sold free of the husband's contingent interest, protecting him in the proceeds. Legislation of this nature was found, however, in only two jurisdictions. In **West Virginia**, the purchaser takes free of the husband's dower if the husband is made a party, but he is entitled to such part of the proceeds as represents the present value of his inchoate right. Under a **Maine** statute, an assignee for benefit of creditors, a trustee in bankruptcy, or any person holding title by levy or sale on execution may bring an action to have the husband's statutory interest divested with compensation. A few jurisdictions, particularly those which have raised the husband's interest to a share in fee, go farther and allow the wife's lands to be appropriated for the payment of her debts free and clear of his contingent interest. Thus, his curtesy is barred by sale on execution if he is a party (**Delaware**) ; and he is not entitled to a statutory share of lands sold on execution or "judicial" sale (**Iowa, Kansas, Minnesota, Nebraska**), or appropriated by general assignment for benefit of creditors or by insolvency or bankruptcy proceedings (**Minnesota**). In this general connection, **Illinois** provides that a mechanic's lien is superior to the husband's dower, if he has knowledge of the improvements and does not give written notice of his objection before the same are made.

V. Miscellaneous

Similar to inchoate dower, the husband's contingent interest in the wife's lands held by her in common is subordinate to the paramount right of a co-tenant to compel partition, and may be defeated by sale under partition proceedings during the marriage. In the absence of

§ 220]

statute, he is probably not a necessary party to the action and is not entitled to share in the proceeds. Judicial partition is regulated in detail by legislation in most jurisdictions. Only those statutes which refer in express terms to the barring of the husband's curtesy or statutory interest are collected here. Five states are express to the effect that his contingent estate is barred by partition sale (**Delaware, Maryland, Minnesota, Virginia, West Virginia**), if he is a party to the action (**Delaware, West Virginia**), or regardless of whether he is a party (**Virginia**). He is entitled to be protected in the proceeds, either by way of immediate compensation or by investment of the proceeds (**Delaware, Iowa, Nebraska, Oregon, West Virginia**) unless his share be less than $1,000, or unless he has abandoned the wife (**Iowa**). That he has an interest in the proceeds is probably true in most jurisdictions by reason of provisions in the partition statutes protecting contingent interests generally.

The common law did not recognize the right of a person to defeat the husband's curtesy by inserting in the conveyance to the wife a provision excluding the same. Occasionally, a court of equity has reached a contrary result. The **Virginia** statute is express to the effect that the husband is not entitled to curtesy in the wife's equitable separate estate if his right thereto is expressly excluded by the instrument creating the same.

Very desirable legislation is found in **Maine** and **West Virginia** under which the husband's dower or statutory interest may be barred with compensation when the wife is under a contract to sell and he refuses to release the same. These statutes are the subject of comment in **Section 201.**

It remains to add that several statutes contain general statements of common-law dower principles to the effect that no judgment or decree confessed or recovered against the wife, no laches, default, covin or crime (**Illinois, Missouri**), or recovery by default or collusion (**Kentucky, Ohio, West Virginia**), shall prejudice the surviving husband's estate.

Citations for the statutory material discussed in this section follow:

I. *Bar by contract, settlement, or jointure:* **Connecticut,** G. S. 1930, Sec. 5156; **Delaware,** R. C. 1915, Sec. 3050, as amended by Sess. L. 1919, Ch. 197, p. 525; **Illinois,** Cahill, R. S. 1931, Ch. 41, Secs. 7–9, 11, 13; **Indiana,** Burns, Ann. St. 1926, Sec. 3366; **Iowa,** C. 1927, Sec. 10447; **Kansas,** R. S. 1923, Sec. 22(238); **Kentucky,** Carroll, St. 1922, Secs. 2136, 2148; **Maryland,** Bagby, Ann. C. 1924, Art. 45, Sec. 7; Art. 93, Secs. 315, 326; **Massachusetts,** G. L. 1932, Ch. 189, Secs. 1, 7–9; **Minnesota,** G. S. 1923, Sec. 8621; **Missouri,** R. S. 1929, Secs. 319, 334–35;

[§ 220

Nebraska, Comp. St. 1929, Sec. 30(106) ; **New Hampshire,** Pub. L. 1926, Ch. 306, Secs. 15, 16; **New York,** Cahill, Consol. L. 1930, Ch. 13, Sec. 18(9) ; **North Carolina,** C. 1927, Sec. 2516; **Ohio,** Complete G. C. 1931 (Page), Supp. 1932, Sec. 10502(2) ; **Oregon,** C. 1930, Secs. 10(314)–10(317), 10(319), 10(330), 33(201) ; **West Virginia,** C. 1931, Ch. 43, Art. 1, Secs. 7, 8.

II. *Bar by deed, etc.:* **Illinois,** Cahill, R. S. 1931, Ch. 41, Sec. 16; **Iowa,** C. 1927, Secs. 10043, 10051–52, 11993; **Kansas,** R. S. 1923, Secs. 22(108), 22(127) ; **Kentucky,** Carroll, St. 1922, Secs. 506, 2135; **Maine,** R. S. 1930, Ch. 74, Sec. 1; Ch. 89, Sec. 9; **Maryland,** Bagby, Ann. C. 1924, Art. 45, Secs. 7, 12; Art. 46, Sec. 3; **Massachusetts,** G. L. 1932, Ch. 189, Secs. 1, 1*a*, 4, 5; **Minnesota,** G. S. 1923, Sec. 8196; **Nebraska,** Comp. St. 1929, Sec. 30(105) ; **New Hampshire,** Pub. L. 1926, Ch. 288, Sec. 4; **New Jersey,** Comp. St., Supp. 1925–30, Secs. 55(66*a*), 124(3*a*), 124(8*w*[1]) ; **Oregon,** C. 1930, Secs. 10(305)–10(306), 10(313), 10(321), 10(330) ; **Tennessee,** C. 1932, Secs. 8365–66; **Virginia,** C. 1930, Secs. 5135, 5338*a*; **West Virginia,** C. 1931, Ch. 37, Art. 1, Sec. 8; Ch. 43, Art. 1, Secs. 3, 4; Ch. 48, Art. 3, Secs. 3–5.

III. *Bar by wife's will:* See **Section 219.**

IV. *Bar by appropriation for wife's debts:* **Delaware,** R. C. 1915, Secs. 4320, 4373, as amended by Sess. L. 1929, Ch. 269, p. 793; **Illinois,** R. S. 1931, Ch. 82, Sec. 1; **Iowa,** C. 1927, Sec. 11990; **Kansas,** R. S. 1923, Sec. 22(108) ; **Maine,** R. S. 1930, Ch. 89, Secs. 9, 19; **Massachusetts,** G. L. 1932, Ch. 236, Sec. 55; **Minnesota,** G. S. 1923, Sec. 8720; **Nebraska,** Comp. St. 1929, Secs. 30(101), 30(105) ; **West Virginia,** C. 1931, Ch. 43, Art. 1, Sec. 5.

V. *Miscellaneous:* **Delaware,** R. C. 1915, Sec. 3286; **Illinois,** Cahill, R. S. 1931, Ch. 41, Sec. 6; **Iowa,** C. 1927, Sec. 12347; **Kentucky,** Carroll, St. 1922, Secs. 2140, 2148; **Maine,** R. S. 1930, Ch. 89, Sec. 19; **Maryland,** Bagby, Ann. C. 1924, Art. 16, Sec. 46; Art. 45, Sec. 7; **Minnesota,** G. S. 1923, Secs. 8720, 9550; **Missouri,** R. S. 1929, Secs. 319, 330; **Nebraska,** Comp. St. 1929, Sec. 20(2198) ; **Ohio,** Complete G. C. 1931 (Page), Supp. 1932, Sec. 10502(6) ; **Oregon,** C. 1930, Sec. 6(628) ; **Virginia,** C. 1930, Secs. 5139*a*, 5281; **West Virginia,** C. 1931, Ch. 43, Art. 1, Secs. 5, 6, 16.

REFERENCES

Books

STIMSON, F. J. *American Statute Law,* Sec. 3304 (1886).

TIFFANY, HERBERT THORNDIKE. *Real Property and Other Interests in Land,* 2d ed., Vol. 1, Sec. 243 (1920).

Note

"Real Property—Protection of Inchoate Right of Curtesy after a Partition Sale," 26 Col. L. Rev. 1037–38 (1926).

Annotations

"Separation Agreements as Affecting Right of Inheritance," 35 A. L. R. 1526 (1925).

"Bar of Curtesy by Adverse Possession," 52 L. R. A. (N.S.) 535 (1914).

§ 220]

"Curtesy as Affected by Conveyance or Mortgage by Wife without Joining Husband," 14 A. L. R. 355–60 (1921).
"Validity of Postnuptial Agreement Releasing or Waiving Rights of Surviving Spouse on Death of Other Spouse," 49 A. L. R. 116–53 (1927).
"Tax Sale of Property as Extinguishing Right of Dower or Curtesy," 75 A. L. R. 430–33 (1931).
"Interlocutory Decree of Divorce as Affecting Marital Rights of One Spouse in Estate of the Other," 76 A. L. R. 284–96 (1932).

Section 221. Curtesy—Forfeiture of

CROSS REFERENCES: Effect of absolute divorce upon wife's property, **Secs. 96–98**; Effect of limited divorce on wife's property, **Sec. 128**; Conveyances, etc., of wife when deserted by husband, **Sec. 143**; Forfeiture of widow's dower or statutory share or of provision in lieu thereof, **Secs. 202, 203**; Barring curtesy, etc., **Sec. 220**; Forfeiture of curtesy for waste, **Sec. 222**

In the absence of legislation to the contrary, the surviving husband's rights in the wife's real and personal property are barred by absolute divorce but left unaffected by limited divorce. Statutes in some jurisdictions treat the matter as one of forfeiture, and preserve the same when divorce is decreed because of the wife's misconduct (see cross references above). If the marriage continues until dissolved by the death of the wife, the fact that the husband has been guilty of serious misconduct during coverture does not operate to deprive him of his curtesy or statutory share at common law. While the Statute of Westminster II, regarded by some courts as a part of the American common law, provided that the wife's adultery should bar her dower, no similar penalty was imposed on the husband.

Legislation was found in sixteen jurisdictions establishing one or more grounds of forfeiture whereby the husband's misconduct operates to deprive him of his curtesy, dower, or statutory share, as follows: adultery (eight); desertion or abandonment (ten); abandonment and failure to provide (one); neglect or refusal to provide (three); felonious killing of wife (three); conviction of bigamy (one). The statutes evidence a considerable variation in detail (see résumé at end of this section). They are subject to the same comment as those which bar the widow's dower, collected in **Section 202**, where a more extended discussion of the problem will be found. Most of them are broad enough to bar the husband's statutory share of personalty as well as his interest in

[§ 221

lands. In two jurisdictions, the forfeiture is dependent upon the wife obtaining a judicial decree to that effect during her lifetime. In all but **Illinois,** the adultery penalized is a living in adultery. **Indiana** seems to require that the adultery exist at the time of the wife's death, but in the others it is sufficient if it has not been forgiven during her life. Three jurisdictions which establish adultery as a ground of forfeiture do not regard desertion without adultery as of sufficient gravity to punish in a similar manner. Of those states which penalize desertion, only three require it to have continued a specified time before the wife's death. The **New Hampshire** statute appears to be the broadest of any found. Under it, the husband loses all of his rights in the wife's property, except such as her will gives him, if at the time of her death she is living apart because of his misconduct constituting cause for divorce.

Viewed as a whole, the legislation which bars the property rights of the surviving spouse because of misconduct during marriage is not impressive. Indeed, a majority of jurisdictions leave the matter as at common law, if the innocent spouse does not pursue the redress offered by the divorce court. Where the lawmaker has acted in the matter, the discrimination between spouses is not substantial; but the antiquated view that adultery by the husband is of less gravity than adultery by the wife finds some support in the statutes. The writer has already expressed his opinion that the principle of the forfeiture statutes should be extended. What was said in **Section 202** will not be repeated here. There is also a need for legislation permitting the husband to convey his lands free of the wife's inchoate interest therein when he has been deserted or is living apart for cause.

A summary of the foregoing statutes by jurisdiction follows:

Arkansas (Crawf. and Moses, Dig., Supp. 1927, Sec. 3514*b*) : If husband kills wife and he is convicted of murder in first or second degree, he forfeits dower or curtesy in her estate (but see **Sec. 216;** husband does not have dower or curtesy, as such).

Connecticut (G. S. 1930, Sec. 5156) : Husband forfeits statutory share of real and personal property when, without sufficient cause, he abandons wife and continues such abandonment to the time of her death.

Illinois (Cahill, R. S. 1931, Ch. 41, Sec. 15) : If husband voluntarily leaves wife and commits adultery, he is barred of dower or benefit of jointure, unless he and wife are afterwards reconciled and dwell together.

Indiana (Burns, Ann. St. 1926, Secs. 3354–55).: If husband leaves wife and is living at time of her death in adultery, he shall take no part of her estate. If he abandons wife without just cause, failing to make provision for her or for his children by her, he shall take no part of her estate.

Iowa (C. 1927, Sec. 12032) : If husband feloniously takes or causes or procures another to take wife's life, he loses all his interest in her estate as surviving spouse or under her will.

Kentucky (Carroll, St. 1922, Secs. 1406, 2133) : If husband voluntarily leaves wife and lives in adultery, he forfeits all right and interest in and to the property and estate of wife, unless they afterward become reconciled and live together as man and wife.

Maryland (Bagby, Ann. C. 1924, Art. 27, Sec. 23; Art. 45, Sec. 7) : If husband is convicted of bigamy, he forfeits his dower, and all his claim or title to any estate he may have in right of his first wife.

Massachusetts (G. L. 1932, Ch. 209, Sec. 35) : If a court having jurisdiction has entered a decree that wife has been deserted or is living apart for cause, she may convey her real property with the same effect as if single, and surviving husband loses right to waive the provisions of her will, and is not entitled upon her death, if she leaves a will, to his curtesy.

Minnesota (G. S. 1923, Sec. 8622) : When wife is deserted by husband for one year, or has cause for divorce, she may bring action for a decree which shall bar husband of statutory share in her lands.

Missouri (R. S. 1929, Sec. 337) : If husband leaves wife and goes away and continues with an adulteress, or abandons her without reasonable cause and continues to live separate for one year next preceding her death, or dwells with another woman in a state of adultery continuously, he is barred of his inheritance, jointure, homestead, curtesy, and statutory allowances in the wife's real and personal estate, unless she is voluntarily reconciled to him and suffers him to dwell with her.

New Hampshire (Pub. L. 1926, Ch. 306, Secs. 18, 19) : If husband has willingly abandoned wife, and has absented himself from her, or has wilfully neglected to support her, or has not been heard from, in consequence of his own neglect, for three years next preceding her death; or if at death wife is living apart because of husband's misconduct constituting cause for divorce, husband is not entitled to any interest or portion in the real or personal estate of wife, except such as is given him in her will.

New York (Cahill, Consol. L. 1930, Ch. 13, Sec. 18) : Husband who has neglected or refused to provide for wife or has abandoned her loses his right to elect to take against her will.

[§ 221

North Carolina (C. 1927, Secs. 10, 12, 2519, 2522, 2524) : Curtesy and all rights in personal property of wife are barred if husband without cause abandons wife, maliciously turns her out of doors, separates from wife and lives in adultery, and such conduct is not condoned by wife, or if he is convicted of felonious slaying of wife or of being an accessory before the fact. In case of adultery and abandonment, wife may convey her property before condonation and bar curtesy.

Ohio (Complete G. C. 1931 [Page], Supp. 1932, Sec. 10502[5]) : Husband who leaves wife and dwells in adultery is barred of dower in lands, unless the offense is condoned by wife.

Pennsylvania (St. 1920 [West], Sec. 8354) : Husband's interest in wife's real and personal estate is forfeited if, for one year previous to her death, he wilfully neglects or refuses to provide for her or wilfully and maliciously deserts her.

Virginia (C. 1930, Secs. 5140, 5277) : If husband wilfully deserts or abandons wife, and such desertion or abandonment continues until her death, he forfeits all interest in her estate as tenant by the curtesy, distributee, or otherwise. If husband leaves wife and lives in adultery, he forfeits his distributive share of personal estate and right to renounce provisions of wife's will, unless before her death they were reconciled and lived together.

West Virginia (C. 1931, Ch. 42, Art. 3, Sec. 3; Ch. 43, Art. 1, Sec. 19) : Husband forfeits dower if he voluntarily leaves wife and lives in adultery and they are not afterward reconciled and live together, or if he voluntarily leaves or abandons wife without cause sufficient for absolute or limited divorce and is so living apart at time of her death. If dower is barred, husband cannot renounce provisions of wife's will, and is not entitled to any part of her estate except such as is given to him by her will.

REFERENCES

Book

Stimson, F. J. *American Statute Law,* Sec. 3307 (1886).

Annotation

"Misconduct of Surviving Spouse as Affecting Marital Rights in Other's Estate," 71 A. L. R. 277–90 (1931).

§ 221]

Section 222. Curtesy—Waste

CROSS REFERENCES: Liability of widow as tenant in dower for waste and repairs, Secs. 192, 193; Forfeiture of husband's curtesy or statutory share for misconduct, Sec. 221

A tenant by the curtesy, as any other life tenant, is impeachable for waste. Most jurisdictions have statutes providing in some detail for the relief which a reversioner or remainderman may obtain against tenants generally. Legislation expressly providing that the husband as tenant by the curtesy or as tenant in dower is liable for waste is found in eight jurisdictions (**Delaware, Illinois, Maryland, Massachusetts, New Jersey, Ohio, Oregon, Wisconsin**). Under these statutes he is subject to treble damages in one (**New Jersey**), to double damages in two (**Delaware, Wisconsin**), and to forfeiture of the premises wasted in five (**Delaware, Illinois, Massachusetts, New Jersey, Ohio**). A tenant by the curtesy is liable for permissive as well as voluntary waste to the same extent as any other life tenant. Five of the jurisdictions above provide that an action lies against the widower when he commits or "suffers" waste (**Illinois, Massachusetts, Ohio, Oregon, Wisconsin**). In **Illinois** and **Oregon,** he is expressly charged with the duty to "maintain the houses and tenements, with fences and appurtenances, in good repair." In **Maryland,** the orphans' court is authorized to apportion the expenses for repairs and improvements when the same have been first sanctioned by the court and the interests of minors are involved. The husband holding a life estate in the widow's lands as survivor must pay the general taxes assessed against the premises. Occasionally his failure to do so has been regarded as waste. Under an **Ohio** statute, he not only is liable for damages sustained by reason of such neglect, but is subject to a forfeiture of his estate if the property is sold for the payment of delinquent taxes and he does not redeem within one year thereafter.

Citations for the statutes above follow:

Delaware, R. C. 1915, Secs. 3323–33; **Illinois,** Cahill, R. S. 1931, Ch. 41, Sec. 45; **Maryland,** Bagby, Ann. C. 1924, Art. 93, Secs. 316, 320–23, 326; **Massachusetts,** G. L. 1932, Ch. 242, Sec. 1; **New Jersey,** Comp. St. 1910, p. 5790, Sec. 3; **Ohio,** Complete G. C. 1931 (Page), Sec. 5688; Supp. 1932, Sec. 10502(7); **Oregon,** C. 1930, Secs. 10(322), 10(330); **Wisconsin,** St. 1931, Sec. 279.02.

REFERENCES
Book
STIMSON, F. J. *American Statute Law,* Sec. 3308 (1886).

[§ 222

Section 223. Curtesy—Miscellaneous Provisions

CROSS REFERENCES: Emblements of a tenant in dower, **Sec. 194**; Failure of provision in lieu of dower, **Sec. 204**; Assignment of dower, **Secs. 208–13**; Dower in partition and executor's sale proceedings, miscellaneous provisions on dower, **Sec. 214**; Curtesy, abolition and statutory substitutes, **Sec. 216**; Amount of curtesy, **Sec. 217**; Barring curtesy by jointure, **Sec. 220**; Curtesy of alien, **Sec. 295**; Barring curtesy of insane husband, **Sec. 311**

Miscellaneous provisions relating to curtesy are not conducive to any measured classification, but, for convenience, may be divided into five groups: (1) assignment of the surviving husband's share; (2) such share in partition and executor's sale proceedings; (3) failure of provisions in lieu of his share; (4) emblements of a tenant by the curtesy; (5) other miscellaneous provisions.

1. ASSIGNMENT OF THE SURVIVING HUSBAND'S SHARE

Common-law curtesy obviously needed no admeasurement, since it existed in all of the wife's land. Today, however, in many jurisdictions some procedure analogous to assignment of dower is necessary because of the statutory changes in curtesy and the substitutes for it (**Sec. 216**). In fourteen jurisdictions the provisions relating to assignment of dower or of the widow's share are applicable to the setting off of the surviving husband's share (**Hawaii, Illinois, Iowa, Kansas, Kentucky, Maryland, Massachusetts, Missouri, New Jersey, Ohio, Oregon, Vermont, Virginia, West Virginia**). The discussion of assignment of dower will not be repeated; the reader is referred to **Section 208** for general comment, and to **Sections 209–13** inclusive for specific provisions on assignment. In **New Hampshire** it is provided that the surviving husband's share of realty in lieu of curtesy, when the wife dies without issue (see Table CV, **Sec. 216**), is to be assigned in the same manner as dower is assigned to a widow. However, if in such case the entire realty left by the wife does not exceed the widower's share (see Table CV), no assignment is necessary unless some party in interest petitions the probate court therefor.

2. SURVIVING HUSBAND'S SHARE IN PARTITION AND EXECUTOR'S SALE PROCEEDINGS

Eleven jurisdictions have the following legislation pertaining to the widower's share in partition proceedings: (1) in seven states the same statutes apply to either the widow's or the widower's interest (**Illinois, Kentucky, Maryland, Missouri, New Jersey, Ohio, Oregon**); (2) in two (**Alaska, Tennessee**) the same provisions apply in general,

§ 223]

except for the compensation, the widower having curtesy in the entire proceeds of the sale; (3) in two (**Delaware, Wisconsin**) the following statutes apply only to the widower. In **Delaware,** if curtesy is in an undivided share of the lands, and if the husband is a party, a sale may be free of curtesy; but if it is in other than an undivided share, there is no partition until curtesy is determined, unless upon the joint petition of the husband and one or more of the other parties entitled. If a sale is made, the proceeds are invested for his benefit, except that upon his petition or upon that of any party the court may order the value of the curtesy paid him and the residue to the other parties. In **Wisconsin,** if curtesy exists in the whole of the premises, judgment of actual partition does not affect the husband. A necessary sale may be free of curtesy if he is a party, and a share is invested for his benefit, or, with his written consent, a gross sum is paid as determined by the law on annuities. An **Oregon** statute provides that all of the proceeds of a partition sale be invested for the husband's benefit; but since curtesy exists only in one-half of the wife's property (C. 1930, Sec. 10[330]), the partition statute is evidently an oversight. Table CIII in **Section 214** contains the details of the provisions referred to above which apply to both husband and wife.

In five jurisdictions the legislation relating to assignment, sale, and compensation of the widow's dower or share, in an executor's or administrator's sale for the husband's debts, applies also to a surviving husband (**Illinois, Maryland, Massachusetts, New Jersey, Ohio**). (See Table CIII.)

3. FAILURE OF PROVISIONS IN LIEU OF SURVIVING HUSBAND'S SHARE

Statutes permitting curtesy to be barred by jointure are collected in **Section 220.** Three states (**Indiana, Ohio, West Virginia**) have express legislation to the effect that if a widower is lawfully evicted from lands settled on him by jointure or other provision he is entitled to a share in the property as if such jointure or provision had never been made. Five other states reach the same result, since similar statutes pertaining to the widow (**Sec. 204**) apply as well to the widower (**Kentucky, Massachusetts, Missouri, New Jersey, Oregon**). A general discussion of this legislation may be found in **Section 204.**

4. EMBLEMENTS OF A TENANT BY THE CURTESY

In the absence of statute, a widower with a life estate in the wife's lands is entitled to emblements in like manner as any other life tenant.

[§ 223

New Jersey and **West Virginia** have provisions recognizing this right; a similar statute in **Virginia,** in terms limited to a widow, may be construed to include a widower. The general subject of emblements is discussed in **Section 194.**

5. OTHER MISCELLANEOUS PROVISIONS

The writer has attempted only to direct attention to the following minor statutory details found in nine states: (1) a collusive assignment of the widower's share by a guardian does not prejudice an infant entitled to the lands (**Kentucky, Missouri, New Jersey, Ohio, Oregon, West Virginia;** see **Sec. 214**); (2) annuity tables are used to compute the present value of his share (**Missouri, Oregon, Virginia, West Virginia, Wisconsin**); (3) a sale under power of sale in a will may be free of his claim if the widower consents to other compensation (**Maryland**); (4) a widower may transfer his interest before his share is set off (**Missouri**); (5) a sale for taxes may be free of curtesy (**New Jersey**); (6) the widower is liable for taxes levied on lands held as his share (**Ohio**); (7) curtesy may be set off in a suit to satisfy any valid lien (**Virginia**). Cross references at the beginning of this section indicate other details which are discussed elsewhere.

The preceding discussion in the five subsections has been drawn in great measure from statutes found in eleven jurisdictions providing, in substance, that the widower's share, called "curtesy," "dower," or merely a "share," is defined and limited by the same rules which apply to the widow's "dower" or "share" (**Illinois, Iowa, Kansas, Kentucky, Maryland, Massachusetts, Missouri, New Jersey, Ohio, Oregon, West Virginia**).

CITATIONS

A great number of the statutes included in this section have already been cited in previous sections on dower and curtesy. It is felt that these citations may easily be found, since the jurisdictions having such statutes are set forth completely in the text above.

1. *Assignment:* Statutes are cited in Table C, **Section 208;** in footnote 2 (pp. 486–87), Table C; and in Table CII, **Section 213.** Additional citations: **Maryland,** Bagby, Ann. C. 1924, Art. 46, Secs. 32–35; **New Hampshire,** Pub. L. 1926, Ch. 305, Sec. 13, as amended by Sess. L. 1933, Ch. 118, p. 171; **Virginia,** C. 1930, Sec. 5139*a*.

2. *Partition and executor's sales:* Statutes applying to both widow and widower are cited in Table CIII, **Section 214.** Additional citations: **Alaska,** Comp. L. 1913,

Sec. 1260; **Delaware,** R. C. 1915, Secs. 3286–87, 3293; **Tennessee,** C. 1932, Sec. 9211; **Wisconsin,** St. 1931, Secs. 276.02, 276.18, 276.22, 276.35, 276.36.

3. *Failure of provisions in lieu of share:* Citations are to be found in **Section 204.**

4. *Emblements:* **New Jersey,** Comp. St. 1910, p. 5864, Sec. 12; **Virginia,** C. 1930, Sec. 5130; **West Virginia,** C. 1931, Ch. 43, Art. 1, Sec. 17.

5. *Miscellaneous:* **Illinois,** Cahill, R. S. 1931, Ch. 41, Sec. 1; **Iowa,** C. 1927, Sec. 11991; **Kansas,** R. S. 1923, Sec. 22(127); **Kentucky,** Carroll, St. 1922, Secs. 2140, 2148; **Maryland,** Bagby, Ann. C. 1924, Art. 45, Sec. 7; Art. 93, Sec. 324; **Massachusetts,** G. L. 1932, Ch. 189, Sec. 1; **Missouri,** R. S. 1929, Secs. 319–20, 353, 359, 3132–34; **New Jersey,** Comp. St. 1910, p. 2046, Sec. 6; p. 2047, Sec. 7; p. 4684, Secs. 24, 25; p. 5202, Sec. 297; Supp. 1925–30, Sec. 63(34a2); **Ohio,** Complete G. C. 1931 (Page), Secs. 5680, 5688, 12016; Supp. 1932, Sec. 10502(10); **Oregon,** C. 1930, Secs. 6(624), 10(329)–10(330); **Virginia,** C. 1930, Secs. 5131–33, 6266a; **West Virginia,** C. 1931, Ch. 43, Art. 1, Secs. 1, 16; Art. 2, Secs. 1–5; **Wisconsin,** St. 1931, Secs. 276.36, 314.06.

REFERENCES

Annotations

"Dower or Marital Rights of Husband or Wife in Respect of Improvements Made by Spouse's Alienee or His Successor after Death of Spouse," 74 A. L. R. 1168–72 (1931).

"Insurable Interest of Husband or Wife in Other's Property," 68 A. L. R. 362–71 (1930), at p. 365.

"Quantum of Estate Acquired by Purchaser at Tax Sale of Property Which Is Subject to Successive Estates or Different Interests," 75 A. L. R. 416–38 (1931), at p. 430.

Section 224. Assignment of Wages by Husband and Wife

CROSS REFERENCES: Other limitations on transfer of property by husband and wife, **Sec. 225;** Exemptions, **Sec. 228;** Assignment of wages by infant, **Sec. 287**

Most jurisdictions have legislation of some kind in respect to the form and effect of wage assignments, either generally or when made for certain special purposes. In particular, the practice of assigning future wages to secure a present loan, together with the expansion of the wage brokerage business, has occasioned special regulatory measures. The purpose of this section is to collect in the table following those statutes which require the concurrence of both spouses in assignments of wages made by one or either of them. Legislation of this kind was found in

[§ 224

twenty-five jurisdictions. Many of these statutes are of limited application, contemplating assignments made to secure loans from licensed moneylenders only. Thirteen apply to the husband's assignment only, and eight to the assignment of future wages only. In twelve jurisdictions, the spouse's written consent must be attached to the assignment; in seven, the two spouses must join in the instrument; and in six, both joinder and acknowledgment are required.

The table and citations follow.

TABLE CVI*

Assignment of Wages by Husband or Wife

Jurisdiction[1] and Citation	Assignment, etc.	Earned or Future Wages, etc.	By Whom Assigned	For What Purpose Assigned	Requirement of Joinder, etc.
Arizona R. C. 1928, Sec. 2012	Wages, commissions, other compensation for services	Earned or to be earned	Married person	To secure small loan from licensed moneylender	Written assent of spouse endorsed or attached thereto[2]
Arkansas Crawf. and Moses, Dig. 1921, Sec. 7134	Wages	To be earned in future	Husband		Written consent of wife attached thereto
California C. C. 1933 (Lake), Sec. 955	Wages or salary		Married person		Written consent of spouse attached thereto
Colorado[3] Comp. L. 1921, G. S., Sec. 3796	Salary or wages	Earned or to be earned	Married person	To secure small loan from licensed moneylender	Signed in person by both spouses[2]
Georgia C. 1926, Pol. C., Sec. 1770(76)	Salary or wages	Earned or to be earned	Married person	To secure small loan from licensed moneylender	Signed in person by both husband and wife[2]
Indiana Burns, Ann. St. 1926, Sec. 9359	Wages or salary		Husband who is head of family residing in state		Signature of wife thereto, executed and acknowledged before proper officer, other than wage broker or one connected with him
Iowa[3] C. 1927, Sec. 9427	Salary, wages, commissions, other compensation for services	Earned or to be earned	Married person	To secure small loan from licensed moneylender	Signed and acknowledged in person by both spouses

* See page 578 for numbered footnotes to this table.

§ 224]

TABLE CVI (*Continued*)

Jurisdiction[1] and Citation	Assignment, etc.	Earned or Future Wages, etc.	By Whom Assigned	For What Purpose Assigned	Requirement of Joinder, etc.
Louisiana ...... Sess. L. 1916, Act 102, p. 223	Wages or salaries	To be earned in future	Husband	(Part of an act to regulate wage brokers)	Written consent of wife attached thereto[2]
Maryland ...... Bagby, Ann. C. 1924, Art. 8, Sec. 11	Wages or salary		Married person		Executed and acknowledged in person by both spouses
Massachusetts .. G. L. 1932, Ch. 154, Secs. 2, 3	Wages or salary	To be earned in future	Husband	To secure small loan, and in general	Written consent of wife attached thereto
Michigan .... Comp. L. 1929, Sec. 12214	Salary, wages, commissions, other compensation for services	Earned or to be earned	Married person	To secure small loan from licensed moneylender	Signed in person by both spouses[2]
Minnesota ...... G. S. 1923, Sec. 4138	Wages	To be earned in future	Husband	To secure a loan of less than $200	Written consent of wife attached thereto
Montana .... R. C. 1921, Sec. 4178	Wages or salary		Husband with wife residing in state	To a wage broker	Signature of wife thereto, executed and acknowledged before a proper officer, other than wage broker or one connected with him
Nebraska[3] ...... Comp. St. 1929, Sec. 45(120)	Wages		Married person	To secure loan from licensed moneylender	Written consent of spouse attached thereto
New Jersey..... Comp. St., Cum. Supp. 1911–24, Sec. 35(19)	Wages	Earned or to be earned	Husband	To secure small loan from licensed moneylender	Written consent of wife attached thereto[2]
New York ...... Cahill, Consol. L. 1930, Ch. 3, Sec. 347	Salary or wages	"Future" salary or wages	Married person not legally separated from spouse	To secure loan from personal-loan company	Not valid unless accompanied by written assent of spouse
Ohio .... Complete G. C. 1931 (Page), Sec. 6346(7)	Salary, wages, or earnings		Married person living with spouse	To secure a loan from licensed moneylender	Signed by spouse
Pennsylvania ... St. 1920 (West), Sec. 21510	Wages or salary	To be earned in future	Husband	To secure a loan	Written consent of wife attached thereto

[§ 224

TABLE CVI (*Concluded*)

Jurisdiction[1] and Citation	Assignment, etc.	Earned or Future Wages, etc.	By Whom Assigned	For What Purpose Assigned	Requirement of Joinder, etc.
Rhode Island ... Sess. L. 1923, Ch. 2312, p. 24, Sec. 16	Salary, wages, commissions, other compensation for services	Earned or to be earned	Married person	To secure small loan from licensed moneylender	Signed in person by both spouses[2]
Texas .... Complete St. 1928, Civ. St., Art. 6165a(6)	Wages		Husband	(Part of an act regulating wage brokers)	Wife must join in assignment, and her separate acknowledgment taken and certified
Utah .... R. S. 1933, 7-8-6	Wages	Earned or to be earned	Husband	To secure small loan from licensed moneylender	Written consent of wife attached thereto[2]
Virginia .... C. 1930, Sec. 4168(54)	Salary, wages, commissions, other compensation for services	Earned or to be earned	Married person	To secure small loan from licensed moneylender	Signed in person by both spouses[2]
Washington .... Remington, Comp. St. 1922, Sec. 7598	Wages	To be earned in future	Husband		Written consent of wife attached thereto
Wisconsin ...... St. 1931, Sec. 241.09	Salary or wages, exempt by law from garnishment	Earned or to be earned	Husband		Signed by wife if she is a member of the family at the time. Her signature must be witnessed by two disinterested witnesses
Wyoming ...... R. S. 1931, Sec. 8(102)	Wages	To be earned in future	Husband	To secure loan of less than $200 (except from banks)	Written consent of wife attached thereto

[1] See also **New Mexico**, Statutes, Annotated, 1929, Section 8(101), for a 1929 statute apparently intended to require that the wife join in the husband's assignment of his wages, and acknowledge her signature, but which seems to have failed in its purpose because of a typographical error.

[2] Assent of spouse is not required in the following jurisdictions if the husband and wife have lived apart for five months prior to the assignment: **Arizona, Colorado, Georgia, Louisiana, Michigan, New Jersey, Rhode Island, Utah, Virginia.**

[3] Three jurisdictions have statutes on the subject in addition to those given in the table. **Colorado**, Compiled Laws, 1921, General Statutes, Section 4251, is similar to the **Indiana** provision outlined in the table; while Section 4259 provides that an assignment of wages not already earned, made by a married person residing with his or her spouse, must be signed by such spouse. It will be observed that these provisions, standing alone, are not entirely consistent one with the other. **Iowa**, Code, 1927, Section 9454, and **Nebraska**, Compiled Statutes, 1929, Section 36(203), are statutes of general application providing that an assignment of wages by "the head of a family" must be executed and acknowledged by both spouses.

§ 224]

REFERENCES

Article

STRASBURGER, ALBERT F. "The Wage Assignment Problem," 19 Minn. L. Rev. 536–55 (1935).

Section 225. Other Limitations on Transfer of Property by Husband and Wife

CROSS REFERENCES: Transfer of property by abandoned wife, **Sec. 143;** Transfer by abandoned husband, **Sec. 144;** Transfer of community property, **Sec. 178;** Conveyances between spouses, **Sec. 182;** Conveyances by wife to third persons, **Secs. 183–85;** Homestead and exempt property, **Sec. 228;** Conveyance by insane spouse, **Sec. 304**

The cross references above contain discussions of the more important questions relating to transfers of property by husband and wife. This section is concerned with miscellaneous limitations on such transfers—statutes dealing with the transfer of homesteads, of exempt personal property, and with other minor details (see **Sec. 228** for a general discussion of homesteads and exempt property).

The security of the home and the other benefits derived from homestead laws would be seriously endangered if the owner of the property from which a homestead has been selected could convey it without the consent of the other spouse. Consequently, forty-one jurisdictions have been found which limit the disposal of such property as follows: (1) in twenty-seven, the consent of both spouses is necessary to an alienation or encumbrance of the homestead (**Alaska, Arizona, California, Colorado, Florida, Georgia, Idaho, Illinois, Iowa, Kansas, Minnesota, Mississippi, Missouri, Montana, Nebraska, Nevada, New Hampshire, New Jersey, New York, North Dakota, Oklahoma, South Carolina, South Dakota, Tennessee, Utah, Vermont, Washington**); (2) ten provide that the "wife" of the owner must consent to a sale or encumbrance (**Alabama, Arkansas, Indiana, Louisiana, Massachusetts, Michigan, North Carolina, Texas, Wisconsin, Wyoming**); (3) in two, a mortgage of the homestead is invalid unless signed (**New Mexico**) of executed (**Ohio**) by the wife of the debtor; (4) and in two, husband and wife must join in a release or waiver of the homestead exemption (**Connecticut, Kentucky**). **Alabama, Arizona, Illi-**

nois, **Louisiana, South Carolina, Washington,** and **Wyoming** also have the latter provision respecting waiver. Strictly speaking, such statutes are not limitations on the transfer of property, but are analogous and serve the same purpose in a limited manner.

It is often possible that a homestead may be selected from the property of the wife (see **Sec. 228**). In such a case, according to the language of the foregoing statutes requiring the consent of the "wife" of the owner, she apparently could transfer her property without the husband's consent. If so, the result can be justified because of the fact that the homestead exemptions are considered to be primarily for the protection of the wife. However, it should also be remembered that in a few jurisdictions the general statutes pertaining to any transfer of her real property may require the joinder of the husband (see **Sec. 183**).

In **Colorado** and **South Dakota**, the conveyance of the homestead may be by the joint or separate deed of the husband and wife; in four states (**Kansas, New Jersey, New York, Tennessee**), the statutes are ambiguous as to joint or separate deeds. A **New Jersey** statute, which provides generally that separate deeds "heretofore made by husband and wife" are as valid as if they had joined in the same deed, seems to imply that the homestead may be conveyed by separate deeds. In **Georgia,** the homestead may be sold jointly by husband and wife with the sanction of the court. But in the remaining thirty-four jurisdictions named above, the statutes seem definite to the effect that the instrument conveying or encumbering the homestead or releasing the homestead right must be signed or executed and acknowledged by both spouses or joined in by the wife of the owner. Three states (**Alabama, North Carolina, Texas**) require the separate or privy examination of the wife (see also **Sec. 184** for broad statutes requiring the separate examination of the wife to conveyances of her property).

Eight states have special statutes. If a homestead of greater value than the exemption allows is sold, the proceeds due the owner receive the same protection the homestead had from the voluntary disposition by the husband (**Nevada, North Dakota, Washington**); receive such protection for six months after the sale (**California, Idaho, Montana, Nebraska**); and the court may order the proceeds paid into court to be paid out only on the joint receipt of husband and wife (**Nevada, North Dakota**). In **New Jersey,** the consideration for a sale of the homestead must be its full, fair value, and such consideration, or one thousand dollars thereof, must be re-invested in other lands to be declared as a homestead.

§ 225]

It is usually held that a conveyance of the homestead by the husband to his wife is not within the contemplation of the foregoing statutes; therefore, the wife need not join (*Kindly* v. *Spraker,* 72 Ark. 228; 79 S. W. 766 [1904]), and **Illinois** and **Wisconsin** have codified such a rule. In six states, by express statute, the wife need not join in a mortgage to secure the purchase price of the property which becomes the homestead (**Arkansas, Michigan, Minnesota, New Hampshire, North Carolina, Vermont**); the same result may be reached in other jurisdictions under broad statutes subjecting the homestead to such mortgages.

Eleven jurisdictions have taken similar steps to protect exempt personal property. It cannot be encumbered without the joint concurrence of husband and wife (**Idaho, Iowa, Kansas, Minnesota, North Dakota, Utah**); a sale or mortgage is not valid unless signed by the wife of the owner (**District of Columbia, Michigan, Wisconsin**); husband and wife may jointly waive a personal-property exemption (**Delaware**); and it is "unlawful" for either spouse to create a lien on the property without the consent of the other spouse (**Kansas**). In **Georgia,** exempt personal property may be sold in like manner as the homestead is sold (see above).

Nine states have analogous statutes concerning "household goods." No mortgage (**Illinois, North Carolina, Ohio**), sale or mortgage (**Colorado, Nebraska, New Hampshire, New Jersey, North Dakota, Texas**), of such goods is valid unless it is executed by both husband and wife (**Colorado, Illinois, New Hampshire, North Dakota, Ohio**); or signed, sealed, executed, and acknowledged (**New Jersey**) like a conveyance of real property (**Nebraska**); or joined in by the wife of the owner and her separate acknowledgment taken (**North Carolina, Texas**). In **Ohio** it is "unlawful" for either spouse to create a lien on household property without the other's consent.

A recent amendment (1933) in **Ohio** provides that any promise, agreement, or contract which seeks to waive the provisions of the exemption laws is void. No decision has been found construing the statutes discussed above in the light of the amendment; but the reader should recognize the possibility of a conflict in such provisions.

Four states have miscellaneous provisions which may be summarized briefly as follows: (1) a wife who joins in her husband's conveyance is not bound by the general covenant of warranty (**Alabama**); (2) in a partition sale, if the owner of a share sold and his or her spouse do not agree on the disposition of the proceeds, the court may order the sum

[§ 225

invested in real estate for their benefit, under control of the court's appointee (**Iowa**) ; (3) each spouse has a right of interment in the other's burial lot which cannot be defeated by conveyance (**Massachusetts**) ; (4) the "home site" cannot be conveyed, except to secure the purchase money, during the life of the wife without her signature and assent shown by her privy examination; except that if she commits adultery or abandons the husband the limitation does not apply (**North Carolina**).

Citations follow:

Alabama, Const., Secs. 205, 210; C. 1923, Secs. 7436, 7883; **Alaska,** Comp. L. 1913, Sec. 499, as amended by Sess. L. 1933, Ch. 107, p. 191; Sec. 1104; **Arizona,** R. C. 1928, Secs. 956, 1733–34; **Arkansas,** Crawf. and Moses, Dig. 1921, Sec. 5542; **California,** C. C. 1933 (Lake), Secs. 1242, 1257; **Colorado,** Comp. L. 1921, G. S., Secs. 5088, 5929; Sess. L. 1927, Ch. 150, p. 592, Sec. 13; **Connecticut,** G. S. 1930, Sec. 5042; **Delaware,** R. C. 1915, Sec. 4330; **District of Columbia,** C. 1929, T. 24, Sec. 312; **Florida,** Const., Art. 10, Secs. 1, 4; **Georgia,** Const., Art. 9, Sec. 3 (in C. 1926, C. C., Sec. 6584) ; C. 1926, C. C., Sec. 3397; **Idaho,** Comp. St. 1919, Secs. 5442, 5457, 6374; **Illinois,** Cahill, R. S. 1931, Ch. 30, Sec. 28; Ch. 52, Sec. 4; Ch. 95, Sec. 26; **Indiana,** Burns, Ann. St. 1926, Sec. 781; **Iowa,** C. 1927, Secs. 10013, 10147, 12347; **Kansas,** Const., Art. 15, Sec. 9; R. S. 1923, Secs. 22(102), 58(312), 60(3501) ; **Kentucky,** Carroll, St. 1922, Sec. 1706; **Louisiana,** Const., Art. XI, Sec. 3 (in Marr, R. C. of Prac. 1927, p. 486) ; Marr, Ann. R. S., Supp. 1926, Act 35, p. 1105; **Massachusetts,** G. L. 1932, Ch. 114, Secs. 32, 33; Ch. 188, Secs. 7, 7*A*; **Michigan,** Const., Art. XIV, Sec. 2; Comp. L. 1929, Secs. 14578, 14609; **Minnesota,** G. S. 1923, Secs. 8340, 8349; **Mississippi,** C. 1930, Secs. 1778, 1780; **Missouri,** R. S. 1929, Sec. 608; **Montana,** R. C. 1921, Secs. 6949–50, 6965; **Nebraska,** Comp. St. 1929, Secs. 36(301), 40(104), 40(113) ; **Nevada,** Const., Sec. 81; Comp. L. 1929 (Hillyer), Secs. 3316–17, 3360; **New Hampshire,** Pub. L. 1926, Ch. 214, Sec. 4; Ch. 288, Sec. 8; **New Jersey,** Comp. St. 1910, p. 469, Sec. 10; p. 4694, Sec. 63; Sess. L. 1931, Ch. 281, p. 710; **New Mexico,** St. Ann. 1929, Secs. 48(111), 48(118) ; **New York,** Civ. Prac. Act 1931, Sec. 678; **North Carolina,** Const., Art. X, Sec. 8; C. 1927, Secs. 2577, 4103; **North Dakota,** Comp. L. 1913, Sec. 5517; Secs. 5607–8, as amended by Supp. 1913–25, pp. 1137–38; Sec. 5608*a*, added by Supp. 1913–25, p. 1139; Sec. 5618; Sess. L. 1933, Ch. 204, p. 321; Ch. 205, p. 322; **Ohio,** Complete G. C. 1931 (Page), Secs. 8565(1)–8565(2) ; Sec. 11729, as amended by Sess. L. 1933, p. 430; Sec. 11739; **Oklahoma,** Const., Art. XII, Sec. 2; St. 1931, Sec. 9661; **South Carolina,** Const., Art. III, Sec. 28; C. of L. 1922, C. C., Sec. 5494; **South Dakota,** Comp. L. 1929, Sec. 451; **Tennessee,** Const., Art. XI, Sec. 11; C. 1932, Sec. 7719; **Texas,** Complete St., Civ. St., Arts. 1300, 5460, 6165*a*(6) ; **Utah,** R. S. 1933, 13-0-3, 38-0-13; **Vermont,** G. L. 1917, Secs. 2715–16, as amended by Sess. L. 1921, No. 74, p. 69; Sec. 2717, as amended by Sess. L. 1921, No. 74, p. 67; Sec. 3523, as amended by Sess. L. 1919, No. 90, p. 98, and by Sess. L. 1929, No. 48, p. 63; **Washington,** Remington, Comp. St. 1922, Secs. 533–34, 549, 571; **Wisconsin,** St. 1931, Secs. 235.01, 241.08; **Wyoming,** Const., Art. XIX, Sec. 9; R. S. 1931, Sec. 97(205).

§ 225]

REFERENCES

Books

STIMSON, F. J. *American Statute Law,* Secs. 85, 1974 (1886).

THOMPSON, SEYMOUR D. *A Treatise on Homestead and Exemption Laws,* Secs. 465–534 (1878).

Notes

"Conveyance of Homestead by Separate Deeds of Husband and Wife," *Hawkins* v. *Corbit,* 83 Okla. 275; 201 P. 649 (1921) ; *Thomas* v. *James,* 84 Okla. 91; 202 P. 499 (1921)—6 Minn. L. Rev. 325–26 (1922).

"Estoppel of Mortgagor of Homestead Who Represents Himself to Be Unmarried," *Bozich* v. *First State Bank of Buhl,* 150 Minn. 241; 184 N. W. 1021 (1921)—6 Minn. L. Rev. 326 (1922) ; 31 Yale L. Jour. 552–53 (1922).

"Homestead—What Property Is Subject to Mortgage Executed by Husband Alone," *First National Bank* v. *Hallquist,* 48 N. D. 263; 184 N. W. 269 (1921)—35 Harv. L. Rev. 342 (1922).

"Right of Mortgagor of Homestead to Marshal Assets," *Booker* v. *Booker,* 225 Ala. 626; 144 So. 870 (1932)—46 Harv. L. Rev. 1035 (1933).

"Right of Non-Resident Alien Wife to Claim Homestead against Alienee of Husband," *Leonetti* v. *Tolton,* 264 Mich. 618; 250 N. W. 512 (1933)—20 Va. L. Rev. 472 (1934).

Annotations

"Reformation of Instrument as against Wife Claiming Homestead," 44 A. L. R. 118–19 (1926).

"Validity and Effect of Alienation or Encumbrance of Homestead without Joinder or Consent of Wife," 45 A. L. R. 395–436 (1926).

Section 226. Husband and Wife as Witnesses for and against Each Other

CROSS REFERENCES : Evidence in action for absolute divorce, **Sec. 86;** Evidence in action for limited divorce, **Sec. 126**

The material in this section logically falls into five main divisions : (1) husband or wife as a witness "for" the other; (2) husband or wife as a witness "against" the other; (3) testimony to communications between husband and wife; (4) exceptions and miscellaneous provisions; (5) a criticism of the statutory situation. It has been necessary to further separate the statutes in the first two divisions on the basis of testimony in civil and criminal actions.

Only a minimum of space will be devoted to the common law, but it must be remembered that all of the statutes are supplemented by judi-

cial decisions based on common-law rules.[1] Several vague statutes have
been classified in the text below according to their interpretation by the
courts; the cases are cited in footnotes to Table CVII following.

1. Husband or Wife as Witness "for" the Other

The common law at an early period definitely refused to permit one
spouse to testify for the other. The most plausible of several reasons
given was that their testimony would be biased because of mutual marital
interest and affection. Such reasoning is indefensible at the present time,
since bias and interest now only affect the credibility of the witness and
do not disqualify. A recent Supreme Court decision, *Funk* v. *United
States,* 290 U. S. 371; 54 Sup. Ct. 212; 78 L. Ed. 369 (1933), recognized
this fact and held that under the present common law a wife is a competent witness for her husband in a criminal action.

A few of the older common-law rules are as follows: (1) the marriage must be legal and both spouses alive and undivorced for the incompetency to apply; (2) in a civil action the testimony is "for" the other
when the other is interested according to the common-law definition,
and the evidence to be given assists him or her; (3) in a criminal action
the general rule seems to be that it is "for" the other only when the
other is the party accused.

Forty-five jurisdictions which have legislation on this subject in civil
actions may be classified as follows: a spouse is (1) privileged—sixteen
(**Alaska, Arizona, California, Colorado, District of Columbia,
Idaho, Michigan, Minnesota, Mississippi, Montana, Nevada,
North Dakota, Oregon, South Dakota, Utah, Washington**); (2)
"competent," "may testify," etc.—thirteen (**Delaware, Iowa, Maine,
Massachusetts, Nebraska, New Mexico, Ohio, Rhode Island, Tennessee, Texas, Vermont, Virginia, Wisconsin**); (3) competent and
compellable — twelve (**Florida, Hawaii, Indiana, Maryland, Missouri, New Hampshire, New Jersey, New York, North Carolina,
South Carolina, West Virginia, Wyoming**); (4) incompetent—
four (**Arkansas, Illinois, Kentucky, Oklahoma**). Of the sixteen
jurisdictions in which privilege obtains, the **District of Columbia** apparently requires the consent of the spouse testifying; the others require
the consent of the spouse testified "for"; thus, in effect, making a spouse
competent and compellable, since consent would usually be given to evidence in his or her behalf.

---

[1] See Wigmore, *A Treatise on Evidence,* Vol. 1, Secs. 600-620; Vol. 4, Secs. 2227-45;
Vol. 5, Secs. 2332-41 (1923), for a full discussion of the common law.

§ 226]

Fifty jurisdictions have statutes applicable to a spouse in criminal actions, and, classified as above, are as follows: a spouse is (1) privileged—twenty-two (see below); (2) "competent" or "may testify"—fifteen (**Delaware, Hawaii, Iowa, Maine, Maryland, Nebraska, New Mexico, New York, North Carolina, Ohio, Oklahoma, Tennessee, Texas, Vermont, Wisconsin**); (3) competent and compellable—nine (**Florida, Indiana, Kansas, Louisiana, New Hampshire, South Carolina, Virginia, West Virginia, Wyoming**); (4) incompetent—four (**Arkansas, Georgia, Illinois, Kentucky**). Of the twenty-two jurisdictions which provide for privilege, ten require the consent of the spouse testified "for" (**Arizona, Colorado, Michigan, Minnesota, Mississippi, Missouri, Nevada, North Dakota, South Dakota, Washington**); six require the consent of both spouses (**Alaska, California, Idaho, Montana, Oregon, Utah**); and six apparently give the privilege to the spouse testifying (**Alabama, Connecticut, District of Columbia, Massachusetts, New Jersey, Rhode Island**).

The jurisdictions already noted in both civil and criminal actions which provide that a spouse is "competent" or "may testify" have been put into a separate classification because their statutes are not definite, and no cases were found to interpret them. Logically, they should place a spouse in the position of a third-person witness, since, at common law, spouses were incompetent to testify "for" each other, and not privileged. It is conceivable, however, that such a statute might be construed to make a spouse competent but not compellable.

2. HUSBAND OR WIFE AS WITNESS "AGAINST" THE OTHER

Authority is divided on the question whether, under the common law, the testimony of one spouse against the other is "incompetent" or "privileged" (*Barber* v. *People, 203 Ill. 543; 68 N. E. 93 [1903]; Wigmore, A Treatise on Evidence, Vol. 4, Sec. 2242 [1923]). Under either theory the spouse is usually prevented from testifying, since the privilege, if there be such, is possessed by the spouse testified against. The reasons usually given for the rule are (*a*) that it is the policy of the law to protect marital peace, and that anti-marital testimony would provoke dissension between spouses; (*b*) that it is not "sporting" to force a spouse to give evidence so repugnant to normal feelings. Rules determining when evidence is "against" a spouse are similar to those relating to testimony "for" the other spouse as given in the preceding subsection.

Forty-six jurisdictions have been found with legislation concerning civil actions, and are as follows: a spouse is (1) privileged—fifteen

(Alaska, Arizona, California, Colorado, District of Columbia, Idaho, Michigan, Minnesota, Montana, Nevada, North Dakota, Oregon, South Dakota, Utah, Washington); (2) "competent" or "may testify"—eleven (Delaware, Maine, Massachusetts, New Mexico, Ohio, Rhode Island, Tennessee, Texas, Vermont, Virginia, Wisconsin); (3) competent and compellable—eleven (Florida, Hawaii, Indiana, Maryland, Missouri, New Hampshire, New Jersey, New York, North Carolina, South Carolina, West Virginia); (4) incompetent — nine (Arkansas, Illinois, Iowa, Kentucky, Mississippi, Nebraska, Oklahoma, Pennsylvania, Wyoming). In the jurisdictions where the testimony is privileged, the District of Columbia apparently requires the consent of the spouse testifying; the remaining jurisdictions require the consent of the spouse testified "against."

According to the classifications already used, the legislation in all fifty-one jurisdictions relating to criminal actions is as follows: a spouse is (1) privileged—twenty-five (see below); (2) "competent" or "may testify," etc.—six (Delaware, Maine, New York, Tennessee, Vermont, Wisconsin); (3) competent and compellable—four (Florida, Indiana, New Hampshire, South Carolina); (4) incompetent—sixteen (Arkansas, Georgia, Hawaii, Illinois, Iowa, Kentucky, Mississippi, Nebraska, New Jersey, New Mexico, North Carolina, Ohio, Oklahoma, Pennsylvania, Texas, Wyoming). Nine of the jurisdictions in which the testimony is privileged apparently require the consent of the spouse testifying (Alabama, Connecticut, District of Columbia, Kansas, Louisiana, Maryland, Massachusetts, Missouri, Rhode Island); eight, the consent of both spouses (Alaska, California, Idaho, Montana, Oregon, Utah, Virginia, West Virginia); and the remaining eight, the consent of the spouse testified "against" (Arizona, Colorado, Michigan, Minnesota, Nevada, North Dakota, South Dakota, Washington).

It should be remembered that the statutes which, in terms, make a spouse "competent," etc., may be interpreted by the courts to mean that the witness is also compellable.

3. COMMUNICATIONS BETWEEN HUSBAND AND WIFE

Husband and wife, at common law, are usually said to be privileged and not incompetent to testify to marital communications. The reason given is that it is good public policy to protect marital confidence; that freedom in the home, and trust between husband and wife, will be promoted. Such an argument has proven persuasive with legislatures, and

§ 226]

statutes have generally retained the supposed protection. A few common-law rules show that this phase of marital testimony is clearly distinct from the questions discussed in the preceding subsections: (1) the privilege is available though neither spouse is a party to, or interested in, the action; (2) the communication must be confidential; (3) the privilege is not terminated by death or divorce; (4) it has been held that "acts" of one spouse are protected by the privilege (*Schreffler* v. *Chase*, 245 Ill. 395; 92 N. E. 272 [1910]), although the cases are not agreed.

In the forty-three jurisdictions in which legislation has been found, there are two general types of statutes. (1) The communication is privileged in twenty-four. The consent of the spouse not testifying is necessary in sixteen (**Alaska, Arizona, California, Colorado, Idaho, Minnesota, Montana, Nevada, New York, North Dakota, Oregon, South Dakota, Utah, Virginia, Washington, Wisconsin**) ; seven merely provide that a spouse is "not compellable," apparently giving the privilege to the spouse testifying (**Hawaii, Louisiana, New Jersey, New Mexico, North Carolina, Pennsylvania, South Carolina**) ; and in **Michigan,** the consent of both spouses is necessary. (2) In sixteen jurisdictions a spouse is said to be "incompetent" or "may not testify" as to communications (**Arkansas, District of Columbia, Georgia, Illinois, Indiana, Iowa, Kansas, Kentucky, Maryland, Missouri, Nebraska, New Hampshire, Ohio, Oklahoma, Texas, Vermont**).

Three states have special statutes. In **Rhode Island,** the statute making a spouse incompetent refers only to civil actions. In **Tennessee,** in all civil actions, neither spouse may testify to any matter which occurred between them by virtue of the marital relation. And in **West Virginia,** one statute uses the term "incompetent," whereas another makes the communications privileged.

Of the foregoing jurisdictions, twelve protect "confidential" or "private" communications; in twenty-seven, the statutes merely say "any communication"; and in four the statutes are ambiguous (see Table CVII following). However, the express terms of such statutes cannot always be relied on, for some courts have held that "any communication" means only a "confidential" one.[1]

4. EXCEPTIONS AND MISCELLANEOUS PROVISIONS

At common law, husband and wife were early permitted to testify for and against each other in certain cases from necessity, where their

---

[1] See Wigmore, *A Treatise on Evidence,* Vol. 5, Sec. 2336, note 1, for a collection of cases on this topic.

testimony usually was the only available evidence. The statutory exceptions which have been made for the same reason may be roughly divided into two classes: (1) broad exceptions (e.g., spouses may testify for and against each other in civil actions between them); and (2) narrow, specific exceptions (e.g., the wife may testify against her husband in prosecutions for his desertion).

The following thirty jurisdictions have the broader exceptions: **Alaska, Arizona, Arkansas, California, Colorado, Georgia, Hawaii, Idaho, Illinois, Iowa, Kentucky, Michigan, Minnesota, Mississippi, Montana, Nebraska, Nevada, New Jersey, New Mexico, North Dakota, Oklahoma, Oregon, South Dakota, Texas, Utah, Virginia, Washington, West Virginia, Wisconsin, Wyoming.** The details of these statutes are given in the last column of Table CVII. Forty-three jurisdictions have the more specific exceptions which include actions for (1) divorce; (2) desertion and non-support; (3) encouraging prostitution of the wife by the husband; (4) various sex offenses of the spouses. These provisions are not given in tabular form, but are cited in footnote 2 of Table CVII (p. 600).

A few miscellaneous statutes may be noted. (1) The privilege or incompetency is limited in criminal actions to those in which the spouse who is testified "for" or "against" (**Alaska, California, Connecticut, Idaho, Montana, New Jersey, Oregon, Rhode Island, Utah**), or "against" (**Mississippi, Missouri, New Mexico, North Carolina**), is the party accused. (2) A failure to call a spouse to testify for the accused spouse creates no presumption or inference against accused (**Kansas, Mississippi, North Carolina, West Virginia**). (3) If the party to the action (**Oregon**) or to a criminal action (**Virginia**) offers himself or herself as a witness, that is deemed a consent to the examination of the other spouse; **New Mexico** has a similar statute relating to privileged communications. (4) In **New Hampshire** and **Vermont** neither spouse may testify against the other as to any statement, conversation, or other communication made to the other or to another person; nor may either testify to any matter which, in the court's opinion, would lead to a breach of marital confidence. Other special statutes are collected in the last column of Table CVII.

It has generally been held that the widespread statutes abolishing interest as a disqualification did not impliedly do away with marital disqualification (*Kelley* v. *Proctor,* 41 N. H. 139 [1860]). On the other hand, it is the weight of authority that a statute permitting a "party" to testify makes a spouse who is a party competent for or against the other.

§ 226]

5. Criticism

An analysis of the statutes which clearly restrict testimony by one spouse for or against the other gives the following result:

	For Other Spouse		Against Other Spouse	
	Civil	Criminal	Civil	Criminal
Incompetent	4	4	9	16
Privileged	16	22	15	25

It is gratifying to see that, in varying degrees, the great majority of jurisdictions have modified the common law; but progress has been checked too quickly. In the writer's opinion, no jurisdiction should restrict in any way testimony of one spouse for or against the other.

The argument in favor of testimony "for" the other spouse being incompetent has already been stated. It has little support among judges and writers, and further discussion seems unnecessary. Jurisdictions which, by statute, require the consent of the spouse testified "for" have, in reality, done away with restrictions. But the statutes requiring the consent of both spouses, or of the witness spouse, are incomprehensible. Why should one spouse be able to withhold evidence "for" the other? It is probable that such testimony has been confused with anti-marital evidence and the two distinct problems thrown indiscriminately together.

It is apparent that in the field of anti-marital testimony the majority of jurisdictions still prefer to attempt the protection of marital peace and the sensibilities of a spouse in this needless and ineffective way, instead of enabling the law to arrive at the truth by all available evidence. Space does not permit further discussion. Suffice it to say that this hoary common-law rule should be abolished.

The third phase of marital testimony, viz., communications between husband and wife, is not so easily put aside and has many proponents. Yet the writer would also do away with this privilege. How many husbands and wives know of it and extend confidences accordingly? If it were gone, how many would suppress such confidences and marital trust in anticipation of future litigation or crime? Are lawyers and their wives more trusting with each other than the laymen who know nothing of such law? It seems that practical reasoning on this subject of privileged communications will lead to their repudiation.

In short, therefore, the writer recommends that husband and wife as witnesses be governed by the same rules of evidence as affect third persons, with the reservation that their credibility be weighed in the light of their relationship.

Citations to the statutes discussed above are given in the table following.

[§ 226

TABLE

HUSBAND AND WIFE AS WITNESSES

Jurisdiction and Citation	For Each Other		Against Each Other	
	Civil Action	Criminal Action	Civil Action	Criminal Action
Alabama .... C. 1923, Sec. 5639		May testify, but not compellable		May testify, but not compellable[3]
Alaska .... Comp. L. 1913, Secs. 1867, 2259	Privileged[4]	Spouse of party accused is privileged[5]	Privileged[6]	Spouse of party accused is privileged[5]
Arizona .... R. C. 1928, Secs. 4412, 5177	Privileged[4]	Privileged[4]	Privileged[6]	Privileged[6]
Arkansas .... Crawf. and Moses, Dig. 1921, Secs. 3125, 4146	Incompetent	Incompetent	Incompetent	Incompetent
California .... C. C. P. 1933 (Lake), Sec. 1881; P. C. 1933 (Lake), Sec. 1322	Privileged[4]	Privileged in action in which one or both are parties[5]	Privileged[6]	Privileged in action in which one or both are parties[5]
Colorado .... Comp. L. 1921, G. S., Sec. 6563	Privileged[4]	Privileged[4]	Privileged[6]	Privileged[6]
Connecticut .... G. S. 1930, Sec. 6480		Spouse of party accused is privileged[8]		Spouse of party accused is privileged[8]
Delaware .... R. C. 1915, Sec. 4216	Lawful for spouse to testify	Lawful for spouse to testify	Lawful for spouse to testify	Lawful for spouse to testify[9]
District of Columbia .... C. 1929, T. 9, Secs. 13, 14	Competent but not compellable	Competent but not compellable	Competent but not compellable	Competent but not compellable[10]
Florida .... R. G. S. 1920, Secs. 2702, 6018	Spouse of a party not excluded as a witness[11]	Spouse of a party not excluded as a witness[11]	Spouse of a party not excluded as a witness[11]	Spouse of a party not 15 excluded as a witness[11]
Georgia .... C. 1926, C. of Prac., Sec. 5785; Supp. 1930, P. C., Sec. 1037		Incompetent		Incompetent

* See pages 600–601 for all numbered footnotes to this table.

§ 226]

CVII*

FOR AND AGAINST EACH OTHER

Marital Communications			
Spouse In-competent?	Spouse Privi-leged?	Need Be Con-fidential?[1]	Exceptional and Miscellaneous Provisions[2]
	Yes[7]	No	Privileges do not apply to civil action by one spouse against other; nor to criminal action for crime by one against other
	Yes[7]	No	Privileges do not apply to civil action by one spouse against other; nor to criminal action for crime by one against other
Yes		No	In criminal prosecution, spouse may testify against other in case in which injury has been done by either to person or property of other
	Yes[7]	No	Privileges do not apply to civil action by one against other; nor to criminal action for crime by one against other, or for crime by one against another person, committed while engaged in and connected with commission of crime by one spouse against other
	Yes[7]	No	Privileges do not apply to civil action by one against other; nor to criminal action for crime by one against other
Yes		Yes	
	See footnote 11	See footnote 11	
Yes		No	Either is competent but not compellable to testify against other in prosecution for offense committed or attempted on person of either by other

[§ 226

TABLE CVII

Jurisdiction and Citation	For Each Other		Against Each Other	
	Civil Action	Criminal Action	Civil Action	Criminal Action
Hawaii .... R. L. 1925, Sec. 2618; Sec. 2619, amd. by Sess. L. 1927, Act 164, p. 163; Sec. 2620	Spouse of party is competent and compellable[12]	Spouse of party accused is competent	Spouse of party is competent and compellable[12]	Incompetent
Idaho .... Comp. St. 1919, Secs. 7937, 8035, 9130	Privileged[4]	Privileged in action in which one or both are parties[5]	Privileged[6]	Privileged in action in which one or both are parties[5]
Illinois .... Cahill, R. S. 1931, Ch. 51, Sec. 5	Incompetent[13]	Incompetent[13]	Incompetent[13]	Incompetent[13]
Indiana .... Burns, Ann. St. 1926, Secs. 549– 50, 556, 2267	Apparently no incompetency or privilege[14]	Apparently no incompetency or privilege[14]	Apparently no incompetency or privilege[14]	Apparently no incompetency or privilege[14]
Iowa .... C. 1927, Secs. 11260–62	May testify	May testify	Incompetent	Incompetent
Kansas .... R. S. 1923, Secs. 60(2805), 62(1420)	See footnote 15	Spouse of party accused is compellable	See footnote 15	Spouse of party accused is competent but not compellable[16]
Kentucky .... Carroll, Civ. C. of Prac. 1906, Sec. 606, amd. by Sess. L. 1930, Ch. 21, p. 69	Incompetent	Incompetent[17]	Incompetent	Incompetent
Louisiana .... Marr, R. C. of Prac. 1927, Act 157, p. 379		Competent and compellable[18]		Not compellable
Maine .... R. S. 1930, Ch. 96, Sec. 114; Ch. 146, Sec. 19	Spouse of party may testify	Spouse of accused is competent	Spouse of party may testify	Spouse of accused is competent
Maryland .... Bagby, Ann. C. 1924, Art. 35, Secs. 1, 4	Spouse of party is competent and compellable[12]	Spouse of accused is competent	Spouse of party is competent and compellable[12]	Spouse of accused is competent but not compellable[19]
Massachusetts ..... G. L. 1932, Ch. 233, Sec. 20	May testify	Not compellable[20]	May testify	Not compellable

(Continued)

Marital Communications			
Spouse Incompetent?	Spouse Privileged?	Need Be Confidential?[1]	Exceptional and Miscellaneous Provisions[2]
	Yes	No	Spouse is compellable against other in criminal action for crime by one against person of other
	Yes[7]	No	Privileges do not apply to civil action by one against other; nor to criminal action for crime of violence upon one by other
Yes		No	No incompetency in cases where wife, if unmarried, would be plaintiff or defendant; or where action grows out of personal wrong by one to other
Yes		No	When one spouse is a party and incompetent in his or her own behalf, the other is also excluded, except in action for wife's seduction, where husband is competent and wife incompetent
Yes		No	Spouses may testify against each other in criminal action for crime by one against other, or in civil action by one against other
Yes		No	Neglect or refusal of wife to testify for husband, accused, raises no presumption of guilt and shall not be referred to in case
Yes		No	In actions which might have been brought by or against wife if she were unmarried, either but not both may testify
	Yes	Yes	
Yes (see last column)		Yes	Provision on communications is only express as to criminal actions
Yes		Yes	

[§ 226

TABLE CVII

Jurisdiction and Citation	For Each Other		Against Each Other	
	Civil Action	Criminal Action	Civil Action	Criminal Action
Michigan .... Comp. L. 1929, Secs. 14217, 14221	Privileged[4]	Privileged[4]	Privileged[6]	Privileged[6]
Minnesota .... G. S. 1923, Sec. 9814	Privileged[4]	Privileged[4]	Privileged[6]	Privileged[6]
Mississippi .... C. 1930, Sec. 1528	May be introduced by each other	May be introduced by each other	Spouse of party is incompetent (see last column)	Spouse of party is incompetent (see last column)[21]
Missouri .... R. S. 1929, Secs. 1728, 3692–93	Not disqualified as witnesses[22]	May testify at option of defendant spouse	Not disqualified as witnesses[22]	Spouse of accused not compellable
Montana .... R. C. 1921, Secs. 10536, 12176	Privileged[4]	Privileged in action in which one or both are parties[5]	Privileged[6]	Privileged in action in which one or both are parties[5]
Nebraska .... Comp. St. 1929, Secs. 20(1201), 20(1203)– 20(1204)	Competent[23]	May be witnesses	Incompetent	Incompetent
Nevada .... Comp. L. 1929 (Hillyer), Sec. 8971	Privileged[4]	Privileged[4]	Privileged[6]	Privileged[6]
New Hampshire[24] ... Pub. L. 1926, Ch. 336, Sec. 31	Competent and compellable	Competent and compellable	Competent and compellable	Competent and compellable
New Jersey .... Comp. St. 1910, p. 1838, Sec. 57; p. 2222, Sec. 5	Spouse of person interested is competent and compellable	Spouse of accused is privileged[8]	Spouse of person interested is competent and compellable	Spouse of accused is incompetent (but see last column)
New Mexico .... St. Ann. 1929, Secs. 45(505), 45(507); Sec. 45(512), amd. by Sess. L. 1933, Ch. 33, p. 35	Spouse of party is competent[12]	Spouse of defendant is competent	Spouse of party is competent[12]	Spouse of defendant is incompetent

§ 226]

(Continued)

Marital Communications			Exceptional and Miscellaneous Provisions[2]
Spouse In-competent?	Spouse Privi-leged?	Need Be Con-fidential?[1]	
	Yes[5]	No	Privileges do not apply where action grows out of personal wrong by one to another. In any action instituted by either in consequence of adultery, neither is competent
	Yes[7]	No	Privileges do not apply to civil action by one against other; nor to criminal action for crime by one against other
			Spouses are competent in own behalf as against each other, in all controversies between them. In instances where they are not introduced by each other, they shall not be required to answer inter-rogatories or make discovery without consent of both
Yes		Yes	No inference is to be drawn from failure of de-fendant to avail himself or herself of testimony of other spouse
	Yes[7]	No	Privileges do not apply to civil action by one against other; nor to criminal action for crime by one against other
Yes		No	Spouses competent against each other in criminal action for crime by one against other
	Yes[7]	No	Privileges do not apply to civil action by one against other; nor to criminal action for crime by one against other
Yes		See last column	Neither may testify against other as to any state-ment, conversation, letter or other communication made to other or to another person; nor may either testify to any matter which in the court's opinion would lead to violation of marital con-fidence
	Yes	Yes	Spouses are incompetent for or against each other in action for criminal conversation, and not compellable for each other in divorce for adultery, except to prove marriage in both cases. Wife may testify against husband in criminal action if she is the complainant against him and offers herself as a witness[25]
	Yes	No	Either is competent to testify against other in prosecution for assault or violence forcibly com-mitted by other on person of witness. If spouse voluntarily testifies to communication made to other spouse, that is deemed a consent to exami-nation of spouse to whom communication was made

[§ 226

TABLE CVII

| Jurisdiction and Citation | For Each Other | | Against Each Other | |
	Civil Action	Criminal Action	Civil Action	Criminal Action
New York .... Cahill, Consol. L. 1930, Ch. 41, Sec. 2445; Civ. Prac. Act 1931, Secs. 346, 349	Spouse of party is competent and compellable[12]	Spouse of accused is competent	Spouse of party is competent and compellable[12]	Spouse of accused is competent
North Carolina ..... C. 1927, Secs. 1801–2	Spouse of party is competent and compellable[12]	Spouse of accused is competent	Spouse of party is competent and compellable[12]	Spouse of defendant is incompetent
North Dakota ...... Comp. L. 1913, Sec. 7871	Privileged[4]	Privileged[4]	Privileged[6]	Privileged[6]
Ohio .... Complete G. C. 1931 (Page), Secs. 11494, 13444(2)	Apparently competent[26]	Competent	Apparently competent[26]	Impliedly incompetent
Oklahoma .... St. 1931, Secs. 272, 3069	Incompetent	May be witnesses	Incompetent	Incompetent
Oregon .... C. 1930, Secs. 9(404)–9(405), 13(930)	Privileged[4]	Privileged when other is the accused[5]	Privileged[6]	Privileged when other is the accused[5]
Pennsylvania ...... St. 1920 (West), Secs. 8169–70, 21837, 21839, 21846–47			Incompetent	Incompetent
Rhode Island ...... G. L. 1923, Secs. 5023, 5029	Spouse of party is competent	Spouse of respondent is privileged[8]	Spouse of party is competent (see last column)	Spouse of respondent is privileged[8]
South Carolina ..... C. of L. 1922, C. C. P., Sec. 708; C. Cr. P., Sec. 98	Spouse of party is competent and compellable[12]	Competent and compellable	Spouse of party is competent and compellable[12]	Apparently competent and compellable (but see footnote 27)

§ 226]

(Continued)

Marital Communications			Exceptional and Miscellaneous Provisions[2]
Spouse Incompetent?	Spouse Privileged?	Need Be Confidential?[1]	
	Yes[5]	Yes	Neither is competent against other in action founded on adultery except to prove marriage, disprove adultery or certain defenses. In action for criminal conversation, plaintiff's wife is incompetent for him, but competent for defendant except as to confidential communications
	Yes	Yes	Spouses are incompetent for or against each other in divorce for adultery, except to prove marriage; and in action for criminal conversation except that wife may refute charges which assail her character. Failure to call spouse for defendant in criminal action is not to prejudice the defense
	Yes[7]	No	Privileges do not apply to civil action by one against other; nor to criminal action for crime by one against other
Yes		Yes (see last column)	Spouses may not testify to a communication between them or act done by either in other's presence, unless communication was made or act done in known presence or hearing of third person competent as a witness (see also footnote 2)
Yes		No	In criminal action for crime by one against other, spouses may testify against each other, and may disclose communications made between them
	Yes[7]	No	Privileges do not apply to civil action by one against other; nor to criminal action for crime by one against other. If party to action offers himself as a witness, that is deemed a consent to examination of other spouse
	Yes	Yes	See footnote 2
Yes (see last column)		No	In civil action spouse cannot criminate other; or disclose communications, except in trials involving their respective property rights (see also footnote 2). Statute relating to communications specifies only civil actions
	Yes	See footnote 28	

[§ 226

TABLE CVII

Jurisdiction and Citation	For Each Other		Against Each Other	
	Civil Action	Criminal Action	Civil Action	Criminal Action
South Dakota ...... Comp. L. 1929, Sec. 2717	Privileged[4]	Privileged[4]	Privileged[6]	Privileged[6]
Tennessee .... C. 1932, Secs. 9777–78	Competent	Competent[29]	Competent	Competent[29]
Texas .... Complete St. 1928, Civ. St., Art. 3715; C. Cr. P., Art. 714	Spouse of party is competent[12]	May be witnesses	Spouse of party is competent[12]	Incompetent
Utah .... Const., Art. I, Sec. 12; R. S. 1933, 104-49-3, 105-45-4	Privileged[4]	Privileged in action in which one or both are parties[5]	Privileged[6]	Privileged in action in which one or both are parties[5]
Vermont .... G. L. 1917, Sec. 1894	Competent	Competent	Competent	Competent
Virginia .... C. 1930, Secs. 6210–12	Competent	Compellable	Competent	Privileged[5] (see last column)
Washington .... Remington, Comp. St. 1922, Sec. 1214	Privileged[4]	Privileged[4]	Privileged[6]	Privileged[6]
West Virginia ..... C. 1931, Ch. 50, Art. 6, Sec. 10; Ch. 57, Art. 3, Secs. 2–4	Competent and apparently compellable[30]	Competent and compellable	Competent and apparently compellable[30]	Privileged[5]
Wisconsin .... St. 1931, Sec. 325.18	Competent	Competent	Competent	Competent
Wyoming .... R. S. 1931, Secs. 89(1702)– 89(1703)	May testify as though unmarried	May testify as though unmarried	Incompetent	Incompetent

§ 226]

(Continued)

Marital Communications			Exceptional and Miscellaneous Provisions[2]
Spouse Incompetent?	Spouse Privileged?	Need Be Confidential?[1]	
	Yes[7]	No	Privileges do not apply to civil action by one against other; nor to criminal action for crime by one against other
See last column	See last column	See last column	In all civil actions spouses are incompetent to testify to any matter which occurred between them by virtue of the marital relation
Yes		See footnote 28	Spouses may testify against each other in criminal action for offense by one against other; and may testify as to communications which extenuate or justify an offense for which either is on trial
	Yes[7]	No	Privileges do not apply to civil action by one against other; nor to criminal action for crime by one against other
Yes		See last column	Neither may testify against other as to statement, conversation, letter or other communication made to other or to another person, nor may either testify in any case to a matter which in the court's opinion would lead to violation of marital confidence
	Yes[7]	Yes	Either is compellable to testify against other in criminal action for offense by one against other. If either is examined for other, in prosecution, the privilege is gone and such witness may then be compelled to testify against accused
	Yes[7]	No	Privileges do not apply in civil action by one against other; nor to criminal action for crime by one against other
See footnote 31	See footnote 31	See footnote 31	Spouses are compellable against each other in criminal action for offense by one against other. Failure of spouse to testify creates no presumption against accused and shall not be the subject of comment
	Yes[7]	Yes	Private communication is not privileged: (a) where both spouses are parties; (b) where it relates to charge of personal violence by one against other; (c) where it relates to matters within scope of agency of one spouse for other
			Spouses may testify against each other in criminal action for crime by one against other; or in civil action by one against other

[§ 226

TABLE CVII (*Continued*)

[1] Jurisdictions are classified in this column according to the wording of the statutes. However, some courts have read into the statute the necessity of confidentiality (see *Leucht* v. *Leucht*, 129 Ky. 700; 112 S. W. 845 [1908]; and *Hagerman* v. *Wigent*, 108 Mich. 192; 65 N. W. 756 [1896]). Cases in particular jurisdictions should be consulted.

[2] Forty-three jurisdictions have specific provisions permitting one or both spouses to testify in certain actions, as exceptions to the general rules set forth in the table above. The importance of these variations, in the writer's opinion, does not justify their inclusion in tabular form; therefore, only citations are given: **Alabama,** C. 1923, Sec. 5638; **Alaska,** Sess. L. 1913, Ch. 57, p. 121, Sec. 2; Ch. 75, p. 292, Sec. 3; Sess. L. 1919, Ch. 49, p. 156, Sec. 5; **Arizona,** R. C. 1928, Secs. 4412, 5177–78; **Arkansas,** Crawf. and Moses, Dig. 1921, Secs. 2416, 2709, 4146; **California,** C. C. P. 1933 (Lake), Sec. 1881; P. C. 1933 (Lake), Secs. 270e, 1322; Deering, G. L. 1931, Vol. I, Act 1906, p. 820; **Colorado,** Comp. L. 1921, G. S., Secs. 2451, 5570, 6846; **Connecticut,** G. S. 1930, Secs. 4865, 5583, 6480; **Delaware,** R. C. 1915, Secs. 3041, 4236, 4791; **Georgia,** C. 1926, P. C., Secs. 104, 116; Supp. 1930, P. C., Sec. 1037; **Hawaii,** R. L. 1925, Sec. 2619, as amended by Sess. L. 1927, Act 164, p. 163; Sess. L. 1925, Act 164, p. 189; **Idaho,** Comp. St. 1919, Sec. 9130; **Illinois,** Cahill, R. S. 1931, Ch. 38, Sec. 8; Ch. 51, Sec. 5; **Indiana,** Burns, Ann. St. 1926, Secs. 556, 2558; **Iowa,** C. 1927, Secs. 11257, 11260, 13231; **Kansas,** R. S. 1923, Sec. 60(1509); **Kentucky,** Carroll, St. 1922, Sec. 1215b(3); Civ. C. of Prac. 1906, Sec. 606, as amended by Sess. L. 1930, Ch. 21, p. 69; **Louisiana,** Marr, Ann. R. S. 1915, Secs. 1650, 2313–14; **Maine,** R. S. 1930, Ch. 73, Sec. 2; Ch. 135, Sec. 24; **Massachusetts,** G. L. 1932, Ch. 233, Sec. 20; Ch. 273, Sec. 7; **Michigan,** Comp. L. 1929, Secs. 12695, 12790, 12793, 14221, 16868–69; Sess. L. 1931, No. 328, p. 656; **Minnesota,** G. S. 1923, Sec. 9814; **Mississippi,** C. 1930, Sec. 1419; **Missouri,** R. S. 1929, Sec. 266; **Montana,** R. C. 1921, Sec. 12176; **Nebraska,** Comp. St. 1929, Secs. 20(1203), 42(306); **Nevada,** Comp. L. 1929 (Hillyer), Secs. 8969, 10165, 10521; **New Jersey,** Comp. St. 1910, p. 1771, Sec. 73b; p. 4714, Sec. 72; p. 2833, Secs. 23, 24; **New Mexico,** St. Ann. 1929, Secs. 45(505)–45(506), 100(219); **New York,** Consol. L. 1930, Ch. 41, Sec. 1091; **North Carolina,** C. 1927, Sec. 1802; **Ohio,** Complete G. C. 1931 (Page), Secs. 11988, 13444(2); **Oklahoma,** St. 1931, Secs. 272, 681; **Oregon,** C. 1930, Sec. 11(1102); Sec. 13(930) as amended by Sess. L. 1933, Ch. 274, p. 421; Sec. 14(851); **Pennsylvania,** St. 1920 (West), Secs. 8169, 9068, 9072, 14571, 14603, 14605, 21837–38, 21840, 21847–51; Cum. Supp. 1928 (West), Secs. 10172a(2), 10172b(1); **Rhode Island,** G. L. 1923, Sec. 5023; **South Dakota,** Comp. L. 1929, Secs. 2717, 2979, 4109; **Texas,** Complete St. 1928, Civ. St., Art. 4633; P. C., Arts. 507, 521, 605; **Utah,** R. S. 1933, 103-51-14, 104-49-3, 105-45-4; **Vermont,** G. L. 1917, Secs. 1894, 3541, 5379; **Virginia,** C. 1930, Sec. 4579; **West Virginia,** C. 1931, Ch. 61, Art. 8, Sec. 7; **Wisconsin,** St. 1931, Secs. 325.18, 351.18; **Wyoming,** R. S. 1931, Secs. 32(808), 35(111), 89(1702).

[3] See *McCoy* v. *State,* 221 Ala. 466; 129 So. 21 (1930), holding that a wife may testify against her husband in a criminal prosecution "if she so desires."

[4] Spouse who is to be testified "for" must consent.

[5] Both spouses must consent.

[6] Spouse who is to be testified "against" must consent.

[7] Spouse other than the one sought to be examined as witness must consent.

[8] Spouse sought to be examined must consent.

[9] In *State* v. *Jaroslowski,* 30 Del. 108; 103 A. 657 (1918), the court held that a wife could testify voluntarily against her husband in a criminal action, over his objection. Whether she was compellable was expressly left undecided.

[10] A similar statute in **Alabama** was held to mean that the spouse testifying possessed the privilege, a natural interpretation (see footnote 3 above).

[11] The court in *Ex parte Beville,* 58 Fla. 170; 50 So. 685 (1909), interpreted the ambiguous statute to mean (a) that a spouse is competent and compellable to testify for and against the other, in criminal as well as civil actions (followed by *Whitfield* v. *State,* 85 Fla. 142; 95 So. 430 [1923]); and (b) that the common law as to marital communications was undisturbed.

[12] Spouse of party, or "person in whose behalf an action is brought or defended."

[13] Illinois (Cahill, R. S. 1931, Ch. 51, Sec. 5): The spouses are incompetent for or against each other "as to any transaction or conversation occurring during the marriage . . . ." (there are numerous exceptions).

§ 226]

TABLE CVII (*Concluded*)

[14] The **Indiana** provisions are not entirely clear, but from the language used in *Vukodono-vich* v. *State*, 197 Ind. 169; 150 N. E. 56 (1926), and *Pritchard* v. *Pritchard*, 93 Ind. App. 89; 177 N. E. 502 (1931), it appears that husband and wife are competent and compellable, for and against each other, in all actions.

[15] The **Kansas** statute does not expressly cover civil actions. However, in *Harris* v. *Brown*, 187 F. 6 (1911), the court gives a full discussion leading to its conclusion that husband and wife are competent for and against each other in civil actions.

[16] See *State* v. *Ralston*, 131 Kan. 138; 289 P. 409 (1930), to the effect that a husband is competent to testify against his wife in a criminal action, but must do so voluntarily.

[17] *Jones* v. *Commonwealth*, 252 Ky. 341; 67 S. W. (2d) 480 (1934), is a late case holding that a wife is not a competent witness for her husband.

[18] *State* v. *Todd*, 173 La. 23; 136 So. 76 (1931), expressly holds that the privilege against being compelled to testify relates only to testimony "against" the other spouse, and that the defendant in a criminal action can compel the spouse to testify for him or her.

[19] *Richardson* v. *State*, 103 Md. 112; 63 A. 317 (1906), held that a wife was competent against her husband, but that she could not have been compelled to testify.

[20] **Massachusetts** (G. L. 1932, Ch. 233, Sec. 20): This ambiguous provision apparently means that a spouse is not compellable for or against the other in a criminal action (see *Commonwealth* v. *Spencer*, 212 Mass. 438; 99 N. E. 266 [1912]; and *Commonwealth* v. *Moore*, 162 Mass. 441; 38 N. E. 1120 [1894]). A similar provision in **Louisiana** was given a different interpretation (see footnote 18 above).

[21] See *Davis* v. *State*, 157 Miss. 669; 128 So. 886 (1930), holding a spouse incompetent as against the other.

[22] In *Tucker* v. *Tucker*, 224 Mo. App. 669; 31 S. W. (2d) 238 (1930), the court said that the restrictions on a spouse testifying for or against the other had all been removed, except as to admissions and confidential communications.

[23] *Smith* v. *Meyers*, 52 Neb. 70; 71 N. W. 1006 (1897), seems to consider a spouse competent and compellable "for" the other.

[24] See *Clements* v. *Marston*, 52 N. H. 31 (1872), for a good review of **New Hampshire** legislation.

[25] *State* v. *Snyder*, 93 N. J. L. 18; 107 A. 167 (1919), held that the wife need not be the "formal" complainant against her husband in order to testify against him.

[26] The **Ohio** statutes are vague as to marital testimony in civil actions, but *Westerman* v. *Westerman*, 25 Ohio St. 500 (1874), held that husband and wife were competent in such actions.

[27] The provision in **South Carolina** (C. of L. 1922, C. C. P., Sec. 708) apparently makes the spouses competent and compellable against each other in criminal actions; and it was so held in *State* v. *Reynolds*, 48 S. C. 384; 26 S. E. 679 (1896). In a later case, however, *State* v. *Bramlett*, 114 S. C. 389; 103 S. E. 755 (1920), it was said that a wife was incompetent against her husband. Authority was cited which had been distinguished by the Reynolds case as being under an earlier and narrower statute; and the Reynolds case was not cited.

[28] In **South Carolina** and **Texas**, the term "confidential communication" is used in speaking of civil actions, while the term "any communication" is used as to criminal actions (see **South Carolina**, C. of L. 1922, C. C. P., Sec. 708; C. Cr. P., Sec. 98; and **Texas**, Complete St. 1928, Civ. St., Art. 3715; C. Cr. P., Art. 714).

[29] *McCormick* v. *State*, 135 Tenn. 218; 186 S. W. 95 (1915), indicates that the spouses are competent and compellable for and against each other.

[30] *Kilgore* v. *Hanley*, 27 W. Va. 451 (1886), stated that in civil actions husband and wife are competent to give evidence, "the same as any other persons."

[31] **West Virginia** (C. 1931): In Chapter 50, Article 6, Section 10, it is said that spouses are "incompetent" to testify concerning "any communication" by one to the other. However, in Chapter 57, Article 3, Section 4, it is said that neither spouse "without the consent of the other" may testify as to any "confidential communication." The discrepancy is an example of the loose language used by many legislatures in dealing with this subject of marital testimony.

REFERENCES

Book

WIGMORE, J. H. *A Treatise on Evidence,* Vol. 1, Secs. 600–620; Vol. 4, Secs. 2227–45; Vol. 5, Secs. 2332–41 (1923).

Articles

HINES, FREDERICK E. "Privileged Testimony of Husband and Wife in California," 19 Calif. L. Rev. 390–414 (1931).

HUTCHINS, R. M., and C. SLESINGER. "Some Observations on the Law of Evidence: Family Relations," 13 Minn. L. Rev. 675–86 (1929).

Notes

"Admissibility of Wife's Adverse Testimony as to Husband's Conduct in Her Presence," *Smith* v. *State,* 198 Ind. 156; 152 N. E. 803 (1926)—26 Col. L. Rev. 897–98 (1926).

"Compellability of Husband and Wife as Witnesses against One Another in Criminal Cases," 94 Just. P. 691–92 (1930).

"Competency of Husband and Wife as Witnesses in Criminal Case in Federal Court," 31 Law Notes 108–12 (1927).

"Privilege of Husband and Wife—Use for Purpose of Impeachment of Testimony Obtained in Violation of Privilege," *Daggett* v. *State,* 86 Tex. Cr. 98; 215 S. W. 454 (1919)—33 Harv. L. Rev. 873 (1920).

"Privilege of One Spouse Not to Testify 'for or against' the Other," *Hunter* v. *State,* 10 Okla. Cr. 119; 134 P. 1134 (1913)—2 Calif. L. Rev. 148–50 (1914).

"Waiver of Privilege of Not Testifying for or against Spouse—Community Property," *Ex parte Strand,* 123 Cal. App. 170; 11 P. (2d) 89 (1932)—6 So. Calif. L. Rev. 336–38 (1933).

"Wife a Compellable Witness on Charge of Personal Violence by Husband," *Rex* v. *Lapworth,* (1931) 1 K. B. 117—47 L. Quar. Rev. 11–12 (1931).

"Competency of Wife to Testify in Defense of Husband in Criminal Case," *Funk* v. *United States,* 290 U. S. 371 (1933)—33 Mich. L. Rev. 306–7 (1934) ; 23 Ky. L. Jour. 190–94 (1934).

Annotations

"Abortion as an Offense against Other Spouse within Exception to Rule Relating to Competency of One as Witness against Other," 16 A. L. R. 490–92 (1922).

"Competency of Husband or Wife to Testify in Suit for Divorce on Ground of Cruelty," 70 A. L. R. 499–506 (1931).

"Crime Directed against Spouse but Taking Effect against Third Person as within Exception to Rule of Incompetency of Husband or Wife," 35 A. L. R. 1132–34 (1925).

"Effect of Marrying a Witness in Order to Prevent Her from Testifying," 67 L. R. A. 499–504 (1905).

"Effect of Statute Making Husband and Wife Competent for or against Each Other, upon Privilege as to Confidential Communications," 27 L. R. A. (N.S.) 273–75 (1910).

§ 226]

"Sexual Offense by One Spouse with or against Third Person as Crime against Other Spouse within Statute Relating to Competency of Husband or Wife as Witness against Other," 4 A. L. R. 1069–73 (1919) ; 35 A. L. R. 138–39 (1925).

"Waiver of Privilege as to Communication between Husband and Wife by Calling One Spouse as Witness for Other," 40 L. R. A. (N.S.) 43–44 (1912).

"Competency or Privilege of One Spouse as a Witness in a Prosecution against Other for an Offense Committed before Marriage," 76 A. L. R. 1088–92 (1932).

"Direction of Verdict Based on Testimony of Spouse of Party," 72 A. L. R. 87 (1931).

"Competency or Privilege of One Spouse as a Witness in Prosecution against Other for Offense Committed before Marriage," 76 A. L. R. 1088–92 (1932).

"Killing or Assaulting Third Person by One Spouse against the Other within Exception to Rule of Incompetency of Husband or Wife," 82 A. L. R. 644–45 (1933).

Section 227. Descent and Distribution

CROSS REFERENCES : Effect of absolute divorce on property rights, **Secs. 96–99;** Effect of limited divorce, **Secs. 128–29;** Antenuptial and postnuptial contracts of husband and wife affecting survivor's property rights, **Secs. 155–56;** Descent and distribution of community property, **Sec. 178;** Statutory changes in dower, **Sec. 189;** Statutory changes in curtesy, **Sec. 216;** Barring rights of surviving spouse, **Secs. 196–99, 220;** Forfeiture of rights of surviving spouse, **Secs. 202, 221;** Election and waiver, **Secs. 189, 205–7, 216, 219;** Homestead, exempt property, and family allowance, **Sec. 228;** Inheritance by children, **Sec. 239;** Inheritance by and from bastards, **Sec. 249;** Inheritance by adopted child, **Sec. 262;** Inheritance from adopted child, **Sec. 263**

A few preliminary distinctions are essential to a proper understanding of the scope of the present section. We are concerned primarily with the factual situation of a deceased spouse who dies completely intestate, secondarily with a decedent who dies partially intestate, and not at all with a decedent who dies completely testate. It is obvious in the latter case that true statutes of descent and distribution do not apply ; the rights of the surviving spouse are governed by provisions on dower, curtesy, and statutory substitutes in the nature of dower and curtesy. Several jurisdictions have provisions which give to a surviving spouse an absolute share of real or personal property whether the decedent dies testate or intestate. Although these statutes apply to the property of an intestate decedent, they are more properly classified as statutory substitutes for dower and curtesy than as true statutes of descent and distribution. Therefore they have been collected in **Sections 189** and **216** and are not repeated in the present section. It is assumed here that the share of the

[§ 227

survivor is given only after the decedent's debts have been satisfied; exempt property is discussed in **Section 228**. The term "intestate share" is hereafter used to indicate the rights of a survivor as a true heir or distributee. It should also be remembered that when the eight community-property states (**Arizona, California, Idaho, Louisiana, Nevada, New Mexico, Texas, Washington**) are referred to only the succession to the decedent's separate property is covered; succession to community property is discussed in **Section 178**. No attempt has been made to incorporate into this section special statutes dealing with inheritance by children, by and from bastards or adopted children, although such provisions have an indirect effect on the share of the surviving spouse.

At common law, husband and wife did not inherit real property from each other, but were confined to rights of dower and curtesy. The extensive marital rights of the husband in his wife's personalty made his rights as distributee unimportant; and even where she infrequently possessed personal property at her death, the practice of appointing the husband as administrator without obligation to account for surplus virtually made him the sole distributee. An early English statute (St. 22 and 23 Car. II, c. 10), generally regarded as part of the common law, gave the widow a right to one-third of the husband's personalty if there were children surviving; to one-half if there were no children.

The common law, however, is no longer of great importance because of the widespread statutes of descent and distribution found in varying forms in all fifty-one jurisdictions. The relevant material has been divided into the following subsections: complete intestacy; partial intestacy; miscellaneous statutes; comment.

COMPLETE INTESTACY

The many statutory variations necessitate a general discussion in this text; for details the reader is referred to Table CVIII following. For the sake of clarity the legislation has been further divided according to the possible factual situation existing at the death of the intestate: (1) children, issue, lineal descendants (see table) survive; (2) no lineal descendants, etc., survive; (3) no blood relatives, kindred, heirs (as stated below) survive. A discussion of election between the intestate share and dower, curtesy, or statutory substitutes comprises a fourth subdivision.

1. *Lineal descendants survive.*—Any measured classification is impracticable, but the fifty-one jurisdictions may be divided into five general groups, complemented by Table CVIII following.

§ 227]

a) Twenty-one jurisdictions: **Alabama, Alaska, Arkansas, Delaware, District of Columbia, Hawaii, Iowa, Kansas, Kentucky, Louisiana, Missouri, New Hampshire, New Jersey, North Carolina, Oregon, Rhode Island, Tennessee, Vermont, Virginia, West Virginia, Wisconsin.** In eighteen of these jurisdictions (**Alabama, Arkansas,** and **Louisiana** excepted), the true statutes of descent of real property do not include the surviving spouse, who is thus confined to marital rights of dower, curtesy, or statutory substitutes. Certain of these jurisdictions do provide a statutory share in fee as a marital portion (see **Secs. 189, 216**), but such share is given whether the deceased spouse dies testate or intestate, and the share does not come within the purview of the present section. In **Alabama** and **Arkansas,** the widow is confined to dower; the widower is said to take under the statute of descent but is not a true heir since the share is only for life (see table). In **Louisiana,** a community-property state, no provision was found which gives the survivor an intestate share of separate property, real or personal. Eight of the foregoing jurisdictions likewise do not include the widow (**Arkansas**) or the surviving spouse (**Hawaii, Iowa, Kansas, Kentucky, Missouri, New Hampshire, Vermont**) in statutes of distribution of personalty. However, an absolute share of personalty is often given as an addition to dower or curtesy (see **Secs. 189, 216**).

b) Twenty-three jurisdictions: **California, Colorado, Connecticut, Florida, Idaho, Maine, Maryland, Massachusetts, Minnesota, Mississippi, Montana, Nebraska, Nevada, New Mexico, New York, North Dakota, Ohio, Oklahoma, Pennsylvania, South Carolina, South Dakota, Utah, Wyoming.** Here the legislation has been simplified in a manner which the writer thinks advisable. No distinction is drawn between real and personal property; and, what is perhaps more important, the widow and widower take equal shares. The writer can perceive no valid reason for giving either spouse a greater intestate share than the other, especially in view of general legislation placing husband and wife on an equality. As might be expected, the amount of the share varies: the survivor is entitled to one-half or one-third depending on whether there is one child or more than one (ten jurisdictions); to one-third (seven jurisdictions); to one-half (two jurisdictions); to a child's share (two jurisdictions); to one-fourth (one jurisdiction); in **Nebraska** the share may be one-fourth, or one-third, or one-half (see table).

c) Five jurisdictions: **Arizona, Illinois, Michigan, Texas, Washington.** In these five states the widow and widower have equal rights, but the share of real property is different from the share of personalty

[§ 227

(see table). Seven of the jurisdictions already enumerated (see group *a* above) which do not provide an intestate share of realty do give the survivor the same share of personalty, obviously distinguishing between the two kinds of property (**District of Columbia, New Jersey, Oregon, Rhode Island, Tennessee, Virginia, West Virginia**).

d) Two jurisdictions: **Georgia, Indiana.** Here the shares of real or personal property are equal in amount, but the widow is entitled to a different and greater share than the widower under specified circumstances (see table).

e) In five states which have been included in group *a* above and which draw a distinction between intestate realty and intestate personalty, the situation is further complicated by the fact that the widow is entitled to a different share than the widower (**Alabama, Arkansas, Delaware, North Carolina, Wisconsin**). (See table for details.)

2. *No lineal descendants, etc., survive.*—Again the term "lineal descendants" is used in a broad sense; the wording of particular statutes is set forth in the table. The fifty-one jurisdictions may be grouped roughly into six categories.

a) Ten jurisdictions: **Alaska, Colorado, Florida, Georgia, Kansas, Minnesota, Mississippi, New Mexico, Oregon, Wisconsin.** The surviving spouse is entitled to the whole of the intestate's estate, whether real or personal property. These provisions have been criticized as being too generous when blood relatives of the decedent survive, but, although specific applications of the statutes may seem unfair, on the whole the question seems one of policy, and the writer feels that the fault, if any, is not sufficiently glaring to justify criticism.

b) Eleven jurisdictions: **Connecticut, Indiana, Iowa, Massachusetts, New York, North Dakota, Pennsylvania, South Dakota, Utah, Vermont, Wyoming.** These states (with perhaps the exception of **Indiana**) have modified the provisions of group *a* above by giving the surviving spouse the entire real and personal property up to a specified value, and, in addition thereto, one-half (three-fourths in **Wyoming**) of the property in excess of such value. The **Indiana** statute similarly gives the survivor the whole up to a stated value, but, if the estate exceeds such value, the survivor apparently is entitled only to three-fourths, and not to three-fourths in addition to the stated sum. The limitation of value varies from one thousand dollars in **Indiana** to twenty-five thousand dollars in **Utah.**

c) Eleven jurisdictions: **California, Hawaii, Idaho, Maine, Maryland, Montana, Nebraska, Nevada, Ohio, Oklahoma, South Caro-**

lina. These jurisdictions provide that the surviving spouse is entitled to one-half of the estate, except in **Ohio** where the share is three-fourths. No distinction is drawn between real and personal property, and they are to be commended for treating husband and wife alike.

d) Five jurisdictions: **Arizona, Illinois, Texas, Washington, West Virginia.** The surviving spouse in these five states is entitled to all of the personal property and to one-half (**Arizona, Illinois, Texas, Washington**), to a specially stated share (**West Virginia**), of the real property.

e) Ten jurisdictions: **Alabama, Arkansas, Delaware, District of Columbia, Michigan, New Jersey, North Carolina, Rhode Island, Tennessee, Virginia.** These states do not lend themselves to any measured classification. In **New Jersey, Tennessee,** and **Virginia,** the survivor is not included in statutes of descent of realty, but he or she takes all of the personalty. **Rhode Island** gives the survivor all of the realty for life and a stated share of personalty. The remaining six jurisdictions differentiate between real and personal property; and five of them (**District of Columbia** excepted) also distinguish between the widow and the widower (see table for details).

f) Four jurisdictions: **Kentucky, Louisiana, Missouri, New Hampshire.** No statutes giving the survivor a true intestate share of real or personal property were found in these states. However, in **Kentucky, Missouri,** and **New Hampshire,** the marital rights provided, whether the decedent is testate or intestate, should be noted (see **Secs. 189, 216**). In **Louisiana,** the survivor apparently is confined to rights in community property.

3. *No relatives, kindred, etc., survive.*—It is obvious that we are not concerned in this subdivision with the ten jurisdictions which provide that the surviving spouse is entitled to the entire estate if there are no lineal descendants (see 2 *a* above). The remaining forty-one jurisdictions may be divided into four groups.

a) Six jurisdictions: **Arizona, Connecticut, Idaho, Indiana, Iowa, Ohio.** With the exception of **Iowa,** the surviving spouse is entitled to the entire real and personal property if there are no surviving descendants or parent of the decedent. In **Iowa,** the same is true provided also that there are no heirs of a parent. In **North Dakota,** the survivor is entitled to the whole estate not to exceed the value of twenty-five thousand dollars and to one-half of the excess if there are no surviving descendants or parent of decedent (see also the next group, *b*).

[§ 227

b) Nineteen jurisdictions: **Alabama, California, Hawaii, Illinois, Maryland, Michigan, Missouri, Montana, Nevada, New York, North Dakota, Oklahoma, South Dakota, Texas, Utah, Virginia, Washington, West Virginia, Wyoming.** In these jurisdictions the widow or widower is entitled to all of the real or personal property if the decedent has left no issue, parent, brother or sister, or descendant of a deceased brother or sister. The same is true of personalty in the **District of Columbia.**

c) Eleven jurisdictions: **Arkansas, Kentucky, Louisiana, Maine, Massachusetts, Nebraska, New Hampshire, Pennsylvania, Rhode Island, South Carolina, Vermont.** The real or personal property descends or is distributed to the surviving spouse if the decedent has left no blood relatives (**Nebraska**), no heirs (**New Hampshire**), no kindred capable of inheriting (in the remaining nine states). In **South Carolina** the survivor takes two-thirds of the real or personal property if the decedent leaves next of kin but no lineal relatives (see the table for a provision respecting "natural children" in **Louisiana**).

d) Five jurisdictions: **Delaware, District of Columbia, New Jersey, North Carolina, Tennessee.** It is difficult to generalize concerning these jurisdictions. In **New Jersey** and **Tennessee** the distribution of all the personalty has been noted (see *2 e* above); in **North Carolina** the widow is entitled to all of the personalty if there be no child, or its representative, and no next of kin; but in all three of the foregoing states the entire real property descends to the survivor if there are no kindred capable of inheriting. The table following gives distinctions between real and personal property and between widow and widower in **Delaware** and the **District of Columbia.**

4. *Election.*—This discussion is limited to the situation of complete intestacy; partial intestacy is covered in the next subsection. Also, election between dower or curtesy and a statutory share in lieu thereof is discussed in **Sections 189, 205–7, 216;** and election between a testamentary provision and dower, curtesy, etc., is discussed in **Sections 199, 205–7, 219.** Whether or not the survivor is entitled to a homestead or family allowance in addition to the intestate share is considered in **Section 228.** Briefly, the present problem is this: Is the survivor entitled to an intestate share in addition to dower, curtesy, etc., or must he or she elect? The question does not arise in the eight community-property states, nor in **North Dakota** or **South Dakota** (see **Secs. 189, 216**); nor in jurisdictions where the survivor, under certain circumstances, is not included in statutes of descent and distribution (see discussion above).

§ 227]

Only eight jurisdictions have been found with express legislation relating to election. In effect, the widow (**Florida, Georgia, Michigan, South Carolina, Utah**), the surviving spouse (**Illinois, Maryland, Massachusetts**), must elect between an intestate share and dower (**Florida, Georgia, Illinois, Maryland, Massachusetts, Michigan, South Carolina**), curtesy (**Massachusetts**), or a distributive share in fee in the nature of a substitute for dower (**Utah**) (see table). **Illinois**, however, further provides that the right to an intestate share does not bar the survivor's right to dower in real estate of which the intestate did not die seized. Statutes have been collected in **Sections 189** and **216** which expressly give a distributive share of personalty in addition to dower, curtesy, etc.

Any general statement concerning the remaining jurisdictions is likely to be misleading because of the many constructions given particular statutes; judicial decisions should be consulted. Where the survivor is entitled to a life estate of dower or curtesy, it seems logical, in the absence of express statute, that he or she is entitled also to an intestate share of the estate (see to that effect *Dahlman* v. *Dahlman,* 28 Mont. 373; 72 P. 748 [1903]). Where, however, the survivor is in the nature of a forced heir, it appears that such statutes are intended to apply when the decedent attempts to dispose of the property by will, and not to the complete intestacy situation. If so, the intestate share would be given.

Partial Intestacy

If the decedent's attempt to devise or bequeath his property fails in part, or if his will does not purport to dispose of the entire estate, a partial intestacy occurs. No statutes expressly applicable to such situations have been found, but the following problems may arise: (1) Does a testamentary provision in favor of the surviving spouse bar his or her share of the intestate property? (2) If dower or curtesy, etc., is claimed where the will contains no provision for the survivor or when he or she dissents from the will (see **Secs. 189, 216**), is a share of the intestate property also given?

1. Fifteen jurisdictions have statutes which may be interpreted to bar the intestate share at least in part if a testamentary provision is given the survivor. Five provide that the "statutory" or "distributive" share of personalty given the widow (**District of Columbia, Kentucky, Montana, Wisconsin**) or the surviving spouse (**Maryland**) as an addition to dower or curtesy is barred by a testamentary provision (see **Sec. 199**). The construction of the terms "statutory" and "distribu-

[§ 227

tive" determines whether or not the survivor's intestate share of personalty is barred. Two jurisdictions provide that the survivor's "statutory share" (**Connecticut**), "distributive share" (**Iowa**), of the estate is barred by a testamentary provision (subject to his or her election). It has been held in **Connecticut** that such terms may mean intestate share; as to the situation in **Iowa**, see *In re Estate of Noble,* 194 Ia. 733; 190 N. W. 511 (1922). Eight states have statutes which, in effect, apparently provide that the share of the partially intestate property (**Indiana, Kansas, Mississippi, Nebraska, New Hampshire, Ohio, West Virginia**), of the partially intestate realty (**Maine**), is barred by a provision in the will for the survivor (see table following and also *Bunker* v. *Bunker,* 130 Me. 103; 154 A. 73 [1931]). The writer, however, does not profess to be dogmatic in the foregoing interpretations.

Variations in the legislative schemes of particular jurisdictions have produced a variety of judicial decisions (see references following this section); but it seems to be held generally that if the decedent has attempted to dispose of the property by will a testamentary provision for the survivor bars his or her right to a share of real property made intestate by failure of a devise.

2. No statutes expressly applicable to the case of partial intestacy were found, but the general statutes in eight states requiring an election between dower, etc., and the intestate share (see subdivision 4 under "Complete Intestacy") apparently apply also to the present situation. In the absence of such statutes, the majority view seems to permit the survivor to take a share of the partially intestate property in addition to dower or curtesy, or statutory substitutes, when he or she is entitled to and does dissent from the will (see *Blatt* v. *Blatt,* 79 Colo. 57; 243 P. 1099 [1926]). The reader is referred to the references following this section for a more extended discussion than can be given here. The statutes should also be noted which give the widow (or the survivor) a statutory share of personalty expressly in addition to dower (see **Secs. 189, 216**).

MISCELLANEOUS STATUTES

Twenty-two jurisdictions have legislation under which the surviving spouse who is responsible for the decedent's death (by murder, etc.) apparently forfeits his or her intestate share. In eighteen the provisions are general in terms, applying to "any person," etc. (see table) (**California, Colorado, District of Columbia, Florida, Indiana, Kansas, Louisiana, Mississippi, Nebraska, North Dakota, Ohio, Oklahoma,**

§ 227]

South Carolina, Tennessee, Utah, Virginia, West Virginia, Wyoming) ; the remaining four states expressly refer to the surviving spouse (Iowa, Minnesota, Oregon, Pennsylvania) (see also a special statute in North Carolina). Such a statute has been held constitutional in spite of a provision that conviction shall not work a forfeiture of estate (*Hamblin* v. *Marchant,* 103 Kan. 508; 175 P. 678 [1918]).

Statutes providing for the barring of dower and curtesy by contract and property settlement, and for forfeiture of the same by misconduct, are collected in prior sections of this volume. A number of these provisions are sufficiently broad in terms to apply as well to an intestate share. They have not here been repeated; the reader is referred to footnote 5 (pp. 626–27) of the table following for such jurisdictions (see also Secs. 155–56). Barring the intestate share by will has already been mentioned above under partial intestacy.

Six jurisdictions provide that an advancement by a decedent to a child, heir, etc. (see table), is not to be considered in computing the widow's intestate share; she takes only from the remaining property (Alabama, Alaska, Kentucky, Massachusetts, Oregon, Washington). North Carolina, on the other hand, expressly provides that children who have received advancements shall account for the same to the widow before her child's part of the intestate property is ascertained.

A few other miscellaneous statutes are collected in the last column of the table. The reader is referred particularly to interesting statutes in California, Georgia, Indiana, Nevada, New Jersey, Ohio, and Oklahoma relating to property which has been acquired in a specified manner.

COMMENT

The clear trend of legislation on descent and distribution has been toward greater simplicity and clarity. Another modern tendency is to treat husband and wife alike, a practice that should be universal. The natural desire to favor a widow is accomplished through dower, homestead, and family-allowance legislation; as heirs, the spouses should be on an equality. A few statutes are needlessly ambiguous and involved (e.g., in Delaware); and the failure of many jurisdictions to define clearly the survivor's rights as heir, as affected by his or her marital rights of dower, curtesy, statutory share, and homestead, has created an undesirable situation easily remedied by a properly drawn statute.

In the writer's opinion, a satisfactory statute should be constructed on the following basic framework: (*a*) an equal share given the widow and widower; (*b*) real and personal property treated in the same manner; (*c*) a varying share in amount, depending on the number of surviving children or their descendants, but to be not less than a defined amount, regardless of the number of children (see **California**); (*d*) when there are no children, etc., a definitely larger share to be given, perhaps the whole (see **Colorado**) or the whole up to a stated value and a proportion of the excess (see **Massachusetts**); (*e*) if there are no children or their descendants, nor parent, brother or sister, or descendant of a deceased brother or sister, the entire estate to be given (see **Illinois**); (*f*) a provision clearly defining the relation of the intestate share to other marital rights; (*g*) a provision clarifying the situation of partial intestacy.

Citations to the statutes discussed above appear in the table following.

TABLE CVIII*

DESCENT AND DISTRIBUTION

Jurisdiction and Citation	When Children, Issue, Descendants, etc., Survive, Surviving Spouse¹ Is Entitled to	When Children, or Other Heirs, etc., Do Not Survive, Surviving Spouse¹ Is Entitled to	Other Rights of Survivor Affecting Intestate Share²	Miscellaneous
Alabama .... C. 1923, Secs. 7365, 7374–76	Whether there are children or not, widower is entitled (*a*) to life estate in the whole, (*b*) to one-half. Widow is entitled (*b*) to one-half if there is only one child, to a child's part if there is more than one and not more than four children, to one-fifth if there are more than four children. (*a*) See footnote 3 as to widow	*a*) The whole if there are no children or their descendants, no parent, no brothers or sisters or their descendants. (*b*) Widow is entitled to the whole if there are no children; widower is entitled as in *a*	*b*) See Table XCV, **Sec. 189**, and Table XCIX, **Sec. 205**	Widow's share is not increased when advancements to a distributee are brought into hotchpot
Alaska .... Comp. L. 1913, Secs. 594–96	*a*) See footnote 3. *b*) One-half if intestate leaves issue	*a*) The whole if intestate leaves no lineal descendants. (*b*) The whole if intestate leaves no issue		*b*) Value of advancement to any of issue is not considered in computing widow's share of one-half

* In this table, *a* indicates descent of real property; *b*, distribution of personal property. See pages 626–28 for all numbered footnotes to the table.

§ 227]

TABLE CVIII (*Continued*)

Jurisdiction and Citation	When Children, Issue, Descendants, etc., Survive, Surviving Spouse[1] Is Entitled to	When Children, or Other Heirs, etc., Do Not Survive, Surviving Spouse[1] Is Entitled to	Other Rights of Survivor Affecting Intestate Share[2]	Miscellaneous
Arizona[4] .... R. C. 1928, Sec. 978	*a*) Life estate in one-third if deceased have a child, children or their descendants. *b*) One-third if there are descendants as in *a*	*a*) One-half if there are no heirs as in preceding column; and the whole if deceased also has no surviving parent. (*b*) The whole if there are no heirs as in preceding column		
Arkansas .... Crawf. and Moses, Dig. 1921, Sec. 3477; Supp. 1927 (Castle), Sec. 3536*a*	Widower is entitled (*a*) to one-third for life, (*b*) to one-third, if wife leaves descendants. See footnote 3 as to widow	*a*) and (*b*) The whole if there be no children or their descendants, parent, nor descendant, or paternal or maternal kindred capable of inheriting. Widower is entitled (*a*) to one-half for life, (*b*) to one-half if wife leaves no descendants		
California[4] .... Prob. C. 1933 (Lake), Secs. 221, 223–24, 229–30, 258	*a*) and (*b*) One-half if decedent leaves only one child or issue of deceased child; one-third if decedent leaves more than one child or one child and lawful issue of one or more deceased children	*a*) and (*b*) One-half if decedent leaves no issue; the whole if decedent leaves no issue, parent, brother or sister or descendant of deceased brother or sister (see last column)		If decedent leaves no issue, surviving spouse is not entitled to share in property of decedent which was separate property of a previously deceased spouse of decedent and came to decedent by gift, descent, devise or bequest. Person convicted of murder of decedent forfeits any portion of the estate
Colorado .... Comp. L. 1921, G. S., Sec. 5151; Sess. L. 1923, Ch. 195, p. 712	*a*) and (*b*) One-half if intestate leaves children or their descendants	*a*) and (*b*) The whole if intestate leaves no child or descendants of any child		Person convicted of murder in first or second degree as principal or accessory shall not take by descent, or any other manner, from decedent
Connecticut .... G. S. 1930, Sec. 5156	*a*) and (*b*) One-third if there are children or their representatives	*a*) and (*b*) The whole to extent of two thousand dollars and one-half of remainder if any, if there are no children or their representatives; the whole of whatever value if there are no children or their representatives and no parent		Testamentary provision for survivor is in lieu of his or her statutory share of real or personal property unless contrary clearly appears from will (subject to election)[5]

[§ 227

TABLE CVIII (*Continued*)

Jurisdiction and Citation	When Children, Issue, Descendants, etc., Survive, Surviving Spouse[1] Is Entitled to	When Children, or Other Heirs, etc., Do Not Survive, Surviving Spouse[1] Is Entitled to	Other Rights of Survivor Affecting Intestate Share[2]	Miscellaneous
Delaware ...... R. C. 1915, Secs. 3267, 3311, 3382	a) See footnote 3. b) Widow is entitled to one-third if there be issue of intestate; widower is entitled to a child's part if wife leaves a child or children (issue of deceased children taking their parent's share)	a) Widow is entitled to one-half for life if there be no child of intestate or lawful issue of such child, and to the whole for life if there be no kin or heir of intestate; widower is entitled to one-half for life if wife dies without having lawful issue by widower. (b) Widow is entitled to one-half if there be no issue and to the whole if there be no kin to intestate; widower is entitled to the whole if wife leaves no children nor descendants of such		See footnote 5
District of Columbia .... C. 1929, T. 14, Sec. 37; T. 25, Secs. 242, 250; T. 29, Secs. 282–84	a) See footnote 3. b) One-third if there is a child or children or descendant or descendants from a child	a) The whole if there are no descendants or kindred of intestate (see statute). (b) One-half if intestate leaves no child or descendants; to the whole if intestate leaves no child, parent, grandchild, brother or sister or child of brother or sister	See Table XCV, Sec. 189; Table XCIX, Sec. 205; Table CV, Sec. 216; Sec. 219	No person convicted of felonious homicide of decedent shall take any part of estate by way of inheritance, distribution, etc. Bequest of personal estate to widow is in bar of distributive share of personalty unless otherwise expressed in will (subject to election)[5]
Florida .... Sess. L. 1933, Ch. 16103, p. 549, Sec. 24; p. 551, Sec. 32; p. 553, Secs. 35, 36	a) and (b) Child's share if intestate leaves lineal descendants	a) and (b) The whole if there be no lineal descendants	Widow may elect to take dower in lieu of her intestate share of real and/or personal property[6]	Person convicted of murder of decedent cannot inherit from decedent

TABLE CVIII (*Continued*)

Jurisdiction and Citation	When Children, Issue, Descendants, etc., Survive, Surviving Spouse[1] Is Entitled to	When Children, or Other Heirs, etc., Do Not Survive, Surviving Spouse[1] Is Entitled to	Other Rights of Survivor Affecting Intestate Share[2]	Miscellaneous
Georgia .... C. 1926, C. C., Secs. 2995, 3929–31	*a*) and (*b*) Child's part if intestate leaves a surviving child or children or descendants from a child or children, such descendants taking per stirpes; provided that if there will be more than five shares widow is entitled to one-fifth[7]	*a*) and (*b*) The whole if intestate leaves no lineal descendants	If widow elects to take dower, she has no further interest in realty of intestate	Acquisitions of wife and children with her, living separate from husband, descend to her children; if none, then to her next of kin. If survivor is under 21 years of age, he or she may take share without intervention of guardian or other trustee
Hawaii .... R. L. 1925, Secs. 3302, 3305	*a*) and (*b*) See footnote 3	*a*) and (*b*) One-half if intestate leaves no issue; the whole if intestate leaves no issue, nor parent, brother or sister, nor descendant of any deceased brother or sister		
Idaho[4] .... Comp. St. 1919, Secs. 7793, 7802	*a*) and (*b*) One-half if decedent leaves only one child or lawful issue of one child; one-third if decedent leaves more than one child or one child and lawful issue of one or more deceased children	*a*) and (*b*) One-half if decedent leaves no issue; the whole if decedent leaves neither issue, father, nor mother		
Illinois .... Cahill, R. S. 1931, Ch. 39, Secs. 1, 2	*a*) See column three. *b*) One-third if there is a child or children of intestate or descendants of such child or children	*a*) One-half and (*b*) the whole when there is no child or children of intestate or their descendants. *a*) and (*b*) The whole when there is no child or children or their descendants, and no parents, brothers or sisters and their descendants	*a*) Survivor is entitled to one-third of each parcel if he or she waives right of dower (see Table XCIX, Sec. 205, for similar details of election between will and dower)	Provisions in preceding columns do not bar right of surviving spouse to dower in real estate of which intestate did not die seized. (*a*) and (*b*) Estate of illegitimate deceased spouse descends in like manner as that of legitimate; provided that if there is no child or descendant of a child, it descends to surviving spouse

TABLE CVIII (*Continued*)

Jurisdiction and Citation	When Children, Issue, Descendants, etc., Survive, Surviving Spouse[1] Is Entitled to	When Children, or Other Heirs, etc., Do Not Survive, Surviving Spouse[1] Is Entitled to	Other Rights of Survivor Affecting Intestate Share[2]	Miscellaneous
Indiana[8] .... Burns, Ann. St. 1926, Secs. 3336–38, 3343–48, 3356–57, 3363, 3376	a) and (b) One-third in any event; provided that widow is entitled to one-half if decedent leaves only one child[9]	a) and (b) The whole to extent of one thousand dollars, and to three-fourths if estate exceeds such value, if decedent leaves no child; the whole regardless of value, if decedent leaves no child and no parent	See Table XCV, Sec. 189; Table XCIX, Sec. 205; Table CV, Sec. 216; Sec. 219	In case of testamentary provision for survivor, he or she shall receive nothing from estate under any law of descent unless otherwise expressed in will (subject to election). If wife dies holding property vested in her by judicial sale of husband's property in which she had an inchoate interest, the whole of such property descends to widower. No person convicted of unlawfully killing another, or who aids or abets therein, shall take by descent from decedent[5, 8]
Iowa .... C. 1927, Secs. 11847, 11860, 11986, 12017, 12023, 12032	a) and (b) See footnote 3	a) and (b) The whole to amount of seventy-five hundred dollars and one-half of estate in excess of such amount, if intestate leaves no issue; the whole if intestate leaves no issue, no parent nor heirs of parent (see statute)[10]	See Table XCIX, Sec. 205	Surviving spouse may select property to amount of seventy-five hundred dollars (see column two). Survivor who feloniously takes or procures another to take decedent's life forfeits all rights in estate. Testamentary provision is presumed to be in lieu of survivor's distributive share unless contrary intention in will is clear and explicit (subject to election)
Kansas .... R. S. 1923, Secs. 22(119), 22(127), 22(130), 22(133), 22(245)	a) and (b) See footnote 3	a) and (b) The whole if intestate leaves no issue	See Table XCIX, Sec. 205	Person convicted of killing, conspiring to kill, or procuring to be killed, decedent forfeits all rights in estate. Survivor is not entitled to take testamentary provision and also under law concerning descent and distribution (subject to election)

TABLE CVIII (*Continued*)

Jurisdiction and Citation	When Children, Issue, Descendants, etc., Survive, Surviving Spouse[1] Is Entitled to	When Children, or Other Heirs, etc., Do Not Survive, Surviving Spouse[1] Is Entitled to	Other Rights of Survivor Affecting Intestate Share[2]	Miscellaneous
Kentucky ...... Carroll, St. 1922, Secs. 1393, 1403–4, 1408	a) and (b) See footnote 3	a) and (b) The whole if there is neither paternal nor maternal kindred	See Table XCIX, Sec. 205	Widow may not receive both testamentary provision and distributable share of personalty unless testator's intent to give both is necessarily inferable from will (subject to election). Advancements to distributee are not considered as personal estate in estimating widow's distributable share (see Table XCV, Sec. 189)
Louisiana[4] ...... C. C., Arts. 924, 930–33, 966		a) and (b) The whole if decedent has left no lawful descendants, ascendants, nor collateral relations; provided that widower is so entitled only when wife, in addition to above, leaves no natural child or children duly acknowledged by her		If heirs are absent, surviving spouse (see column two) may be put into possession of succession on giving security to save rights of heir who comes forward within three years after survivor was put into possession.[11] Person convicted of having killed or attempted to kill decedent is deprived of succession
Maine .... R. S. 1930, Ch. 74, Sec. 8; Ch. 89, Secs. 1, 13, 20	a) and (b) One-third if intestate leaves issue	a) and (b) One-half if intestate leaves no issue; the whole if intestate leaves no kindred	See Table XCV, Sec. 189; Table XCIX, Sec. 205; Table CV, Sec. 216; Sec. 219. See also footnote 12	Survivor is not entitled to both testamentary provision and interest by descent unless it appears from will that testator so intended (subject to election)[5]
Maryland .... Bagby, Ann. C. 1924, Art. 46, Secs. 1–4; Art. 93, Secs. 125–27, 310, 326	a) and (b) One-third if there be a child or children or descendant or descendants from a child	a) and (b) One-half if there be no child or descendant of intestate; the whole if intestate leaves no child, parent, grandchild, brother or sister or child of a brother or sister	Dower is presumed to have been waived in favor of intestate share unless survivor affirmatively elects to take dower (see Table XCV, Sec. 189; Sec. 205; Table CV, Sec. 216; and Sec. 219 for details of such election and also as to election against will)	a) Consent of survivor is unnecessary to sale under decree of court where he or she is entitled to intestate share. Bequest of personal estate is in bar of survivor's share of personalty unless otherwise expressed in will (subject to election)

[§ 227

TABLE CVIII (*Continued*)

Jurisdiction and Citation	When Children, Issue, Descendants, etc., Survive, Surviving Spouse[1] Is Entitled to	When Children, or Other Heirs, etc., Do Not Survive, Surviving Spouse[1] Is Entitled to	Other Rights of Survivor Affecting Intestate Share[2]	Miscellaneous
Massachusetts .. G. L. 1932, Ch. 189, Sec. 1; Ch. 190, Secs. 1, 2; Ch. 196, Sec. 3	*a*) and (*b*) One-third if deceased leaves issue	*a*) and (*b*) The whole to amount of five thousand dollars[13] and one-half of estate in excess of such amount, if deceased leaves kindred and no issue; the whole if deceased leaves no issue and no kindred	Dower or curtesy is presumed to have been waived in favor of intestate share unless survivor affirmatively elects dower or curtesy (see Table XCV, **Sec. 189**; Table XCIX, **Sec. 205;** Table CV, **Sec. 216**; and **Sec. 219** for details of such election and also as to election against will)	Widow is entitled only to intestate share in residue of property after deducting value of advancement made to child or other lineal descendant[5]
Michigan .... Comp. L. 1929, Sec. 13440, amd. by Sess. L. 1931, No. 79, p. 126; Secs. 13451, 15726	*a*) One-third if intestate leaves issue. *b*) One-third if there be children or issue of deceased child or children; one-half if there be but one child or issue of such deceased child surviving	*a*) and (*b*) One-half if intestate leaves no children or their issue; the whole if intestate leaves no issue, nor parent, brother nor sister, nor child of brother or sister. Provided that widow is entitled (*b*) to whole to amount of three thousand dollars and to one-half of excess of such amount, if there be kindred (as above) but no children or their issue	*a*) Intestate share is in lieu of dower and homestead rights of widow unless she otherwise elects (see Table CIX, **Sec. 228,** for details). See also Table XCV, **Sec. 189;** Table XCIX, **Sec. 205**	Rights under statute of descent do not affect dower and curtesy (other than as in preceding column)[5]
Minnesota[9] ..... G. S. 1923, Secs. 8722, 8726, 8734	*a*) and (*b*) One-third in any event	*a*) and (*b*) The whole if there is no surviving child nor lawful issue of deceased child	See Table XCIX, **Sec. 205; Sec. 219**	Surviving spouse who feloniously takes or procures another to take life of decedent shall not inherit from decedent. Testamentary provision in lieu of survivor's rights by statute confines survivor to will (subject to election), and no testamentary provision is treated as adding to his or her rights by statute unless contrary appears from will (see Table XCV, **Sec. 189**)

§ 227]

TABLE CVIII (*Continued*)

Jurisdiction and Citation	When Children, Issue, Descendants, etc., Survive, Surviving Spouse[1] Is Entitled to	When Children, or Other Heirs, etc., Do Not Survive, Surviving Spouse[1] Is Entitled to	Other Rights of Survivor Affecting Intestate Share[2]	Miscellaneous
Mississippi ..... C. 1930, Secs. 1404, 1406, 1413, 3560–61	*a*) and (*b*) Child's part if intestate leaves children or their descendants by the present or a former marriage	*a*) and (*b*) The whole if intestate does not leave children or their descendants (as in preceding column)	See Table XCV, Sec. 189; Table XCIX, Sec. 205; Table CV, Sec. 216; Sec. 219	Person wilfully causing or procuring death of another in any way shall not inherit from decedent. Testamentary provision for survivor bars any share of real or personal estate unless will otherwise expresses (subject to election)
Missouri .... R. S. 1929, Sec. 306	*a*) and (*b*) See footnote 3	*a*) and (*b*) The whole if there be no children or their descendants, parent, brother or sister nor their descendants		See footnote 5
Montana .... R. C. 1921, Secs. 5819, 7072–73	*a*) and (*b*) One-half if decedent leaves only one child or lawful issue of one child; one-third if decedent leaves more than one child or one child and lawful issue of one or more deceased children	*a*) and (*b*) One-half if decedent leaves no issue; the whole if decedent leaves neither issue, parent, brother nor sister nor children of deceased brother or sister	See Table XCIX, Sec. 205	Testamentary provision for widow bars her share in personal estate unless will otherwise expresses (subject to election)
Nebraska .... Comp. St. 1929, Secs. 30(101), 30(103), 30(107), 30(119)	*a*) and (*b*) One-fourth if there be a child or children or issue of deceased child or children and survivor is not parent of all children of deceased; one-third if survivor is parent of all children of deceased and there be two or more children or one child and issue of one or more deceased children; one-half if survivor is parent of all children of deceased and there be only one child or issue of a deceased child surviving	*a*) and (*b*) One-half if there be no children nor issue of deceased child or children surviving; the whole if deceased leaves no relatives of his or her blood	See Table XCV, Sec. 189; Table XCIX, Sec. 205; Table CV, Sec. 216; Sec. 219	No person convicted of unlawfully killing or conspiring to kill another shall take any property from decedent by descent and distribution. Survivor is not entitled to take both testamentary provision and by inheritance, descent and distribution unless such intent plainly appears from will (election provided for)[5]

[§ 227

TABLE CVIII (*Continued*)

Jurisdiction and Citation	When Children, Issue, Descendants, etc., Survive, Surviving Spouse[1] Is Entitled to	When Children, or Other Heirs, etc., Do Not Survive, Surviving Spouse[1] Is Entitled to	Other Rights of Survivor Affecting Intestate Share[2]	Miscellaneous
Nevada[4] .... Comp. L. 1929 (Hillyer), Secs. 9859, 9868, 9883–85	*a*) and (*b*) One-half if there be only one child or lawful issue of one child; one-third if there be more than one child living or one child living and lawful issue of one or more deceased children	*a*) and (*b*) One-half if intestate leaves no issue; the whole if the intestate leaves no issue, no parent, brother or sister or children of any brother or sister		If deceased spouse dies intestate (and if wife dies without issue), leaving heirs in this state, and surviving spouse subsequently dies intestate without heir, leaving property in this state, latter's estate vests in former's heirs
New Hampshire . Pub. L. 1926, Ch. 306, Sec. 17; Ch. 307, Secs. 1, 6; Sec. 7, amd. by Sess. L. 1933, Ch. 136, p. 193	See footnote 3; also Table XCV, **Sec. 189**	*a*) and (*b*) The whole if there be no heir		Testamentary provision is in lieu of rights which he or she has by law in estate unless contrary intention appears from will[5]
New Jersey ..... Comp. St., Cum. Supp. 1911–24, Sec. 57(6); Supp. 1925–30, Secs. 57(13*b*), 146(169), 146(169*a*)	*a*) See footnote 3. *b*) One-third if there be any children or legal representatives of deceased children	*a*) The whole if intestate leaves no issue, brothers nor sisters, parent nor other kindred capable of inheriting (see statute; see also last column). (*b*) The whole if there be no children nor any legal representatives of them		Surviving spouse is entitled to the whole of property of which decedent died seized which was purchased by decedent during coverture
New Mexico[4] ... St. Ann. 1929, Secs. 38(106), 38(109), 154(306)	*a*) and (*b*) One-fourth in any event	*a*) and (*b*) The whole if intestate leaves no issue		

§ 227]

TABLE CVIII (*Continued*)

Jurisdiction and Citation	When Children, Issue, Descendants, etc., Survive, Surviving Spouse[1] Is Entitled to	When Children, or Other Heirs, etc., Do Not Survive, Surviving Spouse[1] Is Entitled to	Other Rights of Survivor Affecting Intestate Share[2]	Miscellaneous
New York ...... C. Cahill, Consol. L. 1930, Ch. 13, Secs. 81, 83	*a*) and (*b*) One-third if deceased leaves a child or legal representatives of a deceased child or children	*a*) and (*b*) Five thousand dollars and one-half of residue if deceased leaves no child or descendant; ten thousand dollars and one-half of residue if deceased leaves no descendant or parent; the whole if deceased leaves no descendant, parent, brother or sister, nephew or niece	See Table XCV, Sec. 189; Table CV, Sec. 216; Sec. 219	
North Carolina .. C. 1927, Secs. 7, 10, 137–38, 1654	*a*) See footnote 3. *b*) Widow is entitled to one-third if there are not more than two children; to a child's part if there are more than two children. Widower is entitled to one-half if intestate leaves one child; to a child's part if intestate leaves more than one child (deceased children are considered as "children"; but see last column)	*a*) The whole if intestate leaves no lineal or collateral kindred who can claim as heirs. (*b*) Widow is entitled to one-half if there is no child nor legal representative of deceased child; to the whole if there is no child nor legal representative of deceased child, nor any next of kin	See Table XCV, Sec. 189; Table XCIX, Sec. 205	Children who have received advancements shall account for the same to widow of intestate in ascertaining her child's part of estate.[5] If wife dies wholly or partially intestate, surviving husband is entitled to administer on her personal estate and hold the same, subject to creditors, to his own use. Spouse convicted of felonious slaying of other, or of being accessory before the fact to slaying, loses right to distributive share of personalty of other
North Dakota .. Comp. L. 1913, Secs. 5683, 5742–43; Supp. 1913–25, Sec. 5743	*a*) and (*b*) One-half if decedent leaves only one child or lawful issue of deceased child; one-third if decedent leaves more than one child living or one child living and lawful issue of one or more deceased children	*a*) and (*b*) The whole not to exceed value of fifteen thousand dollars and one-half of excess of such value if decedent leaves no issue; the whole not to exceed value of twenty-five thousand dollars and one-half in excess of such value if decedent leaves no issue and no parent; the whole if decedent leaves no issue, parent, nor brother nor sister, nor children of deceased brother or sister		No person convicted of feloniously causing death of another shall take benefit by succession or otherwise from such decedent

[§ 227

TABLE CVIII (*Continued*)

Jurisdiction and Citation	When Children, Issue, Descendants, etc., Survive, Surviving Spouse[1] Is Entitled to	When Children, or Other Heirs, etc., Do Not Survive, Surviving Spouse[1] Is Entitled to	Other Rights of Survivor Affecting Intestate Share[2]	Miscellaneous
Ohio .... Complete G. C. 1931 (Page), Supp. 1932, Secs. 10503(1), 10503(4), 10503(5), 10503(17), 10504(61)	*a*) and (*b*) One-half if there be one child or its lineal descendants surviving; one-third if there be more than one child or their lineal descendants surviving	*a*) and (*b*) Three-fourths if there be no children or their lineal descendants; the whole if there be no children or their lineal descendants, and no parent	See Table XCV, Sec. 189; Table XCIX, Sec. 205; Table CV, Sec. 216; Sec. 219	If the relict of a deceased spouse dies intestate without issue, possessed of property which came to relict from any deceased spouse, by gift, devise, bequest, or descent, surviving spouse of relict is entitled to intestate share (as in columns preceding). No person finally adjudged guilty, as principal or accessory, of murder in first or second degree is entitled to inherit from person killed. Survivor's election to take under will bars his or her right to intestate share unless it plainly appears from will that provision was intended to be in addition to intestate share[16]
Oklahoma ...... St. 1931, Secs. 1615–17	*a*) and (*b*) One-half if decedent leaves only one child or lawful issue of one child; one-third if decedent leaves more than one child, living, or one child living and lawful issue of one or more deceased children[15]	*a*) and (*b*) One-half if decedent leaves no issue; the whole if decedent leaves no issue and no parent nor brother nor sister nor children of deceased brother or sister (see also last column)		*a*) and (*b*) Surviving spouse is entitled to the whole of property acquired by joint industry of husband and wife during coverture, if there is no issue. No person convicted of taking, or procuring another to take, life of another shall inherit from decedent
Oregon .... C. 1930, Secs. 10(101)– 10(103), 10(210), 10(213)	*a*) See footnote 3. *b*) One-half if intestate leaves issue	*a*) The whole if intestate leaves no lineal descendants. (*b*) The whole if intestate leaves no issue		*b*) If intestate leaves issue, widow is entitled only to one-half of residue after deducting advancement made to any of the issue. No person who feloniously takes or procures another to take another's life shall inherit from decedent as surviving spouse

§ 227]

TABLE CVIII (*Continued*)

Jurisdiction and Citation	When Children, Issue, Descendants, etc., Survive, Surviving Spouse[1] Is Entitled to	When Children, or Other Heirs, etc., Do Not Survive, Surviving Spouse[1] Is Entitled to	Other Rights of Survivor Affecting Intestate Share[2]	Miscellaneous
Pennsylvania ... St. 1920 (West), Secs. 8342–44, 8385, 8392	*a*) and (*b*) One-half if intestate leaves only one child or no children but descendants of one deceased child; one-third if intestate leaves more than one child or one child and descendants of more than one deceased child	*a*) and (*b*) The whole not to exceed value of five thousand dollars and one-half of residue, if intestate leaves no issue; the whole in default of known heirs or kindred (see statute; see also last column)	See Table XCV, Sec. 189; Table XCIX, Sec. 205; Table CV, Sec. 216; Sec. 219	Surviving spouse is entitled to select the property to value of five thousand dollars (see column two) from estate (*a* or *b*). Such a sum is in addition to widow's exemption as allowed by law.[16] No person finally adjudged guilty, as principal or accessory, of murder in first or second degree can inherit from decedent as surviving spouse[5]
Rhode Island ... G. L. 1923, Secs. 5549, 5553–54	*a*) See footnote 3. *b*) One-half if intestate died leaving issue	*a*) The whole for life if intestate dies without issue;[17] the whole in fee if there be no paternal or maternal kindred. (*b*) Sum of three thousand dollars and one-half of the remainder if intestate died without issue; the whole if there be no paternal or maternal kindred		
South Carolina .. C. of L. 1922, C. C., Secs. 5236, 5237, 5333; Sess. L. 1924, No. 726, p. 1188	*a*) and (*b*) One-third if intestate leaves one or more children or lineal descendants of deceased children	*a*) and (*b*) One-half if intestate leaves no child or other lineal descendant; two-thirds if intestate leaves no child, or other lineal descendant, parent, brother or sister of the whole blood or child of such brother or sister, nor brother or sister of the half-blood, nor lineal ancestor; the whole if intestate leaves none of above heirs and no next of kin	If widow accepts her intestate share, she is barred of her dower[18]	No person convicted of unlawfully killing another shall receive benefit from death of decedent, except in case of involuntary manslaughter, whether by way of intestate succession or otherwise[5]

[§ 227

TABLE CVIII (*Continued*)

Jurisdiction and Citation	When Children, Issue, Descendants, etc., Survive, Surviving Spouse[1] Is Entitled to	When Children, or Other Heirs, etc., Do Not Survive, Surviving Spouse[1] Is Entitled to	Other Rights of Survivor Affecting Intestate Share[2]	Miscellaneous
South Dakota ... Comp. L. 1929, Secs. 700–701	a) and (b) One-half if decedent leaves only one child or lawful issue of one child; one third if decedent leaves more than one child living, or one child living and lawful issue of one or more deceased children	a) and (b) The whole not to exceed value of twenty thousand dollars and one-half of excess of such value, if decedent leaves no issue; the whole if decedent leaves no issue, no parent, nor brother nor sister nor children or grandchildren of deceased brother or sister		
Tennessee ...... C. 1932, Secs. 7753, 8382, 8388–89, 8395	a) See footnote 3. b) Child's share if there are children or descendants of children	a) The whole if decedent leaves no heirs at law capable of inheriting (see statute). (b) The whole if there are no children or descendants of children		Person who kills, conspires to kill, or procures to be killed, another person forfeits all rights in decedent's property
Texas[4] .... Complete St. 1928, Civ. St., Arts. 2571, 2574, 4610	a) One-third for life and (b) one-third, if deceased have a child or children or their descendants	a) One-half and (b) the whole, if deceased have no child or children or their descendants. (a) and (b) The whole if deceased have neither children or their descendants, nor surviving parent, brothers or sisters or their descendants		Prenuptial agreement between spouses cannot alter the legal orders of descent
Utah .... R. S. 1933, 101-3-22, 101-4-2, 101-4-5, 101-4-8	a) and (b) One-half if decedent leaves only one child or issue of one child; one-third if decedent leaves more than one child living and issue of one or more deceased children	a) and (b) The whole not to exceed value of twenty-five thousand dollars, exclusive of debts and expenses, and one-half of excess of such amount, if decedent leaves no issue; the whole if decedent leaves neither issue, parent, brother nor sister, nor children or grandchildren of deceased brother or sister	Widow's intestate share is not additional to her statutory one-third of real property (see also Table XCV, Sec. 189). Value of homestead and exempt personal property set apart to survivor is deducted from survivor's intestate share	No person convicted of feloniously causing death of another may inherit from decedent

§ 227]

TABLE CVIII (*Continued*)

Jurisdiction and Citation	When Children, Issue, Descendants, etc., Survive, Surviving Spouse[1] Is Entitled to	When Children, or Other Heirs, etc., Do Not Survive, Surviving Spouse[1] Is Entitled to	Other Rights of Survivor Affecting Intestate Share[2]	Miscellaneous
Vermont .... G. L. 1917, Sec. 3278; Sec. 3416, amd. by Sess. L. 1919, No. 86, p. 93; by Sess. L. 1923, No. 55, p. 69; and by Sess. L. 1929, No. 46, p. 62	a) and (b) See footnote 3. (b) Wearing apparel, ornaments and such other property as probate court assigns, whether there are heirs or not[19]	a) and (b) Property not to exceed value of four thousand dollars and one-half of excess of such value, if deceased leaves no issue; the whole if deceased has no kindred who may inherit	See Table XCV, Sec. 189; Table XCIX, Sec. 205; Table CV, Sec. 216; Sec. 219	
Virginia .... C. 1930, Secs. 5138, 5264, 5273–74	a) See footnote 3. b) One-third if intestate left surviving children or their descendants[20]	a) The whole if there be no child or its descendant, no parent, or brothers or sisters or their descendants. (b) The whole if no children or their descendants survive		No person shall acquire interest by descent or distribution from estate of one whom he has killed to obtain such interest[5]
Washington[4] .... Remington, Comp. St. 1922, Sec. 1341, amd. by Supp. 1927, Sec. 1341; Secs. 1343, 1364–65	a) One-half if decedent leaves only one child or lawful issue of one child; one-third if decedent leaves more than one child living or one child living and issue of one or more deceased children. (b) One-half if intestate leaves issue	a) One-half if decedent leaves no issue; the whole if decedent leaves no issue, parent, brother or sister, nephew or niece. (b) The whole if there be no issue		b) If intestate leaves issue, widow is entitled only to one-half of residue after deducting value of advancement to any relation
West Virginia .. C. 1931, Ch. 42, Art. 1, Secs. 1, 3; Art. 2, Sec. 1; Art. 3, Sec. 2; Art. 4, Sec. 2	a) See footnote 3. b) One-third if intestate leaves issue	a) Share, per capita, one moiety of estate with intestate's brothers and sisters, if there be no child nor descendants of any child and only one parent; share (as above) the whole estate if there be no child nor its descendant and no parent (descendants of deceased brother or sister represent such deceased). (b) The whole if intestate leaves no issue	See Table XCV, Sec. 189; Table XCIX, Sec. 205; Table CV, Sec. 216; Sec. 219	No person convicted of feloniously killing or conspiring to kill another shall take from such decedent by descent or distribution. Testamentary provision for survivor bars his or her statutory share of personalty, and (subject to election) is all that survivor shall take of estate, unless contrary intention clearly appears from will and proper attendant facts[5]

[§ 227

TABLE CVIII (*Continued*)

Jurisdiction and Citation	When Children, Issue, Descendants, etc., Survive, Surviving Spouse[1] Is Entitled to	When Children, or Other Heirs, etc., Do Not Survive, Surviving Spouse[1] Is Entitled to	Other Rights of Survivor Affecting Intestate Share[2]	Miscellaneous
Wisconsin ...... St. 1931, Secs. 233.13, 237.01, 318.01	*a*) See footnote 3. *b*) Widow is entitled to one-half if deceased leaves only one child; in all other cases, to one-third	*a*) and (*b*) The whole if intestate leaves no lawful issue	See Table XCV, **Sec. 189**; Table XCIX, **Sec. 205**	Widow is not entitled to both testamentary provision and statutory share of personalty unless it plainly appears from will that such was intended (subject to election)
Wyoming .... R. S. 1931, Secs. 88(4001), 88(4009)	*a*) and (*b*) One-half if intestate leaves children or their descendants surviving	*a*) and (*b*) All of estate up to sum of twenty thousand dollars after payment of debts and expenses of administration, and three-fourths of remainder, if intestate leaves no child nor its descendants; the whole if intestate leaves no child or its descendants, no parents, brothers and sisters, nor descendants of deceased brother or sister		No person who feloniously takes or procures to take life of a person shall inherit from such decedent

[1] The surviving spouse takes the share set forth in the table, and, where the rights of the widow and widower are the same, the words "surviving spouse" are not repeated; where their rights differ, the proper spouse is specified.

[2] The present section does not give a true picture of the rights of a surviving spouse unless it is read in connection with statutes concerning dower, curtesy, statutory substitutes in the nature of dower and curtesy, and rights in homestead, exempt property, and family allowance (see Secs. 189 *et seq.*, 216 *et seq.*, and 228). Many statutes provide that the survivor may dissent from the decedent's will and take as if the decedent had died intestate. These are not properly included in the present section, but reference is made in column three of the table above to sections dealing with the widow (**Secs. 189, 205**), and with the widower (**Secs. 216, 219**).

[3] The surviving spouse (widow in **Alabama** and **Arkansas**), under circumstances stated in the table above, is apparently not included in statutes of descent of real property (*a* in table), or in statutes of distribution (*b* in table). In some jurisdictions this means that the survivor is confined to rights of dower or curtesy; in others, to a statutory substitute which is often similar to an intestate share but which is given whether the decedent dies testate or not (see **Secs. 189** and **216**).

[4] The provisions in the table refer only to the separate property of the decedent (see **Sec. 178** for community property).

[5] Details of statutes providing for barring or the forfeiture of dower, curtesy, or statutory substitutes have been set forth in preceding sections. Some of these provisions apply expressly to the survivor's intestate share or seem broad enough to include it. To avoid duplication, the reader is referred particularly to the tables or summaries in the following sections where these

TABLE CVIII (*Continued*)

statutes of the jurisdictions here listed are set forth: Section 196, for **Indiana, Kentucky, Maine, New Hampshire;** Section 197, for **Connecticut, Delaware, Maine, Nebraska, North Carolina;** Section 198, for **Connecticut, North Carolina;** Section 202, for **Connecticut, Delaware, Indiana, Kentucky, Maine, Maryland, Massachusetts, Michigan, New Hampshire, North Carolina, Pennsylvania, South Carolina, Virginia, West Virginia;** Section 220, subsection I, for **Connecticut, Delaware, Indiana, Kentucky, Maine, Nebraska, New Hampshire, North Carolina;** Section 221, for **Connecticut, Indiana, Kentucky, Maryland, Missouri, New Hampshire, North Carolina, Pennsylvania, Virginia, West Virginia.**

[6] **Florida:** Widow's election to take dower must be written, signed, and acknowledged by her and filed with the county judge in whose court the estate is being administered within nine months after the first publication of the notice to creditors. Such election is recorded by the judge.

[7] **Georgia:** The provisions in the table as they apply to the surviving husband refer to the wife's property when "she dies intestate leaving a separate estate without remainder, or limitation over, which can and does take effect."

[8] **Indiana** (Burns, Ann. St. 1926): If widow is a childless, second, or subsequent wife of deceased, and there are children or their descendants alive by a previous wife, widow takes only life estate in intestate real property (Sec. 3339). If widow marries a second or subsequent time, holding real estate by virtue of any previous marriage, on her death such property descends to her children or their descendants by the previous marriage (Sec. 3342).

[9] The statutes of **Indiana** and **Minnesota** apply to a testate decedent as well as to an intestate, but they have been included in the present section because they are express to the effect that the survivor takes by inheritance, even though such term is not used in its ordinary sense (see **Secs. 189, 216**).

[10] **Iowa** (C. 1927, Sec. 12026): If intestate has had more than one spouse who died or survived in lawful wedlock, portion of estate uninherited when there are no parents or their heirs is equally divided between living spouse and heirs of dead spouse.

[11] **Louisiana** (C. C., Secs. 1005–6, 1019): Acceptance of inheritance by wife is not valid without authorization of husband or of judge. If wife refuses to accept, husband may do so for her at his risk, in order to increase revenues he enjoys during matrimony; provided that, if husband refuses to allow wife to renounce inheritance, judge may allow it.

[12] See *Bunker* v. *Bunker,* 130 Me. 103; 154 A. 73 (1931).

[13] **Massachusetts:** If estate exceeds five thousand dollars in value, such sum is paid first out of the personal property; if that is insufficient, real property may be sold or mortgaged by court order to provide the amount.

[14] **Ohio** (Complete G. C. 1931 [Page], Supp. 1932): When surviving spouse dies within three days after decedent's death, or within thirty days after decedent's death if death resulted from a common accident, estate of first decedent descends as though he had survived the surviving spouse; and above prevails over survivor's right of election (Sec. 10503[18]). (Similar general statutes referring to an "heir" in other jurisdictions probably apply to surviving spouse.)

[15] **Oklahoma:** If decedent has married more than once, spouse surviving at time of death inherits only a child's part of property not acquired during coverture with such survivor, when decedent leaves children or lawful issue of deceased child.

[16] **Pennsylvania** (St. 1920 [West], Secs. 8347–49): If survivor claims said five thousand dollars from real estate which cannot be divided feasibly, the entire parcel is set apart to him or her, conditioned on his or her paying value in excess of share to which he or she is entitled. If survivor refuses or fails so to pay, land is sold and proceeds paid those entitled; provided that a proportionate part of income received by survivor from such property is deducted from five thousand dollars. In all cases where property, real and/or personal, is set apart to survivor, he or she is entitled to income from it from decedent's death (see also Secs. 8345–46 for procedural details).

[17] **Rhode Island:** If there be no issue, probate court, in its discretion, may set off to survivor realty in fee not exceeding value of five thousand dollars over and above all encumbrances, if not required for decedent's debts. If real estate is in a single parcel of greater value not feasible to divide, it may be sold and above sum paid survivor.

[18] **South Carolina:** The converse is also true; acceptance of dower bars the widow's right to an intestate share (see *Glover* v. *Glover,* 45 S. C. 51; 22 S. E. 739 [1895]).

[§ 227

TABLE CVIII (*Concluded*)

[19] **Vermont:** This share is given the survivor "according to his or her circumstances and the estate and degree of the deceased," and shall not be less than a third after the payment of debts, expenses of funeral and administration. The statute is similar to those discussed in Section 228, but has been included in this section because such a share is subject to the decedent's debts.

[20] **Virginia:** Widower's share of personalty is only one-third if deceased wife left only illegitimate children or their descendants.

REFERENCES

Book

STIMSON, F. J. *American Statute Law,* Secs. 6425, 3105–6, 3109, 3400–3405 (1886).

Articles

EAGLETON, WILLIAM L. "Introduction to the Intestacy Act and the Dower Rights Act," 20 Ia. L. Rev. 241–43 (1935).

——. "The Intestacy Act," 20 Ia. L. Rev. 244–60 (1935).

SAYRE, PAUL L. "Husband and Wife as Statutory Heirs," 42 Harv. L. Rev. 330–64 (1929).

Note

"Descent and Distribution—Community Property—Construction of Word 'Widow' under Civil Code, Section 1386, Subdivision 8," *Estate of McArthur,* 210 Cal. 439; 292 P. 469 (1930)—19 Calif. L. Rev. 313–23 (1931).

Annotation

"Husband or Wife as Next of Kin within Provision of Will," 59 A. L. R. 1407–14 (1929).

Section 228. Homestead, Exempt Property, and Family Allowance

CROSS REFERENCES: Effect of absolute divorce on homestead, **Sec. 102;** Effect of limited divorce on general property rights, **Secs. 128–29;** Barring dower, curtesy, and property rights, **Secs. 196–99, 220;** Forfeiture of dower, curtesy, and property rights, **Secs. 202, 221;** Limitations on transfer of homestead, **Sec. 225;** Descent and distribution, **Sec. 227;** Miscellaneous exemptions, **Sec. 230;** Allowances to children, **Sec. 267**

The wealth of material relevant to the present section has been placed in three subdivisions: (*a*) homestead; (*b*) family allowance (as appli-

§ 228]

cable to a surviving spouse) and exempt property; (c) comment and suggestions.

HOMESTEAD

Homestead, in this section, means the statutory exemption from attachment and execution of real property. Unknown at common law, it has spread over the United States from its inception in 1839 in the old Republic of Texas (see *Roco* v. *Green,* 50 Tex. 483 [1878]). Legislatures, recognizing the family home as the bulwark of the state, have protected it from creditors; and although the exemption has been used at times to defraud creditors, its general beneficial effect has been universally admitted. Complete discussion of the many phases of the homestead would require volumes; here the writer is concerned only with special rights of husband and wife (see references following for material relative to other questions). Furthermore, the multitude of statutes on marital rights permits only a very general discussion in the text; Table CIX following should be consulted for details. Homestead legislation will be discussed under two heads: (1) homestead rights during coverture; and (2) homestead rights of a surviving spouse.

1. *Homestead rights during coverture.*—The statutes are often indefinite in specifying the person who may select the homestead, and from what property it may be claimed. Since the husband is ordinarily the head of the family and owns the property, he usually is given the primary right of selection during coverture. The following persons in the following number of jurisdictions, in general, may select or claim the homestead: a householder or head of the family—fifteen; the owner of the property—fifteen; the husband as head of the family—nine; the husband—three; four states have special statutes (**Nevada, Pennsylvania, Utah, Vermont** [see Table CIX]); and the remaining five jurisdictions apparently have no specific provisions. Of the foregoing jurisdictions, thirteen protect the wife; if the husband fails to claim the homestead, she may do so. Similarly, five jurisdictions provide that the owner of the property or his or her spouse may claim the exemption; and six states have special statutes relating to a claim of the homestead by the wife (**Indiana, Mississippi, Missouri, South Carolina, Tennessee, Wyoming**).

Under some circumstances the homestead may be selected from the property of the wife, e.g., where that is the only available land, or where she qualifies as a general head of the family. Since the wife is usually not liable for the husband's debts (**Sec. 159**), selection of the homestead

[§ 228

from his property is more beneficial to the family; but where she is liable for family expenses though incurred in his name (**Sec. 160**), it may be advisable and is usually permissible to claim the homestead from her property. Five community-property states have statutes respecting their special system of marital property. Four (**Arizona, California, Idaho, Washington**) provide that the homestead may be selected from community property, from the husband's separate property, or from the separate property of the wife with her consent and joinder in the selection. In **Nevada** both spouses must join in a declaration from either's separate property. In four non-community–property states the wife's consent is essential to a valid selection of the homestead from her separate property (**Montana, Nebraska, North Dakota, Utah**).

Limitations on the value of the homestead have a broader application than to husband and wife; but it is interesting to note their wide variation (see table). For example, in **Maine** and **New Hampshire** the limit is five hundred dollars, whereas in seven states (**California, Idaho, Nevada, North Dakota, Oklahoma, South Dakota, Wisconsin**) the maximum value is five thousand dollars (for further discussion see "Comment" below).

After a homestead has been declared, one of the most important incidents is the restriction on its destruction. Numerous statutes requiring the joinder of the spouses in a conveyance or encumbrance are collected in **Section 225**. The following additional protections have been given marital rights: (1) seven states require a declaration of abandonment of the homestead to be signed (**Arizona, Louisiana**), executed and acknowledged (**California, Idaho, Montana, Nevada, Washington**), by husband and wife; (2) in three states neither spouse can remove the other or the children from the homestead without the other's consent (**Illinois, Iowa, Utah**), unless another suitable homestead is provided (**Illinois, Utah**); (3) in **Iowa** and **South Dakota** no change in the homestead limits made without the consent of the other spouse affects his or her rights therein.

It is the general rule that after a homestead has been selected from the property of the owner the other spouse (usually the wife) has no interest in the property, other than the protections discussed above, or the protected expectancy discussed in the next subsection. In **Nevada,** however (a community-property state), it is expressly provided that the spouses hold the homestead as joint tenants.

2. *Homestead rights of surviving spouse.*—It is obvious that the family's need for protection from creditors is as great (or greater) on

§ 228]

the death of the head of the family or owner of the homestead as it is during coverture. Therefore forty-four jurisdictions have provided in varying degrees for a right of the surviving spouse or widow in the family homestead or for a right to have the court set apart a homestead as part of the administration of the estate. **Indiana** and **Pennsylvania** have somewhat similar provisions, although the term "homestead" is not used. Relevant statutes were not found in **Delaware, District of Columbia, Maryland, Rhode Island;** and in **West Virginia,** the rights in the decedent's homestead are vested solely in the surviving minor children. A distinction should be noted between the survivor's (or widow's) right (*a*) to take all or part of the decedent's realty, exempt; and (*b*) to hold an exempt homestead from the survivor's property. It is with the former that we are concerned; the latter depends on whether or not the survivor can qualify under the general homestead statutes applicable to a head of a family, householder, etc. (see references following this section). A complete enumeration of the debts or claims which may or may not be enforced against the homestead right of the survivor or widow is not attempted. The usual provision is to the effect that such right is exempt in like manner as the homestead was exempt in the decedent's hands (for qualifications see table). It should be remembered that the rights of surviving children do not properly come within the scope of the present volume, although it has been necessary to include them very briefly in connection with the survivor's rights. Unless otherwise indicated, the term "children" is used to mean "minor children."

Since rights in the homestead are affected by the system of marital property peculiar to community-property states, such states are considered apart from other jurisdictions. Their more important statutes follow. A homestead selected from community property (**Arizona, California, Idaho, Nevada, Washington**) during coverture (**Arizona, California, Idaho**), or selected from the separate property of the spouse who made or joined in the selection (**California, Idaho**), vests absolutely in the survivor. One selected from the separate property of a decedent (**Nevada, Washington**) or of a decedent who did not join in the selection (**Arizona, California, Idaho**) vests in the decedent's heirs, subject to the power of the court to set it aside for a limited time to the family (**Arizona, California, Idaho**), not to exceed the lifetime of the survivor and/or the minority of the children (**California, Idaho**). In **Arizona,** if the decedent joined in the selection from his or her separate property, the homestead vests in the heirs, subject to a life estate in

[§ 228

the survivor. In all of the foregoing states, if the homestead were selected from the separate property of the survivor, it apparently remains
his or her property. In such case in **Nevada,** the homestead exemption
ceases; the survivor would then have to qualify for the exemption under
the general statute specifying a "head of a family."

The so-called "probate homestead" (i.e., one selected by the court)
is also provided for. If no homestead has been selected before the decedent's death as above, the court is to select one from community property (**Arizona, California, Nevada**), from land held by the spouses
as tenants in common (**California**), from the decedent's property
(**Idaho**); or if there is no such property as above, from the decedent's
separate property (**Arizona, California**) for a period not to exceed
the lifetime of the survivor and the children's minority (**California**).
Washington has a unique statute providing a generous probate homestead for the survivor (see the table following). With the exception of
California and **Washington** the jurisdictions above seem to provide
definitely that the probate homestead so set apart is limited to the same
value as the homestead selected during coverture. In **California,** the
statute is not express but the rule appears well established that the value
of the homestead is left in the discretion of the probate court without
arbitrary limitation (*Estate of Barkley,* 91 Cal. App. 388; 267 P. 148
[1928]). The **Washington** provision is set forth in Table CIX.

The three remaining community-property states (**Louisiana, New
Mexico, Texas**) have statutes dissimilar to the provisions discussed
above (see table and notes thereto). The probate-homestead provision
in **Texas** should be specially noted. The statutes found in the community-property states relating to the decedent's exempt property other
than the homestead are discussed in the next subsection in connection
with the family allowance.

The lack of uniformity in the remaining thirty-six jurisdictions
makes any measured classification impracticable and a detailed discussion would merely be a repetition of the material in the table. The statutes may be grouped roughly as follows: (1) the surviving spouse may
have an interest in the homestead for life—twelve jurisdictions (**Connecticut, Illinois, Iowa, Kansas, Kentucky, Montana, Nebraska,
New Hampshire, North Dakota, Ohio, Oklahoma, South Dakota**);
(2) the widow may be entitled to a life interest—twelve jurisdictions
(**Arkansas, Georgia, Maine, Massachusetts, Michigan, Missouri,
New Jersey, New York, North Carolina, South Carolina, Tennessee, Virginia**); (3) the surviving spouse may receive an interest in

§ 228]

fee—five states (**Mississippi, Oregon, Utah, Vermont, Wyoming**);
(4) the widow may be given the homestead absolutely (**Alaska**); (5)
six jurisdictions (**Alabama, Colorado, Florida, Hawaii, Minnesota,
Wisconsin**) have statutes which cannot readily be classified (see table).
It is important that Table CIX and the notes thereto be read in connection with the foregoing statements, for there are many qualifications
which, in particular instances, will produce entirely different results.
For example: in **South Carolina** the husband apparently may defeat
the widow's homestead rights, although the statute is not express; in
North Carolina, Virginia, and a few other jurisdictions it is held that
the widow is not entitled to the homestead if the husband left no creditors. In **Vermont** the surviving spouse takes the same estate in the
homestead of which the decedent died seized. In this connection it
should be noted that, although it is the general rule that a homestead may
be claimed in an estate less than a fee, it is obvious that any right of
the surviving spouse can be no greater in interest than the quantity of
the estate held by the decedent.

The failure of the deceased spouse to select or declare a homestead
during coverture should not prejudice the rights of the surviving spouse.
The logical thing would be to permit the probate court to set apart a
homestead with like effect as though one had been selected. Such "probate homestead" statutes in community-property states have already
been mentioned; other similar statutes are as follows: (1) the court is
to select a homestead in whole or in part for the benefit of the survivor
(**Montana, North Dakota, South Dakota**) or the widow (**Alabama,
North Carolina, Virginia**); (2) the surviving spouse and other heirs
entitled to inherit from the decedent (**Mississippi**), the widow (**Ohio**),
may claim a homestead from the decedent's property; (3) in three jurisdictions, whether or not a homestead has been selected by the decedent,
the court is to set apart one to the survivor (**Oregon**), in part to the
survivor (**Utah**), or the widow is entitled to the home absolutely (**Alaska**). Ordinarily the probate homestead is limited in value in like manner as the homestead during coverture, either expressly or by clear
implication.

Where the surviving spouse is entitled to dower, curtesy, or a statutory share (**Secs. 189, 216**), or to an intestate share (**Sec. 227**), the
question arises as to whether the homestead right is cumulative to the
other marital rights or is an alternative provision. The following fifteen
jurisdictions have relevant statutes: (1) concerning dower—eleven
(**Florida, Illinois, Kentucky, Massachusetts, Michigan, Missouri,**

[§ 228

New Hampshire, Ohio, Tennessee, Virginia, Wisconsin); (2) concerning a share by descent—four (Massachusetts, Michigan, North Dakota, South Dakota); (3) concerning a "distributive" share—three (Iowa, New Hampshire, Utah). In the absence of definitely express statutes, it is generally held that since the homestead is for the benefit of the family, and for the survivor as a constituent member, the homestead right is cumulative, at least to dower (see also *In re Druhl's Estate,* 61 N. D. 168; 237 N. W. 697 [1931]). Where the homestead right is interpreted merely as an exemption protecting property the survivor (or widow) receives under the statute of descent, the question would not arise (e.g., see South Carolina).

With the exception of two jurisdictions, the statutes discussed in this subsection indicate that the homestead rights cannot be defeated by a devise of such property, for a contrary result would permit the decedent to abrogate these beneficent provisions. In Mississippi, however, the statute apparently applies only to intestate property; and in South Carolina the statute has been construed in like manner (see Table CIX, footnote 52 [p. 662]; and see also footnote 55 [p. 662] for a special interpretation of the Utah statute). A further troublesome question arises when the decedent provides for the survivor in the will. Only four states have been found with express statutes relating to homestead. Iowa, Kansas, and Wisconsin provide for election between the testamentary provision and the homestead rights; a Wyoming statute states that the widow's rights in the homestead are not affected by her renouncing or failing to renounce the provision of the will. Other general statutes relating to election between the will and the survivor's rights by law may be construed to cover homestead rights (see Mississippi, New Hampshire, North Carolina, Ohio, in summary in Sec. 199).

In the absence of express statute, it is commonly said that the general rules regarding election between the will and dower apply to election between the will and homestead. It is apparently the common-law rule that the survivor need elect only when the devise is clearly inconsistent with homestead rights or expressly in lieu thereof (*O'Rourke* v. *Cleary,* 104 Vt. 312; 163 A. 583 [1933]); but judicial decisions in particular jurisdictions should be consulted as to the effect of the general statutes relating to election against the will.

Included in the next subsection are statutes relative to (*a*) rights in the decedent's exempt personal property; and (*b*) the setting off of small, entire estates. Such provisions are usually considered as allowances for the family's support after the decedent's death.

§ 228]

Exempt Property and Allowances

The same benevolent legislative spirit which has prompted the protection of the family homestead has also provided for the support of the family after the decedent's death. The statutes are varied and detailed, and for a complete treatment Table CIX must be consulted. For purposes of discussion they may be roughly classified as follows: (1) statutes relating to possession of the home temporarily during administration; (2) statutes giving an allowance in money or property for a stated period of time; (3) statutes disposing of the general exempt personalty of the decedent; (4) statutes disposing of specified articles or other personal property within limitations; (5) statutes providing for the disposal of the entire estate when it is not of great value; (6) miscellaneous statutes. The purpose of all such statutes is the same—support of the decedent's family—and therefore they frequently overlap. The court having jurisdiction over administration usually may exercise considerable discretion under many of these statutes (see table).

1. In nine jurisdictions the surviving spouse (**Wyoming**), surviving spouse and children (**California, Oregon**), widow and children (**Alaska, Arizona, Hawaii, Idaho, Montana, Nevada**), are entitled to the homestead, family furniture, apparel, and other household effects until letters are granted and the inventory of the estate filed. Seven other states (**Connecticut, Iowa, Massachusetts, Tennessee, Utah, Virginia, West Virginia**) have somewhat similar statutes (see table). Several of the foregoing jurisdictions also give a reasonable provision for support, if necessary, during such interim. The provisions above are commendable. They do not interfere with rights of creditors and do give a certain amount of support to the family.

2. If the family is in need of support during the settlement of an estate, some form of an allowance should be given to them. Accordingly, twenty jurisdictions provide for such allowance to the widow and children (**Arizona, California, Hawaii, Idaho, Michigan, Minnesota, Montana, Nevada, North Dakota, South Dakota, Vermont, Washington, Wisconsin, Wyoming**; and **Oregon** if the estate is solvent), to the surviving spouse and children (**Nebraska, Oklahoma, Utah**), to the widow (**Alaska, Connecticut**). (See Table CIX, footnote 7 [p. 659] as to limitation on allowance in case of an insolvent estate.) Twelve jurisdictions have similar statutes giving property or money for support for one year from the decedent's death, applicable to the surviving spouse (**Missouri**) or to the widow and children (**Alabama,**

[§ 228

Arkansas, Florida, Georgia, Illinois, Iowa, Mississippi, North Carolina, Ohio, Tennessee, Texas). Two jurisdictions limit such allowance to six months from the decedent's death, to be given to the surviving spouse and children under fifteen years of age (New Mexico) or to the family (Rhode Island). The allowance in the foregoing jurisdictions is generally paid to the widow (or the surviving spouse) to be used for the benefit of such spouse and the children.

3. When the decedent dies leaving exempt personal property, it seems just that the family should be entitled to it, free from creditors. Nineteen jurisdictions have been found which, in varying degree, so provide (Alaska, Arizona, California, Connecticut, Idaho, Iowa, Mississippi, Montana, Nebraska, Nevada, New Mexico, North Dakota, Oklahoma, Oregon, South Dakota, Texas, Utah, Virginia, West Virginia). The table following should be consulted for details, for any measured classification of these statutes is impracticable.

4. Somewhat similar statutes were found in thirty-one jurisdictions recognizing the family's right to certain specified articles from the estate (e.g., household furniture, wearing apparel, etc.), or providing for the setting apart to the family of personal property for support. Many of these provisions supplement other allowances; some are given to the surviving spouse, some to the family, some to the widow. Furthermore, the limitations on value in some states vary widely. Space will not permit an extended discussion; the details may be found in Table CIX (see therein Alabama, Alaska, Arkansas, Colorado, Connecticut, Delaware, District of Columbia, Florida, Georgia, Illinois, Indiana, Kansas, Kentucky, Maine, Maryland, Massachusetts, Michigan, Minnesota, Missouri, Nebraska, New Jersey, New York, Ohio, Pennsylvania, Rhode Island, South Dakota, Tennessee, Vermont, Virginia, West Virginia, Wisconsin).

5. A further provision for support is found in twenty-two jurisdictions. It is provided that, if the entire estate does not exceed a stated value (comparatively small) or does not exceed the amount of the allowances for support, it is set apart without further administration: to the widow (Alaska, California, Idaho, Illinois, Indiana, Pennsylvania); to the widow and children (Arizona, Florida, Georgia, Michigan, Minnesota, Montana, Vermont); to the surviving spouse (Missouri, North Dakota); to the surviving spouse and children (Nebraska, Nevada, Utah); to the family (Arkansas). The widow and children likewise receive: the entire intestate estate (Oregon), the entire personal estate (Oklahoma), the entire intestate personalty (South

Dakota), if it does not exceed a certain value. The maximum values vary from four thousand two hundred dollars in **Alaska** to three hundred dollars in **Vermont** (see table for details).

6. Many of the statutory allowances discussed above are declared to be subject to the expenses of the last illness and of the funeral, and to administration charges. Footnotes 6, 9, 19, and 30 to Table CIX indicate the distribution of these provisions in the several jurisdictions. With the exception of such statutes, the allowances are ordinarily and rightly given whether the estate is solvent or not, although the insolvency may affect the amount of the allowance.

The purpose of the allowances shows that the decedent should not be able to defeat them by will, and such is the general rule. However, where there is a testamentary provision for the beneficiary of an allowance, an election may be required; and nine jurisdictions have statutes which recognize that fact (**Alaska, Georgia, Kentucky, Maine, Michigan, New Hampshire, North Carolina, Ohio, Tennessee**). Other general statutes requiring an election between rights under the will and rights given by law may have a similar effect. But five states have statutes which apparently give certain of the allowances in addition to the testamentary provision (**Illinois, Minnesota, Nebraska, Wisconsin, Wyoming**) (see table). In the absence of statute, the majority view is that no election is required unless the will is clearly inconsistent with an allowance.

Eight states have legislation to the effect that if the widow (**Arizona, California, Montana, Nevada, Oklahoma, South Dakota, Texas**), or the surviving spouse (**Utah**), has a described amount of separate maintenance or property she (or he) may be excluded from all or part of the allowances (see table). A similar result is presumably reached in many other jurisdictions, because the allowance is to be given only if reasonably necessary in the court's discretion.

COMMENT

The attempt of legislatures to provide a protection for the family by means of the statutes discussed above is praiseworthy in spirit, but in practice it has resulted: (*a*) in a hodgepodge of legislation which is often ambiguous; (*b*) in a serious impairment of the rights of creditors in a few jurisdictions; and (*c*) in rather niggardly benefits to the family in others. A variance in the statutes is inevitable because of the different conditions in the several jurisdictions, but, within limits, uniform legislation is greatly needed. The writer has already indicated his approval

[§ 228

of much of the legislation, but cannot approve the following: (*a*) the practice in several states of fixing the value of the homestead permitted, by constitutional provision (the difficulty of changing the value to meet new conditions outweighs the benefit of a check on too generous legislatures); (*b*) the practice of enumerating specific articles of personalty to be exempt (limitation on value would seem preferable); (*c*) the piecemeal character of the legislation (the various provisions should be co-ordinated); (*d*) the maximum value of five hundred dollars on the homestead in **Maine** and **New Hampshire** (such a provision is little better than none).

However, despite the minor faults referred to, the statutes included in this section pay tribute to the generosity of our legislation.

TABLE CIX*

HOMESTEAD AND EXEMPT PROPERTY—WIDOW'S ALLOWANCE[1]

Jurisdiction and Citation	Marital Rights during Coverture[2]	Rights of Surviving Spouse[2,3]	Allowance to Widow—to Family (Analogous Provisions)[2,3]
Alabama .... Const., Secs. 206, 208; C. 1923, Secs. 7882, 7911, 7918–25, 7942–44, 7951–52	Any resident may claim two thousand dollar homestead from his property	Widow and/or children entitled: (*a*) to homestead until estate is ascertained to be solvent or insolvent; and (*b*) to homestead exempt from administration and debts except those enforceable against it in husband's lifetime, share and share alike, in general, during her life and/or their minority; but (*c*) to homestead absolutely, and exempt as above if estate is insolvent or if homestead is all of real property in state;[4] or (*d*) to remain in possession of excess-value homestead until it is sold or divided; and (*e*) to homestead rights in proceeds of such sale if division is not feasible, or in proceeds of sale made during husband's life if he did not receive them; or (*f*), if he had no homestead and they have not received benefits of *e* above, to have homestead set apart by court, or, if necessary, real estate sold and homestead purchased with proceeds to be held as above. Devisee of property may clear it of homestead rights by payment of two thousand dollars for purchase of another homestead. Widow and/or children do not forfeit rights by removal from homestead. Homestead of deceased wife passes to her children, so far as is practicable, in like manner as above	Widow entitled to have set apart to her: (*a*) specified apparel and household goods (see statute) necessary for family's support for twelve months after decedent's death, to be selected by her; and (*b*) other personal property not to exceed value of one thousand dollars.[5] Above property, exempt from administration and debts, is to be used for support of widow and children; and any child leaving family is entitled to equal share of such property then on hand. Title to property vests, share and share alike, in widow and/or children, absolutely if estate does not exceed exempt property; during her life and their minority if it does so exceed. Before it is set apart, they may use it, and widow may sue and be sued concerning it, to same extent as if it had been set apart. Property of deceased wife is exempt to her children as above

* See pages 659–62 for all numbered footnotes to this table.

§ 228]

TABLE CIX (*Continued*)

Jurisdiction and Citation	Marital Rights during Coverture[2]	Rights of Surviving Spouse[2,3]	Allowance to Widow—to Family (Analogous Provisions)[2,3]
Alaska .... Comp. L. 1913, Secs. 595, 1104, 1647; Secs. 1648–50, amd. by Sess. L. 1919, Ch. 12, pp. 24–26, Secs. 1–3	Owner of property or his or her spouse may claim twenty-five hundred dollar family homestead	See next column as to home and exempt property	Until inventory is filed, widow and children are entitled to homestead, apparel, household furniture and reasonable provision for support. Widow is then entitled: (*a*) to her apparel and ornaments; and (*b*) to absolute title to property not exceeding value of four thousand dollars, exclusive of liens, to include home, household goods, and all exempt property of deceased, to be used for support of herself and children; and (*c*), if necessary, to further reasonable allowance during settlement of estate; or (*d*) to entire estate if value does not exceed two hundred dollars over value in *b*. Above property is not subject to further administration.[6] Widow entitled as above when she waives testamentary provision as when husband dies intestate
Arizona .... R. C. 1928, Secs. 1731–32, 1734, 3973–80	Husband, as head of family, or his wife may claim four thousand dollar homestead from the community property; from separate property of husband; or from separate property of wife if she joins in selection. Declaration of abandonment must be signed by husband and wife	Homestead selected (*a*) from community property during coverture vests absolutely in surviving spouse; (*b*) from separate property of either spouse vests in his or her heirs, but, if decedent joined in selection, it is subject to use of survivor for life; if decedent did not join, it is subject to court's power to set it aside to family for limited period (see below). If none was selected as in *a,* or if selected as in *b* and decedent did not join, court may select homestead for family's use from community property; if none, then from decedent's separate property for limited period (see above as to descent). All exempt property of decedent is set apart to family's use; and is property of survivor, if no children; if children, then one-half to survivor and one-half to children. Homestead above is exempt from debts of husband and/or wife, except those enforceable against homesteads generally. Excess-value homestead is divided if feasible; if not, is sold and proceeds paid parties entitled (see statute)	Widow and/or children entitled: (*a*) to homestead, apparel, household furniture, and reasonable provision for support until inventory is returned; and (*b*) to exempt property (see preceding column); and (*c*), if necessary, to further preferred allowance[9] for support during settlement of estate;[7,8] or (*d*) to entire estate for support if value does not exceed two thousand dollars, subject to liens valid at husband's death.[6] If widow has separate property equal to portion given above and in preceding column, entire property, other than her one-half of homestead, goes to children (see preceding column for division of exempt property between widow and children)

[§ 228

TABLE CIX (*Continued*)

Jurisdiction and Citation	Marital Rights during Coverture[2]	Rights of Surviving Spouse[2, 3]	Allowance to Widow—to Family (Analogous Provisions)[2, 3]
Arkansas .... Const., Art. IX, Secs. 4–6; Crawf. and Moses, Dig. 1921, Secs. 80, 83, 84, 86, 90, 5523–24, 5530, 5539–41, 5543	Resident debtor may claim twenty-five hundred dollar homestead from his property; if husband fails to claim one, wife may do so	Widow not having separate homestead of her own,[10] and/or children, entitled to husband's homestead exempt; one-half of rents and profits vest in widow for life, one-half to children; if none, then all in widow; and on majority of youngest child, all vest in widow. They need not reside on homestead. Excess-value homestead is sold and another, as selected by widow, is purchased with twenty-five hundred dollars of sale proceeds	Widow and/or children entitled absolutely to personal property not to exceed value of three hundred dollars, subject only to funeral expenses not to exceed twenty-five dollars. Widow is entitled: (*a*) as above; and (*b*) absolutely to specified apparel, furniture, provisions, etc. (see statute), necessary for family's support for twelve months; and (*c*) to other personal property not to exceed value of one hundred and fifty dollars, provided estate is solvent. If entire estate does not exceed above allowances, it is set apart to family without administration. Such allowances are cumulative to homestead or other property rights of widow and children in estate
California ...... C. C. 1933 (Lake), Secs. 1238–39, 1243–44, 1260–62, 1265; Prob. C. 1933 (Lake), Secs. 645, 660–65, 667–82	Husband, as head of family, or, if he fails to do so, wife may claim five thousand dollar homestead from community property; from separate property of husband; or from separate property of wife with her consent and joinder. It may be abandoned only by declaration or grant thereof, executed and acknowledged by husband and wife	Homestead selected (*a*) from community property during coverture, or from separate property of spouse who made or joined in selection, vests absolutely in survivor; (*b*) from separate property of decedent who did not so join vests in his or her heirs or devisees subject to court's power to set it aside for limited period to family (see below). If none was selected as in *a* or if selected as in *b*, court must select one for use of survivor and children from community property, or from property held in common by decedent and survivor; if none, then from decedent's separate property, but, if so, only for limited period not beyond lifetime of survivor and/or minority of children. All exempt property may be set apart to family's use (except see above as to homestead); if so, with exception of homestead selected during decedent's life, it is the property—one-half of survivor, one-half of children; if none, then all of survivor. Either homestead above is subject only to those of decedent's debts enforceable against it in decedent's lifetime. Excess-value homestead is divided if feasible; if not, is sold and proceeds paid parties entitled	Surviving spouse and children entitled to homestead, apparel, household furniture and other exempt property until inventory is filed. Widow and children entitled to reasonable allowance necessary for their support during settlement of estate;[6, 7] it may be granted before inventory is filed and modified afterward.[8] If either widow or child has maintenance from other property, allowance is given to others who have no separate maintenance. If entire estate does not exceed net value of twenty-five hundred dollars over encumbrances of record at husband's death, title to it vests absolutely in widow subject to encumbrances on it, and exempt from further administration;[9] but widow having other estate of five thousand dollars in value is not so entitled

§ 228]

TABLE CIX (*Continued*)

Jurisdiction and Citation	Marital Rights during Coverture[2]	Rights of Surviving Spouse[2, 3]	Allowance to Widow—to Family (Analogous Provisions)[2, 3]
Colorado .... Comp. L. 1921, G. S., Sec. 5331; Sec. 5347, amd. by Sess. L. 1929, Ch. 184, p. 640; Secs. 5919–20, 5924–25, 5927	Householder, head of family, may claim two thousand dollar homestead; if owner of land fails to claim one, his or her spouse may do so	On death of person seized of homestead, surviving spouse or children are entitled to it, exempt from decedent's debts;[11] and decedent's family is then entitled to same homestead exemption as deceased had as head of family. Specified personal-property exemptions (see statute) exist for benefit of widow and family on husband's death	Resident widow entitled to preferred allowance[6] of two thousand dollars in cash; or, at her election, to its equivalent in value of real and/or personal property. Real estate may be sold to pay cash sum, if personal estate is insufficient
Connecticut ..... G. S. 1930, Secs. 4954–56, 5042–43, 5156	Any owner of dwelling may claim one thousand dollar homestead	Surviving spouse and children entitled to occupy decedent's homestead, for his or her life and their minority, exempt from decedent's liabilities except expenses of last illness and funeral and exempt from their liabilities. It may be sold for decedent's debts subject to such right of occupation. Survivor may release such right by instrument executed and recorded like deeds of land	Widow entitled: (*a*) to such allowance as probate court thinks necessary for support of herself and family during settlement of estate; and (*b*), if personal estate exclusive of exempt household goods is insufficient for debts, to such goods; and court may set out to her any other of decedent's exempt property. Decedent's family may remain in dwelling house and appurtenant buildings until same are disposed of according to law. Widow shall not take her statutory share during time that allowance in *a* is given
Delaware .... R. C. 1915, Sec. 3363; Sec. 3415, amd. by Sess. L. 1933, Ch. 185, p. 651; Sess. L. 1923, Ch. 238, p. 680; Sess. L. 1933, Ch. 187, p. 653	Personal-property exemptions may be claimed by both spouses jointly, or by either with other's written consent; or half by each spouse, but both are not entitled each to all exemptions allowed a head of family	Specified personal-property exemptions of household goods, etc. (see statute), exist for widow's benefit, in like manner as they did for benefit of husband[12]	Specified apparel, provisions, etc. (see statute), not to exceed value of thirty dollars, are not assets of estate but may be set apart for family's support. Widow of any decedent is entitled to cash up to amount of five hundred dollars, which sum takes priority over all unsecured claims, expenses, legacies, and taxes; such provision does not affect any other of her rights under husband's will or under intestacy laws
District of Columbia.... C. 1929, T. 21, Sec. 3; T. 29, Sec. 176			Specified articles of personal property, apparel, etc. (see statute), of head of family on his death are excepted from inventory, exempt from debts, and distributed to family as court may decide

[§ 228

AMERICAN FAMILY LAWS

TABLE CIX (*Continued*)

Jurisdiction and Citation	Marital Rights during Coverture[2]	Rights of Surviving Spouse[2,3]	Allowance to Widow—to Family (Analogous Provisions)[2,3]
Florida .... Const., Art. 10, Secs. 1, 2; Sess. L. 1933, Ch. 16103, pp. 544 *et seq.*, Secs. 6, 28, 35, 37, 124, 162, 165, 198	Head of family may claim homestead of one hundred and sixty acres from his rural property; or homestead of one-half acre from his urban property	Homestead of intestate decedent descends as other property (see Table CVIII, Sec. 227), except that if decedent is survived by widow and lineal descendants she takes life estate in it, with remainder to them. Homestead of decedent leaving widow and/or lineal descendants cannot be devised, but descends as above. Homestead is not to be included in property subject to dower, but descends as above. Exemptions of homestead and personal property given head of family inure to benefit of widow and heirs on his death[13]	If necessary, widow is entitled to family allowance of one year's support for herself and/or children, in addition to homestead and exempt personalty; allowance may be modified or discontinued but in no event shall it exceed value of twelve hundred dollars;[6] it is paid first from property or funds as designated by will if they are sufficient; if not, then from other property as specified (see statute). Widow of intestate is entitled to apparel, household goods, etc. (see statute), necessary for maintenance of herself and family; articles are not part of her dower or inheritance. During administration, if it appears that estate does not consist of more than homestead and exempt personalty, it may be distributed to persons entitled, without further administration
Georgia .... C. 1926, C. C., Secs. 3377, 3393, 3396–97, 3414, 3416–17, 3424–25, 4041–42, 4044–45, 4048–51	Husband, as head of family (or, if he refuses, wife or her next friend), may claim constitutional homestead for benefit of wife and children of sixteen hundred dollars, or may claim statutory, short homestead for their benefit (see statute). (See also next column)	*a*) Property set apart for benefit of wife as constitutional exemption reverts to estate on her death or marriage, unless sold or reinvested; and same reversion follows reinvestments unless fee simple is sold.[14] (*b*) Statutory or "short" homestead right is for benefit of debtor's family, and ceases as to a wife on her death or marriage. Such homestead is extended to intestate insolvent estate if widow or child survives[15]	Widow and/or children entitled: (*a*) to property or money for support for twelve months from administration, and, if there is a widow, to necessary household furniture, allowance to be not less than one hundred dollars and to be an expense of administration; or (*b*) to entire estate if value does not exceed five hundred dollars and widow may pay such estate debts as she thinks proper; or (*c*) to support, as in *a*, for every year estate is kept together in administration, if there are no debts. Above property vests in widow and children share and share alike, subject to purchase-money mortgages and crop liens for rent and supplies. If husband provides for support by will, widow may elect between will and above allowance
Hawaii .... R. L. 1925, Secs. 493, 505, 519, 2487	Husband and wife cannot both apply for homestead lease[16]	On death of owner of homestead lease, his or her interest passes first to surviving spouse, any conveyance, devise, or bequest notwithstanding. If survivor remarries and deceases, his or her interest passes to issue of first marriage[16]	Widow or children entitled: (*a*) to homestead, apparel, household furniture and reasonable provision for support until inventory is returned; and (*b*) to reasonable allowance for support during settlement of estate,[7] if allowance in *a* is insufficient[8,9]

§ 228]

TABLE CIX (*Continued*)

Jurisdiction and Citation	Marital Rights during Coverture[2]	Rights of Surviving Spouse[2,3]	Allowance to Widow—to Family (Analogous Provisions)[2,3]
Idaho .... Comp. St. 1919, Secs. 5438–39, 5443, 5460–62, 5465, 7564–67; Secs. 7565 and 7568–69, amd. by Sess. L. 1927, Ch. 34, pp. 45–47; Secs. 7571, 7573	Husband, as head of family, or, if he does not do so, his wife may claim five thousand dollar homestead from community property; from separate property of husband; or from separate property of wife with her consent and joinder. It may be abandoned only by declaration or conveyance, executed and acknowledged by husband and wife	Homestead selected during coverture (a) from community property or from separate property of spouse who made or joined in selection vests absolutely in survivor; (b) from separate property of decedent who did not join vests in his or her heirs, subject to court's power to assign it for limited period to family but not to exceed lifetime of survivor and/or minority of children. If none was selected, court must set apart one for use of survivor and children from decedent's property (see b, above), but property vests in heirs. All exempt property may also be set apart to survivor or children. Above property set apart is decreed to survivor if any. Excess-value homestead is divided if feasible; if not, is sold and proceeds paid parties entitled. Homesteads given as above are subject only to debts enforceable against them in decedent's lifetime	Widow or children entitled: (a) to homestead, apparel, household furniture and provision for support until inventory is returned; and (b) to exempt property (see preceding column); and (c), if property in b is insufficient, then to reasonable allowance during settlement of estate;[7,8,9] or (d) to entire estate for support if value does not exceed fifteen hundred dollars.[6] Above allowances are decreed to widow if there be one
Illinois .... Cahill, R. S. 1931, Ch. 3, Secs. 60, 71, 75–77; Ch. 41, Secs. 37, 44; Ch. 52, Secs. 1, 2, 15; Ch. 82, Sec. 3; Ch. 106, Sec. 22	Householder with family may claim one thousand dollar homestead. Neither spouse can remove other or their children from homestead without other's consent, unless owner of property in good faith provides another suitable homestead	On death of householder, homestead exemption continues for benefit of survivor so long as he or she occupies homestead; and specified personal-property exemptions for decedent (see statute) continue for family's benefit. Allotment of homestead or dwelling house to survivor as dower does not affect his or her homestead right therein; but if dower is allotted from other lands, acceptance of such allotment is a waiver of survivor's homestead estate unless court orders otherwise. Homestead may be set off in partition action, in proceeding to sell estate for decedent's debts, to sell real estate of ward,[17] or to sell under power of sale in will	Resident widow is entitled as her absolute property: (a) to family pictures, jewels, and ornaments of herself and children; and (b) to sum of money reasonable for support of herself and children for one year after husband's death, or to its equivalent, in whole or in part, in personal property selected by her; year's award is to be not less than five hundred dollars with additional sum not to exceed two hundred dollars for each child under eighteen at husband's death;[9] award is not affected by her renouncing or failing to renounce provisions in will for her benefit. If personal property and assets of estate after deducting expenses of funeral and administration do not exceed allowance above, entire estate is given her without further administration

[§ 228

TABLE CIX *(Continued)*

Jurisdiction and Citation	Marital Rights during Coverture[2]	Rights of Surviving Spouse[2, 3]	Allowance to Widow—to Family (Analogous Provisions)[2, 3]
Indiana Burns, Ann. St. 1926, Secs. 769, 780, 3104–5, 3112, 3276–79, 8746	Resident householder or, if he is absent from state or from his home, his wife may claim six hundred dollar exemption of his real and/or personal property. Resident married woman, whether householder or not, is entitled to same exemptions of her property as householder	See preceding and next columns	Widow and/or children entitled: (a) to specified household goods (see statute); and (b) to possession of dwelling house and appurtenant messuage not to exceed forty acres for one year after husband's death, free of rent. Widow is entitled: (a) to personal property not to exceed value of five hundred dollars, or to that sum in cash;[18] or (b) to entire estate absolutely without further administration if it does not exceed value in a, exclusive of encumbrances(subject to mortgages on real property[19, 20]
Iowa C. 1927, Secs. 10135–38, 10141, 10145–46, 10148–51, 11847, 11918, 11923–24, 11969, 12002, 12012–13	Owner of property may claim homestead (five hundred dollars of land; three hundred dollars of buildings. Changes in limits of homestead without consent of other spouse do not affect his, her, or child's rights therein. Neither spouse can remove other or children from homestead without other's consent. Homestead for family may be owned by either spouse	Surviving spouse entitled: (a) to homestead until it is disposed of according to law; (b) to homestead for life as a homestead while occupying it as such, in lieu of distributive share of realty,[21] but affirmative election to take homestead must be made, in like manner as that between will and dower;[22] failure to do so is waiver of homestead right. If survivor's distributive share is sold by court order, new, exempt homestead may be purchased with share of proceeds. Subject to above rights, homestead may be devised; but, if survivor is named as a devisee in will, it is presumed, unless contrary intention is clear, that devise is in lieu of homestead and exemptions. Homestead, in survivor's hands, is subject only to those of decedent's debts enforceable against it during decedent's life[20]	Widow and/or children under age of fifteen entitled, if necessary, to sufficient property for support for twelve months after husband's death; allowance may be increased or diminished.[6] Widow is entitled to all exempt personal property of deceased head of family, exempt in her hands as it was in his
Kansas R. S. 1923, Secs. 22(102)– 22(107), 22(127), 22(245)– 22(246), 22(511)– 22(512), 22(514), 60(3501)– 60(3502)	Owner of property or, if householder fails to do so, his wife may claim family homestead of one hundred and sixty acres of rural property, or of one acre of urban property	Surviving spouse and/or children (apparently either adult or minor) of intestate entitled to homestead occupied as residence at decedent's death, as their absolute property; if there are no children, survivor takes all. When survivor remarries or children are all of age, homestead may be partitioned —one-half to survivor, one-half to children. If more land was left than law allows as homestead, survivor may select part to be taken. It is exempt from decedent's debts as it was in his or her hands. Surviving spouse of testate decedent, who dissents from will, is entitled to same homestead rights as spouse of intestate[23]	Widow and/or children entitled absolutely: (a) to specified apparel, household goods, etc. (see statute); and (b), if property in a does not amount to value of two hundred fifty dollars, to the difference in cash or other property. If there are no children, widow takes all of above. Property is selected by widow and appraised at value over and above legal prior liens to which it is subject; but is liable for no other debts

TABLE CIX (*Continued*)

Jurisdiction and Citation	Marital Rights during Coverture[2]	Rights of Surviving Spouse[2, 3]	Allowance to Widow—to Family (Analogous Provisions)[2, 3]
Kentucky .... Carroll, St. 1922, Secs. 1403, 1702, 1706-8	Resident house-keeper with family may claim one thousand dollar homestead	Surviving spouse and unmarried children entitled to joint occupancy of homestead and benefit of such exemption; survivor's right continues while he or she occupies homestead; children's right until youngest is of age. Necessary sale for decedent's debts may be had, subject to above homestead rights. Homestead right is estimated in allotting dower[24, 25]	Widow of intestate or widow who renounces testamentary provision and children are entitled to personal property or money on hand or in bank to amount of seven hundred and fifty dollars, exempt from distribution and sale. Widow may select such property[6, 26]
Louisiana ...... Const., Art. XI, Sec. 1, in Marr, R. C. of Prac. 1927, p. 486; Marr, Ann. R. S., Supp. 1926, Act 35, p. 1105, Secs. 2, 4; C. C., Art. 2374; Art. 2382, amd. by Sess. L. 1926, Act 113, p. 176; Arts. 2422, 3252, 3254	Owner of property may claim two thousand dollar homestead; from benefit of home-stead to husband is deducted value of property owned and enjoyed by wife. If husband refuses to claim exempt family home, wife living with him may do so.[27] Declaration of abandonment must be signed by both spouses	Benefit of specified exemptions (see statute), including homestead, may be claimed by surviving spouse or chil-dren of deceased beneficiary[28]	Widow entitled: (*a*) to habita-tion and to mourning dresses dur-ing year of mourning, value not to be deducted from interests due her; and (*b*) to maintenance during delays given her to make inventory and deliberate as to renouncing community of gains; and (*c*), if in necessitous circum-stances, to usufruct during wid-owhood of a sum which, with her own property, totals one thousand dollars in value; such sum pre-ferred except as to vendor's priv-ileges and expenses of selling property to obtain sum. When wife has brought no dowry or an inconsiderable dowry with re-spect to husband's condition, if either spouse dies rich, leaving survivor in necessitous circum-stances, survivor is entitled: (*a*) to one-fourth of the succession in full property if there be no children (apparently adult or minor); or (*b*) to such portion in usufruct if there are no more than three children; or (*c*) to child's share in usufruct if there are more than three children. Survivor is bound to include in such portion a legacy left him or her by decedent[29]

[§ 228

TABLE CIX (*Continued*)

Jurisdiction and Citation	Marital Rights during Coverture[2]	Rights of Surviving Spouse[2, 3]	Allowance to Widow—to Family (Analogous Provisions)[2, 3]
Maine .... R. S. 1930, Ch. 76, Sec. 48; Ch. 78, Secs. 14–16, 19; Ch. 95, Secs. 68, 69, 71	Householder may claim five hundred dollar homestead from his property	Widow and/or children entitled to debtor's homestead during her widowhood and/or their minority, exempt from his debts except liens of mechanics or materialmen[12]	Specified articles of personality (see statute) are not estate assets but are given to widow and children. Widow of intestate, of insolvent testate, or of testate who did not provide for her in will, or widow who waives testamentary provision, is entitled: (*a*) absolutely to so much personalty, besides her ornaments and apparel, as judge deems necessary; allowance may be increased if further property is discovered; and (*b*) to temporary allowance from personal estate, in addition to *a*, during litigation of will (not provided for if testate is insolvent). Widower may be given allowance as above if estate is solvent
Maryland ...... Bagby, Ann. C. 1924, Art. 93, Secs. 228–29, 317–18, 326			Provisions on hand at decedent's death remain for family's use and are exempt. Widow entitled to husband's apparel if there is no child nor grandchild, exempt from appraisement. Surviving spouse entitled to allowance from personal estate: (*a*) of one hundred and fifty dollars in money, household articles or kitchen furniture, if there is a child of survivor and decedent surviving; or (*b*) of seventy-five dollars as above, if there is no such child[30]
Massachusetts .. G. L. 1932, Ch. 188, Sec. 4; Ch. 196, Sec. 1; Sec. 2, amd. by Sess. L. 1933, Ch. 36, p. 43	Householder with family may claim eight hundred dollar homestead from his property	Homestead estate existing at death of householder continues for benefit of widow and children, if one of them or a purchaser[31] occupies premises, until youngest child is of age and until widow's death or remarriage; it may be set off in same manner as dower. Premises subject to above homestead rights are subject to laws relating to devise, descent, dower and sale for debts and legacies	Widow entitled: (*a*) to her apparel and ornaments; and (*b*) to use of decedent's house and furniture therein, for six months after his death (also see preceding column); and (*c*) to such personalty as court deems reasonable for support of widow and family; allowance is not subject to debts, legacies, or administration charges; and if personal property is exhausted, real property may be sold or mortgaged to provide allowance, by decree, in same manner as it is sold or mortgaged for debts; petition for decree is to be made by any party in interest within one year after approval of executor's or administrator's bond

TABLE CIX (*Continued*)

Jurisdiction and Citation	Marital Rights during Coverture[2]	Rights of Surviving Spouse[2, 3]	Allowance to Widow—to Family (Analogous Provisions)[2, 3]
Michigan .... Const., Art. XIV, Secs. 2–4; Comp. L. 1929, Sec. 13440, amd. by Sess. L. 1931, No. 79, p. 126; Secs. 14608, 15553–56, 15659, 15726, 15847	Resident may claim fifteen hundred dollar homestead from his property	Homestead of family is exempt from decedent's debts during minority of children; if no children, is exempt and rents and profits accrue to widow during her widowhood unless she owns homestead in her own right (homestead is to be occupied by one of above persons). Intestate share of realty is in lieu of widow's dower and homestead rights unless within one year after administration is granted she claims dower and homestead; if so, dower and homestead are in lieu of intestate share.[32] Excess-value homestead is divided if feasible; if not, it is sold and fifteen hundred dollars invested with court's approval in another homestead or in securities, exempt for benefit of widow or family. Possession of estate by executor or administrator shall not interfere with possession of homestead (as above)[33]	Widow and/or children entitled to reasonable allowance for maintenance during settlement of estate, but not after shares of estate are assigned them,[7] to be paid according to will if provision is adequate, otherwise from property not devised, or if necessary from devises and legacies in proportion to their amounts.[34] Widow of intestate or widow who waives testamentary provision is entitled to apparel and ornaments of herself and decedent, to household furniture, and to other personal property selected by her not to exceed value of two hundred dollars. If entire intestate estate does not exceed value of one hundred and fifty dollars over above allowances, court may set it apart for use of widow and children[9]
Minnesota ...... G. S. 1923, Secs. 8337–39, 8341, 8719, 8726, 8825, 8834–35	Owner of property may claim homestead of eighty acres of rural property; or of one-third acre in town of five thousand inhabitants or over; or of one-half acre in town of less than five thousand. Homestead title may be vested in either spouse and exemption extend to debts of either or both	Homestead descends free from will or other disposition to which surviving spouse did not consent in writing, and exempt from all debts which were not valid charges on it at decedent's death, as follows: (*a*) to survivor if there is no child (apparently adult or minor), or lawful issue of deceased child; or (*b*) otherwise to survivor for life, remainder to children and issue of deceased children.[35] Probate court may order decedent's homestead sold if (*a*) personal estate is insufficient for debts, legacies and administration expenses, and (*b*) court deems it to be for best interests of parties, and (*c*) life tenant consents in writing. Proceeds of sale are treated and distributed as real estate. If in interests of those concerned, court may order it mortgaged or leased instead of sold	Widow of intestate or widow who takes testamentary disposition is entitled to deceased's apparel, household furniture not to exceed value of five hundred dollars, and to other personalty not to exceed same value, both to be selected by her. Widow and/or children entitled: (*a*) to such reasonable allowance for support during settlement of testate or intestate estate as court deems necessary;[7] or (*b*) to entire intestate estate if value does not exceed one hundred and fifty dollars over above allowances. Above property and allowance are exempt from decedent's debts. If personal estate is insufficient, real estate may be sold to pay allowance in *a*

[§ 228

TABLE CIX (*Continued*)

Jurisdiction and Citation	Marital Rights during Coverture[2]	Rights of Surviving Spouse[2,3]	Allowance to Widow—to Family (Analogous Provisions)[2,3]
Mississippi ..... C. 1930, Secs. 1410–12, 1654, 1656, 1664, 1667, 1765–66, 1770, 1779	Resident householder with family may claim three thousand dollar homestead from his property. When wife owns homestead and occupies it with her family, it is exempt in like manner as that of householder above	Exempt real and personal property descends exempt (a) to decedent's children (adult or minor), grandchildren of deceased children, and surviving spouse, as tenants in common (grandchildren inheriting share of deceased parent); or (b) to survivor if there are no children, etc.[36] But if it descends as in a, to widow, it is not subject to partition during her widowhood as long as occupied or used by her, without her consent. Title, as above, vests by operation of law. Survivor and/or other heirs may select and have set apart a homestead from any real property of which decedent died seized and possessed, whether decedent selected one or not	Widow and/or children (apparently adult or minor) supported by decedent are entitled: (a) to necessary year's provisions and apparel, to be included in them so much thereof as is embraced in exempt property (see preceding column); or (b), if amount of provisions or apparel available is insufficient, to a sum of money to supply the same for one year. Chancery court may apportion allowance according to rights and interests of children and widow
Missouri .... R. S. 1929, Secs. 2, 108–10, 250, 608, 612, 614, 2998; Sess. L. 1933, p. 164, Sec. 107	Housekeeper or head of family may claim homestead from his property of fifteen hundred dollars in rural property or in towns or cities with less than forty thousand inhabitants; of three thousand dollars in larger cities. Married woman is entitled to homestead and all exemptions given head of family, except where husband has claimed such protections for his property	Widow and children entitled to joint occupancy of homestead, respectively, until her remarriage or death and/or their majority. If there are no children, widow is sole occupant as above. Such homestead is exempt from husband's debts except those enforceable against it during his life; but if his heirs are other than his children, it may be sold for valid debts subject to widow's rights. Homestead is first set out, then dower from residue, amount of dower being diminished by widow's homestead interest[37] (see next column as to exempt property)[20]	Surviving spouse entitled absolutely: (a), in addition to dower, to specified household articles, apparel, etc. (see statute), and to such sums of money in exclusion of debts, charges, legacies, and bequests as court deems reasonable for support of survivor and children under age of eighteen, for one year after decedent's death; if personalty is insufficient to pay allowance, court may order necessary real estate sold, or mortgaged for not longer than one year, to provide deficiency, such sale to be subject to homestead rights and existing liens; and (b) to personal property in addition to a, not to exceed value of four hundred dollars, its value to be deducted from dower in personalty; or (c), if above property is not received, but is sold, then to sale money before it is applied to debts or is distributed; or (d) to entire estate without administration if court is satisfied that its value will not exceed above allowances

TABLE CIX (*Continued*)

Jurisdiction and Citation	Marital Rights during Coverture[2]	Rights of Surviving Spouse[2, 3]	Allowance to Widow—to Family (Analogous Provisions)[2, 3]
Montana .... R. C. 1921, Secs. 6946–47, 6951, 6968–70, 6973, 10144–53	Husband, as head of family, or, if he does not do so, his wife may select twenty-five hundred dollar homestead from his property, or from wife's separate property with her consent and joinder. It may be abandoned only by declaration or grant thereof, executed and acknowledged by both spouses	Homestead selected during coverture from separate property of decedent goes to his or her heirs or devisees, subject to life estate in surviving spouse. If none was selected, court must select one for use of survivor and children as a life estate in survivor. Homestead above is exempt from decedent's debts except those enforceable against it during decedent's lifetime.[38] Survivor and/or children entitled to all other exempt property of decedent, one-half to survivor, one-half to children; if there are no children, then all to survivor (see next column as to separate maintenance of widow). Excess-value homestead is divided if feasible; if not, is sold and proceeds paid parties entitled	Widow and/or children entitled: (*a*) to homestead, apparel, household furniture and reasonable provision for support until inventory is returned; and (*b*) to exempt property (see preceding column); and (*c*), if property in *b* is insufficient, to reasonable allowance for maintenance of family during settlement of estate;[7, 8] or (*d*) to entire intestate estate without further administration if value does not exceed fifteen hundred dollars.[6] Above property for family's use is divided as is exempt property (see preceding column), except that if widow has separate maintenance equal to her above portions whole allowance or property, other than homestead, goes to children[9]
Nebraska .... St. 1929, Secs. 30(103), 30(230), 30(404), 40(101)– 40(102), 40(115), 40(117)	Husband as head of family may select two thousand dollar homestead from his separate property, or from wife's separate property with her consent	Homestead selected from separate property of decedent vests in surviving spouse for life, with remainder to decedent's heirs or devisees; it is exempt from debts of husband and/or wife existing at death, except those enforceable against it during decedent's lifetime. If survivor wilfully fails to provide home and maintenance for children or elects to partition homestead, above right terminates. Surviving spouse of intestate or spouse who receives testamentary provision is entitled: (*a*) to apparel, etc. (see statute); and (*b*) to all exempt property; and (*c*) to other personalty not to exceed value of two hundred dollars. Property above is not an estate asset (see next column as to allowance to surviving spouse)	Surviving spouse and children (family) of intestate, widow and/or children of testator,[39] entitled: (*a*) to such reasonable allowance from personalty or from income of real estate as court deems necessary for their support during settlement of estate but not after their shares of estate are assigned (see footnote 7 as to intestate estate); or if above sources of allowance are insufficient, allowance is a debt against estate, preferred after debts due in this state, but before general creditors; or (*b*) to entire estate if value does not exceed five hundred dollars[9] (see preceding column as to allowance of exempt property)

[§ 228

TABLE CIX (*Continued*)

Jurisdiction and Citation	Marital Rights during Coverture[2]	Rights of Surviving Spouse[2, 3]	Allowance to Widow—to Family (Analogous Provisions)[2, 3]
Nevada .... Comp. L. 1929 (Hillyer), Secs. 3315–18, 3365, 9699–9705	Five thousand dollar homestead may be selected by husband and/or wife; after declaration, they hold as joint tenants. Both must join in declaration from the separate property of either. Homestead may be abandoned only by declaration signed and acknowledged (separately by wife) by both spouses	Homestead selected (*a*) from decedent's separate property ceases on death, property vests in his or her heirs; (*b*) from survivor's separate property ceases on death and property remains in survivor; (*c*) from community property is set apart by court as sole property of survivor for benefit of survivor and legitimate children (apparently adult or minor) and is exempt from decedent's debts (provided that in *a* and *b* above the separate property must continue as separate property until decedent's death). If none has been selected, court sets one apart for use of family.[40] All other exempt property is set apart as in *c* above	Widow and children entitled: (*a*) to homestead, apparel, etc. (see statute), and reasonable provision for support;[41] and (*b*) to all exempt property (see preceding column); and (*c*), if property in *b* is insufficient, to reasonable allowance necessary for support during settlement of estate;[7, 30] or (*d*) to entire estate if value does not exceed one thousand dollars (widower also so entitled), but it may all be given children if, in court's discretion, their best interests would be served. Above property is apportioned one-half to widow, one-half to children; if none, then all to widow; but if she has separate maintenance equal to her portion, whole property or allowance goes to children
New Hampshire. Pub. L. 1926, Ch. 214, Secs. 1, 2, 5, 11; Ch. 306, Secs. 1, 11, 13, 15–17	Owner of property may claim five hundred dollar homestead, and, during his or her life, his or her spouse is entitled to share occupancy of it. If excess-value homestead is sold, owner and spouse must agree to division of sale proceeds, otherwise they are distributed by court	Surviving spouse and children are entitled to occupy homestead right during his or her lifetime and their minority, respectively, unaffected by devise of it. It is exempt in their hands in like manner as any homestead right. Surviving spouse must release homestead right (also dower or curtesy) to be entitled to distributive share of realty. Devise by decedent to survivor is in lieu of latter's rights by law in estate unless contrary intent exists in will. Antenuptial settlement made upon survivor, stipulated to be in lieu of homestead, bars survivor's homestead right[20]	Widow of intestate, widow not mentioned in will, or widow who waives testamentary provision may be given by court reasonable allowance from personal estate for her present support. Whole or part of allowance, as court deems reasonable, is accounted part of her distributive share of personal or real estate
New Jersey ..... Comp. St. 1910, p. 3819, Sec. 22; p. 3831, Secs. 60, 61; p. 4693, Sec. 57	Householder having a family may claim one thousand dollar homestead	Homestead exemption continues after owner's death for benefit of widow and family during her life and until majority of youngest child, but one of them must occupy homestead. No release or waiver of such exemption is valid	Resident widow and/or children entitled: (*a*) to allowance from estate income for support during contest of husband's will, allowance to include expense of contest and such expenses paid from income or from corpus of estate if necessary; and (*b*) to decedent's apparel and other chattels, money, etc., to value of two hundred dollars; such articles may be selected by widow and are reserved against all creditors (family of testate or intestate are so entitled), but giving such property shall not conflict with will

TABLE CIX (*Continued*)

Jurisdiction and Citation	Marital Rights during Coverture[2]	Rights of Surviving Spouse[2,3]	Allowance to Widow—to Family (Analogous Provisions)[2,3]
New Mexico .... St. Ann. 1929, Secs. 38(107), 47(510), 48(101), 48(111), 48(113)– 48(114), 48(119), 154(301), 154(306)	Husband or, if he fails to do so, his wife may claim family homestead of one thousand dollars; but neither spouse may claim homestead if other has one	Surviving spouse and unmarried children are entitled to have homestead set apart to them on petition of executors or administrators to sell to pay debts. It remains exempt so long as unmarried child resides thereon. No homestead provision shall impair dower rights. Surviving spouse is entitled to all exempt personalty of deceased head of family, exempt as in decedent's hands. Specified personal-property exemptions (see statute) given head of family likewise exist for benefit of widow	Surviving spouse, and children under fifteen years of age, are entitled to allowance, if necessary, for maintenance for six months from decedent's death[6]
New York ...... Civ. Prac. Act 1931, Secs. 671, 673–74; Surrogate's Court Act 1931, Sec. 200	Householder having a family, or a married woman, may claim one thousand dollar homestead	Homestead exemption on husband's death continues for benefit of widow and children until her death and/or their majority, but ceases if premises are not occupied by person for whose benefit it continues[42]	Surviving spouse or children entitled to specified household goods, apparel, etc. (see statute); such property is the property of survivor and is not considered an estate asset
North Carolina .. Const., Art. X, Secs. 2, 5; C. 1927, Secs. 3, 443, 748, 4108–10, 4112–13, 4115, 4120, 4124–25	Owner of property may claim one thousand dollar homestead	If there are no children (adult or minor), widow is entitled: (*a*) to husband's homestead during widowhood, exempt from his debts, unless she owns homestead in her own right; or (*b*) to have homestead set apart as in *a* if none was selected by husband[43,44]	Family may use crops, stock, provisions on hand, as necessary, until year's support (see below) is assigned. Widow of intestate or widow who dissents from will is entitled to allowance from personal property on hand; if that is insufficient, then from other personalty, for support of herself and family for one year after husband's death; property to be exempt from any lien claimed against it; and it is in addition to distributive share in personalty. She must apply for allowance within one year after husband's death (see footnote 45 as to its value)

[§ 228

TABLE CIX (*Continued*)

Jurisdiction and Citation	Marital Rights during Coverture[2]	Rights of Surviving Spouse[2, 3]	Allowance to Widow—to Family (Analogous Provisions)[2, 3]
North Dakota... Comp. L. 1913, Secs. 5622, 5626–29, 5631–32, 7736, 8723, 8725, 8727–29; Supp. 1913–25, Sec. 5606	Husband, as head of family, or, if he does not do so, his wife may select five thousand dollar homestead from his separate property, or from her separate property with her consent. Only one spouse may claim such homestead	Surviving spouse is entitled: (*a*) to homestead estate of decedent for life or until remarriage; or (*b*) to homestead as above, selected by court if none was selected during decedent's life; and (*c*) absolutely to decedent's exempt personal property and to other property selected by survivor not to exceed value of fifteen hundred dollars (property in *a, b,* and *c* is exempt from decedent's debts except those enforceable against it during his lifetime); or (*d*) absolutely to entire intestate estate for family's support, if value does not exceed fifteen hundred dollars, subject only to encumbrances on it at decedent's death.[6] Subject to above homestead rights, real property constituting homestead descends or may be devised like other realty[46]	If personal property set apart to survivor (see *c* in preceding column) is insufficient, widow and/ or children entitled, in court's discretion, to reasonable allowance for family's maintenance during settlement of estate[7, 8, 9] (see preceding column as to entire estate for support)
Ohio .... Complete G. C. 1931 (Page), Secs. 10795–96, 11591, 11730, 11732–34, 11738, 11740; Supp. 1932, Secs. 10504(61), 10509(54), 10509(55), 10509(74), 10509(75), 10509(77), 10509(121), 10509(122)	Husband or, if he fails to do so, his wife may claim family homestead of one thousand dollars; neither spouse may claim homestead if other has one. Married woman is entitled to all exemptions given heads of families. In case of assignment for benefit of creditors, with written, filed consent of husband and wife, homestead may be sold subject to dower and homestead rights	On petition of executors or administrators to sell to pay debts, homestead (see preceding column) is assigned widow,[47] to remain exempt so long as she remains unmarried. If homestead is sold to pay a superior lien, residue of proceeds not to exceed five hundred dollars is paid widow in lieu of homestead. If husband has not claimed homestead, widow may do so at any time before sale of property (see preceding column), but lands may be sold subject to such homestead right. Nothing in homestead provisions impairs dower rights; homestead is set off, and then dower. Widow may claim chattel exemptions and, in addition, may hold real or personal property in lieu of homestead, exempt to value of five hundred dollars. Widow or widower living with unmarried daughter or unmarried minor son may hold family homestead of one thousand dollars, exempt	Surviving spouse entitled: (*a*) to specified household goods, apparel or sum of money[48] (see statute) during time he or she lives with and provides for children and, when he or she ceases to do so, to his or her own apparel, ornaments, bed and bedding; or (*b*) to articles in *a* absolutely if there are no children. Widow is entitled to provisions or property for support of herself and for necessary support of children under fifteen years, for twelve months from decedent's death; property consumed by them before allowance given is considered in fixing allowance; if property is insufficient, sum of money is given for deficiency; and such allowance may be increased or diminished as necessary.[6] Election by widow to take under will does not bar her right to year's allowance unless will expressly directs otherwise[48]

§ 228]

TABLE CIX (*Continued*)

Jurisdiction and Citation	Marital Rights during Coverture[2]	Rights of Surviving Spouse[2, 3]	Allowance to Widow—to Family (Analogous Provisions)[2, 3]
Oklahoma ...... St. 1931, Secs. 1223–30, 1642–43	Owner of property may select family homestead of five thousand dollars. Family home comprises family homestead whether title is in husband or wife	Surviving spouse entitled: (*a*) to whole homestead for life without administration, until it is otherwise disposed of according to law;[49] and (*b*) to specified family personalty (see statute) which is not an estate asset; and (*c*) to exempt personalty of estate, exempt from decedent's debts.[6] Homestead above is exempt from debts of husband and/or wife prior to or at death, except those secured by liens valid against homesteads in general. Personal property set apart belongs one-half to survivor, one-half to child; if more than one child, one-third to survivor, two-thirds to children; if none, then all to survivor (see also next column as to widow's separate maintenance)	If property given surviving spouse and/or children (see preceding column) is insufficient, they are entitled, in court's discretion, to reasonable allowance necessary for their maintenance during settlement of estate.[7, 8, 9] Property, if set apart, is divided as in preceding column. Widow and/or children entitled to entire personal estate, if value does not exceed fifteen hundred dollars, for their support.[6] However, if widow has separate maintenance equal to above portions and property given as in preceding column, entire property so set apart, other than her right in homestead, goes to children
Oregon .... C. 1930, Secs. 3(201)–3(202), 3(204)–3(206), 11(401)– 11(404), 63(378)	Owner of land or his or her spouse may claim three thousand dollar homestead	Surviving spouse is entitled to have court set apart to him or her all estate property exempt from execution at decedent's death, including homestead; such property to belong to survivor and to be used for support of survivor and children[50]	Surviving spouse and children are entitled to homestead, family apparel and household furniture until inventory is filed. Widow and children are entitled: (*a*) to reasonable allowance for support during above period; and (*b*) to further allowance, in court's discretion, if exempt property set apart (see preceding column) is insufficient, but only if estate appears solvent; or (*c*) to entire intestate estate if value does not exceed one hundred and fifty dollars over and above exempt property[9]
Pennsylvania ... St. 1920 (West), Secs. 8446–47; Sec. 8452, amd. by Sess. L. 1931, No. 86, p. 116; Sec. 8455	Debtor is entitled to three hundred dollar exemption on his real property	See next column	Widow is entitled: (*a*) to real or personal property of estate or proceeds thereof to value of five hundred dollars exempt from husband's debts, but subject to purchase-money liens on real estate; or (*b*) to entire estate if value does not exceed five hundred dollars; and (*c*) to net rents, income, etc., from above property set apart, from decedent's death[51]

[§ 228

TABLE CIX (*Continued*)

Jurisdiction and Citation	Marital Rights during Coverture[2]	Rights of Surviving Spouse[2, 3]	Allowance to Widow—to Family (Analogous Provisions)[2, 3]
Rhode Island ... G. L. 1923, Secs. 5484–87			Widow is entitled for her support: (*a*) to her apparel; and (*b*) to household effects, supplies and other personal property as court deems necessary, exempt from attachment; and (*c*) to suitable portion of real estate not required for husband's debts, if there be no issue of husband living at his death, to be held in addition to and under same conditions as dower. Court shall also order necessary allowance for family's support for period not to exceed six months from husband's death; real estate may be sold to pay such allowance after personalty is exhausted. Personal property given above is not an estate asset
South Carolina.. Const., Art. III, Sec. 28; C. of L. 1922, C. C., Secs. 5490, 5493, 5496; Sess. L. 1925, No. 59, p. 93	Resident head of family may claim one thousand dollar homestead. Wife is entitled to homestead from her separate property if husband does not have enough property for one; but their joint exemptions shall not exceed those given generally to head of family	If husband is dead, widow and children (adult or minor) are entitled to family homestead exempted in like manner as if husband were living. Homestead is subject to partition among children of head of family in like manner as if no debts existed; provided that no partition or sale shall be made until youngest child is of age, unless such sale is deemed best for interests of minor children[52]	If intestate estate of personalty does not exceed value of five hundred dollars, it shall be paid out by probate judge to distributees without administration (see Table CVIII, Sec. 227)
South Dakota ... Comp. L. 1929, Secs. 450, 461, 463, 466–67, 469, 2658, 2665, 3345–53	Owner of land or his or her spouse may select five thousand dollar family homestead. No change of homestead made without concurrence of spouse affects his or her children's rights therein. Debtor's wife may claim personal property exemptions if he fails to do so	Surviving spouse is entitled: (*a*) to decedent's homestead for life, until it is otherwise disposed of according to law,[53] exempt from decedent's and survivor's debts except those enforceable against homesteads generally; or (*b*) to have court select homestead to be held as above by survivor, if none was selected in decedent's lifetime; and (*c*) to specified household effects (see statute) and provisions for one year; and (*d*) to money or personal property to amount of seven hundred and fifty dollars exempt.[6] When personal property is set apart to family's use, it belongs one-half to survivor, one-half to child; if more than one, one-third to survivor, two-thirds to children; if none, then all to survivor. Subject to survivor's rights in homestead, it descends or may be devised like other real property	Widow and/or children entitled: (*a*) to further reasonable allowance, in court's discretion, during settlement of estate[7, 8, 9] if amount set apart as in preceding column is less than that allowed by law, and is insufficient; or (*b*) to entire intestate estate of personal property if value does not exceed fifteen hundred dollars without further administration.[6] If widow has separate maintenance equal to portion above and given in preceding column, whole property set apart other than her right in homestead goes to children (see preceding column as to apportionment of personal property)

§ 228]

TABLE CIX (*Continued*)

Jurisdiction and Citation	Marital Rights during Coverture[2]	Rights of Surviving Spouse[2, 3]	Allowance to Widow—to Family (Analogous Provisions)[2, 3]
Tennessee ...... Const., Art. XI, Sec. 11; C. 1932, Sec. 7706; Sec. 7719, amd. by Sess. L. 1933, Ch. 72, p. 166; Secs. 7728–29, 7733, 8320–32, 8234, 8236, 8357	Husband may claim one thousand dollar homestead. If debtor is incapacitated from filling out schedule of personal-property exemptions, his or her spouse may do so. Homestead is allowed to wife only when husband does not have sufficient property from which to claim one	Widow is entitled to decedent's homestead for life, exempt from debts and regardless of will, for benefit of herself and family while residing with her. Homestead is set apart in same manner as dower is assigned. If widow is entitled to homestead and dower out of the same lands, homestead is set apart first, then dower from remaining lands. If dower and homestead cannot be set apart in kind, realty is sold, one thousand dollars[54] of proceeds invested in another homestead for benefit of widow and children, and dower is assigned from residue	*a*) Widow of intestate is entitled to provisions, crops, etc. (see statute), for family's support until letters are granted; (*b*) widow of intestate or widow who dissents from will is entitled absolutely to provisions, etc., or other assets for support for one year after husband's death, absolutely exempt; (*c*) widow is entitled to husband's exempt property for herself and in trust for children; such property does not go to executor or administrator
Texas .... Const., Art. XVI, Sec. 52; Complete St. 1928, Civ. St., Arts. 3476–78, 3480–91; Art. 3492, amd. by Supp. 1931, Sec. 3492; Arts. 3493–3501, 3833	Head of family may claim homestead (*a*) of two hundred acres from rural property; or (*b*) of five thousand dollars from urban property	On decedent's death homestead vests in like manner as other real property but shall not be partitioned during lifetime of surviving spouse or so long as he or she elects to use or occupy it as a homestead. Rights of widow and children are the same whether homestead is from decedent's separate property or from community property. Homestead is exempt from estate debts except those enforceable against homesteads generally. Widow is entitled after inventory is returned: (*a*) to all exempt property (except one year's provisions), if there are no children (adult or minor) or if children are her own; if not hers, then to one-half (see above as to homestead); and/or (*b*) to allowance in money or property selected by her, in lieu of any exempt property existing in estate; allowance is not to exceed five thousand dollars in lieu of homestead, nor five hundred dollars in lieu of other property; and is divided as in *a;* estate may be sold to provide allowance. If estate finally proves solvent, exempt property (except homestead), or allowance, is subject to partition and distribution as other property; if estate is insolvent, title of widow is absolute and property is exempt from estate debts but subject to valid liens.[19] In ascertaining whether estate is solvent or not, exempt property, allowance in lieu of it, and year's allowance are not considered as estate assets	Widow and children are entitled: (*a*) to allowance, in court's discretion, for maintenance for one year from husband's death; or (*b*) to personal property selected by widow or children's guardian, respectively, in lieu of above allowance. Estate may be sold, if necessary, to pay allowance; it is not subject to estate debts;[19] and it is apportioned like exempt property (see preceding column); provided that, if widow or child has adequate separate maintenance, such one is not entitled to allowance

TABLE CIX (*Continued*)

Jurisdiction and Citation	Marital Rights during Coverture[2]	Rights of Surviving Spouse[2, 3]	Allowance to Widow—to Family (Analogous Provisions)[2, 3]
Utah .... R. S. 1933, 38-0-1, 38-0-5, 38-0-6, 38-0-8, 38-0-11, 40-2-10, 101-4-3, 101-4-6, 101-4-7, 101-4-8, 102-8-1, 102-8-2	Husband or wife, as head of family, may claim homestead of two thousand dollars, with additional values of seven hundred and fifty dollars for his wife and three hundred dollars for each other member of family, from husband's separate property or from wife's separate property with her consent. If debtor fails to claim homestead, his or her spouse may do so. Neither spouse may remove other from homestead without other's consent, unless another suitable one is provided	Surviving spouse and/or children are entitled to a homestead and all exempt personal property of decedent; such property belongs one-half to survivor, one-half to children; if none, then all to survivor; it is subject only to debts enforceable against it during decedent's life, and may be partitioned only when survivor remarries or all children become of age. Value of survivor's share is to be deducted from his or her distributive share[55]	Surviving spouse and children are entitled: (*a*) to homestead and exempt property until court directs otherwise; and (*b*) to reasonable allowance, in court's discretion, during administration; if estate is insolvent, allowance is not to continue any longer than one year;[6] or (*c*) to entire estate absolutely if value does not exceed fifteen hundred dollars, one-half to survivor, one-half to children; if none, then all to survivor;[6] or (*d*) to property, in court's discretion, as in *c* from estate of greater value.[6] However, provisions in *c* and *d* do not affect decedent's right to dispose of property by will. Court, in its discretion, may exclude from above portions person who has separate property or income
Vermont .... G. L. 1917, Sec. 2710, amd. by Sess. L. 1927, No. 47, p. 51; Secs. 2725–26, amd. by Sess. L. 1921, No. 74, p. 70; Secs. 3281–82, 3287	Natural person may claim one thousand dollar homestead	Surviving spouse takes same estate in homestead of which decedent died seized, subject only to those of decedent's debts legally charged thereon in his or her lifetime.[56] If severance of homestead would adversely affect parties interested, probate court may order estate sold and portion of proceeds invested in new homestead or paid survivor or trustee of court	Widow residing with husband at his death is entitled to household goods, furniture, etc. (see statute), in addition to distributive share. Widow and/or children entitled, in court's discretion: (*a*) to reasonable allowance for maintenance during settlement of estate, but not after their shares in estate are assigned, or, if estate is insolvent, not after eight months from date administration is granted; or (*b*) to entire estate if value does not exceed three hundred dollars; or (*c*) to three hundred dollar share of estate which is not sufficient to pay debts and expenses of settlement and leave balance of three hundred dollars. Allowance in *a* may be paid from personal estate or income from real estate

§ 228]

TABLE CIX (*Continued*)

Jurisdiction and Citation	Marital Rights during Coverture[2]	Rights of Surviving Spouse[2, 3]	Allowance to Widow—to Family (Analogous Provisions)[2, 3]
Virginia Const., Sec. 190; C. 1930, Secs. 6531, 6536–38, 6541–43, 6546, 6550, 6554, 6562	Householder or head of family may claim exemption on real and/or personal property to value of two thousand dollars	Widow and children are entitled: (*a*) to hold homestead and exempt personalty of deceased householder exempt from his debts as it was during his life and exempt from their debts until widow's death or remarriage[57] and until children reach age of twenty-one (or marry if they do so while minors); or (*b*) to have homestead and personal property set apart as above by court, if decedent did not have exemptions as allowed by law (see preceding column); and (*c*) to petition and, in court's discretion, to have above property sold; proceeds to be invested in other property to be likewise exempt. If widow receives dower or jointure, she cannot take homestead rights; and value of dower or jointure is deducted from benefits of exempt personalty. When exemptions cease (see above) above property passes as other real or personal estate[51]	Widow and/or children and unmarried daughters constituting husband's family at his death entitled: (*a*) to use dead victuals on hand, or to kill livestock before distribution or sale, as necessary for food; and (*b*) absolutely to specified household articles, apparel, etc. (see statute), which were exempt to decedent; articles are exempt as in his lifetime and also from funeral or administration charges
Washington Remington, Comp. St. 1922, Secs. 530–31, 535, 552–53, 558, 561, 1364; Secs. 1473–74, amd. by Supp. 1927, Secs. 1473–74; Sec. 1476	Husband, as head of family, or, if he does not do so, his wife may claim two thousand dollar homestead from his separate property, or from her separate property with her consent, shown by her making declaration of homestead. It may be abandoned only by declaration or grant thereof, executed and acknowledged by husband and wife	Homestead selected (*a*) from community property vests in survivor, exempt as before death; (*b*) from decedent's separate property vests in his or her heirs, subject to court's power to assign it for limited period to family (but see probate homestead below). Surviving spouse is entitled, without further administration: (*c*) to have probate court set aside to him or her in fee simple, homestead selected during decedent's life, if value does not exceed two thousand dollars exclusive of liens enforceable against it; and (*d*) to have court set apart absolutely other property (community or separate) which added to *c* will not exceed value of three thousand dollars exclusive of liens, if expenses of last illness, funeral and administration are provided for; or (*e*) to property set apart as in *d*, not to exceed three thousand dollars, if no homestead has been claimed, such award to include home and household goods.[58] Awards in *c, d*, and *e* are in lieu of further homestead and exemption provisions; they shall not be taken from decedent's separate property otherwise devised, if there is no child, issue or adopted, of decedent and survivor, living[58]	Widow of intestate or widow who takes under will is entitled to her apparel or ornaments and such provisions or other necessaries for use of herself and family as may be allowed under any law; to be preferred over debts, charges of funeral and of settling estate. In addition to awards given in preceding column, court may make further reasonable allowance of cash, necessary for family's maintenance during settlement of estate[6]

[§ 228

TABLE CIX (*Continued*)

Jurisdiction and Citation	Marital Rights during Coverture[2]	Rights of Surviving Spouse[2, 3]	Allowance to Widow—to Family (Analogous Provisions)[2, 3]
West Virginia .. C. 1931, Ch. 38, Art. 8, Secs. 1, 3, 10, 11; Art. 9, Sec. 1; Ch. 44, Art. 1, Sec. 17	Husband may hold one thousand dollar homestead. If owner of personal property fails to claim exemptions, his or her spouse may do so	Widow and/or children entitled to select personal estate of deceased not to exceed two hundred dollars in value, and to hold it exempt from his debts or other execution or process, but not from claims for purchase money or taxes. If property is not selected, it is not exempt[51, 59]	Decedent's family is entitled to provisions and fuel on hand at his or her death, or to kill live stock for food before distribution or sale, as necessary for its use, without account being made (see also preceding column)
Wisconsin ..... St. 1931, Secs. 233.01, 233.14, 233.16, 237.02, 238.04, 272.20, 276.14, 313.15, 313.26, 314.05	Owner of property may claim five thousand dollar homestead from it; it may also be claimed from land held by husband and wife jointly or in common	Homestead of intestate passes to widow if no issue; if issue, to her until her death or remarriage with remainder to heirs. Widow of testate may elect dower and homestead rights as against testamentary provision;[60] if so, or if will contains no provision for her, homestead descends to her as if husband had died intestate leaving issue (see above). If she takes as above or as devisee of homestead, it is exempt from decedent's debts except lawful mortgages, laborers' and mechanics' liens. Widow is not entitled to dower in homestead, and homestead may not be sold under power of sale in will or for partition without her consent; but if consent is given, she takes dower in proceeds in lieu of homestead rights. Undisputed homestead right may be assigned in like manner as dower; and homestead may be set off in partition action	Widow is entitled whether she waives or accepts will or whether husband is intestate: (a) to specified apparel, furniture, etc (see statute); and (b) to other personal property selected by her not to exceed value of two hundred dollars. Widow and/or children entitled: (a) to reasonable allowance, in court's discretion, necessary for maintenance during settlement of estate but not after their shares are assigned; it may be paid from personal property or from income from real property;[7] and (b) to a sum not to exceed one thousand dollars for support, if personalty exceeds apparel, furniture, allowance, as above[9]
Wyoming ...... R. S. 1931, Secs. 88(2901)– 88(2904), 88(3002), 89(2212), 89(2984), 89(2986), 89(2993)	Householder, head of family, may claim twenty-five hundred dollar homestead. Married woman is entitled to all exemptions given heads of families	Surviving spouse is entitled absolutely: (a) to all exempt property of decedent, including homestead; and (b) to value of exempt property allowed by law to decedent but which he or she did not have at death, in money or other property. Property in a and b is exempt from decedent's debts.[6] Widow's rights as above are not affected by her renouncing or failing to renounce testamentary provision (see also next column). Excess-value homestead is divided if feasible; if not, it is sold and proceeds paid parties entitled. On death of head of family, family is entitled to exemptions generally given head	Surviving spouse is entitled to homestead, family apparel and decedent's furniture until inventory is returned. Widow and/or children entitled: (a) to reasonable allowance for support until inventory is returned; and (b) to allowance necessary for support during settlement of estate if amount of estate set apart to them is insufficient. Above allowances are not to invalidate any record mortgage or lien against decedent's property[9]

§ 228]

TABLE CIX (*Continued*)

[1] The term "children" when used in this table means minor children unless otherwise indicated.

[2] The material in the text and table of the present section has been limited to specific problems relating to husband and wife. No attempt has been made, therefore, to include statutes relating to the following: (*a*) general rights to personal-property exemptions (in the first column); (*b*) essentials to the retention of the homestead not expressly applicable to a spouse (e.g., residence on the homestead by the family); (*c*) limitations on the area of the homestead in jurisdictions which also have a limitation on value (**Alabama, Alaska, Arkansas, Georgia, Iowa, Louisiana, Michigan, Mississippi, Missouri, Montana, Nebraska, North Dakota, Oklahoma, Oregon, South Dakota, Wisconsin**); (*d*) procedural details even though they expressly apply to husband or wife; their extent and diversity make their inclusion in tabular form inadvisable. Certain of the procedural provisions have been cited incidentally in the table with statutes relating to substantive rights; the following citations may be consulted in addition thereto: **Alabama,** C. 1923, Secs. 7912, 7927–59; **Arizona,** R. C. 1928, Secs. 3981–82; **Arkansas,** Crawf. and Moses, Dig. 1921, Secs. 81, 85, 87, 88, 5525–29, 5531–38; **California,** Prob. C. 1933 (Lake), Secs. 640–44, 646, 666; **Idaho,** Comp. St. 1919, Secs. 7572, 7574–77; **Iowa,** C. 1927, Sec. 12018; **Kansas,** R. S. 1923, Sec. 22(513); **Michigan,** Comp. L. 1929, Secs. 15844–46; **Minnesota,** G. S. 1923, Secs. 8796–97; **Missouri,** R. S. 1929, Secs. 618–19; **New Hampshire,** Pub. L. 1926, Ch. 293, Sec. 5; Ch. 306, Sec. 14; **New Jersey,** Comp. St. 1910, p. 3832, Sec. 62; **North Carolina,** C. 1927, Secs. 1244, 3900, 4114, 4116–19, 4121–23, 4126–27; **North Dakota,** Comp. L. 1913, Secs. 5630, 8724, 8726; **Ohio,** Complete G. C. 1931 (Page), Secs. 10658, 10660; **Pennsylvania,** St. 1920 (West), Secs. 8448–49, 8453–54, 8456–57; **Texas,** Complete St. 1928, Civ. St., Sec. 3479; **Wyoming,** R. S. 1931, Secs. 88(2905), 88(3001), 88(3003)–88(3004).

[3] The writer has attempted to segregate the material in columns two and three of the table according to the tenor of the statute. However, because of the similarity between provisions giving exempt property to the surviving spouse and those giving an allowance for support, each column should be read in conjunction with the other.

[4] **Alabama:** When homestead is all of real estate, title of widow and children, as against heirs, does not vest until judicial proceedings; but as against creditors, title is presumed absolute until judicial determination that homestead is not all of real estate (see also *Little* v. *Simmons,* 222 Ala. 206; 131 So. 561 [1930]). Homestead which is absolute property of widow and children shall not be sold or partitioned by court order until her death and majority of youngest child, except for reinvestment with widow's consent.

[5] See *Jackson* v. *Wilson,* 117 Ala. 432; 23 So. 521 (1897): Specified household articles are not part of distributive share; but one thousand dollar allowance of property is in anticipation of distributive share or legacy, if estate is solvent.

[6] Allowance or property (see table) is paid after, or subject to, expenses of last illness, funeral, and administration.

[7] If estate is insolvent, settlement of it must not take longer than one year after letters are granted.

[8] Allowance may, in court's discretion, take effect from decedent's death.

[9] Allowance or property (see table) is paid after, or subject to, expenses of funeral and administration.

[10] See *Stone* v. *Stone,* 185 Ark. 390; 47 S. W. (2d) 50 (1932).

[11] *Union National Bank of Greeley* v. *Wright,* 78 Colo. 346; 242 P. 54 (1925): Rights of surviving spouse are not enlarged or diminished by fact of decedent's death.

[12] See **Section 197; Section 202,** summary.

[13] See *Hinson* v. *Booth,* 39 Fla. 333; 22 So. 687 (1897), interpreting the Constitution, Article 10, Section 2.

[14] **Georgia:** See Code 1926, Sections 3400–3403, 3405–8, as to sales of exempt property free from reversion to estate, the fee simple being sold.

[15] See *Donalson* v. *Yeates,* 173 Ga. 30; 159 S. E. 856 (1931): Title to homestead property vests in heirs of intestate subject to use of widow and children during her life and their minority.

[16] The statutes of **Hawaii** refer to homestead leases of public lands, but such homesteads are somewhat analogous to the homesteads, referred to elsewhere in this section, declared or selected by the owner of property.

[17] **Illinois** (Cahill, R. S. 1931): In a partition action (*a*) premises allotted as homestead may be partitioned among claimants, subject to homestead right; and (*b*) homestead estate of

[§ 228

TABLE CIX (Continued)

party to action may be sold with other property with party's assent, written and filed with court; value in gross is then paid, or proportion of proceeds invested for party's benefit (Ch. 106, Secs. 22, 32, 34). In action to sell decedent's estate for debts or in sale under power of sale in will, homestead may be sold and compensated under same rules as in partition action above (Ch. 3, Sec. 102). See *Dinquel* v. *Dacco, 273* Ill. 117; 112 N. E. 337 (1916): Homestead interest is estate in land and passes to surviving spouse.

[18] **Indiana:** If widow does not take such personal property, she is paid equivalent in cash after expenses of last sickness, funeral and administration have been paid; or if estate is clearly solvent, from first money received by representative. If personal property is insufficient to pay cash due her, deficit is a lien on real estate, enforceable as other liens and superior to judgment liens against decedent.

[19] Property (see table) is subject to expenses of last illness and funeral.

[20] See **Section 202,** summary; **Section 221,** summary.

[21] See *Ehler* v. *Ehler,* 214 Ia. 789; 243 N. W. 591 (1932): Taking homestead of deceased husband in **California** did not bar widow's distributive share in **Iowa** property.

[22] **Iowa:** Within six months after written notice to survivor given by heir or by administrator if a sale is necessary for debts, survivor may elect to take distributive share or the right to occupy homestead (as to formalities, see **Sec. 205,** Table XCIX).

[23] See *Dayton* v. *Donart,* 22 Kan. 256 (1879), and *Breen* v. *Breen,* 102 Kan. 766; 173 P. 2 (1918): Homestead is exempt until widow dies or remarries and children become of age; or until they abandon it. See also *Campbell* v. *Durant,* 110 Kan. 30; 202 P. 841 (1921): Widow of testate decedent who dissents from will is entitled to the same homestead rights as widow of intestate.

[24] See *Shields* v. *Parsons,* 230 Ky. 143; 18 S. W. (2d) 961 (1929): Homestead right of surviving husband is for life; title is in the heirs. See also *Overby* v. *Williams,* 170 Ky. 140; 185 S. W. 822 (1916): Widow may occupy homestead by tenant, but sale by her works an abandonment of homestead right.

[25] See **Section 196,** Table XCVII; **Section 202,** summary; **Section 220,** subdivision I; **Section 221,** summary.

[26] See *Weddington* v. *Adkins,* 245 Ky. 747; 54 S. W. (2d) 331 (1932): Widow given devise of realty and also seven hundred and fifty dollar share of personalty undisposed of by will.

[27] **Louisiana** (Marr, Ann. R. S., Supp. 1926, Act 35, p. 1105, Secs. 1, 2): If husband fails to declare homestead within six months after he acquires the property, wife may do so; but her declaration is limited to community property occupied as a home—if from urban property, not to exceed lots on which family residence is situated; if from rural property, not to exceed twenty acres on which family residence is situated.

[28] For a good discussion of homestead right of surviving widow, see *Succession of White,* 170 La. 403; 127 So. 883 (1930): Widow may claim decedent's homestead (*a*) exempt from his debts or community debts whether she is head of family, has dependents, or not; but (*b*) exempt from her debts only when she is a head of family or has dependents.

[29] **Louisiana:** If survivor is entitled to such marital portion (see table), he or she is entitled to periodical allowance, during pendency of proceedings, of five per cent interest on the apparent marital portion; if portion when finally fixed does not yield revenue equal to allowance, amount of such deficiency is deducted from marital portion. (See *Succession of Bancker,* 154 La. 77; 97 So. 321 [1923], to the effect that the marital portion is not a right of inheritance, but is in the nature of a bounty given by the sovereign.)

[30] Allowance is subject to funeral expenses.

[31] **Massachusetts** (G. L. 1932, Ch. 188, Sec. 8): Widow may sell homestead estate if there are no children; or she may join in sale with children's guardian if he has license to sell from probate court. Purchaser is entitled to premises for full time that widow and/or children would have been entitled; probate court may apportion sale proceeds among parties.

[32] **Michigan** (Comp. L. 1929, Sec. 13440, as amended by Sess. L. 1931, No. 79, p. 127): (*a*) Probate judge, if he thinks proper, may at any time before estate is closed, on widow's petition and after notice to all persons interested, permit her to begin proceedings and have dower and homestead set off as though she had done so within the year (see table); judge shall limit the time so available to her. (*b*) If administrator, after expiration of year and before court order as in *a,* has sold real estate, widow's dower and homestead shall be set off from lands not conveyed, if so much remains unsold. (*c*) Widow may appear voluntarily in proceeding for

§ 228]

TABLE CIX (*Continued*)

license to sell real estate, and waive dower and homestead; if she does not do so, notice to appear and elect shall be served personally upon her at least ten days prior to such hearing. Thereafter, if she does not elect, she is deemed to have waived dower and homestead; except that probate judge may give her additional time in which to elect, if he thinks it proper.

[33] See **Section 202**, summary.

[34] **Michigan:** Court may exempt specific devises and legacies from contribution to family allowance if there is other sufficient estate.

[35] **Minnesota** (G. S. 1923, Sec. 8722): See **Section 199**, summary, as to election between will and rights by statute. It is further provided that, if the title to the homestead is in litigation and is not determined within the six months given for election, survivor may elect within thirty days after such litigation is concluded (see also **Sec. 205, Table XCIX**).

[36] **Mississippi:** If surviving spouse owns residence equal in value to homestead, and decedent has no surviving children or grandchildren of last marriage, but has children or grandchildren of former marriage, homestead does not descend to survivor.

[37] See *Martin* v. *Martin,* 313 Mo. 476; 285 S. W. 92 (1926): ".... While dower may be merged in the homestead, the homestead cannot be merged in the dower."

[38] **Montana:** If decedent's homestead does not exceed twenty-five hundred dollars in value, secured claims enforceable against it are paid from other estate funds, if funds are adequate to pay all claims against estate; if inadequate, secured claims share proportionally with other claims and are enforced against homestead only for deficiency.

[39] See *In re Estate of O'Shea,* 85 Neb. 156; 122 N. W. 881 (1909): The concurring opinion of Root, J., indicates that Compiled Statutes 1929, Section 30(230), referring to "widow" of testator, is probably an oversight and should read "surviving spouse."

[40] See *In re Cook's Estate,* 34 Nev. 217; 117 P. 27 (1911): No homestead had been selected during decedent's life; *held,* that court could not set apart to widow homestead from decedent's separate property; *dictum,* that court must set apart homestead from community property, if any, to surviving spouse.

[41] **Nevada:** Compiled Laws 1929, Section 9699, does not specify how long a widow and children may retain homestead, etc. However, the following section and similar statutes in other states (see **California**) indicate that it is intended for their use until inventory is filed.

[42] **New York** (Civ. Prac. Act 1931, Sec. 675): Homestead exemption does not cease (see table) if residence is suspended for period not to exceed one year because of injury to dwelling house.

[43] See *Caudle* v. *Morris,* 160 N. C. 168; 76 S. E. 17 (1912): Even though there are no children, widow is not entitled to homestead if deceased husband left no creditors; she is confined to dower.

[44] See **Sections 197–98; Section 202**, summary.

[45] **North Carolina:** Value of allowance in general is three hundred dollars and one hundred dollars additional for each member of family besides widow; and if it is assigned through application of personal representative to justice of peace, and if estate is insolvent or does not exceed two thousand dollars, above is maximum value. But if allowance is assigned through widow's application to superior court, she may be given amount actually necessary, not to exceed one-half of annual net income of deceased for three years next preceding his death. Value of articles consumed by family before assignment is deducted from allowance.

[46] See *In re Druhl's Estate,* 61 N. D. 168; 237 N. W. 697 (1931): Homestead right of surviving spouse is separate from and not affected by the right of survivor to take real property subjected to homestead, either as heir or under will.

[47] **Ohio** (Complete G. C. 1931 [Page], Supp. 1932, Sec. 10510[30]): In action brought by executor or administrator, if deceased left family homestead and surviving spouse and/or children are entitled to have homestead set off, court shall order appraisers to do so. In lieu of homestead, survivor and/or children may elect to waive homestead and receive from proceeds of sale five hundred dollars in money.

[48] **Ohio** (Complete G. C. 1931 [Page], Supp. 1932): Value of specified articles which are not estate assets (see statute) is not to exceed twenty per centum of appraised value of property, real and personal, in inventory (gross estate); but is not to be more than twenty-five hundred dollars if there be a surviving spouse, nor less than five hundred dollars if inventory contains so much. If personal property selected is of less value than above, surviving spouse is entitled to sum of money equal to the difference, which sum is a charge on all estate property and is

TABLE CIX (*Concluded*)

prior to claims of unsecured creditors (Sec. 10509[54]). Court may, in its discretion, set off year's allowance to widow and children of non-resident decedent from his **Ohio** property, but not if the state of his residence provides such allowance to them (Sec. 10509[78]).

[49] See *Holmes* v. *Holmes,* 27 Okla. 140; 111 P. 220 (1910); and *Belt* v. *Bush,* 74 Okla. 94; 176 P. 935 (1918): It is apparently held in **Oklahoma** (*a*) that "disposed of according to law" (see table) means a disposition arising from enforcement of valid claims against homestead; and (*b*) that title to real estate passes to heirs subject to homestead right.

[50] See *Banfield* v. *Small,* 139 Ore. 134; 8 P. (2d) 779 (1932): Surviving spouse in **Oregon** now apparently takes homestead in fee simple, after it is set apart by court. Decisions contra were reached under earlier, different statutes.

[51] See **Section 202,** summary.

[52] See *Dorn* v. *Stidham,* 139 S. C. 66; 137 S. E. 331 (1926): Right of widow and/or children is not an interest in land; it is apparently only an exemption from decedent's debts, protecting property they receive under statute of descent or under will; but husband may defeat such right by otherwise devising property. See also *Kennedy* v. *Kennedy,* 74 S. C. 541; 54 S. E. 773 (1906).

[53] See footnote 49 above as to interpretation of similar phrase in **Oklahoma.**

[54] **Tennessee:** The statute, in terms, provides for investment of two thousand dollars but is evidently an oversight, for the homestead exemption has been amended to one thousand dollars (see Sess. L. 1933, Ch. 72, p. 166).

[55] **Utah:** In *In re Schenk's Estate,* 53 Utah 381; 178 P. 344 (1919), it was held that the homestead right of the surviving spouse could be defeated by the will of the decedent. The statute upon which the court relied provided that the section conferring the homestead right should ". . . . not be construed to prevent the disposition by will of the homestead and exempt personal property" (Comp. L. 1917, Sec. 6409). However, the clause quoted has been deleted from the present homestead statute (R. S. 1933, 104-4-6); and, presumably, the homestead right, in accord with the great weight of authority, cannot now be defeated by the decedent's will (see also *In re Syndergaard's Estate,* 31 Utah 490; 88 P. 616 [1907]).

[56] **Vermont:** See General Laws 1917, Section 2710, as amended by Session Laws 1927, Number 47, page 51, for details respecting forfeiture of survivor's homestead rights resulting from separation or from absence when estate is administered.

[57] See *Barker* v. *Jenkins,* 84 Va. 895; 6 S. E. 459 (1888): If husband leaves no debts, reason for widow's homestead ceases, and she has no right to his homestead or to have one set apart. See also *Davis* v. *Davis,* 101 Va. 230; 43 S. E. 358 (1903): If homestead has been awarded to widow, she cannot be deprived of it by payment of decedent's debts by heirs.

[58] **Washington:** By feloniously killing deceased spouse survivor forfeits right to award provided for in *e* of column two of the table. Provisions in *a* and *b* of column two are the ones usually found in community-property states, but those in *c, d,* and *e* are innovations adopted subsequently to *a* and *b* and presumably overrule the latter in case of conflict. Such later provisions are regarded as being given for family's support.

[59] See footnote 1 (p. 493) to Table CI in **Section 209** for a provision partially protecting family home.

[60] See **Section 205,** Table XCIX, for details of election.

REFERENCES

Books

STIMSON, F. J. *American Statute Law,* Secs. 87, 6253 (1886).

THOMPSON, SEYMOUR D. *A Treatise on Homestead and Exemption Laws* (1878).

WOERNER, J. G. *A Treatise on the American Law of Administration,* 3d ed., Vol. I, Secs. 94–104 (1923).

Articles

COLE, BRADY. "The Homestead Provisions in the Texas Constitution," 3 Tex. L. Rev. 217–33 (1925).

§ 228]

Foster, Henry H. "The Nebraska Homestead," 3 Neb. L. Bull. 109–59, 353–435 (1924–25).

Lewis, J. H. "Principles of Exemption Laws," 2 Dak. L. Rev. 140–47 (1928).

Notes

"Bankruptcy—Homestead Exemption—When Declaration of Homestead Is Effective," *White* v. *Stump,* 266 U. S. 310 (1924)—25 Col. L. Rev. 492–93 (1925).

"Frauds on Creditors—Disposal of Assets to Acquire Homestead," 13 Calif. L. Rev. 499–501 (1925).

"Homestead—Alienation, Abandonment, Estoppel," *Krueger* v. *Groth,* 190 Wis. 387; 209 N. W. 773 (1926)—11 Marquette L. Rev. 59–61 (1926).

"Homestead—Exemption of Property Homesteaded by Grantee from Attachment Existing at Time of Grant—Effect of Wife's Failure to Acknowledge or Join in Declaration of Homestead," *Jacobin* v. *Pope and Talbot,* 214 Cal. 758; 7 P. (2d) 1017 (1932)—20 Calif. L. Rev. 569–71 (1932).

"Nature and Extent of Homestead Rights," *Brandenburg* v. *Petroleum Exploration Company,* 218 Ky. 557; 291 S. W. 757 (1927)—16 Geo. L. Jour. 122–24 (1927).

"Right of Non-Resident Alien Wife—Conflict between State Homestead Statute and Treaty," *Engen* v. *Union State Bank of Harvard,* 121 Neb. 257; 236 N. W. 741 (1931)—10 Neb. L. Bull. 485–89 (1932).

"The Todok Case," *Todok* v. *Union State Bank of Harvard,* 281 U. S. 449 (1930)— 26 Amer. Jour. Int. Law 144–46 (1932).

Annotations

"Debtor's Marriage after Levy or Service of Process to Reach Property, as Entitling Him to Exemption Enjoyed by Married Debtor," 82 A. L. R. 739–42 (1933).

"Estate or Interest in Real Property to Which Homestead Claim May Attach," 89 A. L. R. 511–63 (1934).

"Exemption of Proceeds of Voluntary Sale of Homestead," 1 A. L. R. 483–88 (1919).

"Failure of Head of Family to Claim Homestead Exemption as Affecting Other Members of the Family," 33 A. L. R. 611–14 (1924).

"Homestead Right in Community Property," 89 A. L. R. 554–55 (1934).

"Homestead Rights of Wife as Affected by the Fact That She Does Not Live in State," 92 A. L. R. 1054–56 (1934).

"Inclusion of Different Tracts or Parcels in Homestead," 73 A. L. R. 116–48 (1931).

"Mechanic's or Materialman's Lien on Homestead," 65 A. L. R. 1192–1213 (1930).

"Misconduct of Surviving Spouse as Affecting Marital Rights in Spouse's Homestead," 71 A. L. R. 283, 286 (1931).

"Rights and Remedies of One Whose Funds Are Fraudulently Used in the Purchase or Improvement of Homestead," 43 A. L. R. 1446–47 (1926) ; 48 A. L. R. 1269 (1927).

"Right of Wife to Exclude Husband from Possession, Use or Enjoyment of Family Residence or Homestead Owned by Her," 21 A. L. R. 745–52 (1922).

"Scope and Import of Term 'Owner' in Homestead Exemption Statutes," 2 A. L. R. 793–94 (1919).

"Time as of Which, and Extent to Which, Homestead Exemption Attaches to Property Received in Exchange for Homestead," 83 A. L. R. 54–62 (1933).

"Waiver by Contract of Homestead Exemption," 47 A. L. R. 303–5 (1927).

[§ 228

Section 229. Statute of Limitations

CROSS REFERENCES: Suits by the wife, **Sec. 179**; Suits between spouses, **Sec. 180**; Infants and statutes of limitations, **Sec. 276**; Insane persons and statutes of limitations, **Sec. 306**

In the great majority of jurisdictions, the wife may now sue as if sole (**Sec. 179**). Logically, statutes of limitations should run against her as against other persons. However, this is not true in some of the states which allow her procedural freedom. The explanation lies in the historical situation.

At a time when the wife could not sue alone, statutes were passed in most jurisdictions providing for suspension of limitations when her causes of action accrued during coverture, as it was felt that she should not be barred with the same strictness applicable to persons who could sue alone. Such enactments either gave her a specified time in which to sue after discoverture or provided that in computing the period of limitations time of disability should not be considered.

The special privilege accorded the wife was without a valid reason when she was permitted to sue alone, and only twelve jurisdictions have been found with legislation which retains such privilege in varying forms. The statutes in **Nevada** and **Texas** have a legitimate purpose in so far as they apply to actions in which the husband must be joined (Table XC, **Sec. 179**); and in four states the provisions by their own terms are practically inoperative (**California, Connecticut, Idaho, North Carolina**). In the remaining six jurisdictions, the effect of the statutes has been left to the courts (**Colorado, Delaware, Maine, Missouri, New Jersey, Pennsylvania**). The cases are divided, but the apparent weight of authority has taken a logical view, viz., that the procedural emancipation statutes have impliedly repealed the wife's privilege (for arguments to that effect and also contra, see *McIrvin* v. *Lincoln Memorial University*, 138 Tenn. 260; 197 S. W. 862; L. R. A. 1918C 191 [1917]). The situation in **Kentucky** is stated in footnote 3 of the Table CX following.

There is a curious inconsistency in the statutory situation. The six jurisdictions mentioned above allow the wife to sue in general as if unmarried, yet, in terms, still suspend statutes of limitations. On the other hand, of the few jurisdictions which do not permit the wife to sue alone in all actions (**Sec. 179**), the majority have apparently repealed any privilege as to limitations because of coverture.

Five states have definite legislation to the effect that in certain enumerated actions (**Louisiana, Missouri**) or in all actions (**Maryland,**

Rhode Island, Tennessee) limitations run against the wife as against a feme sole. These statutes are admirably direct, although the difficulty discussed above can perhaps more easily be remedied by the method of the majority of jurisdictions, namely, omission of any reference to disability of married women in statutes of limitations.

No legislation has been found on the related question of limitations on actions between spouses. Where such actions are permitted (**Sec. 180**), it would seem logical that without express statutes to the contrary limitations should apply as in actions against third persons. However, some cases and text writers have said that actions between spouses are not to be encouraged and that delay in bringing them should not be penalized (see references at end of this section). The weakness of such reasoning is patent; furthermore, the modern recognition of husband and wife as separate legal entities for most purposes makes it desirable to apply the usual limitations as a bar to marital litigation. If, in a particular jurisdiction, a statute is necessary to accomplish that result, it is the writer's opinion that it should be adopted.

Citations are given in the table below.

TABLE CX

WIFE AND STATUTES OF LIMITATIONS

Jurisdiction and Citation	Suspension of Limitations as a Privilege of Wife[1]	No Exception Because of Coverture[1]
California .... C. C. P. 1933 (Lake), Sec. 352	In actions other than for recovery of real property, if husband is a necessary party, and if right of action accrued during marriage, time of disability of wife is not a part of time limited for commencement of action	
Colorado .... Comp. L. 1921, G. S., Sec. 6406	If person entitled to sue in certain enumerated personal actions is a married woman when cause of action accrues, limitations as specified for those actions begin to run only on removal of disability[2]	

[1] It is impossible in the available space to set forth the great numbers of actions covered by the statutes of limitations. Where the term "enumerated actions" is used, the statute must be consulted for particular actions.

[2] An annotation following Section 6406 in Compiled Laws of 1921 indicates that the section is considered obsolete.

TABLE CX *(Continued)*

Jurisdiction and Citation	Suspension of Limitations as a Privilege of Wife	No Exception Because of Coverture
Connecticut .... G. S. 1930, Sec. 6004	Wife married prior to April 20, 1877, and married when cause of action first accrues, may sue for or enter into lands or tenements within five years after discoverture	
Delaware .... R. C. 1915, Secs. 3336, 4664, 4679, 4683–84, 4689, 4693	If right of action accrues during marriage, wife may sue as follows: For lands or tenements (or may enter upon same)—within ten years after removal of disability; in enumerated personal actions — within specified periods after removal of disability; to review a will — within three years from removal of disability; on appeal from decree of chancellor — within two years from ceasing of disability; on exceptions to account of executor, administrator, or guardian—within three years after ceasing of disability	
Idaho .... Comp. St. 1919, Secs. 6606, 6623	If right of action accrues during marriage, and husband is a necessary party, wife may sue as follows: For real property (or to enter on same), or for rents and services out of same—within five years after disability ceases; in actions other than for recovery of real property—time of disability is not part of time limited for commencement of action	
Kentucky³		

³ Until recently, **Kentucky** statutes of limitations reserved a privilege to the wife. However, by an enactment effective as of January 1, 1937, such privilege has been expressly omitted; and at that time the wife will be in the same position as a single woman (see Sess. L. 1934, Chs. 43, 44, p. 150; Ch. 45, p. 151).

§ 229]

TABLE CX *(Continued)*

Jurisdiction and Citation	Suspension of Limitations as a Privilege of Wife	No Exception Because of Coverture
Louisiana .... C. C., Art. 3541, amd. by Marr, Ann. R. S., Supp. 1926, p. 249; Art. 3555; Supp. 1926, Act 23, p. 1140		Prescription runs against wife: on enumerated actions; for credits brought by her to marriage, or for what was promised her in dower. Limitations of six months on action to annul adjudication of minor's property apply to wife
Maine .... R. S. 1930, Ch. 95, Sec. 96	If person entitled to sue in certain enumerated personal actions is a married woman when cause of action accrues, limitations as specified for those actions begin to run on removal of disability[4]	
Maryland .... Bagby, Ann. C. 1924, Art. 53, Sec. 27; Art. 57, Sec. 7		Period of limitations on any suit or action shall not be extended because plaintiff is or shall be a feme covert
Missouri .... R. S. 1929, Secs. 853, 868, 1528	If right to sue in enumerated personal actions accrues during marriage, specified limitations run from removal of disability. Wife may enter motion to open proceedings to perfect land titles, within two years after removal of disability[5]	Action by wife to recover real estate, or concerning any interest or right therein, must be brought within ten years after right accrues
Nevada .... Comp. L. 1929 (Hillyer), Secs. 8533, 8539–40	In action other than for recovery of real property, if right of action accrues during marriage, time of disability of wife is not a part of time limited for commencement of action. When two or more disabilities co-exist at time right of action accrues, limitation does not attach until all are removed	

[4] The privilege is no longer in force in **Maine:** *Brown* v. *Cousens,* 51 Me. 301 (1864). This case contains a good discussion of the reasons involved.

[5] In **Missouri** the wife may take advantage of the exception to limitations: *Brunnert* v. *Boeckmann's Estate,* 226 Mo. App. 494; 258 S. W. 768 (1924); *Kneuven* v. *Berliner's Estate* (Mo. App.); 54 S. W. (2d) 494 (1932).

[§ 229

TABLE CX (*Continued*)

Jurisdiction and Citation	Suspension of Limitations as a Privilege of Wife	No Exception Because of Coverture
New Jersey .... Comp. St. 1910, p. 3172, Sec. 29	If right of action for land, tenements or other real estate accrues during marriage, action may be brought within five years after discoverture	
North Carolina .... C. 1927, Sec. 408	Time constituting period of adverse possession does not include any possession had against a feme covert during coverture prior to February 13, 1899	
Pennsylvania ...... St. 1920 (West), Secs. 13860, 13881, 13890	If right of action accrues during marriage, wife may sue as follows: In enumerated personal actions — corresponding statutes of limitations begin on discoverture; for recovery of land (or entry upon)—within ten years after discoverture, but action must be within thirty years after right first accrued[6]	
Rhode Island ...... G. L. 1923, Sec. 4207		In all causes of action or cases of adverse possession, accruing hereafter, no exception to running of statute of limitations shall be made in favor of wife because of coverture
Tennessee .... C. 1932, Sec. 8462		Statutes of limitations apply in favor of or against a wife and her property, as against a feme sole and her property

[6] *Nissley* v. *Brubaker*, 192 Pa. St. 388; 43 A. 967 (1899), expressly held that the wife's privilege was impliedly repealed by the procedural emancipation statute.

§ 229]

TABLE CX (*Concluded*)

Jurisdiction and Citation	Suspension of Limitations as a Privilege of Wife	No Exception Because of Coverture
Texas .... Complete St. 1928, Civ. St., Arts. 932, 1064, 5535, 5544	Wife has two years after removal of disability to apply for a revision of proceedings on estate of decedent or ward. Real estate of wife sold for taxes may be redeemed at any time within one year after removal of disability. If right of action in enumerated personal actions accrues during marriage, specified limitations begin to run on removal of disability. Disabilities may not be tacked; nor will an intervening disability interrupt the running of limitations[7]	

[7] Suspension of limitations in the wife's favor is still in force in **Texas**: *Garza* v. *Kenedy* (Tex. Comm. of App.); 299 S. W. 231 (1927).

REFERENCES

Book

WOOD, H. G. *Limitation of Actions,* 4th ed. (rev. by D. C. Moore), Vol. 2, pp. 1107–34 (1916).

Notes

"Limitation of Actions—Action by Married Woman for Personal Injuries Sustained after Marriage Held Not Barred by One-Year Statute of Limitations," *Dowell* v. *Gray Von Allmen Milk Company,* 221 Ky. 780; 299 S. W. 965 (1927) —16 Ky. L. Jour. 360–61 (1928).

"Limitation of Actions—Saving Clause in Statute—Removal of Disabilities," *Higgins* v. *Stokes,* 116 Ky. 664; 74 S. W. 251 (1903)—17 Harv. L. Rev. 61 (1903).

"Statutes of Limitations as between Husband and Wife in Wisconsin," 1 Wis. L. Rev. 378–84 (1922).

"Suspension of Limitations during Coverture," *Morris* v. *Pennsgrove National Bank and Trust Company,* 115 N. J. Eq. 219; 170 A. 16 (1934)—33 Mich. L. Rev. 128–30 (1934).

Annotation

"Statutory Removal of Disability of Coverture as Repealing Exception in Statute of Limitations in Favor of Married Women," L. R. A. 1918C 193–204.

[§ 229

Section 230. Miscellaneous Provisions

Statutes of a miscellaneous nature dealing with certain marital rights not discussed elsewhere in this volume may be conveniently classified under four heads: (1) statutes relating to insurance; (2) statutes expressly removing certain common-law disabilities of married women, thus affecting a wife's right to act as executrix, as administratrix, as a bank depositor, or as a shareholder or stockholder in associations or corporations; (3) statutes relating to miscellaneous rights of a surviving spouse on the death of the other spouse; (4) a few other interesting statutes which cannot readily be classified. Because of the diverse character of these statutes, their details have not been discussed; the writer has attempted merely to call attention to them and to provide a collection of citations.

1. *Statutes relating to insurance.*—It is generally true that the life of the husband may be insured for the benefit of the wife in the absence of statute, or under broad statutes of insurance; moreover, twenty-seven jurisdictions have been found with express legislation to that effect. Sixteen of these jurisdictions (**Alabama, District of Columbia, Maryland, Massachusetts, Michigan, New Hampshire, New Jersey, North Carolina, Ohio, Oklahoma, South Carolina, Tennessee, Vermont, Washington, West Virginia, Wisconsin**) recognize that his life may be insured for her benefit by either husband or wife. Seven (**Arkansas, Delaware, Hawaii, Illinois, Missouri, Nebraska, New York**) recognize that it may be so insured by the wife; and two (**Georgia, Indiana**) that the husband may make the wife the beneficiary of the policy on his life. Special statutes in **Iowa** and **South Dakota** are discussed below.

Eighteen jurisdictions provide that the insurance proceeds of which the widow is the beneficiary on the husband's death are free from the claims of his representatives, and, in varying amounts, are exempt from the claims of his creditors (**Arkansas, Delaware, District of Columbia, Hawaii, Illinois, Maryland, Massachusetts, Michigan, Missouri, New Hampshire, New Jersey, New York, North Carolina, Ohio, South Carolina, Vermont, West Virginia, Wisconsin**). Eight states have statutes which similarly exempt all or part of the proceeds from the claims of the husband's creditors, apparently assuming that the widow is entitled as against his representatives (**Alabama, Arizona, Indiana, Minnesota, North Dakota, Oklahoma, Pennsylvania, Tennessee**). Other jurisdictions have provisions generally exempting life insurance proceeds to a certain extent from the debts of the assured. Under such statutes the widow would be protected although not specifically mentioned. However, in the writer's opinion, the exemption should also extend to the widow's debts; otherwise, creditors can reach the proceeds in her hands in all cases where she is also liable for the husband's debts. Thus, the proceeds are exempt in varying amounts (see statutes) from the debts of the surviving spouse (**South Dakota**), from the debts of the widow (**Iowa, Wisconsin**) if the debts were contracted by her prior to the death of the assured (**Iowa**); and are apparently exempt from her debts (**Arizona, Minnesota, Oklahoma**).

The theory of an insurance exemption is a commendable one and in many states is used as a practical substitute for the homestead exemption. Of course, the exemption should not be available as a means of defrauding creditors, but the statutes, in general, limit the amount of the insurance which is exempt and also enable creditors to attach the proceeds to an amount equal to premiums paid from the husband's property to defraud them.

Three states have specially phrased statutes. In **Iowa** a policy of life insurance, in the absence of an agreement or assignment to the contrary, inures to the separate use of the husband or wife and children of the assured, independently of his creditors. In **South Dakota** such policy in the absence of an agreement, etc., to the contrary, to the extent of five thousand dollars, inures to the benefit of the surviving spouse and children, exempt to such amount from the debts of assured and those of the survivor. A **Tennessee** statute provides that any life insurance effected by either spouse on the husband's life inures to the widow and children to be divided among them according to the statutes of distribution and to be exempt from his debts.

In addition to the exemption of the insurance upon the death of the assured, many of the foregoing statutes also provide that the policy inures to the benefit of the wife during the husband's lifetime and cannot be attached for his debts. Other statutes exempt insurance procured by a third person for the benefit of the wife or assigned to her. Also, many provide for the payment of the proceeds to the children if the wife predecease the husband. For these and other details, the statutes should be consulted.

Citations follow:

Alabama, C. 1923, Sec. 8277; **Arizona**, R. C. 1928, Sec. 1738; **Arkansas**, Crawf. and Moses, Dig. 1921, Sec. 5579; **Delaware**, Sess. L. 1931, Ch. 52, p. 212,

[§ 230

Sec. 620(47); Sess. L. 1933, Ch. 43, p. 233, Sec. 2; **District of Columbia,** C. 1929, T. 14, Secs. 47, 48; **Georgia,** C. 1926, C. C., Sec. 2498; **Hawaii,** R. L. 1925, Secs. 3011–13; **Illinois,** Cahill, R. S. 1931, Ch. 73, Sec. 342; **Indiana,** Burns, Ann. St. 1926, Secs. 9034–35; **Iowa,** C. 1927, Sec. 8776, as amended by Sess. L. 1933, Ch. 150, p. 183; Sec. 11921; **Maryland,** Bagby, Ann. C. 1924, Art. 45, Secs. 8, 9; **Massachusetts,** G. L. 1932, Ch. 175, Secs. 125–26; **Michigan,** Comp. L. 1929, Sec. 12451, as amended by Sess. L. 1931, No. 170, pp. 262–63; Secs. 12452–53; **Minnesota,** G. S. 1923, Sec. 9447(14); **Missouri,** R. S. 1929, Secs. 5736–37, 5739; **Nebraska,** Comp. St. 1929, Sec. 44(804); **New Hampshire,** Pub. L. 1926, Ch. 277, Sec. 1; **New Jersey,** Comp. St. 1910, p. 2850, Secs. 35–37, 39; **New York,** Cahill, Consol. L. 1930, Ch. 14, Sec. 52; **North Carolina,** Const., Art. 10, Sec. 7; C. 1927, Sec. 2512; **North Dakota,** Comp. L., Supp. 1913–25, Sec. 8718*a*; **Ohio,** Complete G. C. 1931 (Page), Secs. 9393, 9395, 9397, 9399; Secs. 9394, 9398, as amended by Sess. L. 1933, No. 458, pp. 340–41; **Oklahoma,** St. 1931, Sec. 10518; **Pennsylvania,** St., Supp. 1928 (West), Sec. 1038*a*; **South Carolina,** C. of L. 1922, C. C., Sec. 4099; **South Dakota,** Comp. L. 1929, Sec. 2661; Sec. 9310, as amended by Sess. L. 1931, Ch. 170, p. 216; **Tennessee,** C. 1932, Secs. 8456–58; **Vermont,** G. L. 1917, Secs. 3531, 3533–34; **Washington,** Remington, Comp. St., Supp. 1927, Sec. 569(2); **West Virginia,** C. 1931, Ch. 48, Art. 3, Sec. 23; **Wisconsin,** St. 1931, Sec. 246.09, as amended by Sess. L. 1933, Ch. 320, p. 675; Sec. 246.11.

2. *Statutes relating to disabilities of married women.*—These statutes relate to (*a*) a wife as executrix or administratrix; (*b*) bank deposits of married women. In general, they have expressly emancipated married women from certain common-law disabilities.

Fifteen states provide that a married woman may be appointed and act as executrix or administratrix (**Arkansas, Delaware, Georgia, Kentucky, Maryland, New Jersey, Ohio, Rhode Island, South Dakota, Wisconsin, Wyoming**) or as executrix (**Idaho, Montana, North Dakota, Utah**) in like manner as if unmarried. Six jurisdictions provide that she may act as administratrix or executrix (**Florida, Hawaii, Massachusetts**), as executrix (**Alabama, Iowa**), as administratrix (**Montana**), without the consent of her husband. And five have statutes to the effect that marriage does not disqualify her or that she may act as administratrix or executrix (**California, Nevada, Oregon, Vermont**), or as administratrix (**Idaho**). Of the foregoing twenty-four jurisdictions, ten have statutes to the effect that a subsequent marriage of a woman who has been appointed as administratrix or executrix does not revoke her authority (**Georgia, Idaho, Montana, Nevada, New Jersey, Ohio, Rhode Island, South Dakota, Vermont, Wyoming**). Apparently the same is true in **California.** Four other states (**Maine, Missouri, New Hampshire, West Virginia**) have provisions analogous to those of the ten noted above. In those jurisdictions which

§ 230]

possess broad equal-rights statutes (**Sec. 150**), presumably a married woman may act as executrix or administratrix in like manner as if unmarried; furthermore, such a result may be implied from statutes which, in specifying those persons incapable of so acting, do not include married women.

Three of the foregoing jurisdictions and six others have statutes which draw a distinction between a married and an unmarried woman. In the **District of Columbia, Indiana,** and **Maryland** a feme sole is to be preferred over a married woman of equal degree in the granting of letters of administration. A married woman cannot be appointed administratrix (**Indiana, Utah**) or executrix (**Louisiana**) without her husband's consent (**Indiana, Louisiana**), or if any person interested in the estate objects (**Utah**). If an unmarried woman has been appointed as an executrix or administratrix (**Indiana, Utah**) or as administratrix (**Nevada**), her authority is revoked by her subsequent marriage unless her husband consents to becoming bound (**Indiana**); or the court may revoke her authority upon her subsequent marriage on the petition of other persons entitled to administration (**Nevada**) or on the motion of any person interested in the estate (**Utah**). In **Virginia,** if an unmarried woman who has been appointed personal representative marries, the court shall, on motion of her surety, and may, on motion of any person interested, or may, when it shall seem proper to the court, revoke her authority. And in **South Carolina,** upon the subsequent marriage of a widow who has been granted administration of her husband's estate, the judge has power to revoke her authority or to join one or more of the next of kin with her. **Illinois** provides that when a wife is an executrix her husband may give bond with her for her faithful performance of the trust, "as in other cases."

In further express recognition of the emancipation of married women, twenty jurisdictions provide that a wife may make and withdraw deposits in banks; and according to most of the statutes, the deposits are expressly free from the husband's control (**Arkansas, California, Delaware, District of Columbia, Florida, Idaho, Indiana, Iowa, Kentucky, Louisiana, Maine, Maryland, Missouri, New Jersey, North Carolina, Pennsylvania, Rhode Island, Texas, Washington, Wisconsin**). A similar result presumably is reached under the general statutes empowering a wife to contract (**Sec. 152**) and under the equal-rights statutes (**Sec. 150**). It is clear that she should have such a right.

Citations to the statutes discussed under subdivision 2 follow:

[§ 230

Alabama, C. 1923, Sec. 5733; **Arkansas,** Crawf. and Moses, Dig. 1921, Secs. 5577, 5583; **California,** Prob. C. 1933 (Lake), Secs. 401, 420; Deering, G. L. 1931, Act 652, p. 231, Sec. 15*a*; **Delaware,** R. C. 1915, Secs. 2114, 3053, 3339; **District of Columbia,** C. 1929, T. 14, Sec. 50; T. 29, Secs. 113, 268; **Florida,** R. G. S. 1920, Secs. 4177, 4196; Sess. L. 1933, Ch. 16103, p. 576, Sec. 84; **Georgia,** C. 1926, C. C., Secs. 3944–45; **Hawaii,** R. L. 1925, Sec. 2996; **Idaho,** Comp. St. 1919, Sec. 5265; Sec. 7479, as amended by Sess. L. 1921, Ch. 174, p. 369; Sec. 7492, as amended by Sess. L. 1921, Ch. 174, p. 370; **Illinois,** Cahill, R. S. 1931, Ch. 3, Sec. 3; **Indiana,** Burns, Ann. St. 1926, Secs. 3068–69, 3096, 3888; **Iowa,** C. 1927, Secs. 9193, 11871; **Kentucky,** Carroll, St. 1922, Sec. 591; Supp. 1926, Sec. 3845; **Louisiana,** Marr, Ann. R. S. 1915, Secs. 322, 394, 4468; C. C., Art. 1664; **Maine,** R. S. 1930, Ch. 57, Sec. 24; Ch. 76, Sec. 27; **Maryland,** Bagby, Ann. C. 1924, Art. 11, Sec. 74; Art. 45, Sec. 11; Art. 93, Secs. 27, 28, 59; **Massachusetts,** G. L. 1932, Ch. 209, Sec. 5; **Missouri,** R. S. 1929, Secs. 42, 5502; **Montana,** R. C. 1921, Secs. 5808, 10059, 10073; **Nevada,** Comp. L. 1929 (Hillyer), Sec. 9641; **New Hampshire,** Pub. L. 1926, Ch. 299, Sec. 9; **New Jersey,** Comp. St. 1910, p. 4702, Sec. 26, as amended by Sess. L. 1932, Ch. 41, p. 60; p. 4718, Sec. 91; Supp. 1925–30, Secs. 72(17*a*), 146(142); **North Carolina,** C. 1927, Sec. 2508; **North Dakota,** Comp. L. 1913, Sec. 8651, as amended by Sess. L. 1927, Ch. 221, p. 375; **Ohio,** Complete G. C. 1931 (Page), Supp. 1932, Sec. 10506(66); **Oregon,** C. 1930, Sec. 11(231); **Pennsylvania,** St. 1920 (West), Secs. 1366, 19761, 21354*c*; **Rhode Island,** G. L. 1923, Secs. 4194, 4202, 5426; **South Carolina,** C. of L. 1922, C. C., Sec. 5382; **South Dakota,** Comp. L. 1929, Secs. 3241, 3254; **Texas,** Complete St. 1928, Civ. St., Art. 409; **Utah,** R. S. 1933, 102-3-17, 102-4-5; **Vermont,** G. L. 1917, Secs. 3245, 3522; **Virginia,** C. 1930, Sec. 5373; **Washington,** Remington, Comp. St. 1922, Sec. 3250; **West Virginia,** C. 1931, Ch. 44, Art. 1, Sec. 10; **Wisconsin,** St. 1931, Secs. 221.44, 319.36; **Wyoming,** R. S. 1931, Secs. 88(1604), 88(1704).

3. *Statutes relating to miscellaneous rights of a surviving spouse on the death of the other spouse.*—**Delaware** is the only one of the fifty-one jurisdictions in which no statute was found respecting the granting of letters of administration to the surviving husband or wife on the death of the other spouse. In thirty-two jurisdictions it is provided that, in general, a surviving spouse is to be preferred as an administrator (**Alabama, Arizona, California, Colorado, Florida, Georgia, Hawaii, Idaho, Illinois, Indiana, Iowa, Kentucky, Massachusetts, Mississippi, Missouri, Montana, Nevada, New Mexico, New York, North Carolina, North Dakota, Ohio, Oklahoma, Pennsylvania, South Carolina, South Dakota, Texas, Utah, Virginia, Washington, West Virginia, Wyoming**). In eleven, letters of administration are to be granted first to the surviving spouse (**Connecticut, Maine, Michigan, Minnesota, New Hampshire, Rhode Island, Vermont, Wisconsin**) or widow (**Kansas, Nebraska, New Jersey**) and the next of kin, or to either of them, usually in the discretion of the court. In the **District of Columbia** and **Maryland,** administration is granted first

§ 230]

to the surviving spouse and a child or children, or either of them, in the court's discretion. In three jurisdictions the surviving husband (**Alaska, Oregon**) or the widow (**Tennessee**) is to be preferred, but, in **Alaska** and **Oregon,** if the decedent was the husband, the widow or next of kin or both are preferred, in the court's discretion. In **Arkansas,** the preference is given to a surviving spouse or to a distributee of the estate, in the court's discretion. And in **Louisiana,** in "contestations" concerning the curatorship of vacant successions and of absent heirs, preference is given the surviving spouse after a surviving partner and after an heir, but before creditors. Whether the widow's authority is revoked upon her subsequent marriage has been considered above in subdivision 2.

Nine states have legislation which, in varying degrees, permits a surviving spouse to collect, without administration, certain moneys owing the deceased spouse at his or her death (**Alabama, Arizona, California, Connecticut, Delaware, Florida, Massachusetts, New Jersey, New York**). The statutes are too varied to permit details to be given here; but it may be noted that, in general, they extend such a right to wages and bank deposits due the decedent. The citations to these statutes follow, together with citations to the provisions relating to the surviving spouse as administrator of the decedent's estate:

Alabama, C. 1923, Secs. 5742, 7923; **Alaska,** Comp. L. 1913, Secs. 1606, 1608; **Arizona,** R. C. 1928, Secs. 264, 3922, 4167; **Arkansas,** Crawf. and Moses, Dig. 1921, Sec. 8; **California,** Prob. C. 1933 (Lake), Secs. 422, 630, 630.5; **Colorado,** Comp. L. 1921, G. S., Sec. 5222; **Connecticut,** G. S. 1930, Secs. 4885, 4904, 4970; **Delaware,** R. C. 1915, Sec. 3380; **District of Columbia,** C. 1929, T. 29, Secs. 104–5; **Florida,** R. G. S. 1920, Secs. 4979–80; Sess. L. 1933, Ch. 16103, p. 574, Sec. 80; **Georgia,** C. 1926, C. C., Sec. 3943; **Hawaii,** R. L. 1925, Sec. 2483; **Idaho,** Comp. St. 1919, Sec. 7487; **Illinois,** Cahill, R. S. 1931, Ch. 3, Sec. 18; **Indiana,** Burns, Ann. St. 1926, Sec. 3067; **Iowa,** C. 1927, Secs. 11883; **Kansas,** R. S. 1923, Sec. 22(312); **Kentucky,** Carroll, St. 1922, Sec. 3896; **Louisiana,** C. C., Sec. 1121; **Maine,** R. S. 1930, Ch. 76, Sec. 18; **Maryland,** Bagby, Ann. C. 1924, Art. 93, Secs. 18, 19; **Massachusetts,** G. L. 1932, Ch. 193, Secs. 1, 2; Ch. 194, Secs. 5, 7; Sess. L. 1932, Ch. 175, p. 229; **Michigan,** Comp. L. 1929, Sec. 15586; **Minnesota,** G. S. 1923, Sec. 8772, as amended by Sess. L. 1925, Ch. 135, p. 122, Sec. 1; **Mississippi,** C. 1930, Sec. 1629; **Missouri,** R. S. 1929, Sec. 7; **Montana,** R. C. 1921, Sec. 10068; **Nebraska,** Comp. St. 1929, Sec. 30(314); **Nevada,** Comp. L. 1929 (Hillyer), Secs. 9637, 9649, 9651; **New Hampshire,** Pub. L. 1926, Ch. 299, Sec. 2; **New Jersey,** Comp. St. 1910, p. 3051, Sec. 126; p. 3822, Sec. 27; **New Mexico,** St. Ann. 1929, Sec. 47(110); **New York,** Cahill, Consol. L. 1930, Ch. 3, Sec. 149; Surrogate's Court Act 1931, Secs. 118, 133; **North Carolina,** C. 1927, Secs. 6, 7, 31; **North Dakota,** Comp. L. 1913, Sec. 8657, as amended by Sess. L. 1927, Ch. 221, p. 376; **Ohio,** Complete G. C. 1931 (Page), Supp. 1932, Sec. 10509(3); **Oklahoma,** St. 1931, Secs. 1135, 1150, 1153; **Oregon,** C. 1930, Secs. 11(208), 11(210);

[§ 230

Pennsylvania, St., Supp. 1928 (West), Sec. 8400; Rhode Island, G. L. 1923, Sec. 5428; South Carolina, C. of L. 1922, C. C., Sec. 5382; South Dakota, Comp. L. 1929, Sec. 3249; Tennessee, C. 1932, Sec. 8151; Texas, Complete St. 1928, Civ. St., Arts. 3357, 3359; Utah, R. S. 1933, 102-4-1; Vermont, G. L. 1917, Sec. 3231, as amended by Sess. L. 1919, Ch. 83, p. 91; Virginia, C. 1930, Sec. 5360; Washington, Remington, Comp. St. 1922, Sec. 1419; Supp. 1927, Sec. 1431; West Virginia, C. 1931, Ch. 44, Art. 1, Sec. 4; Wisconsin, St. 1931, Sec. 311.02; Wyoming, R. S. 1931, Sec. 88(1701).

4. *Other miscellaneous statutes.*—Nineteen jurisdictions expressly provide that a spouse is not criminally liable as an accessory after the fact if the principal concerned is the other spouse, or reach the same result by specifically excepting the spouse from the definition of an accessory after the fact (Alabama, Delaware, Florida, Hawaii, Illinois, Indiana, Kentucky, Maine, Massachusetts, Minnesota, Missouri, Tennessee, Texas, Vermont, Virginia, Washington, West Virginia, Wisconsin, Wyoming). Three of the foregoing jurisdictions, however, do not extend such immunity to a spouse who breaks prison (Delaware, Kentucky) or uses force (Delaware, Kentucky, Tennessee) to aid the offending spouse. It is likewise provided in three states that a spouse is not guilty of concealing the criminal spouse (Indiana), of knowingly harboring or relieving the criminal spouse (Rhode Island), or of misprision of treason for concealing the treason of the other spouse (Pennsylvania).

In two states the killing of a paramour who is in the act of carnal knowledge with the wife of the killer is justifiable; provided, that such husband and wife are living together as man and wife (New Mexico) or that there has been no connivance or assent to the act by the husband (Texas). An interesting Ohio statute makes it criminal for a married man to represent himself fraudulently to be unmarried and propose marriage, repeatedly call on, or keep company with a single female of good character upon such representations. In Connecticut, the surviving spouse is given the control and custody of the remains of a deceased spouse unless the survivor has abandoned and is living apart from the decedent at the time of death.

The writer does not purport to include in the present section all miscellaneous statutes relating to marital rights, for there are many to be found in one or two states only and their importance does not justify their inclusion. Citations to the miscellaneous statutes discussed under subdivision 4 follow:

Alabama, C. 1923, Sec. 3197; Connecticut, G. S. 1930, Sec. 4957; Delaware, R. C. 1915, Sec. 4807, as amended by Sess. L. 1927, Ch. 230, p. 630; Florida, R. G. S.

1920, Sec. 5010; **Hawaii,** R. L. 1925, Sec. 3920; **Illinois,** Cahill, R. S. 1931, Ch. 38, Sec. 613; **Indiana,** Burns, Ann. St. 1926, Secs. 2029, 2587; **Kentucky,** Carroll, St. 1922, Sec. 1129; **Maine,** R. S. 1930, Ch. 143, Sec. 9; **Massachusetts,** G. L. 1932, Ch. 274, Sec. 4; **Minnesota,** G. S. 1923, Sec. 9918; **Missouri,** R. S. 1929, Sec. 4447; **New Mexico,** St. Ann. 1929, Sec. 35(315); **Ohio,** Complete G. C. 1931 (Page), Sec. 13146; **Pennsylvania,** St. 1920 (West), Sec. 8053; **Rhode Island,** G. L. 1923, Sec. 6252; **Tennessee,** C. 1932, Sec. 10766; **Texas,** Complete St. 1928, P. C., Secs. 18, 1220; **Vermont,** G. L. 1917, Sec. 7120; **Virginia,** C. 1930, Sec. 4765; **Washington,** Remington, Comp. St. 1922, Sec. 2008; **West Virginia,** C. 1931, Ch. 61, Art. 11, Sec. 6; **Wisconsin,** St. 1931, Sec. 353.08; **Wyoming,** R. S. 1931, Sec. 32(1102).

REFERENCES

Articles

IRWIN, HAROLD S. "Joint Banking Account of Husband and Wife in Pennsylvania," 34 Dick. L. Rev. 156–68 (1930).

PATTEN, FRANCIS B. "Insured Wife's Rights under General Exemption Statutes," 3 B. U. L. Rev. 75–108 (1923).

Notes

"Insurance Effected by One Spouse on His or Her Life in Favor of the Other," *Cousins* v. *Sun Life Assurance Society,* (1933) 1 Ch. 126; 174 L. Times 339–40 (1932); 67 Ir. L. Times 103–5, 109–10 (1933); 76 Sol. Jour. 571–72 (1932).

"Liability of Husband and of Wife's Estate for Funeral Expenses of Wife," *Lee* v. *Hempy,* 35 Ohio App. 402; 172 N. E. 421 (1929)—4 U. of Cinn. L. Rev. 486–91 (1930).

"Widow Not Liable at Common Law for Husband's Funeral Expenses," *O'Hagan* v. *Fraternal Aid Union,* 144 S. C. 84; 141 S. E. 893 (1927)—5 Notre Dame Lawy. 51–52 (1929).

Annotations

"Executrix's and Administratrix's Authority as Terminated by Marriage," 8 A. L. R. 181–82 (1920).

"May Adverse Possession Be Predicated upon Use or Occupancy by One Spouse of Real Property of Other?" 74 A. L. R. 138–48 (1931).

INDEX TO VOLUME III

[References are to sections]

Accessories, husband and wife as, 230

Acknowledgment, of conveyance by wife, 184

Actions (*see* Suits)

Administrator, husband as, 230

Administratrix, married woman as, 230

Alienation of affections, suit for, 158

Allowance to widow, 228

Amount—
of dower, 190
of curtesy, 217

Annuity tables—
dower, 214
curtesy, 223

Antenuptial agreements, between husband and wife, 155

Antenuptial debts, 151

Assignment—
of dower, 208–12
of wages, by husband or wife, 224

Bank deposits, of husband and wife, 230

Barring curtesy, 220

Barring dower—
methods of, in general, 195
by jointure, 196
by settlement of property before marriage, 197
by settlement of property after marriage, 198
by will, 199
by deed, 200
by other means, 201

Coercion, of wife by husband—
torts, 157
crimes, 165

Community property, 178

Confidential communications, between husband and wife, 226

Consortium, suits for loss of, 158

Contracts, of wife—
before marriage, 151
after marriage, 152–54
with husband, 155, 156

Conveyances—
by husband to wife, 182
by wife to husband, 182
by wife to third persons, 183
of homestead, 225

Courts—
domestic relations, 163
family, 163

Creditors, fraud on, in conveyance between husband and wife, 182

Crimes—
by wife, 165
by one spouse, injurious to other, 166

Criminal conversation, 158

Curtesy—
in general, 215
abolished or modified, 216
amount, 217
property subject to, 218
election, 219
how barred, 220
forfeiture of, 221
waste, 222
miscellaneous provisions, 223
collusive assignment, 223

Death (*see* Wrongful death)

Debts—
antenuptial debts of wife, 151
postnuptial debts of wife, 152–54
of husband, 159

Deed (*see also* Conveyances)—
barring dower by, 200

Deposits (*see* Bank deposits)

Desertion—
civil liability for, 161
criminal liability for, 162

Descent and distribution (*see* Inheritance)
Domestic relations courts, 163
Domicile, of wife, 164
Dower—
  in general, 188
  abolished or modified, 189
  extent, 190
  property subject to, 191
  waste, 192
  repairs, 193
  emblements, 194
  barring, in general, 195
  barring by jointure or settlement, 196
  barring by contract or settlement before marriage, 197
  barring by contract or settlement after marriage, 198
  barring by will, 199
  barring by deed, 200
  barring by other means, 201
  forfeiture of, 202
  forfeiture of provision in lieu of, 203
  failure of provision in lieu of, 204
  election and waiver, in general, 205
  election and waiver, time and manner, 206
  election and waiver, miscellaneous provisions, 207
  assignment, in general, 208
  assignment, possession of dwelling, etc., pending, 209
  assignment, by non-judicial action, 210
  assignment, by summary proceedings, 211
  assignment, action to compel and damages for withholding, 212
  assignment, method of, 213
  miscellaneous provisions, 214
  collusive assignment, 214

Earnings, of wife, 173
Election—
  of dower, or statutory share, 205–7
  of curtesy, or statutory share, 219
Emblements, right of tenant by dower to, 194

Equal-rights statutes, 150
Evidence (*see* Witnesses)
Executrix, wife as, 230
Exemptions, family allowance and exempt property, 228

Family allowance, 228
Family courts, 163
Family desertion, 162
Family expenses, 160
Forfeiture—
  of dower, 202
  of provision in lieu of dower, 203
  of curtesy, 221
Fraud, on creditors, by conveyance between husband and wife, 182

Homestead, 228
  conveyance of, 225
Household goods, transfers of, 225
Husband (*see* Husband and wife)
Husband and wife (*see also* Curtesy, Dower, Wife)—
  introductory, 149
  general principles, 150
  wife's antenuptial debts, 151
  wife's postnuptial debts, 152–54
  necessaries, 153
  marriage settlements, 155
  antenuptial contracts, 155
  postnuptial contracts, 156
  wife's torts, 157
  torts by third persons, 158
  husband's debts, 159
  family expenses, 160
  civil liability for support, 161
  criminal liability for support, 162
  family courts, 163
  courts of domestic relations, 163
  domicile of wife, 164
  crimes by wife, coercion, 165
  crimes by one spouse injurious to the other, 166
  wife's property, 167–75
  paraphernalia, 170
  wife's earnings, 173
  husband's property, 176

Husband and wife (*continued*)—
property acquired outside the state,
177
community property, 178
suits by and against the wife, 179
suits by one spouse against the other,
180
wife's power to make a will, 181
conveyances between husband and
wife, 182
wife's conveyance of real property to
third person, 183–84
wife's transfers of personal property,
185
power of attorney of husband and
wife, 186
wife as sole trader, 187
dower, 188–214
curtesy, 215–23
assignment of wages by husband or
wife, 224
other limitations on transfers of property by husband or wife, 225
witnesses for and against each other,
226
descent and distribution, 227
homestead, exempt property, and family allowance, 228
statute of limitations, 229
miscellaneous provisions, 230

Inheritance, by husband and wife, 227
Insurance on husband's life for benefit
of wife, 230

Jointure, 196
Jurisdiction—
of family courts, 163
over assignment of dower, 208
over assignment of statutory curtesy,
223

"Lazy husband" laws, 162
Limitations (*see* Statute of limitations)

Marriage settlement, 155
Married women (*see* Husband and wife)

Mortgages—
of wife's land, 183
dower in mortgaged land, 191
of homestead and exempt property,
225

Necessaries, wife's contracts for, 153

Paraphernalia, 170
Partition suits—
dower in, 214
curtesy in, 223
Personal property—
possessed by wife at marriage, 169
paraphernalia, 170
acquired by wife after marriage, 172
earnings, 173
wife's transfers of, 185
succession to, 227
Postnuptial agreements between husband and wife, 156
Postnuptial debts, 152–54
Power of attorney, of husband or wife,
186
Property (*see* Husband and wife, Personal property, Real property)
Punishment, right of husband to inflict
on wife, 166

Real property (*see also* Husband and
wife)—
of wife, at marriage, 168
of wife, acquired after marriage, 171
of husband, 176
community interest in, 178
conveyance of, between husband and
wife, 182
conveyance of, by wife to third person, 183
dower in (*see* Dower)
curtesy in (*see* Curtesy)
inheritance of, 227
homestead in, 228
Recording—
of separate property of wife, 174
effect of, 175
Repairs, by dowress, 193

Separate examination, of wife, **184**
Separate property—
 liability of, for husband's debts, **159**
 of wife, in general, **167**
 recording of, **174**
 effect of recording of, **175**
 of husband, **176**
Services, of wife, **173**
Settlement—
 antenuptial, **155**
 postnuptial, **156**
 barring dower by, **196–98**
Sole trader, wife as, **187**
Statute of limitations—
 in actions for dower, **212**
 in suits by and against wife, **229**
Suits—
 by and against wife, **170**
 by one spouse against the other, **180**
Support, of one spouse by the other,
  150, 161, 162

Torts—
 of wife, **157**
 by third persons to husband or wife,
  158

Wages, assignment of, **224**

Waste—
 by dowress, **192**
 by tenant by curtesy, **222**
Widow's allowance, **209**
Wife (*see also* Husband and wife)—
 contracts of, **151–56**
 torts of, **157**
 support of family by, **160–62**
 domicile of, **164**
 crimes by, **165**
 property of, **167–75**
 earnings of, **173**
 suits by and against, **179**
 will of, **181**
 conveyances by, **182–83**
 separate examination of, **184**
 transfers of personal property by, **185**
 powers of attorney of, **186**
 as sole trader, **187**
 assignment of wages by, **224**
 as executrix or administratrix, **230**
Will—
 of wife, **181**
 barring dower by, **199**
Witnesses, husband and wife as, **226**
Wrongful death, of spouse, right of
  other to sue for, **158**